COURVOISIER'S BOOK OF THE BEST

TRAVEL

Courvoisier's connection with Napoleon dates back to 1811, when Napoleon I visited Emmanuel Courvoisier's warehouses in Bercy, Paris. Napoleon III proclaimed the company official purveyor to his court in 1869, making Courvoisier the only true Napoleon cognac.

To mark the connection, not only does a bust of Napoleon appear on the bottles, but also, on the Three Star and VSOP grades, his personal bee motif. Two theories prevail as to the Bee's origin.

One is that the curtains in Napoleon I's Elysée Palace were turned upside-down (an economy measure) which gave their fleur-de-lys pattern the appearance of bees. Napoleon regarded these as a symbol of the benign head of state – himself, the natural leader, around whom the French army and people gathered.

The other theory goes back to 1682, when the grave of Childeric I, 5th-century founder of France as a unified state, was opened. Inside were golden cicadas that had been buried with him to represent the immortality of his soul. Napoleon interpreted the cicadas as bees and adopted them as symbols of the unification of France under his own rule.

The Bee has been used in this book to denote a person or establishment that has been highly recommended by several of our contributors. Such entries head, in order of merit, the otherwise alphabetical listings.

COURVOISIER'S BOOK OF THE BEST

Edited by
Lord Lichfield

Compiled and written by
Sue Carpenter

SALEM HOUSE PUBLISHERS
TOPSFIELD, MASSACHUSETTS

First published in the United States by Salem House Publishers, 1986, 462 Boston Street, Topsfield, MA 01983

Published in the United Kingdom by
Ebury Press
Division of The National Magazine Company Ltd
Colquhoun House
27–37 Broadwick Street
London W1V 1FR

ISBN 0 88162 216 8

Library of Congress Catalog Card Number 86–60818

Editorial Direction	Yvonne McFarlane
Art Direction	Frank Phillips
Project Editor	Anne Charlish
Project Co-ordinator	Sarah Bailey
Researchers	Chantal Revell-Smith Katy Jones
Australian Editor	Charles de Lisle
Paris Editor	Anne-Elisabeth Moutet
Tokyo Editor	Claudia Cragg
Additional written material	Alexandra Artley Susan Irvine Andrew Jefford
Illustrations	Natacha Ledwidge
Design	William Mason

Computerset in Great Britain by
MFK Typesetting Ltd, Hitchin, Herts
Printed in Great Britain at the University Press, Cambridge

Courvoisier's Book of the Best will be an annually updated guide. We would welcome your views in writing to Courvoisier's Book of the Best, Ebury Press, 27–37 Broadwick Street, London W1V 1FR.

The information contained in this book was checked as rigorously as possible before going to press. The publisher accepts no responsibility for any changes which may have occurred since, nor for any other variance of fact from that recorded here in good faith.

CONTENTS

FOREWORD

by LORD LICHFIELD

There is really no such thing as the best, as what is best for me is going to differ from what is best for you. Best for *me* represents quality and uncompromising attention to detail. As a result of an upbringing in a very large country house – Shugborough in Staffordshire – I had the advantage of seeing things beautifully done, not only upstairs, but downstairs too. From the age of seven, each holiday was spent as understudy to a different member of staff. The idea was not only to teach me how things ought to be done, but also to ensure that I would never demand anything unreasonable of an employee. I became adept at ironing newspapers to remove the ink before the grown-ups' fingers did, boning shoes, and cleaning the inside of decanters.

Now, as a travelling photographer, I constantly have the opportunity to judge standards, particularly of airlines, hotels and restaurants, since I travel 250,000 miles a year, spend 150 nights in hotels and eat out virtually every day. My choice is, of course, personal. However, if several people, whose views are informed and respected, recommend the same things – Annabel's nightclub in London, Manolo Blahnik's shoes, the Mandarin hotel in Hong Kong, British Airways, Roederer Cristal champagne – you can begin to take notice.

Where most guide books are rather dreary and egotistic (who wants to be doused in one person's opinions?), this book is not, because I have asked 200 style-setters and experts to nominate their personal "bests", in the major cities, resorts and country areas of Europe, the Americas, Australasia and the Far East. Their views alone make riveting reading. You will discover, for example, why Bruce Oldfield wears Giorgio Armani, Diana Vreeland's recipe for feeling good, Brooke Shields's recipe for looking good, the first chef to serve kangaroo, the buzz about Spago, Le Cirque and Chez Oz, which restaurant packs its pans for the summer and moves town, the importance of Royal Ascot, how to play stomach roulette, and why Robert Sangster flies Aer Lingus.

But this *is* a guide, and so each entry has been thoroughly researched, and full addresses and telephone numbers are supplied. We cover the best of Food and Drink, Nightlife, Fashion, Health and Beauty, Sporting Life, Travel, and Homes and Property. Each section is introduced by an expert on the subject: respectively, Paul Levy, David Shilling, Jasper Conran, Leslie Kenton, Stirling Moss, René Lecler and David Mlinaric. The world and continental ratings in each section have been reached by the consensus opinion of our 200 contributors, and entries that have received a large number of recommendations are awarded the Courvoisier bee.

Some of our contributors are recognized experts in their field, such as Hugh Johnson or Michael Broadbent on wine; some are well-known in another context (actors such as Peter Ustinov, models such as Marie Helvin, writers and personalities such as Jackie Collins). All are well-travelled connoisseurs who have experienced the best things around the world.

LORD LICHFIELD, 47, great nephew of the Queen Mother, was educated at Harrow and spent seven years in the Grenadier Guards. He left to become an assistant photographer in London in the Sixties. He worked for *Life*, *Queen* and many newspapers before taking up a five-year contract with American *Vogue* at the behest of Diana Vreeland. Advertising work followed, taking him all over the world. His books include *Lichfield – The Most Beautiful Women*, *Lichfield – A Royal Album* and *Lichfield on Travel Photography*.

"Best" means the most commended or fitting; it is by no means the grandest or most expensive (although I have generally found that quality does come at a price). It is a matter of avoiding mediocrity when there is an alternative. The Duke of Windsor used to have his trousers made in Italy and his coats made in Britain – he took the time and trouble to find the best.

Quality is certainly available to everyone. Take Marks & Spencer. You don't need a bulging wallet or expensive tastes to buy really excellent food there, but people with *discerning* tastes swear by it. I know of one MP who sends out from the House of Commons for Marks & Spencer's sandwiches.

There are some "bests" in this book which cost nothing at all. In the Travel section, for example: in Africa and Australia, you will find the best beaches, in Sydney the best views, in India the best festivals (in the eyes of actor Victor Banerjee) – plus the odd "worst", such as why Eric Newby *doesn't* like cruises.

Long-standing "bests" are balanced with what is trendsetting, innovative and currently fashionable. It is boring simply to trot out the same old establishments that everyone *knows* are excellent. All the time wonderful places are cropping up – new young chefs and fashion designers emerge. Our experts have their ears to the ground. They spot the latest trends. In all spheres, the best way to find out what is "in" is by word of mouth, and this book provides you with news and views from the best mouths. Almost all our contributors were interviewed (rather than writing their recommendations), which adds tremendous spontaneity.

Though this guide is compiled in London, its view is far from Eurocentric. We judge Australian, American and Far Eastern restaurants, for example, by asking local food and wine writers, restaurateurs and style leaders to nominate what they consider the best. The views of the European jetsetter who passes through Sydney, New York or Tokyo twice a year would not be a fair barometer.

As the producers of the best and most stylishly presented cognacs in the world, it was only natural for Courvoisier to initiate and support this book with such enthusiasm. Connoisseurs in one area are able to appreciate fine things on a broader scale: those who savour Courvoisier's fine cognacs are attuned to the best things in life.

Courvoisier's Book of the Best will be an annually updated guide. While some establishments are undoubtedly timeless, many fluctuate. What is the best restaurant today may not be next year. We will constantly be assessing what is best, rating new entries and sifting out dead wood. From now on, instead of a suitcaseful of Michelins, Gault Millaus, Fodors, Good Food and Hotel Guides, you'll need only one, all-encompassing guide: *Courvoisier's Book of the Best*.

CONTRIBUTORS

PRUE ACTON, OBE Australian fashion designer.

AZZEDINE ALAIA Paris-based Tunisian fashion designer, still wowing the fashion scene with sculpted forms in leather and synthetics (he studied sculpture in Tunis). He has worked with Dior and dressed famous women from Garbo to Grace Jones.

KAY ALSOP Canadian journalist, TV hostess and radio commentator. Ex-fashion editor of *Vancouver Province*.

LADY ELIZABETH ANSON Sister of Lord Lichfield and founder of Party Planners which has organized parties for most British royals, as well as international clients from Mick Jagger to Baron Thyssen.

GENERAL SIR JOHN ARCHER, OBE Chief executive of the Jockey Club in Hong Kong. Ex-General Commander in Chief of the UK Land Forces.

GIORGIO ARMANI Top Italian fashion designer of women's and menswear, a master of tailoring. He worked with Cerruti and Ungaro before setting up alone.

LUDOVIC AUTET French-born, New York-based president and founder of the Junior International Club. He has just opened new clubs in Boston and Los Angeles.

VICTOR BANERJEE Star of the award-winning film *A Passage to India*. Born and educated in Calcutta, he has a house there and a cottage in the Himalayas. He plays the lead role in the new comedy film *Foreign Body*.

VIVIENNE BECKER Jewellery historian from London, specializing in Art Nouveau. Her latest book is *Art Nouveau Jewelry*.

SHARI BELAFONTE-HARPER Top American model, and star of the television series *Hotel*. Her father is singer Harry Belafonte.

NICOLAS BELFRAGE, MW British expert on Italian wines, author of *Life beyond Lambrusco* on fine Italian wines. Regular contributor to specialist wine magazines.

LORD PATRICK BERESFORD Former top British polo player who was a member of Prince Philip's high-goal team from 1966–71.

TONY BILSON Australian restaurateur who set up Australia's best restaurant, Berowra Waters near Sydney. He now runs Kinselas theatre-restaurant in Sydney.

JANE BIRBECK British health and fitness expert who runs the fashionable health club, Bodys in Chelsea, which she founded with her former boyfriend James Hunt.

MARK BIRLEY Proprietor of Annabel's in London, the world's top nightclub, which attracts the global glitterati. Part-owner of Harry's Bar and Mark's Club in Mayfair, London.

MANOLO BLAHNIK Voted by *The New York Times* the most influential shoe deisgner in the world. A Spaniard living in London, he has designed for Perry Ellis, Calvin Klein and Yves Saint Laurent as well as for his own Chelsea shop.

RAYMOND BLANC French chef-owner of the acclaimed Le Manoir aux Quat' Saisons in Oxfordshire. A self-taught cook, he also owns the Oxford pâtisserie, Maison Blanc, and bistro, Le Petit Blanc.

BILL BLASS Top American fashion and furnishings designer, and one of the most fashionable people to be seen with in New York.

HENRY BLOFELD British cricket writer with *The Guardian*, BBC cricket commentator and reporter for Australian radio.

KYM BONYTHON Australian art gallery owner in Adelaide.

FRANK BOWLING British-born General Manager of the Ritz-Carlton in New York.

SEYMOUR BRITCHKY American author of the annual guide *The Restaurants of New York*, now in its 12th edition, and of the restaurant periodical *Seymour Britchky's Restaurant Letter*.

MICHAEL BROADBENT, MW Head of Christie's Wine Department in London, he is an international wine auctioneer, president of the International Wine and Food Society and author of the *Great Vintage Wine Book*.

JOHN BROOKE-LITTLE British heraldry and genealogy expert at the College of Arms in London.

CONTESSA ARISTEA BRUGUIER Italian landowner and society figure. Her Tuscany farm produces the well-known wine Il Luchesiano.

MARIAN BURROS Restaurant critic for *The New York Times*, former food editor of the *Washington Post* and author of several food books.

JOAN BURSTEIN Owner and top buyer of Browns, London's foremost fashion store, which houses the finest international designers for men and women.

ROBERT BURTON Australian fashion designer. He learned his trade in London and ran the Yves Saint Laurent shop in New York before returning to Australia.

HERB CAEN American gossip columnist for the *San Francisco Chronicle*, author, and key social figure in the city.

SHAKIRA CAINE Guyanan beauty and wife of Michael Caine. Based in Beverly Hills and London, she writes a travel diary for US *Elle*.

PAT CANTOR American fashion editor of *Harper's Bazaar*.

EDMOND CAPON British-born director of the Art Gallery of New South Wales in Sydney.

SONJA CAPRONI Fashion buyer for the prestigious San Francisco fashion store, I Magnin.

EDWARD CARTER Widely travelled American multi-millionaire who owns The Point hotel at Saranac Lake, NY.

MARINA CHALIAPIN Daughter of the Russian bass singer, Fiodor Chaliapin, she lives in Rome and is Rome editor of *Harpers & Queen*.

JEAN-PHILIPPE CHATRIER A French actor, he appears in Claude Lelouche's latest film *20 Years Later*. Son of Philippe Chatrier, president of the World Federation of Tennis.

TINA CHOW Japanese-born model married to top restaurant owner Michael Chow. Recently voted one of the best dressed women in the world, she is based in California.

GLYNN CHRISTIAN New Zealand-born food writer and broadcaster, now living in England. A direct descendant of Fletcher Christian who lead the mutiny on the Bounty, his most recent book is *Edible France*.

CRAIG CLAIBORNE American food writer who studied at the Ecole Hôtelière in Switzerland. Food editor of *The New York Times* for nearly 30 years, his books include *The New New York Times Cook Book*.

FELICITY CLARK Beauty director of British *Vogue*, she joined Condé Nast in 1964.

NICHOLAS COLERIDGE Features Editor of *Harpers & Queen*. An intrepid traveller, his last book, *Around the World in 78 Days*, took him in the steps of Phileas Fogg.

JACKIE COLLINS British novelist and author of blockbuster novels including *Hollywood Wives* and *Hollywood Husbands*. She is married to Oscar Lerman who owns the Tramp nightclubs in Los Angeles and London.

RICHARD COMPTON-MILLER British newspaper columnist and social observer, he is editor of the William Hickey column in the *Daily Express* and wrote the alternative *Who's Really Who*.

JASPER CONRAN See Fashion.

PATRICIA COPPLESON British-born journalist living in Sydney. She writes for *Vogue Australia* and is contributing editor to *Vogue Living Australia*.

OLIVIER COQUELIN Paris-born hotelier and club owner. Lives in New York and Haiti, where he co-owns Le Relais de L'Empereur and Plantation Cocoyer hotels and the Imperial Cocoyer Yacht Club.

HOWARD COSELL American sporting broadcaster for ABC since 1956. A former lawyer, he is the author of *Cosell* and *Like It Is*.

CANDIDA CREWE British journalist party-giver and -goer, she is the daughter of Quentin (see below) and has written 2 novels, *Focus* and *Romantic Hero*.

QUENTIN CREWE British writer, restaurateur and traveller. A partner in the Brasserie St Quentin and Spécialités de St Quentin in London, his books include *Great Chefs of France*, *In Search of the Sahara* and *The Last Maharaja*. He is currently writing a book on the Caribbean.

STEVEN CRIST *The New York Times* sports reporter specializing in racing.

SCOTT CROLLA Young British fashion designer and owner of the Crolla fashion shops in London and Tokyo.

ALAN CROMPTON-BATT British food expert and writer, a former Egon Ronay inspector. He is now a leading food consultant and PR and is working on books with Lady Elizabeth Anson and Nico Ladenis.

BARBARA DALY Top British make-up artist and Managing Director of Colouring Cosmetics. Her latest book is *New Looks*.

JOYCE DAVIDSON Canadian television personality living in New York. She hosts a daily news and current events programme, the *Joyce Davidson Show*, on CBC.

DAVID DAVIES Top British banker in Hong Kong, where he is Managing Director of the Hong Kong Land Co.

JUSTIN DE BLANK British restaurateur and grocer whose food shops in London are known for their high-quality produce.

MARC DE GONTAUT BIRON French-born socialite living in New York. Ex-Junior International Club, he broke away to form Club Biron, organizing smart social events.

INES DE LA FRESSANGE French house model for Chanel, the inspiration for many of Karl Lagerfeld's designs.

VANESSA DE LISLE A fashion editor of *Harpers & Queen* for 12 years, and now with British *Vogue*.

NIGEL DEMPSTER British journalist, gossip columnist and royal biographer. A former Grovel columnist for *Private Eye*, he is editor of the *Daily Mail* Diary.

COMTESSE DE PARIS Born Princesse Isabelle d'Orléans-Bragance, she is the wife of the Comte de Paris and has edited a book on class, *Haut de Gamme*.

ROBIN DERRICK British art director and fashion co-ordinator for *The Face* magazine. He spends about 4 nights a week nightclubbing in London.

RODNEY DILLARD British-born senior vice-president of Sotheby's in Palm Beach, USA.

PRIMROSE DUNLOP Australian social columnist for the *Sunday Telegraph*, she also contributes features to *The Australian*.

JAKE EBERTS Canadian founder and chief executive of the London film company, Goldcrest.

MEREDITH ETHERINGTON-SMITH An American fashion journalist living in England. Special correspondent to *W* magazine and London correspondent for Paris *Vogue*.

LEN EVANS British-born wine producer, writer and restaurateur based in Australia, where he co-owns Rothbury Estate winery in the Hunter Valley.

NICHOLAS FAITH British financial journalist and wine expert. He writes for *The Sunday Times*. His latest book is *Cognac*.

GEORGE FALKINER Australian property owner whose 4 properties are worth A$20 million. These include Haddon Rig in New South Wales, one of Australia's top 3 Merino sheep studs.

SERENA FASS British founder-director of Serenissima, the exclusive tour company. She travels extensively and loves India.

MICHAEL FISH British menswear designer who created jazzy shirts and kipper ties in the Sixties. He has made robes for Mohammed Ali and has been a TV fashion commentator on Royal Ascot.

DIANA "Bubbles" FISHER British-born social writer, television and radio personality based in Sydney. An ardent royalist, she has been an air stewardess and a ringmaster.

LILLIAN FRANK, MBE Australian hairdresser and journalist born in Burma. She has held hair shows in Paris, London, Rome and New York and is a regular social columnist for the *Melbourne Herald*.

LYNNE FRANKS Chairman of her own highly successful PR company in London, specializing in fashion. The main force behind Fashion Aid, her clients include Katharine Hamnett and the Labour Party.

DIANE FREIS American fashion designer based in Hong Kong. Managing Director of her own fashion company, her international clients include Elton John, Liza Minnelli and the Pointer Sisters.

MARCHESA BONA FRESCOBALDI Italian aristocrat whose Tuscany estate yields some of Italy's best wines.

DAVID FROST, OBE British film and television producer and presenter, a director of TV-am. Reputed to be the world's most travelled man, his books include *Who Wants to be a Millionaire?* and *I Could Have Kicked Myself (David Frost's Book of the World's Worst Decisions)*.

ANIKO GAAL Fashion buyer for the top fashion store Garfinckel's in Washington.

ANDREW GIBBONS Top Australian real estate agent, based in Sydney. He handled the A$8 million Toison d'Or sale in 1985.

CHRISTOPHER GIBBS Top British antique dealer who owns a respected New Bond Street shop.

JOHN GOLD British co-founder and host of Tramp nightclub in London.

SONDRA GOTLIEB Wife of the Canadian ambassador to Washington, she writes a column for the *Washington Post*.

DAVID GOWER Ex-England cricket captain, born on April Fool's Day. He has played in over 80 tests and scored more than 5000 test runs.

LUCINDA GREEN British 3-day eventer, 6 times champion of the Badminton Horse Trials and a member of the gold medal team at the 1984 Los Angeles Olympics. An elephant polo enthusiast.

GAEL GREENE Restaurant critic for the influential *New York Magazine* and contributor to their Best of New York issue. Her latest book is *Delicious Sex*.

TONY GREIG South African-born cricketer living in Sydney. Captained England's cricket team in the mid-Seventies and the World XI in Kerry Packer's World Series Cricket. Now Managing Director of an insurance company and cricket commentator for Channel 9.

AIDA GREY French-born beauty scientist living in Los Angeles. Author of the *Aida Grey Beauty Book*, she invented natural cosmetics, sold through her 75 salons in the US and Europe.

JENNY GUCCI Married to Paolo Gucci of the Gucci empire, Jenny is an opera singer, fashion expert and "professional shopper".

MICHEL GUERARD Top French chef and restaurateur. He created cuisine minceur for his health-conscious guests at Les Prés et les Sources spa at Eugénie-les-Bains, where he also runs his world-famous restaurant.

KATHARINE HAMNETT Trendsetting British fashion designer. She studied at St Martin's School of Art in London and founded her own company in 1979. Famous for her blatant T-shirts-with-a-message, such as "Stay alive in '85."

MARCELLA HAZAN Italian food expert, she has a cookery school in Bologna, runs courses in Venice and lives mainly in New York. Her books include *The Classic Italian Cookbook* and *The Second Classic Italian Cookbook*.

MARIE HELVIN An American top model, her mother is Japanese and she grew up in Hawaii. Now based in London, separated from photographer husband David Bailey, she writes on fashion and beauty and is the author of *Catwalk*.

MARGAUX HEMINGWAY Actress turned documentary film-maker and granddaughter of the legendary Ernest, about whom she has just made a film. She likes "grouse-hunting", helicopter skiing and, in her native Idaho, fishing.

ANOUSKA HEMPEL Australian-born beauty of Russian-German descent. A sometime actress, she owns the glamorous Blakes Hotel in London and is also a fashion and interior designer with her own showroom in Chelsea.

BILL HERSEY British socialite living in Tokyo, where he is advisor to some 30 nightclubs. His favourite is Lexington Queen. He writes a social column for *The Tokyo Weekender*.

DON HEWITSON New Zealand-born wine expert and writer who owns several top London wine bars.

DAVID HICKS The doyen of English interior design, his international assignments have ranged from Gatcombe Park, Princess Anne's house in Gloucestershire, to the Aeroflot offices.

STANLEY HO Hong Kong property magnate who runs most of Macao's casinos and hotels. He loves tennis and ballroom dancing.

ROMILLY HOBBS Owner of the top class grocers and caterers, Hobbs of Mayfair, London. Married to Lord McAlpine, she entertains on a grand scale.

WARREN HOGE Foreign editor on *The New York Times*, which he joined in 1977. He travels widely, often to his favourite country, Brazil.

DAVID HOLAH British co-founder (with Stevie Stewart) of the trendsetting fashion label, Body Map, and a keen nightclubber.

KEN HOM American-born Chinese cookery expert. He runs a food consultancy and has a cookery school in Hong Kong. His books include *Ken Hom's Encyclopaedia of Chinese Cookery Technique*.

SIMON HOPKINSON British head cook at the top London restaurant Hilaire. An ex-Cambridge chorister, he was an Egon Ronay inspector for 2 years.

IAN JAMIESON International authority on German wines, he has been in the trade for 28 years. Author, wine writer, lecturer and broadcaster, his books include the *Pocket Guide to German Wines*.

JEAN-MICHEL JAUDEL International businessman based in Paris, where he is a member of all the best clubs. He has a fine contemporary art collection.

HUGH JOHNSON International expert on wine and author of the definitive *Wine*, *World Atlas of Wine*, and the annual *Pocket Wine Guide*. Wine editor of *Cuisine* and president of the Wine Club, his other love is gardening and trees. He is currently researching a book on the history of wine.

CHRISTINE JONES Australian publisher of *Stiletto*, a leading Sydney youth lifestyle magazine.

STEPHEN JONES British milliner whose clients range from the Princess of Wales to model Yasmin Parvaneh, wife of Simon Le Bon. He creates hats for designers Jean-Paul Gaultier and Benny Ong.

BARBARA KAFKA American food expert and president of her own

New York food consultancy. Author of *Food for Friends* and a food column in US *Vogue*.

JENNY KEE Australian fashion designer who specializes in fabrics and knitwear. Owner of her own clothes shop, Flamingo Park, she loves painting.

LESLIE KENTON See Health and Beauty.

BETTY KENWARD Social editor of *Harpers & Queen*, she lives in Mayfair, London. At 80, she still attends every social event in Jennifer's Diary, which she has written since 1945. She regards the Queen's coronation as the most memorable occasion of her career.

JENNIFER KRAMER Travel Editor of *Town & Country*, based in New York.

NICO LADENIS Half-Greek, Tanzanian-born chef-owner of Chez Nico in Berkshire and owner of Chez Nico in London. A former economist, the volatile Nico is a self-taught chef.

MAX LAKE Australian writer and owner of Lakes Folly winery in the Hunter Valley. A former surgeon, he lives in Sydney, is a keen cook, and has written several books on Australian wine.

ELEANOR LAMBERT Head of her own top fashion PR company based in New York, she initiated the Best Dressed Lists. Top designer Donna Karan is one of her many clients.

ELISABETH LAMBERT ORTIZ London-born Latin American food writer of award-winning cookery books such as *The Book of Latin American Cooking*. She contributes regularly to *Gourmet* magazine.

WILLIE LANDELS Half-Italian half-Scottish editor and art director of *Harpers & Queen*, he also designs furniture, and was once a stage painter for La Scala in Milan.

WINSOME LANE Hong Kong journalist, ex-women's editor of the *South China Morning Post*.

ALEXANDRE LAZAREFF Lives in Paris where he works for the Ministry of Finance. An expert on Parisian nightlife, his book *Paris Rendez-Vous* gives ideas on what to do between 5 pm and 5 am.

RENE LECLER See Travel.

PRUE LEITH South African-born food expert living in London where she runs the prestigious Leith's School of Food and Wine, Leith's Restaurant and Leith's Good Food caterers. Cookery editor of *The Guardian*, she is author of *Leith's Cookery Course* and the *Cook's Handbook*.

DOREEN LEUNG Hong Kong food writer, director of Food World Advertising, programme hostess on Radio Hong Kong and a columnist for *The Metropolitan Weekly*.

PAUL LEVY See Food and Drink.

ALASTAIR LITTLE One of the new batch of top British chefs whose namesake restaurant is among the most fashionable in London.

JOHN LLOYD British tennis player who has twice won the Wimbledon mixed doubles championship with Australia's Wendy Turnbull. Married to Chris Evert, he travels the world on the tennis circuit.

KAI-YIN LO Top Chinese jewellery designer, educated in England and based in Hong Kong. Former head of PR at Mandarin Hotel, she is a well-known society figure.

SAUL LOCKHART Educated in Britain and France, he has lived in Hong Kong for 15 years and writes the *Insight Guide to Hong Kong* and the *Hong Kong Good Food Guide*.

SIMON LOFTUS Inspired director of Adnams of Southwold wine merchants and author of their wine list (compulsive reading *and* drinking).

FRANK LOWE British chairman and founder of top international advertising group Lowe Howard-Spink & Bell. He organizes the Stella Artois tennis tournament in London.

YUKI MAEKAWA Tokyo-born fashion expert. Living in London since 1976, she is currently researching antique costumes and contributes to Japanese fashion magazines.

MARIUCCA MANDELLI Italian head of design at Krizia in Milan. A former primary school teacher, she founded Krizia in the 1950s, and has worked with Karl Lagerfeld.

STANLEY MARCUS American Chairman emeritus of top Dallas store Neiman-Marcus. He is also a lecturer, marketing consultant and publisher of minature books.

LORD McALPINE OF WEST GREEN Conservative Party Treasurer in Britain and a director of Sir Robert McAlpine construction. He owns an antiquities business in London and a wildlife park in Australia.

PATRICK McCAUGHEY Australian Director of the National Gallery of Victoria where his father is Governor.

ANNE McNAIR-WILSON Young socialite who works for a photographic agency and the Comedy Store cabaret venue. She spends most nights clubbing and is involved in the London Limelight.

CLIFF MICHELMORE Widely travelled British television and radio broadcaster and producer, and presenter of BBC's *Holiday* programme.

HARRY M MILLER New Zealand-born impresario, theatrical agent and promotor of numerous theatrical and musical productions in Australia. A keen polo player.

KAILASH MISHRA Indian shoemaker based in New Delhi who fits royal feet all over the world, from Princess Anne to the Maharajah of Udaipur.

DAVID MLINARIC See Homes and Property.

ROBERT MONDAVI Internationally renowned California wine expert, he left the family winery, Charles Krug, in 1966 to found his own. He is now regarded as the moving spirit of the Napa Valley.

BRYAN MONTGOMERY London-based Managing Director of the Andry Montgomery group that organize major exhibitions worldwide.

DEBBIE MOORE Founder of the Pineapple Dance Studios, a British former model and Businesswoman of the Year. She has one studio in New York and three in London.

HANAE MORI A Japanese fashion designer, graduate in Japanese literature and theatrical costume designer. She has shops in Tokyo, Paris and New York.

BERNADINE MORRIS American chief fashion writer for *The New York Times* for 23 years, previously with *Women's Wear Daily*.

ANTON MOSIMANN Swiss-born Maître Chef des Cuisines at the Dorchester Hotel in London, considered one of the best chefs in the world. He travels round the world regularly to give lectures. Author of *Cuisine à la Carte*.

STIRLING MOSS See Sporting Life.

ANNE-ELISABETH MOUTET French correspondent for British *Elle* and *The Sunday Times*, she lives in Paris.

PEGGY MULHOLLAND Top American party planner, she divides her time between Newport Rhode Island, Palm Beach and New York. She is co-writing a book with Sandi Britton called *Perfect Parties*.

JEAN MUIR, CBE Top British fashion designer. She started her career as a designer for Jaeger in 1956 and is now internationally acclaimed. She is a Fellow of the Royal Society of Arts.

GEORGE NEGUS Australian radio and television broadcaster. One of the original presenters for *60 Minutes* in Australia, he now has a peak morning slot on Packer's radio network, and is a political interviewer on Channel 9.

ERIC NEWBY British travel editor of *The Observer* and author of a number of highly acclaimed, amusing travel books, including *A Short Walk in the Hindu Kush*, *Slowly Down the Ganges* and *On the Shores of the Mediterranean*.

ROBERT NOAH American food writer living in Paris. He runs Paris en Cuisine, a company specializing in gastronomic tours of France.

LORD OAKSEY OF TREVETHIN British racing expert and correspondent to *The Daily Telegraph*, *Sunday Telegraph* and *Horse and Hound*.

BRUCE OLDFIELD British fashion designer whose clients include the Princess of Wales, Charlotte Rampling and Joan Collins. Brought up in a Barnardo's home, he went on to train at St Martin's School of Art. He designed for Dior and Saint Laurent before opening his own shop in London.

BENNY ONG Chinese fashion designer brought up in Singapore. He now lives in London, running his own fashion business.

CATHERINE OXENBERG Daughter of Princess Elizabeth of Yugoslavia, one of the world's most successful models and star of the television series *Dynasty*. She was born in New York, educated in London and now lives in Beverly Hills.

SIR PETER PARKER British millionaire and highly successful businessman, best known for his 8 years as chairman of British Rail. In 1951 he stood for parliament for the Labour Party, and he is now chairman of Mitsubishi.

MICHAEL PARKINSON A television personality from Yorkshire, he presented his own BBC chat show, *Parkinson*, for 11 years, until 1982. He now divides his time between Sydney, where he does TV interviews and documentaries, and London, where he presents BBC Radio 4's *Desert Island Discs*.

ELISE PASCOE Australian cookery writer and consultant. A regular television and radio broadcaster, she also lectures and writes a weekly cookery column.

BOB PAYTON Larger-than-life Chicagoan based in London, where he owns several restaurants, including the Chicago Pizza Pie Factory. A keen huntsman with the Cottesmore.

ROBERT PERENO Young Anglo-Italian social figure and actor based in London. He organizes 2 party nights each week at Crazy Larry's nightclub in London.

NERIDA PIGGIN Australian fashion designer of resort wear. A former model (once ranked in the world top 10), she now divides her time between London and Sydney.

WOLFGANG PUCK Innovative Californian chef-owner of Los Angeles restaurants Chinois on Main and Spago and a regular on TV shows like *Good Morning America*.

CHARLOTTE RAMPLING British actress and former model, she lives in Paris with her children and musician husband Jean-Michel Jarre. Her films include *Georgy Girl*, *The Verdict* and *Stardust Memories*.

BILL RANKEN Australian country property PR for Andrew Gibbons Real Estate. A well-known social figure and property owner.

FREDERIC RAPHAEL British novelist and writer of screenplays, biographies, television plays and reviews. Novels include *The Glittering Prizes* and *Heaven and Earth*. He lives in England and the Dordogne in France.

JAN READ Leading British expert on Spanish and Portuguese wines. His books include *The Wines of Spain* and *The Wines of Portugal*.

JANET REGER British doyenne of lingerie, she revolutionized the undies industry in the Sixties by introducing beautifully made designs in natural fabrics. She is now working on a range of bed-linen and tableware.

SUSAN RENOUF Well-known social figure from Melbourne, the daughter of a politician. She commutes between Australia, New Zealand and England.

GEOFFREY ROBERTS Pioneer of California wines in the UK, he runs Les Amis du Vin in London. The exclusive agent for over 20 California wineries, he also has a selection under his own label.

JANCIS ROBINSON, MW British wine expert, *Sunday Times* wine correspondent, author of *Masterglass* and the *Great Wine Book*, television presenter of her own wine course, and contributor to magazines such as *A la Carte*.

BEVERLEY ROCKETT Expert on Canadian fashion, she has won awards for her fashion presentations on stage, film, TV and in the press. Fashion director of a large advertising company.

SALLY ROSSI FORD Australian travel agent. She works in Perth for the family travel company, Mary Rossi Travel.

CLAUDIA ROSSI HUDSON Sister of Sally Rossi Ford, a travel consultant specializing in tours outside Australia. She is a director of Mary Rossi Travel.

ROBERT SANGSTER British racehorse owner and breeder whose wins include the Derby and Prix de l'Arc de Triomphe. Son of pools founder Vernon Sangster and director of the family business, he lives in the Isle of Man.

VIDAL SASSOON Haircut supremo and founder of the worldwide hairdressing empire, now based in California. Born in London, he revolutionized the hair industry in the Sixties by inventing easy-to-manage "wash and wear hair".

ARNOLD SCAASI A Canadian fashion designer, he moved to the US in 1955 and is now their only couturier. He has dressed 2 First Ladies, Joan Rivers and Mrs Adnan Khashoggi.

LEO SCHOFIELD Australian PR and advertising expert, food and travel writer. He writes a weekly restaurant review and a Saturday column on Sydney for the *Sydney Morning Herald*.

SEBASTIAN SCOTT Co-editor of Eye-Q for *Harpers & Queen*, reporter for *Women's Hour* and researcher for the BBC. He is a keen clubber and passionate party giver.

JOAN SEVERANCE Top US model whose many magazine and TV appearances include the commercials for Revlon cosmetics.

BROOKE SHIELDS Ravishing actress who first appeared on television in a commercial at 11 months. Now 21, her films include *Pretty Baby*, *Blue Lagoon* and *Sahara*.

DAVID SHILLING See Nightlife.

DREW SMITH British food writer, editor of *The Good Food Guide* and co-editor of *The Good Food Directory*.

YAN-KIT SO London-based Chinese cookery expert from Hong Kong. Among her bestselling books are the award-winning *Yan-kit's Classic Chinese Cook Book* and *Wok Cookbook*. She also teaches cookery and writes for magazines.

STEVEN SPURRIER British wine expert who moved to Paris in 1970 to buy the highly regarded wine shop, Caves de la Madeleine. Founder of L'Académie du Vin, Paris's first wine school, his books include *Wine Course* and *French Country Wines*.

BLYTH AND GLORIA STALEY Australia's premier restaurateurs, they own Fanny's and Glo Glo's in Melbourne and Chez Oz in Sydney.

ARIANNA STASSINOPOULOS Greek author brought up in London and Athens, now living in California. Former president of the Cambridge Union, she has written biographies of Maria Callas and Pablo Picasso.

JOHN STEFANIDIS Leading interior designer based in London, he was born in Alexandria, Egypt. An Oxford graduate, he is renowned for his use of light and space.

TERRY TAN An Asian food expert, born in Singapore. A former journalist, he is now a food consultant in London, and author of *Strait's Chinese Cooking* and the *Complete Asian Cookbook*.

MOM RATCHAWONG THANADSRI SVASTI A Thai Prince born in Bangkok. Vice-president of the World Gastronomic Council, he also composes music, sings and hosts a cookery show for television and a daily radio programme.

TAKI THEODORACOPULOS Greek journalist and former karate champion known for his acerbic column in the *Spectator*. Based in London, he travels frequently around Europe and to New York, where he writes for *Esquire*.

DAN TOPOLSKI British journalist and former Olympic rower, he now coaches the Oxford University Boat Race crew. Son of Polish artist Feliks Topolski, he has travelled extensively in South America and Africa and has written several books on his expeditions.

JEREMIAH TOWER Top American chef, a pioneer of new Californian cuisine. Brought up in Europe, he owns the acclaimed Santa Fe Bar and Grill in Berkeley and Stars in San Francisco.

SHIZUO TSUJI Japanese head of the prestigious cookery school, Ecole Technique Hôtelière Tsuji in Osaka. He has written many books on food, travel and music, including *Japanese Cooking: A Simple Art*.

MURRAY TYRRELL Australian wine expert who owns a top winery in the Hunter Valley. His vineyard contains some of the oldest producing grapes in the area.

PETER USTINOV Multi-talented international actor, author, director and producer, star of countless films and plays. A gifted linguist, he lives in Switzerland and Paris.

GIANNI VERSACE Milan-based top Italian fashion designer renowned for developing new fabrics and for his designs in leather.

DIANE VON FURSTENBERG Belgian-born fashion designer now living in the US., She is president of her own companies dealing with clothes, jewellery and cosmetics.

PRINCE ALFONSO VON HOHENLOHE-LANGENBERG A Lichtensteiner educated in Switzerland and the US. He founded and built the Marbella Club, of which he is president, and now runs the new Anchorage Club in Mallorca.

DIANA VREELAND Respected former fashion editor of US *Harper's Bazaar* and US *Vogue*. Born in Paris and educated in Britain, she lives in New York where she is a consultant at the Costume Institute of the Metropolitan Museum of Art.

LESLIE WALFORD Leading Australian interior decorator and social figure.

SYLVIO WANG Hawaiian-born entrepreneur who owns a nightclub empire in the Far East, including the Casablanca club in Hong Kong.

ANTONY WATSON One of the richest men in Jamaica, he was educated in England and now runs the top hotel Plantation Inn at Ocho Rios.

AUBERON WAUGH British author, wine expert and editor of the *Literary Review*. Son of Evelyn Waugh and former diary writer for *Private Eye*.

DORIAN WILD English-born gossip columnist for the Sydney *Daily Telegraph*. A former political journalist in Canberra, he is well-known on the social scene.

ANNE WILLAN British food expert, writer and founding director of l'Ecole de Cuisine La Varenne in Paris. She lives in Washington.

CAROL WRIGHT British travel, cookery and health writer. She is travel correspondent for *House and Garden*.

LYNN WYATT Dynamic Texan socialite and patron of the arts, she dominates the Texan – and international – social and charity scene.

FRANCIS YEOH Young millionaire owner of My Place discothèque in Singapore. He has recently opened a resort hotel in Pangkor in Malaysia.

PETER YORK Cult British style writer, journalist and marketing consultant. Co-author, with Ann Barr, of *The Official Sloane Range Handbook*.

YUKI Japanese fashion designer based in London. He worked for Hartnell and Cardin before launching his own collection.

FOOD AND DRINK

by PAUL LEVY

WORLD'S BEST RESTAURANTS

1
ROBUCHON,
Paris

2
GIRARDET,
Crissier, Switzerland

3
MICHEL GUERARD,
Landes, France

4
KICCHO,
Tokyo

5
L'ESPERANCE,
Burgundy, France

6
SONG HE LOU,
Suzhou, China

7
TROISGROS,
Roanne, France

8
LE MANOIR AUX QUAT' SAISONS,
Oxfordshire, England

9
CHEZ PANISSE,
Berkeley, California

10
BEROWRA WATERS INN,
near Sydney

When it comes to food and drink, it is easy – in one sense – to identify the best. There are seldom any grounds for complaint about Petrossian's caviare; Mouton Rothschild is good even in indifferent years; and Krug Grande Cuvée has no bad ones.

This applies even to the humbler foodstuffs: the best haricot beans in the world are called Belles de Soissons just as certainly as the luxurious white truffle comes from Alba. Such knowledge, however, is not enough. Foodie perfection does not depend on Monsieur Poîlane's bread alone. The beans can be cooked badly, the truffle sliced too thickly. The champagne and the claret can be spoiled by serving them at the wrong temperature; and even Monsieur Petrossian's caviare is less enjoyable if eaten in the wrong surroundings or in disagreeable company.

That, of course, is why divine providence instituted restaurants – to remove these elements of haphazardness from the only pleasure most people experience three times a day. Yet no one could deny that some of the best gastronomic experiences happen outside the restaurant.

I still savour the memory of the foie gras I had in Julia Child's dining room near Grasse; a barbecue at Anton Mosimann's country cottage; a soufflé in Raymond Blanc's north Oxford kitchen; supper eaten off the silver thalis belonging to the Maharajah of Udaipur; and tasting a hitherto unknown California Chardonnay with Danny Kaye in his Beverly Hills living room.

Restaurants themselves don't have to be grand to provide experiences. I have seldom eaten better than at the hawkers' stalls of Singapore. My best ever breakfast was a bowl of rice porridge, congee, garnished with chillies and fried pig. And the best fish I've ever eaten was caught by a fisherman at Lau Fau Shan in the New Territories of Hong Kong, and cooked in little more than a shack – the restaurant Oi Man. In China itself, some of the best meals can be had in coaching inns in Sichuan, and some of the most elaborately confected dishes

I've ever tasted are served in the brutal concrete surroundings of the Song He Lou restaurant in Suzhou. One of the best is Mandarin fish in the shape of a squirrel, party trick of the great chef Liu Chih.

But finally, of course, it all boils down to France. At my first three-star meal, at Charles Barrier's restaurant in Tours, I was bowled over equally by my first taste of foie gras de canard and by the absurdity of the Donald Duck terrine in which it was served. On another occasion, a Lyons restaurateur detected the symptoms of crise de foie from our demeanour, and sent us a whole raw black Périgord truffle with a knife and salt cellar. And no gastronomic experience has matched up to Paul Bocuse himself making purée de pommes de terre for my 10-month-old daughter, who was hidden away in a Moses basket in his restaurant.

Perhaps the best meal I've ever had was designed specially for us by the great Michel Guérard at Eugénie-les-Bains. To the Foodie, anything more than the names of the dishes will be superfluous: salade à la grive de vigne, coquille Saint-Jacques à la coque, foie gras grillé aux navets confits, millefeuille à la reinette sauce caramel. We drank a Condrieu with the first two courses and a Château d'Yquem with the last two. Now *that's* perfection.

King Foodie PAUL LEVY was born in Kentucky in 1941. A graduate of the Universities of Chicago, London, Harvard and Oxford, his all-consuming passion is food and drink, the pursuit of which regularly leads him around the globe. Food and wine editor of *The Observer*, and co-author of *The Official Foodie Handbook*, he lives – and cooks – in a farmhouse near Oxford with his wife and two daughters.

EUROPE

BEST RESTAURANTS

★

1 ROBUCHON, Paris
2 GIRARDET, Crissier, Switzerland
3 MICHEL GUERARD, Landes, France
4 L'ESPERANCE, Burgundy
5 TROISGROS, Roanne, France
6 LE MANOIR AUX QUAT' SAISONS, Oxfordshire, England
7 L'OASIS, La Napoule, France
8 LUCAS CARTON, Paris
9 DORCHESTER GRILL ROOM, London
10 DIE AUBERGINE, Munich, Germany

ENGLAND

LONDON

BEST RESTAURANTS

ENGLISH

CONNAUGHT HOTEL, Carlos Place, W1 ☎ (01) 499 7070. The first great English hotel kitchen to be resurrected by a European – Michel Bourdin, whose style is classic and immaculate. The restaurant and Grill serve both trad English and French food. *"It has tremendous elegance and interesting people around you as you eat – there is usually a cabinet minister, usually someone you know. The clientele and atmosphere are great. The best restaurant in the country"* (Richard Compton-Miller). *"The Grill Room still has the quality, that magic: if you go there for Sunday lunch, there is always somebody wonderful, looking beautiful in a black hat, or some fat old art dealer – it's a lovely left-over bit of London which hasn't changed"* (Anouska Hempel). The croustade d'oeufs de caille Maintenon (quail's egg yolks in a pastry boat) is Lord Lichfield's all-time favourite hors d'oeuvre.

DORCHESTER HOTEL, Park Lane, W1 ☎ (01) 629 8888. The Terrace Restaurant is what all the gallic fuss is about, while the Grill Room serves supreme English dishes, including *"the best bread and butter pudding"* (Jancis Robinson) and *"the best smoked salmon available in any restaurant in England"* (Paul Levy). The old joke "Q: What's the difference between God and Anton Mosimann? A: Anton Mosimann is everywhere EXCEPT in the Dorchester kitchens" may have to be taken with a pinch of sodium-free salt, but it is wise to check that this Swiss phenomenon is cooking before going along to sample some of the most accomplished and carefully considered dishes in town. His new style is "cuisine naturelle" – no cream, butter, the minimum of sugar, salt – all part of the Keep Britons Clean campaign.

GREEN'S CHAMPAGNE AND OYSTER BAR, 36 Duke St, SW1 ☎ (01) 930 4566. Fine oysters, salmon, beef, ham and English school food are consumed by pinstriped St James's and racing types, such as Robert Sangster, in gentlemen's clubby surroundings.

WILTON'S, 55 Jermyn St, SW1 ☎ (01) 629 9955. After its bombing and subsequent closure, Wilton's, the haunt of peers and clubmen, has reopened in elegant new premises. Emphasis on seafood, fish and game. *"For good plain eating – high-quality fish and chips"* (Michael Parkinson). *"If I'd been away in the desert, I would most want to eat a dozen oysters from Wilton's – the best"* (Quentin Crewe).

ECLECTIC

Foodies traditionally used to look down their noses at anything less than pure French cuisine. "International" suggested unoriginal, cribbed cuisine. Now it's fashionable and daring to draw on and develop the best ideas and flavours of other great cuisines of the world. *"There has been a change in outlook because there is so much written about food now that it has totally opened up the field. But although I love fiery flavours and have different dishes like gravad lax on my menus, I still think you can't beat French traditional cooking, because it is so deeply satisfying and comforting"* (Simon Hopkinson).

ALASTAIR LITTLE, 49 Frith St, W1 ☎ (01) 734 5183. This is where food's at – modern Anglo-French cuisine, placed in front of an appreciative image-conscious crowd. Having made his name in smooth refuges of London's media meritocracy, such as L'Escargot and 192 (192 Kensington Park Rd, W11 ☎ (01) 229 0482, which, under Angela Dwyer's reign, still features fondly in the lives of the Notting Hill set), Alastair Little went on to open his own, brilliantly successful restaurant. It instantly scooped up the cream of the local designer/advertising/PR set at lunchtime, while attracting all sorts for dinner (*"I hate restaurants where the customers are all from one age group or one section of society"* – Alastair Little).

“ The state of eating out has never been greater or more glorious in the history of the country. The clientele is becoming Yuppy-ized, as in America. There is a new class of restaurant-goer ... Hairdressers and people in advertising are keeping it alive – although you won't want to sit next to them and listen to their conversation ”

(PAUL LEVY)

BLAKES HOTEL, 33 Roland Gardens, SW7 ☎ (01) 370 6701. Anouska Hempel's ritzy hotel has an outstanding restaurant: *"I was one of the first to mix Japanese, French and Indian food on the same menu and now everybody's doing it. I go to great pains with my presentation and the sauces I invent. I design and decorate food as much as I design and decorate everything"* (Anouska Hempel). She's right, of course – this is dining in exotica, gorgeously black and mirrored, with oriental lacquer and bamboo, and tables laid alternately in black and white with contrasting plates that offset couture dishes perfectly. *"The best caviare"* (David Frost).

LE CAPRICE, Arlington House, Arlington St, SW1 ☎ (01) 629 2239. The most fashionable dinery in town. The L-shaped room of black and chrome offsets a glittering international crew of film, fashion (Bruce Oldfield loves it) and media stars. *"A better place than Langan's to see the crème de la crème these days. Really high, heavy fashion people"* (Bob Payton). *"Very comfortable and the food is of a very high standard"* (Felicity Clark).

CLARKE'S, 124 Kensington Church St, W8 ☎ (01) 221 9225. Brilliant restaurant cooked up by inspired young chef Sally Clarke, who trained at Michael's in Los Angeles. The influence is nouvelle Californie – much marinating, charcoal grilling and experimental partnering of flavours.

L'ESCARGOT, 48 Greek St, W1 ☎ (01) 437 2679. The upstairs restaurant has long been a retreat for pleading-poor publishers, agents, filmy folk and other media types, though some regulars have defected to the Groucho. Downstairs is cheaper, relaxed and fashionable, with a decent – though not always reliable – brasserie menu. Appreciative habitués include grapies Steven Spurrier, Auberon Waugh and Jancis Robinson (wife of Nick Lander, who runs the place).

HILAIRE, 68 Old Brompton Rd, SW7 ☎ (01) 584 8993. Simon Hopkinson is one of the culinary stars of today. His style, which has been described as "cuisine éclectique", is influenced by French (presentation, panache), English, Thai and other cuisines, all whizzed up in the food processor to his own modern recipe, using the best of what's in season. His keenest fan, Sir Terence Conran, will soon be his new boss at the new Conran restaurant in the Michelin building.

LANGAN'S BRASSERIE, Stratton St, W1 ☎ (01) 493 6437. Think of glitz and you think of Langan's, though the glamour is sometimes tarnished by a brassy sub-pop-star set and, for novices, by the rumbustious proprietor Peter L. *"I probably enjoy being in Langan's as much as anywhere. It's the combination of people, and it's a big room which I love. But don't ever go during Ascot Week because all the East Enders go in their tails and 4-day stubble ..."* (Bob Payton). Nevertheless, a *face* is bound to be there: paparazzo Richard Young checks in most evenings for gossip column fodder. Part-owner Michael Caine is no

❝ The best service is service gladly given. If something's wrong with the food, you want to be able to complain without some stroppy waiter going away in high dudgeon. Most people are so frightened of waiters now, they daren't complain about anything ❞ (MARK BIRLEY)

Young bloods

PHILIP BRITTEN (London's Chez Nico), SALLY CLARKE (Clarke's), NICK GILL (Hambleton Hall), SIMON HOPKINSON (Hilaire) and ALASTAIR LITTLE (Alastair Little) are the brightest stars of the new generation of chefs. *"Chefs like these represent a young fusion between French and British influences. The future belongs to them"* (Paul Levy). *"They are incredibly talented. They follow the modern trend of lightness and simplicity"* (Nico Ladenis).

news – he *lives* in the place when in town: clock Mick Jagger, Jerry Hall, David Bowie, Bryan Ferry or Catherine Oxenberg instead: or Michael Parkinson, tucking into his favourite starter – spinach soufflé with anchovy sauce.

“The best lamb comes fresh from South Wales, the best scallops from Cornwall, ice cream and tomatoes from Italy, oranges from Spain, grapes from Belgium, pineapples from Hawaii, pink grapefruit from Texas, cos lettuce, Cox's apples and asparagus from England – and nothing can beat English strawberries” (ANTON MOSIMANN)

“It's silly to bring things from right round the world when you can get good fresh food here in Britain, like samphire [sea asparagus – the latest hip ingredient], a European marsh plant that can be served fresh or pickled with oysters. Some of the best comes from Norfolk. We have excellent Somerset plums and apples, and the best berries” (ALASTAIR LITTLE)

FRENCH

LE GAVROCHE, 43 Upper Brook St, W1 ☎ (01) 408 0881. Fantastically complex cuisine under the skilled thumb of Albert Roux. Steep prices make you savour every precious mouthful. The set lunch menu at £19.50 (US$28) allows you a few bargain swallows. Both Lord Lichfield and Anouska Hempel think the Soufflé Suissesse is heaven on earth: Stanley Marcus enjoys it all.

TANTE CLAIRE, 68 Royal Hospital Rd, SW3 ☎ (01) 946 4431. A really superb, innovative, modern French menu. Fish and seafood reign supreme, attended by luscious sauces: every plate is a picture. *"I still think this is the best cooking in London"* (Prue Leith). Gloria Staley agrees. *"The best foie gras on toast"* (Auberon Waugh).

L'ARLEQUIN, 123 Queenstown Rd, SW8 ☎ (01) 622 0555. It seemed as though Christian Delteil's fearsomely French restaurant would rule the roost when Nico Ladenis cut for the country, but neighbouring Chez Nico has maintained its standards. Charming terrace setting, terrific puddings – and waiters who are wont to patronize. *"Top-quality French food"* (Steven Spurrier).

ST QUENTIN, 243 Brompton Rd, SW3 ☎ (01) 589 8005. Quentin Crewe's restaurant (and his favourite restaurant) is trendy and busy. Brasserie food at restaurant prices.

CHEZ NICO, 129 Queenstown Rd, SW8 ☎ (01) 720 6960. Although Nico has gone to Shinfield (see Country restaurants), he has left his London restaurant in the capable culinary hands of Philip Britten. Starry regulars are loyal, some wickedly suggesting that the place is better for the crazy Greek's absence.

NINETY PARK LANE, Grosvenor House Hotel, 90 Park Lane, W1 ☎ (01) 499 6363. The godchild of Louis Outhier, under the auspices of Trust House Forte, is a civilized Foodie haven. *"You sit on chintz sofas at a table with Lord Forte's family portraits looking down on you. One of the most agreeable restaurants in London"* (Paul Levy). *"Unusual ideas – John Dory with mango, the French fish St Pierre – gorgeous food"* (Elisabeth Lambert Ortiz).

LE SUQUET, 104 Draycott Ave, SW3 ☎ (01) 581 1785. A cheerful little place where *"It's as if you're sitting in Monte Carlo or Cannes harbour hearing the clinking masts. The best and my most favourite for French fish and seafood. Their plateau de fruits de mer would rival any, even in France – a cork platter covered in seaweed, scallops, winkles, oysters, crab – every seafood imaginable"* (Richard Compton-Miller). *"I love it here"* (Catherine Oxenberg).

ITALIAN

CECCONI'S, 5a Burlington Gdns, W1 ☎ (01) 434 1509. The most authentic and second most expensive Italian restaurant in Britain (Harry's takes the biscotti). Patronized largely by visiting Italian newspaper and publishing magnates and American millionaires. *"They make very good minestrone and very good pasta with truffles – it's outstanding. I was surprised to find such a very fine restaurant in London"* (Robert Mondavi).

HARRY'S BAR, 26 South Audley St, W1 ☎ (01) 408 0844. Private dining club, owned jointly by Mark Birley and James Sherwood (Orient Express/Cipriani chief). Carefully designed à la Harry's in Venice, with all the hallmarks of Birley's taste, it has an idolatrous clientele of jetsetters – business tycoons and smartly turned-out women. *"If I had to eat in one place for the rest of my life, it would be in Harry's Bar. It has the best food, day in, day out"* (Stanley Marcus). A favourite of Prue Leith, Susan Renouf, Anouska Hempel, Michael Parkinson, Joan Burstein, Robert Sangster and Romilly Hobbs, who loves the bitter chocolate ice cream.

CHINESE

CHUEN CHENG KU, 17 Wardour St, W1 ☎ (01) 437 1398. On Sundays, 4 storeys' worth of mainly Chinese eaters tuck into the best dim sum in London. One of Chinese food lover Anton Mosimann's top 3.

DIAMOND, 23 Lisle St, W1 ☎ (01) 437 2517. Cheap, classic Cantonese. The Diamond is Anton Mosimann's best friend.

KEN LO'S MEMORIES OF CHINA, 67 Ebury St, SW1 ☎ (01) 730 7734. Upmarket restaurant, where subtle, creative combinations are achieved under the direction of the venerable Ken Lo, who introduced Britain to the heights of oriental cuisine. Another Mosimann favourite.

TAI PAN, 8 Egerton Garden Mews, SW3 ☎ (01) 589 8287. Lord Lichfield's Chinese restaurant attracts the ritzy Knightsbridge set. The Princess of Wales has been spotted here, perhaps attracted by the Tiger's Whiskers on the menu. If these don't tickle your fancy, there is plenty more to tempt your palate.

JAPANESE

SUNTORY, 72 St James's St, SW1 ☎ (01) 409 0201. The grandest Japanese restaurant, divided in 3. In the Teppan-Yaki room, you sit round a table-cum-griddle, where the chef performs the cooking rites on tender steaks and fish before your eyes. *"Their method of cooking is light, alive, fresh. They use very little butter, so the flavour of the delicacies comes through"* (Raymond Blanc).

INDIAN

♨ **BOMBAY BRASSERIE, Bailey's Hotel, Courtfield Close, Courtfield Rd, SW7 ☎ (01) 370 4040.** The best Indian restaurant in Britain. A slice of old colonial life with ceiling fans and a conservatory. All the Raj with smart and fashionable Indophiles. Set-price buffet lunch: brilliantly refined dishes from a variety of regions in the evening. Anton Mosimann loves the Mango Bellini.

BEST TEAS

"My favourite meal of all is tea, eaten from my own china tea set (Interlude, by Coalport), complete with toast rack and muffin dishes to keep crumpets warm. You shouldn't eat too much for tea, or you'll get fat, but I love home-made jam and Jackson's Earl Grey tea" (David Shilling).

Very genteel English teas are served in the salons of the best London hotels: Indian or China teas, mere slivers of cucumber sandwiches that make the daintiest of eaters seem ham-fisted, light scones, fresh cream and jam, delicate cakes and smooth, old-fashioned service. The best are: the RITZ, London, at £8.50 (US$11) a head the most expensive, the most famous and, inevitably, the most tourist-ridden (so book); BROWN'S, 20–24 Dover St, W1 ☎ (01) 493 6020; CLARIDGE'S, Brook St, W1 ☎ (01) 629 8860 and the DORCHESTER, Park Lane, W1 ☎ (01) 629 8888. The best tea shop, according to Paul Levy, is WHITTARD & CO, 111 Fulham Rd, SW3 ☎ (01) 589 4621, who stock around 50 teas and tisanes.

BEST VALUE FOOD

LA BERSAGLIERA, 372 King's Rd, SW3 ☎ (01) 352 5993. Tiny, terrifically trendy, always packed. Garlicky pizzas, fresh pasta, great house white.

CHICAGO PIZZA PIE FACTORY, 17 Hanover Sq, W1 ☎ (01) 629 2669. One of the original American restaurants in London, the first of Bob Payton's empire. Authentic deep dish pizzas, crispy potato skins, wise-guy menus.

CHICAGO RIB SHACK, 1 Raphael St, SW7 ☎ (01) 581 5595. A Payton fast fooderie: the meatiest (and messiest) ribs in town (bibs are supplied); crowd-pulling crispy onion loaf.

BEST CAFES AND BARS

LA BRASSERIE, 272 Brompton Rd, SW3 ☎ (01) 584 1668. Chelsea café society sit outside on the pavement. Best for Sunday brunch with the papers – freshly squeezed orange juice, kippers, piping croissants and brisk aproned waiters.

CRITERION BRASSERIE, 222 Piccadily, W1 ☎ (01) 839 7133. Food is not the point, it's just one of the most fabulous pieces of architecture in London – grand, lofty, mosaic'd ceilings and tiled floors – a bit like a Roman baths, with round café tables and newspapers in the front half. *"The most beautiful building in town, and the bar and brasserie end are nice"* (Prue Leith).

DOME, 354 King's Rd, SW3 ☎ (01) 352 7611. French-style café-bar, buzzing with aware young film/pop people – one of the hippest meeting points in town.

MARINE ICES, 8 Haverstock Hill, NW3 ☎ (01) 485 2528. The best ice cream in London, according to Drew Smith.

RANOUSH SNACK BAR, 43 Edgware Rd, W1 ☎ (01) 723 5929. *"One of London's funniest café-bars. Brilliant fruit cocktails served until 2 am. There's a duck pond in the middle of the room with plastic ducks"* (David Shilling).

TRADER VIC'S, London Hilton, Park Lane, W1 ☎ (01) 493 8000. Famous for their Scorpion, a cocktail invented by Trader himself that hangs over the consciousness of smarties in the know. Lemon and orange juice, orgeat syrup, brandy and light Puerto Rican rum blended with crushed ice and garnished with a fresh gardenia form the deadly beast.

BEST CATERER

LEITH'S GOOD FOOD, 1 Sebastian St, EC1 ☎ (01) 251 0216. It is Prue Leith's catering firm that feeds the hungry travellers on the Venice Simplon-Orient-Express. Superb personal service for weddings, banquets and cocktail parties; they can arrange the whole party package – marquees, bands, florists.

BEST FOOD SHOPS

♨ **CHARBONNEL ET WALKER, 28 Old Bond St, W1 ☎ (01) 629 4396; 2 Knights Arcade, Brompton Rd, SW1 ☎ (01) 581 3117.** Masters of presentation, the royal chocolatiers were established in 1875 and patronized by Edward VII. Top-quality dark chocs come in floral mini hat-boxes or the famous boîte blanche, which gives you carte blanche to fill the box to your whim: when it's chock-full, it's surrounded by a message of chocolate letters and tied with one of 48 coloured ribbons. The Knightsbridge branch contains a library where, coffee in hand, you can be guided, longingly, through their complete range. Speciality: a chocolate champagne bottle filled with Heidsieck-flavoured truffles.

Tea leaves

They wouldn't swop their brews for all the tea in China: *"Twinings Lapsang; tisanes like lemon mist made by Celestial Seasoning herb teas – a blend of rosehip, hibiscus, etc"* (Justin de Blank); *"Twinings Earl Grey"* (Craig Claiborne); *"Twinings"* (Paul Levy); *"I've been drinking Jackson's Earl Grey ever since they stopped putting Black Russian into tea bags: a very black day"* (David Shilling).

HARRODS, Knightsbridge, SW1 ☎ (01) 730 1234. Still regarded as home of the most beautiful and comprehensive food halls in existence. *"The best place for cheese – in fact it has the best food hall in the world. It's even better than places like Fauchon in Paris"* (Bob Payton). *"The best fresh fish – they have wonderful displays"* (Lord Lichfield). *"Food you can eat right away – the definition of a good food shop"* (Marcella Hazan). *"Very good – you can't beat it"* (Robert Mondavi). Stanley Marcus, Ken Hom and Alan Crompton-Batt hold it in equally high esteem.

R ALLEN & CO, 117 Mount St, W1 ☎ (01) 499 5831. Old-fashioned Mayfair butcher, widely regarded as the best. A striking array of joints, with white rabbits and pheasants in the window.

BERNIGRA ICE CREAM PARLOUR, 69 Tottenham Court Rd, W1 ☎ (01) 580 0950. Superb smooth Italian ices in rich, tangy fruit flavours or creamy coconut, hazelnut, etc.

BOUCHERIE LAMARTINE, 229 Ebury St, SW1 ☎ (01) 730 4175. Owned by the Roux brothers. Paul Levy recommends their fine French cuts of meat; also bread from Maison Blanc.

CAMISA & SON, 61 Old Compton St, W1 ☎ (01) 437 4686. The best Italian deli in London – a ceiling full of salamis and parma hams, fresh pasta, cheeses and all the trimmings. Hardened tortelloni testers Drew Smith, Auberon Waugh and Alan Crompton-Batt give it their seal of approval.

FORTNUM & MASON, 181 Piccadilly, W1 ☎ (01) 734 8040. Hushed, carpeted food hall, locked in a time warp, with a liveried doorman and black morning-coated attendants. Traditional English foods – Stilton (*"the best cheese in the world"* – Craig Claiborne), hams, good vegetables – plus packaged goods, such as mustard, preserves and chocolates under their own suave wraps. Anton Mosimann and Steven Spurrier are just 2 Fortnum's fans.

HOBBS & CO, 29 South Audley St, W1 ☎ (01) 409 1058. Romilly Hobbs's shop stocks provisions from all over the world, plus home-made dishes of the day, chocolate cakes and truffles. Memorable hampers. *"They have a lovely selection of French cheeses, and wonderful Australian lime juice"* (Felicity Clark).

H R HIGGINS, 42 South Molton St, W1 ☎ (01) 499 5912. The best coffee suppliers, full of beans from around the world; roast-to-measure service.

JEROBOAMS, 24 Bute St, SW7 ☎ (01) 225 2232. A Prue Leith favourite, specializing in unpasteurized French cheeses and English farmhouse cheeses. Up to 120 varieties, including some from Androuet in Paris. Wines to suit the cheeses, too.

JUSTIN DE BLANK, 42 Elizabeth St, SW1 ☎ (01) 730 0605. A highly favoured deli for ready-made dishes – goulash, quiches, salads, meringues, tarts – special sausages, cheeses and home-baked breads from his Hygienic Bakery.

LA MAISON DES SORBETS, 140 Battersea Park Rd, SW11 ☎ (01) 720 8983. *"Run by a marvellous guy, Julian Tomkins, whose sorbets turn up at posh shops"* (Prue Leith). Tomkins learnt to make sorbets in France and now produces exquisite flavours – from passion fruit to tomato to Earl Grey tea – in sorbet or soufflé form, presented, if you wish, on a crisp nougatine basket.

MARKS & SPENCER at branches nationwide. *"The best every-day foods, because they buy their goods from the best*

Coffee nuts

These are the favourites of committed coffee drinkers: *"Jamaican Blue Mountain"* (Lord Lichfield); *"Columbian"* (Drew Smith); *"a blend of Robusta and Arabica – I always take my own blend with me to restaurants"* (Raymond Blanc); *"Arabic coffee, not too strongly roasted; we have our own blend at the restaurant"* (Michel Guérard); *"the best coffee I've had in my life was brewed in a tin kettle with cardamom in the Sinai desert at 3 in the morning, just under the walls of St Catherine's monastery – nothing has ever tasted that good since"* (Anne-Elisabeth Moutet).

producers. Their kippers come from Lock Fyne and their pork pies from Pork Farms. It's hard to beat Marks" (Lord Lichfield). Their ready-made gourmet dishes, particularly fish and seafood, slip down a treat and their fruit and vegetables are good quality if expensive. Votes go to their chocolate mousse (just like the real, home-made, thing), gooseberry fool (ditto) and fresh cream chocolate truffles.

PANZER, 24 Notting Hill Gate, W11 ☎ (01) 229 0822. *"The best smoked salmon in London"* (Lynne Franks); *"Best smoked salmon and cream cheese bagels"* (Jancis Robinson).

PAXTON & WHITFIELD, 93 Jermyn St, SW1 ☎ (01) 930 9892. 200-year-old purveyors of choice cheeses. Went through a crumbly phase but now has the cream of English and continental cheeses. *"Wonderful shop, a beautiful selection"* (Anton Mosimann); Drew Smith concurs.

ROCOCO, 321 King's Rd, SW3 ☎ (01) 352 5857. Trendy shop with cherub frescoes, run by Chantal Coady. Classic English chocs and fresh cream truffles nestle next to imported smooth Swiss and Pyrenean chocolates.

ROSSLYN DELICATESSEN, 56 Rosslyn Hill, NW3 ☎ (01) 431 2309. *"The best shop in England for ready-prepared, smoked and preserved foods, and cheese – over 120 types, at their peak because there is such a high turnover. It's French-owned, by M Bellier, but uninhibited by regionalism. The best Jewish foods in England"* (Paul Levy). *"The best grocer's in London"* (Jancis Robinson).

LES SPECIALITES ST QUENTIN, 256 Brompton Rd, SW3 ☎ (01) 225 1664. Quentin Crewe's terribly French pâtisserie sells exquisite tartlets and flans that tug on the purse strings. *"Once you try the shop you'll regret it – you'll spend an awful lot of money in it! It really is good – everything is home-made and French. The chocolate cake is the best thing"* (Quentin Crewe).

STEVE HATT, 88 Essex Rd, N1 ☎ (01) 226 3963. A family business with the best-quality fresh and home-smoked fish (*"The best salmon come from the Tay – my father has a love affair with the Tay"* – Steve Hatt). Alert them a day in advance, and your fish is their command: they'll scale the market next morning for anything you desire, and prepare it any way you ask – for sushi, say. Also Beluga caviare and other delicacies.

COUNTRY

BEST RESTAURANTS

The best dining in the country is generally at country-house hotels. Exemplary standards at GRAVETYE MANOR, HAMBLETON HALL, MILLER HOWE, CROMLIX HOUSE and INVERLOCHY CASTLE (see TRAVEL).

ECLECTIC

CARVED ANGEL, 2 South Embankment, Dartmouth, Devon ☎ (08043) 2465. The best of British ingredients prepared with French flair by Joyce Molyneux.

GIDLEIGH PARK, Chagford, Devon ☎ (06473) 2367. Real food in a superb country-house hotel. Innovative handling of the freshest of ingredients, from lobster and foie gras to leeks and brains. *"A cosy country house with the additional splendours of imaginative, tasty menus and an outstanding wine list"* (Michael Broadbent). *"The best cream tea – their clotted cream and strawberry jam are to die for"* (Bob Payton).

SHARROW BAY, Howtown Rd, Ullswater, Cumbria ☎ (08536) 301. A lakeside hotel whose kitchens produce delicious, gastronomic, calorific feasts – rich, wondrous sauce combinations of wine, cream, butter, spirits and stocks; fine fish and game, sinful puddings.

FRENCH

♔LE MANOIR AUX QUAT' SAISONS, Church Rd, Great Milton, Oxfordshire ☎ (08446) 8881. This 15th century manor is a calming, pastel-toned showcase for one of the best restaurants in the world, with Raymond Blanc at the helm. It's also a small hotel, so that purring punters can make a weekend of it. *"I think the best meal I've had anywhere was at Le Manoir"* (Bob Payton). It's also Jancis Robinson's best in Britain. Michael and Shakira Caine's too.

"The prettiest and most dramatic dessert we do is Petit Paquet Surprise du Manoir – Mandarin ice cream with flakes of caramel inside, wrapped in a parcel of finest pastry, with sugar ribbons, sealed with a sugar flower, served in passion fruit juice. It has everything – the sweet juice, melting refreshing ice, the crunch of the sugar and the pretty pastel colours – you would kill yourself for another one" (Raymond Blanc).

CHEZ NICO, The Old Vicarage, Church Lane, Shinfield, Berkshire ☎ (0734) 883783. Sensational cuisine from Nico Ladenis, but rather too sensational in other repects – it is no secret that if you insult Nico by asking for

❝ Under a Conservative government everything is tighter – people think in terms of investing money instead of spending it on food. Conservative people are the worst customers. Socialists are more intellectual and sophisticated; they love wine. The more Conservatives there are in England, the worse it is for the restaurant trade ❞ (NICO LADENIS)

❝ The best French restaurants in the world in the next 10 years are not going to be in France, because with the socialist government they've got and the way they're running the country, everyone is getting out. Bocuse has a restaurant in Japan and he's involved in this thing down at Disneyworld, Raymond Blanc's over here [England], another guy's in Dallas – they're everywhere. They're all jumping ship. *All* the great French chefs are going to be cooking in other places ❞ (BOB PAYTON)

melba toast or Irish coffee, say, it could result in the swift termination of your dinner and your coats in a heap by the door. Nico's culinary expertise remains unchallenged. Raymond Blanc's best in Britain. Menus change with the seasons.

WATERSIDE INN, Ferry Rd, Bray, Berkshire ☎ (0628) 20691. In what is perhaps the most expensive restaurant in Britain, Michel Roux rules as his brother rules in London. The Waterside holds 3 Michelin stars; food and clientele are on the nouvellish side. *"Delicious food, fine dining; very romantic being by the river with swans floating by"* (Lynn Wyatt). *"Michel Roux's charm and deftness of touch and a beautiful riverside situation"* (Michael Broadbent). *"Amazing professionalism – typical grand French food, enormously impressive"* (Justin de Blank).

BEST FOOD SHOPS

MAISON BLANC, 3 & 3a Woodstock Rd, Oxford, Oxfordshire ☎ (0865) 54974. The best bread and croissants in the world according to Paul Levy, Jane Grigson, and, unsurprisingly, Raymond Blanc. *"The croissants are better even than French ones – flaky and light, buttery but not oozy, not sticky, and they don't fall apart in your lap. You'd never butter – or better – them; wonderful to look at, too. And because they're so buttery, they freeze perfectly"* (Paul Levy). *"Seriously the best bakery. We supply all the best hotels in London and there is quite simply nothing to beat it."* (Raymond Blanc).

COLCHESTER OYSTER FISHERY, North Farm, East Mersea, Colchester, Essex ☎ (0206) 384141. The best English oysters and clams. Smarties get them sent in the post.

FITZBILLIES, 52 Trumpington St, Cambridge, Cambridgeshire ☎ (0223) 352500. Sticky cakes (*"The best coffee sponge"* – Justin de Blank), brioches, buns, bread, croissants and 32 varieties of chocolates, all home-made.

MINOLA SMOKERIES, Filkins, Lechlade, Gloucestershire. Oak-smoked wild Scottish salmon with an almost buttery melt-in-the-mouth consistency. Try it at the Lords of the Manor hotel (see TRAVEL).

TOFFEE SHOP, 7 Brunswick Rd, Penrith, Cumbria ☎ (0768) 62008. The best fudge in England, according to Jancis Robinson, and *"easily the best in the world"* (Lord Lichfield). People in the know arrange mail order.

WELLS STORES, Bull Corner, Reading Rd, Streatley-on-Thames, Berkshire ☎ (0491) 872367. Patrick Rance (now retired) is renowned for his finely tuned nose which has sniffed out a brilliant and expansive range of superb cheeses. His son Hugh now runs the shop. *"The ripest smelling shop in Europe. Rance not only knows the names of the cheesemakers, but sometimes even the names of the cows"* (Paul Levy). He also sells the best olive oil in the country.

SCOTLAND

BEST RESTAURANTS

CHAMPANY INN, Champany Corner, Linlithgow, W Lothian ☎ (050683) 4532. The best steak and beef in Great Britain. Clive Davidson upholds an entire philosophy of meat – cut, breed, thickness and cooking.

PUMPING IRON

Perrier launched the Designer Water fad, only to be drowned in a fountain of superior splashes:

BADOIT *"Sparkling, full of iron"* (Steven Spurrier). *"I like it because it is not too fizzy"* (Peter Ustinov).

GRAVETYE MANOR's own, East Grinstead, Sussex – Drew Smith.

MALVERN WATER – Lord Lichfield.

SCOTTISH HIGHLAND – Anton Mosimann

KINLOCH LODGE HOTEL, Isle of Skye, Sleat ☎ (04713) 214 and 333. People in the know come here for peace and traditional dishes, including venison and fabulous puddings. Delightful atmosphere, more like a private house than a hotel.

PEAT INN, Peat Inn, Fife ☎ (033484) 206. This whitewashed pub is the sum of the crossroads village. Drew Smith is just one punter who recognizes the fabulous real food and the enviable wine list. Feuilleté of fresh fish, scallops poached in Barsac, wild duck, grouse and pigeon are regulars on the menu: fine sauces of herbs or fruit with spirits: killer puddings.

BEST FOOD SHOPS

GEORGE CAMPBELL & SONS, 18 Stafford St, Edinburgh ☎ (031) 225 7507. Founded in 1872, they hold the royal warrant as fishmongers (about 30 different types of fish), poulterers and game dealers. Home-smoking of what's on the slab, or of your own fish, which they'll then send back to you anywhere in the UK.

PINNEY'S OF SCOTLAND, Brydekirk, Annan, Dumfries and Galloway ☎ (05763) 401. Superb salmon go through a subtle smoking process and are finely carved by hand. No colouring or preservatives, *naturally*. Suppliers to all the best shops – Harrods, Fortnum's, Marks & Spencer – and a mail order service.

WALES

BEST RESTAURANT

WALNUT TREE INN, Llandewi Skirrid, Gwent ☎ (0873) 2797. Another surprising little pub with a French-trained Italian chef, who creates eclectic gourmet dishes. Home-made pasta, superb seafood, fresh Piedmontese truffles, salmon and wild game followed by rich European puddings, washed down with a rare Italian or French wine. Drew Smith heartily recommends.

BEST FOOD SHOP

VIN SULLIVAN, 11 High St, Abergavenny, Gwent ☎ (0873) 2331. A special fishmonger, gamery and grocer (very fine fruit and veg) that supplies fish to many top-class restaurants in Britain, from Miller Howe to the Walnut Tree. A Parisian agent sends fresh and unusual supplies across the Channel twice a week. Here's where to get Isle of Man scallops, baby crayfish, Kenyan and Turkish crayfish, Cornish and Canadian lobster, Wye salmon, and live sea urchins (collected during a full moon when the roes are at their best).

FRANCE

PARIS

BEST RESTAURANTS

FRENCH

♛ROBUCHON, 32 rue Longchamp, 75016 ☎ (1) 4727 1227. Formerly Jamin, the restaurant is now named after the brilliant chef Joel Robuchon, who has made this restaurant the best in the world. When he dishes up pig's head and mash his way, or more traditional truffle, foie gras and seafood masterpieces, Paul Levy (*"the most elegant cooking in the world . . . surest touch in bringing old-fashioned food up to date"*), Michel Guérard, Gloria Staley, Ken Hom, Leo Schofield and the Michelin men dish out accolades.

♛LUCAS CARTON, 9 place de la Madeleine, 75008 ☎ (1) 4265 2290. New life has been breathed into this restaurant by the great chef Alain Senderens (late of l'Archestrate). Steven Spurrier, David Shilling, Michel Guérard and Gloria Staley warm to the place.

♛CARRE DES FEUILLANTS, 14 rue de Castiglione, 75001 ☎ (1) 4286 8282. Formerly of Au Trou Gascon, the brilliant Alain Dutournier is inspired by the cuisine of the south-west of France. Delicacies include ravioli stuffed with foie gras and truffles or with lobster, and wild salmon cooked with smoked bacon. *"A strange combination of purity and originality"* (Paul Levy).

♛TAILLEVENT, 15 rue Lamennais, 75008 ☎ (1) 4561 1290. Consistently rated as one of the best. Among the experts who say so are: Steven Spurrier (*"the best grand restaurant in Paris – one I'd cancel all appointments for"*), Craig Claiborne (*"the greatest restaurant in the world"*), Michael Broadbent (*"excellent food, faultless wine selection and immaculate service"*), Justin de Blank and Gloria Staley.

ANDROUET, 41 rue d'Amsterdam, 75008 ☎ (1) 4874 2693. De Gaulle is supposed to have reflected on the impossibility of governing a nation that produced more than 350 kinds of cheese. They can all be found here, to buy or to eat in a 7-course fromage feast (not *all* at one sitting), accompanied only by bread and Bordeaux.

LE BERNARDIN, 18 rue Troyon, 75017 ☎ (1) 4380 4061. Parisian and international theatre, film and other gossip column-worthy stars flock to eat superb salmon and other fish. Olivier Coquelin recommends.

BRASSERIE LIPP, 151 blvd St Germain, 75006 ☎ (1) 4548 5391. Fashionable and vibrant late into the night. *"My favourite café in the world. It maintains terrific standards and has a wonderful crowd of people – the most glamorous people, artists, politicians, designers . . ."* (Leo Schofield). One of Charlotte Rampling's favourites, too. In the same chain are the equally fashionable, value-for-money, classic art deco brasseries FLO (*"Traditional, great ambience – the best brasserie in Paris"* – Raymond Blanc), TERMINUS NORD, JULIEN, VAUDEVILLE and the newest, LE BOEUF SUR LE TOIT.

BRISTOL, 112 Faubourg St Honoré, 75008 ☎ (1) 4266 9145. Elegant hotel restaurant, said by some to be gastronomically superior to the Ritz.

CHEZ L'AMI LOUIS, 32 rue du Vertbois, 75003 ☎ (1) 4887 7748. Old-fashioned, a landmark in Paris, for foie gras, roast poultry and game, and gargantuan quantities of allumettes (matchstick chips). Mimi Sheraton is very keen on it. *"The best restaurant in Paris, home ground for Foodies, but neglected by the guides. But go before 83-year-old chef Magnin dies, to enjoy the finest of honest food"* (Anne Willan). *"He fires the oven with oak chips and cooks the best meat in the world. There are only 12* *tables. If he doesn't like the look of you, you won't get in"* (Meredith Etherington-Smith).

LE COCHON D'OR, 192 ave Jean-Jaurès, 75019 ☎ (1) 4208 3981. Some of the best steaks – and foie gras – in Paris. Huge 4-inch (10 cm) wedges of meat, scorched on the outside, red but warm inside. Serious eating in a working-class quartier.

LA COUPOLE, 102 blvd Montparnasse, 75014 ☎ (1) 4320 1420. A cavernous brasserie with row upon row of tables and waiters traditionally attired in long white aprons. This is seeing and being seen made easy. Full of spirit, still terrifically trendy, and a set menu that won't break la banque. Steven Spurrier, Bob Payton and Barbara Kafka recommend.

DODIN-BOUFFANT, 25 rue Frédéric Sauton, 75005 ☎ (1) 4325 2514. To its credit: 2 toques, 2 rosettes and 2 sittings full of diners, which have included President Mitterand and Karl Lagerfeld. A grand bistro atmosphere and *"the most glorious raspberry soufflé – a dream"* (Anne-Elisabeth Moutet).

L'ESPACE CARDIN, 1 ave Gabriel, 75008 ☎ (1) 4266 1170. Modish but casual café-restaurant, designed by Pierre Cardin and frequented by glamorous actors from Christopher Lambert to Valerie Kaprisky; Princess Caroline pops in from time to time.

ESPADON, Ritz, 15 place Vendôme, 75001 ☎ (1) 4260 3830. The most famous of the 3 hotel restaurants. All in all, one of the most wonderful dining experiences, though la carte may be a little dog-eared, inspiration-wise. Recommended by Steven Spurrier for their fraises et framboises des bois.

FAUGERON, 52 rue Longchamp, 75016 ☎ (1) 4704 2453. *"My favourite restaurant. An agreeable place where the food is extraordinarily good. You don't feel you are in a museum and that every mouthful is watched to see if you are appreciating it"* (Peter Ustinov).

LA GAUDRIOLE, 33 rue Monpensier, 75001 ☎ (1) 4297 5549. *"A nice small restaurant which always has free tables. In summer, you can eat out in the garden. I have simple food such as parma ham and melon"* (Inès de la Fressange).

GUY SAVOY, 28 rue Duret, 75016 ☎ (1) 4500 1767. The eponymous chef is much toqued about for his fine combinations of poultry, fish and offal, served in unusual ways. Gloria Staley recommends.

JACQUES CAGNA, 14 rue Grands Augustins, 75006 ☎ (1) 4326 4939. A still-rising star, based in an old Parisian mansion. Fish is a speciality. *"Inventive, light, well thought out and worked out. I like the honest aspect of the cooking – there is great attention to taste as well as presentation – very often elsewhere it is* all *presentation"* (Raymond Blanc).

MAXIM'S, 3 rue Royale, 75008 ☎ (1) 4265 2794. Exorbitant prices and improved cooking, but, most importantly, the art nouveau elegance of one of the world's best dining rooms, and the glitzy clientele.

RESTAURANT LES AMBASSADEURS, Hotel Crillon, 10 place de la Concorde, 75008 ☎ (1) 4265 2424. Opulently hung with tapestries and kitted out in marble, this is probably the greatest of the 3 best hotel restaurants.

LA TOUR D'ARGENT, 15 quai Tournelle, 75005 ☎ (1) 4354 2337. The best view, over the Notre Dame; the best wine cellar in Paris, if not the world; the most elegant, civilized setting, with antiques, silver and linen – and a thoroughly good menu. Walls are graffiti-stricken with autographs of tout le monde – Princes of Wales past and present, Sir Winston Churchill, de Gaulle, Roosevelt, Barbra Streisand, Woody Allen ... Anne Willan plays safe: *"The worst restaurant to be seen at with the best food"*, but it's next-best-thing-to-royalty Jacques d'Orléans's favourite without qualification.

LE VOLTAIRE, 27 quai Voltaire, 75007 ☎ 4261 1749. The couturiers' canteen. Hubert de Givenchy, Yves Saint Laurent, Diane von Fürstenberg, Karl Lagerfeld and Pierre Cardin have discovered the charms of vieille cuisine – boeuf bourguignon, escargots, game and decent wines. *"My favourite restaurant. The décor is simple and old, the cuisine traditional. Unpretentious and the people are nice. I like to have the special of the day – it's a matter of seasons and the weather"* (Azzedine Alaïa).

VIETNAMESE

TAN DINH, 60 rue Verneuil, 75007 ☎ (1) 4544 0487. *"The most exquisitely flavoured food I have ever tasted, though it was its wine list that drew me there in the first place. It was my first taste of Vietnamese cooking and I let one of the proprietors choose our meal"* (Michael Broadbent). *"The best ethnic restaurant in Paris, with the best list of Pomerols"* (Jancis Robinson).

BEST CAFES AND BARS

AUX DEUX MAGOTS, 170 blvd St Germain, 75006 ☎ (1) 4548 5525. Very obviously on the tourist beat, but it's a fabulous place to sit and watch the world strut by, where buskers, mime and circus acts often perform on a summer's evening.

CAFE DE FLORE, 172 blvd St Germain, 75006 ☎ (1) 4548 5526. La même chose, next door: equally teeming with life, and preferred by Steven Spurrier (and formerly by Picasso).

HEMINGWAY BAR, Ritz, 15 place Vendôme, 75001 ☎ (1) 4260 3830. The barman used to hunt with his old habitué, "Papa" Hemingway lui-même, and will tell you wonderful stories if he takes a liking to you. One of Charlotte Rampling's haunts.

LE VIEUX BISTROT, 14 rue du Cloitre Notre-Dame, 75004 ☎ (1) 4354 1895. A family restaurant, remarkable for its kir royal à la mure. Wonderful curved zinc bar.

Best Teas

MAXIM'S, 3 rue Royale, 75008 Paris ☎ (1) 4742 8846. The most expensive afternoon tea in the world – not in the restaurant, but in the flower shop next door. Only 3 tables, so book.

HOTEL LANCASTER, 7 rue de Berri, 75008 Paris ☎ (1) 4359 9043. The *best* tea in Paris, elegantly served in the drawing room, or en plein air in summer.

BEST CAVIARE

"Caviare is one of those foods which makes you feel it is good for you" (Peter Ustinov); Appreciated or not, the very best is: Royal Beluga *"as grey as possible, almost pearl-white. The finest, most delicate flavour"* (Anton Mosimann). Try it at CAVIAR KASPIA, 17 place de la Madeleine, 75008 ☎ (1) 4265 3352, which is *"Wonderful for its Russian atmosphere, everything done regardless of price, right in the gastronomic centre of the world"* (Steven Spurrier). Smarties secure a table and sample an ounce of Beluga, Sevruga or Osietra (from FF 5,960 per kilo or US$382 per pound) with a chilled glass of Sancerre or champagne. If you can't afford that, *"the most affordable Malossol caviare falls off the back of Bulgarian lorries when they reach Paris"* (Anne Willan).

BEST FOOD SHOPS

ANDROUET, 41 rue d' Amsterdam, 75008 ☎ (1) 4874 2690. A fabulous fromagerie. Cheeses from all over the country are aged in cellars below the shop. About 10,000 lb (4,545 kg) of 200 varieties are sold a month. You can also sit down to a grand cheese dégustation.

BARTHELEMY, 51 rue de Grenelle, 75007 ☎ (1) 4548 5675. The grandest cheese shop in town serves the cream of Paris society, including the Palais d'Elysée. It's le meilleur, according to Azzedine Alaïa, Steven Spurrier and Don Hewitson.

BELL VIANDIER, 25 rue du Vieux Colombier, 75006 ☎ (1) 4548 5783. Beautiful, historic surroundings place this a cut above the other boucheries. *"A minuscule shop. The window display is so fabulous you have to stop, and you'll want to buy everything in it"* (Steven Spurrier).

BERTHILLON, 31 rue St Louis en l'Ile, 75004 ☎ (1) 4354 3161. The ice cream's a dream, although the queues and offhandedness of the staff can make it a nightmare. Azzedine Alaïa and Michel Guérard have been known to grin and bear it, but those who can't may taste the ices at the nearby café. **Le Flore en l'Ile, 42 quai d'Orleans, 75004 ☎ (1) 4329 8827.**

BETJEMAN & BARTON, 23 Boulevard Malesherbes, 75008 Paris ☎ (1) 4265 3594. The best teas in Paris. Smoked Suchong is a speciality.

LA BRULERIE, 89 Boulevard de Charonne, 75011 Paris ☎ (1) 4370 2892. The best coffee in Paris: they'll make up a blend to order and keep a record of the recipe for you.

CHRISTIAN CONSTANT, 26 rue du Bac, 75007 ☎ (1) 4296 5353. Don Hewitson's choix for chocolates; superb sorbets and ice creams; magnificent cakes and pastries.

COLOM, 150 ave Victor Hugo, 75016 ☎ (1) 4727 9030. The finest fruit and vegetables in town.

DALLOYAU, 101 rue du Faubourg St Honoré, 75008 ☎ (1) 4359 1810. Established in 1802, they make the best croissants (drools Steven Spurrier) and extravagant gâteaux, the best of which are the mogador – chocolate cake, chocolate mousse and a fine layer of raspberry jam – and the coffee macaroons. Exotic chocolates and caramels, and catering to order. Favoured and savoured by Charlotte Rampling.

DEBAUVE & GALLAIS, 30 rue des Saints-Pères, 75006 ☎ (1) 4548 5467. The famous pharmacie (running since 1818) turned chocolatier, where pralines and truffles are stacked in pharmacists' jars. The old sign still hangs outside: *"Fine and hygienic chocolates."*

FAUCHON, 26 place de la Madeleine, 75008 ☎ (1) 4742 6011. The grandest and most famous food hall in Paris, although it's fashionable to think it's not the best. Over 20,000 products from home and abroad – exotic groceries, pastries, chocolates (Charlotte Rampling's favourites), coffee, tea, spices and charcuterie.

HEDIARD, 21 place de la Madeleine, 75008 ☎ (1) 4266 4436 and branches. A tremendous array of goods, down to their own spices, oils and vinegars. *"The best pâtes de fruits – the best present to give your hostess for a country weekend"* (Anne-Elisabeth Moutet).

LAMAZERE, 23 rue de Ponthieu, 75008 ☎ (1) 4359 6666. The best foie gras in town. A restaurant, too, with fine cuisine from the south-west.

LA LANGOUSTE, 8 place des Victoires, 75002 ☎ (1) 4260 9653. Specialists in lobsters from Brittany, they are the main supplier to top restaurants.

LENOTRE, 44 rue d'Auteuil, 75016 ☎ (1) 4524 5252. Inès de la Fressange's favourite traiteur: outrageously expensive ready-made dishes to take away, catering to order, confectioner, baker, chocolate-maker.

LIONEL POILANE, 8 rue du Cherche-Midi, 75006 ☎ (1) 4548 4259. His handmade sourdough pain de campagne, baked in wood-fired ovens, is known and loved the whole world over. It's exported to America and Japan, while Parisians can buy it now from any one of 600 shops. Expert palates (Justin de Blank, Paul Levy and René Lecler) cannot fault it.

LA MAISON DU CHOCOLAT, 225 rue du Faubourg St Honoré, 75008 ☎ (1) 4227 3944. Robert Linxe is unanimously voted the premier chocolatier in France. His fame has grown largely by word of (full) mouth. Golden platters piled high with sinful wafers, truffles and filled chocs have tempted Michel Guérard for one.

LA MAISON DE LA TRUFFE, 19 place de la Madeleine, 75008 ☎ (1) 4265 5322. The best and most expensive truffles can be sniffed out here between November and March.

PAUL CORCELLET, 46 rue des Petits Champs, 75002 ☎ (1) 4296 5182. Sells 60 varieties of tea, 15 kinds of honey, 25 varieties of vinegar, 25 different mustards, and specializes in North African spices. *"A wonderful shop"* (Steven Spurrier).

PETROSSIAN, 18 blvd Latour-Maubourg, 75007 ☎ (1) 4551 5973. Cult caviare of the very best quality, sold in picturesque tins: Christian Petrossian pops over to the Caspian Sea regularly to make sure his caviare is being processed properly. Also very fine smoked salmon, foie gras, truffles, fresh blinis and Russian pastries.

LA POULARDE ST HONORE, 9 rue du Marché St Honoré, 75001 ☎ (1) 4261 0030. Formerly known as Chez Victor, until his recent death. *"Without a doubt, the best poulterer in Paris. The chickens and ducks come from the best parts of France"* (Steven Spurrier).

ROBERT & COESNON, 30 rue Dauphine, 75006 ☎ (1) 4326 5639. The best charcuterie in town – a small affair with the finest pâté en croûte, cervelas, rosette de Lyon, home-smoked bacon, foie gras cru, game terrines and a range of boudins noirs (black sausage).

COUNTRY

BEST RESTAURANTS

FRENCH

MICHEL GUERARD, Les Prés et les Sources d'Eugénie-les-Bains, 40320 Geaune, Landes ☎ (58) 511901. Restaurant Michel Guérard is a showpiece for Guérard's cuisine minceur and classic nouvelle cuisine. *"A grand master of cuisine in a top country house"* (Raymond Blanc). None-too-slender recommendations from Paul Levy and Robert Mondavi.

L'ESPERANCE, St Père, 89450 Vezelay, Yonne ☎ (86) 332045. A classic restaurant tucked away in a small hotel. *"It's so beautiful. The drive is magnificent, down the hills of Burgundy, and it lies at the foot of the hills in the most wonderful surroundings. A late 18th-century stone house – very friendly, and not the typical style or atmosphere of a 3-star restaurant. M Meneau is a very innovative chef. His best dishes are fricassée de champignons des bois, cromesqui de foie gras (cooked in light, crunchy pastry), and for dessert, just warm raspberries with vanilla ice cream"* (Raymond Blanc).

TROISGROS, place de la Gare, 42300 Roanne, Loire ☎ (77) 716697. A long-standing family-run hotel-restaurant that has consistently been awarded the top foodie accolades. Unpretentious, fine bourgeois cooking at its very finest.

L'OASIS, rue Jean-Honoré-Carle, La Napoule, 06210 Mandelieu, Alpes-Maritimes ☎ (93) 499552. The quintessential Côte d'Azur restaurant, with perfectly presented dishes that please Paul Levy (*"Louis Outhier is one of the 6 best chefs in the world: he understands seasoning better than any other chef in the West"*), Leo Schofield and Frederic Raphael. *"There is nothing more romantic than taking a boat across to La Napoule from Antibes and having lunch in the wonderful courtyard. The dessert trolley would blow your mind"* (Frank Lowe).

ALAIN CHAPEL, Mionnay, 01390 St-Andre-de-Corcy, Ain ☎ (7) 891 8202. *"The best food in the world when he is cooking up to standard. It's very much aligned to local food, la cuisine Bressane – things like ragout of cocks' combs and kidneys with truffles: absolutely delicious"* (Tony Bilson).

CHANTECLER, Hotel Negresco, 37 promenade des Anglais, 06000 Nice, Alpes-Maritimes

“ The most exciting things are happening outside Paris today. The quality of food is better. All the famous chefs are outside Paris ” (ROBERT NOAH)

☎ (93) 883951. *“An incredible restaurant, well put together. Jacques Maximin is really superb; you get really wonderful food there”* (Ken Hom). One of the leading hotel chefs in the world.

MOULIN DE MOUGINS, Quartier Notre-Dame de Vie, 424 chemin de Moulin, 06250 Mougins, Alpes-Maritimes ☎ (93) 757824. Holds 3 rosettes from Michelin, 19/20 from Gault Millau, and now a bee. Rich, gourmet extravaganzas are served to a very rich, ritzy clientele from the coast. *“A fantastic auberge, where the food is superb and the cadre divine”* (Olivier Coquelin). Lord Lichfield recommends.

PAUL BOCUSE, 50 quai de la Plagne, 69660 Collonges-au-Mont-d'Or, Lyons, Rhône ☎ (7) 822 0140. An inspired master of cuisine ancienne – home cooking exquisitely executed. A favourite of Michel Guérard (*“His roast chicken is one of the best I know of”*), Craig Claiborne and Robert Mondavi.

L'AMANDIER DE MOUGINS, place de Commandant Lamy, 06250 Mougins, Alpes-Maritimes ☎ (93) 900091. Restaurant-only retreat owned by Roger Vergé in the same town as his 3-rosette Moulin. Superb quality and value for money. *“If I could only have one meal, I'd go here. It's a spectacular mill with spectacular food”* (Frank Lowe).

AUBERGE DE L'ILL, rue de Collonges, Illhaeusern, 68150 Ribeauville, Haut-Rhin (89) 718323. By the river Ill, with a lovely flower garden full of willows. A sophisticated combination of haute cuisine and Alsatian regional cooking by the Haeberlins. Recommended by Craig Claiborne.

JEAN BARDET, 1 rue J-J Rousseau, 36000 Châteauroux, Indre ☎ (54) 334 8269. The provincial chef of the year in the 1985 Gault Millau, celebrated for his featherlight touch and gastronomic surprises. *“An up-and-coming chef who is very good and going to get better. The food is light and tasty, and since the town is not very fashionable, it's never too crowded”* (Frederic Raphael).

LEON DE LYON, 1 rue de Pléney, 69001 Lyons, Rhône ☎ (7) 828 1133. Lyonnaise ambience and specialities that please the well-worn palates of Paul Levy and Drew Smith.

OUSTAU DE BAUMANIERE, Le Vallon, Les Baux-de-Provence, 13520 Mausanne-les-Alpilles ☎ (90) 973307. Pretty hotel and restaurant with antique furniture and a flowery terrace. *“Another fantastic auberge ...”* (Olivier Coquelin).

PIC, 285 ave Victor Hugo, 26000 Valence, Drôme ☎ (75) 441532. *“The one French chef who never stirs from his restaurant and concentrates only on his restaurant. The best pudding in the world is his soufflé orange glacé, halfway between ice cream and sorbet – I'd go miles for that”* (Quentin Crewe).

BEST FOOD SHOP

LA FROMAGERIE DE PHILIPPE OLIVIER, 43 rue Thiers, Boulogne, Normandy 62200 ☎ (21) 319474. A small fromagerie, renowned in Europe for the quality and extensive range of its cheeses. His brother Claude has a more select range at **EPICERIE OLIVIER, 18 rue St Jacques, Dieppe, Normandy 76200 ☎ (35) 842255.**

ITALY

ROME

BEST RESTAURANTS

ITALIAN

LE RALLYE, Grand Hotel, via Vittorio Emanuele Orlando 3, 00185 ☎ (06) 4709. The best hotel restaurant in Italy. Outstanding classic Italian and international cuisine.

ALBERTO CIARLA, piazza Cosimata 40, 00183 ☎ (06) 581 8668. Brilliant fish restaurant, probably the finest in Italy.

DAL BOLOGNESE, piazza del Popolo 1, 00186 ☎ (06) 361 1426. Bolognese specialities, pasta, truffles, beautiful meats, savoured by Romilly Hobbs and fashionable Italians.

HOSTARIO DELL'ORSO, via Monte Brianzo 93, 00186 ☎ (06) 656 4250. The grandest restaurant in Rome, in a magnificent Renaissance building. Moltissimo chic for Roman nobility and other well-heeled diners.

PIPERNO, Monte de' Cenci 9, 00186 ☎ (06) 654 0629. One of Romilly Hobbs's favourites for Roman specialities.

EL TOULA, via della Lupa 29, 00186 ☎ (06) 678 1196. Moneyed and movie people sparkle at this rising Roman landmark. Old-style Italian cooking. Giorgio Armani likes the branch in Milan.

BEST CAFES AND BARS

ALLEMAGNA, via del Corso 181, 00186 ☎ (06) 679 2887. The best sandwiches in Rome – crusty or wholemeal bread and rolls filled with parma ham and melon or cream cheese, etc. Superb fruit milkshakes and panetone.

ANTICO CAFFE GRECO, via Condotti 86, 00187 ☎ (06) 679 1700. Founded in 1742, with long-standing intellectual and literary connotations, it now plays host to an older establishment clientele. *“I like cafés to have historical or literary associations, like this one. But it's so full that it's unbearable”* (Peter Ustinov).

BARETTO DI VIA CONDOTTI, via Condotti 55, 00187 ☎ (06) 678 4566. So smart and exclusive, there's no sign to tell you this is Baretto. Only those in the know go.

DONEY'S, via Vittorio 145, 00187 ☎ (06) 493405. Not as

“The best regional cuisine comes from Emilia, cooked by my mother” (GIORGIO ARMANI)

“I adore fish but there is nowhere to eat it. Even in Venice it is starting to be frozen. I love the idea of catching a fish off Sardinia and cooking it myself” (CONTESSA ARISTEA BRUGUIER)

aristocratic as its Florentine counterpart, but more trendy, one of the best vantage points for the best everyday fashion parade in the world (at its zenith around 6 pm). Best after the tourists have gone in late autumn. *“I do like Doney’s. It has excellent croissants and outstanding goodies”* (Robert Mondavi).

HARRY’S BAR, via Vittorio 150, 00187 ☎ (06) 474 5832. Almost as famous and just as fashionable as the Venice Harry’s.

ROSATI, piazza del Popolo 5, 00187 ☎ (06) 360 5859. For generations, the summer meeting place of rich young Romans.

SAN FILIPPO, via de Villa San Filippo 8, 00197 ☎ (06) 879314. The best ice cream in town: their ice cakes are what the cognoscenti dish up for pudding; worth a pilgrimage for their zabaglione.

MILAN

BEST RESTAURANTS

GUALTIERO MARCHESI, via Bonvesin della Riva 9, 20129 ☎ (02) 741246. The best restaurant in Milan. Serious, expensive Foodie stuff, with menus composed of historical dishes.

BICE, via Borgospesso 12, 20121 ☎ (02) 702572. *“Without a doubt, the best restaurant in Milan. Simple, unaffected Italian cookery”* (Gianni Versace).

BEST FOOD SHOP

PECK’S, via Spadari 9, 20123 ☎ (02) 871737. *“The best deli in Italy. It’s absolutely beautiful. The displays are stupendous. Wonderful pastas, cheeses, a charcuterie, an amazing rotisserie and tavola calda”* (Romilly Hobbs).

FLORENCE

BEST RESTAURANTS

ENOTECA PINCHIORRI, via Ghibellina 87, 50122 ☎ (055) 242757. One of the best ristorantes in Italy. Superb cellars; very chic, very expensive. Marchesa Bona Frescobaldi and Paul Levy pay the price for elegantly presented fish and duck, and an equally elegant glass of vino.

COCO LEZZONE, via Parioncino 26, 50123 ☎ (055) 287178. Genuine Tuscan trattoria, teeming with cool types from the realms of film, finance and fashion: favourite of Giorgio Armani.

TAVERNA DEL BRONZINO, via delle Ruote 25, 50129 ☎ (055) 495220. Current smash hit in Tuscany, discovered by Denholm Elliott during the filming of *Room With a View* and canonized by Simon Callow, a gastronome par excellence, who makes serious foodies look like junk-food freaks.

BEST CAFES AND BARS

DONEY’S, via Tornabuoni 46, 50123 ☎ (055) 214348. In the best position for the evening parade. Terrifically smart, a traditional writers-and-artists hangout since the early 19th century. *“The café with the most relaxing atmosphere”* (Giorgio Armani).

GIACOSA, via Tornabuoni 83, 50123 ☎ (055) 296226. Exclusiv café-bar for the young élite. Birthplace of the Campari-based Negroni.

BEST FOOD SHOPS

VIVOLI, via Isola delle Stinche 7, 50122 ☎ (055) 292334. A gelateria of world renown – the very best creamy-textured Italian ice cream, tasting acutely of the fruit or chocolate that it’s meant to taste of.

VENICE

BEST RESTAURANT

OSTERIA DA FIORE, San Polo calle del Scaleter 2202, 30125 ☎ (041) 721 308. Venetian seafood and fish specialities. *“Fresh, simple, Venetian, modest, elegant”* (Barbara Kafka). *“Wonderful for grilled seafood – cappe lunge, razor clams; coquilles St Jacques and risotto”* (Marcella Hazan).

BEST CAFES AND BARS

HARRY’S BAR, Calle Vallaresso 1323, 30124 ☎ (041) 523 6797. The most famous bar in the world, home of the Bellini (champagne and fresh peach juice). *“The best food and the most amusing place to go in Venice. You can just drink – if you can get near the bar”* (Mark Birley). *“. . . for their speciality, Carpaccio, the best dish in Venice”* (Giorgio Armani). Lord (*“wonderful Tizianos”*) Lichfield, Steven Spurrier, Anton Mosimann, Jeremiah Tower, Stanley Marcus, Romilly Hobbs and Frank Bowling fight their way in.

CAFE FLORIAN, piazza San Marco, 67, 30125 ☎ (041) 528 5338. Established in 1720, the gilded and frescoed café-bar (rather than the restaurant part) is the other hub of Venetian social life, when you can’t get near Harry’s. Frothy cappuccinos and scrumptious pastries. *“An exclusive café under the colonnades of San Marco – beautiful; wonderful hot chocolate”* (Romilly Hobbs).

GRITTI PALACE, Campo Santa Maria del Giglio 2467, 30124 ☎ (041) 26044. A beautiful bar where you can sit outside overlooking the canal. *“A princely palazzo – what more could you want? Their Bellinis are excellent”* (Anne Willan). Barbara Kafka is equally taken.

BOLOGNA

BEST RESTAURANTS

🏵 **SAN DOMENICO, via Sacchi 1, 40026 Imola ☎ (0542) 29000.** Just outside Bologna, this is reckoned to be one of the best restaurants in Italy at the moment. Old-style and refined, serving duck, game, truffle pâté and Bolognese specialities.

DANTE, via Belvedere 2b, 40121 Bologna ☎ (051) 224464. A wonderful, dimly lit, avant-garde restaurant hidden in the maze of streets. Beautiful presentation in nouvelle cuisine style of Bolognese favourites.

AUSTRIA

VIENNA

BEST CAFES

CAFE SPERL, Gumpendorfstrasse 11, 1016 ☎ (0222) 564158. *"My favourite café – old marble tables, endless rows of newspapers, including* The Times, *a billiard table, and it's full of artists and chess players . . . it's a great meeting place, open all day"* (Cliff Michelmore).

DEMEL'S, Kohlmarkt 14, 1010 ☎ (0222) 635516. What was Franz Josef's favourite cake shop offers tea in an elegant salon. The Sachertorte and Dobostorte lure Romilly Hobbs and Frank Bowling back for more.

HOTEL SACHER, Philharmonikerstrasse 4, 1010 ☎ (0222) 525575. Founded as a hotel-cum-pâtisserie in 1876, it is world-famous for its Sachertorte, a chocolate gâteau made from a secret recipe. At Christmas, they send out up to 3,000 tortuously scrummy Sachertortes around the globe.

BELGIUM

BRUSSELS

BEST RESTAURANT

🏵 **COMME CHEZ SOI, 23 place Rouppe, 1000 ☎ (02) 512 2921.** A 19th-century auberge with expensive but brilliantly orchestrated food. Pierre Wynants competes with Girardet for the title of best chef outside France.

BEST FOOD SHOPS

GODIVA CHOCOLATIER, Grande Place, 1000 ☎ (02) 511 2537 and **MAISON LEONIDAS, 46 Blvd Anspach, 1000 ☎ (02) 720 5980.** Globetrotting chocolate-lovers rate them the best in the world.

GERMANY

MUNICH

BEST RESTAURANT

🏵 **DIE AUBERGINE, Maximiliansplatz 5, 8000 Munich 2 ☎ (089) 598179.** The very best of the new French-influenced German nouvelle cuisine, based on trad national favourites, from game and mushrooms to quark. A 3-rosetter.

SWITZERLAND

ZURICH

BEST RESTAURANT

KRONENHALLE, Ramistrasse 4, 8001 ☎ (01) 251 0256. *"One of the very best restaurants. They have an exceptional collection of pictures, the restaurant is over 100 years old and it's still run in the old-fashioned way. You hang your coat in the middle of the room instead of being given a ticket for it. The tables are nice and wide and people sit properly. All the staff have been there for donkeys' years and they're just satisfied – the service is absolutely effortless. It's very Zurich, with excellent zuriçoise cooking"* (Mark Birley).

BEST CAFES

CAFE SCHOBER, Napfcasse 4, 8001 ☎ (01) 251 8060. *"One of my favourites. Absolutely sensational because it rambles all over the place. This kind of café develops a special kind of waitress who is maternal and feminine at the same time. Here you get the best chocolate cakes in the world (although I am not allowed to eat them). It's full of students and dour burghers reading newspapers on sticks, pretending the students aren't there"* (Peter Ustinov).

CONFISERIE SPRUNGLI, Am Paradeplatz, Bahnhofstrasse 21, 8001 ☎ (01) 221 1772. The biggest chocolatiers in Switzerland *"The best chocolate in the world has to be Swiss. You can't beat it. Its quality, made with fresh Swiss milk and cream – it's just gorgeous. Famous for their white truffles"* (Anton Mosimann). Bob Payton echoes that. The truffes du jour are sold only on the day they are made. A celebrated coffee house and restaurant too.

LAUSANNE

BEST RESTAURANT

🏵 **GIRARDET, 1 rue d'Yverdon, Crissier, 1023 ☎ (021) 341514.** Wrestling with Robuchon, Paris, for No 1 restaurant. Super-fresh ingredients, brilliant inventiveness and perfectionist execution. Showered with approval from one and all – Paul Levy (*"Girardet's precision is amazing, yet he has an element of spontaneity that conflicts with the Swissness of it all"*), Alan Crompton-Batt (*"the chefs' and critics' restaurant"*), Drew Smith, Barbara Kafka, Robert Mondavi, Ken Hom (*"Out of this world"*) and Michel Guérard (*"He does an extremely good chocolate soufflé"*).

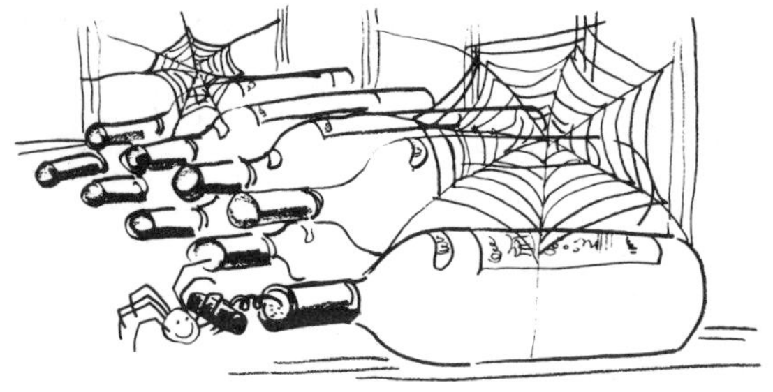

FRENCH WINE

CHAMPAGNE

TOP 3

★

1 ROEDERER CRISTAL
2 KRUG GRANDE CUVEE
3 DOM PERIGNON

ROEDERER CRISTAL. Most people find the world looks best through a Cuvée de Prestige Cristal glass. *"I love Cristal"* (Robert Mondavi); so do Lord Lichfield, Quentin Crewe, Jeremiah Tower, Barbara Kafka, Margaux Hemingway and Contessa Aristea Bruguier, while Raymond Blanc enjoys the pink, in company with Azzedine Alaïa (though he likes practically everything else in black and white).

KRUG The non-vintage Grande Cuvée is a match for anyone else's Cuvée de Prestige: *"The size of bubbles is very small and they almost seem to disappear as you taste – outstanding. It has a beautiful after-taste. I don't like champagnes that are too acid. Krug is beautifully harmonious and delicate"* (Robert Mondavi). *"I prefer it to vintage champagnes: it's the accepted best"* (Paul Levy). *"The best-made champagne – about the only one left of the grand marques that is made with proper hand-turning of the bottles. Magnificent"* (Leo Schofield). *"Their Blanc de Blancs, Clos du Mesnil, is* fantastic" (Hugh Johnson). Margaux Hemingway's No 1.

DOM PERIGNON The first-born among these dizzy unequals – to Moët & Chandon. Favoured by Anne-Elisabeth Moutet (she particularly likes the 1970) and Contessa Aristea Bruguier, and *"never turned down"* by Francis Yeoh.

BOLLINGER Non-vintage favourite, for its majesty and balance; it regularly has grapies reaching for their flutes.

LANSON BLACK LABEL Frederic Raphael finds inspiration in its freshness and fruitiness. He was not the first. In the days of their courtship, Edward, then Prince of Wales, and Wallis Simpson would crack a bottle of Lanson '15; nowadays, it's in to drink pink.

LAURENT-PERRIER Admired for its floweriness, lightness and delicacy. The rosé was chosé by Lady Elizabeth Anson: under her own label, it adds froth to clients' parties. Auberon Waugh is *"very fond"* of the Cuvée Grande Siècle.

PERRIER-JOUET The luxury Belle Epoque comes in a painted bottle; together they please the eye and palate of Robert Mondavi.

POL ROGER Much support, including that of Hugh Johnson (*"My favourite champagne since I was born – their Cuvée de Prestige is the 'Sir Winston Churchill', but I think their rosé is fabulous. Very à la mode, the chic-est thing in town"*); Steven Spurrier (*"delicious, elegant, perfect – lots of tiny bubbles"*) and Lady Elizabeth Anson.

SALON LE MESNIL The original Blanc de Blancs. Only appears about once every 5 years. *"The snobbiest of the lot"* (Hugh Johnson).

TAITTINGER Cuvées de Prestige arrive nowadays in ever-more outrageous party attire: the latest is the skin-tight gold lamé outfit worn by Taittinger Collection Champagnes (designed by Victor Vasarely and sealed by laser beam). Consumed by Inès de la Fressange for one. Must be served on a black lacquer tray.

VINTAGE CHAMPAGNES Made from grapes picked in a single year and rich with the character of that year. (Non-grapies are sometimes disappointed by the un-bubbliness of their venerable beads.) Much fancied are BRUNO PAILLARD 1973, BESSERAT DE BELLEFON 1975, MONTAUDON 1976 and BILLECART SALMON BLANC DE BLANCS 1979.

USTINOV ON VIN

"My wife and I have a running battle because she prefers Bordeaux and I prefer Burgundy. But really I like most wines as long as they don't have antifreeze in them.

"The French are still in a league of their own when it comes to wine, like the Germans in music. They have the most catholic range and more ingredients than anybody else both in their wines and in their food. The French must have put more things in their mouths than any other race.

"I think it is important that you do not become too much of an expert … or you become really obsessed about whether the wine is at the right temperature, and every little flaw becomes an irritation."

BORDEAUX

Thinkers pause over claret to sip and reflect; irrationalists and sensation-seekers gulp at burgundy. There are four main growing areas for red Bordeaux.

THE MEDOC

A small number of beautiful châteaux. (Margaux is the finest: *"I'd love to have a small vineyard and my own Château Margaux in Tuscany,"* fantasizes *la* Hemingway) and a large number of valuable grapes redeem an otherwise dull landscape. The four *grands* – Baron Eric's LAFITE-ROTHSCHILD, Baron Philippe's MOUTON-ROTHSCHILD, Laura Mentzecopoulos's MARGAUX and the English-owned LATOUR (Harveys of Bristol have a share) – dominate, and these are the wines that top the best lists. *"I think Latour has come up top more often than any other claret during my lifetime"* (Hugh Johnson). Michael Broadbent (whose gold-plated taste buds deserve mention in their own right: the world's best papillae) lists 2 vintages of each among his greatest wines: 1899 and 1953 for Lafite, 1900 and 1961 for Margaux, 1924 and 1949 for Mouton, and 1929 and 1945 for Latour. Lafite and Mouton are both admired by Azzedine Alaïa; Inès de la Fressange is in the Lafite camp, while Robert Mondavi flocks to Mouton (*"the best maintained château in the world"*). Jancis Robinson fancies Margaux 1953 and 1979, Lafite 1976 and Latour 1978.

THE GRAVES

HAUT-BRION Although surrounded now by suburban Bordeaux, it maintains its long-held dominance. Michael Broadbent is haunted by 1945 and 1961; an Impériale of the 1899 was *"the most spell-binding claret I have ever drunk."* (Hugh Johnson).

ST-EMILION

CHEVAL-BLANC Along with AUSONE (the name is associated with Roman poet and tippler Ausonius), this is the best in the region, producing soft, rich wines. Among those who dream of Cheval-Blanc are Lord Lichfield, Jancis Robinson (*"the most successful wine of the 1980 vintage"*) and Michael Broadbent (*"the 1921 and the 1947"*). *"The '47 is one of the great classic vintages of all time: it is the marker for all claret lovers, a monolithic wine, like a pillar of marble. The moment you meet it, it grabs your attention and explodes with flavour. You just think: 'What is this thing?' Anybody would know that it was something quite out of the ordinary."* (Hugh Johnson).

POMEROL

PETRUS *Hors concours*, and nearly everything else. Tiny quantities of fabulous wine (*"out of this world"* – Margaux Hemingway) sell at double the price you first thought of and more. Pétrus '61 is the finest wine Auberon Waugh has ever tasted. Michael Broadbent sticks his neck out over the '45 and '71.

BEST CLARETS

★

1. **CHATEAU PETRUS, Pomerol**
2. **CHATEAU LATOUR, Médoc**
3. **CHATEAU LAFITE-ROTHSCHILD, Médoc**
4. **CHATEAU MOUTON ROTHSCHILD, Médoc**
5. **CHATEAU MARGAUX, Médoc**
6. **CHATEAU CHEVAL-BLANC, St-Emilion**

Yquem – je t'aime

As Pétrus to Pomerol, so Château d'Yquem to Sauternes: definition and epiphany in one. Lord Lichfield, Steven Spurrier (*"the 1945"*), David Shilling (*"1925, iced, is my absolute favourite drink"*), Charlotte Rampling and Romilly Hobbs sip away. Michael Broadbent votes the 1921 the finest he's tasted: Leo Schofield the 1927.

BURGUNDY

Red burgundy is an unreasonable, irrational wine. The climate in the Burgundy region is of almost British unpredictability, and the grape they use (pinot noir) is a prima donna. The best red burgundies are wildly expensive. White burgundy is more reliable (though no less expensive), a sage queen to its mad red consort.

RED BURGUNDY

LA ROMANEE-CONTI This is the best red burgundy and prices are in the Pétrus league. Michael Broadbent cites the 1937 vintage as the one to sell your house to buy, while Steven Spurrier thinks the 1934 the best wine he's ever tasted. *"Burgundy is my favourite, and Romanée-Conti is the best. I'd be very happy drinking that for the rest of my life"* (Quentin Crewe). *"Really the very best burgundy, still made in the traditional way – bare feet, treading the grapes"* (Raymond Blanc).

LA TACHE Michael Broadbent recalls the 1945 with reverence; Murray Tyrrell the 1962: *"The best wine I've ever tasted. There is no fault in it. It has that lovely soft, attractive nose. The length of palate is unbelievable."* It would see Quentin Crewe happily through life if the Romanée-Conti ran dry.

Both vineyards, unfairly enough, are owned by the Domaine de la Romanée-Conti, a partnership between vivacious Mme "Lalou" Bize-Leroy, and Aubert de Villaine, urbane, scholarly, meticulous. In 1983 de Villaine had damaged grapes picked by tweezer.

WHITE BURGUNDY

LE MONTRACHET Hugh Johnson, Raymond Blanc, Michel Guérard and Anne Willan are united and positive: this is the best, *"all 9 acres of it"* (Anne Willan). Michael Broadbent thirsts after a 1952 (Laguiche) or a 1966 (Domaine de la Romanée-Conti). It is in this context that Quentin Crewe recalls Lalou: *"I think Madame Bize-Leroy produces the most beautiful wine. She also has a very beautiful daughter, and I wanted my son to marry her so that I could drink her Montrachet for the rest of my life."* (Cruel fate: she has just married another.)

THE RHONE VALLEY

For those that like red wines that are big and unbridled, smell of earth, animals and leather, and taste of fruit and spice, the Rhône has at least three best wines.

HERMITAGE The king. (It sold at 5 francs a bottle even in 1835, 1 franc more than Mouton and Latour.) The best names are Paul Jaboulet Aîne (Hermitage La Chapelle) and Gérard Chave. Impatient imbibers are warned away: no good Hermitage should even be approached before its 10th birthday, and the best of the best only begin to learn manners at 20. (Knowing grapies are buying all the CORNAS they can lay their hands on, especially Jaboulet's or Clape's: it's Hermitage's considerably cheaper country cousin, though it needs nearly as long to mature.)

CHATEAUNEUF-DU-PAPE The knave: at its worst, infernal and head-splitting; at its best (like the 1969 Château Rayas that Michael Broadbent thinks the best Rhône wine he's ever tasted) rich, herby and head-turning.

COTE-ROTIE The queen: it has a delicacy foreign to Hermitage that makes it "*the finest of all Rhône wines*" for Hugh Johnson. Etienne Guigal, Robert Jasmin and René Rostaing are the best names: Steven Spurrier reckons Guigal's 1978 "La Landonne" to be one of the finest wines he's ever tasted.

Best Cognacs

Cognac Courvoisier XO
Delamain's Grande Champagne Pale and Dry
Gourmel's L'Age des Epices
Hennessy XO
Martell Cordon Bleu
Ragnaud Sabourin Grande Champagne

REST OF THE BEST

THE LOIRE VALLEY

MUSCADET is perhaps the best *petit vin* for seafood (a favourite of Lady Elizabeth Anson's) and POUILLY-FUME, the best for smoked food of all sorts (Anne-Elisabeth Moutet doesn't like to be without it). The best Loire wines *tout court* are the sweetest: the ANJOU RABLAY 1928 that Prunier's released on to the market several years ago.

ALSACE

These are far and away the best wines to order in a restaurant when nothing else on the list beckons: the finest – like the GEWURZTRAMINER of Théo Faller that Justin de Blank so enjoys – deserve ordering in their own right. Adventurous palates should seek out Hugel's Vendange tardive and Sélections de Grains Nobles: Michael Broadbent thinks the 1971 Vendange tardive wine the best Alsace he's sipped.

XO-LENCE

The palate-teasing Cognac Courvoisier XO draws rich, fluid comments from the cognacenti: "*Courvoisier XO is one of the most fascinating and complicated experiences when drunk European-style in a balloon glass [as against Hong Kong-style over ice]. Some of the XO cognacs have been aged in the cask for more than 60 years*" (Glynn Christian). "*Courvoisier XO is rich, a style that I like*" (Nicholas Faith). "*The finest and noblest bouquets come from the Charente region, and from Jarnac in particular where Courvoisier is based. Their products are of legendary quality. Each bottle bears a signature guaranteeing the uniqueness of the product*" (Jacques Chirac).

ITALIAN WINE

Until recently, Italian wines have been the world's most maligned (and currently the most spiked), but the best are indeed as extraordinary as any work of art in Florence. Take CERATTI'S GRECO DI BIANCO. One of the world's best sweet aperitif wines, it is made by immersing freshly picked grapes in boiling water prior to crushing them: "*Clean as a whistle, as ancient as wine and about the nearest thing to divine nectar that I have come across anywhere*" (Nicolas Belfrage).

PIEDMONT

"*For uninhibited exploration of the varieties of grape juice and what can be made of them, no part of Europe can compare with Piedmont*" (Hugh Johnson). Most of the grape juice is red, and the best ends up as Barolo and Barbaresco. The differences between the best of these are less important than their similarities: big wines, rich in fruit, extract and mysterious woodland smells, for long ageing.

BARBARESCO One name dominates: GAJA. The label is the world's most megalomaniac: the name hits the eye, "Barbaresco" is lost among the small print. All of Gaja's wines are good: the best is the single-vineyard Sorì San Lorenzo ("*great wine*" sighs Belfrage). The 1961 was one of the two best Italian wines Michael Broadbent has tasted.

BAROLO "*I think there are some frightfully good Barolos coming in*" (Auberon Waugh). The best is Pio Cesare's all-conquering version ("*nothing in excess, marvellous harmony, amazing complexity*" – Nicolas Belfrage).

TUSCANY

SASSICAIA A cabernet red, and "*a fantastic wine – it has been the best red wine in Italy for the past 10 years*" (Hugh Johnson). In part responsible is Piero Antinori. "*the*

“ Italy is the most exciting part of the Old World at the moment. Lots of people are putting money into wine production there: it's the California of Europe. The best thing about Italy is that their best wines are not based on clones of French varieties, but their own ancient grapes ” (SIMON LOFTUS)

best and most interesting wine-maker in Italy. He has made the top reds in Tuscany" (Hugh Johnson). His own triumph is TIGNANELLO *"a watershed wine"* – Nicolas Belfrage).

BRUNELLO DI MONTALCINO Outprices any other wine in Italy (partly because, in poor years, the whole crop is declassified). Michael Broadbent thinks their BIONDI-SANTI is, along with Gaja's Barbaresco, the greatest Italian wine. Robert Mondavi eyes their vineyards enviously: *"Montalcino has some very fine growing areas."*

VENETO

The best wine-makers of the Veneto all have big attics. In a good year, that's where they take their prize bunches of red grapes to have them wizen slowly in the warmth of the autumn. The resulting wines can be either very dry and very strong (AMARONE) or sweet and slightly less strong (RECIOTO DELLA VALPOLICELLA). In either case, the wine is one of the world's most extraordinary: *vini da meditazione*, something to think about when the *turiste* have gone home. The best visitors have taken some bottles of TEDESCHI'S RECIOTO CAPITEL MONTE FONTANA (*"like a low-strength port but much more interesting"* – Simon Loftus), as well as any bottles of GIUSEPPE QUINTARELLI'S AMARONE MONTE CA' PALETTA (*"undoubtedly one of the half-dozen most superb wines I have ever tasted"* (Nicolas Belfrage) they could lay their hands on.

GERMAN WINE

Look for these key names.

MOSEL-SAAR-RUWER

DEINHARD One of the best Mosel names, thanks initially to its 1900 acquisition of a portion of the Mosel's best vineyard: the Doctor at Bernkastel. All its wines meet a very high standard, though: *"classic"* is the favoured description. Der Bischöflichen Weingüter (based in Trier) may be a mouthful, but a sip of any of its *"superbly elegant and characterful wines"* (Ian Jamieson) would be ample compensation for attempting to pronounce it in the first place.

EGON MULLER The best name in the Saar whose Scharzhofbergers-Schwarzhof have, for Hugh Johnson, *"as much penetrating perfume, vitality and 'breeding' as any wine in Germany."*

MAXIMIN GRUNHAUS The best name in the Ruwer has a more musical ring: von Schubert is the owner. Much loved for their fairytale label (more Perrault than Grimm: *"incredibly beautiful"* waxes Jancis Robinson) and for their magically haunting wines.

J J PRUM Their Sonnenuhr wines are among the Mosel's most voluptuous: Hugh Johnson enjoys their *"glorious honeyed ripeness."* It was their Wehlener Sonnenuhrfeinste Beerenauslese of 1949 that Michael Broadbent noted in golden ink.

RHEINGAU

SCHLOSS VOLLRADS One of the two best names in the Rheingau (and their labels harbour, in smaller print, one of the wine world's best names: owner Graf Matuschka-Greiffenclau). This is one of Germany's best private estates, and one of the greatest in extent and influence. From its cellars came the best Rhine wine ever enjoyed by Michael Broadbent: a 1947 Trockenbeeren-auslese (TBA) – the sweetest and rarest grade of German wine. His sentiments are echoed by Max Lake: *"The great TBA is the best sweet wine in the world,"* and by Hugh Johnson (*"I never write anything about German wine without saying they should forget everything except Riesling"*).

Among the other great Rheingau estates are the STATE DOMAINE (*"one of the greatest wine estates on earth, historically amazing, going back to the Cistercian monks"* – Hugh Johnson): SCHLOSS SCHONBORN: VON SIMMERN and WEGELER-DEINHARD (again): all recommended by Johnson. The Steinberg is the finest vineyard, *"its name holds magic"* (Hugh Johnson).

NAHE

The best Nahe wines are often said to be between those of the Mosel and Rhine in character. This they are – with something more: *"To me, the great Nahe wines often have a hint of ethereal Sancerre, a delicate hint of the blackcurrant leaf with a delicious mineral undertone. In their delicacy yet completeness they make hypnotic sipping, far into the night"* (Hugh Johnson). Most hypnotic of all are Crusius, Hans and Peter (*"among the best in Germany"* for Johnson) and the State Domaine of Niederhausen-Schlossböckelheim, mighty rival to Eltville.

RHEINPFALZ

Germany's sunny back garden produces much wine best drunk in sunny back gardens. The finest, though, are dining or drawing room affairs, and the three "Bs" – VON BUHL, BASSERMANN-JORDAN and BURKLIN-WOLF – are the names to go for. Bürklin-Wolf is perhaps the best: Hugh Johnson can imagine drinking their Riesling Kabinett for breakfast: *"so pure and refreshing"*.

SPANISH WINE

RIOJA

MARQUES DE MURRIETA The best: *"powerful and altogether more serious stuff than the Marqués de Riscal"* (Hugh Johnson). Its white Rioja is the best of all. Spanish connoisseurs duel over the rare Castillo Ygay Reserva, made only once every 25 years or so.

MARQUES DE RISCAL The best-known name, especially

among claret-lovers, but its elegant modern wines are almost too light to take seriously. However, Jan Read has described the 1922 as reminding him of "*nothing so much as one of the best old crus from St-Emilion*".

PENEDES

TORRES In terms of the best table wines, Penedès means Torres. Every year, Torres produces a portfolio of wines from different classic and native grape varieties, in different styles, that would leave a Californian breathless – and he then rushes off to the family's vineyards in Chile to do the same thing there.

The best Torres wine is undoubtedly the GRAN CORONAS "BLACK LABEL".

VEGA SICILIA This wine is 10 years in the making "*a rare beauty*" (Jan Read). "*It's living dangerously – it's kept in the wood almost* too *long*" (Hugh Johnson). Valbuena, the junior version, makes less absolute demands on time and wallet, and according to Hugh Johnson, "*it's also better wine*".

SHERRY

Just as mouldy grapes make some of the world's best sweet wines, so mouldy white wine makes one of the world's best apéritifs: dry sherry. The thicker the fur of *flor* across the wine in cask, the drier the finished sherry. Few of those who have quickened their appetites on Barbadillo's Sanlúcar Manzanilla would disagree with Justin de Blank's declaration that it's "*a marvellously elegant start to a meal*".

"*The truly great wines of Jerez, wines that can stand comparison in their class with great white burgundy or champagne, are absurdly undervalued. There is no gastronomic justification for the price of Montrachet being four times that of the most brilliant fino – nor, at the other end of sherry's virtuoso repertoire, of the greatest olorosos selling at a fraction of the price of their equivalent in Madeira*" (Hugh Johnson).

JAN READ'S BEST SPANISH WINES

TIO PEPE "*The world's biggest selling dry sherry, and one of the best*"

MARQUES DE RISCAL, 1922 "*A superb old red Rioja*"

TORRES GRAN CORONAS "BLACK LABEL" 1976 "*The best of the red wines from Catadonia*"

VEGA SICILIA 1966

SCHOLTZ SOLERA, 1855 "*A fine dessert wine*"

PORTUGUESE WINE

The Portuguese red wines are the best forgotten wines of Europe. The Portuguese forget about them, too, for as long as 10 years at a stretch, which is why, when they come to sell them, they're so good.

Almost anything that leaves the country will be worth trying. One of the best wines, though, can only be tried in Portugal, and then only in 5 hotels: the Palace Hotel in Buçaco and 4 others in the d'Almeida family group (including Lisbon's Metropole). It is BUÇACO TINTO. Nothing has changed in the way that the wine is made for hundreds of years. Hugh Johnson notes its "*exquisite hand-made quality, great fragrance and depth*".

MADEIRA

Vintage Madeira is among the world's best fortified wines, and it will outlive vintage port. Vintages, though, are rarer.

The best – like the 1795 Terrantez enjoyed by Michael Broadbent, or even the non-vintage Cossart Gordon Sercial Duo Centenary so liked by Hugh Johnson – command love, respect, devotion ... and further purchases.

PORT

TAYLOR'S The best: still foot-trodden, their wines are of "*unrivalled ripeness, depth and every other dimension*" (Hugh Johnson). Michael Broadbent thinks their 1935 the best he's ever tasted, while Anton Mosimann favours the 1945. Their top vineyard is the Quinta de Vargellas, released in lesser years as a single vineyard port and eagerly snapped up by Auberon Waugh ("*about half the price of Taylor's vintage port and just as good, I think*"). Other houses worth a vintage detour are Grahams, Dow, Fonseca, Cockburn and Quinta do Noval (of which Michael Broadbent enjoyed the 1955, 1963, 1908 and 1931 respectively). Of recent years, 1977 is the one to invest in: just the thing for New Year's Eve 1999.

Jan Read's Best Portuguese Wines

TAYLOR'S VINTAGE PORT, 1970 "*A classical port, rich and sumptuous*"

FERREIRA'S DUQUE DE BRAGANZA "*A tawny port, for those who prefer something lighter than vintage*"

COSSART GORDON BUAL SOLERA, 1822 "*A rare and exquisite old (Madeira) dessert wine*"

BARCA VELHA, 1966 "*A velvety red table wine from the Douro*"

PALACIO DE BREJOEIRA "*A light and refreshing, young green wine*"

Best Single Malt Whiskies

Glenlivet
Glenmorangie
Lagavulin
Longmorn
Macallan
Talisker

THE AMERICAS

UNITED STATES

BEST RESTAURANTS

★

1 CHEZ PANISSE, Berkeley, California
2 QUILTED GIRAFFE, New York
3 LUTECE, New York
4 STARS, San Francisco
5 ROUTH STREET CAFE, Dallas
6 LE FRANCAIS, Wheeling, Illinois
7 ARCADIA, New York
8 K'PAUL'S LOUISIANA KITCHEN, New Orleans
9 MAX AU TRIANGLE, Los Angeles
10 MICHAEL'S, Los Angeles

The Nancy girls

When Nancy Reagan's in town, she meets up with her pals over exorbitant though meagre lunches to arrange the social calender for the cream of New York. Top-drawer diners who attend these summits include Nan Kempner, Pat Buckley, CZ (that's Seezee to non-yankees) Guest, Mica Ertegun, Lynn Wyatt and Evangeline Bruce. Impeccably groomed as ever, they lunch at Le Cirque, Arcadia, Four Seasons, La Grenouille, Harry's Bar and Mortimer's.

NEW YORK

The Big Apple is the eating out core of the world. TV suppers are not a New York habit, and apartments seldom have enough room for entertaining. Lunch is the main see-and-be-seen spot of the day, and smarties will pay any price for what smacks of quality and exclusivity." (Marc Biron)

BEST RESTAURANTS

AMERICAN

QUILTED GIRAFFE, 955 2nd Ave, NY 10009 ☎ (212) 753 5355. New American cuisine favoured by Marian Burros, who loves their beggar's purses – tiny crêpes filled with best caviare and sour cream with a twist of lemon. *"Splendour and surprise delivered without fail by Barry and Susan Wine"* (Gael Greene). *"Barry Wine is the best of a new generation of American chefs"* (Alan Crompton-Batt). In Craig Claiborne's top 3.

ARCADIA, 21 E 62nd St, NY 10021 ☎ (212) 223 2900. Real new American cuisine, using rich, strong flavours such as smoked lobster, home-made duck sausage, gorgonzola, American caviare, quail and venison. Cool New Yorkers book to sit in the main dining room at the back – by the walls, not in the centre. One of Gloria Staley's favourites.

FOUR SEASONS, 99 E 52nd St, NY 10022 ☎ (212) 754 9494. *The* lunch spot for media heads and captains of industry – and it costs nigh on a tanker of oil to eat here. It's trendiest to eat not in the grander Pool Room (that's for tourists), but in the Bar Room, as the queues testify. *"The Bar Room is the best luncheon club in town, certain habitués phone only when they won't be using their table that day"* (Gael Greene). This seasonally changing restaurant is now an international celebrity, thanks to owners Paul Kovi and Tom Margittai. *"I like it a great deal. Anything the chef makes is great. It's hard to choose from a menu you like so much"* (Ken Hom). Both Craig Claiborne and David Frost rate it in their top 3 New York restaurants.

GOTHAM BAR & GRILL, 12 E 12th St, NY 10003 ☎ (212) 620 4020. Newish, glamorous and successful, appealing to glitterati and Yuppies alike. An eclectic menu in the hands of a gifted chef, who wields the best of American ingredients around his own inventive dishes (lobster pasta, spaetzle in mustard and chive butter, grilled tuna with lemon-basil pasta). *"Irresistible good taste"* (Gael Greene).

JAMS, 154 E 79th St, NY 10021 ☎ (212) 772 6800. Original but conventional cooking (steak and fries still sell like hot cakes) appeals to the best Upper East Siders. *"I like it because it's very American"* (Leo Schofield). *"Of the many stars of great American cooking I'll pick Jams. Jonathan Waxman's kitchen spins forth supernal foie gras on exotic greens, jalapeño corn cakes with American caviares, perfect venison and the best French fries in town. It's wildly expensive, but worth saving for"* (Gael Greene). *"We're Jammin',"* say Gloria Staley, Barbara Kafka and Paul Levy, *"and we hope you like Jammin' too."*

MAURICE, Parker Meridien, 119 W 56th St, NY 10019 ☎ (212) 245 7788. Comfortable, club-like hotel dining room with seriously different modern cooking, a delight to imbibe. *"They have a great starter – Maine Sea scallops ravioli made with light won ton skin and cooked in a beurre blanc sauce. Really quite fabulous"* (Ken Hom). *"An inventive kitchen"* (Gael Greene). Now that the great Jean Louis Palladin is consultant chef, the standard of cuisine could rise to even dizzier heights.

MORTIMER'S, 1057 Lexington Ave, NY 10021 ☎ (212) 517 6400. *"It's very amusing – the social side is great"* (Marc Biron). *"You can't get in if you're not known. Glenn Bernbaum, the owner, is always there ... I love*

"In America, there's nothing much between haute cuisine with tremendous formality, and college kids saying 'Have a nice day, Sir' and 'Good choice, Sir'" (NICHOLAS COLERIDGE)

him, but I'd hate to be a stranger" (Eleanor Lambert). *"It's good for ambience more than the food – it's like a private club"* (Lynn Wyatt).

"Members" include Taki, Pat Buckley, Ken Lane, Nan Kempner, Carolina Herrera and Bill Blass, but the list of celebs who have dined there is endless, Jackie Onassis, Shirley MacLaine, Gloria Vanderbilt, Princess Margaret, King Juan Carlos, Joan Collins, George Hamilton, Claudette Colbert . . . The most desired table for two in town is 1B, by the window.

OYSTER BAR, Grand Central Station, Lower Level, NY 10163 ☎ (212) 490 6650. *"The best counter in town"* (Gael Greene). From their bar stools beneath white-tiled vaulting, customers become rapt watching white-coated waiters whip oysters from their shells. You can order one each of a dozen different kinds of oyster. *"The best, and an extraordinary variety, noted for their freshness"* (Craig Claiborne). *"The best range of oysters, incomparable scallop stew and great California Chardonnay. My idea of bliss"* (Michael Broadbent).

MEXICAN

ROSA MEXICANO, 1063 1st Ave, NY 10022 ☎ (212) 753 7407. Reputed to be the best Mexican restaurant in the United States. A highbrow Mex mix – from red snapper in cilantro (coriander) to fresh tortillas and burritos, and plantains with ground beef, black beans and rice. Elisabeth Lambert Ortiz advises going down Rosa Mexicano way.

FRENCH

LUTECE, 249 E 50th St, NY 10022 ☎ (212) 752 2225. The best French restaurant in town. Like all top dineries in New York, it has its cosseted regulars (Bill Blass is one happy luncher) but for everyone, *"the welcome is pleasantly unintimidating. The chef-owner, André Soltner, is a master of the grand tradition, with innate taste: innovative but incapable of committing nouvelle silliness"* (Gael Greene). *"Like Chanterelle, it's a true restaurant, the food is varied and served with great care, using the finest ingredients"* (Seymour Britchky). *"Up-to-date French cooking – creative and imaginative."* (Marian Burros).

LE BERNARDIN, 155 W 51st St, NY 10111 ☎ (212) 489 1515. The newest addition to the dining scene, this seafood restaurant was awarded an almost-unheard-of 4 stars by the *New York Times*. So haute is their cuisine that they'll tickle live scallops at your table to get a reaction (from the scallops rather than you). No twitch and they'll ditch 'em.

LA CARAVELLE, 33 W 55th St, NY 10019 ☎ (212) 586 4252. The grand old lady (or, as Seymour Britchky prefers, the sweet old aunt) of New York's smarter French restaurants. She's still one of David Frost's top 3, but has lost a little of her old verve.

CHANTERELLE, 89 Grand St, NY 10013 ☎ (212) 966 6960. In the top league – the Waltucks, who run it, show *"perfection and style"* (Gael Greene). *"A true restaurant, not a show place or theatre"* (Seymour Britchky).

LA GRENOUILLE, 3 E 52nd St, NY 10022 ☎ (212) 752 1495. Superb classic French haute cuisine, up there at le sommet for over 20 years. A favourite of Stanley Marcus, Joan Burstein, and Bill Blass, who says: *"One of the places I go regularly for lunch."*

ODEON, 145 W Broadway, NY 10013 ☎ (212) 233 0507. A revamped cafeteria with tons of tubular chrome and fine French food. A streetwise young crowd cram into *"the best late-night spot downtown"* (Gael Greene).

LE RELAIS, 712 Madison Ave, NY 10021 ☎ (212) 751 5108. A high-toned café that burgeons out on to the sidewalk in summer. Foreign and native notables eat in Parisian brasserie style. *"It's cramped and frenetic. Zeffirelli might be on the next table, and usually all the people that you saw at the party the night before are there – it's great"* (Bruce Oldfield).

DOING LE CIRQUIT

LE CIRQUE, 58 E 65th St, NY 10021 ☎ (212) 794 9292. The buzzest restaurant in town. Important regulars such as Richard Nixon, Bill Blass, Ken Lane, Jerry Zipkin and Nancy Reagan have their tables earmarked – by the door is best. *"Deeply hilarious, completely ghastly. A tremendously grand head waiter hands you a menu written in the most complicated French, and 90 per cent of the customers haven't a clue what it means. They sit there in their incredibly expensive Bill Blass and Oscar de la Renta outfits – very slim women and immensely fat men whose suits fit them like baked potato jackets – and end up having whatever the head waiter wants them to have."* (Nicholas Coleridge). *"My favourite restaurant in New York because of Sirio, the maître d'. He knows what you like"* (Lynn Wyatt). As well as rather wonderful French cuisine, there are sensational Italian dishes, including the famous spaghetti primavera (*"they invented it; the food and the restaurant are fantastic"* – Margaux Hemingway) and the best crème brûlée in town.

LA TULIPE, 104 W 13th St, NY 10011 ☎ (212) 691 8860. Très français, très chouette. The Parisian scene, set by a zinc-topped bar and tables, is completed by Sally and John Dare's artfully arranged dishes. Herby, succulent snapper, creamy-sauced seafood, game with spinach and pine kernels, typical French tarts and gâteaux. Paul Levy and Elisabeth Lambert Ortiz recommend.

ITALIAN

ELAINE'S, 1703 2nd Ave, NY 10022 ☎ (212) 534 8103. An institution, packed with publishers and literati who love-hate the matronly Elaine and her Italian fare. *"Elaine's such a great woman. The place is full of writers. You can drink late at night, but the food's not so good"* (Taki). Barbara Kafka vouches for it, however.

HARRY CIPRIANI, 783 5th Ave, NY 10022 ☎ (212) 759 9047. An instant and ongoing success since its opening less than a year ago. Harry (well, Arrigo) transplanted his son and some staff from Venice to run things in the slick but vibrant Harry's Bar manner. As well as fresh pastas, there are whopping sirloin burgers and pizza bread stuffed with chicken, bacon, lettuce and tomato – which elegantly manicured and ringed fingers decline to get involved with. Stars come out en force, however: Paloma Picasso, Estée Lauder, Kirk Douglas, Nancy Kissinger, Carolina and Reinaldo Herrera, Valentino, and Ali McGraw. *"I enjoy lunching here – it's very good"* (Bill Blass) and *"A lot of fun"* (Eleanor Lambert).

PARIOLI ROMANISSIMO, 24 E 81st St, NY 10028 ☎ (212) 288 2391. Conscious chic, marvellous pasta. *"My favourite Italian restaurant"* (Lynn Wyatt). *"No one has rack of veal or baby birds as magnificent and no restaurant is quite so pretentious"* (Gael Greene).

PRIMAVERA, 1578 1st Ave, NY 10028 ☎ (212) 861 8608. Popular with Nancy and her entourage, it's one of the smartest Italians in New York, with superb modern cuisine. *"Sublime porcini, intense white truffles, irresistible baby artichokes and crisp goat"* (Gael Greene).

SPANISH

EL INTERNACIONAL, 219 W Broadway, NY 10013 ☎ (212) 226 8131. Funky downtown Catalan restaurant where craze-conscious New Yorkers toy with tapas – picky, snacky things.

RUSSIAN

PETROSSIAN, 182 W 58th St, NY 10019 ☎ (212) 245 2214. The grander restaurant counterpart to the Parisian caviare bar. An art deco symphony in pink, with banquettes of mink-trimmed kid. This elegance offsets superlative Beluga, Sevruga and Osietra (Christian P gets first pickings direct from the USSR). *"The best foie gras in New York"* (Craig Claiborne), and a *mighty* bill.

PETROUSCHKA, 435 E 86th St, NY 10028 ☎ (212) 876 3800. Opened recently by Prince Obolensky, it's like going back in a time machine to pre-Bolshevik Russia. *"The White Russians are the greatest hosts the world has ever known. Between the vodka, the broken glasses, the singing and the crying, you have for one night the nostalgia of being an autocrat, removed and inaccessible, part of a semi-divine class, where your slightest desire is law"* (Olivier Coquelin).

RUSSIAN TEA ROOM, 150 W 57th St, NY 10019 ☎ (212) 265 0947. Exotic, bustly café-restaurant where the café society – people like Liv Ullman – sip Russian tea or swig vodka (one of 20 different types). *"The nicest place to eat caviare – glamorous, faded plush ... bad taste but beautifully done"* (Alan Crompton-Batt). *"The best place to have tea – you must go downstairs for the best atmosphere, where it's gay and convivial"* (Seymour Britchky).

CHINESE

AUNTIE YUAN, 1191a 1st Ave, NY 10029 ☎ (212) 744 4040. Taiwanese/Cantonese food and jet black décor. David Keh plays with crisp and spicy vegetables, rich chicken with garlic, mussel broth ... nouvelle Chinoise. *"I love it. The cooking is quite pure and clean and wonderful"* (Ken Hom). *"The best Chinese restaurant for adventurous palates"* (Gael Greene).

SHUN LEE PALACE, 155 E 55th St, NY 10022 ☎ (212) 371 8844. The best Chinese, according to Craig Claiborne. *"I like it a great deal. Their Sichuan specialities are nice"* (Ken Hom).

JAPANESE

NISHI, 325 Amsterdam Ave, NY 10023 ☎ (212) 799 0117. *"The best Japanese food ever – really fantastic"* (Margaux Hemingway).

INDIAN

DARBAR, 44 W 56th St, NY 10019 ☎ (212) 432 7227. *"The best Indian food in New York. A high-class restaurant with linen on the tables"* (Seymour Britchky).

BEST BARS

21 CLUB, 21 W 52nd St, NY 10019 ☎ (212) 582 7200. The restaurant is gentlemen's clubby expense-account chic, but *"the bar is one of the best there can be – you get very good drinks and there is always someone there to serve you. A huge selection of whiskies and brandy. They're courteous and highly professional"* (Seymour Britchky).

WESTERN PLAZA HOTEL, 768 5th Ave, NY 10019 ☎ (212) 759 3000. Two noteworthy bars. OAK BAR: *"A very old bar with great murals of old New York on the walls and a tall mahogany ceiling. It has a very friendly atmosphere"* (Craig Claiborne). TRADER VIC'S: The usual formula, and *"the best Scorpions"* (George Falkiner).

See also ELAINE'S and ODEON (Restaurants) and ALGONQUIN (TRAVEL).

BEST CATERER

GLORIOUS FOOD, 172 E 75th St, NY 10021 ☎ (212) 628 2320. Run by Sean Driscoll, this is the first name in catering, sweeping up all the best galas. Pat Buckley uses them a great deal, and they do the food for the grand openings at the Metropolitan Museum of Art. *"Definitely the best. Everything they do is exquisite"* (Peggy Mulholland).

BEST FOOD SHOPS

BALDUCCI'S, 424 Ave of the Americas, NY 10011 ☎ (212) 673 9483. Brilliant deli-grocer with superb fresh produce, herbs, pasta, candies, home-made take-away dishes and hampers. Exotic displays, exorbitant prices. *"Better than Fauchon in Paris because there is not the culinary chauvinism – a wider selection of foods, produce from more countries and traditions"* (Paul Levy). *"Excellent vegetables, whether in or out of season"* (Marian Burros).

BLOOMINGDALES, 1000 3rd Ave, NY 10021 ☎ (212) 355 5900. Imports the cream of European foods; excellent bakery: *"Wonderful crusty, coarse grain loaves"* (Marian Burros).

CHARLOTTE'S, 146 Chambers St, NY 10007 ☎ (212) 732 7939. Charlotte Bonnier's excellent fishmonger's – her own smoked salmon, gravad lax, quenelles, mousses and other inspired fish dishes from her French chef.

COUNTRY HOST, 1435 Lexington Ave, NY 10016 ☎ (212) 876 6525. English-style baker's and grocer's, run by a Cheshire woman: country ham, steak and kidney pie, Eccles cakes, shortbread and Shrewsbury biscuits. Also pickles and preserves made on her Connecticut farm.

DEAN & DELUCA, 121 Prince St, NY 10012 ☎ (212) 254 7774. Chief rival to Balducci's and Zabar's. Glamorously presented Italian and general deli foods, plus specialist temptations such as edible ferns (4 different types), lure serious Foodies and tourists alike. Paul Levy recommends.

EAT, 867 Madison Ave, NY 10021 and **1064 Madison Ave, NY 10028 ☎ (212) 879 4017.** Owned by Eli Zabar, brother of Saul and Stanley of Zabar's. He left the family biz to set up his own experimental fantasy food outlets. He tests recipes again and again to get them right, makes fabulously slender baguettes, and may even whizz off to France for the day to find the right cheese.

SANT AMBROEUS, 1000 Madison Ave, NY 10021 ☎ (212) 570 2211. A branch of a confiteria of the same name in Milan. Inside are Murano glass chandeliers and window displays of sweets, cakes, gelati, plus savouries such as seafood salads. Food can be eaten there or taken away. *"Wonderful rich, full-flavoured ice-cream"* (Marian Burros). *"It's heaven to stand at the counter nibbling a slice of chilled Delizia, a superb, perfect sweet – a meringue-crust torte with a rice-chestnut mousse filling and a thick, soft top layer of semi-sweet chocolate mousse"* (Gael Greene).

WILLIAM POLL, 1051 Lexington Ave, NY 10021 ☎ (212) 288 0501. Old-established deli-caterer, the first to make fine take-away dishes. Marcella Hazan's favourite chocolatier, Barbara Kafka's source of smoked salmon.

ZABAR'S, 2245 Broadway, NY 10024 ☎ (212) 787 2000. *"The best delicatessen, with the world's greatest variety per square inch"* (Anne Willan). *"The best Jewish deli in the world"* (Paul Levy). An institution – you can barely move for the crowds. Each week at least 30,000 customers get through the same number of croissants, 10,000 lb/4,545 kg of coffee (tasted and roasted by Saul Zabar himself) and 2,000 lb/909 kg of smoked salmon (hooked not netted). Zabar's stock 26 kinds of salami, 30 types of honey, 42 of mustard, and chicken roasted in 5 different ways.

WASHINGTON DC

BEST RESTAURANT

JEAN-LOUIS AT WATERGATE, Watergate Hotel, 2650 Virginia Ave, DC 20037 ☎ (202) 298 4488. The most elegant diner in the capital. Renowned for its wonderful, eponymous French chef Jean-Louis Palladin (one of the best in the country), and its multi-course, prix fixé meals (though they are fixed pretty high). A winner with Ronnie and friends.

BOSTON

BEST RESTAURANTS

LE MARQUIS DE LAFAYETTE, 1 Ave de Lafayette, MA 02150 ☎ (617) 451 2600. The American outpost of Michelin 3-rosette chef Louis Outhier, who acts as consultant over Jean-George Vongerichten. New and full of mouth-watering promise.

RITZ-CARLTON DINING ROOM, 15 Arlington St, MA 02117 ☎ (617) 536 5700. A trademark in Boston, known as the place which would not let Joseph Kennedy set foot in it. The clientele is discreet, elegant, old-style – no glitzy rock-star stuff.

“ The best ice cream in the world is Valah's packed ice cream from Chicago. Their chocolate fudge marshmallow ice cream you'd take off your clothes for. And they used to have it stamped on the bottom, handpacked by Agnes, or handpacked by Dorothy. It's wonderful ” (BOB PAYTON)

PHILADELPHIA

BEST RESTAURANT

LE BEC-FIN, 1523 Walnut St, PA 19102 ☎ (215) 567 1000. Grandiose French restaurant run by Georges Perrier. Gorgeous Louis XV décor, superlative food and service. *“One of the best 3 in America”* (Craig Claiborne).

CHICAGO

BEST RESTAURANTS

AMERICAN

BUTCH McGUIRE'S, 20 W Division, IL 60610 ☎ (312) 337 9080. *“Important because it was the first singles bar in America. Now you see all these guys who have married and divorced. It's a second-time-round singles bar. But their coleslaw is unbeatable and their coleslaw and pork sandwich is terrific”* (Bob Payton).

CARSON'S, 612 N Wells, IL 60610 ☎ (312) 275 5000. Barbecued baby back ribs, steaks, prime rib and chicken, with Carson's own inimitable sauce. *“The best barbecue in Chicago”* (Bob Payton).

CRICKETS, Tremont Hotel, 100 E Chestnut St, IL 60611 ☎ (312) 280 2100. Clubby restaurant where the commercial and financial big boys congregate at lunchtime. Honest steaks, lamb, fish and liver.

ED DEBEVIC'S, 640 N Wells, IL 60610 ☎ (312) 664 1707. Like a Fifties movie set – and everyone plays the part. *“The best American theme restaurant ever. It's a 1980s version of a 1950s diner, and it serves cheese fries and meat loaf and blue plate specials like we had in the Fifties – that's the special of the day”* (Bob Payton).

MORTONS, 1050 N State St, IL 60610 ☎ (312) 226 4820. The best-quality meat in Chicago, chomped in company with the prime cut of the eating population. “The *place for really good steaks”* (Bob Payton).

FRENCH

LE FRANCAIS, 269 S Milwaukee Ave, Wheeling, IL 60606 ☎ (312) 541 7470. Seasonal Foodie masterpieces prepared by owner-chef Jean Banchet. One of Craig Claiborne's top 3 restaurants in America.

RITZ-CARLTON DINING ROOM, 160 E Pearson St, IL 60611 ☎ (312) 266 1000. As sumptuous and impressive as its Boston sister. Impeccable French cuisine coupled with slick American service.

ITALIAN

AVANZARE, 161 E Huron St, IL 60611 ☎ (312) 337 8056. Eclectic, progressive Italian cooking, as its name suggests . . . raw tuna and grilled rolled eggplant, pan-fried baby artichokes with mustard sauce, baked polenta with goat cheese. *“Great Italian food. The owner, Rich Melman (who also owns Ed Debevic's and a new seafood restaurant, Shaw's Crab House) is the most influential man in American eating today”* (Bob Payton).

LOS ANGELES

BEST RESTAURANTS

AMERICAN

SPAGO, 1114 Horn Ave, CA 90069 ☎ (213) 652 4025. Wolfgang Puck's cult palm-studded and tented parlour *“started the avant-garde pizza craze – high-energy pizzas with smoked duck sausage, etc. Frequented by showbiz people”* (Barbara Kafka). *“The best pizza joint in LA. It's very Italian-looking really. It's run brilliantly, there's great service, and it has great ambience and a terrific mix of people. Any night you could see Joan Rivers or Dudley Moore or Michael Caine or Billy Wilder”* (Jackie Collins). *“I like it because it's very American, not just a transplanted European restaurant”* (Leo Schofield). *“Their pasta and pizza dishes are 5-star and more. They do pizzas with wild mushrooms, say – whatever they can get that's fresh. They are innovative with new tastes but not strange – dishes are well put together and well thought out. Their roast duck is fabulous too, done the Chinese way”* (Ken Hom). *“I love it”* (Catherine Oxenberg). Loved too by Gloria Staley, it was the main inspiration for her Sydney restaurant Chez Oz.

BEVERLY HILLS HOTEL, 9641 W Sunset Blvd, Beverly Hills, CA 90210 ☎ (213) 276 2251. *“For the best Neil McCarthy salads”* (David Frost).

CHASEN'S, 9039 Beverly Blvd, CA 90048 ☎ (213) 271 2168. Impressive, expensive, grown-up Thirties starlet. *“The best hobo steak with a side order of chilli”* (David Frost); he's not the first to think it – Howard Hughes, Richard Burton and Elizabeth Taylor used to relish the chilli, and Richard

“ California is next to France as the best and most perfect place for variety in cooking and climate. Californian cuisine is about using our own ingredients in our own way with mixed influences from all over the world. Grilling is particularly American because of our climate. We've always had the barbecue, but usually with large slabs of meat. Now we just do it in a more refined manner ” (WOLFGANG PUCK)

Nixon loves to plough through a hobo – a divine slab of sirloin, cooked to Chasen's own special 50-year-old recipe, sliced finely and served with melting butter on sourdough bread.

THE IVY, 113 N Robertson Blvd, CA 90048 ☎ (213) 274 8303. Masters of mesquite grilling – a New Californian cuisine trademark – and a menu rich in fish, chicken and veal. *"I love it"* (Catherine Oxenberg).

MORTONS, 8800 Melrose Ave, CA 90069 ☎ (213) 276 5205. The place to see a galaxy of stars, would-bes and has-beens. Delicious marinated and grilled meats; scrumptious puddings such as chocolate truffle cake. *"An industry restaurant – a lot of studio heads and agents and a lot of business people. It has a great ambience"* (Jackie Collins). Catherine Oxenberg, Jake Eberts and Frank Bowling join the throng.

REGENCY CLUB, 10900 Wilshire Blvd, CA 90024 ☎ (213) 208 1443. Founded by David Murdoch, an exclusive dining club and bar on top of the Murdoch Plaza. $5,000 initial membership fee plus $95 a month to get your foot in the door. *"It is a wonderful place for lunch, like an English club. It has an incredible view of LA. A lot of business people go there – it is not very well known, so it's nice and quiet"* (Arianna Stassinopoulos).

TRUMPS, 8764 Melrose Ave, CA 90069 ☎ (213) 855 1480. Another hit with celebs, whose cultivated tans show up against white walls. Light, airy, modern base for adventurous cuisine – Pacific Western salmon tartar and other creations. Jake Eberts recommends.

FRENCH

♔ **MAX AU TRIANGLE, 233 N Beverly Drive, Beverly Hills, CA 90210 ☎ (213) 550 8486.** The kitchen of the legendary Joachim Splichal draws gourmets and gourmands from the Hills and beyond. A la carte or set menus and a fine wine list. Paul Levy hails it as one of the best in the West.

♔ **MICHAEL'S, 1147 3rd St, Santa Monica, CA 90403 ☎ (213) 451 0843.** Michael McCarty's Foodie restaurant is a byword in southern Californian gourmet circles and a gigantic hole in their pockets. Spectacular New Californian-cum-French creativity, with the very best ingredients imported, if necessary – scallops from France, fish from New Zealand. A training ground for top chefs.

THE BISTRO, 246 N Canon Drive, Beverly Hills, CA 90210 ☎ (213) 273 5663. Golden oldies glow within the ersatz walls of the Paris bistro from *Irma la Douce*, given to the restaurant by one of its original backers, Billy Wilder. It has played host to Frank Sinatra, Jack Lemmon, Tony Curtis, the Reagans and some marvellous Hollywood hooleys.

BISTRO GARDEN, 176 N Canon Drive, Beverly Hills, CA 90210 ☎ (213) 550 3900. A Bistro clone, with a racier image than the original. Movie greats lunch in the Riviera-style garden, picking at a little seafood, salad or soufflé. A favourite of Robert Sangster, Lord Lichfield and David Shilling.

CHINESE

CHINOIS ON MAIN, 2709 Main St, Santa Monica, CA 90405 ☎ (213) 392 9025. The Franco-Oriental brainchild of that eclectic sorcerer Wolfgang Puck, who has unusual ingredients grown specially for him. Here he does for Peking duck, sashimi, satay and curried cucumber what he did at Spago for pizza. Dishes like salmon with black and gold noodles dazzle on the plate.

BEST BARS

LE DOME, 8720 Sunset Blvd, CA 90069 ☎ (213) 659 6919. Bar-bistro that pulls a razzy pop-star set round its circular bar. Robert Sangster recommends.

EL PADRINO, Beverly-Wilshire Hotel (see TRAVEL).

POLO LOUNGE, Beverly Hills Hotel, 9641 W Sunset Blvd, CA 90201 ☎ (213) 276 2251. Still playing to packed houses – any international star who's passing through, be it from Bel Air to Hollywood or Sydney to London, will check in at the pretty Polo Lounge for a cocktail. A favourite of Lord Lichfield.

SAN FRANCISCO

BEST RESTAURANTS

AMERICAN

♔ **STARS, 150 Redwood Street, CA 94102 ☎ (415) 861 7827.** Sister of Berkeley's Santa Fe Bar and Grill, Jeremiah Tower's new star is an equally successful exponent of the New American dream cuisine. He led sharks and lambs alike to the mesquite grill, he combined oysters with spiced lamb sausage, he fried black bean cake with chillies and sour cream, and he dished up James Beard's apple pie to a guzzling audience. *"I absolutely love it. Terrific. Marvellous"* (Leo Schofield). *"Excellent grilled food"* (Marcella Hazan).

CAMPTON PLACE, Campton Place Hotel, 340 Stockton St, CA 94108 ☎ (415) 781 5155. Fresh, modern Californian cuisine. *"The best downtown for lunch"* (Herb Caen).

ROSALIE'S, 1415 Van Ness Ave, CA 94102 ☎ (415) 928 7188. *"The most Hollywood of restaurants"* (Herb Caen). Unusual food and mad décor – a cavernous room with white upholstery, chrome palms and mannequins hanging upside down from the ceiling.

ECLECTIC

TRADER VIC'S, 20 Cosmo Place, CA 94109 ☎ (415) 775 6300. The original. This is the only restaurant where HRH the Queen has eaten out since her coronation. It happened in 1983, when the bay was too rough to stomach lunch on board *Britannia*. The most eclectic menu in the world, with dishes from the South Sea Islands, Indonesia, Europe and America, in a Polynesian setting. *The* place is the Captain's Cabin, *"where much yoohoo-ing takes place"* (Herb Caen).

FRENCH

LE CENTRAL, 453 Bush St, CA 94108 ☎ (415) 391 2233. *"The best bistro"* (Herb Caen). A little slice of Paris, with typical bistro dishes such as cassoulet and choucroute.

L'ETOILE, Huntington Hotel, 1075 California St, Nob Hill, CA 94108 ☎ (415) 771 1529. A pre-opera meeting-place, or where music lovers of a different sort go *"for pianist Peter Mintum"* (Herb Caen). Superb food in delicate sauces. *"A dish I like there is Chicken Forestienne, prepared fantastically well – as good as any I've had in the world"* (Robert Mondavi).

FOURNOU'S OVENS, Stanford Court Hotel, 905 California St, CA 94108 ☎ (415) 989 1910. A charming place where the huge provençale-tiled ovens do their magic to duckling, fillets of beef and rack of lamb. Recommended by Barbara Kafka.

FRENCH ROOM, Four Seasons Clift Hotel, 495 Geary St, CA 94102 ☎ (415) 775 4700. Consistently the best classic French cuisine in San Francisco, with faultless service to match.

JACK'S, 615 Sacramento St, CA 94111 ☎ (415) 986 9854. An institution, around since the earthquake (and before – though it looked different then). *"The best oysters on the West Coast. Their Olympic oysters are the tiniest in the world. It takes 100 to make a cocktail"* (Craig Claiborne). *"Very San Francisco"* (Herb Caen).

ITALIAN

MODESTO LANZONE'S, 601 Van Ness Ave, CA 94102 ☎ (415) 928 0400. Modern art gallery-cum-ristorante: high quality on both counts, viewed and consumed by an appreciative Herb Caen.

CHINESE

IMPERIAL PALACE, 919 Grant Ave, CA 94108 ☎ (415) 982 4440. Old-established smart San Francisco landmark. Traditional Chinese food includes superb Maine lobster, Imperial-style. Regulars such as Robert Mondavi swear by the consistent elegance of the restaurant.

MANDARIN, Ghirardelli Square, 900 N Point St, CA 94109 ☎ (415) 673 8812. Owner Madame Chiang has peppered the place with her antiques, giving it an air of nobility. Robert Mondavi savours specialities such as smoked tea duck and minced squabs; beggar's chicken and mandarin duck must be ordered in advance.

BEST BARS

BUENA VISTA, 2765 Hyde St, CA 94109 ☎ (415) 474 5044. The best bar-restaurant in San Francisco, particularly *"for Irish coffee"* (Herb Caen) – this is where it was introduced to America – and for eggs benedict. Robert Mondavi enjoys it, too, despite the crowds.

PERRY'S, 1944 Union St, CA 94123 ☎ (415) 922 9022. The best bar-bar: *"A good place to hang out; they make the best Ramos gin fizz"* (Bob Payton). Drink, talk and be elbowed among tourists and stars alike.

TRADER VIC'S see Best restaurants).

BERKELEY

BEST RESTAURANTS

♔ **CHEZ PANISSE, 1517 Shattuck Ave, CA 94709 ☎ (415) 548 5525.** The best restaurant in America, run by the pioneering Alice Waters. Downstairs, there is a different one-off 5-course fixed-price menu every night. Upstairs is CAFE CHEZ PANISSE, her wonderful trattoria-cum-bistro. *"Truly one of the best restaurants in America. You eat whatever's on the menu of the day – it's always different. It's always a surprise and always extremely good"* (Ken Hom). Marian Burros is also a fan.

SANTA FE BAR AND GRILL, 1310 University Ave, CA 94702 ☎ (415) 841 4740. Jeremiah Tower's original mesquite-grilling mecca. Once part of a railway station, it's the end of the line for gourmets and cool North Californians, who keep it constantly packed to rush-hour capacity. Fresh pasta and unusual salads complement the famous grilled offerings.

NAPA VALLEY

BEST RESTAURANTS

♔ **MUSTARD'S GRILL, 7399 St Helena Highway, Napa, CA 94558 ☎ (707) 944 2424.** More fine Californian cooking; especially good seafood. *"Young and fresh, with a woman chef"* (Barbara Kafka).

AUBERGE DU SOLEIL, 180 Rutherford Hill Road, Rutherford, Napa, CA 94573 ☎ (707) 963 1211. Sophisticated Californian-French cuisine. *"They use local ingredients and concentrate on that . . . fresh garden vegetables and fresh fish"* (Robert Mondavi).

MIRAMONTE, 1327 Railroad Ave, St Helena, Napa, CA 94574 ☎ (707) 936 3970. *"Very good – typically Californian-French cuisine. The wines are very, very good"* (Robert Mondavi).

NEW ORLEANS

BEST RESTAURANTS

♔ **K'PAUL'S LOUISIANA KITCHEN, 416 Charters St, LA 70130 ☎ (504) 524 7394.** Cult centre of Cajun cuisine, cooked up by Paul Prudhomme, himself an Acadian (from which the word

"New Orleans is the best eating city in America. It has a unique kind of cooking. You just can't go wrong there; no matter where you go the food is great" (BOB PAYTON)

"Cajun" derives), descended from the southern French who settled in Louisiana. Cajun encompasses the spices of the Bayou kitchen, the fish and stews of Creole, the best and freshest local ingredients and the eclectic polish of New American cuisine. K'Paul's is informal and downbeat, but the food inspired enough to lure the most exalted of eaters. Lord Lichfield loves their blackened red fish. *"One of the best 3 restaurants in America"* (Craig Claiborne). *"A meal of a lifetime; it's just wonderful"* (Bob Payton). In summer K'Paul's packs its bags (read cookers, fridges, everything including the proverbial kitchen sink) and moves to another town, where the queues mark its arrival. In recent years it has opened in San Francisco and New York; Paris and London are being mooted for next time.

BRENNANS, 417 Royal St, LA 70130 ☎ (504) 525 9713. Even 12 dining rooms can't contain the tourist throng in comfort, but you have to go, *"for the most comprehensive breakfast in the world – absinthe frappé, eggs benedict, grits ..."* (Lord Lichfield).

DALLAS

BEST RESTAURANTS

ROUTH STREET CAFE, 3005 Routh St, TX 75201 ☎ (214) 871 7161. Fine American South-Western food under French wraps. Real Foodie stuff; prix fixé menu which changes daily. *"Native American chauvinist nouvelle cuisine"* (Paul Levy).

MANSION ON TURTLE CREEK, 2821 Turtle Creek Blvd, TX 75219 ☎ (214) 559 2100. The stuff soap operas are made of: hair-dos and high heels slither out of chauffeur-driven cars to be escorted along the carpet to the front door. Superb food – American regional specialities – in the most elegant setting in town.

MEXICO

MEXICO CITY

BEST RESTAURANTS

HOSTERIA SANTO DOMINGO, Belisario Dominguez 72 ☎ (525) 510 1434. A 19th-century restaurant, mercifully unaffected by the earthquake. *"All traditional Mexican dishes. The best is chillis in nogada. Its colours are that of the Mexican flag – red, white and green. It is Poblano pepper stuffed with a mixture of mince, fresh walnuts and cream, decorated with pomegranate seeds – an astonishing flavour, very rich"* (Elisabeth Lambert Ortiz).

CANADA

TORONTO

BEST RESTAURANTS

FRENCH

PANACHE, 1112 Yonga St, M5E 1V8 ☎ (416) 921 4468. Where bank presidents and other power people lunch, squeezed up at the bar. Nouvelle cuisine.

WINSTON'S, 104 Adelaide St W, M5H 1D5 ☎ (416) 363 1627. Gourmet French cuisine and a wine list beyond reproach. Lots of politicos, who earmark their own tables for future meals.

ITALIAN

IL POSTO, York Square, 148 Yorkville Ave, M4W 1L2 ☎ (416) 968 0469. The best and most imaginative Italian food in Toronto – dishes such as sautéed fresh sardines stuffed with parmesan, spinach, eggs, garlic and parsley. Clubby atmosphere; a great favourite of Peter Ustinov.

MONTREAL

BEST RESTAURANTS

LES HALLES, 1450 Crescent St, H3G 2B6 ☎ 844 2328. Very French; a hive of activity at night.

LA MAREE, 404 place Jacques Cartier, H2Y 3B2 ☎ (514) 861 8126. Brilliant, old-established seafood restaurant.

VANCOUVER

BEST RESTAURANTS

UMBERTO'S, 1380 Hornby St, V6Z 1W5 ☎ (604) 687 6316. The original in a chain of restaurants set up by Umberto. Foodie king of Vancouver. This one specializes in northern Italian cuisine – veal permutations and pasta. Umberto spreads his net to **1376: LA CANTINA DI UMBERTO ☎ (604) 687 6621** – for fresh local seafood – and to **1392: IL GIARDINO ☎ (604) 669 2422** – for fowl and wild game.

WINE

CALIFORNIA

Although the great winemakers such as André Tchelistcheff got there first, it was Robert Mondavi who, in building his Napa Valley winery in 1966, uncorked the torrent, and for 15 years wine splashed and foamed in every corner of California. Trying to keep in touch with what was happening was, as Bob Thompson has said, like taking a census in a rabbit warren. Many of the rabbits have left now, fortunes made and lost: the working burrows, though, keep producing better wines every year, as those in the know testify: *"Top quality is what California can offer the world. On the whole, California wines are still getting better, and 1985 is going to be a really exciting vintage. When the wines are released they will be stunning"* (Simon Loftus). *"I like California wines. They are the best-made wines in the world, for California has the world's best winemakers. It's very unlikely you'll get a bad California wine. The climate is perfect, and their wines combine the best of European techniques, yet maintain a consistency of style that is the envy of the Europeans. And their labelling is so informative. They put a back label on; everything you need to know is there"* (Geoffrey Roberts).

Styles have changed. The original idea was to make the Great American Wine, the one that had the most of everything. France was going to have to learn Californian. The power game is now over though: subtlety's the new buzz. The best California wines of today have acidity, complexity and an alcohol level that means you can still remember your name after a glass or two.

When Geoffrey Roberts nominated California's 5 best wineries, he said: *"Look for the maker's name and not the geography: if you go to any of these makers, you'll get a good wine."* His votes go to ROBERT MONDAVI (for Fumé Blanc), JOSEPH PHELPS (for Cabernet Sauvignon), TREFETHEN (for Chardonnay), RIDGE (for Zinfandel) and HEITZ (for Martha's Vineyard).

"Over the last decade California has proved itself the most exciting wine region in the world" (JANCIS ROBINSON)

"Napa Valley and Bordeaux are, in my estimation, the top wine-growing areas in the world, though our climatic conditions are definitely better than they are in Bordeaux. Once you get accustomed to tasting our wine and French wine, you'll appreciate both of them. I can't say that one is better than the other ... they have very different characteristics. They are equally pleasing. Each and every one is different" (ROBERT MONDAVI)

Opus 1 (Symphonie de Sauvignon?)

The name finally chosen for the wine with the best pedigree in the world. A joint venture between Robert Mondavi and Baron Philippe de Rothschild, whose 1979 and 1980 vintages were London-launched in 1984. Rumour has it that 1979 is the Baron's favourite (elegant, *plus bordelais*), and 1980 maestro Mondavi's (bigger, more Californian). Prices are at first-growth level: the best cellars simply must have it. 1979 is the best quaff now.

NAPA VALLEY

ROBERT MONDAVI is the current best in the Napa Valley, and therefore California, Mondavi *is* Napa: his family *made* Napa. *"He is the acknowledged king of Napa, a worthy Californian counterpart to Baron Philippe de Rothschild"* (Jancis Robinson). *"He fits the description of genius better than anyone I know. His aim is top quality on an industrial scale. Inspiration and perspiration have taken him there"* (Hugh Johnson). *"One of the highest-ranking winemakers in the world"* (Simon Loftus). *"The best red wine? California and Bob Mondavi every time!"* (Anne Willan). His best wines are from the grape variety the Napa Valley is chiefly famous for: Cabernet Sauvignon. *"The real excitement is in his Reserve wines"* (Simon Loftus): the Reserve is *"a gentle Titan you can drink after dinner with relish but would do well to keep for 20 years"* (Hugh Johnson). The coup de grâce is Opus 1.

ANDRE TCHELISTCHEFF – Dean of the Napa Valley. *"The greatest winemaker that ever turned up in the Napa Valley. He's in his eighties and looks like a schoolboy. Worshipped in the area"* (Hugh Johnson). The Georges de Latour Private Reserve Carbernets (Beaulieu vineyard) of the Fifties and Sixties are thought to be his masterpieces: Simon Loftus puts the 1968 *"in the same league as many great French wines: a sensational wine by any standard."* Jeremiah Tower, though, prizes the first – 1937 – above all. Michael Broadbent singles out the 1946 Beaulieu Pinot Noir as being the best Californian version of this grape he's tasted.

JOE HEITZ heists accolades, too. He buys his grapes from friends, and the ones Martha May sells him go to make the famous Martha's Vineyard Cabernet Sauvignon. The 1974 was California's epic Cabernet for Michael Broadbent, a wine Hugh Johnson describes as *"dense and gutsy, with spicy, cedary and gumtree flavours, unmistakably the Mouton of the Napa Valley, even at the teeth-staining stage."* Simon Loftus's favourite is the 1977.

GRAPES OF FROTH

SCHRAMSBERG produces California's best sparkling wine. For Geoffrey Roberts, their Blanc de Blancs is California's *"finest sparkling wine – as good, if not better, than most champagnes,"* while Simon Loftus prefers looking through a glass of Blanc de Noirs darkly.

Rarely caught napping on the Cabernet front are CHAPPELLET (*"staggering, immortal Cabernet"* – Hugh Johnson); Bernard Portet's CLOS DU VAL (Bernard was brought up at Lafite, where his father was manager); FREEMARK ABBEY and STAG'S LEAP.

TREFETHEN, meanwhile, earns rosettes from Simon Loftus and Hugh Johnson among others for *"beautifully long-lived, well-balanced Chardonnay, one of the best Rieslings in the Valley, and the best winery building, in the best old barn"* (Hugh Johnson).

SANTA CLARA

A small but important wine-producing area, with the RIDGE vineyard way out on top. *"We really are trying to make the finest wine not just in California but in the world,"* Paul Draper has said, and his Monte Bello Cabernet Sauvignon (*"often regarded as California's answer to Château Latour"* – Simon Loftus) is what he's aiming to convince the world with. *"There's nothing like the Monte Bello"* (Hugh Johnson). Some have already been convinced: at a blind tasting of Latour and Monte Bello arranged for New York wine writers, no one spotted that the wines were from different wineries. Ridge's York Creek Cabernet Sauvignon is nearly as good, and their Zinfandels (the best indigenous grape variety) are the best in their own right (*"fine grape, marvellous wine,"* enthuses Geoffrey Roberts).

SONOMA VALLEY

SONOMA-CUTRER is the best vineyard, for Chardonnay only. *"It wangles unbelievable flavours from different vineyards; Les Pierres is its Montrachet"* (Hugh Johnson). CHATEAU ST JEAN still has a great name. White wine specialists whose Chardonnay (with *"few peers as consistent"* – Jancis Robinson) is one of California's leaders (but has just been bought by Suntory: watch this space). It's one of the best wineries to visit. JORDAN vineyard is California's answer to Eden (*"beautiful even by Sonoma standards"* – Hugh Johnson) while IRON HORSE leads the field for Sonoma Cabernet Sauvignons. HENZELL produces the best Pinot Noir.

"The measure of a good cocktail bar is by their Bloody Marys. It's a serious cocktail for serious drinkers"

(BOB PAYTON)

REST OF AMERICA

Wine fever is sweeping America: Texan Traminer and Michigan Merlot are realities: vines are replacing lonesome pines coast-to-coast. Vineyards and winemaking are now a mandatory part of The Great American Dream. Two areas – the Pacific North-West and New York State – have turned dream into drink on a commercial scale. Operations are at an early stage in Washington and Oregon, but both areas look set to produce fine white wines within 10 years (*"lovely whites from Washington State"* – Hugh Johnson), and Oregon has already made a name for its Pinot Noir deemed *"fantastic"* by Hugh Johnson. Idaho is producing *"a great Chardonnay"* (Hugh Johnson): Ste Chappelle.

Winemaking is old-established in New York State: the shock of the new here is the invasion of European grape varieties. Gold Seal Vineyards get the Lone Star award for persistent innovation: in particular, their Chardonnay and Riesling show the way forward.

COCKTAILS

CARIBBEAN COCKTAIL *"My favourite cocktail when in the Caribbean: cut a fresh coconut in half and remove most of the juice. Score the flesh (this is the secret of the magic cocktail maker), take a measure of very old rum – brown, powerful Barbados rum – and one measure of the lightest most sophisticated white rum. Mix in a dash of Cointreau, the juice of a lime, fresh orange, pineapple and grapefruit, and add canned syrup to sweeten. 2 straws and a bit of sunshine – you can't beat it!"* (Raymond Blanc).

RAMOS GIN FIZZ *"Everyone drinks Ramos gin fizz in San Francisco – the best come from Perry's. It's a very West Coast brunch-time drink, made with egg white, cream, gin and lemon. The best ones are made with orange flower water"* (Bob Payton).

MARGARITA *"The best margarita on balance of ingredients comes from New York's Gotham Bar & Grill: really fresh lime and a great glass"* (Gael Greene).

HAIR OF THE DOG

"The best hangover cure, if you are in the country, is to get up and go shooting or hunting with a dog. Having worked up a sweat, drink freezing champagne. If you are in the city, have a warm seafood Bloody Mary – warm shrimp cocktail, garlic, hot chilli peppers and shrimp stock. But, most importantly, there should be no noise at all" (Jeremiah Tower).

"Drink 1 thing all evening, don't mix, and then at 1 or 2 am, start with 2 Alka Seltzers in a drop of champagne. Otherwise, next morning, drink what you had the night before to put you back in the same state. For a really pounding headache with the eyes bulging, take 3 Alka Seltzers" (Raymond Blanc).

"Take 2 Actron – wonderful medicine available over the counter in France – before you go to bed" (Anne-Elisabeth Moutet).

AUSTRALASIA

AUSTRALIA

BEST RESTAURANTS

★

1. BEROWRA WATERS INN, near Sydney
2. FANNY'S, Melbourne
3. TWO FACES, Melbourne
4. STEPHANIE'S, Melbourne
5. PERRY'S, Sydney
6. CHEZ OZ, Sydney
7. JEAN JACQUES, Melbourne
8. PEGRUM'S Sydney
9. SUNTORY, Sydney
10. KELVIN HOUSE, Brisbane

“I think we have at last grown up and we're now confident enough and sensible enough to approach food in a more intelligent way. The food is going to be allowed to speak for itself, make its own statement, not be a mishmash of ingredients which don't go together. Thank God nouvelle cuisine never really got its act together in Australia. But it did leave some good things behind and the legacies were lightness and freshness” (ELISE PASCOE)

SYDNEY

BEST RESTAURANTS

AUSTRALIAN

PERRY'S, 495 Oxford St, Paddington, NSW 2021 ☎ (02) 333377. Neil Perry's latest venture. *“My favourite restaurant in Sydney. It's stylish, uncluttered – just fine glasses, fine cutlery, lovely plain china, and no flowers to distract you. But, knockout! – hundreds of dollars' worth of flowers on the mantelpiece. The food is light, never over- or underseasoned, using the best and freshest ingredients”* (Elise Pascoe). Tony Bilson and Len Evans join the Perried ranks.

BARRENJOEY HOUSE, 1108 Barrenjoey Rd, Palm Beach, NSW 2108 ☎ (02) 919 4001. Although owner Neil Perry now cooks at his other, newer, namesake restaurant, this one remains delightful. Best on a summer's evening, dining under a white awning on a plant-filled terrace. Inventive meaty dishes; scrummy puddings such as chocolate millefeuille with blackcurrant sauce or fresh strawberry shortcake with crème fraîche. One of Bryan Brown and Rachel Ward's favourite locals.

DOYLE'S ON THE BEACH, 11 Marine Parade, Watsons Bay, NSW 2030 ☎ (02) 337 2007. A glorified fish 'n' chippy in an old waterfront house. Visitors love to love it. The problem is there's too many of them loving it at once. Massive platefuls of exotic fish and seafood – barramundi, red snapper, John Dory and royal reds (*“to fight over”* – Michael Parkinson) – uniformly battered. *“My favourite fish is tregalin, like a small jew fish, cooked in fine batter so the fish is moist; then I peel the batter off”* (Len Evans). *“The main thing is it's by a little beach and it's very pleasant to be there”* (Mark Birley). Lord Lichfield, Prue Leith, Romilly Hobbs and Diane Freis are fans.

REFLECTIONS, 1075 Barrenjoey Rd, Palm Beach, NSW 2108 ☎ (02) 919 5893. *“One of the best restaurants in Australia.”* (Len Evans). *“An absolute must to fly up to Reflections (or to Berowra Waters) for lunch”* (Patricia Coppleson). Top-flight cuisine, with refined flavours and textures – hare and pistachio terrine; scallop and basil tart with champagne sauce. Heartier meat dishes are pursued by wicked chocolate/fig/raspberry concoctions. Tony Bilson, Gloria Staley and author Morris West rate it.

ECLECTIC

BAYSWATER BRASSERIE, 32 Bayswater Rd, Kings Cross, NSW 2011 ☎ (02) 357 2749. Lively, interesting, media-style clientele. One of the best dishes is fresh pasta with whole baby vegetables in a cream sauce. *“A fun, noisy place to be”* (Elise Pascoe).

BEROWRA WOW

BEROWRA WATERS INN, Berowra Waters, NSW 2082 ☎ (02) 456 1027. Known universally as the finest restaurant in Australia. Inventive cuisine – variations-on-a-veal-sweetbread school – under the direction of Gay Bilson. *“A brilliant menu with lovely contrasts: ascending and descending palate flavours”* (Elise Pascoe). *“The only restaurant of international class in the country. It has no road access – you have to go by boat or fly in. Really innovative Australian cooking that doesn't have too much of an international cringe about it”* (Leo Schofield). *“The best dining experience in Australia – fine cuisine bourgeoise”* (Jancis Robinson). *“A magnificent restaurant – people fly there specially”* (Len Evans). *“An unparalleled achievement, but I'm exhausted when I get there”* (Max Lake).

Oz BUZZ

☃ CHEZ OZ, 23 Craigend St, Darlinghurst, NSW 2010 ☎ (02) 332 4866. The latest restaurant from the stable of Blyth and Gloria *"I called it Oz because I love Australia, and I put the Chez in to give it a fancy touch"* Staley: a hybrid out of Fanny's and Glo Glo's, crossed with the much-admired Spago in Los Angeles. *"The most atmospheric and chic restaurant in Sydney. A good-looking crowd: captains of industry, Yuppies, celebs like Lauren Bacall. It's* the *place to go"* (Leo Schofield). *"The food is delicate, intelligent. Very stylish – I love the darling little courtyard at the back"* (Elise Pascoe). *"The best restaurant in Sydney. Bright and cheerful, with more attractive people than in any other restaurant"* (Patricia Coppleson). *"You always see a Melbourne face, which is great for me being a Melbourne girl"* (Susan Renouf).

BUTLER'S, 123 Victoria St, Potts Point, NSW 2011 ☎ (02) 357 1988. An elegant setting for Frenchish food with an Asian slant. *"The only place I go to consistently for French-style food. They work a lot with Michel Roux; it's a similar style – not too heavy, extremely interesting"* (Max Lake).

ELIZA'S GARDEN RESTAURANT, 29 Bay St, Double Bay, NSW 2028 ☎ (02) 323656. Where the rich, European, Double Bay set go. Buzzing at lunchtime, when elegant shoppers drape themselves around a little something from the smorgasbord. One of Robert Sangster's hot tips.

FRENCH

☃ PEGRUM'S, 36 Gurner St, Paddington, NSW 2021 ☎ (02) 357 4776. One of the very best – Len Evans, Gloria Staley and Wilton Morley are among those who drop in for, say, a warm seafood salad followed by duck breast, pheasant or lamb à la Pegrum's. *"The Armstrongs deserve a lot of accolades. Their restaurant always looks lovely. I like the way Lorinda comes round and explains the dishes. She's such a charmer"* (Elise Pascoe).

CLAUDE'S, 10 Oxford St, Woollahra, NSW 2025 ☎ (02) 331 2325. Superb, intimate little restaurant that plays to packed houses. Lots of interesting ways with rabbit or wild duck or local fish, and the obligatory sinful chocolate special. Len Evans and Gloria Staley are among Claude's ardent fans. *"One of the best restaurants in Australia"* (Leo Schofield). *"Superb food, and we can take wine from our cellar there"* (Elise Pascoe).

KABLE'S, Regent of Sydney, 199 George St, NSW 2000 ☎ (02) 238 0000. Just about the grandest restaurant in town. Rather stiffly formal with slick, attentive service and nouvellish dishes that are little short of perfection. *"The best hotel restaurant in Australia. Elegant, lovely table settings, a wonderful wine cellar and the best service. And they make the best soups in Australia – incredibly wonderful combinations – a warm apple soup with curry, the clearest, finest duck consommé with beads of Beluga caviare ..."* (Elise Pascoe). *"Excellent for people who are visiting town"* (Susan Renouf).

Bring your own

Many restaurants, even top-class ones, are unlicensed, so you bring your own grog. *"BYO is lovely because you can take the appropriate wines – to the Dumpling Inn, for example, we take a very dry rosé"* (Elise Pascoe).

KINSELAS, 383 Bourke St, Darlinghurst, NSW 2010 ☎ (02) 331 3100. A trendy theatre-restaurant, artfully converted from an old funeral parlour. A brasserie-style restaurant downstairs with piano, a cocktail bar on the 2nd floor, and the theatre part at the top, where you can also eat and drink. Part-owned by Tony Bilson.

LE TRIANON, 29 Challis Ave, Potts Point, NSW 2011 ☎ (02) 358 1353. *"The only equivalent to Melbourne's grandest restaurants"* (Tony Bilson). Décor is Fifties plush; service is faultless.

ITALIAN

DARCY'S, 92 Hargrave St, Paddington, NSW 2021 ☎ (02) 323706. Rather English in feel, with William Morris wallpaper and a muddle of antiquey furniture. Traditional salads and meat dishes, and a sea of Packer media faces such as Sam Chisholm, Jana Wendt, Mike Gibson and Tony Greig – it's the Channel 9 canteen. *"We always start and finish with a bottle of Cristal – it's the congratulations or the commiserations (you're either about to be carpeted or given a raise). It also happens to be a very good restaurant"* (George Negus).

DONINI, 45–51 Cross St, Double Bay, NSW 2028 ☎ (02) 328 7142. Chic little restaurant, humming with multi-credit-carded Double Pay persons. Superb fresh pasta dishes. *"Terrific. Go out on the terrace. It's* the *place to go if you're shopping in Double Bay"* (Patricia Coppleson).

MARIO'S, 73 Stanley St, Darlinghurst, NSW 2010 ☎ (02) 331 4945. *"Wonderful, good, noisy place where you always run into people you know. Mario's has an air of currency about it. It's modish, not* silly *modish,* nice *modish, and there is decent food"* (Leo Schofield). *"The best Italian food in Sydney"* (Harry M Miller). Fashion types Carla Zampatti, Maggie Tabberer and June McCallum join the mêlée.

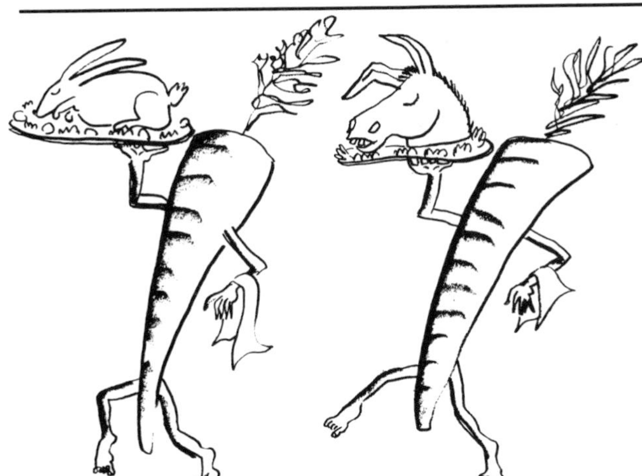

“I think you'll probably eat better at dinner parties here than anywhere else in the world, with the possible exception of France. I once hosted Paul Bocuse and Michel Guérard at Rothbury. I put on an enormous plateau de fruits de mer, 6 ft long and tiered on heaps of seaweed. They were just stunned ... All the freshwater fish and seafood had been flown in from all parts of Australia ... The scallops were so fresh that Bocuse ate them raw saying they were the best scallops he'd ever seen, thank you very much!” (LEN EVANS)

LA STRADA, 95 Macleay St, Potts Point, NSW 2011 ☎ (02) 358 1160. More luxurious and, if anything, more glamorous than Mario's. As well as local celebs, Spandau Ballet, Wham! and Julian Lennon have eaten here. “*One of my favourite restaurants in Sydney. The meal is cooked and served at the table, which to me is very important*” (Susan Renouf).

TAYLOR'S, 203–205 Albion St, Surry Hills, NSW 2010 ☎ (02) 335100. Based in a pair of colonial houses with a pretty garden. “*Very good, beautifully prepared Italian food from various regions*” (Elise Pascoe). “*The best Italian restaurant we've got*” (Max Lake). “*The restaurant I enjoy most. Exceptionally good food, excellent, unobtrusive service, probably the most interesting wine list in Sydney, plus it's indoor/outdoor – as any restaurant worth its salt in Australia should be*” (George Negus).

CHINESE

DUMPLING INN, 5/65 Strathallen Ave, Northbridge, NSW 2063 ☎ (02) 950389. “*It's Pekinese – I'm very tired of Cantonese – and the great thing is, when you walk in, it's two-thirds filled with Chinese. Stunning value, and BYO*” (Elise Pascoe).

IMPERIAL PEKING HARBOURSIDE, 15 Circular Quay West, The Rocks, NSW 2000 ☎ (02) 277073. A grand Chinese affair, expensive and superb, as Len Evans and Michael Parkinson will vouch.

“*If I'm with international guests of some repute I take them to the Imperial Peking. The best dishes are the shellfish – mud crab, yabbies [crayfish] or lobster – either highly spiced with chillies, or in black bean sauce, or in ginger and shallot sauce, or poached and simple*” (Tony Bilson).

LEAN SUN LOWE CAFE, 54 Dixon St, NSW 2000 ☎ (02) 211 4617. “*We go here at least once a week. Their best dishes are the combination sort – Chinese ravioli, with a scoop of stock; steamed beef; dry-fry black-bean chicken; and a dish that Archie does specially for Joy and me – a seafood combination with a separate dish of crispy noodles.*” (Max Lake).

PEACOCK GARDENS, 100 Alexander St, Crows Nest, NSW 2065 ☎ (02) 439 8786. “*This and the Imperial Peking are my favourite Chinese restaurants – my favourite type of food is Chinese*” (Michael Parkinson).

JAPANESE

🏆 **SUNTORY, 529 Kent St, NSW 2000 ☎ (02) 267 2900.** The best Japanese restaurant in Australia, savoured by Edmund Capon and Len Evans. “*I've had some fine, fine dinners there. Their lobster sashimi is stunning. The lobsters are kept alive in a tank until you order. They cut the lovely tail meat into small pieces, arrange it back in the shell and mount it on a board so it has a lovely curve. They put beautifully carved vegetables and wasabi around it – it's a lobster in a sea garden*” (Elise Pascoe). “*A fantastic restaurant. I really like their presentation of kaiseki. It's a tea ceremony type of Zen food that can be a really sunny experience*” (Tony Bilson).

HAYANA, 42 Kellett St, Kings Cross, NSW 2011 ☎ (02) 356 4222. Individual Japanese epicure, rated by Edmund Capon. Stylishly based in a renovated Victorian terrace.

THAI

BANGKOK, 234 Crown St, Darlinghurst, NSW 2010 ☎ (02) 334804. Elegant, upmarket and very stylish. “*We're mad about Thai food, nuts about it. The Bangkok's very good*” (Elise Pascoe).

JITTRA, 22 Victoria Parade, Manly, NSW 2095 ☎ (02) 977 7220. “*The best Thai food in Sydney*” (Max Lake).

U-THONG, 433 Miller St, Cammeray, NSW 2062 ☎ (02) 922 6087. Another contender for the best Thai food in town, according to Elise Pascoe: “*The restaurant's quite hideous, with green stucco walls, plastic roses, and grandmother's lace tablecloths. It's BYO and has the best Thai food. They do a stunning whole fish dish with chillies.*”

BEST CAFES AND BARS

BAR ROMA, 189 Hay St, NSW 2000 ☎ (02) 211 3909. *"Wonderful coffee and Italian munchies. I go there a lot"* (Max Lake). Superb iced coffees, made with coffee ice cream.

BOURBON & BEEFSTEAK, 24 Darlinghurst Rd, Kings Cross, NSW 2011 ☎ (02) 357 1215. A raunchy late-nighter where young nightclubbers drop in for drinks and/or breakfast in the early hours – it's open from 7 am to 3 am.

CAPPUCCINO CITY, 12 Oxford St, Paddington, NSW 2021 ☎ (02) 334543. For the best cappuccino and iced coffee.

COSMOPOLITAN, Cosmopolitan Centre, Knox St, Double Bay, NSW 2028 ☎ (02) 327 1866. Conspicuous sipping of cocktails and coffee on a terrace set back from showy Knox Street, with its high-heeled parade of wealthy fashion victims.

DEAN'S, 7 Kellett St, Kings Cross, NSW 2011 ☎ (02) 358 3357. Late-night café that attracts post-nightclub trendies. Small courtyard out front where coolies sip the best hot chocolates in town. Open until 6 am on Friday and Saturday, 3.30 am weekdays.

GELATO BAR, 140 Campbell Parade, Bondi Beach, NSW 2026 ☎ (02) 304033. *"I consistently go to the Bar. They do an excellent cup of coffee, pastries out of this world, and an excellent menu which not many people know about – middle-European dishes, the best osso buco in Sydney, and it's BYO"* (Max Lake).

GEORGE STREET BAR, Regent of Sydney, 199 George St, NSW 2000 ☎ (02) 238 0000. A busy bar with a separate entrance from the hotel, for some of the best cocktails in town. Also in the hotel is the Club Bar, where you can have refined afternoon tea. *"Very civilized, and good hot chocolate late at night"* (Elise Pascoe).

KINSELAS (see Restaurants).

LAMROCK CAFE, 72 Campbell Parade, Bondi Beach, NSW 2026 ☎ (02) 306313. Edmund Capon's favourite café. Very casual, as close to the beach as you can be. Great Bloody Marys. Trendies like Stuart Membery and the Double Bay Ferrari set come here for breakfast on Sunday morning – fabulous eggs benedict.

SEBEL TOWN HOUSE (see TRAVEL). *"The best Bloody Marys in town"* (Elise Pascoe). *"A voyeur's paradise – you see all the stars"* (Dorian Wild).

BEST CATERER

ANDERS OUSBACK, 120 Ocean St, Woollahra, NSW 2025 ☎ (02) 329056. Unquestionably the best caterer. An ex-maître d', *"he puts together the finest ingredients in a simple but intelligent way; he started by catering out of Leo Schofield's kitchen, and has built up a lovely business"* (Elise Pascoe). *"You can rely on extremely good food"* (Patricia Coppleson).

BEST FOOD SHOPS

BON BON CHOCOLATES, 12 Cross St, Double Bay, NSW 2028 ☎ (02) 327 4046; Shop 38c, MLC Centre, Castlereagh St, NSW 2000 ☎ (02) 233 8074. *"The best imported chocolates. I admire their set-up. The girls wear white cotton gloves so they never transfer their blood temperature to the chocolates"* (Elise Pascoe).

LA BRETAGNE, 15 Plumber Rd, Rose Bay, NSW 2029 ☎ (02) 327 3646; 516 Old South Head Rd, Rose Bay, NSW 2029 ☎ (02) 371 8575. A marvellous display of pastries and gâteaux, created by owner Jean Apert, who trained in Marseilles. *"The best brioche in Sydney. I present little baby brioches with Tasmanian smoked trout with a sour cream cheese mix for cocktail parties."* (Elise Pascoe).

CYRIL'S DELICATESSEN, 183 Hay St, NSW 2000 ☎ (02) 211 0994. A delectable array of poultry, cold meats, preserves and European specialities. *"The finest imported produce; the finest quality fresh smoked geese and the best fresh goose livers for making pâté de foie gras"* (Elise Pascoe).

DAVID JONES, Market St, NSW 2000 ☎ (02) 266 5544. *"The finest upmarket supermarket in Australia. A good selection of teas"* (Elise Pascoe). *"The best food hall in the world. Superb, with white tiles, brass, glass and little bars all round where you can eat, say, a dozen oysters. They have a menu each week, and they give you directions as to how to go round buying all the food on the menu in the right order"* (Glynn Christian).

GELATO BAR, 140 Campbell Parade, Bondi NSW 2026 ☎ (02) 304033; CBA Centre, 60 Margaret St, NSW 2000 ☎ (02) 273698. The best almond croissants – oozing, light, nutty, irresistible: equally sinful pastries, slices, cakes and tarts and a particularly good apfel strudel.

LA GLACERIE, 164 Campbell Parade, Bondi, NSW 2026 ☎ (02) 304995. Fruit sorbets and ice creams that distil the exact taste of the fruit. *"The best ice cream in Sydney, and watermelon is the best flavour"* (Leo Schofield).

INTERNATIONAL CHEESE & GOURMET, 114 Willoughby Rd, Crows Nest, NSW 2065 ☎ (02) 433250. *"Fantastic King Island Brie. It's run by a young Greek family who are so knowledgeable and sensible, they won't let me have a cheese if it's not mature enough"* (Elise Pascoe).

NATURALLY ICE CREAM, Shop 1, Eastgate Shopping Centre, Spring St, Bondi Junction, NSW 2022 ☎ (02) 387 5259. Some of the same ices as they have at La Glacerie, made in Mittagong. Deliciously rich Vienna chocolate, slurpworthy blueberry, in decent crispy sugar cones.

OTELLO, Shop 19, Cremorne Plaza, 336 Military Rd, Cremorne, NSW 2090 ☎ (02) 901119. *"Millie Sherman makes the freshest, finest handmade chocolates in Australia. She puts out her Easter display on Saturday before Easter week … that ensures they are as fresh as they can be. I wouldn't miss the unveiling of the Easter chocs for the world"* (Elise Pascoe). She is also a fine pâtissier and runs a little café with excellent coffee and galactic chocolate gâteaux for those who can't wait.

THE IDIOTS OF GASTRONOMY

"Australia's gastronomy has gone through a dynamic period of change over the past 25 years. It's come a long way since the day when I was given a cup of tea by a girl in a country pub, 'Do you take sugar in your tea?' she asked. 'No thanks,' I said, to which she replied: 'You had better not bloody stir it then!' That's the whole idiom of gastronomy" (Len Evans). As is this little rhyme by Evans's favourite comedian, George Wallace Snr:

What will you have, said the waiter,
Thoughtfully picking his nose,
I'll have two boiled eggs, you bastard,
You can't put your fingers in those.

PARIS CAKE SHOP, 91 Bondi Rd, Bondi, NSW 2026 ☎ (02) 387 2496. The best pâtisserie – glazed fruit tarts and various creamy, crumbly delicacies – and the best croissants. Both Leo Schofield and Elise Pascoe can be seen indulging in a spot of lèche-vitrine, followed by lèche-doigts.

PENNY'S BUTCHERY, 401 New South Head Rd, Double Bay, NSW 2028 ☎ (02) 327 3826. Old-fashioned and old-established – by great-grandfather Penny in 1870. *"A beautiful butcher's. Their display is just knock-out. You'd be thrilled to see that in any capital city in the world"* (Elise Pascoe).

SYDNEY FISH MARKETS, Gipps St, Pyrmont, NSW 2009 ☎ (02) 692 9376. For the best fish and seafood. *"They deserve a special mention"* (Max Lake).

MELBOURNE

BEST RESTAURANTS

AUSTRALIAN

JEAN JACQUES, 502 Queensberry St, N Melbourne, VIC 3051 ☎ (03) 328 4214. Wonderful fish and seafood with a French flair. *"The best seafood restaurant in Australia"* (Len Evans).

TANSY'S, 555 Nicholson St, N Carlton, VIC 3054 ☎ (03) 380 5555. A Victorian terrace with iron fretting. Fresh, light, modern cuisine – deliciously frail mousses, warm salads; duck, quail and hare doused in scintillating sauces . . . flavours that charm Gloria Staley.

VLADO'S, 61 Bridge Rd, Richmond, VIC 3121 ☎ (03) 428 5833. *"Hearty and very, very meaty – absolute hell for vegetarians"* (Patrick McCaughey). Run by Vlado Gregurek, *"an absolute meat fanatic to the nth degree. He buys his beef on the hoof, has it killed his way, then hangs the beef for different periods of time. After the meal, you must discuss the steak you have just eaten with Vlado – it's very serious. He also makes the finest sausages in Australia."* (Len Evans).

ECLECTIC

TWO FACES, 149 Toorak Rd, South Yarra, VIC 3141 ☎ (03) 266 1547. Swiss-French cuisine using unusual top-quality ingredients. *"A very good restaurant with great wines"* (Tony Bilson). Don Hewitson, Prue Leith, Len Evans and Gloria Staley join the queue of admirers.

CHAMPAGNE CHARLIE'S, 422 Toorak Rd, Toorak, VIC 3142 ☎ (03) 241 5936. Run by Francophile New Zealander Iain Hewitson; no bookings, BYO, open late. *"A permanent cocktail party with loads of reasonably priced champagnes and innovative food – an intriguing mixture of nouvelle French and tandoori. The customers are very easy-going – and it's owned by my brother!"* (Don Hewitson). *"I enjoy it here – it's very casual"* (Gloria Staley).

TSINDOS BISTROT, 100 Bourke St, VIC 3000 ☎ (03) 663 3076. A fashionable bistro that is *"marvellous for its food. They make sausages and that's real courage and style."* (Patrick McCaughey).

FRENCH

FANNY'S, 243 Lonsdale St, VIC 3000 ☎ (03) 663 3017. Internationally renowned, one of the best-loved restaurants in Melbourne. *"Small and cosy, and the food is just out of this world. The best food I've ever eaten in my whole life"* (David Hicks). Upstairs is rather chic and smart, downstairs is a bistro with an open kitchen serving cheaper food. A favourite of Harry M Miller, Len Evans and Prue Acton. Lauren Bacall and Marlene Dietrich have visited.

STEPHANIE'S, 405 Tooronga Rd, Hawthorn East, VIC 3123 ☎ (03) 208944. Based in a beautifully restored, grand Victorian mansion, with one of the most innovative chefs in Australia. Len Evans and Gloria Staley back the accolades already showered upon Stephanie Alexander.

CLICHY, 9 Peel St, Collingwood, VIC 3066 ☎ (03) 417 6700. Chef Andrew McIldowney has kept up the standards of his mentor, Iain Hewitson, with a superb, original menu. *"A tiny little place, and still very good"* (Max Lake).

FLEURIE, 40 Ross St, Toorak, VIC 3142 ☎ (03) 241 5792. BYO. Exquisite, light French cuisine, from the Iain Hewitson kitchen. *"I've eaten there and been bored rigid because the food was* marvellous, *but everyone was waiting to find fault. You feel they're almost disappointed when they can't"* (Don Hewitson). But Len Evans leaves sated and happy.

GLO GLO'S, 3 Carters Ave, Toorak, VIC 3142 ☎ (03) 241 2615. Glamorous, formal, expensive, a dressy affair for very special occasions. Faultless modern French cuisine.

“Melbourne is still, to me, the restaurant capital of Australia. Fanny's and Two Faces are still my favourites. Better than any in Sydney. Better food, better wine, better managed”

(MURRAY TYRRELL)

HAGGER'S, 14 Watson Place, off 180 Flinders Lane, VIC 3000 ☎ (03) 639944. Elegant and special. Habituated by rag traders and fashionable sorts, who flock to sample fine fish and seafood, and the best chocolate soufflés in town.

MIETTA'S MELBOURNE, 7 Alfred Place, VIC 3000 ☎ (03) 654 2366. The grand, century-old setting and elegant seasonal epicure make for an excellent evening with plenty of waiters hovering. It is very much to Len Evans's taste. *"Renowned for its fabulous wines – incredibly expensive"* (Tony Bilson).

PETIT CHOUX, 1007 High St, Armadale, VIC 3143 ☎ (03) 208515. A pretty pink and white setting for chef Hans Buddungh, late of Glo Glo's, to present his marvellous fixed-price menu.

ITALIAN

CAFE LATIN, 55 Lonsdale St, VIC 3000 ☎ (03) 662 1985. A shot of modern Italian cuisine has been injected into the old Café Latin by Bill and Cheryl Marchetti. *"One of the best Italians – and posh. If you believe that garlic will save your life, go to the Café Latin. I think I'm going to die from garlic fumes. It also has the best Italian wine I've found outside Italy"* (Patrick McCaughey).

FLORENTINO'S, 80 Bourke St, VIC 3000 ☎ (03) 662 1811. The most proper restaurant in town, with old-fashioned service. Reminiscent of the dining room of a gentlemen's club – wood panelling and ramrod-stiff linen tablecloths.

CHINESE

FLOWER DRUM, 103 Little Bourke St, VIC 3000 ☎ (03) 663 2531. One of the best Chinese restaurants in Australia. Spacious, upmarket, expensive, with extra-special specials – shark's fin soup, abalone, and wonderful Peking duck. Len Evans finds it sweet, never sour.

MIDDLE KINGDOM, 197 Smith St, Fitzroy, VIC 3065 ☎ (03) 417 2438. The best Sichuan restaurant – mind-blowing, mouth-shattering dishes that leave an after-taste pleasant enough for le tout Melbourne to come back and back.

SHARK FIN INN, 50 Little Bourke St, VIC 3000 ☎ (03) 662 2552. More Chinesey than Flower Drum, always packed, with the best yum cha (dim sum) in town.

JAPANESE

KENZAN, Lower Ground Floor, Collins Place, 45 Collins St, VIC 3000 ☎ (03) 662 2933. Food you'd commit harakiri for: the gourmet delights of kaiseki, all 12 courses of it: melt-in-the-mouth sushi. Traditional Japanese service, discreet and kimono'd.

INDIAN

TANDOOR, 517 Chapel St, South Yarra, VIC 3141 ☎ (03) 241 8247. Wonderful tandoori chicken and other hot specials from the clay ovens.

BEST CAFES

SODA SISTERS, 382 Chapel St, Prahran, VIC 3181 ☎ (03) 241 4795. A Fifties style soda fountain with rollerskating waiters, crooning Andrews Sisters and mountainous ice creams.

STARDUST CAFE, 97 Brighton Rd, Elwood, VIC 3184 ☎ (03) 531 2926. A Thirties cafe with milkshakes to shake all others to their knees – chocker with cherries, chunks of chocolate, ice cream and other knock-out goodies.

BEST FOOD SHOPS

CHEESE, 173 Commercial Rd, S Yarra, VIC 3141 ☎ (03) 241 8795. *"The best shop for French cheese"* (Lillian Frank).

LE CROISSANT, 1204 Toorak Rd, Burwood, VIC 3125 ☎ (03) 299 2263. *"The best bakery in Melbourne"* (Lillian Frank).

FLEISCHER'S, 586 Chapel St, S Yarra, VIC 3141 ☎ (03) 241 9606. The best continental cake shop in Melbourne, lined with lusciously calorific delicacies.

GEORGES, 162 Collins St, VIC 3000 ☎ (03) 630411. *"The most beautiful food department, with things from Fortnum & Mason"* (Lillian Frank).

HAIGH'S, 521 Toorak Rd, Toorak, VIC 3142 ☎ (03) 241 8713. The best chocolates. *"They do marvellous oranges or lemons cut in half and dipped in chocolate"* (Lillian Frank).

LIX, 396 Chapel St, S Yarra, VIC 3141 ☎ (03) 241 8396. *"The best ice cream in the whole world"* (Lillian Frank).

MYER'S, 314 Bourke St, VIC 3000 ☎ (03) 66111. *"Probably the best food shop in Australia"* (Max Lake). *"Very good cheese"* (Lillian Frank).

VICTORIA MARKET, Corner of Elizabeth and Victoria Sts, VIC 3000 ☎ (03) 658 9800. An exotic open-air mélange of stalls and stallholders – Turkish, Greek, Italian, Chinese, Indian, plus the odd Aussie. *"It's a sin to shop for food in Melbourne and not to go here"* (Patrick McCaughey).

ADELAIDE

BEST RESTAURANTS

AUSTRALIAN

BARBECUE INN, 196 Hindley St, SA 5000 ☎ (08) 513033. *"My favourite – great for a rump steak"* (Kym Bonython). Cheapish food cooked on an open barbecue, and devoured happily on occasion by Max Lake.

MISTRESS AUGUSTINE'S, 161 O'Connell St, N Adelaide, SA 5006 ☎ (08) 267 4479. *"The best restaurant in Adelaide"* (Kym Bonython). Decorative dishes are downed in smart, surroundings.

FRENCH

CHLOES, 36 College Rd, Kent Town, SA 5067 ☎ (08) 422578. A new restaurant in an old-style house that has shot to the top of the chomping charts. Run on nouvellish lines by well-known restaurateur Nick Papazahariakis, late of Le Paris. He bones his own pheasant, quail and chicken and makes a marvellous yabbie (crayfish) soup. Impressive, trendy and masterly presentation.

GREEK

ELLENI'S, 69 Grote St, SA 5000 ☎ (08) 212 6794. "*A real find. The atmosphere's terrible – dark, panelled, hideous! You go there to eat fresh food, beautifully prepared and sensitively cooked in an Australian-Greek way.*" (Elise Pascoe).

ORIENTAL

DYNASTY, 26 Gouger St, SA 5000 ☎ (08) 211 7036. The best Chinese, with yummy yum cha (dim sum) feasts on Sundays.

TAJ MAHAL, 513 Main North East Rd, Holden Hill, SA 5088 ☎ (08) 261 8665. "*One of my favourites – I've always been a great curry man*" (Kym Bonython).

PERTH

BEST RESTAURANTS

AUSTRALIAN

ESTABLISHMENT, 35a Hampden Rd, Nedlands, WA 6009 ☎ (09) 386 5508. Both the restaurant and the clientele are well established, but they're anything but stuffy. Constantly changing, inventive cuisine: home-smoked meats, delicious salads. A Len Evans hot favourite.

JESSICA'S FINE SEAFOOD, Shop 1, Merlin Centre, 99 Adelaide Terrace, WA 6000 ☎ (09) 325 2511. The trendiest restaurant in Perth. A brilliant newish fish and seafood restaurant – marvellous shark, whole fresh Western Rock lobster, and chowder. "*One of the best things is grilled dhufish, which is unique to the west, a firm, very sweet fish with a delightful flavour*" (Sally Rossi Ford). Good views over the Swan River.

ORD STREET CAFE, 27 Ord St, W Perth, WA 6005 ☎ (09) 321 6021. The best restaurant in Perth; light modern cuisine is served in the drawing rooms of this old house or on the verandah. "*Superb atmosphere, small, cosy, romantic if you want it to be, yet great for business*" (Sally Rossi Ford).

BRISBANE

BEST RESTAURANTS

KELVIN HOUSE, 252 Kelvin Grove Rd, Kelvin Grove, QLD 4059 ☎ (07) 356 8605. "*Unquestionably the best restaurant in Brisbane. The chef is an amazing 20-year-old called Tracey Christensen. She produces panfried duck liver served with raspberry pie – there's a darling little pastry pie on the side. It's* so *good. She does a dessert called Triple Silk – layers of dark, milk and white chocolate bavarois served with a special coulis – magnificent*" (Elise Pascoe).

MICHAEL'S, 164 Queen St, QLD 4000 ☎ (07) 229 4911. "*A very elegant restaurant with one of the best wine lists in Australia*" (Elise Pascoe).

CANBERRA

BEST RESTAURANTS

FRENCH

CHARLIE'S, Bunder St, ACT 2600 ☎ (062) 488338. Nouvelle-style epicure in an unusually dark setting. Interesting soups and simple dishes, all beautifully done. Politicos dine here when parliament is sitting.

JEAN-PIERRE'S CAROUSEL, Red Hill Lookout, ACT 2600 ☎ (062) 731808. Stunning views over the town, lake and surrounding hills, best experienced at sundown. Classic French cuisine matches the view.

TASMANIA

SPECIALIST FOODS

KING ISLAND DAIRY PRODUCTS, North Rd, King Island, TAS 7256 ☎ (004) 621348. Foodies come here for the best dairy products. "*The King Island butter, cream and Brie are the finest I've ever tasted outside of Normandy.*" (Elise Pascoe).

TASMANIAN SMOKE HOUSE, RSD 860, Beloraine, TAS 7304 ☎ (003) 622539. For special Tassie smoked trout and other fish.

NEW ZEALAND

BEST RESTAURANTS

AUCKLAND

FRENCH

ANTOINE'S, 333 Parnell Rd, Parnell 1 ☎ (09) 799756. Top-quality restaurant in an old colonial house; it's like arriving for a private dinner – you ring the doorbell and the maître d' greets you. "*Brilliant – nouvelle without being ridiculous*" (Don Hewitson).

LE GOURMET, 1 Williamson Ave, Grey Lynn 2 ☎ (09) 769499. The chef, Warwick Brown, is among the most celebrated in the country. "*There I've had the best things I've ever eaten in New Zealand*" (Glynn Christian).

WELLINGTON

PIERRE'S, 342 Tinakori Rd, Thorndon ☎ (04) 726238. The best restaurant in Wellington (also polled the best BYO in NZ). "*A great French bistro – really good food*" (Don Hewitson).

AUSTRALIAN WINE

Australian vineyards are peppered (grapeshot, of course) across the bottom of the continent. Anywhere further north and the grapes become raisins. Western Australia and Tasmania have a few wine growing areas: South Australia, New South Wales and Victoria pouch the kangaroo's share. Grapies pull the cork on Oz wines not by learning regions and vineyards (trucking grapes across deserts or flying them huge distances is commonplace) but by knowing their grapes.

CHARDONNAY

The great white wonder. It's done for Australian wine what waltzing did for Matilda. "*The typical Australian Chardonnay is richly, ripely, vibrantly and unmistakably Australian. These are wines for gulping almost as soon a they're in the bottle, sometimes smoky, sometimes oaky – just like white burgundy – but always much fruitier and more obviously full-bodied than the French prototype*" (Jancis Robinson). The HUNTER VALLEY, New South Wales, is one of the finest producers of Chardonnay, as Hugh Johnson will vouch. Particularly good are LINDEMAN'S, ROSEMOUNT and TYRRELL'S: Murray Tyrrell (known as "*The Mouth of the Hunter*") stakes his reputation on the 1986 – "*I have no doubt that the 1986 Chardonnay is the greatest ever from this winery.*" Simon Loftus backs Brian Croser at PETALUMA, South Australia (part-owned by Bollinger): "*He is moving in the direction of elegance in Australian wine.*" Meanwhile, the rest of the best's in the west. Chardonnay from the LEEUWIN ESTATE, Margaret River, Western Australia, rubs corks with Château d'Yquem as Romilly Hobbs's favourite wine, and Gloria Staley drinks to that: "*Very, very good.*" Denis Horgan, the brains (and wallet) behind Leeuwin's, chose the site on Robert Mondavi's recommendation. "*Leeuwin Estate Chardonnays have been sensational, with aromas, liveliness, richness and grip to outdo anything in Australia and most in California*" (Hugh Johnson).

The strength of the Hunter

"*The '86 Hunter wines are going to be fairly big, a lot of colour, a lot of strength, reasonably high in alcohol – but not too high – and they've got great acid, which means they're going to keep for years and years if they're properly cellared. Tremendous fruit character, great bouquet and great length of palate – they fill your mouth and go right across your tongue, and, as you swallow them, that fruit remains. The best time to drink the reds will be from 1992*" (Murray Tyrrell).

CABERNET SAUVIGNON

Bordeaux, with a heavy Australian accent. These are the wines the best cellars are cautiously losing for a year or two, just to see. "*The best Cabernets come from Clare and Coonawarra*" croons Murray Tyrrell. "*That's the way it was,*" says an up-to-the-minute Hugh Johnson, "*until tiny wineries such as IDYLL and MOUNT MARY, near Melbourne, started producing beautifully delicate French-style Cabernets.*"

Meanwhile, back at South Australia's big 2 Cs, WYNN'S, ROUGE HOMME, PENFOLD'S, HILL-SMITH, BRAND'S LAIRA and WOLF BLASS fight for the crown. Grapies give Brand's Laira the Golden Mouton award; Wolf, too, likes to be seen in Mouton's clothing. In the Hunter, the small barrels used by Max Lake for his LAKES FOLLY wines earn Hugh Johnson's approval ("*splendid*"). Max Lake thinks 1969, 1972, 1978, 1980, 1981 and 1985 his best vintages.

SHIRAZ

Also known as Hermitage, and the same red grape as that used in the Rhône. The Rambo of the wine world: finds muscles in your mouth you never knew were there. Much admired by the best palates. Penfold's Grange Hermitage is Australia's best of the best for Hugh Johnson: "*The one true first-*

Murray Tyrrell's 10 best Hunter Valley wines

1952 McWilliams Stephen Hermitage
1954 Tulloch Hermitage
1959 Lindeman's 5924 Red
1967 McWilliams Hermitage
1967 Lindeman's Chablis (Semillon)
1972 Rothbury Semillon-Chardonnay
1973 Tyrrell's Chardonnay
1974 Tulloch Verdelho-Semillon
1976 Tyrrell's Pinot Noir
1979 McWilliams Semillon

“ I enjoy serving Australian white wines at a dinner party, and seeing the surprise and delight on the faces of international guests. I've discovered some very select wines in Victoria – particularly whites. And I will be putting down some young reds and building up a cellar ” (SUSAN RENOUF)

“ I'm a great believer in drinking the wines and eating the produce of the country you're in. Great Sauternes like Château d'Yquem are unbeatable, but an Australian sticky like Peter Lehmann's Riesling is nice and unctuous and goes well with pudding ” (LEO SCHOFIELD)

growth of the southern hemisphere", while Auberon Waugh has described it as "*Australia's equivalent of Château Latour*". It is one of the two finest Australian wines Michael Broadbent has ever tasted: he remembers the 1955 vintage. Sparring partners include the Rothbury Estate (Hunter Valley), Taltarni (Victoria) and Seppelt (Barossa Valley).

SEMILLON

A white grape variety the French use for Sauternes and Graves. Australia has done something to it. No one quite knows what, but it works: "*A total triumph,*" says Hugh Johnson, "*light, dry, soft wine, Chablis-green when young, ageing superbly for up to 20 years.*" The best area for these is the Hunter Valley: the catch is that the Semillon gets called Riesling there (no one quite knows why). Tyrrell's Vat 1 is the one to drown in. If you get pulled out, make for Lindeman's Ben Ean.

RHINE RIESLING

The Real Thing, this time. Its relatively undemanding flavour has always pleased punters. "*The best*", says Hugh Johnson, "*are excitingly flowery, just off dry, satisfyingly acid and well worth several years ageing.*" True Riesling does best when there's a nip in the air and where the grass stays green all summer: Tasmania's PIPER'S BROOK and MOORILLA are tipped and tippled by the best money. Petaluma's Rhine Riesling (trucked home to the Adelaide Hills by Brian Croser) is "*intense, noticeably richer than a German wine, and more elegant and vibrant than most California counterparts*" (Jancis Robinson): "*Clare in South Australia produces the best Rhine Riesling in Australia*" says Murray Tyrrell.

MUSCAT

Comes in two styles: light and aromatic (applauded by knowing antipodeans) and thick and sticky (which has new and old world grapies gurgling with delight). The best comes from Victoria. "*I don't think there is a better drink than the Muscats from North Victoria which are equal to the best ports*" (more Lake lore): "*the best ones are Morris, Baileys, Chambers Rosewood, Brown Bros and Stanton & Killeen.*" Murray Tyrrell's praise is equally restrained: "*Victoria certainly makes the greatest ports and muscats comparable to anywhere in the world. Baileys and Brown Bros and Campbells all produce fabulous wines.*" To which Michael Broadbent would add All Saints Very Old Rutherglen Muscat: on a par with Penfold's great Grange.

TAKE A PAIR OF SPARKLING OZ

There is great snob value in "French champagne" (a sweeping term used by Aussies), but connoisseurs recognize the virtues of the sparklers from two local wineries.

TALTARNI, Victoria. A fine pedigree – set up by Dominique Portet, brother of Bernard of Clos du Val, Napa in California and son of André of Château Lafite. The "champagnes" are recommended by Max Lake and Len Evans. "*The best sparkling wines in the country. There is nowhere else in the world so adventurous. They do a Brut Royal, a sparkling wine with cassis in the bottle; or Brut Tache, an ordinary champagne stained with red wine*" (George Negus.)

YELLOWGLEN, Victoria. Run by French-trained Dominique Landragin. Recommended by Max Lake, George Negus and Gloria Staley.

NEW ZEALAND WINE

"*New Zealand's natural gift is what the winemakers of Australia and California are constantly striving for: the growing conditions that give slowly ripened, highly aromatic rather than super-ripe grapes.*

"*At the north end of the South Island in the Marlborough, or Blenheim region, there is a new estate, the HUNTER ESTATE, whose Chardonnay and Sauvignon are staggeringly good and will be talked about in the future*" (Hugh Johnson). They plant as far south as Christchurch. The other best areas, according to Don Hewitson, are "*on the east coast of the islands*". And the best wines produced are their whites: the top New Zealand Sauvignon Blancs are the "*best white wines*" Don Hewitson knows. Names to watch for are the TE MATA ESTATE and MISSION VINEYARDS (both in Hawkes Bay), and MATUA VALLEY WINES (Waimauku). Cooks' version "*shows promise*" (Hugh Johnson). Look out, too, for the Gewürztraminer of MATAWHERO WINES ("*It seems rather as if the British wine trade has been talking about Dennis Irwin's Gewürztraminer for decades, but in fact it is only a matter of years,*" notes Don Hewitson) and the MORTON ESTATE (on the Bay of Plenty: supplies are always good). MONTANA'S spicy Riesling is appreciated by Hugh Johnson, and Morton's Chardonnay is appreciated by everyone who tastes it. The best reds are the Te Mata Cabernet Sauvignon/Merlot blend ("*a very fine wine,*" approves Hugh), McWILLIAMS Cabernet Sauvignon and NOBILO's Pinot Noir. The Montana Lindauer is, for Glynn Christian, "*the best champagne-style wine.*"

"There is enormous potential in New Zealand. In the next 5 years, we'll see New Zealand as the white wine producer challenging the very best in the world" (SIMON LOFTUS)

FAR EAST

TOP 10

★

1 KICCHO, Osaka
2 SONG HE LOU, Suzhou
3 FOOK LAM MOON, Hong Kong
4 MAN WAH, Hong Kong
5 DONG FENG, Sichuan
6 GADDI'S, Hong Kong
7 NODAIWA, Tokyo
8 NORTHERN VILLAGE SEAFOOD, Singapore
9 SUNNING UNIFORN, Hong Kong
10 PIERROT, Hong Kong

JAPAN

TOKYO

BEST RESTAURANTS

JAPANESE

NODAIWA, 1-5-4 Higashi Azabu, Minato-ku ☎ (03) 583 7852. Established at the end of the Edo era, it has always fed a stash of celebrities. Its speciality is kaba-yaki (broiled eel). A favourite of Shizuo Tsuji, who admires their ability to find obscure ingredients.

DAIGO, 2-4-2 Atago, Minato-ku ☎ (03) 431 0811. A great vegetarian restaurant, particularly for shojin ryori (Japanese vegetarian food, served on special occasions). Recommended by Tina Chow, who says it was formerly annexed to a temple in Shiba Koen. Idyllic setting in the temple garden.

FUKUDAYA, 6 Kiocho, Chiyoda-ku ☎ (03) 261 8577. Getting a reservation in this place requires a series of complex negotiations (it *is* refined and exclusive) and the bill is also in the higher realms of experience. But it is still an experience not to be missed. You and your partner dine alone in an olde cottage set a short distance away from the main inn (the kimono-d waitress runs back and forth along a flagstoned garden path to serve you). An intriguing series of miniature mouthful-sized delicacies (including a superb squid) follows and goes on-and-on-and-on.

GOEMON, 1-1-26 Hon-Komagome, Bunkyo-ku ☎ (03) 811 2015. The best place in Tokyo for traditional tofu cuisine. (Most people make a bee-line for the little tea-houses seating 5 or 6, set high in the garden.) This restaurant puts tofu in the top echelons of cooking and not just the worthy health-food slabs of putty we know in the West (try tomoe dangaku, for example, which is a kind of tofu kebab). In winter, food is cooked over a brazier at your table to warm you as well.

HOUMASA, 3-2-21 Moto-Azabu, Minato-ku ☎ (03) 479 2880. Tiny restaurant (two tables, one private room for 4 and a counter that seats 10) offering kaiseki ryori (a delicate imperial food designed to be eaten before the tea ceremony). The chef of this quiet, refined little place is Mr Hara, who, despite clamouring businessmen, refuses to open at lunchtime. No prices on the menu but expect to pay about 10,000 yen (US$56).

INAGIKU, 2-9-8 Nihonbashi Kayabacho, Chuo-ku ☎ (03) 669 5501. Japanese equivalent of the Tour d'Argent in Paris (and in New York there's a branch at the Waldorf). The height of Japanese luxury with delicate hovering hand 'n' foot service, understated design, the best tempura in Tokyo and, for psyched-up businessmen, old-fashioned Japanese peace. After hors d'oeuvres (such as one teriyakied scallop, marinated chestnuts and bits of crisp vegetables in a mysterious sauce) you move on to dobinmushi (an autumn broth). Then comes the magnificent tempura sequence (you are given a list of the 18 types that might be served).

ISEGEN, 1-11-1 Kandusada-cho, Chiyoda ☎ (03) 251 1229. Wonderful old-fashioned restaurant specializing in one perfect special dish – anko-nabe (monkfish, tofu and Japanese vegetable stew). This dish is in season from September to March and this very friendly, noisy restaurant acts like a magnet on a cold winter's day. The anko-nabe comes with strange crunchy pickles and afterwards (if you ask her) the waitress will make an ojiya at your table (a sort of chunky rice-broth omelette spiked with fresh herbs and chopped scallions). You all sit on tatami mats around small tables in one big room.

ISEJU 14-9 Kodenmacho, Nihonbashi ☎ (03) 663 7841. Founded in 1869 by the Takamiyama family, this is the longest established (and the very best) place for sukiyaki in Tokyo. The restaurant specializes in beef dishes using meat from its own butcher's shop (a big meat counter faces out on to the street). Speciality of the house is their gyu-nabe, a superb stew cooked at your table in antique copper-lined lacquer basins full of water. Authentic and no frills: a genuine

"In Japan, oysters are regarded as a poor man's food, but persuade a fisherman to give you some in a jam jar, take them home and bake them in a pie, and it's absolutely delicious. Very good, very cheap oysters." (QUENTIN CREWE)

"My favourite food is sushi. There are many kinds, but I mean nigirizushi – sushi shaped by hands. It's made by adding a dab of wasabi to a bite-size rice ball, on to which is firmly pressed fresh raw seafood such as filletted sea-bream, tuna, shrimp or abalone." (SHIZUO TSUJI)

sukiyaki dinner costs a modest 10,000 yen (US$56) per head (including sake).

KICCHO, 8-17-4 Ginza, Chuo-ku ☎ (03) 541 8228. A branch of the great Kiccho in Osaka. "*The best restaurant for kaiseki in Tokyo with food served on exquisite dishes*" (Tina Chow). Strictly invitation only (even Prime Minister Nakasone needs one) to taste kaiseki ryori, to be eaten before the tea ceremony. Food is just part of the total experience (your eyes are also supposed to eat the design of the room, the *art*, the colour and texture of serving dishes).

KIZUSHI, 6-17-2 Hongo, Bunkyo-ku ☎ (03) 811 5934. Good place to go to dazzle the blasé seen-it-all sushi crowd. On first sight Kizushi looks like any other sushi spot (you can't miss it near the huge red gates of Tokyo university). But one phone call changes all that. With advance notice, the restaurant's sushi whizz, Yamaguchi-san, will lay on a stunning sushi banquet. New York and Californian sushi bores leave *amazed.*

KOMAGATA DOJU, 1-7-12 Komagata, Taito-ku ☎ (03) 842 4001. Top place for minimalist fish cuisine, going since 1801 and rebuilt 3 times after 2 earthquakes and 1 war. The menu is centred around the sardine-sized fish called dojo (roach), served in a score of imaginative ways, such as Yanagawa nabe (sliced dojo in a thin omelette). Thick boards serve as (very) low tables and you sit on thin cushions on the split-bamboo floor.

KYOAJI, 3-3-3 Shinbashi ☎ (03) 591 3344. Recommended by Tina Chow for kaiseki. The owner hails from the home of ceremonial food, Kyoto – the old capital.

SHIRUYOSHI, 6-2-12 Akasaka, Minato-ku ☎ (03) 583 0333. Tokyo's limo and table-telephone folk congregate here to toy with the tempura and kaiseki after a hard day's power-broking. The main branch of this top person's eatery was founded in Osaka in 1947 (the seasoning is definitely of the Kyoto/ Osaka school – less obvious, less salty than Tokyo palates are used to). Although the kaiseki is first class, purists may not like this place because it tries to combine the Japanese food ethic with Western Noov luxe (fitted carpets, crystal tumblers, buttoned leather loungers, yes, even Martinis).

TENMI, Shizen Shokuhin Centre, 1-10-6 Jinnan, Shibuya-ku ☎ (03) 496 9703. The best health-food restaurant in Tokyo. Its imaginatively presented food draws the macrobiotic showbiz crowd, models and foreigners in the know. Scrubbed tables, shoji screens, simple chairs and a tatami-mat alcove add up to a natural Japanese simplicity which makes you feel r-e-l-a-x-e-d the minute you walk in. Star attraction is the health-food hamper or Makunoushi (a fantastic health-food meal with seaonal ingredients presented in a handsome lacquered box).

TONKI, 1-1-2 Shimo-Meguro, Meguro-ku ☎ (03) 491 9928. The best robotic dining experience in Tokyo (provided you like pork as

THE GOOD FUGU GUIDE

The best (and the most expensive) gastronomic fright in Japan is to play stomach roulette with fugu (poisonous blow-fish). The raw flesh of the fugu is usually okay, but the innards are 500 times more lethal than cyanide. This is the place where gastronomy and martial arts meet – and it's the absolute pinnacle of Japanese cuisine. (They also worship it and make a decorative cult out of it.) Today, fugu cooks in Japan need an official licence to practise, which they only earn after years of training, but around 30 fugu-eaters still die every year (mostly amateur cooks who took a fugu home to have a go). If uncertainty adds to your fun in eating out, there's fuguashi (an exquisite pattern of raw flakes eaten with a soy, bitter orange and green chive sauce); or fuguchiri (a rather more dangerous soup) or birezake (sun-dried fugu fins) which you dip in hot sake. And like the innocent oyster, you eat fugu only when there's an aaargh in the month …

that is all there is). The ultimate pork chop (tonkatsu) is to be found here, resulting in 800 people battering the door to get in every day. Robotic décor means a blaze of white lights, a frighteningly clinical assembly-line *"eating bar"* and fifteen white-shoed assistants slotting you and your order in with breathtaking timing. As well as tonkatsu, pork also comes as rosu (roast), hire (scrumptious fillet) and kushikatsu (Japanese pork kebab). A long wait – up to half an hour – but no matter: this is a glimpse of the Future.

ECLECTIC

A TANTOT, Axis Bldg, 3rd Fl, 5-17-1 Roppongi, Minato-ku ☎ (03) 586 4431. You've heard of the Axis Building, Tokyo's chic-est shopping spot: if you seriously want kangaroo-skin driving shoes from Le Garage, goose-down pillows or the most minimal-ever furniture from Cassina, the Axis shopping arcades will provide, from the best of Japanese design. In the middle of all this, A Tantot is the ultimate designer's restaurant (everything down to the stainless steel swizzlestix is perfectly designed). Food is a bit designed, too – French/japonais (nouvellish in other words).

KURUMAYA DOWNSTAIRS, 2-37-1 Kabukicho, Shinjuku-ku ☎ (03) 232 0301. This is a cult restaurant among Western visitors to Tokyo. Chef Kiyoshi Ozawa has hit on the daring idea of treating Western ingredients with Japanese sensitivity to come up with yofu kaiseki – Western food prepared as if for a tea ceremony. East marries West is the theme throughout (forks and chopsticks, lacquerware and Limoges).

LOBSTER INN, 1-4-50 Nishi-Azabu, Minato-ku ☎ (03) 478 1261. Best place in Japan for fresh North American lobster. This place is tucked away near a US Army area and looks like a Maine coast clam bar on the outside (white clapboard 'n' ivy) and ultra-modern Italian inside. Lobster in every way – bisque: blanched: split and grilled: dipped in melted butter and lemon juice (New England style): dipped in light soy and vinegar sauce (Japanese style) or poached in champagne and served with champagne butter. Competitively priced French white Burgundy and a highly reckoned blackcurrant sorbet.

PRUNIER, Tokyo Kaikan, 2nd Fl, 3-2-1 Marunouchi, Chiyoda-ku ☎ (03) 215 2111. Very grand, very subdued, very Western fish restaurant (packed at midday by the out-to-lunch international banking set). 40 tables with huge window overlooking the Imperial moat, plus swish opera boxes to dine in and the Grill Rossini downstairs sets the scene. Prunier's offers Beluga caviare at a bargain price (5,200 yen/US$29 for 1 oz/28 g) and keeps the cuisine French bourgeoise in tone.

FRENCH

JOEL, Kyodo Building, 2nd Fl, 5-6-24 Minami-Aoyama, Minato-ku ☎ (03) 400 7149. Despite the external dinge (tatty plastic sign, faded Club Méditerranée poster etc), this is widely voted one of the best French restaurants in Tokyo. Chef-owner Joel Bruants worked with Paul Bocuse at Collonges-au-Mont-d'Or before sweeping on to be chef de cuisine at the Tokyo Rengaya. 15 is their maximum number.

L'ORANGERIE, Hanae Mori Bldg, Omote Sando, 3-6-1 Kita Aoyama ☎ (03) 407 7461. A vast, understated white room, very French, with Georgian-style chairs. *The* place to be seen for brunch in Tokyo. Fashion designers, architects, anyone who's in town, crowd informally here. Food is from a buffet (sliced salmon with sour cream, a fine selection of cheeses rarely found in Japan).

Designer Hanae Mori (see FASHION) opened this restaurant above her offices in the Seventies to save time rushing off for business lunches. *"At that time there were no restaurants run on strictly continental lines with a certain ambience for the diner. I'd become used to such places in New York and Paris and wanted to re-create it here. I adore food and because I work so hard, I need to eat a lot for energy. I don't watch my weight!"* (Hanae Mori).

MAXIM'S, Sony Bldg, 3rd Basement, 5-3-1 Ginza, Chuo-ku ☎ (03) 571 3621. Glitzy replica of the fin-de-siècle Parisian restaurant installed by Sony tycoon Akio Morita in 1966 (all Tokyo staff still spend 6 months training in Paris). Paquet is the chef and a packet is what it costs when you get stuck into items like his Caneton Rôti aux Pêches. One of his own creations is the Poëlon des Pécheurs Breton (a yumptious, slightly japonais fish stew). Some travellers reckon this to be the best French restaurant in Japan (and everyone agrees it has the best wine list in Tokyo).

CHINESE

BODAIJU, Bukkyo Dendo Center Bldg, 2nd Fl, 4-3-14 Shiba, Minato-ku ☎ (03) 456 3257. The official restaurant of the Buddhism Promotion Foundation (the only place in Tokyo where you can dive in for some ancient Chinese vegetarian cuisine). The food is excitingly different from the established Chinese cuisines known in the West (weeny sautéed vegetable sandwiches, for example). This style of cooking has only just hit Japan (the cooks all hail from Hong Kong) and is tipped to follow Sichuan as the new cult cuisine in the West. When it's time to feed your soul, there's a meditation hall in the restaurant complex.

LE CHINOIS, Bianca Bldg basement, 3-1-26 Jinguamae, Shibuya-ku ☎ (03) 403 3929. Tokyo's most strangely glamorous restaurant, drawing late-night city sleekers. Décor is art deco plus Italian leather squashy sofas (it inspired Wolfgang Puck's Chinois on Main in LA). The food is not wildly authentic Chinese, just clever-Zennish, but remember you go here for the Restaurant-As-Theatre Experience.

HAI WHAN, Akasaka Floral Bldg, 4/5 Fls, 3-8-8 Akasaka, Minato-ku ☎ (03) 586 5666. If cruelty to fish makes you cry, avoid this one-and-only example of Chinese haixian restaurant. Haixian is the ultimate in very simple and elegant Chinese food (everything is so fresh there is almost no cooking involved). Here the emphasis is on LIVE fish. There is a marble pool with every known type of fish in the entrance hall; then a wooden bowl jumping with it is brought for your attention. The chef cuts and serves the live fish and a few minutes later you could be eating an amazing "carp tartare" with the head and tail still quivering.

KEIKA, 3-25-6 Shinjuku, Shinjuku-ku ☎ (03) 352 4836. There are those who say that the very best ramen (robust Chinese-style noodles) are to be found on a street stall under a red lantern as a late-night snack. However, if there is no red light in your district, there are 3 branches of Keika in Japan, a restaurant that specializes in ramen. If you are absolutely starving (and can't face another tiny delicate mouthful) make for this branch – the original ramen headquarters. Best thing on the menu is the taromen (a huge bowl of al dente noodles, garlic cabbage, a rich soup that could stand up on its own, plus big chunks of pork). And all for 650 yen (US$4).

AMERICAN

SPAGO, 5-7-8 Roppongi, Minato-ku ☎ (03) 423 4025. A branch of the LA original and Japan's best American restaurant, where the Tokyo Yuppies, known as Tuppies, hang out. Décor is one vast peachy-pastel aircraft hangar full of fresh flowers and garden furniture, designed by Barbara Lazaroff. Star culinary attractions are the marinated fresh tuna, capelli di angeli (pasta with goat cheese and asparagus), calf's liver with red onion marmalade, and grilled tuna with mint sauce. This is also the place to hit for the best Californian Cabernet Sauvignons in Tokyo.

BEST CAFES AND BARS

CHIANTI, Ikuma 3-1-7, Azabadia, Minato-ku ☎ (03) 583 7546. *"The only decent espresso to be found in Tokyo,"* says Tina Chow of the ground-floor coffee bar in this restaurant which also serves *"rather decent Italian food and the best chocolate mousse in Tokyo"* (Claudia Cragg).

FRANK LLOYD WRIGHT BAR, Imperial Hotel, 1-1-1 Uchisaiwai-cho, Chiyoda-ku ☎ (03) 504 1111. Like Hong Kong's Captain's Bar at the Mandarin: expats and other smarties crowd in for pre-prandials.

LOS PLATOS, Terrace Akasaka, 6-13-11 Akasaka, Minato-ku ☎ (03) 583 4262. Wonderfully authentic Spanish bar where you slip straight into the tapas habit (small plates of hot or cold appetizers to while away hunger pangs before the Very Late Spanish Dinner). 35 Andalusian tapas are on offer plus Cerveza (beer) and, of course, a wide choice of Spanish wine.

RUNDELL, 8-3-7 Ginza, Chuo-ku ☎ (03) 572 3843. Wildly expensive cocktail club catering to Tokyo's male expense-accounters (a few hours for a party of 4 means a bill for 100,000 yen/US$560). Limos wait to take execs and guests home (the bill is sent to the office).

STOVE ROOT, 1-26-16 Minami-Aoyama, Minato-ku ☎ (03) 401 2876. Nice, comfortable rambling caff where you can flop over a cup of coffee all day. Big salads, pasta and interesting piped jazz.

COUNTRY

BEST RESTAURANTS

JAPANESE

♔ **KICCHO, 3-23 Koraibashi, Higashiku, Osaka ☎ (06) 231 1937.** *"My most favourite restaurant in Japan, because of its absolute perfection in all respects. Mr Teiichi Yuki is an exceptionally skilled chef held in the highest esteem. Superb quality food. Also renowned for the tableware and furniture – many are art treasures"* (Shizuo Tsuji). Paul Levy is just one other admirer.

ARAGAWA, 2-15-18, Naka-yamate-dori, Chuo-ku, Kobe ☎ (078) 221 8547. Stupendous steakery using only first-class Sanda beef, from specially bred cattle. *"The tenderness and flavour of the meat is top qualty; it's seasoned only with salt and pepper and broiled on special grills – a truly perfect steak dinner"* (Shizuo Tsuji).

CHIHANA, Nawate-higashi-iru, Shi jo-dori, Higashiyama-ku, Kyoto ☎ (075) 561 2741. Small kappo (top-grade restaurant for authentic Japanese cuisine) which serves Kyoto's traditional dishes. *"The standard surpasses that of a first-class ryotei [usually bigger and more expensive than a kappo]. Beautiful presentation of food served on plates of super quality. In front of the clean cypress counter [for 9 at most], you can watch the itamae [chef] deftly perform his art"* (Shizuo Tsuji).

FUJIWARA, 3-6-14 Motomachi-dori, Chuo-ku, Kobe ☎ (078) 331 3373. Immaculate restaurant for some of

SAKE PARTY

"The best sake is summer sake from a small producer – white, not clear, served chilled" (Barbara Kafka). And the best time to taste the best sake is when you're in Japan. Sample what's on offer in a nomiya (sake-house). The best one is **SASASHU, 2-2-2 Ikebukuro, Toshima-ku ☎ (03) 971 9363.** Sake-tasting sessions here are spaced out with palate-clearing nibbles (or for hungries, a big slice of charcoal-grilled salmon). The famous old theatrical sake-house, **CHICHIBU NISHIKI, 2-13-14 Ginza, Chuo-ku ☎ (03) 541 4777** is a conservationist's dream: a beautifully preserved wooden town-house, plus antique fittings and Shinto altar room. (Actors flock in from the magical Kabuki Theatre next door.) If you want to take away, buy your sake from **YANIGAYA SAKETEN, Kaiji-cho, Kanda ☎ (03) 265 5001.**

the most perfect tempura in Japan. *"The golden, thin-fried coating is a true delight to the senses"* (Shizuo Tsuji).

SANKO-IN-TEMPLE, 3-1-36 Hon-machi, Koganei-chi ☎ (0423) 811116. A spiritual experience through vegetarian food. It offers ancient Buddhist temple food (shojin ryori to those in the know) in a peaceful temple surrounded by trees and moss. The equivalent of vegan food, it contains no animal or dairy products. You sit down quietly in your private room and wait to be served every 20 minutes or so with understated mouthfuls. The only restaurant in the world to serve robai – fresh wheat gluten on a bed of konbu kelp.

TAKO UME, 1-1-8 Doton-bori, Minami-ku, Osaka ☎ (06) 211 0321. Renowned oden restaurant. Clients sit at a counter for about 18 people. You can't book, so look – and wait.

TAMIYA, 2-4 Kakuda-cho, Kita-ku, Osaka ☎ (06) 361 7513. Fish specialists. *"The owner is so careful about selecting the freshest fish possible that he closes after a storm"* (Shizuo Tsuji).

CHINA

"The most exotic food market in the world is the People's Free Market in Canton, at 6 am, just a few steps from the White Swan Hotel on Pearl River" (Anne Willan).

BEST RESTAURANTS

BEIJING

CHINESE

FENGZE YUAN, Zhushikou, No 83 ☎ 332828. Expensive, prestigious place famed for its fine seafood and chicken.

HUAIYANG FANZHUANG, Xidan N, No 217 ☎ (660521. Good rich seafood – crabs, prawns, eels and more.

"I have tried gourmet delicacies in China like elephant's trunk and bear's paw (which is supposed to be an aphrodisiac). They are braised and cooked for a long time. I do not really recommend the elephant" (YAN-KIT SO)

SHAGUO JU, Xisi Kaijie, No 60 ☎ 663206. This 300-year-old restaurant is the oldest in Beijing. Its Manchurian specialities centre around pork (sometimes cooked in ceramic pots).

SHOUFENG HUIMEN KAOROU, Xuanwumennei, No 102 ☎ 330700. Charming old Mongolian restaurant where you cook your own meat on a barbecue.

SICHUAN FANDIAN, Rongxian Hutong, No 51 ☎ 336356. A nine-courtyard house with beautiful décor (one of the few restaurants in China where you can also feast your eyes). Offers excellent hot peppery dishes including Sichuan duck.

TINGLI GUAN, Summer Palace ☎ 281276. This place was once the private theatre of the Dowager Empress Tz'u Hsi. Set on the north shore near the Marble Boat, it's a stunning place to eat Velvet Chicken, fish from the lake and other Imperial dishes.

XIANGJIANG FANZHUANG, Xidan, No 135 ☎ 661414. The best place to eat dog (if you really want to). Also does good peppery Dongan Chicken.

XIANGSHAN FANDIAN, Hunting Park (go in the main gate, turn left, then right, up the hill for 75 yards/68 m) **☎ 819244.** By the time you get there, you deserve the excellent soft-fried duck liver, spring rolls, noodles.

COUNTRY

BEST RESTAURANTS

CHINESE

SONG HE LOU, 141 Guangqian St, Suzhou ☎ 2066. What this restaurant lacks in décor it makes up for in quality of food with chef Liu Chih tipped as one of the best in the world by Paul Levy.

DONG FENG, Dong Feng Lu, Chengdu, Sichuan ☎ 7012. Also hailed by Paul Levy as one of the best restaurants in the world. Zhou Bai Meng is the chef (he and Liu Chih are the 2 best in China). Both are elderly, great teachers and walking encyclopedias of their culinary tradition.

PANXI, Li Wan Rd E, Canton ☎ 85655. Charming restaurant complex built on a series of artificial lakes with interconnecting pavilions. *"The complete shoddiness of 40 years of neglect but nonetheless very agreeable"* (Paul Levy).

HONG KONG

BEST RESTAURANTS

CHINESE

FOOK LAM MOON, 459 Lockhart Rd, Causeway Bay ☎ (5) 891 2644. *"Outstanding genuine local food but very expensive"* (Paul Levy). *"Come here for dried superior abalone which is excellent and reasonably priced"* (Doreen Leung).

MAN WAH, Mandarin Hotel, 5 Connaught Rd, Central ☎ (5) 220111. Hong Kong is food city and that goes for the hotels too. (This is one of the few cities in the world where you don't steer clear of the hotel restaurants.) Perched high on top of the Mandarin, this place is famed for its scrumptious Cantonese cuisine. Voted by Lord Lichfield and Paul Levy as one of the best restaurants in the world.

SUNNING UNICORN, 1 Sunning Rd, Causeway Bay ☎ (5) 776620. Highly recommended by Hong Kong's gastronomes, you will find yourself in an elegant traditional Chinese setting to enjoy exceptional Chinese and Sichuan cuisine. Don't miss the speciality of the house – drunken prawns.

❝ At Aberdeen, there is a wonderful market where you can buy live langoustine, crab and all sorts of exotic fish ❞
(YAN-KIT SO)

FUNG LUM, 45-47 Tsuen Nam Rd, Taiwai, Shatin, New Territories ☎ (0) 621175. Best place in HK for pigeon.

GREAT SHANGHAI, 26 Prat Ave, Tsimshatsui, Kowloon ☎ (3) 668158. Tina Chow chows the freshwater crabs here (and also goes for the "*drunken Shanghai crabs*". Star attractions of this Shanghainese restaurant are the Mandarin fish (carp to you), Shanghai-bred eels in garlic sauce and the world-famous crabs. (HK's crab season is Oct–Nov.)

NORTH SEA FISHING VILLAGE RESTAURANT, Basement Auto Plaza, Tsimshatsui E, Kowloon ☎ (3) 723 6843; 445 King's Rd, Ground Fl, N Point ☎ (5) 630188. Two of the finest restaurants in the Hong Kong area (they owe their name to the fact the host company also owns a fishing village which supplies fresh seafood to both restaurants). At the centre of each restaurant, there is an authentic Chinese junk stacked and floodlit with tanks of fishy victims (you choose your own). Excellent prawns, octopus, crab, shark fins plus good dim sum.

OI MAN, 4 Ching St, Lau Fau Shan, New Territories ☎ (0) 721504. This is recommended by Paul Levy as a great fisherman's restaurant (it is set bang in the middle of a seething fish market). You buy your own live fish and shellfish straight from the fisherman, take it into the restaurant, and they cook it.

SICHUAN GARDEN, 3rd Fl, Gloucester Tower, Central ☎ (5) 214433. "*Authentic food, and accommodating staff. The thing I like especially is the smoked tea duck which I have rarely had so good even in China. The chefs were trained in Sichuan province and are some of the best chefs in Hong Kong. This is one of the few Chinese restaurants which also does great desserts. They have a coconut and honeydew melon soup which is a great ending for a spicy meal*" (Ken Hom).

SUN TUNG LOK'S SHARK'S FIN RESTAURANT, Phase 3, Harbour City, 25-27 Canton Rd, Kowloon ☎ (3) 722 0288. "*The place for expensive and unusual southern Chinese food*" (Paul Levy). "*What I like about this place is it's art deco-ish and looks like a setting for a Fred Astaire and Ginger Rogers film – you expect them to come running into the restaurant and start dancing. They have all kinds of wonderful shark's fin dumplings which are superb*" (Ken Hom).

ECLECTIC

GADDI'S, Peninsula Hotel, Salisbury Rd, Kowloon ☎ (3) 666251. One of the best HK restaurants serving Western food. "*I love Gaddi's. Really fabulous food. Their roast pigeon breasts and salads are really wonderful – especially the foie gras salad. They also do a wonderful watercress ginger soup which is out of this world*" (Ken Hom). Also terrine du chef, oyster soup, stuffed quail, etc. A favourite of Lord Lichfield.

KEN HOM'S FAVOURITE MEAL

"*I like really simple things – vegetables like flowering Chinese cabbage, stir-fried with salt and garlic, plain rice, chicken simply steamed with a dipping sauce of ginger and salt and oil. I would have a perfect steamed fish – nothing beats that, finished off with soy sauce, spring onions and hot oil. Roast duck – roasted in 2 styles – Cantonese (with a marinade inside the cavity of bean sauce, a little stock, fresh coriander . . .) and Peking (dried in a certain way and served with pancakes). I'd be greedy and have both. It sounds so simple and wonderful, but to me, that's an ideal meal*" (Ken Hom).

HONG COGNAC

More cognac is drunk in Hong Kong than anywhere else in the world. Here it is a symbol of style and here it is "*the most expensive place in the world to drink cognac – a bottle of the top of the range, such as Courvoisier's XO, can cost well over £100. It's a surprise to Europeans to learn that superior cognac is often drunk over ice or with water – that's how the Chinese like it and often with their meals. The Chinese perhaps more than anyone know and appreciate their cognac. The older generation in particular believe that foods are either chilling or warming to the blood or spirit. Cognac is believed to be one of the most warming, particularly to a man's virility. This is why you will see groups of quite poor Chinese eating with a bottle of cognac in front of them*" (Glynn Christian). The historical reason for Hong Kong's cognac lust is variously ascribed to a shortage of good rice wine before World War II and to the perspicacity of the Chinese, who noticed that while foreign sailors drank rum, their officers always drank brandy, and the captain, cognac.

FRENCH

PIERROT, Mandarin Hotel, 5 Connaught Rd, Central ☎ (5) 220111. The best French restaurant in Hong Kong, frequented by bejewelled and fashionable Chinese. A favourite of Diane Freis.

MARGAUX, Shangri-La Hotel, 64 Mody Rd, Tsimshatsui E, Kowloon ☎ (3) 721 2111. First-class French cuisine in luxurious surroundings.

BEST CAFES AND BARS

CAPTAIN'S BAR, Mandarin Hotel (see NIGHTLIFE).

DRAGON BOAT BAR, Hilton, 2 Queen's Road, Central ☎ (5) 233111. The best place in HK for strange cocktails such as a Big Bamboo.

L'APERITIF, Peninsula Hotel, Salisbury Rd, Kowloon ☎ (3) 666251. Chic piano-bar for quiet sophisticated music.

PEAK TOWER COFFEE SHOP, Victoria Peak ☎ (5) 849 7381. The best café giving the best panorama of HK.

YAM SING BAR, Lee Gardens Hotel, Hysan Ave, Causeway Bay ☎ (5) 767211. The best place in HK to spend the happy hour. The name means "bottoms up". Intimate atmosphere and live music.

THAILAND

BANGKOK

BEST RESTAURANTS

THAI

BANKAEW RUENKWAN, 212 Soi 12 Sukhumvit Road ☎ (2) 251 8229. One of the best restaurants in Bangkok for traditional Thai seafood dishes (but don't expect any concessions to feeble European taste buds).

CHITPOCHANA, 62 Soi 20, Sukhumvit Rd ☎ (2) 258 6401. Some of the best authentic Thai food in the world is available here in a restaurant where you can eat indoors (in air-conditioned splendour) or outdoors (in lovely gardens splashing with fountains). The branch at the Oriental Hotel is also recommended.

INDRA REGENT HOTEL, Rajprarob Rd ☎ (2) 251 1111. A Thai-style theatre-restaurant, similar to Piman (see below).

PIMAN, 46 Soi 49, Sukhumvit Rd ☎ (2) 258 8107. Best restaurant in Bangkok for décor (if not for food). The theatre-restaurant is an ancient Thai institution (you watch classical dancing while you eat). This theatre-restaurant is a replica of the 14th-century Sukothai-period house in which you can watch the show and eat toned-down Thai food. Unashamedly touristy.

FRENCH

FIREPLACE GRILL, President Hotel, 135–26 Gaysorn Rd, ☎ (2) 253 0444. Best grill room in Bangkok, for dishes such as steak au poivre and agneau provençale.

NORMANDIE GRILL, Oriental Hotel, 48 Oriental Ave ☎ (2) 234 8621. Superb French cuisine in one of the best hotels in the world (see TRAVEL). Beautifully presented, delicately sauced fresh local fish and seafood are specialities. You also feast your eyes on a rooftop view of the Chao Phya River. Prince Thanadsri recommends it for its atmosphere. The Prince also munches on to the LORD JIM'S restaurant in the old part of the Oriental, which he couldn't put higher in the cuisine stakes: *"It's got the most lavish buffet in South-east Asia."*

SCANDINAVIAN

TWO VIKINGS, 2 Soi 35, Sukhumvit Rd ☎ (2) 258 1470. Many people vote this the best European restaurant in Bangkok. Set in an old Thai house, this elegant six-roomed restaurant is just the place to think of cool northern forests and the whole Norse code when the Far-Eastern colour and heat get to be just too much ...

CHINESE

JADE GARDEN, Montien Hotel, 54 Suriwongse Rd ☎ (2) 234 8060. Hot-spot for Cantonese cooking with one of the best buffet lunches on offer in Bangkok.

JAPANESE

AOYAMA, 960 Rama IV Rd ☎ (2) 233 4832. The best Japanese restaurant in Bangkok with some luxurious touches (you can order a Japanese bath before dinner and, after it's all over, enjoy a leisurely walk in an exquisite garden). Geishas waft around to add to the air of imperial luxury. Pricy.

INDIAN

CAFE INDIA, 460/8 Suriwongse Rd ☎ (2) 233 0419. North Indian and tandoori specialist – some of the best Indian food in SE Asia.

BEST BAR

ORIENTAL HOTEL (see TRAVEL). Chic quaffing, indoors or out on the terrace. *"I love their Oriental Slings, made of Thai whisky and lime juice"* (Auberon Waugh).

COUNTRY

BEST RESTAURANT

PAE KRUNG KAO, K 4 U-Thong Rd, Ayutthaya ☎ (35) 257236. The name means "floating restaurant" and it's the *"best restaurant in Thailand"* (Prince Thanadsri). Ayutthaya is the ancient capital of old Siam (founded in 1350 by Prince U-Thong) and it lies in a loop of the Chao Phya River (driving takes one and a half hours from Bangkok). Drink in the Pagoda of Sri Suriyothi, the Buddha Mongkol, the Poo Khao Thong Monastery and other fantastic ruins and then move on to the best dishes of the Pae Krung Kao. Prince Thanadsri recommends the grilled freshwater lobster with rice and nahm pla (the famous Thai fish sauce) and tom yum kung (a spicy prawn soup).

MALAYSIA

KUALA LUMPUR

BEST RESTAURANTS

INN OF HAPPINESS, Kuala Lumpur Hilton, Jalan Sultan Ismail ☎ (03) 422122. Highly recommended for Chinese cuisine.

LE COQ D'OR, 123 Jalan Ampang ☎ (03) 429732. French – one of the best European restaurants in Kuala Lumpur.

PENANG

BEST RESTAURANT

MING PALACE, Ming Court Hotel, 202a Macalister Rd ☎ (04) 26131. Very good Cantonese food.

BEST BAR

EASTERN & ORIENTAL HOTEL, 10 Farquhar St ☎ (04) 375322. The dear old colonial survivor has the best bar service in SE Asia. Go to the E&O for the open-air G&Ts (waiters streak back and forth with drinks as you sit under the palms next to a charming seaside swimming pool).

FOREIGNER'S MILE

The best open-air barbecues in Malaysia are to be found along Batu Ferringhi (Foreigner's Mile), the blissful beach strip of Penang. Check before you book into any of the hotels here that you can dine beneath-the-palms-beneath-the-stars.

SINGAPORE

BEST RESTAURANTS

CHINESE

NORTHERN VILLAGE SEAFOOD RESTAURANT, 124–134 Ground Fl, Orchard Plaza, 150 Orchard Rd ☎ 733 4211. Terry Tan votes this the best Cantonese restaurant in Singapore (with a huge menu). *"Cantonese classics that hark back to Manchu China, plus sumptuous décor reminiscent of imperial China, with blackwood furniture in the best Qing tradition and sculptured gardens. Incredible stewed whelks and esoteric yak meat. Pricy but not out of this world. Definitely for the affluent (or the will-pay-anything gourmand) is the stuffed pigeon with superior bird's nest. Excellent braised tench and crystal prawns. More than an eating experience, a trip into history"* (Terry Tan).

PINE COURT, Mandarin Hotel, 333 Orchard Rd ☎ 737 4411. Highly recommended for Pekinese food (specialities include Peking duck and baked tench).

SHANG PALACE, Shangri-La Hotel, 22 Orange Grove Rd ☎ 737 3644. Fantastic dim sum.

INDIAN

BANANA LEAF APOLLO, Race Course Rd ☎ 293 8682. Simple, excellent place where you eat with your fingers and food is served on a banana leaf plate. This place offers excellent Indian, fish and meat dishes.

OMAR KHAYYAM, 55 Hill St ☎ 336 1505. *"A smallish but lavishly presented North Indian establishment. Dine like a Moghul prince here. Menus are hand-painted with scenes from Indian mythology and the best tandoori chicken in town is served with chunks from the epic of Omar Khayyam. Wadhu Sakrani, the proprietor, is a courtly Indian gentleman who belongs more to the gentry than behind a stove. Hard to beat for sheer splendour in the best Indian tradition"* (Terry Tan).

ECLECTIC

ELIZABETHAN GRILL, Raffles Hotel, 1–3 Beach Rd ☎ 337 8041. Excellent food in opulent surroundings. You can eat Italian or Singapore-ish specialities in the PALM COURT restaurant (an open-air restaurant set in a lush tropical garden), plus (yes) a palm court trio to gently feast your ears after dark.

FRENCH

LA ROTONDE, Marco Polo Hotel, Tanglin Rd ☎ 474 7141. First-class French cuisine.

JAPANESE

UNKAI RESTAURANT, Century Park Sheraton, Nassim Hill ☎ 737 9677. Reputed to be the best Japanese restaurant in Singapore (very expensive).

THAI

CHAO PRAYA, 4272-A, Block 730 Ang Mo Kio Ave 6 ☎ 456 0119. First-rate Thai restaurant in a less salubrious part of town *"amid grotty factories and high-rise flats.*

"You choose your fish or shellfish from tanks and vegetables straight from the counter. They are whisked away to the kitchen behind huge glass windows and you see your dinner being broiled, fried, steamed ad infinitum.

"The food is first-rate Thai and the ambience reminiscent of Bangkok's bustling markets. Specialities are the thom yam soup, hot and sour fish and the green fish curry. You can buy Thai pottery like theirs from the corner shop" (Terry Tan).

NIGHTLIFE

by DAVID SHILLING

WORLD'S BEST NIGHTSPOTS

1
ANNABEL'S, London

2
AREA, New York

3
CASTEL'S, Paris

4
DOUBLES, New York

5
PALLADIUM, New York

6
LEXINGTON QUEEN, Tokyo

7
ROGUES, Sydney

8
CASABLANCA, Hong Kong

9
TRAMP, London

10
INFLATION, Melbourne

If your idea of a great evening is a TV dinner, then this book should change your mind if not your life. There's so much going on: nightclubs vie with charity balls, openings of ballet and opera, art previews, restaurants that are more meet than eat, and lavish private parties.

Nightlife used to mean discothèques. Now there is everything from formal nightclubs to nocturnal theme parks with live music, videos, ever-more vigorous lightshows, and cabaret reminiscent of the Sixties-style "happening". At Palladium in New York, a castle descends onto the dance floor as you gyrate. Some boîtes have private bars for the chosen few, some have membership but let you in if you're sufficiently beautiful, eccentric or rich. Some, like hermit crabs, take temporary homes and then – to retain their elusive, exclusive image – just as you rumble them, slope off to another home.

The best way to find what's "in" is to keep your ears open. However, if you tour the nightclub district and spy a crowd trying to get in somewhere, it's a clue that something's happening in that dirty old basement. The rule is never to join the queue – go to the head of it and charm your way in.

The best nightlife occurs in cities that never sleep. Clubs beget late-night cafés, only known to the clubbing cognoscenti. In Monte Carlo, everyone winds up at the Tip Top, in London you might go on to Brick Lane for a bagel, in Sydney, you move on to Dean's or the Bourbon & Beefsteak in the Cross. In New York, nothing ever seems to close, so when you finish in one club, you go on to the next. The whole point is your attitude to a nightclub: it shouldn't be the end of the evening, it should be the start of something better.

Start off at a smart club like Annabel's in London or Castel's in Paris when you look your best, then move on to let your hair down. I once designed a dress that had a detachable full-length taffeta tulip skirt over a mini dress for women to wear on just that sort of evening. At Annabel's you feel special even before you enter because of its reputation.

Bachelor DAVID SHILLING is British, and best-known for his spectacular hats. At 12, he began designing hats for his mother to wear at Ascot. He went on to become a Lloyd's underwriter and a merchant banker before heading back to hats, and now also designs clothes, fabrics and china. He travels extensively ("in the last month I've been to New York, Los Angeles and Stoke-on-Trent") and clubs frenetically. "Being single, I don't want to go to bed with a hot water bottle, so people tend to point me in the direction of late nightlife and I love it! I even manage to tire New Yorkers out."

It's the same with Jimmyz in Monte Carlo in summer, which has the added bonus of a beautiful location with fountains overlooking the sea. My favourite nightclub in the world is in Gozo, in a castle by the water. The music's good, drinks are cheap, the lights are great and the stars help. The police raid every other night at 1am and it reopens at 1.30. The test of a good club is whether it's worth hiring a helicopter to get you there – and for this one, it is.

In the end, there is no formula for a successful nightclub. Some spend a fortune on décor, lighting and sound equipment and fail. A nightclub is all about mood (one of the saddest sights is a club during the day with the lights up). A good host is important to co-ordinate the moods created by music, décor and drink, to decide who to let in, who to pamper.

It's the same with charity balls. Good organization is essential. First look at the pedigree of the committee (charity begins at home – but whose home have those meetings been in?) and then the venue and theme. I've been to some pretty extraordinary events, from a circus party to one where they showed Valentino movies across the swimming pool. Pools are great for adding mood, but it's not terribly funny to throw somebody in. The same goes for rivers: if the host hasn't supplied breakfast, he doesn't expect you to go down to the trout farm and catch it.

Always remember the golden rule: if you suddenly think you'd rather be in bed, it's time to go home.

EUROPE

"A good club is not just a flashy lighting system, it's about attracting the right membership, and giving them the right facilities. The right mix of people in surroundings they find comfortable" (JOHN GOLD)

BEST NIGHTSPOTS

TOP 5

★

1 **ANNABEL'S, London**
2 **CASTEL'S, Paris**
3 **TRAMP, London**
4 **NO ROCK, Monte Carlo**
5 **LIMELIGHT, London**

ENGLAND

LONDON

ANNABEL'S, 44 Berkeley Square, W1 ☎ (01) 629 3558. Without question, the best in the world. A conventional club that is exclusive in the true sense of the word (prospective members must be proposed and seconded for the £250/US$362-a-year membership). It's the only one where all British royals feel safe. A stream of admirers puts its success down to Mark Birley himself, who opened the club in 1963, naming it after his then wife, and has consistently paid the finest attention to detail in the realms of décor, food and service. *"There is only one nightclub in the whole world and that is Annabel's. The best service, the best people, in the best city. Anywhere you go people will tell you Annabel's is the best"* (Nigel Dempster). *"It would be very hard to beat it or Mark Birley's taste – he's a perfectionist. It's so much a club rather than just a nightclub"* (Lord Lichfield). *"It has stood the test of time. I go at least once a month. I was eating there once when my 4 sons walked in with their girlfriends. It's still a good meeting place to have fun – you see people you know. Service is fantastic – they know what you want and how to treat you"* (Robert Sangster). *"It has a nice atmosphere and you don't feel like a sardine as with so many clubs. You have space to breathe; it's a bit more elegant and a bit more élite"* (Denice Lewis). *"The smartest and most çivilized of nightclubs; also the best service, best food and the finest wine. I would only go midweek – at the weekends there are too many people"* (Richard Compton-Miller). *"I love it because it's a complete change from the Soho clubs – it's an incredibly polite way to spend an evening, so lush and comforting – though the music's not so hot, I mean Lena Martell's probably a bit boppy for them"* (Sebastian Scott). *"Clearly the best. It's in a complete class of its own. There's nothing to come within a hundred miles of it"* (Nicholas Coleridge). No surprises, no disappointments.

TRAMP, 40 Jermyn St, W1 ☎ (01) 734 0565. In the same mould as Annabel's, only less discreet, less geriatric, less expensive (£100/US$145 a year membership), but more star quality. Owned by Oscar Lerman, hubby of Jackie Collins, and Johnnie Gold. *"Really a lot of fun. Much more casual than Annabel's. You see tons of well-known people and nice faces"* (Denice Lewis). Faces such as Prince Andrew's, Lady Sarah Armstrong-Jones's, Lady Helen Windsor's, Michael Caine's, Rod Stewart's and Duran Duran's.

LIMELIGHT, 136 Shaftesbury Ave, WC2 ☎ (01) 434 1761. The newest club in London, owned by New York Limelighter Peter Gatien, and similarly based in an old church. This one's ex-Welsh Presbyterian: the vaulted roof, original stonework and church trimmings remain intact, but there is an added veneer of comfort. Lots of one-nighters and special events. 800 unorthodox, cosmopolitan, glamorous citizens congregate at the hallowed portals, praying that the doorman will consider them select enough to enter. Once in, the impious mob bop and groove the night away, watched over by their heavenly host.

CAFE DE PARIS, 3 Coventry St, W1 ☎ (01) 437 2036. The latest one-nighter to storm London, held in an old-fashioned red and gold restaurant with a gallery (good for people-watching). Run by photographer Sterling, with Albert from Le Balajo in Paris, who wings his way across the channel every Wednesday. Laid-back jazz, blues and cha cha cha entice the likes of Jasper Conran, Duggie Fields, Nick Ashley, Stephen Jones and a posse of cowgirls (boleros, frayed denims, mean felt hats) on to the floor. Best before midnight, before the transvestite invasion.

TABOO, Maximus Club, 14 Leicester Square, WC2 ☎ (01) 734 4111. The kitschest, hippest, weirdest, tackiest, freakiest hang-out of the moment (at least, it was 6 months ago). Host Leigh Bowery abuses and amuses the likes of Boy George, Bryan Ferry, Paul Young, Michael Clark, John Galliano, Stevie "It's wonderful for a fling on the disco floor" Stewart, David "The club I go to most" Holah, Antony Price, Duggie Fields, Andrew Logan… and they all come running back for more. *"It's London's premier camp site, with the best of kitsch and bitch and a flamboyant host. The longest guest list in town"* (Sean Macaulay). *"Pure hedonism. It was called Taboo as a joke because there's nothing you can't do there. A good-time trash disco"* (Robin Derrick). *"Taboo is outrageous, where everywhere else is quite staid. It's fashionable in the extreme"* (Robert Pereno). *"It's just completely amazing. It's the best. If you're not dressed properly you don't get in. The DJ is the best in London"* (Candida Crewe). The DJ is Jeffrey Hinton, scratch video maker; so inspired is he, that he sometimes puts the record needle on the turntable and plays the

ONE-NIGHT WONDERS

There's Annabel's and there's Everywhere Else. The coolest kids slink along to the one-nighters (once-a-week party nights) Everywhere Else. There is little to distinguish each club – they are mostly cramped, seedy, downbeat dives – it's the people who turn up on the night in question that matter. These ones hold a certain allure for the streetwise Soho set and the charmed Chelsea set (*and* cost under £5/US$7).

Monday	Jungle
Tuesday	Crazy Larry's; 3rd Street
Wednesday	Café de Paris
Thursday	Gaz's Rockin' Blues; Taboo; Mud Club
Friday	WAG; La Cage
Saturday	A warehouse or bus depot, Jongleurs
Sunday	Limelight (♫ consecrated rhythm ♫)

"I think what people do now is look for where the party is. Nobody can say where it's happening. They just find out by word of mouth. There is no constant club which people go to – I don't think that exists. I think the best clubs are the ones that can be busy by having a hard core of friends" (Robert Pereno). Seek and ye shall find – in *Time Out*, which lists what's on and what's in each week.

rubber mat. *"The music is brilliant and the atmosphere is fun and there's no cameras and no art. There's always something new to look at and old friends to meet. I read somewhere that you have to wear your knickers on your head to get in. I've never had that problem. It's nice to read in the papers that you have to put your knickers on your head to get in, but if somebody does turn up with their knickers on their head, you know they are there for the wrong reason. The trouble is that when everybody gets to know about it, it will move on"* (David Shilling).

CRAZY LARRY'S, 533 King's Rd, SW10 ☎ (01) 352 3518. A smartish club with raised dance floor and candlelit tables for dinner. Master of the one-nighters Robert Pereno injects a shot of pzazz on Tuesdays (funky disco) and Thursdays (live bands). *"I don't consider us very street. If you set a particular fashion or sound, you get trapped and it doesn't last long. We just make sure we have a good party. The core of what we do is Chelsea – we get our ideas from Chelsea. It's more Sloany. I prefer that kind of thing"* (Robert Pereno). The young, affluent bourgeoisie downplay it in black polos and rolled up jeans; hero(ine)s like Marilyn have been known to saunter in.

GAZ'S ROCKIN' BLUES, Gossips, 69 Dean St, W1 ☎ (01) 734 0201. Thursdays. *"Gaz's might be regarded as the best counter-culture club"* (Nicholas Coleridge). The only one that's stood its ground. Gary (Gaz) Mayall plays ska, rhythm 'n' blues and rockabilly. *"Very trendy, has been for years. Nice people, good music"* (Candida Crewe).

HEAVEN, Under the Arches, Villiers St, WC2 ☎ (01) 839 3852. The gayest nightspot in town, and the vastest gayspot in Europe. *"A nice place. They've revamped it. You've got to be gay to enjoy the scene"* (Josh Astor). *"Some people won't drink out of the glasses. They'll either bring their own plastic cups or they'll drink out of bottles, and then they're quite suspicious. The women's loo may as well be a matchbox in the middle of a motorway – they don't encourage women at all. But there are a lot of fashion shows and things going on there"* (Anne McNair Wilson). Thursday is straights' night.

HIPPODROME, corner Leicester Square, WC2 ☎ (01) 437 4311. Peter Stringfellow's gaping, high-tech club has the best light show in London – piercing laser beams, swirling mists and clouds, lots of colour, movement and energy. But London can't fill massive flashy discos with fascinating people in the way New York can. Tourists and passers-by (given free invites) are the mainstay. A stream of attractions includes drag shows and one-off balls. *"It's quite fun to be there when the stage moves up and the lights move down and you see Lady Teresa Manners boogieing on down"* (Sebastian Scott).

JONGLEURS, The Cornet, Lavender Gardens, SW11 ☎ (01) 971 2498. Fergie's old haunt. Very groovy cabaret of singers, jugglers, tap-dancers and young comedians, held on Friday and Saturday evenings; the latter is a warm-up for *Saturday Night Live*. 250 people watch the rising stars. Fascinating Aida started out here.

JUNGLE, Busby's, 157 Charing Cross Rd, WC2 ☎ (01) 734 6963. Mondays. Gay and ravy – the best gay night in London. *"Good if you like Tina Turner and Diana Ross, quite funky"* (David Holah).

151 CLUB, 151 King's Rd, SW3 ☎ (01) 351 6826. Membership club frequented by young City boys (still pinstriped) and their molls (going for the mean-Sloane look, pouting and dishevelled). Just one, small, moderately plushy basement room and, at weekends, a queue of hopefuls bandying double-barrelled names of acquaintances who are pretty well bound to be members and must have missed them off the guest list, but…

MUD CLUB, Busby's, 157 Charing Cross Rd, WC2 ☎ (01) 734 6963. Fridays. A double-decker room with a balcony running round the top: big and buzzing. Philip Sallon hosts this Sixties/rockabilly night for a quiffed crowd plus pop stars – Boy George, Marilyn, Bronski Beat. *"A funk night for wide boys and muds – the crew-cut crew"* (Sean Macaulay). *"It's packed out every week. Whereas lots of club owners say 'please come to my club,' Philip Sallon says 'yeah, I think you're trendy enough to pay £5 to come to my club.' People are so pleased he thinks they're trendy enough. There are still traces of the old Buffalo Girls. It's very nice"* (Anne McNair Wilson).

RAFFLES, 287 King's Rd, SW3 ☎ (01) 352 0191. Hooray Henry's first club. A pseudo-gentlemen's club in appearance – the fake library books on fake shelves look – with disco room. Lots of private debby parties. *"Junior Annabel's – lots of 'Come on Eileen', a great Sloane favourite, quite a bit of Frankie Goes to Hollywood, and* quite *a bit of 'When the going gets tough, the tough get going' – get 'em on the floor music"* (Sebastian Scott).

3RD STREET, 3 Cromwell Rd, SW7 ☎ (01) 584 7258. Sebastian Boyle and Robert Pereno's post-Crazy Larry's Tuesday-night party, complete with go-go girls and strippers. On 3 floors, the top one being for very special friends, such as Lady Sarah Armstrong-Jones and Cosmo Fry. *"When it first started, the real friends didn't pay, the semi-friends paid £1 and the others paid £3. It was like a speakeasy. Then the Sloany crowd thought 'This is really trendy' and picked up on it. All things which start out trendy end up Sloany"* (Anne McNair Wilson). Rest assured that by now, Taboo will be solid gold Sloane.

Cage aux folles

LA CAGE The best club-without-a-home. The brain-child of a clandestine sub-culture from the Chelsea, Soho and Notting Hill sets, it now attracts stars-in-the-know from all over the world. Whoever's in town meets at whatever venue is free – always cramped and smoky, it draws a cosmopolitan bunch of media kids and eccentrics. Best night is Friday, when it carries on frenetically until breakfast time – all-night videos, cabaret (black humour: Tom Lehrer songs etc), brilliant disc jockey who plays continuously, champagne cocktails on the house for regulars. *"Fridays are* brilliant. *It's all a matter of who you know – you could be speaking to some American film star one minute, or an Italian fashion designer the next. You just keep plugging all night, you never want to go home"* (David Shilling). Almost impossible to contact: only the best know where to find it.

WAG CLUB, 35 Wardour St, W1 ☎ (01) 437 5534. *"Makes a pretty similar statement to the Cat in the Hat [black, funky, soulful, James Brown* ad nauseam*] on Fridays, but on Saturdays, it's – trashier music, more glitter"* (Robin Derrick). Any other night of the week *"it's guaranteed to have a packed dance floor with a decidedly hip crowd dancing to jazz and Latin"* (Sean Macaulay). *"It's dark, dingy, funky, a bit gay, really trendy, a fun place – I like it"* (Sebastian Scott).

■ BEST CASINOS ■

English casinos are private clubs.

ASPINALL'S, 20-21 Curzon St, W1 ☎ (01) 629 4400. *"The best casino by far. The only one which is run on a gentlemen's club basis. The service is impeccable, and the honesty. You can go upstairs for 4 hours and your money will be placed for you if you give orders. There is absolutely no cheating. Gentlemen don't normally go into the casino business, but Aspinall is a gentleman. It's as good as Annabel's, and you have action too – as much action as you want in one throw of the dice. The limit is extremely high. In other casinos they just chip away at you, so you get bored. It's also the most beautiful house in London"* (Taki). *"It's select and by that I mean it doesn't allow in every rich Arab. Excellent food, a very good wine list, and general smart allure"* (Richard Compton-Miller).

CROCKFORD'S, 30 Curzon St, W1 ☎ (01) 493 7771. A civilized club, established 150 years ago, with none of the usual scrabble round the tables that mars flashier gaming joints. Mostly foreign clientele since it moved from St James's to Mayfair. Rod Steiger held his most recent wedding party here, and it's the haunt of many opera singers.

BEST CLUBS

TOP 5

★

1 WHITE'S
2 BOODLE'S
3 BROOKS'S
4 BUCK'S
5 TURF

The true gentlemen's club exists for no other reason than to provide a non-working, non-sportive sanctuary for its members. If anyone is seen to be scanning anything more taxing than *The Times* (that is, papers to do with his *work*, God forbid), he will be out on his ear. The original clubs are almost identical in appearance and atmosphere – the only way you know you're in the right one is by *whose* pinstriped legs are protruding from the leather armchairs.

WHITE'S, 37 St James's St, SW1 ☎ (01) 493 6671. The gentlemen's club of Evelyn Waugh's novels. Incredibly selective and chock-full of peers: a hushed "Certainly, your Lordship" is to be heard rather more than a clipped "Right away, Sir". Members, even newly elected youngsters, are thought by outsiders to be arrogant. Getting in is a matter of who you are: who you *know* is no guarantee: Rocco Forte is just one recent blackballee. *"The oldest and best club in England, according to foreigners"* (Taki). Members include Lords Lichfield, Tryon, Cawdor and Soames.

BOODLES, 28 St James's St, SW1 ☎ (01) 930 7166. One of the 3 grand Regency clubs, along with Brooks's and White's. Old habits prevail, although they probably no longer boil all coins before giving them to members. Getting in is a case of family only and a 5-year wait. Its famous bow window looking on to St James's Street satisfies people-watchers from within and without. A remarkable winelist (the cellars are enormous) and the best cuisine of all the gentlemen's clubs. In the main dining room, only members may dine at the central table. Members *with guests* must sit at side tables. To attempt to sit at high table would be horrifyingly bad form, and could well send inmates to an early grave.

BROOKS'S, 61 St James's St, SW1 ☎ (01) 499 0072. Founded in 1764 as the Whig rival to White's, it's like a country house with lots of wood panelling. Women are allowed in as guests in the evening. The Great Subscription Room is scene of many a 21st birthday cocktail party. Members include Sir James Goldsmith, Lord Oaksey, and a strong wine-trade contingent who savour some of the best wines available in London here – bigwigs from Berry Bros & Rudd and the wine departments of Christie's and Sotheby's.

BUCK'S, 18 Clifford St, W1 ☎ (01) 734 2337. A mere fledgling, started after World War I, when *voluntary* American officers were admitted as members. A strong US contingent remains today. It was here that Buck's Fizz was invented (by Captain Buckmaster): when ordering one at the club, it is screamingly ignorant to ask for anything more than a Fizz.

TURF CLUB (see SPORTING LIFE).

ATHENAEUM, 107 Pall Mall, SW1 ☎ (01) 930 4843. Plodding intellectuals, civil servants, men of the cloth, and a few oddballs such as Alistair Cooke. *"I've never seen the Athenaeum. I'd like to know if it really is full of stuffed bishops"* (Peter York). *"In the gents, the nail and clothes brushes are chained to the wall..."* (Lord Lichfield).

GARRICK, 15 Garrick St, WC2 ☎ (01) 379 6478. For Bohemian grandees – members from the media, stage, literary and legal worlds wear a green and salmon striped tie. It used to be uncontested king of the bookish world until the hipper Groucho's and Moscow came along with their non-sex-discrimination policy. Members such as Viscount Norwich, Cliff Michelmore and Peter Ustinov are not about to defect.

THE GROUCHO CLUB, 45 Dean St, W1 ☎ (01) 439 4685. Founded by a mixed foursome of publishing luminaries for like minds, it's put all other business luncheries and drinking haunts in the shade. Civilized and unflashily glamorous, it attracts an upbeat liter-arty set – publishers, agents, major bylines and media kids like Patsy Kensit – rather than brown serge Fleet Street hackery. Bestsellers, papers and mags are scattered round and the shiny bar stays open until 1 a.m. *"Drawing room atmosphere with wonderful dark blue velvet sofas and red brocade chairs. Really smiley waiters. It's a bit too cool now, but I still love it"* (Candida Crewe). *"One club I go to regularly. It looks as if it's been made out of some defunct Italian restaurant [upstairs, the dining room is anything but defunct], like a hotel in Torquay gone absolutely mad. It's quite pretty, but the main thing is, there are more hacks per square inch than anywhere else in London. It's not a treat but it's* nice, *a good place to meet friends"* (Peter York). *"It's really nice, and the good thing is there are lots of mirrors, so you don't have to crane your neck to see who's walking in"* (Sebastian Scott).

MOSCOW CLUB, 62 Frith St, W1 ☎ (01) 434 1871. Groucho's new and racier rival has a more creative/pop video/advertising/design leaning; actors and pop stars rock up after their shows (the club's open till 1 a.m.). The narrow, black and white, nouvellish room feels like a train, with its rows of chairs and little tables designed by founders Ian Hoath and his pals. The red square in the centre of each white menu is intended as a graphic rather than political statement. *"A bit more user-friendly than Groucho's. It's all part of the revamping of Soho"* (Sebastian Scott).

RAC, 89 Pall Mall, SW1 ☎ (01) 930 2345. A yuppy version of the gentlemen's club that manages to maintain a grand and civilized air while keeping up with the times. Women join in their own right. Good sporty facilities, steam rooms, and the most beautiful swimming pool in London – lapis lazuli and gold, mosaics and pillars. Officers on guard at St James's Palace swim here. Reciprocal arrangements with L'Auto club in Paris.

REFORM, 104 Pall Mall, SW1 ☎ (01) 930 9374. Rather dour, church-like and *brown*, in true Victorian tradition: dark wood, dark leather, lots of brownish marble pillars. It was from here that Phileas Fogg set off on his fabled 80-day non-stop round-the-world trip. *"I see it through the eyes of fogeys I know, over dinners and jollies. It obviously appeals like crazy to the fogey sensibility"* (Peter York).

SAVILE CLUB, 69 Brook St, W1 ☎ (01) 629 5462. *"Very pretty, small club with a blue and silver ground room. It's a bit like the Garrick, very writerly, with lots of senior TV editors"* (Peter York). Frederic Raphael belongs.

2 BRYDGES PLACE, WC2 ☎ (01) 836 1436, aka Alfredo's, after the proprietor. Comfy, laid-back club with a mishmash of furniture and an even greater mishmash of members, from young arty trendies like Charlotte Faber, Cosmo Fry, Michael Clark, Layla d'Angelo and Craigie Aitchison, to members of the English National Opera, plus the odd crumbly. Special lunches on the first Sunday of the month. *"It's very nice, with an open fire, like someone's drawing room. There's a bar and a dining room upstairs. It's nice to get away from things. You can dance when everyone else has gone"* (David Holah).

■ BEST EVENTS ■

The English season kicks off with a bevy of coming-out balls in May, continues with the summer run of sporting sprees (Ascot, Henley, Wimbledon…see SPORTING LIFE), drifts off to Scotland (The Glorious Twelfth) for August, collects its thoughts in September, then bounces back with a fresh round of charity balls in October, rising to a dizzying crescendo around Christmas. Jennifer's Diary in *Harpers & Queen* records the lot.

COVENT GARDEN ROYAL OPERA HOUSE GALA, Bow St, WC2 ☎ (01) 240 1066. Occasional combined gala performances by the Royal Ballet and Royal Opera companies to celebrate a state visit or a special (often royal) event.

Sweet Charity I

Charity events are conducted in typically British fashion by rather grand-sounding double-barrelled women, who work largely on a voluntary basis. No one dares push the boat out American-style on extravagant décor or gimmicky extras, because few people will pay more than £50 (US$72) a ticket (even less in the country). Neither will ball-goers dress up in anything more ritzy than the trusty taffeta (one of the great institutions of the 1980s). It's not a matter of stinginess or dinginess: all the readies are channelled back into school fees and stopping the manor falling down, and old families don't need Saint Laurent to put them on the social map. Dowdy or not, charity balls are high social points in the country calendar, when a local grandee will magnanimously throw open the gates of his stately, always for a *good* cause, which means diseases or disabilities or cruelty to children or animals. The best charities, functions-wise, are those with a royal patron.

One of the best galas ever was held for the Queen's 60th birthday in April this year, with a galactic gathering of stars on stage. *"I love Covent Garden galas. When it's all dressed up it's a very special thing"* (Felicity Clark). *"I do enjoy a gala performance at the Royal Opera House – always so gracious. It's a very good venue"* (Betty Kenward). In order to catch the Princess of Wales doing high kicks with

Wayne Sleep, or playing Juliet to PC's Romeo, you'll have to become a Friend of Covent Garden and go to their private parties.

ROSE BALL, 1 Castelnau, Barnes, SW13 ☎ (01) 748 4824. May. A hardy annual held in a pink blossom-filled Grosvenor House, for Queen Alexandra Rose Day. Unofficially, it takes the place of the former Queen Charlotte's Ball, where debutantes were launched into society. Green young girls arrive in the perennial strapless silk taffeta, accompanied by hopeful parents. *"The best ball of the year"* (Betty Kenward).

ROYAL CALEDONIAN BALL, 94 Elms Rd, SW4 ☎ (01) 622 6074. May. A braw Scots affair, where reel men wear kilts, or white tie and facings, and their ladies dig out the heirloom jewels and clan sashes. The dance opens with set reels in which one has to be invited to participate. Dancers descend the stairs accompanied by pipers and drums of the Scots Guards. The Duke of Atholl traditionally leads them on to the floor for the No. 1 reel, often with Princess Margaret.

PARTIES OF THE YEAR

YOUNG ROYALS' 21ST BIRTHDAY PARTY, held at Windsor Castle for Prince Edward, Lady Helen Windsor, Lady Sarah Armstrong-Jones and James Ogilvy. Guests were greeted with a laser display saying "Welcome to Windsor" in glorified Butlin's fashion. There were no other gimmicks, no speeches – it was a thoroughly informal formal do. Wherever you looked there was a royal face grinning back. While shrinking violets sat out in the rose arbours that were flourishing in one room, Ladies Sarah and Helen and Princess Diana went wild on the dance floor. The best sight, in the blackness of the Batcave-like disco, was a radiant Queen Mother bopping between the laser beams with Prince Edward.

BIRTHDAY BALL, Royal Albert Hall, held in aid of Birthright in the presence of a scarlet-sheathed Princess of Wales, whose brother Viscount Althorp chaired the junior committee. The inspired Paul Dyson decorated the hall with swags of fruit and flowers in keeping with the red and gold theme, and glowing lights interspersed with laser beams. Tiers of dinner tables, all spruce in white linen, circled the activities below. The Roux brothers did the menu, the Three Degrees, gilded and rouged, sang, and masks designed by celebs from Sir Sidney Nolan to Joan Collins were auctioned. A wealth of aristos and media celebs – Lady Teresa Manners, David and Lady Carina Frost, Mark and Anouska Weinberg, Alan Jay Lerner.

VISCOUNT ALTHORP'S 21ST BIRTHDAY PARTY at Spencer House, the family's splendid neo-classical mansion in St James's, with its lovely balcony view over Green Park. Charlie Althorp organized it all himself with gimmicks galore – robots and transvestites wandering round and a satellite connection to LA in order to receive far-flung birthday greetings. *"A good mixture of guests, not too stuffy – from Charles and Diana to Peter Stringfellow and various pop stars. Phyllis Nelson flew in for the cabaret"* (Richard Compton-Miller).

COUNTRY

BEST EVENT

GLYNDEBOURNE FESTIVAL OPERA, Lewes, E Sussex ☎ (0273) 812321. A season of the very best opera in a lovely country house and grounds, from May to August. *"I love Glyndebourne. It is very specifically English, especially the idea of getting into evening dress in the middle of the day. If it's a lovely evening, the light is extraordinary, and the gardens are beautiful. There is a wonderful mixture of people in long dresses sitting around having drinks and picnics and enjoying the music and the light and the scenery. It's much more of a social event than just an evening for opera lovers"* (Felicity Clark).

BEST HOSTS

Brilliant private party-givers include **Lady Sonia Melchett**; the **Countess of Burford**; the **Emanuels**: *"Good party-givers because they unreservedly love show business, and show business loves them"* (Peter York); Iranian socialite **Kokoly Fallah**, whose annual fancy-dress summer ball at her Datchet villa on the Thames is *"the best private party. The music and cabaret are fantastic"* (Richard Compton-Miller); **John Aspinall**: *"When he entertains in his own house. No one goes to more trouble or spends more money. Last time I went there, he had 1,000 Boy Scouts carrying torches"* (Taki). Charity gala-organizing supremos are **Una-Mary Parker** and **Iris Banham-Lee**, whose cultural soirées, People and Places, are *"terribly well done – thematic in a clever way"* (Peter York): famous people perform a special recital or masque in a notable house. *The Enigma of George Sand* was specially written for a soirée at the French Embassy residence and performed by Alexandra Bastedo

“Colour is the safest and the cheapest theme. I've done some stunning black and white parties, and at Christmas time red and gold, black and silver etc. It's simple for people to dress up. I'm anti fancy dress – it simply terrifies me. It adds about £30 to everyone's bill, and some people feel very uncomfortable in it – me for one” (LADY ELIZABETH ANSON)

and John Julius Norwich: at a Duff Cooper evening in the grounds of Mrs Banham-Lee's own house in Wiltshire, Tamara Ustinov played Lady Diana. Mrs B-L also organized Lady Diana Cooper's 90th birthday bash, and gives an annual Pink Party in the summer, to which the local Archdeacon wears a special pink stock.

BEST PARTY ORGANIZERS

PARTY PLANNERS, 66 Ladbroke Grove, W11 ☎ (01) 229 9666. Lady Elizabeth Anson is the undisputed queen of party planning throughout the world. In the business for 25 years, she is involved in up to 14 parties *a day*, from a mammoth gala down to a child's birthday cake. Recent years have seen her hosting 2 Royal Wedding parties, a ball in the presence of the Duchess of Kent at the Regent Hotel in Hong Kong and in gumboots halfway up a Swiss mountain, arranging a thrash for Freddie Heineken. Betty Kenward and Diane Freis are among her ardent fans.

PARTY PARAGON, 8 Hereford Square, SW7 ☎ (01) 370 7743. Run by American heiress Marchesa Nicole de Francisci and Iranian Olfat Esfandiari, who started the craze for breakfast parties in England. *“Because they're so new, they try harder than Lady Elizabeth Anson's well-established outfit”* (Richard Compton-Miller).

BEST VENUES

THE BELFRY, 11b W Halkin St, SW1 ☎ (01) 235 9625. A private dining club in a Scottish Presbyterian church, with wood panelled rooms decorated by Nina Campbell. The best room is in the vaulted Belfry itself, frescoed with flocks of birds against a heavenly sky.

LEIGHTON HOUSE, 12 Holland Park Rd, W14 ☎ (01) 602 3316. A lovely museum-piece of high Victoriana, filled with paintings of the era; room for cocktails and dinners, up to 150 people.

LONDON DUNGEON, 28–34 Tooley St, SE1 ☎ (01) 403 0606. A little apéritif under the gallows, a snack on the rack … this will be the most tortuous drinks party you've ever endured. Cocktails among life-size medieval tableaux in 35,000 sq ft (3,252 sq m) vaults cost £800 (US$1,157) for 100; a full gruesome evening costs £1,525 (US$2,206) for 300. Added attractions include branding, flogging, beheading, and perhaps a little scorching at the stake.

MADAME TUSSAUD'S, Marylebone Rd, NW1 ☎ (01) 935 6861. Hollywood hooleys in company with Joan Collins and Michael Caine, state dinners with world leaders, or one of those grisly evenings down at the Chamber of Horrors.

THE ORANGERY, Holland Park, W11 c/o Town & County Catering, Manor House, Manor Farm Rd, Alperton, Middlesex ☎ (01) 998 8880. Classy and glassy: cocktails in the airy conservatory, or a ball in a marquee in the grounds.

30 PAVILION ROAD, SW1, c/o Searcy Tansley & Co, 136 Brompton Rd, SW3 ☎ (01) 584 3344. An elegant Georgian house behind Sloane Street – lots of coming out cocktails and wedding receptions.

BEST TENTS

BLACK & EDGINGTON HIRE, 29 Queen Elizabeth St, SE1 ☎ (01) 407 3734: have been making tents for royals since Queen Victoria's day. Supply the works for garden parties at Buckingham Palace, for Henley and Wimbledon.

TG & TS PEPPER, Crosshill, Snaith, Goole, N Humberside ☎ (0405) 860249. Frame tents, not conventional marquees with poles: brilliant lighting.

PARIS

Clubland is not hyperactive in Paris, but the hippest kids go to one-nighters, as they do in London. The best are:

Monday	Le Balajo
Tuesday	Royal Lieu
Thursday	Le Palace

BEST NIGHTSPOTS

CASTEL'S, 15 rue Princesse, 75006 ☎ (1) 4326 9022. Paris's answer to Annabel's. *“It has stood the test of time and fashion, though it is for the older generation”* (Jean-Philippe Chatrier). *“It has charm; funny little rooms on different levels, not that terrible purpose-built look. They pick and choose who they would like to have in the place – it's run more on a friends-of-Jean-Castel basis than Annabel's, where membership is rather strictly observed”* (Mark Birley). *“Castel's and Annabel's are* grands seigneurs *of the night. Here you meet the most interesting people in the world. Starting a conversation or butting in on one is absolutely expected. Here are the most famous, the not-so-famous and the once famous – but everybody is part of the same fraternity and whatever tongue is being used it is the same language spoken”* (Olivier Coquelin).

LES BAINS, 7 rue du Bourg l'Abbé, 75003 ☎ (1) 4887 0180. Still known as the Bains-Douches to many. Along with Palace, it's the most *branché* young club, based in an old public baths, brimming with notables. It has a dinky pool downstairs, which keeps punters cool even when they don't swim in it. Azzedine Alaïa and Joan Severance regularly dip in.

LE PALACE, 8 rue du Faubourg Montmartre, 75009 ☎ (1) 4236 8398. *“Like Les Bains, it belongs to the history of Paris and has been trendy for years [apart from a sticky patch when the former owner died of AIDS]. Best now for* *private parties"* (Alexandre Lazareff). Staff in Gaultier get-ups, Paris models, film stars and the *jeunesse dorée* ooze glamour alongside the likes of Azzedine Alaïa, Charlotte Rampling and Joan Severance. Masses of attractions – magicians, jugglers, performing animals …

LE TANGO, 11 rue Au-Maire, 75003 ☎ (1) 4272 1778. An Afro-Latin club run by Serge Kruger, a young designer in Les Halles. *"The best club. Very black, jammed and sweaty; lots of white trendies go"* (Alexandre Lazareff).

APOCALYPSE, 40 rue Colisée, 75008 ☎ (1) 4225 1168. Membership club with smoochy piano bar/high-tech discothèque/*trompe l'oeil* Roman restaurant. Wednesdays are party nights, frequented by ageing trendies.

ATMOSPHERE, 45 rue François I, 75008 ☎ (1) 4720 4924. Black, mirrored St Tropez-type club for a Castel's-style clientele and their children. Princess Stéphanie, Paul Belmondo, Ursula Andress and Alain Delon lap it up, while *mecs sportifs* such as Alain Prost and Bjorn Borg watch themselves on video.

LE BALAJO, 9 rue de Lappe, 75011 ☎ (1) 4700 0787. Fabulous art deco club in the Moulin Rouge tradition (and designed by the same man, Henri Mahe). It peaked in the 1950s and is now trendy once more. Monday nights are as streetwise as Paris gets. You can hire it for parties. *"Very Front Populaire, '30s, Jean Gabin and all that"* (Alexandre Lazareff).

NEW MORNING, 7-9 rue des Petites Ecuries, 75010 ☎ (1) 4523 5141. Live music from Europe and America – the best jazz club in town.

REGINE'S, 49 rue de Ponthieu, 75008 ☎ (1) 4359 7300. Hangover jetsetty stuff, where Barbra Streisand, Liza Minnelli, Julio Iglesias add a touch of international stardom to an otherwise rather grotesque set of dissolute old men and over-made-up floozies that have been poured into their jeans. Régine herself shows her face when she's not in Monte or Marbella. One clubber says: *"She is as tough as old boots, but can be warm. She's never used a bouncer in her clubs – she likes to reject the undesirables herself. She works like mad and only needs 3 hours' sleep – in the beginning you could see her counting up the cash register. But no customer can resist her."*

ROSE BIRD, 11*bis* rue Delambre, 75014 ☎ (1) 4335 3854. A roomy jazz bar that stays open till all hours.

ROYAL LIEU, 2 rue des Italiens, 75009 ☎ (1) 4824 4388. A hip little club on Tuesday nights.

RUBY'S, 31 rue Dauphine, 75006 ☎ (1) 4633 6816. The Castel's of Paris noir, where you might meet Diana Ross, or even Mick Jagger and Jerry Hall one Ruby Tuesday.

LES TROTTOIRS DE BUENOS AIRES, 37 rue des Lombards, 75001 ☎ (1) 4160 4441. Live Argentinian tango music – very alternative Paris. *"Not young or fashionable, but fascinating and really authentic. A great sound"* (Jean-Philippe Chatrier).

BEST CLUBS

CERCLE INTERALLIE, 33 rue du Faubourg St Honoré, 75008 ☎ (1) 4265 9600. An enlightened club that admits women members of which Catherine Deneuve is one. Set in a beautiful 18th-century town house with a grand garden (where you can dine) backing on to the Champs Elysées, it has a hidden outdoor swimming pool, squash courts, sauna and whirlpool bath. The presidents are the Comte de Beaumont and, on the ladies' side, the Duchesse de Rochefoucauld. Created during World War I as a meeting place for Allied Officers (de Gaulle, Churchill, Eisenhower), it now attracts all top diplomats. *"If one were to choose to be a member of one club in Paris, this would be it. Very comfortable and relaxed. The club has 2 parts: the morgue, where the average age is 103, with a bar, dining room, library etc; and the downstairs part, where it is younger, more informal and relaxed"* (Jean-Michel Jaudel).

L'AUTOMOBILE CLUB DE FRANCE, 8 place de la Concorde, 75008 ☎ (1) 4380 6858. Large and aristocratic, L'Auto takes men only. The dining room overlooks Concorde. Glittering '20s mosaic pool. Affiliated to the RAC in London (see London Clubs).

JOCKEY CLUB, 2 rue Rabelais, 75008 ☎ (1) 4359 8563. The stuffiest club with the most nobles per square centimetre: edging on the anti-semitic. Affiliated to White's in London (see London Clubs).

TRAVELLERS', 25 ave des Champs Elysées, 75008 ☎ (1) 4359 7500. *"The only club in Paris which resembles an English gentlemen's club. Women are allowed in on Thursdays, but they are hardly recommended to come. Very straight and traditional – you can still be blackballed"* (Jean-Michel Jaudel). A town house with Napoléon III décor and mainly American and European members. Evelyn Waugh used it when he was in Paris; Sam White can be seen there now, pondering his next column over a gin; Sir James Goldsmith belongs. Lots of gambling – high stakes on backgammon. The best place to view the Bastille Day military march.

BEST EVENT

VERSAILLES FESTIVAL OPERA, c/o Syndicat d'Initiative, 7 rue des Réservoirs, Versailles 78000 ☎ (1) 3950 3622. As part of the Versailles Festival in June, a beautiful baroque opera is staged at the Château de Versailles in the original setting and costumes. Its tiny jewel of an opera house was built for the future Louis XVI's marriage to Marie-Antoinette.

BEST HOSTS

Pierre Cardin: *"He gets all sorts of different people together – those who live in Paris, those passing through, opera singers, fashion and showbiz people – I love his parties"* (Charlotte Rampling). **Princess Caroline of Monaco**: *"A great hostess"* (Inès de la Fressange). **Baroness Marie-Hélène de Rothschild**: a brilliantly imaginative hostess (one of her best

“ The best compliment you can have in Paris is to be invited to supper in someone’s private home ”
(MEREDITH ETHERINGTON-SMITH)

parties was a surrealist ball at the Château de Ferrières, where the grand staircase was lined with sleeping footmen wearing cats’ heads. Dali paintings were re-created as centrepieces on every table, the guests included President Pompidou, Audrey Hepburn and Baron de Rede, and the Baroness wore a deer mask with tears of real diamonds flowing down its soft furry jowls). Publisher **Nicole Wisnik**: *“She is so good at mixing people. Her party for Helmut Newton had all sorts – Karl Lagerfeld, Françoise Sagan, people in politics, arts…”* (Inès de la Fressange). **Régine**: a charming, eccentric dinner-party hostess – she once received early-comer André Malraux in curlers and made him sit with her in the bathroom while her hairdresser finished her set. He said her conversation fascinated him. **Karl Lagerfeld**: *“His parties are something because he has the most spectacular 18th-century dining room and candlelit chandeliers. You are entertained royally, with exquisite food and always marvellous people”* (Meredith Etherington-Smith).

COUNTRY

BEST VENUES

CHATEAU VAUX-LE-VICOMTE, Seine et Marne ☎ (16) 066 9709. Designed by Mansard with gardens by Le Nôtre, the château was built for Fouquet, financial superintendent to Louis XIV. Fouquet’s splendiferous parties there were so much superior to the King’s that Louis had Fouquet clapped in irons, and promptly commissioned Mansard, Le Nôtre and artist Le Brun to build a château for himself at Versailles. Vaux-le-Vicomte is hirable for parties (such as the Dior Poison launch) and was Drax’s pad in *Moonraker*.

CHATEAU DE VERSAILLES, ave de Paris, Versailles. Hirable via Mme Buffalan, Pavillon Mollien, Palais du Louvre, 75001 ☎ (1) 4260 3926. The best venue of all. Dances are held in the Galerie des Batailles (up to 700 people) or the Salle des Croisades (about 250), at a cost of 50,000 francs (US$7,047) plus 15,000 francs (US$2,114) for the caretaker.

Best Riviera hosts

Eddie Barclay, whose weddings (7 to date) are among the best parties in the South of France; Michelle Halberstadt, whose annual garden party at Cannes Festival time is a must; French Cultural Minister Jack Lang.

MONACO

MONTE CARLO

BEST NIGHTSPOTS

NO ROCK, 11 rue du Portier, 98000 ☎ (93) 250925. Mariana Borg’s trendy new club, the in place to be (it must be – Princess Stéphanie and Prince Albert drop in of an evening). A piano bar-disco with the atmosphere of an English club – warm and cosy, done up in blues and reds, with dark little nooks for discreet tête-à-têtes. In South of France style, drinks are bought by the bottle: a litre of Scotch costs around £90 (US$130). Mariana is great mates with Régine, and after a hard night, the 2 of them have been seen with their feet in champagne buckets full of ice.

JIMMYZ D’HIVER (winter), **place du Casino, 98007 ☎ (93) 508080; JIMMYZ D’ETE** (summer), **Monte Carlo Sporting Club, ave Princesse Grace, 98000 ☎ (93) 509090.** Movable seasonal pleasure, started by Regine. Princess Caroline adds presence but some glitzy clients have moved on to the No Rock.

LIVING ROOM, 7 ave de Spilugues, 98000 ☎ (93) 508031. A piano bar with a singer most nights. Dark, smallish and noisy, a less pretentious version of Jimmyz with an oldish clientele.

BEST CASINO

MONTE CARLO SUMMER CASINO, Monte Carlo Sporting Club, ave Princesse Grace, 98000 ☎ (93) 509090. The most glamorous gamblers hang out at this modern complex, leaving the more obvious delights of the old year-round casino (place du Casino ☎ (93) 506931) to visitors, who find it: *“Mind-blowing! It’s the best of the best. The style is old and ornate, with chandeliers and gold braid and carved walls and pillars. When you walk in, it’s like going into Buckingham Palace”* (Nigel Oakes).

BEST EVENT

INTERNATIONAL RED CROSS GALA, Monte Carlo Sporting Club, ave Princesse Grace, 98000 ☎ (93) 509090. *“The No 1 event of the season, part of the long affair of summer”* (Lynn Wyatt). One of the glossiest, most international events in the world. *Le monde* jets or floats in for a week of private, commercial and charitable partying, culminating in this extravaganza. The bejewelled crowd include the Monégasque royals, Roger Moore, Audrey Hepburn, Princess Michael of Kent, the di Portanovas (all the way from Houston), and cabaret stars Frank Sinatra, Elton John, Liza Minnelli and Sammy Davis Jnr.

ITALY

Florence sets the style for the rest of Italy. The trendy and the aristocratic move in Florentine circles. Milan and Rome are far more classical.

BEST NIGHTSPOTS

BELLA BLU, via Luigi Luciani 21, 00197 Rome ☎ (06) 360 8840. The Annabel’s of Rome, started by socialite Marina Lante della Rovere. Small, classic and smart, with blue-tinted mirrors. Actors, film stars and Roman nobility slink across the half-moon dance floor.

♔ **MANILA, piazza Matteucci, Campi Bisenzio, 50013 Florence ☎ (055) 894121.** An avant garde club for the hip and chic, with beautiful graffiti. Also a venue for fashion shows and exhibitions.

♔ **PLASTIC, viale Umbria 120, 20135 Milan ☎ (02) 743674.** The trendiest club in Milan, teeming with young fashion designers. Modern, black and slick, apart from the incongruous Venetian glass chandeliers which hang from the ceiling.

♔ **TENAX, via Pratense 47, 50145 Florence ☎ (055) 373050.** A restored warehouse, vast and sparse, on 2 floors. The upper floor has train seating and videos. The utterly cool clientele wear Comme des Garcons and John Galliano.

ACROPOLIS, via Luigi Luciani 52, 00197 Rome ☎ (06) 870504. Large disco, revamped in Grecian style. The cool young yuppy crowd wear jeans and Timberland shoes. All the big rock and pop stars play here when in Rome.

GIL'S, via Romagnosi 11a, 00196 Rome ☎ (06) 361 1348. A disco run by the make-up artist Gil, who knows the whole of Italy. Glitzier, flashier and lately not as trendy as Bella Blu, despite its exotic Arabian tent-style décor.

IL TARTARUGHINO, via della Scrofa 2, 00186 Rome ☎ (06) 678 6037. A piano bar where smart older Romans and politicians gather. It closes in Rome and follows its regulars to Sardinia for July and August.

NEPENTHA, piazza Armando Diaz 1, 20123 Milan ☎ (02) 873652. Straight and simple, where all the smart middle-of-the-via Milanesi feel safe.

OPEN GATE, via San Nicola da Tolentino 4, 00187 Rome ☎ (06) 475 0464. Gleaming all-white piano bar/club/restaurant, recently renovated by its new owner. Frequented by aristocratic Rome.

RUDI'S GOGO, via Pandolfini 34, 50122 Florence☎ (055) 296998. A smart private club that looks classic until you realize most of the ravishing Dynastic girls are transvestites. The mirrored dance floor is always packed.

BEST CLUB

CLUBINO DADI, via Omenoni 3, 20135 Milan ☎ (02) 862977. A gentlemen's club for the aristocracy. Difficult to get in. Those who have may use the stairs if they are male, but only the tiny lift if they are female. The old aristocracy go to play bridge.

BEST EVENTS

FOX HUNT BALL, c/o Società Romana Caccia alla Volpe, via Montoro 8, 00186 Rome. Held in a different élite venue each year – the last was at the Circolo della Caccia in the Palazzo Borghese. *Strictly* by invitation. *"The most exclusive ball. You have to be somebody to get in, or something to do with fox hunting. It's all very beautifully done, and people in the most wonderful outfits flock from all over Italy and from abroad"* (Marina Chaliapin).

LA SCALA, Teatro alla Scala, via Filodrammatici 2, 20121 Milan ☎ (02) 88791. The opening night of the opera, always on 7 Dec, is the most important date on the Italian social calendar. The greatest social gaffe is to invite someone out on the 7th. Everyone from the Head of State down attends, not only from Milan, but from Rome and Florence too. Marchesa Bona Frescobaldi and Mariuccia Mandelli love it to death.

BEST HOST

Marta Marzotto: she lives on Rome's Piazza di Spagna (among other residences) and *"has the most amusing parties, if a bit wild. She's not at all stuffy, she's just fun. She arranges wonderful parties because she's got so much money she just can't count it – which always helps for big parties. She's a little bit Bohemian, even a bit fast, a bit of a mad cat. Her guests are artists and singers and pop stars and actors and high society – anyone she thinks amusing. Barbecues, dances, masked balls, fun parties, intellectual parties – she loves parties"* (Marina Chaliapin).

SPAIN

REGINE'S, Hotel Puente Romano, Carretera de Cadiz, Marbella ☎ (052) 770100. Those who float around Puerto Banus by day drop anchor at Régine's for the evening. A basement *boîte* where le tout Marbella strut their funky stuff – Gunther Sachs, Alain Delon, Princess Margaret, the King of Saudi Arabia, the Duchess of Seville, Gunilla von Bismarck.

THE AMERICAS

AMERICA'S BEST NIGHTSPOTS

★

1 AREA, New York
2 DOUBLES, New York
3 PALLADIUM, New York
4 TRAMP, Los Angeles
5 LE CLUB, New York

BEST EVENTS

★

1 METROPOLITAN MUSEUM OF ART Costume Institute opening dinner, New York, Dec
2 WHITE HOUSE STATE DINNER, Washington, any time
3 CONSUL'S BALL, Boston, Jan
4 BACHELORS COTILLION, Baltimore, Nov
5 DONOR'S BALL, Chicago, Nov
6 BLACK AND WHITE BALL, San Francisco, April/May
7 OPERA BALL, San Francisco, Sept
8 COCONUTS, Palm Beach, New Year's Eve
9 COMUS and REX BALLS, New Orleans, Mardi Gras
10 CRYSTAL CHARITY BALL, Dallas, Dec

UNITED STATES

NEW YORK

BEST NIGHTSPOTS

AREA, 157 Hudson St, NY 10013 ☎ (212) 226 8423. Still at the top for the beautiful and the weird, its modest size in comparison to that of Palladium allows it to retain some semblance of exclusivity. Charlotte Rampling, Brooke Shields and Inès de la Fressange add chic. *"Area is the perfect name – you travel through different zones of the club. The live sculptures are amazing – a chap will stand motionless for hours amid the chaos and confusion of dancing bodies, and then move his pose just slightly"* (Victor Banerjee). Fake portraits also disconcert onlookers when the eyes suddenly dart sideways.

DOUBLES, Hotel Sherry-Netherland, 783 5th Ave, NY 10022 ☎ (212) 751 9595. The most exclusive private club in New York, interior-designed (all red) by Valerian Rybar, a haven for older Establishment families. Very Upper East side. *"The only place you can have some privacy and meet an elegant set of people – the best of the Americans"* (Marc Biron). Popular for private parties. Good cuisine and cocktails.

PALLADIUM, 123 E 13th St, NY 10003 ☎ (212) 473 7171. A wildly extravagant and ambitious Steve Rubell and Ian Schrager venture, constructed within a 1920s theatre and splashing big art names on walls. Andrée Putman on interiors and Azzedine Alaïa on get-ups. Space for 3,500: *"A big bag of people – princes from Europe, the best New York families, people from Brooklyn and the Bronx"* (Ludovic Autet): *"A mix of funky, arty, downtown people and formal, traditional clientele"* (Marc Biron). Margaux Hemingway and Charlotte Rampling join the mêlée when in town.

LE CLUB, 313 E 58th St, NY 10022 ☎ (212) 355 5520. Enduring, dignified private club, possibly even more exclusive than Doubles because it's smaller, based in a town house. *"It's very charming. The décor is European with lots of flowers and wood, designed by Pierre Scapula"* (Ludovic Autet). Dark suits and ties rule. A young intercontinental crowd injects a bit of life into old backgammoners.

CLUB A, 333 E 60th St, NY 10020 ☎ (212) 308 2333. Brazilian Ricardo Amaral's plushy membership club is not in with the really in, but remains near the top for the smart older European crowd plus younger Eurotrash – children of the European élite – and Arabs. Extortionate drinks (over $20 for 2) and an image so clean it's almost washed out. Clientele wear suits even on a Saturday night, which Area fans find bogus since they can't have come on from work.

HEARTBREAK, 179 Varick St, NY 10014 ☎ (212) 691 2388. Daytime caff, night-time oasis on the dingy fringe of SoHo. Attracts the artsy/model set on Mondays and Tuesdays (one of the few clubs open) who neatly avoid the weekend influx of undesirable Bridge & Tunnel people (from the wrong side of the Brooklyn Bridge and Lincoln Tunnel), aka the BBQs (Brooklyn, Bronx and Queens *Saturday Night Fever* types). *"I only go clubbing 1 night a week. On Monday it's Heartbreak, Frankie's night. I love the music – they play '50s music all night long"* (Joan Severance).

STRINGFELLOWS, 35 E 21st St, NY 10010 ☎ (212) 254 2444. Under the Peter S umbrella, but a different beast from his London club. A new concept for New Yorkers in that you can *eat* here. Prices are double the norm ($40) and they don't give out invitations.

❝ The only thing which makes a good club is the people. The décor must not be too slick, it should be warm and unpretentious. You must be able to go alone or with some people. I think the move will be towards smaller, more private nightclubs ❞

(MARK BIRON)

THE WORLD, 254 E 2nd St, NY 10009 ☎ (212) 674 3348. At the time of writing, the hottest place in town, based in an old Polish wedding palace. Tacky but enormous fun. Live music.

CHINA CLUB, 2130 Broadway, NY 10023 ☎ (212) 877 1166. Nightclub for ageing rock 'n' rollers and those in the music biz. A best for its occasional jamming sessions with the greats – Jagger, Bowie, *et al.*

DANCETERIA, 30 W 21st St, NY 10010 ☎ (212) 620 0515. Seedy and punky it may be, but it achieved desperately sought-after fame in *Desperately Seeking Susan*. Small bands, great boppery.

LIMELIGHT, 660, 6th Ave, NY 10011 ☎ (212) 807 7850. Based in a deconsecrated church, you can't ignore this one. *"Eerie, outrageous, vast, just as you think it's going out, it's in again"* (David Shilling).

EL MOROCCO, 307 E 54th St, NY 10022 ☎ (212) 752 2960. Revamp of the former rave meeting place for European café society, now visited by the next generation – Sabrina Guinness, Anthony Delon.

RITZ, 119 E 11th St, NY 10003 ☎ (212) 254 2800. An old dance hall where touring and up-and-coming bands play to hip young kids (and grown-up kids like Warhol). Record companies talent spot from upstairs tables.

SURF CLUB, 415 E 91st St, NY 10128 ☎ (212) 410 1360. Yup-Prep club for nice all-American Ivy Leaguers. Kitted out to conjure up a beach club in a Long Island summer resort, jitterbugging can turn it swiftly into the Sweat Club.

ZULU LOUNGE, 1584 York Ave, NY 10028 ☎ (212) 722 0556. Clearly a case of robbing Peter to pay Paul: Surf Club owners Toby and Angus Beavers (plus brother Nick and mother Patricia) and John Muller have dragged their own tribe with them into the depths of Africa, amid palm trees, bamboos and Zulu masks. Small and tightly packed.

NOCTURNAL THEME PARKS

Area

"It's so decadent – I walk in there and shake off my civilization. I dance on my own, I allow the music to flow right through me. It's a wonderful pulsing sensation. Decadence to me is really a sensuous way of life, so close to primitiveness" (Prue Acton).

Models, businessmen in tuxedos and outrageous punks jostle behind theatre ropes to capture the doorman's eye and approval, for it's purely his whim that lets you in. Successful applicants look original, act arrogant. Once in, $18 apiece poorer, hipsters file down the long passage with glass cases displaying theme oddities of the month. Clubs normally have a year or two's lifespan before they bore fickle New Yorkers silly. Area skirts this problem by redecorating at least 6 times a year. A theme which strengthened the commitment of the club's disciples was "religion", covering not just WASPish christianity, but religions worldwide, throughout history. Long-suffering models stood among temples and whitewashed Greek archways, in the uneasy attitude of Christ on the cross, or of Saint Sebastian, loinclothed and punctured with arrows.

Palladium

Similar crowds champ at the black velvet ropes, hoping zany doorpeople Haoui Montaug and Sally Randall will pretend to check their names off on their make-believe lists. This charade is purely to taunt the have-nots. However, a spot of rent-a-crowd (the right sort, from model agencies, magazines, Morgans – see TRAVEL) does go on. The privileged – people like Bianca Jagger, Norma Kamali, Calvin Klein, Andy Warhol – sail past the riff-raff with their invitations. The main dance floor is rigged with backdrops, mobile lights and theatrical devices. Hollow stage sets lower on to the floor to create a room within a room; things *happen*. At Madonna's party, rose petals cascaded from the ceiling. The Mike Todd Room at the top (the impresario's old office) is eerie and candlelit. Very decadent, very wartime Berlin. From the sub-sublime to the grotesque: the basement is a frenzy of Sixties psychedelia, Day-Glo squiggles courtesy of hip graffiti-merchant Kenny Scharf. If you could paint a hangover, this would be it.

BEST CLUBS

All across America, gentlemen's clubs and societies tend to be paranoidally secretive. Some instruct their staff not to reveal the club address to telephone callers (even when it appears in the telephone directory).

♔ **THE BROOK, 111 E 54th St, NY 10022 ☎ (212) 753 7020.** 1,000 ageing members, with lots of East Coast blue blood. John F. Kennedy belonged. Based in a little town house. *"For people who know each other, from the same background and the same families – you have to be connected. Membership is closed – you have to wait for someone to die to get in"* (Ludovic Autet).

♔ **RACQUET CLUB, 370 Park Ave, NY 10022 ☎ (212) 753 9700.** Squash and tennis courts and an elegant dining room. For the young élite. *"Very social – it's a perfect place for a younger set. Most of the members are in the Junior International Club"* (Ludovic Autet). *"The club where most of my friends would go – you can do sports, but it's mainly a place to drink and see friends"* (Marc Biron).

♔ **UNION CLUB, 101 E 69th St, NY 10021 ☎ (212) 734 5400.** The most prestigious of the gentlemen's clubs, founded in 1836. Members include Astors, Roosevelts, Delafields and other old upper-crust families. Superb catering; squash and tennis. Women allowed in only for social gatherings.

CENTURY ASSOCIATION, 7 W 43rd St, NY 10036 ☎ (212) 744 0090. Club for intellectuals, founded in 1847 for authors, artists and amateurs of the arts. This maxim has extended to include modern statesmen and all-round smarties.

COLONY CLUB, 564 Park Ave, NY 10021 ☎ (212) 838 4200. Exclusive ladies' club. Achievers from the Social Register.

KNICKERBOCKER CLUB, 2 E 62nd St, NY 10021 ☎ (212) 838 6700. More of the old élite – Vanderbilts, DuPonts, Pells, Rockefellers – plus an international set. Elegant rooms, fabulous Central Park setting.

THE LINKS, 36 E 62nd St, NY 10021 ☎ (212) 838 8181. This Georgian house was originally a golf club, but the only links now are those family ones needed to get in. It helps if you're a Ford, Mellon, Whitney, DuPont or Rockefeller.

RIVER CLUB, 447 E 52nd St, NY 10022 ☎ (212) 751 0100. Smart club overlooking the East River, with tennis courts and swimming pool. *"Very American, very New York. All the top names in America belong. It's really charming"* (Ludovic Autet).

UNIVERSITY CLUB, 1 W 54th St, NY 10021 ☎ (212) 247 2100. An old-established club with a literary air. 4,000-strong all-male membership.

EUROBONDS

JUNIOR INTERNATIONAL CLUB, 575 Madison Ave, NY 10022 ☎ (212) 605 0363. A glorified 18–30s club to launch Eurotrash, children of the European élite, into Manhattan society. The intention was to mix aristocratic Europeans with old-established Americans, but the whole thing has become essentially Eurocentric (ex-JIC man Marc Biron broke away to form Club Biron, a similar set-up for leading young Americans). Young people with a title, or at least a *name* (such as Prince Charles de Bourbon, Lord William Cavendish, Prince Albert de Monaco, Andrew Carnegie Rose, the Princess of Yugoslavia, Anne Eisenhower, Godfrey von Bismarck and Marchese Alessandro Manfredini) are sponsored in by Eurograndees such as Gianni Agnelli, and scooped up by chairman Ludovic Autet, who may even throw a formal hooley in the newcomer's honour. If you don't fit the gold-edged bill, you're refused membership (which costs $800 a year, or $350 to 'Junior Members' – those with strings to pull rather than extreme youth). The Club has no premises, but arranges twice-weekly soirées to restaurants and nightclubs (from the ilk of Area and Palladium to that of Doubles and Club A), and holidays: ski trips to Vail or Aspen, a week in Port Antonio, Jamaica, or a jaunt to the coast of Mexico.

BEST EVENTS

The biggest and best bonanzas are by invitation only, but a few can be penetrated. *Town & Country* chronicle the lot. There is a mini-season in May, but the big bashes start in October, running up to Christmas. *"It's crazy – you have 5 or 6 parties a night. There are lots of charitable events"* (Marc Biron).

♔ **METROPOLITAN MUSEUM OF ART OPENING, 5th Ave/82nd St, NY 10028 ☎ (212) 879 5500.** Diana Vreeland's Costume Institute has one show a year, lasting 9 months. An invitation to the opening night in December (with a bill for $750) is the deepest honour Manhattan can bestow upon a person. *"The opening of the Metropolitan really starts the season. Fashion designers come from all over the world. When you have a party in a large room with 20 Rubens on the wall, it simply has to be the best"* (Ludovic Autet). *"We give wonderful, wonderful shows. The Indian exhibition is* wonderful *– costumes and jewels from royal India, from the maharajahs of the past. The opening is a great formal dinner, with very carefully selected guests*

– about $50 – and placement. *This has nothing to do with me. This has to do with Mrs William Buckley, who organizes the dinner. It's very chic and very attractive. The whole room is done over"* (Diana Vreeland). Done over indeed it was, by John Funt, who created a summer's night in India, with opulent red and gold silks, colonial ceiling fans, trees, and a starlit sky. All the Indian royals from Jaipur and Jodhpur were there, the Kissingers, Bill Blass, Arnold Scaasi, Carolina Herrera, Brooke Astor, Estée Lauder, Ann Getty, Norman Parkinson, Oscar de la Renta – the entire cast of fashionable New York.

APRIL IN PARIS BALL, American French Foundation, 250 Park Ave, Suite 624, NY 10177 ☎ (212) 986 2060. Oct. A full-time committee runs this ball, which benefits 24 different charities. Always a theme, such as the memorable year when it was "Circus" and Marlene Dietrich rode in on an elephant. This year's theme was Fête des Vendanges, the ballroom turned vineyard, with baskets of grapes *partout*. Guests, who pay $400 a head, get $300 worth back in prezzies (though companies donate these) – an immense stripy box packed with wine, liqueurs, champagne and cologne (his) and scent, silk scarves and liqueurs (hers).

METROPOLITAN OPERA HOUSE, Lincoln Center, NY 10023 ☎ (212) 870 7412. For opera, classical music and ballet (Mikhail Baryshnikov is artistic director of the company). The Metropolitan Opera opens with a splash in September. The gala (☎ (212) 870 7428) will set you back about $1,000 for the performance, a black-tie dinner and thrilling extras (last year it was a Chanel couture show). The more private OPERA BALL closes the season in May.

OPERA IN THE PARK, c/o Metropolitan Opera (see above). A handful of free concerts and operas a year in Central Park, with the orchestra, chorus and soloists from the Met. People bring elaborate picnics from Balducci's (see FOOD AND DRINK). A great favourite is Tchaikovsky's 1812 Overture with fireworks.

“ The New York season is very fatiguing. Everything is so commercial – I don't think you ever go to New York to have a good time in that sense. If you're lucky and have some friends there, then it can be really wonderful ” (TINA CHOW)

BEST HOSTS

Mrs William (Pat) Buckley. *"Mrs William Buckley's dinners at the Met and for Memorial Sloan-Kettering are the best – she's a great organizer"* (Lynn Wyatt). At the helm of all the major New York charity extravaganzas (and a few of her own), she is wizard at whipping up enthusiasm, a relentless doer, and mistress of the seating plan. Her right-hand women, who add gloss to any gala by their very presence, include **Mica Ertegun, Chessy Rayner, Nan Kempner, Lynn Wyatt, Paloma Picasso, Carolina Herrera** and **Susan Gutfreund** (notable hostesses themselves).

SWEET CHARITY II

Charity is a whopping great industry in the States – the largest in fact – and high society revolves around its money-spinning circuit. Over $65 billion a year is reaped in tax-deductible contributions and gala takings. Money buys social status when it is dropped (in fantastically large dollops) into the coffers of some deserving trust, or when it creates some entire foundation or centre (as when Winton Blount of Alabama chiselled $21.5 million out of his savings to build a 750-seat Shakespeare Theater on his estate). The arts rate high on the charitable hit list: opera, theatre, ballet, museums and galleries are maintained by bequests, donations and galas, and it is *their* galas that carry the most cachet (openings at the Metropolitan Museum of Art in New York, Opera balls in San Francisco, New York, Chicago and Washington, the lavish opening of the Treasure Houses of Britain exhibition in Washington, to which only British treasure-lenders and those American philanthropists who had donated heavily to the National Gallery of Art in 1985 were invited). Events in aid of the Memorial Sloan-Kettering Cancer Center are always glamorous, and the Center is showered with contributions (in 1985, $36.25 million from Laurence Rockefeller, $10 million from the Milton Petries).

The doyennes of American society shine in the name of charity – Nancy Reagan, Ann Getty, Brooke Astor, Leonore Annenberg, Betty Ford, Dolores Hope, Barbara Sinatra, Lynn Wyatt, Carroll Petrie, Barbara Davis, Katharine Graham... the list, like the funds, is endless.

"The New York season used to be wonderful, but now it's only these charity things. It's a way Americans have found to social climb. They're all on committees so nobody gives parties any more. You don't see anyone you know. You just see hundreds of thousands of New Yorkers pushing" (Taki).

BEST VENUES

The METROPOLITAN MUSEUM OF ART (see Best Events) is available for private parties – Gordon Getty held his 50th birthday bash there.

PLAZA BALLROOM, 768 5th Ave, NY 10019 ☎ (212) 759 3000. *"You can never go wrong with the Plaza Ballroom. When you come out you can always stick your head in a fountain"* (Taki).

RADIO CITY MUSIC HALL, 1260 6th Ave, NY 10020 ☎ (212) 246 4600. A fabulous art deco theatre, the largest in the USA. You can hire the Grand Foyer and mezzanine with balconies for 900 pals (stand up and shout) or 450 (sit down and nibble). $5,000.

BEST PARTY ORGANIZER

PEGGY MULHOLLAND, 245 E 37th St, NY 10016 ☎ (212) 953 9105. Creates wildly imaginative settings and fills them with the right combination of food, music and props. Mainly private parties. Did a pink party for the Farrish family in Kentucky (friends of the Queen of England), with pink panthers serving pink champagne, and girls in pink body stockings with hula hoops lining the drive. She also did a mad gala for Jack Heinz's 75th birthday, entitled "A salute to the Tomato King", in which 57 varieties of vegetable stretched from 57th to 58th Street.

The season is all the time except August and January, when even the gossip columnists clear out. May to July and Christmas are frenetic. Washington society thrives on business meetings in the guise of formal receptions and gala dinners. With the right diplomatic contacts, you could attend 5 functions a night. This is greatly due to the Reagans, who love nothing better than a knees-up.

BEST NIGHTSPOTS

BAYOU CLUB, 31/35 Kay St NW, DC 20007 ☎ (202) 333 2897. A club and a concert hall for rhythm and blues – mainly established groups. Comedy acts too. A university hangout – Georgetown buzzes with uni kids at night.

BLUES ALLEY, 1 Blues Alley, DC 20007 ☎ (202) 337 4141. *The* jazz club. Small in area, big in reputation: Sarah Vaughan, Wynton Marsalis and Ella Fitzgerald have all played here.

DESIREE, 1111 29th St NW, DC 20007 ☎ (202) 342 0820. A private club in the Four Seasons Hotel, where rich diplomatic offspring hang out. Getting in involves being sponsored, being approved at a reception for prospective members, and then paying your $250 dues.

9.30 CLUB, 930 F St, NW, DC 20004 ☎ (202) 393 0930. A London-style new wave club where many lesser-known English bands play: lots of new acts and underground films.

BEST CLUBS

COSMOS CLUB, 2121 Massachusetts Ave NW, DC 20008 ☎ (202) 387 7783. To qualify for membership, you must be distinguished in the areas of art, literature or science. Most members have written 2 recognized literary

Country clubs

CHEVY CHASE CLUB, 6100 Connecticut Ave, Chevy Chase, MD 20815 ☎ (301) 652 4100. A family retreat for a spot of golf, tennis and swimming, with facilities for private parties.

CONGRESSIONAL COUNTRY CLUB, 8500 River Rd, Bethesda, MD 20817 ☎ (301) 365 1600. Senators and congressmen converge on the 2 18-hole golf courses and tennis courts (with underground heaters to stop them frosting over).

works. It is customary to give the President and the Foreign Secretary honorary membership. A man was once lunching there with a senior member in Kissinger's day, when the very man walked past. "Who *is* that?" demanded the senior member. "I have a feeling I've seen him somewhere before."

METROPOLITAN CLUB, 1700 H St NW, DC 20006 ☎ (202) 835 2500. The dean of men's clubs. *Very* private.

BEST EVENTS

KENNEDY CENTER HONORS, c/o JF Kennedy Center, DC 20566 ☎ (202) 737 5858. A gala weekend to honour a handful of greats in the movie world – last year included Bob Hope and Alan Jay Lerner. Gold medals are presented at the ceremony – the highest honour America can give: there's a White House reception and a dance at the Opera House. *"The best event – it's such an honour to be invited. It was done in the best possible taste, very glamorous – a real thrill to be a guest"* (Brooke Shields).

OPERA BALL, c/o Office of Development, Washington Opera, JF Kennedy Center, DC 20566 ☎ (202) 822 4730. June. The most sought-after do in Washington, a 3-day event, commencing with a congressional reception on Thursday, followed by dinners at various embassies on Friday, moving on to the ball at the host embassy (Sweden this year), and culminating in brunch at a top hotel on Saturday. This year, Mrs Caspar Weinberger sat in the chair – it's all *très diplomatique*.

SYMPHONY BALL, c/o National Symphony Offices, JF Kennedy Center, DC 20566 ☎ (202) 785 8100. Held in aid of the Symphony and attended by any old established 'cave-dweller' who is anyone.

A WHITE HOUSE STATE DINNER, The White House, 1600 Pennsylvania Ave, DC 20500 ☎ (202) 456 1414. An invitation to a White House dinner held in honour of a head of state (there are 1 or 2 a month) is the best you could ever muster. (The most coveted invitation ever was to the highlight of the Royal Roadshow [part of the Treasure Houses show festivities], when the likes of Clint Eastwood and John Travolta turned up to shake hands with Charles and a leg with Diana). *"A state dinner is a thrilling thing. A wonderful mixture of people – you could put all the names into a hat, and whoever you pulled out would be wonderfully stimulating and interesting – a CEO, a member of the government, a foreign diplomat, a scientist, a sportsman or someone in showbiz – all people you hear about, read about and know about. The White House is beautiful, decorated with masses of flowers – with the Reagans it's all so elegant. After dinner, there's entertainment – Frank Sinatra or Perry Como – and everyone sits round, in a private, cosy way"* (Lynn Wyatt).

BEST HOSTS

Roy Pfautch's parties see politicos doing the shuffle, singing silly songs and generally letting their hair down. Roy is a lobbyist for such causes as the American Medical Association. **Pamela** and **Averell Harriman** arrange lots of fund-raisers. **Katharine Graham**, of the *Washington Post*, is a grand party-giver.

BEST VENUES

Apart from the KENNEDY CENTER and WHITE HOUSE, the foreign embassies are top venues. The British and French are the best (though the Frog food has gone downhill during Mitterand's administration) and can be hired if the cause is worthy enough. BRITISH EMBASSY, 3100 Massachusetts Ave NW, DC 20008 ☎ (202) 462 1340. You can hire a room for 250 via Mrs Alison Fitzer. FRENCH EMBASSY, 4101 Reservoir Walk NW, DC 20007 ☎ (202) 944 6000.

BALTIMORE

The Baltimore social mentality is similar to that of Boston: traditional, gilt-edged, ceremonious.

BEST EVENT

BACHELORS COTILLION, c/o Mrs Laura Bortle, 3rd Floor, Legal Dept, Equitable Bank Center, 100 S Charles St, MD 21201 ☎ (301) 547 4109. The most formal and prestigious debutante ball. White-gloved paternal gentlemen, virginal young girls. Very *Gone With The Wind*. Gone too, are some of the old customs – girls used to be chaperoned by fathers, uncles and godfathers, and permitted only to dance with them and alcohol was strictly forbidden – now you may dance with a young man and sip champagne.

BOSTON

Bostonians need their beauty sleep. Virtually the only time they emerge is for old society balls, many of which take place at the Copley Plaza in its stunning ballroom.

BEST NIGHTSPOTS

LINKS, 120 Boylston St, MA 02116 ☎ (617) 423 3832. New club set up by brill DJ Michael Crane, late of the Surf Club in New York. Modelled after a turn-of-the-century country club, it draws Beacon Hill yuppies.

METRO, 15 Lansdowne St, MA 02215 ☎ (617) 262 2424. For trainee New Yorkers. The best – only – place for bopping, with live music.

BEST CLUBS

♣ **SOMERSET CLUB, 42 Beacon St, MA 02108 ☎ (617) 227 1731.** The grandest and most patrician of the gentlemen's clubs, based in a pale grey granite building on Beacon Hill. Very select – Lodges, Lowells and Cabots feel quite safe here.

THE COUNTRY CLUB, 191 Clyde St, Brookline, MA 02146 ☎ (617) 566 0240. *The* country club, with one of the oldest golf clubs in the country.

BEST EVENTS

CONSUL'S BALL, Copley Plaza, 138 St James Ave, MA 02216 ☎ (617) 267 5300. Jan. Held in honour of the consular corps of Boston, it's jammed with politicians and dignitaries. By invitation only. $100 a head. About 40 hostesses organize a table each. Excellent international cuisine.

DEBUTANTE COTILLION, Copley Plaza (see above). June. Old-fashioned entrée into society, white gloves, presentations and all.

BEST HOST

Mrs Harris Fahnestock, who is on the Board of Trustees for the Symphony Orchestra.

CHICAGO

BEST NIGHTSPOTS

JAZZ SHOWCASE, 636 N Michigan St, IL 60605 ☎ (312) 427 4300. Home of bebop jazz, based in the Blackstone Hotel.

RACOON CLUB, 812 N Franklin St, IL 60610 ☎ (312) 943 1928. The most elegant and fashionable club in Chicago. Real *Cotton Club* stuff with '30s décor, small tables and music of the era – jazz, swing, and cabaret. For private affairs, some people go the whole hog and dress as gangsters and flappers; most of the time it's anything from black tie to blue jeans.

BEST CLUBS

RACQUET CLUB, 1365 N Deerborn Parkway, IL 60610 ☎ (312) 787 3200. Very exclusive and choosy. Old money, great cachet to belong. Sports-orientated.

SADDLE AND CYCLE CLUB, 900 W Foster Ave, IL 60640 ☎ (312) 275 6600. The best country club, set in 15 acres (6 hectares) with 9 tennis courts, 2 swimming pools and an ice rink. Getting in is a case of knowing as many members as possible, and waiting till one pops off.

TAVERN CLUB, 333 N Michigan St, IL 60601 ☎ (312) 263 1166. A private club where men meet for lunch on the 25th floor, and women on the 26th (*that's* oneupwomanship).

BEST EVENTS

DONOR'S BALL, Historical Society, Clark St at North Ave, IL 60614 ☎ (312) 642 4600. Nov. Proceeds go to the Costume Collection of the Society – one of the best in the country – and 450 of the most fashionable Chicagoans pay $300 to doll themselves up in some splendid outfit that they may later donate to the collection. Abra Anderson is on the committee (dressed last time in Jacqueline de Ribes). Jere Zenko chairs.

PASSAVANT COTILLION, c/o Women's Board, North Western Memorial Hospital, 250 E Superior St, IL 60611 ☎ (312) 908 3313. Dec. Very Social Register. Held in the Grand Ballroom of Chicago Hilton Towers. Debutantes are hand-picked by committee – ex-debs choose about 30 daughters of other ex-debs to be presented.

BEST HOSTS

Abra Prentice Anderson – a Rockefeller, and benefactor of the Prentice Women's Hospital. Has a beautiful penthouse on Lake Shore Drive; **Renée Crown** – on the board of WTTV (Chicago's public broadcasting station), active in the opera and daughter of the late Henry Crown, former owner of the Empire State Building.

LOS ANGELES

BEST NIGHTSPOTS

There are a handful of trendy live music clubs that appeal to the non- starstruck young (who don't have to be up with the lark) plus there are haphazard hangouts like Powertools and Dirtbox which open and shut as often as Joan Rivers's mouth.

TRAMP, Beverly Center, 8522 Beverly Blvd, CA 90048 ☎ (213) 659 8090. Owned by Jackie Collins's husband Oscar Lerman, the Original Tramp of London, as it is properly called, costs $1,000 to join plus $1,000 a year. A hardy Hollywood hit, much larger than its London counterpart, with cinema and private dining room. *"It's the kind of place where you can be comfortable if you are a movie star or a rock star or a lawyer or someone who works in a hairdressing salon"* (Jackie Collins). Regulars include Quincy Jones, Eddie Murphy, Prince, Michael Caine, Michael Douglas, Michael J. Fox, Sylvester Stallone, Barbra Streisand, Rod Stewart and Julian Lennon.

CLUB LINGERIE, 6507 Sunset Blvd, CA 90028 ☎ (213) 466 8557. The club puts on up to 4 bands a night – anything from punk rock to reggae. Occasional arty/fashion evenings. Mostly college kids in their mid-20s, but on punk poker nights the average age soars.

PALACE, 1735 N Vine St, Hollywood, CA 90028 ☎ (213) 462 8135. Based in Merv Griffen's old TV chat show set, renovated in '30s style. Trendy nightclub/ concert hall/restaurant. At

> **"Nobody goes out after 9.30 because it's all casting calls at 7 o'clock in the morning. Not *everybody* in Los Angeles is involved in the movie business, but that's the mentality and style of LA"**
> (BOB PAYTON)

> **"A lot of these little clubs come up like little starlets – very bright starlets, which shine for a while, then fade"**
> (JACKIE COLLINS)

weekends, jazz bands play upstairs while a country or punk or rock concert blares away downstairs. Classy hip kids' stuff.

ROXY, 9009 Sunset Blvd, CA 90028 ☎ (213) 276 2222. *The* rock venue, a showcase for major touring bands. *"Very in at the moment – so in, it's practically impossible to get in"* (Jackie Collins).

BEST CLUB

BEL AIR BAY CLUB, 16801 Pacific Coast Highway, Pacific Palisades, CA 90272 ☎ (213) 454 1391. In Marion Davies's old beach house, built for her by W Randolph Hearst. Smart, social local in a stunning setting on the beach.

BEST EVENTS

Private parties are held in restaurants like SPAGO'S, CHINOIS ON MAIN and THE BISTRO (see FOOD AND DRINK). The best beanos are filmbiz-orientated, naturally – charity movie premières such as *Rocky IV* and *Out of Africa* – but LA society is bored to tears with the same old celebrity faces. Cary Grant rolls up to every do, and the Gabor sisters will go to the opening of a filing cabinet. The Reagans are about the only names to cause a tremor in the Hollywood Hills.

SWIFTY LAZAR'S OSCAR NIGHT PARTY in March, held in a fashionable restaurant. Swifty is *the* agent. Oscar nominees and those with direct connections go to the awards ceremony at the Dorothy Chandler Pavilion: afterwards they hot-foot it to Swifty's to join everyone else who is anyone. *"It's the most important party. It's the people that make it. He manages to get everybody, from the young rock stars to the oldest movie stars – Michael Jackson to George Burns"* (Jackie Collins).

BEST HOSTS

Wallis Annenberg, daughter of Walter, is the best. **Pamela Mason**, **Jackie Collins** and **Marsha Weisman** are hot stuff too.

SAN FRANCISCO

The hippest town on the West Coast. Lots of late-night activity, though drinking stops at 2 a.m. SoMa (South of the Market) is the young, arty, clubby SoHo-cum-Rive Gauche area: NoMa is more Rive Droite. A highly arts-orientated social life.

BEST NIGHTSPOTS

CLUB 9, 399 9th St, CA 94103 ☎ (415) 863 3290. An "art motel" with food, dancing, a performing arts area and exhibitions, run by SoMartie Mark Rennie. Draws a select young art/museum crowd plus lots of visiting New Yorkers.

L'ETOILE, 1075 California St, CA 94108 ☎ (415) 771 1529. An elegant bar where the wealthy go to hear Peter Mintum tinkle the ivories in vintage '40s and '50s style.

THE OASIS, 1369 Fulsom St, CA 94117 ☎ (415) 863 9178. A groovy dance club in an old motel. The swimming pool is covered over to make the dance floor.

ROCK 'N' BOWL, 1855 Haight St, CA 94117 ☎ (415) 826 2695. Pool room, bowling alleys, and large screens showing music videos. A New York fad that has bowled 'em over on the West Coast.

SAN FRANCISCO MUSEUM OF MODERN ART, 401 Van Ness Ave, CA 94102 ☎ (415) 863 8800. Not a nightclub, but a meeting place for cool people on Thursday nights, when the SFMMA has open house, with late-night viewing of ever-changing exhibitions from 6 to 10 p.m.

SESAR'S LATIN PALACE, 3140 Mission St, CA 94110 ☎ (415) 648 6611. An authentic Latin ballroom in the heart of the South American district, where all ages converge to salsa.

THE STONE, 412 Broadway, CA 94113 ☎ (415) 391 8282. Though it's in NoMa, it has bags of street cred. Local hard rock and punk bands. Open till 6 a.m (by that time it's fruit juice and a DJ).

WOLFGANG'S, 901 Columbus Ave, CA 94133 ☎ (415) 474 2995. Owned by Bill Graham, father of rock and roll concerts in the US – he organizes all the star turns in San Francisco and attracts some big names to his club. You go for the band, not the club. Less head-banging, more cerebral goings-on take place in the basement at NOMA, where artsies gather for poetry readings, and 18-year-olds are allowed to gather for a juice until they come of age.

BEST CLUBS

♁ **BOHEMIAN CLUB, 624 Taylor St, CA 94102 ☎ (415) 885 2440.** The club started in a bar where journalists sat tapping their fingers, waiting for hot news. They'd play the piano, have a sing-song and it became the best meeting place in town. Eventually even the railway barons would join the party on the way home from work, and the Bohemian Club was born. Now you may join if you "carry a spear" – connected with the arts or media – and/or are sponsored in. Members include presidents (of the US as well as of major companies) and their right-hand men – such as Ronald Reagan, George Schultz, Caspar Weinberger. Highlight of the year is the mysterious, highly confidential, Masonic-style 2-week Encampment at their own Bohemian Grove, in the redwood forests north of San Francisco. Invitations are like gold dust. A bunch of eminent, influential bigwigs get together to share experiences: it's all based on comradeship, camaraderie, with lectures and music, no talking shop (but you can bet they do), no TV, no radio, no telephone. One source speculates that it's a case of "frustrated artists dancing round redwood trees". Whatever it is, the boys *can't wait*.

BEST EVENTS

BLACK AND WHITE BALL, c/o SFMMA, Davies Symphony Hall, CA 94102 ☎ (415) 552 8000. April/May. A biennial extravaganza in aid of the San Francisco Symphony. The originator, Anna Logan Upton, felt that as symphonies usually have 4 movements, so the ball should have 4 concurrent venues, and since sheet music is black and white, the theme would match. Charlotte Mailliard has taken over the running, and it is held in City Hall, the Opera House, the Museum of Modern Art and Davies Symphony Hall, with continuous music in each – classical (the symphony orchestra play), jazz (Bobby Short), big band (Peter Duchin, Count Basie) and pop (Boz Scaggs, Tower of Power). Special events, indoor fireworks, achromatic dress and food. $150 a head, or $75 for 21 to 30s.

OPERA BALL, Opera House, 301 Van Ness Ave, CA 94102 ☎ (415) 861 4008. Sept. The Opera is at the apex of high society in San Francisco, and is strongly supported by Ann and Gordon Getty. The Fall Season commences with a grand dinner, a gala performance and a glittering ball. Something of an endurance test, but no socialite would dare miss it.

VALENTINE BALL, c/o SFMMA (see above). An extravagant dinner-dance plus fashion show – last year's was Karl Lagerfeld's (and tickets disappeared before they were put on sale). Trader Vic's provide the victuals, dress is romantic.

BEST HOSTS

Charlotte "Tex" Mailliard: No. 1 in both public and private entertaining. Deputy Chief of Protocol for the city, she often acts as hostess for the Mayor and chairs parties for visiting dignitaries. **Ann Getty** is also a seriously good entertainer.

PALM BEACH

Hardly Sin City, Palm Beach conducts its social life in a gentle, civilized manner. There are no nightclubs, but in season (Nov–Easter), there may be as many as 100 charity receptions and balls.

BEST CLUBS

Country clubs are exclusive and secretive, membership is closed. The two most selective and snooty are the BATH AND TENNIS CLUB, 1170 S Ocean Blvd, FL 33480 ☎ (305) 832 4271 and the EVERGLADES COUNTRY CLUB, 356 Worth Ave, FL 33480 ☎ (305) 655 7810.

BEST EVENTS

COCONUTS, 1021 N Ocean Blvd, FL 33480 ☎ (305) 844 6659. New Year's Eve. The Coconuts is a men's club without a clubhouse. The originals were a group of bachelors who banded together and held a New Year's Eve party to repay all their social obligations. The tradition continued and a select beano is still thrown in a different location each year. Each proposed guest has to be approved by a secret committee.

PRESERVATION FOUNDATION BALL, c/o Preservation Foundation, Seagull Cottage, 58 Coconut Row, FL 33480 ☎ (305) 832 0731. March. Held at Mar-a-Lago, the late Marjorie Merriweather Post's madly OTT mansion, now owned by Donald and Ivana Trump. An incredible setting – 110 gilded grotto-like rooms of European Baroque inclination, a mass of archways, carvings and frescoes, everything dizzily embossed and patterned. Ivana threw herself winningly into the role of hostess this year.

BEST HOSTS

Mary Sanford is one of the *grandes dames* of Palm Beach: **Sue Whitmore** and **Lewis Weidener** give tremendous bashes, too.

NEW ORLEANS

The most liberal drinking laws in the States. Although clubs shut at some point in the night to clean up or reorganize, you can drink 24 hours a day.

BEST NIGHTSPOTS

BLUE ROOM, University Place, LA 70140 ☎ (504) 529 4744. A jazzy supper club, based in the old Roosevelt Hotel. Live music: everyone from Fats Domino to Andy Gibb plays.

NAPOLEON BAR, 500 Chartre St, LA 70130 ☎ (504) 524 9752. A respite from the trumpets and clarinets. Late-night drinking in the French Quarter to classical music.

PRESERVATION HALL, 726 St Peter St, LA 70116 ☎ (504) 522 2238. Earthy home of New Orleans jazz – small, with sawdust on the floor, wrinkled black musicians, and sadly too many tourists. Nevertheless, it's captivating stuff. + Preservation Hall bands alternate playing 7 nights a week.

SNUG HARBOR, 626 Frenchmen St, LA 70116 ☎ (504) 949 0696. On the edge of the French Quarter, a better place to hear local jazz.

❝ The best club I have ever been to is one in LA which is so private that there are only ever two other people there. It is called On The Rocks. It's a tiny club with a big video screen. You might find only Jack Nicholson there, sitting in the corner and watching basketball. It's uncrowded and nice, very quiet. ❞

(MARIE HELVIN)

BEST CLUB

BOSTON CLUB, 824 Canal St, LA 70112 ☎ (504) 523 2241. Desperately secretive and discriminatory. For fourth generation-plus families.

BEST EVENTS

MARDI GRAS Exclusive and ultra-clandestine gentlemen's carnival organizations, known as "krewes" (clubs so secret that members are only known to fellow members), go through time-honoured rituals, electing kings and queens, arranging parades and masked balls. Of a week of luncheons, dinners, pageants and about 90 carnival balls, the best events are the REX and COMUS balls, both held on Mardi Gras evening itself. Both very formal, the Rex is perhaps slightly more accessible and the Comus more élite (its krewe is the oldest, formed in 1857).

DALLAS

Society revolves around the oil well. The caste system may be based on business success, but the way you make the money is of paramount importance: it must be through honest hard graft.

BEST NIGHTSPOTS

STARCK CLUB, 703 McKinney St, Suite 107, TX 75202 ☎ (214) 720 0130. Designed by Philippe Starck (see HOMES AND PROPERTY), part-owned by Stevie Nicks of Fleetwood Mac, opened by Grace Jones, it attracts young wealth. Unusual for Dallas, a Palladium-style doorman picks the clientele. Hip dance music played by some of the top DJs in America.

BILLY BOB'S TEXAS, 2520 N Commerce St, Fort Worth, TX 76106 ☎ (817) 429 5979. The bar where Jenna first kissed Bobby during the bull-riding competition in *Dallas*. Real hick Western stuff – Country and Western music played by the greats (Willie Nelson, Waylon Jennings, Merle Haggard) and real live bull-riding.

BEST CLUBS

DALLAS COUNTRY CLUB, 4100 Beverly Drive, TX 75205 ☎ (214) 521 2151. In Park Cities territory, it's one of the stuffiest, most exclusive clubs in the US: 15-year waiting list: discriminatory on grounds of race and religion. Old(ish), white Texan money is what it likes.

DALLAS PETROLEUM CLUB, 4786 Interfirst One Building, 1401 Elm St, TX 75202 ☎ (214) 7547 7053. The oil boys' club. Membership by invitation only – and it's only those with buckets of money who are asked: it sure won't drill a hole in their pockets. An entity unto itself: no reciprocal arrangements with any other clubs. Women admitted in the evenings only.

Social Bibles

The *Social Register*: the "Stud Book" is a black and orange annual directory of people who count – old, non-showy New York, as decided by the Social Register Association; *Forbes 400*, published in a thick gold-edged edition of *Forbes* magazine: a run-down on the 400 richest people in the USA; *Social 400*, a one-off published in the *Washington Dossier* – a run-down on the top 400 people in Washington society; *Town & Country*: the back-patting social magazine which has regular soft-focus photographic features on worthwhile people – the best dinner party-givers, the most important polo/croquet players and clubs, rolls of honour for donors to charities and institutions, and a chronicle of all the forthcoming events you'd ever need to know about.

BEST EVENTS

CRYSTAL CHARITY BALL, 47 Highland Park Village, Suite 5, TX 75205 ☎ (214) 526 5868. Held each December in a downtown hotel. Clearly in the top 2 of the many, many Dallas hooleys. Madly extravagant décor and dress. Tickets at around $600 a head are sold out to the oil society before they even hit the printers. Outsiders don't stand a chance. Money raised for children's charities.

CATTLE BARONS' BALL, c/o Mrs Billy Baneaton, 6342 McCommas, TX 75214 ☎ (214) 827 5475. June. Held outdoors on a local ranch, it's the real-life version of the Oil Barons' Ball in *Dallas*. Big money (old and new), big-name entertainment, a funfair, and a lavish auction where people bid for each others' furs, cars and diamonds. The biggest single fund-raiser for the American Cancer Society.

BEST HOSTS

Caroline Hunt Schoellkopf: the best-liked and most expert hostess in Dallas (it is, after all, her speciality – see TRAVEL). Known for her brilliant thrashes – good guests, good food, good fun. **Nancy Brinker**: wife of fast foodie polo player Norman B., she is in the top 10 Dallas Best Dressed, and organizes a host of charity balls.

BEST VENUES

MANSION ON TURTLE CREEK (see TRAVEL);

DALLAS COUNTRY CLUB (see above).

AUSTRALIA

"People who say there is no society in Australia are absolutely wrong. There's snobbishness in society about everything, whether you're talking sport, theatre or partygoing. You get in either by starting with a good name, or if you're young and pretty and are seen at events, or if you work for a charity, or if you're really good at something. If you're a champion runner, or the star of a show, *lovely* to have you" (DIANA FISHER).

BEST NIGHTSPOTS

TOP 5

★

1 ROGUES, Sydney
2 INFLATION, Melbourne
3 ARTHUR'S, Sydney
4 BERLIN CLUB, Sydney
5 PALACE, Melbourne

SYDNEY

ROGUES, 10 Oxford Square, Darlinghurst, NSW 2010 ☎ (02) 336924. The nearest Sydney gets to Annabel's, although the crowd most nights smacks more of Stringfellow's, slotting in with society matrons who turn up for regular black-tie drinks parties and young movers and shakers of the Eastern Suburbs. Fairly strict membership is enforced by man-about-town owner Peter Simpson. Dark and slick, the club has 3 bars including a piano bar, a high-profile dance floor, one of the best restaurants in Sydney and some of the most glamorous waitresses. *"The best in Sydney. Small, fun, amusing – a nice intimate club. It's in some old wine cellars, so you can make as much noise as you like and nobody cares. The food is excellent and the people are young"* (Diana Fisher). *"It's terrific to have dinner there and go into the nightclub part afterwards. It's got a lot better since the membership was reduced last year and undesirables were kept out. You see friends there"* (Patricia Coppleson).

ARTHUR'S BAR AND RESTAURANT, 155 Victoria St, Potts Point, NSW 2011 ☎ (02) 358 5097. A club sandwich of staggered steel platforms – like a glorified fire escape. The filling consists of bars, a restaurant, a garden and a balcony, and the topping, a tiny dance floor. *"Arthur's is a fantastic club – the décor is wonderful and the staff are so rude, which is very, very cool. The waiters are very aloof – that sets the right tone: you've got to be somebody before a waiter will acknowledge you"* (Christine Jones). TV and film personalities such as Kate Fitzpatrick and Bryan Brown, artist Brett Whiteley, and visiting rock stars like Iggy Pop and the Pointer Sisters, sit on a level at the back away from the throng. Offspring of the affluent, trendy bourgeoisie are the mainstay clientele.

BERLIN CLUB at Jamison St Club, 11 Jamison St, NSW 2000 ☎ (02) 271937 (Tuesdays only). It's the best place in town to go raging (the rest of the week it's businessmen and gold chains). All the spaciousness and charm of a tram terminal – which is exactly what it was before it turned into a loud, hip dance club. This is where Grace Jones discovered the 7-foot muscle man who became Sylvester Stallone's Russian opponent in *Rocky IV*. Spandau Ballet and Duran Duran have been here when in Antipodean straits, as have most touring bands. Masses of models too. Above the main dance floor is a platform for exhibitionists. *"Lots of lasers, confetti, videos. The Berlin Club is very glossy – rich kids, fashion industry, hairdressers, people dressing beyond their means, glamorous girls of 17 and 18 who are stunning, very smart cool boys – sophisticated children of the rich professionals. It's too intimidating for me – I'm a young fogey!"* (Christine Jones).

THE CAULDRON, 207 Darlinghurst Rd, Darlinghurst, NSW 2010 ☎ (02) 331 1523. Steamy pick-up joint bubbling with girls in mini skirts that rise to dizzying heights, even by local standards. In the sleazy Kings Cross area ("the Cross"), which real trendies avoid. *"A brilliant disco and one of the best meat-markets in town. As long as they like the look of you on the door, you're in. Easily the favourite nightclub for rock stars"* (Dorian Wild). The straighter set go there earlier to dine in its rather good restaurant.

IL FIASCO, 34 Bayswater Rd, Kings Cross, NSW 2011 ☎ (02) 358 1881. The newest nightclub/restaurant in Sydney is so far living up to its name. People go there for the sheer pleasure of whining about the restaurant service, which is slow largely because the staff consists mainly of MAWs (model-actor-waiters). However, the club has wonderful post-modern visuals – glass bricks, polished granite surfaces, art deco lights and seats – and a vibrant subterranean bar/disco. Teenies love it, and it's always a challenge to pass the scrutiny of the doorman, whose criteria remain undefined, judging by the crowd some nights. *"It's where people like to be seen – lots of models and advertising people, the sort who go somewhere only if it's absolutely spanking new"* (Dorian Wild).

BENNY'S BAR-RESTAURANT, 12 Challis Ave, Potts Point, NSW 2011 ☎ (02) 358 2454. Where ragers with stamina wind up: *"Horrible, smelly and smoky but tacky in the way the rock industry loves"* (Christine Jones). You could find David Bowie or the Spandaus here after a long, hard evening.

HIP HOP CLUB, 11 Oxford St, Paddington, NSW 2021 ☎ (02) 332 2568. Smallish intimate club with a mix of live shows, jazz, the New Blues and a disco downstairs. It's in the fashiony-arty-gay area, though the gay scene is far less spectacular than it used to be. A jumble of trendy art students who dress down, and *"older people from the social scene"* [read 28] (Christine Jones).

HOPETOUN HOTEL, 416 Bourke St, Surry Hills, NSW 2010 ☎ (02) 335 257. Small, steamy club with a tiny stage where excellent bands from all over Australia play to raging 300-strong audiences.

KINSELAS, 383 Bourke St, Darlinghurst, NSW 2010 ☎ (03) 331 6399. Theatre-cabaret-restaurant (see FOOD AND DRINK) run by Tony Bilson. Sophisticated young to middle-aged arty/theatrical types. TV stars, newsreaders, jazz players and Paddington Yuppies – and that's just in the bar. Comedy acts, bands, fringe plays. Performers include George Melly, and the Cambridge Buskers.

SELINA'S, Coogee Bay Hotel, 253 Coogee Bay Rd, NSW 2034 ☎ (02) 665 0000. The best venue for live music – 3,000 people go to see touring and Australian bands. Music addicts and trendies.

WILLIAMS, Boulevard Hotel, 90 William St, NSW 2000 ☎ (02) 357 2277. Women don every sequin they ever owned and their partners a suit, but the club remains soulless. *"Very swish indeed, probably the best* disco *in town, but you can be there at 11 pm, 12, 1 am and there aren't a huge number of people there. It's the nightclub with the atmosphere most* approaching *that of Annabel's – elegant, a particularly good restaurant – but you can sit there and look at 4 walls"* (Dorian Wild). And on the restaurant again: *"The best taste in Sydney"* (Harry M Miller). Few people even bothered to turn up for its first birthday early this year. However, fashion designers find it the ideal spot for parading their wares to the fashion glitterati.

BEST CLUBS

TATTERSALL'S, 157 Elizabeth St, NSW 2000 ☎ (02) 264 6111. *"Terrific: old-fashioned, masculine, no-nonsense, no frills, with the most fabulous facilities. It has the most beautiful indoor pool in Sydney, built in the '20s – you can do laps there, and they have terrific masseurs. It's a proper old gentlemen's club. Everybody belongs to it – young merchant bankers, jockeys, old-time Sydney identities. It's not difficult to get into – you have to be nominated, but it's not starchy like the business clubs because it has a racing bias. It's the most interesting club in Sydney"* (Leo Schofield).

AMERICAN, 129 Macquarie St, NSW 2000 ☎ (02) 271615. *"The only club I go to regularly, because it has the best views – the men's has a view down over the top of the Opera House – the best loo view in Australia!"* (Max Lake).

AUSTRALIAN, 165 Macquarie St, NSW 2000 ☎ (02) 221 1533. The best club in Sydney according to Dorian Wild, but others reckon it has some "dodgy characters". Large and hotel-like. *"I find the Australian and the Union insufferably arch. Silly, pretentious, sub-English nonsense going on in the colonies. They're pretending to be the Reform or White's" (Leo Schofield).*

QUEEN'S, Corner Elizabeth and Market Sts, NSW 2000 ☎ (02) 264 1171. A women's club with a non-trouser-wearing tradition that irks younger members. However, *"It's a very pretty club inside and has wonderful reciprocal rights overseas [Cosmopolitan, New York; In and Out, London, etc] – a very good reason to belong. They're getting a lot of younger people in now, injecting new life into it"* (Patricia Coppleson).

UNION, 25 Bent St, NSW 2000 ☎ (02) 232 8266. *"Good accommodation and dining room, and a good clientele"* (Dorian Wild). What knights there are in Australia are members, such as former prime minister, Sir Billy McMahon. Politicians, businessmen, and country stock – who descend in herds at Easter and make remarks about the "clerks" (members who are bankers).

BEST EVENTS

BLACK AND WHITE BALL, c/o Mrs Charles Parsons, 402 New South Head Rd, Double Bay, NSW 2028 ☎ (02) 327 5698. Held every October at Sydney Town Hall, for the Royal Blind Society. *"Easily the premier charity committee – it's the oldest; the chairman Marno Parsons is a tireless worker and a very charming woman"* (Dorian Wild). *"They have a tremendous committee which works extremely hard. The Town Hall is much better than the hotels – more room to dance, 1,000 people and bigger bands"* (Diana Fisher). However, brilliant committee plus brilliant venue does not *always* equal brilliant occasion: some complained that last year's A$65 (US$46) affair was overbooked, not everyone was dressed in black and white and, *"for some curious reason, they had a horse race after dinner which completely broke up the atmosphere"* (Dorian Wild).

“Sydney has a pulse, and you feel the pulse as you are about to land. The adrenalin flows. People who are posted there love Sydney, whereas Melbourne's a bit of a drudge. By the time they're getting in on the social scene in Melbourne, they're practically on their way out to another posting. You can come to Sydney and pretend you're anyone. In Melbourne, they might just check your credentials. Sydney is more casual, a cosmopolitan, international city. Melbourne is a little staider, more set and rigid – dinner parties there usually require formal dress, whereas in Sydney it's suits and men may take their jackets off” (SUSAN RENOUF)

CAUSE BALL, c/o Leo Schofield & Associates, 10th Floor, 100 William St, E Sydney NSW 2010 ☎ (02) 357 2122. An irregular ball held by advertising agencies for a cause that fires their imagination. *"Fabulous – they always have a brilliant theme"* (Diana Fisher). The last one, "In the Pink at the Wharf", saw 400 media socialites, dressed in pink with matching pink rinses, sipping pink champagne at the Sydney Theatre Co, in aid of the National Institute of Dramatic Art. There was a theatre, disco, 3 bands, cabaret, laser and fireworks displays, and food by Anders Ousback.

LORDS' TAVERNERS BALL, c/o John Darling, 56 Pitt St, NSW 2000 ☎ (02) 233 5358. Bubbles Fisher helps organize this ball at the Regent Hotel, around October. Lots of pro-celeb fun and games … a mock cricket match in which the Taverners' team always has to win, or a competition in which Olympics stars perform their respective sports and the Taverners, again, beat them. This year, they are expected to have the TV dating game that Aussies sit glued to with morbid fascination, *Perfect Match*. *"I like balls to have something different. You can't just have a band and a dance and a dinner. You've got to have a cabaret or razzle-dazzle or something that surprises people"* (Diana Fisher). *"A cut above the other balls"* (Patricia Coppleson).

OPERA IN THE PARK, The Domain Jan. Part of the Festival of Sydney. Using the New York Central Park blueprint, a series of free opera and classical music concerts, accompanied by the chomping of picnics. The *1812* forms a stunning grand finale, complete with resounding explosions from fireworks and cannons, and the ringing of real cathedral bells from nearby St Mary's. *"I happen to be mad about opera, and it's a lovely big peaceful get-together of 100,000 people on a beautiful balmy night"* (Leo Schofield).

PETER PAN BALL, c/o Mrs Peter Collett, 265 Edgecliff Rd, Woollahra, NSW 2025. At the Sheraton-Wentworth, Saturday before Easter, in aid of Dr Barnado's. The only ball that isn't a free-for-all – it's by invitation only, and the names of guests making up a party are vetted by the committee. A fine blend of the best city and country families (who are up from Tassie and Victoria for the Easter Show). *"Together with the Black and White, the most prestigious ball in Sydney"* (Primrose Dunlop).

SYDNEY OPERA HOUSE OPENING NIGHT, Bennelong Point, Circular Quay, NSW 2001 ☎ (02) 20588. Opening nights draw old society names such as Sir James and Lady Rowland, and Lady Fairfax. Dressiness levels vary. Champagne in the interval. The most memorable evenings are when the *grande dame* ("Wonderlungs") is performing: *"There will never be a better thing than Joan Sutherland in* Lucia di Lammermoor. *This was truly the most breathtaking thing for me. The set has been cut down now but originally it was built for the Concert Hall at the Opera House. They had 300 Newington schoolboys as gladiators. The extras were phenomenal. But Sutherland was just this towering vision falling down these huge steps – she was brilliant, absolutely brilliant!"* (Robert Burton).

BEST HOSTS

Lady Mary Fairfax. Wife of Sir Warwick, stepmother of media/publishing baron James, is the undisputed queen of private and fund-raising parties – in the role of

BEST GUESTS I

Sydneysiders who sing for their supper: **Glen-Marie North** (*"utterly divine to look at, a great sense of humour, and much more than that"* – Dorian Wild). **Lady (Mary) Fairfax**, **Harry M.** and **Wendy Miller** (he: *"controversial, interesting"*, she: *"intelligent, a lovely lady to sit next to for a one-to-one conversation"* – Patricia Coppleston). **Kerry Packer** (*"will tell you how he's beating the pants off the cricket establishment with his pyjama (night) cricket. The most charming man,* utterly *charming, but can be an absolute bore when he wants to be"* – Dorian Wild). **Joe** and **Marlene Bugner** (*"good fun, genuinely nice: a spade is a spade"* – Primrose Dunlop). **Barry Humphries** and **Michael Parkinson** when in town (*"if you have either, you're off with a bang – they won't allow people to stay stuffy for long"* – Diana Fisher). **Sir James** and **Lady Rowland** (he: Governor of NSW – *"has quasi-royal status"* – Primrose Dunlop). **Sir Roden** and **Lady Cutler** (he: former Governor of NSW – ditto). **Johnny Baker** (every woman's favourite walker: *"great company"* – Primrose Dunlop; *"if there's a lull in conversation he'll come to the rescue"* – Patricia Coppleson), radio star **John Laws** (*"gives me a buzz"* – Primrose Dunlop: *"a charming man, accepted at the best tables in town"* – Dorian Wild), artist **Tim Storrier** (*"provided the guests are not too stuffy – he's unpredictable, you never know what the hell he's going to say next"* – Patricia Coppleson). **Sir William** and **Lady (Sonia) McMahon** (he: former Prime Minister of Australia; great social figures about town), editor of *Cosmopolitan* and *Harper's Bazaar* **Sylvia Rayner**.

both giver and goer (when she rolls up in her 1964 Phantom V Roller, driven by a uniformed chauffeuse). *"She gets an incredible mixture of people together. The food is also always very good.* **Len Evans:** *"Fabulous, boisterous dinner and lunch parties. In the Hunter Valley, he has the longest, most beautiful refectory table you've ever seen. He always has the most interesting guests. He's ebullient, a great vigneron and great fun."* (Diana Fisher). **Glen-Marie North** and **Robert Frost**: *"She came to prominence doing PR for De Beers. She has excellent taste and more open houses and a wider variety of people at her functions than anyone, with the best of everything"* (Dorian Wild). **Kerry** and **Ros Packer**: An infallible combination of Ros's friends – the old squatocracy (country aristos) and Kerry's, from racing, golf, cricket and Channel 9. **Diana** and **Simon Heath**: *"A beautiful mixture of people, good food, French champagne, great environment and good conversation. Her party after the opening of* La Bohème *at the Opera House when Pavarotti was here was just divine"* (Primrose Dunlop).

PARTIES OF THE YEAR

BOB FROST AND GLEN-MARIE NORTH's WEDDING. *"It was like a scene from Dynasty, it really was. Some people were quite over the top with their sequins. Glen-Marie looked gorgeous in satin with a hat. The food was good, the champagne marvellous, and it went on all night"* (Patricia Coppleson). *"The telegrams were read by Phil Harry, who just can't stop telling jokes. He read one out from the Meteorological Office, a weather report saying 'Frost up North'"* (Dorian Wild).

INTER-CONTINENTAL HOTEL opening party: *"The best hotel opening I've ever been to. Rooms were devoted to a theme of food. In the ballroom there were islands that cascaded with a river of oysters, prawns tumbled over mountain tops and the flower arrangements were done with lobster claws. In the next room, chefs in tall hats were carving turkeys and every other sort of meat, in the next there were puddings, and the next was Covent Garden with stalls of fresh fruit and a lake with the Opera House carved in ice. The whole thing was dazzling"* (Diana Fisher).

ODYSSEY HOUSE BALL This was the first ball held at the new Inter-Continental Hotel; that, and all the thrilling faces and activities brought in by committee head Glen-Marie North, provided enough excitement to keep even a jaded Primrose Dunlop there till 3 am. Joe and Marlene Bugner were there, Marlene looking unruffled in a *Hello Dolly*esque feathered creation. *"Every function and banqueting room in the joint was used. Everybody had a magnificent time. All-in tickets, unlimited drink, efficient and courteous staff. Amazingly well-organized"* (Dorian Wild).

OPERA SWING BALL, Hyde Park Barracks. Hoped to be the first of many. A glamorous opera/fashion crowd wafted in and out of open-sited marquees. *"I had a fabulous time there. It's the first party I can remember for a long time in Sydney where you were mixing with people your own age. That was the one thing that stood out. Full of hot spunks, young people who had made an effort to go out – not one member of the blue rinse set"* (Robert Burton).

■ BEST VENUES ■

LINDESAY, 1 Carthona Ave, Darling Point, NSW 2027 ☎ via National Trust (02) 332 3308. The earliest neo-Gothic house in Australia, built in 1834. Hirable at a price. A knock-out venue, as some people found at the prestigious opening of the annual Lindesay Antiques Fair last year, when the ceiling fell in.

ROYAL SYDNEY GOLF CLUB (see SPORTING LIFE). A smart venue if you're a member and have some A$35,000 (US$24,730) to blow. Lady Potter has held parties there, and Sinclair Hill threw a hooley for the Prince of Wales. *"A great place to have a party. You can make a hell of a racket, there's good food, and lovely old-fashioned surroundings – it works very well"* (Primrose Dunlop). *"Make sure you're properly dressed"* (Lord Lichfield).

SYDNEY OPERA HOUSE, Bennelong Point, Circular Quay, NSW 2001 ☎ (02) 20588. A ball for 500 can be held in the Northern Foyers, overlooking the harbour with gloriously romantic views at night. Exclusive dinner parties for 20–60 in the upper level of the Bennelong Restaurant cost A$50 (US$35) per head for the room alone.

SYDNEY THEATRE CO, Pier 4, Hickson Rd, Millers Point, NSW 2000 ☎ (02) 250 1700. A converted warehouse near the Bridge, available on Sundays only. Brilliant venue with lots of different rooms. Food by Anders Ousback.

"The wonderful thing about Melbourne is it goes on all night. Not many people realize that. It comes second in the world after New York. The young can be out every night of the week at a different place till 7 in the morning. There is a *huge* nightlife here" (PRUE ACTON)

MELBOURNE

BEST NIGHTSPOTS

INFLATION, 60 King St, VIC 3000 ☎ (03) 623674. The best club in Melbourne. Giant video screens and electronic razzmatazz attract a hip and lively crowd – on weekdays more than weekends. *"It's just been renovated and upstairs there's a marvellous cocktail/dance/video bar which is good fun, and then downstairs there's a huge dance floor – it's wonderful"* (Prue Acton). *"Amazing décor on 3 levels, much more like New York than any of the Sydney clubs, very sophisticated cool Melbourne"* (Christine Jones).

PALACE, Lower Esplanade, St Kilda, VIC 3182 ☎ (03) 534 0655. *"It's enormous – I love the spaciousness of it. Palace and Inflation are my favourites in Melbourne and 2 of the best in the world for me"* (Prue Acton).

CHASER'S, 386 Chapel St, S Yarra, VIC 3141 ☎ (03) 241 6615. New, trendy, currently wowing the Melbourne scene. Lots of one-nighters – Vertigo on Wednesdays, funk music on Fridays.

MELBOURNE UNDERGROUND, 22–24 King St, VIC 3000 ☎ (03) 624701. A refined, comfortable, but trendy club in a renovated bluestone warehouse. Masses of room, good food, and screening at the door. The likes of radio personality Derryn Hinch pass the scan.

THE CLUB, 132 Smith St, Collingwood, VIC 3066 ☎ (03) 417 4039. Run by ex-Skyhooks musician Bob Starkey, it's the best nightly venue for prominent local bands.

SUB TERRAIN, 453 Swanston St, VIC 3000 ☎ (03) 663 6471. Groovy underground club.

BEST CLUBS

"Of women's clubs, it's a competition of the dowdy. By a short head, the Lyceum beats the Alexandra for dowdiness. Women's clubs ought to be dowdy. I don't think they ought to be smart or slick or anything like that. They should have that terribly dull look to them" (Patrick McCaughey).

ALEXANDRA CLUB, 81 Collins St, VIC 3000 ☎ (03) 636051. *"A beautiful old premises, just being done up. It's all Victoriana, with a wonderful wedding cake façade, sadly at the moment painted battleship grey – but perhaps, considering the dowagers that frequent the place, that's an appropriate thing"* (Primrose Dunlop).

MELBOURNE CLUB, 36 Collins St, VIC 3000 ☎ (03) 634941. A bastion of old-style society with members such as the Darlings, Carnegies and Baillieus (but no Myers). *"Like stepping into the last century. A private, closed club. No one talks about it; you just know it exists"* (Max Lake). *"The best club in the city, in the best building. It's like Barry's Reform Club in London – absolutely the marque of the great London club architecturally, but much bigger than most London clubs. The interior looks like an Ealing comedy of the 1940s. The wood of the fireplaces in the dining room is an example of some of the most spectacular ugliness ever created by the mind of man. Young bloods used to scale the wood and go round it without touching the floor"* (Patrick McCaughey).

BEST EVENTS

ELLERSLIE HUNT BALL, c/o Ballangeich Run, nr Ellerslie, Mortlake, VIC 3265. John Goold, Joint-Master of the Ellerslie Hunt goes to endless effort to turn on a bash well worth travelling 3 hours from Melbourne for. Held on his property, with catering by Rowland, and flowers by O'Neill, it's the most glamorous occasion in the Western Districts of Victoria.

OAKS DAY cocktail party, in the garden of the Melbourne Club (see Best Clubs), Thursday of Melbourne Cup week, November. Flowerbed-to-flowerbed well-shod society, all on best behaviour.

BEST GUESTS II

Melbourne Magnets: **Sir Ian** and **Lady (Primrose) Potter**, **Andrew Peacock** (*"Australia's most colourful politician – hugely good company, great raconteur"* – Dorian Wild), *Mode* columnist and biographer of Princess Michael of Kent, **Barry Everingham** (*"waspish, social conversation"* – Primrose Dunlop), **Douglas** and **Margaret Carnegie** (*"wonderfully stimulating, such varied interests"* – Primrose Dunlop), **Hugh Morgan** (MD of Western Mining Corp), Fine Arts professor at Melbourne University **Sir Joseph Bourke** (whose style is 1948 London set in aspic), restaurateur **Jannie Goss**, eccentric extrovert **Captain Peter Janson**, **Sir Rupert** and **Lady Clarke** (he has been described as an Australian Etonian; she as very jolly), arties **Jenny Chapman** (of Powell Street Gallery), **Christine Abrahams** (of her own gallery), **Pauline Wrobell** (of Realites Gallery in Toorak).

"In Melbourne, we do social events better than any other country except France, in the sense of doing things with panache and style and a lot of thought. Unlike America, we take enormous trouble to make sure guests don't get bitten by mosquitoes – we have carpets put on the lawn inside the marquee, or have the lawn in the marquee sprayed. Our marquees are beautifully decorated and pretty. There are always new ideas being brought into parties" (LILLIAN FRANK)

ODYSSEY HOUSE BALL, c/o Odyssey House, 10 Bondi Rd, Lower Plenty, VIC 3093 ☎ via Lillian Frank **(03) 241 9179.** A lavish bash held in April, at the new Park Royal Hotel, St Kilda Rd. Beluga caviare, Krug, fireworks to music, 2 bands and a disco. A$100 (US$71) a head. Attended by a who's who of Melbourne. *"All the pretties and beautiful men come to my parties"* (Lillian Frank).

BEST HOSTS

"There are 200 families in Melbourne who give good parties ... Lady Clarke, the Walkers, the (Lindsay) Foxes, the Gandels, the Wenzels, the Baillieus, the Carnegies, Lady (Primrose) Potter, Lady Southey, Sarah and Baillieu Myer ... Some of the 200 families are new, but it makes no difference. People accept you for what you achieve and what you can give" (Lillian Frank). Fund-raiser extraordinaire Lillian Frank herself is in the upper section of the 200.

BEST VENUES

ALEXANDRA CLUB (see Clubs).

VICTORIAN ARTS CENTRE, 100 St Kilda Rd, VIC 3004 ☎ (03) 617 8211. Superb venue with foyers and theatres, lavishly – if gaudily – decorated by John Truscott. Grand balls; dinners in the ANZ Pavilion.

BEST PARTY ORGANIZER

PETER ROWLAND, 3 Tivoli Rd, S Yarra, VIC 3141 ☎ (03) 240 1353. A grand concern. *"I think people feel that if they can't say to their friends that they had Peter Rowland, then it wasn't quite up to standard"* (Elise Pascoe).

Parties of the year

MELBOURNE CLUB BALL, at the Melbourne Club. A one-off private ball, very well organized and civilized. *"It was stunning; everybody raved about it"* (Primrose Dunlop).

LADY (PRIMROSE) POTTER's private party at the Victorian Arts Centre. *"The best of the year. About 100 people from Sydney, Melbourne, Adelaide and abroad were there. Beautifully done, Kevin O'Neill did the flowers"* (Patricia Coppleson). *"Best frocks were worn, all the family diamonds were dragged out, you had a disco in one room, a band in the other, and John Truscott did the whole décor in pale gold and red. It was an absolutely beautiful evening"* (Primrose Dunlop).

RANALD AND PATRICIA MACDONALD's party for Prince Charles and Princess Diana was *"one of those wonderful private parties nobody ever quite knew about. Pure society"* (Primrose Dunlop).

ADELAIDE

"Adelaide is frightfully establishment. They cling to English traditions and are all terribly nice and charming. Like Melbourne, society is hard to get in to" (Primrose Dunlop)

BEST NIGHTSPOTS

SCHMIDT'S, 66 Unley Rd, Unley, SA 5061 ☎ (08) 271 6722. The Rogues of Adelaide – black walls, strict dress code; more conservative and upmarket than Limbo.

LIMBO, 30 Fenn Place, SA 5000 ☎ (08) 211 7117. The only hip spot in town. '50s milkbar-style with curved tables and bright colours. *"It's really cool – more sophisticated than Arthur's in Sydney. American Memphis décor. A good scene for Adelaide"* (Christine Jones).

BEST CASINO

ADELAIDE CASINO, North Terrace, Adelaide, SA 5000 ☎ (08) 212 2811. This A$160 million (US$113 million) casino-hotel is a handsome cross between Monte Carlo and Las Vegas; it will be raking in the takings at Grand Prix time.

BEST CLUBS

ADELAIDE CLUB, 165 North Terrace, SA 5000 ☎ (08) 513348. The best gentlemen's club, in the most attractive building of all the clubs in Australia, opposite Government House. Traditional, conservative; city and country Establishment. Fearfully under-used – only 30 or 40 for lunch each day, though there are 500 members.

QUEEN ADELAIDE, Stevens Place, SA 5000 ☎ (08) 212 3461. The women's answer to the Adelaide Club. Genteel, establishment ladies, some from the country. Useful for an inter-shopping break.

BEST HOSTS

Lady (June) Porter, widow of Sir Thomas Porter, former Lord Mayor of Adelaide. **Lady Downer**, widow of the former High Commissioner: *"Her garden is beautiful and the house divine – she brings back that British polish"* (Primrose Dunlop). **Joe** and **Jessica Dames**: *"They do parties very well and informally"* (Kym Bonython). **Mrs Bardie Simpson** of Simpsons industrial company. **Ian Cocks**: his Grand Prix party last year was a roaring success.

PERTH

BEST CASINO

PERTH CASINO, Burswood Island Resort, 8 St George's Terrace, Perth, WA 6000 ☎ (09) 362 7777. Part of a A$270 million (US$191 million) resort complex, the casino has been described as a cross between a squat Sydney Opera House and a supermarket. Its loss leaders, in the form of inexpensive drinks (combined with windowless rooms, dim lighting and an absence of clocks), encourage punters to play on. The hotel will be ready in December 1986 just in time for the America's Cup final influx.

BEST CLUB

WELD CLUB, 3 Barrack St, WA 6000 ☎ (09) 325 2677. The best in the city, in a wonderful central position.

BEST HOSTS

Eileen "Red" Bond wins hands down. She adores party-giving: her daughter's wedding only gave her a taste for more (which has already meant a bash for the 30th birthday of the younger Bondlet, John, at their Rose Bay residence in Sydney). Now the Bonds are limbering up for the long affair of an America's Cup summer. Other givers and goers are merchant banker **Laurie Connell**. **Lang** and **Rose Hancock**. **Kerry Stokes** and **Denis** and **Trish Horgan**.

BUSH BASHES

The days of lavish country parties are sadly over – they just don't have the disposable dollars. The young, however, have their own little whirl of B&Ss – informal Bachelors' and Spinsters' dances. These are held on country properties, often after Picnic Races (similar to British point-to-points) and are followed by a Recovery (another day of serious drinking).

"The old families maintain a consistency, order and quietude, in English county style; they are not materialistic, not showy, go to the right school, belong to the right club and marry similar people. I lament their demise – people who belong, people with style. They had wonderful house parties. I went to them all in my youth, took out the daughters, went to all the polo and picnic races ..." (Bill Ranken). *"There are some fabulous weddings in the country. But who's got the money to throw all-out glamour soirées with the economic recession, particularly in the country?"* (Primrose Dunlop). *"The Victorian squatocracy – Malcolm Fraser* et al *– is really heavy duty. It's definitely important, old money"* (Dorian Wild).

Country catches: Malcolm and **Tamie Fraser** (*"Get him off his subject and he's a delightful man; she may well be the wittiest and most charming woman in Australia"* – Dorian Wild); **George Falkiner** (high eligibility factor); **Sinclair Hill; Michael** and **Judy White.**

BRISBANE

BEST CASINO

JUPITER'S CASINO, Gold Coast Highway, Broadbeech, QLD 4551 ☎ (075) 502546. The nearest thing to Las Vegas – only better. The A$186 million (US$131 million) complex, houses 2 gargantuan gaming rooms lined with over 100 tables and blackjack machines for which the jackpot is over A$100,000 (US$70,661). *"The opening of Jupiter's Casino was wonderful. They spent A$1 million over 3 days on entertaining. Celebrities and millionaires were flown in from all over the world"* (Lillian Frank).

BEST CLUB

QUEENSLAND CLUB, Alice St, QLD 4000 ☎ (07) 221 7072. A gracious white colonial building at the leafy Parliament House end of George Street. The most exclusive club in Brisbane, city address of the Queensland squatters (landowners) and social haunt of doctors, lawyers and politicians.

CANBERRA

BEST CLUB

CANBERRA CLUB, West Row, ACT 2600 ☎ (062) 489000. *"The great political club. Every public servant of some standing aspires to be, or is, a member – the Head of the Treasury, the Head of Foreign Affairs etc. A leading public servant once said the Australian bureaucracy was conducted over lunches in the Canberra Club. A great place for political gossip. The club is where the power is"* (Dorian Wild).

FAR EAST

BEST NIGHTSPOTS

TOP 5

★

1 **LEXINGTON QUEEN, Tokyo**
2 **CASABLANCA, Hong Kong**
3 **AREA, Tokyo**
4 **PASTELS, Hong Kong**
5 **INK STICK, Tokyo**

JAPAN

TOKYO

The social scene is in the midst of change. Hong Kong Jardine Johnnies are gradually shifting across the East China Sea to Tokyo, where more expatriate jobs are opening up. The posts they have vacated are no longer being filled automatically by the next influx of expats. Meanwhile, having checked out the market in Hong Kong, the fishing fleet – fresh young English girls out to catch their man – move on to Tokyo pronto before the dishy men get hooked up with pretty Japanese girls. Nightspots formerly patronized by impecunious English teachers are now full of broking Brahmins and bankers.

BEST NIGHTSPOTS

ROPPONGI and AKASAKA are the smart centres of nightlife. SHINJUKU and GINZA have the greatest number of nightspots, but these are Japanese business class to Roppongi's first class. Ginza is hostess bars and Japanese restaurants. Shinjuku is glossy gay and transvestite clubs: this is Japanese-style family entertainment. The trendy area is Omote Sando in Shibuya – with its boutiques and a wealth of clubs.

LEXINGTON QUEEN, B1, 3rd Goto Building, 3-13-14 Roppongi, Minato-ku, ☎ (03) 401 1661. The grooviest late-night club. Proprietor Bill Hersey knows everyone – groovers include Whitney Houston, Tina Turner, Rod Stewart, David Bowie, the Carradine Brothers, sleek models, celeb hangers-on and paparazzi.

AREA, Nittaku Building, 3-8-15 Roppongi, Minato-ku, ☎ (03) 479 3721. The disco of the moment. Entrance fee: 4,000 yen (US$22) for men; 3,500 yen (US$19.50) for women. Dress code must be followed. An extraordinary light show – state of the art disco technology. Japanese and international: serious dancing.

INK STICK, B1, Casa Grande Miwa Building, 7-5-11 Roppongi, Minato-ku, ☎ (03) 401 0429. The best nightclub-bar. The *Merry Christmas Mr Lawrence* mates David Bowie and fellow cult musician Ryuichi Sakamoto hit it in a big way when in town. Occasional impromptu performances given by visiting rock stars.

CHARLESTON, 3-8-11 Roppongi, Minato-ku, ☎ (03) 402 0372. A café-bar for pre- or post-prandial drinks. A great expat hangout with a clubby atmosphere.

LATIN QUARTER, 2-13-8 Nagata Cho, Chiyoda-ku, ☎ (03) 581 1326. One of the few old-fashioned geisha-style clubs, with kimono-clad hostesses.

LIVE HOUSE LOLLIPOP, Nittaku Building, 3-8-15 Roppongi, Minato-ku, ☎ (03) 478 0028. A fun late-night bar: excellent venue for live music.

BEST CLUBS

FOREIGN CORRESPONDENTS' CLUB OF JAPAN, 20th Floor, Yurakucho Denki Building, 1-7-1 Yurakucho, Chiyoda-ku ☎ (03) 211 3161. An important club for businessmen and journalists, with visiting speakers such as George Bush and Geraldine Ferraro.

The Gakushuen Girls

Like other allegedly classless societies, Japan – Americanized as it is – has its own social structure. The most powerful family are the Tokugawas, the original Shoguns. The most revered family, however, are still the Imperials. As the final curtain draws near for Emperor Hirohito (who is to most Japanese a living god, whose name they dare not even utter), speculation over the marriage of his grandson, Hiro, who will succeed as Crown Prince, grows to fever pitch. The question is, will he do the right thing and marry a Gakushuen Girl? Gakushuen is the (mixed) school for Japanese nobility, and the girls are the Eastern embodiment of the Sloane Ranger. They are recognizable only for their inconspicuousness – their second-hand Rolleis (no Nikons here) and their lived-in cashmeres. Hirohito's son, the present Crown Prince, married a Seishin girl, from the lowlier rival school to Gakushuen, and Gakushuen Girls are determined to get back into the Imperial class. The Prince and Princess of Wales's recent visit and Prince Andrew's marriage to Sarah Ferguson have added fuel to the Gakushuen fire.

TOKYO AMERICAN CLUB, 212 Azabudai ☎ (03) 583 8381. TAC by name and verging on tack by nature, with bevies of Crimplened Americans, but it's where it all happens – the Capitol Hill of Tokyo.

TOKYO CLUB, 3-2-6 Kasumigaseki, Chiyoda-ku ☎ (03) 580 0781. Very hard to get into, but reciprocal rights with clubs such as London's Oxford & Cambridge enable many Brits to sail in. Eminent and distinguished membership, similar to White's in London. A prestigious place to eat.

BEST EVENTS

BLACK AND WHITE BALL, c/o Japanese Animal Welfare Society, Tanizawa Building, 3-1-8 Moto Azabu ☎ (03) 405 5652. Oct. The smartest people in Japan turn out in studied black and white Azzedine Alaïa or Katharine Hamnett creations for the B&W Ball held at the Capital Tokyu Hotel.

Party of the year

FENDI PARTY at the Moonchild Club in the Hilton. A fabulous thrash held by Koko Volpicelli. *La richesse* of Tokyo were more concerned about looking elegant in front of the fine turn-out from the Imperial family than with the charity angle, but it was undoubtedly a fine affur.

CHERRY BLOSSOM BALL, c/o Tokyo American Club, 212 Azabudai ☎ (03) 583 8381. International Ladies' Benevolent Fund. April. The most splendid event of the season, held at the Okura (see TRAVEL). A proliferation of cherry blossoms fills the venue, and the élite roll up in extravagant ballgowns.

BEST HOSTS

Fashion designer **Hanae Mori** and her husband Ken host about 20 parties a year for all kinds of visiting celebs plus many international fashion events. A great doer with her finger on the fashion pulse, anything she does is a big social event. It was she who brought Stephen Jones and Body Map over to Japan, and paved the way for Issey Miyake (see FASHION). Actor **Toshiro Mifune**: a great entertainer. Head of Cartier, **Bernard** (and **Tamiko**) **Cendron**, and head of Christian Dior, **Nicole Depeyre**, give wonderful corporate parties. **Koko Volpicelli** organized the Fendi party. Dress designer **Jun Ashida**: fabulous parties – everyone goes, including the royals. Grande dames of society, **Fumiko Tottori**, mother of Princess Takamado; **Mrs Aso**, daughter of former Prime Minister Shigeru Yoshida; and **Reijiro Hattori**, of Seiko watches. **Aki** and **Yoshiko Morita** (Aki is head of Sony) entertain on a lavish scale. Fashion designers **Matsuda** and **Yukiko Hanai** both throw marvellous international parties. **Tetsuko Kuronagi** – known as "Tamanegi Chan" (the Onion Lady) because of her hairstyle – author, TV presenter and chief money-raiser in Tokyo for Ethiopia. **Paul** and **Nancy Ma**, a Chinese couple who will have to change the menu of their annual dinner party – the star dish was bear paws, but importation has now been banned. Prize guest: **Prince Takamado,** grandson of the Emperor and Hiro's cousin.

Satisfaction guaranteed

To ensure your party goes with a bang, you enlist the help of one of the gossip gurus. The doyen is Bill Hersey, who writes grippingly for a local giveaway news-sheet, *The Tokyo Weekender*. Always surrounded by glamorous young Japanese men and foreign models, he takes a special interest in Lexington Queen among other nightclubs. Gloria Noda writes for the *Japan Times*. Jane Rees, from San Francisco, who has been in Tokyo for aeons, contributes to the *Asahi Evening News*. These 3 know who's in town, who to invite, where to place them – and then, to prove that it *was* a sensational evening, they scribble about it for the benefit of the rest of Tokyo.

HONG KONG

BEST NIGHTSPOTS

CASABLANCA, 9th Floor, Marina Tower, 8 Shum Wan Rd, Aberdeen ☎ (5) 540044. The smartest club in Hong Kong for dinner and dancing, on top of the Aberdeen Marina Club. Owned by nightclub magnate Sylvio Wang and Malaysian millionaire Robert Kuok. Elegant Moroccan décor, shades of Bogart and Bergman. A belly dancer was carted over from Casablanca to wobble her way through the opening.

PASTELS, Basement, 12 Pedder St, Central ☎ (5) 218421. The newest addition to the Wang stable. (He is the only club-owner in HK to enforce a dress rule – Walter Mondale and Rod Stewart were once turned away from his old club, Manhattan, for violating the no-jeans rule.) Beautifully designed, comfortable enough to take the edge off what would otherwise be severe minimalism. Very good food, elegant, room to breathe; you are cosseted more than in other clubs. The membership rule is usually waived for overseas visitors.

CAPTAIN'S BAR, Mandarin Hotel, 5 Connaught Rd, Central ☎ (5) 220111. *The* place to begin the evening – weekdays only. David Davies (the Taipan of Hong

Kong Land Co– which owns the Mandarin). Viscount Evelyn Errington. Bill Wyllie. Harry Wells. Michael Parry (when he's not tending to his own wine bar) and practically everyone who works in Central hit it between 6 and 7.30. The maître d' finds regulars a place to sit. Many deals are done here.

♕ **RAFFLES, 2nd Floor, Bank of America Tower, Harcourt Rd ☎ (5) 218131.** Civilized British-style membership day and night club. Sitting room with buttonback armchairs, large restaurant, health club – aerobics, sauna, whirlpool bath – and a dance floor. Also a sailing yacht members can hire for the weekend.

Colonial kicks

Typical of any community living abroad, certain expats feel they ought to do all the things their homeland would do, though they would never do them at home. There's a ST GEORGE'S BALL, a ST PATRICK'S BALL, a ST ANDREW'S BALL, a BURNS NIGHT DINNER (all male – gets completely out of hand) and no end of foot-tappers and MUCKLE-SHUNTERs: if you can't reel, you are a social outcast. There's no St David's Ball, but Welsh boys can console themselves down at the Rugby Sevens. This is a tremendous occasion for which people fly in from Tokyo and Singapore – *everybody* goes. All the big companies take boxes and you spend the weekend stumbling from box to box. Ceremonious consumption of lavish picnics is *de rigueur*. No one watches the rugger – it's the Henley of Hong Kong. David Davies gives a brilliant party afterwards.

CANTON, 164 Canton Rd, Tsimshatsui, Kowloon ☎ (3) 721 0209. Sophisticated, funky disco, with super-space age videos and lighting, and the best sound system in Hong Kong, masterminded by Richard Long, who handled the Palladium in New York. Like all discos on the Kowloon side, it's packed out with Chinese trendies with cool haircuts (on the opening night, 10,000 squeezed into a space for 2,000). Hong Kongsiders can't stand the crush.

FACES, New World Hotel, Salisbury Rd, Kowloon ☎ (3) 694111. Civilized club where you can drink champagne in a quiet nook with a group, and not be trapped in the thick of it.

HOLLYWOOD EAST, Hotel Regal Meridien, Mody Rd, Tsimshaitsui, Kowloon ☎ (3) 722 6620. Part of the Wang empire, a razzy Chinese disco.

NINETEEN 97, 9 Lan Kwai Fong, Central ☎ (5) 260303. Still the favourite hangout for well-heeled, cliquish young expats, it's run and staffed by Europeans – most of the fishing fleet have put in here for a stint of waitressing. Eating, dancing and occasional arty happenings. The bistro upstairs holds modern art shows, and travelling thespians sometimes stage fringe plays for small audiences in the basement club. The rest of the time it's bop till you drop at 3 or 4 in the morning.

BEST CLUBS

♕ **ABERDEEN MARINA CLUB, 8 Shum Wan Rd, Aberdeen ☎ (5) 558321.** A ritzy, newish complex with the best marina in Asia. Billiards, bridge, a marvellous mahjong room, sports – swimming, tennis – the works. Super pool parties. It has a restaurant, and there's Casablanca on the top floor (see Best Nightspots). *The* place for cruising yacht-owners – the club runs room service to the yachts, packed champagne lunches, and a junk or a sampan for short-haul voyages.

New Year gweilo-style

Highlight of the year is New Year's Eve, when colonials wind up after dressy dinners at Jardine's outdoor party for the Gun. Kilted gweilos reel frenetically to stave off the frost, helped by mulled wine (though not by the champagne). At midnight the cannon fires and the Chinese police break into a wailing Auld Lang Syne on their pipes. Everyone goes wild for 10 minutes and then hops thankfully on to a ferry which transports them back to Central and the warmth of a nightclub. At 4 am they repair to the Mandarin for breakfast. It's hardly worth going home, since New Year's Day starts with eggnogs at the Mandarin (a private party), followed by eggnogs at the Peninsula (ditto), always in that order.

♕ **AMERICAN CLUB, 47th Floor, Edinburgh Tower, Connaught Rd, Central ☎ (5) 842 7400.** A perfect position on the top floor in Exchange Square, with one of the best panoramas in Hong Kong. It's now more *in* to belong here than the Hong Kong Club, partly for convenience (most blue-chip companies have moved to Exchange Square), and partly in recognition of the shift of power towards the Americans (and it's not all pumpkin pies and barbecues).

♕ **FOREIGN CORRESPONDENTS' CLUB, 2 Albert Rd, Central ☎ (5) 211511.** Lots of characters, such as Clare Hollingworth of the English *Daily Telegraph*. Her big scoops were World War II (she saw tanks waiting at the Polish border) and

Philby's flight to Odessa. Some correspondents are left over from the Vietnam days. 400 journalists, plus those in business and the legal profession. Eminent people passing through often give speeches at the FCC.

HONG KONG CLUB, Jackson Rd, Central ☎ (5) 258251. Former strict rulings against Chinese and anyone under 30 have been relaxed after some of the old stalwarts left the colony in 1984 and the club moved into brand new premises. It still has super-cachet, but members disapprove of the new airport lounge-style surroundings. It's also on the wrong side of Connaught Rd now that everyone works in Exchange Square: it's easier to jump in the lift up to the top floor than get caught up in the flyover jungle.

NAUTILUS, 45-49 Repulse Bay Rd ☎ (5) 812 2204. The banana club – yellow on the outside and white inside: members may be Chinese, but they are very Caucasian in their outlook and behaviour. Primarily a dining club, owned by Sir Kenneth Fung Ping Fan, one of Hong Kong's great entrepreneurs, who also owns McDonalds. His son once hosted a dinner there with caviare, truffles and then, on silver platters, McDonalds hamburgers.

Community Chest

To save arguments, all charities are lumped together under one umbrella and the goodies are parcelled out equally. Running a committee holds little kudos – women have a dozen better things to do with their time. Chinese men channel a portion of their fortune into the Chest over a good many years in order to secure a place on the honours list. The only smart committee to be on is the Hong Kong Philharmonic Ladies' Committee.

ROYAL HONG KONG JOCKEY CLUB. See SPORTING LIFE.

■ BEST EVENTS ■

In Hong Kong, as in Tokyo, social life equals business life. There is no divide. Every conversation, even if it's talking about cucumber sandwiches, has a business slant. Pure socialites do not exist in the Chinese book. The most socially high-profile Chinese women are also top-flight businesswomen, mothers, and dynamos for their husbands. Nevertheless, there is a season, which runs from September to December. Colonials lie low or flee after the Rugby Sevens in April, when the going starts to get hot and muggy, and revive in September to do the party rounds.

HONG KONG ACADEMY OF PERFORMING ARTS, 1 Gloucester Rd, Wan Chai ☎ (5) 282 6622. An annual ball at the Regent with little ballerinas lining the stairs and a ballet performance after dinner. Very smart – anything done by the Academy is brilliantly arranged.

HONG KONG PHILHARMONIC ORCHESTRA, 20th Floor, Harbour View Commercial Building, 2–4 Percival St, Central ☎ (5) 832 7121. A special annual gala event – last year's spectacular, in the atrium of the Landmark, had the theme of A Night in Monte Carlo.

■ BEST HOSTS ■

Chantal and **Bob Miller**: the top party-givers in Hong Kong. Mistress of the grand entrance, she appeared on an elephant at her party for Bob's birthday at the Oriental Bangkok (and she took 30 of Hong Kong's élite along for the ride); for her Carnival in Rio party for 800, Chantal arrived in a hot-air balloon. **Barbara Thomas**: of the famous laquered hairdo; when she arrived from Washington, she held a Champagne and Sweets party to launch herself into Hong Kong society. Fashion businesswoman **Joyce Ma** and her sister **Bonnie Fung**. **Kai-Yin Lo**: the best dinner parties in HK, with big international names. **Lydia Dunn** and sister **Mamie Howe** (both Shanghainese who have anglicized their names). **David** and **Linda Davies**: their best party is during Macao Grand Prix, on top of the Oriental. Property tycoon, **Stanley Ho**: he gives a select banquet in Macao each year, with delicacies such as freshly decapitated monkeys' brains and snake soup. **Philippe** and **Annick Charriol**: American-style no-holds-barred extravaganzas.

Kung Hay Fat Choy

Chinese New Year: In mid-February, the Chinese-populated countries shut down for New Year. Gweilos escape to Bangkok or Macao for the long weekend, leaving bustling streets packed with herb and flower sellers and extraordinary food-stalls. Red and golden lanterns line roads where darting lions and dragons (the Asian version of the pantomime horse) perform their jerky dances. You can watch acts as diverse as Chinese wrestling or opera on makeshift roadside stages. The festivities continue until 2 am for an entire month.

■ BEST GUESTS ■

David Li: more English than the English, educated at Uppingham and Cambridge, a great mucker of Kai-Yin Lo's (they were undergrads together). **David** and **Susanna Tang**: frightfully pukka Shanghainese. **David Davies** (you'd invite but you might not get him). **Amanda Croucher**: attractive, bright; international chatter. **Bill Wyllie**: Aussie business whizz kid. **Lord Kadoorie**, head of Hong Kong Electric, and his playboy son **Michael**. **Dickson Poon**, the most eligible man in Hong Kong.

"My social world centres on Hong Kong and Macao, where business frequently dominates leisure. Entertainment is, more often than not, centred around business or a multitude of civic activities – charity, culture, sport – that commercial leaders are expected to promote. In a full working week, there is little time for other diversions – a stolen half day to shoot teal (for the pot, of course) in China, the occasional game of bridge with family or close friends, tennis – the real passion of my life, and dancing – usually confined to the charity balls that regularly punctuate the social calendar" (STANLEY HO)

BEST CASINO

MACAO CASINO, Lisboa Hotel, Avenida de Amizade ☎ 77666. The best casino in the Far East – with the best fung shui. Money makes Macao go round, and hordes of Chinese speed over from Hong Kong to keep the roulette wheel spinning. Unswayed by glamour, everyone brandishes HK$1,000 notes (HK$1,000 is about US$128), in the hope of becoming an instant millionaire (just as casino owner Stanley Ho has made – and lost – his fortune, several times). For light relief, the winners chink over to Ho's CRAZY PARIS show, still in the Lisboa, where European showgirls kick high.

BANGKOK

BEST NIGHTSPOTS

DIANA'S, Oriental Hotel, 48 Oriental Ave, 10500 ☎ 234 9920. At the other end of the spectrum, an exclusive club for those who can't stand the pace. The Annabel's of Thailand, it's chock-full of Bangkok royals (and theirs is the largest royal family in the world). A barrage of old school Thais from Harrow and Eton have accents so pukka that old colonials imagine they *are* in Annabel's.

PATPONG is the centre of all hustling, blaring, colourful, crazy, oriental nightlife – straight or kinky, from jazz clubs, discos and bars to sex shops and massage parlours, with plenty of deviations in between: all you ever dreamt of or dreaded doing.

SINGAPORE

BEST NIGHTSPOTS

Since the anti-corruption crackdown that stamped out the Bugis Street transvestite area and some avant-garde clubs, the residual night scene has become rather staid.

ATLANTIS, 200 Grange Rd, 0923 ☎ 734 3288. Current No 1 in Singapore, designed at a cost of S$2.5 million (US$1,164,958) by Daniel Flannery (who staged the closing ceremony for the Los Angeles Olympics). Filipino show bands imitate Western groups.

PEPPERMINT PARK, 80 Marine Parade Rd, 04-08 Parkway Parade, 1544 ☎ 344 5888. A café-theatre with live music and various acts that play to Singapore yuppies, both native and expat.

SHANGRI-LA HOTEL, 22 Orange Grove Rd, 1025 ☎ 737 3644. The entire hotel vibrates with movers and shakers in its 3 nightspots. Waft through the Xanadu disco, parade in the Peacock Lounge and sparkle in the Tiara Room, which holds the best late-night cabaret in town.

TOP TEN, 400 Orchard Rd ☎ 732 3077. A converted cinema with the Manhattan skyline scudding across the walls. Disco and live music of the José Felicianos and Commodores kind. Superlative lighting. Since Atlantis arrived, the club has slipped to No 2 in the Top Ten.

FASHION

by JASPER CONRAN

WORLD'S BEST DESIGNERS

1

YVES SAINT LAURENT, Paris

2

AZZEDINE ALAIA, Paris

3

KARL LAGERFELD, Paris

4

GIORGIO ARMANI, Milan

5

JEAN-PAUL GAULTIER, Paris

6

ROMEO GIGLI, Milan

7

CLAUDE MONTANA, Paris

8

DONNA KARAN, New York

9

REI KAWAKUBO, Tokyo and Paris

10

CHRISTIAN LACROIX, Paris

Buying the best in fashion anywhere around the world is the same story – you have to have great dollops of self confidence when entering those hallowed, scented and carpeted (or polished stone) interiors. For designer salespeople are not the type you are likely to meet at C&A; they are trained to assess your bank balance with a flick of the eye. However, he who does not dare does not win, and if it is your desire to see, touch or possess the best, read on.

When in London, go first for the things the British do best – traditional menswear. Lock's in St James's is a very old and English shop, where men buy their Coke (bowler) hats. A reverential hush still pervades, and the only noise to rise over the polite whispers of the salesmen is the tick, tick, tock of the grandfather clock. Lobb's is where the world's royalty have their footwear made. Here it is vital to wear a clean pair of socks. Your feet will be on display for quite some time while they are being measured in minute detail for your last (a pair of wooden feet just like yours). At Fortnum & Mason, the frock-coated gentlemen are sadly not for sale, but will propel you gently past foie gras, port and Stilton to Jean Muir's dresses: masterpieces of navy blue jersey, scattered liberally with solid silver buttons.

Paris is the most daunting prospect of all. Parisiennes are the doyennes of the withering look; a hair out of place is a positive sin, and check your beige slingbacks for anything malodorous before you sally forth to your first stop, which must be Chanel in the rue Cambon: mirrors everywhere, perfumed air, red lips and black bows. Teeter out a great deal poorer, and sashay on down to Kenzo, a riot of colour. But be careful not to depart looking like the Chelsea Flower Show in full bloom – a little goes a long way here.

Milan, it has to be said, is not a very pretty city. However, what it loses in beauty, it makes up for by being the home of Giorgio Armani, king of Italian fashion, whose fabrics, cut and simplicity of style are unparalleled.

British fashion designer JASPER CONRAN is part of the multi-talented Conran dynasty. Son of Sir Terence (of the design empire that includes Habitat) and Shirley of *Superwoman* and *Lace* fame, Jasper Conran trained in art and design in New York, and produced his first independent fashion collection in 1978. He soon rose to receive international acclaim for his chic, beautifully cut womenswear – and now menswear too. Now 26, he has his own ultra-spacious showroom in London, and outlets all over the world.

Tokyo is a different kettle of sushi altogether. Having been unceremoniously crammed like any other old sardine into the underground, burst onto the street seeking desperately a square inch in which to breathe, you dive into a shop and stand dazed and subdued, for this is a practically empty room. There must be some mistake. But no – you have arrived at Comme des Garçons. This is fashion at its most intellectual: black, architectural shapes, worn largely by architects. Your eye settles on one dress? jacket? pair of trousers? – you are not quite sure. Walk towards it for closer inspection, but, your Western eyes have disarranged/sullied/surveyed the garment at ten paces, a sweet little bag-lady-kewpie-doll throws herself at it to tidy it up.

In New York, shopping is a religion. Vast limousines sweep up Fifth Avenue, immaculate women stagger under the weight of beribboned boxes and shiny, coloured bags. Department stores resemble elegant sitting rooms: Bergdorf's, Bendel's, Saks, Bloomingdales, Macy's and, of course, Tiffany's – for twisted ropes of baroque pearls, huge emeralds, discreet sapphires, chain mail bracelets and aqua-coloured boxes tied exquisitely with yet more bows.

EUROPE

EUROPE'S BEST DESIGNERS

★

1. AZZEDINE ALAÏA, Paris
2. GIORGIO ARMANI, Milan
3. JEAN-PAUL GAULTIER, Paris
4. ROMEO GIGLI, Milan
5. CLAUDE MONTANA, Paris

EUROPE'S BEST COUTURIERS

★

1. YVES SAINT LAURENT
2. KARL LAGERFELD at Chanel
3. CHRISTIAN LACROIX at Jean Patou

ENGLAND

LONDON

BEST COUTURIERS

London has some couture and rising stock in ready-to-wear. The couture is good but not "haute", for haute couture, you go to Paris. London street fashion ebbs, but tailors of the new chic are in flood. *"The best suits and coats come more from London and Milan than Paris"* (Meredith Etherington-Smith).

JEAN MUIR, 59–61 Farringdon Rd, EC1 ☎ (01) 831 0691. *"I think she's fabulous ... her eye for detail is marvellous, very understated, and she's very underestimated too. Her clothes are a joy to wear. You can still be your own person in them rather than have something take you over"* (Joan Burstein). Cuts silk jersey on the bias with a puritanical perfectionism, adds little knits and some leather. Her clothes have a strong identifiable look and so does she (*always* to be seen in navy blue).

BRUCE OLDFIELD, 27 Beauchamp Place, SW3 ☎ (01) 584 1363. The one-time Dr Barnardo's boy who is now couturier to the Princess of Wales. Glam, glitz, pzazz. You won't go unnoticed in an Oldfield number, but his shimmering Joan Collins-esque attention-grabbing gowns are often too showy for play-it-down Brits. Marie Helvin dresses up here, as do Joan herself, Charlotte Rampling and other screen and society stars.

EMANUEL, 26 Brook St, W1 ☎ (01) 629 5569. The only married couple ever to be accepted at the Royal College of Art. Their careers took off on the crazed curiosity surrounding their big number for The Royal Wedding (Diana's). Fantasy ballgowns and wedding dresses are still their forte. They do the follow-up to perfection too, with fulsome post-wedding garb for the coming event. Diana Vreeland ventures rare approval: *"Jerry Hall looked wonderful in her maternity dresses from Emanuel ... with their wonderful luxury of colour, cut and materials."*

HARDY AMIES, 14 Savile Row, W1 ☎ (01) 734 2436. The Queen's couturier. Does the upper-crust English thing to a nicety, with little tweed suits, the works. Ken Fleetwood has done the women's collection here for some time now. Betty Kenward, Lady Elizabeth Anson and other traditionalists buy here.

VICTOR EDELSTEIN, 314 Stanhope Mews W, SW7 ☎ (01) 244 7481. *"A real gent. Does wonderful, extravagant gowns"* (Tomasz Starzewski). Eleanor Lambert murmurs mysteriously that Edelstein *"represents the way people want to look at court"*. He conjures up dream evening dresses in sensuous, jewel-coloured fabrics. If there's such a thing as subtle glamour, these clothes have it. He dresses Princesses Diana and Michael.

BEST DESIGNERS

JASPER CONRAN, 37 Beauchamp Place, SW3 ☎ (01) 589 4243. Golden boy of British style – he's just so *wearable.* Lynne Franks says, *"Really the best for tailored clothes. I wear other designers, but I know JC is the most flattering."* She wore his velvet jacket and skirt to Fashion Aid. Margaux Hemingway rates him tops after Armani. Women of means come to him for well-judged, up-to-the-minute clothes. This season's bests: big black petticoats peeping from under pepper-red silk skirts, shantung silk evening coats, ladylike little suits. Stocked at Lucienne Phillips.

RIFAT OZBEK, 18 Haunch of Venison Yard, W1 ☎ (01) 408 0625/491 7033. A Turk turned dressmaker and hot fit to burn. Doing a whole ballet thing this autumn (he's very theme-orientated) with swirly bias-cut dresses, Principal Boy ballet pants, cropped and frogged jackets, Dying Swan head-dress. Manolo has done little dancing slippers to toe in with the look. Marie Helvin, Paula Yates, Charlotte Lewis shop here.

ALISTAIR BLAIR at Gallery 28, 28 Brook St, W1 ☎ (01) 408 0304. New-minuted Scottish designer back from playing a sharp second fiddle to Lagerfeld on the Continent. His first collection is in the shops now. Lynne Franks is keen: *"He's just starting up a collection now which is virtually couture."* Blair has picked up a strong sense of tailoring from his continental sojourn. Best in his collection: sweeping greatcoats with detachable top-capes.

ANTONY PRICE at Gallery 28, 28 Brook St, W1 ☎ (01) 408 0304. Well known for his rockstar glam rags; he did the whole look for Bryan Ferry & Co. He's one of Marie Helvin's top dogs and dresses Jerry Hall in clothes with a life of their own. Not always in the best paaah-sible taste, but strong on high-profile party dressing.

BENNY ONG, 3 Bentinck Mews, W1 ☎ (01) 487 5954. Charming Chinese designer with sensuous sense of colour. *"My favourite colour currently is emerald green. I like to throw it out with either black or bright orange, a flame orange"* (Benny Ong). Pampering, luscious evening wear and day wear with a glamorous edge.

GEORGINA GODLEY at Browns, 25 S Molton St, W1 ☎ (01) 491 7833. Brand-new British high priestess of body-dressing. She was Scott Crolla's silent partner in the hugely successful "Crolla", then she went and did a "Body and Soul" collection on her own this summer, muted in colour, female in form, inspired, she says, by Egyptian hieroglyphics. It's the opposite of Crolla's peacock rococo. Her 2-part autumn collection is called "Lumps and Bumps" (changing the body shape with farthingales) and "Time and Place" (fey focus on occasion dressing ... morning suits, cocktail dresses, as never before seen).

JOHN ROCHA at Gallery 28, 28 Brook St, W1 ☎ (01) 408 0304 and **The Beauchamp Place Shop, 55 Beauchamp Place, SW3 ☎ (01) 589 4155.** A new talent in grown-up but imaginative clothes. Lynne Franks likes him best along with Jasper: *"He's got a shop called China Town which is one of the best shops in Dublin – he's actually Chinese – and now he's in England, too. Does really interesting things with linens and wools."*

KATHARINE HAMNETT, 124b King's Rd, SW3 ☎ (01) 225 1209 and at **50 S Molton St, W1 ☎ (01) 629 0827.** The woman who rednecked Mrs Thatcher with her bold typeface "Anti-Cruise" T-shirt has an upbeat Fifties feel this season. Fitted black jersey day suits, catsuits, Grace Kelly skirts, and cool black mohair suits for the boys all strutted down the catwalk at her show to music from "Thunderbirds". She's Lynne Franks's second UK fave: *"I've got a big black blazer of hers with a lace collar that I've worn and worn. It's right for day or evening."* Hamnett votes herself Best Fashion Designer because *"my range of clothes have both quality and style – and are the best!"* Setting up on her own this autumn with a new shop designed by Norman Foster, no less.

NORMAN HARTNELL, 26 Bruton St, W1 ☎ (01) 629 0992. You thought HM's couturier was long-gone? You're right, but this season, a first collection with day wear by Sheridan Barnett, full-blown evening regalia by Victor Edelstein, and a fantastical element in the shape of costumier Allahn McRae proved an encouraging reincarnation. It's the first ever prêt-à-porter at po-faced Hartnell (they're still "couturiering", of course).

PATRICIA LESTER at Lucienne Phillips, 89 Knightsbridge, SW1 ☎ (01) 235 2134. London's answer to Mary McFadden (who is New York's answer to Mariano Fortuny). Column dresses in crinkly pleating. Wonderfully clinging, wonderfully expensive.

BEST OF THE STREET FLEET

Street fashion, the London success story of the early Eighties, is dead. Haute couture is reborn. This is the thrust of the fashionable year, and, with it, in comes tailoring, out goes decayed Dickensian dishevellment. Spare, pare-wear is the order of the day, fulgent excesses of whimsicality, self-indulgence and sheer weight of cloth are passé, though the legacy remains in more stringent form: wit can still wash, but out-and-out anarchy is out.

The up-and-coming young Brits are now into chic, sharp tailoring influenced by the new hauteur in dress: **John Rocha, Alistair Blair, Rifat Ozbek** are all doing grown-up clothes that depend on cut. **Jasper Conran** spear-headed the dressy edge over here.

Undisputed pearly king of the streets is still **John Galliano,** the man who brought neo-romanticism to historic pitch. He cuts with kudos and bags of style, followed by street stylists **English Eccentrics, Richmond & Cornejo, Culture Shock, Amalgamated Talent** and more. Galliano's autumn '85 show was a key to the new mood. It starred breast-muffs on women's sweaters and corresponding willie-muffs on trousers for men.

JOHN GALLIANO at Bazaar for Men, 4 S Molton St, W1 ☎ (01) 629 1708. Still King of Street Cred. He took the Miss Haversham look to its limit and is now doing a big number on high-waisted early England. Cuts brilliantly and with an original edge. This season he has lots of layers and ruching, shaped tweeds and cream knits with flower peepholes.

WHO ARE THE EUROYUPPIES?

"There is now this generation of people – and I think Courvoisier's Book of The Best *is something they'll go for – who identify through fashion, food and movies and music, and it's all international. So you'll find some of the Sloanes wear Brooks Bros and Ralph Lauren, and Charvet from Paris or whatever is fashionable, French women wear Hermès scarves, and they all identify. The Yuppy exists here. 10 years ago you could walk into a place and say, well, that's an American, that's an Englishman, that's a Frenchman. Now the people who are on the fast track, the successful professionals in their early thirties, all look alike. They all wear horn-rimmed glasses, they all wear Bass Weejuns, at the weekend they all wear beige trousers and blue blazers, blue Oxford shirts of one kind or another and cravats."* (Bob Payton).

Bowery Power

"I usually make something special every time I go out" (Leigh Bowery). To be seen and not worn, on his own instructions. The true spirit of street lives on in Leigh, fashion personality and sources of inspiration,. who says *"I don't produce a single garment in terms of selling."* The bald-headed clown, clad in beautiful trash of his own devising, won't travel on the Tube in case people spot him and copy his designs, but he will create electrifying dream-dress for friends and underground stars, especially dance diva Michael Clark. Runs the club, Taboo (see NIGHTLIFE, and did the famous bruise make-up on the cheeks of friend Trojan.

ENGLISH ECCENTRICS at Harvey Nichols, 109–125 Knightsbridge, SW1 ☎ (01) 235 5000. Wacky and wearable with some totally over-the-top ideas. Highly original prints and silk screening from Helen Littman in a Dadaist vein (their polar bear print was on everyone's backs last year). Virulent colour: poison green, biting violet, iridescent blues and pure white tempered by a new feel for mushroom and black.

RICHMOND & CORNEJO at Bazaar for Women, 34 Brook St, W1 ☎ (01) 629 5262. Used to do the jumpers for Joseph Tricot … and started something big. Now they have their own clutch of canny knits in black, charcoal and spice-brown with powder blue and sage. This autumn is their first step into shoes and tights.

■ BEST STORES ■

HARVEY NICHOLS, 109–125 Knightsbridge, SW1 ☎ (01) 235 5000. The best for wide-ranging international fashion. A broad sweep includes Soprani, Krizia, Sonia Rykiel, Complice, Cacharel, Ellis Flyte. Zone, the trend-spot in the basement, was revamped last year and restocked with English Eccentrics, Marco Polo, Barbara de Vries, Stephanie Cooper *et al.*

LIBERTY, Regent St, W1 ☎ (01) 734 1234. Jewel-like, panelled interior and knockout pastiche façade – part-Hollywood (the Regent St bit), part-gigantic Tudor cottage (the Gt Marlborough St bit). Best in London for sumptuous fabrics. It has an Aladdin's cave quality that makes it the most appealing. Eastern shot silks and crewelwork, also fabulous antique Eastern clothes are in the famous Oriental dept, plus fashion on other floors. And, of course, it's the British Mecca for scarves. At sale time Liberty sells 13½ miles (21.7 km) of scarves in one day.

FORTNUM & MASON, 181 Piccadilly, W1 ☎ (01) 734 8040. The gourmet stopover for famished Americans with several wedding cake floors piled on top, loaded with surprisingly good fashion. Women find Jean Muir, Jasper Conran, Jean and Martin Pallant, Alistair Blair, Maxmara and, arty-smarty, they even stock Paris street cred duo Prémonville et Dewarin. Accessories run to hot New York jeweller Eric Beaman. In the men's department: Tommy Nutter and Ermenegildo Zegna.

HARRODS, Knightsbridge, SW1 ☎ (01) 730 1234. The Top People's Store and The World's Most Famous. Acres of what you're after: the Italians (Soprani, Missoni); the Brits (Emanuel, Benny Ong, Paul Costelloe, John Rocha); and best of all for the upper-crust French designers (YSL, Dior, Givenchy). Way In has been re-styled for style by Joseph's interior designer, Eva Jiricna, and stocks the likes of Pam Hogg, Barbara de Vries, Die For It, for the younger set. Most of us, though, like Bruce Oldfield, come here for things like *"their cotton lisle socks, very cool, very nice; navy blue, light grey and white"*.

SIMPSON'S, 203 Piccadilly, SW1 ☎ (01) 734 2002. Regularly stock up the sock drawer of the top drawer, including the Queen and Prince Philip and Charles. It celebrates its golden jubilee this year. MD Georgina Simpson is married to dishy Anthony Andrews (who buys all his DJs here).

Best Streets

The Old School – Yves, Karl, the Italians, smart-suiting Brits – are on and around *Bond Street*.

Style-conscious *South Molton Street* is losing ground to tackier shops as rents rise – but the bastion of Browns remains.

The new fashion buzz-word is Draycott Avenue, Brompton Road, which Joseph, Issey and friends are colonizing in the name of Design.

BEST SHOPS

JOSEPH BIS, 23 Brompton Arcade, SW3 ☎ (01) 584 1857. Clothing for the body only, garnered by London's most talked-about, most unshaven, most successful, style-stocking shopkeeper. He takes the cream of young London (Culture Shock, Richmond & Cornejo) and adds foreigners like Montana and Martine Stibon. *"I love Joseph's stuff, I'm mad about that. He just takes the best of what's available"* (Anouska Hempel).

JOSEPH POUR LA MAISON, 16 Sloane St, SW1 ☎ (01) 235 9868 and 124 Draycott Ave, SW3. *"Clothing for the home"*, Joseph calls it – including the body. The whole design phenomenon: plates and tablecloths by Timney & Fowler, wafer-thin lighters, Filofax, all the matt black and steel accessories, watches, Swatches, the coffee pot that goes with the coat. The coat? By Azzedine Alaïa, who else? Joseph lets him reign here in solitary splendour among the bowls and vases because, he says, his clothes have to be seen in isolation to be fully appreciated.

BAZAAR FOR WOMEN, 34 Brook St, W1 ☎ (01) 629 5262. The women's shop, carelessly strewn with John Webb's ethereally silversmithed furniture, is a poetical shrine to John-Paul Gaultier, Richmond & Cornejo, John Galliano, Stephen Jones, Eric Beaman. Playing musical shoppers among the chairs are Sade, Siouxsie and the Duran Duran wives.

THE BEAUCHAMP PLACE SHOP, 55 Beauchamp Place, SW3 ☎ (01) 589 4155. A melting pot of talents: Jasper Conran, John Rocha, Betty Jackson, Tom Bell, Ally Capellino, Jacques Azagury, Marion Foale, Emmanuelle Khanh, Ventilo, Edina Ronay and Wendy Dagworthy. Liza Minnelli and several Duchesses, including Westminster and Kent, have been seen shopping here.

BROWNS, 23–27 S Molton St, W1 ☎ (01) 491 7833. Purveyors of high fashion to London's cognoscenti; owned by Joan Burstein and her hubby. High-profile stuff at prices to match for the chic section of both sexes. The large stock of thoroughbreds includes Azzedine Alaïa, Sonia Rykiel, Norma Kamali, Donna Karan, Romeo Gigli, Comme des Garçons, Byblos, Missoni. Clients include stars such as Barbra Streisand, Liza Minnelli, Joan Collins, Faye Dunaway, Twiggy, Marie Helvin, Lee Remick and Jacqueline Bisset.

BURBERRY, 165 Regent St, W1 ☎ (01) 734 4060. The shop with a single success (and how) – Burberry's means raincoats. Joan Burstein likes it. She's not alone, so do most Japs and Yanks on the run from the English rain. Lord Lichfield used to model for them in *"an advertising campaign that made real people look as if they actually owned them, creases and crumples and all"* (Lord Lichfield). Other aristo models include Lady Charlotte Anne Curzon, Lady Denbigh, Lady Annunziata Asquith and Lady Kenilworth.

GALLERY 28, 28 Brook St, W1 ☎ (01) 408 0304. An amalgam of the brash, the beautiful and the newly tailored. Effected by ace entrepreneur Peter Bertelsen, who owns a rash of one-designer shops in Sloane, Bond and Brook Streets. Stocks Angelo Tarlazzi (fabulously feminized men's suits), John Rocha, Piero Panchetti, Pellini, Valentino, Antony Price and Robert Clergerie shoes.

LUCIENNE PHILLIPS, 89 Knightsbridge, SW1 ☎ (01) 235 2134. Practically the full pack of the upper-crust, well-established British designers: Jean Muir, Jasper Conran, Victor Edelstein, Arabella Pollen, Jean and Martin Pallant and more with David Hicks-designed décor. The list of clients outshines even the designers: the Duchess of Kent, the Countess of Lichfield, Lady Attenborough – all very much the upper-crust Brits – plus Mrs Larry Hagman, Joan Plowright, Diana Rigg, Glenda Jackson, Lady Teresa Manners.

POND PLACE, 2 Pond Place, SW3 ☎ (01) 589 4191. Anouska Hempel's broodingly magnificent showcase for her own-designed clothes. An Ali Baba and the Forty Thieves shop where everything from the moss arrangements to the 18th-century Florentine oak bed to the demure sheath dresses in stunning fabrics is for sale. While Joseph Pour La Maison has clothes for the barefaced living-room, Anouska has garments for the boudoir and the salon.

She's part ready-to-wear, part "semi-couture" – *"If you've got a size 10 top and a size 14 botty where on earth are you going to get the whole thing organized? You'd have to have it sorted out, and that's what we're all about"* (Anouska Hempel).

REGINE, 92a Brompton Rd, SW1 ☎ (01) 589 2933 and 43 New Bond St, W1 ☎ (01) 499 0788. The Brompton Road shop is a designer emporium, a guide to world style with the likes of Kamali, Soprani, Ferre, Versace, Montana, Liza Bruce's aggressively erotic swimwear, Ghinea, Chloë, Fabrice, Bill Blass, Oscar de la Renta, Nancy Heller and shoes by Diego de la Valle ... mostly Italians with foreign elements flung in for flavour.

BEST KNITWEAR

JOSEPH TRICOT, 18 Sloane St, SW1 ☎ (01) 235 2719. That clever Mr Ettedgui cashing in on the Eighties' passion for 1-size, big-size knitting. Anyone can wear it, it's young, it's fun, it's knitting top to toe (hats, leggings, jumpers) and they have an exclusive on Martin Kidman's handknitted

"I hate cashmere, primarily because it feels so good. Cashmere must be the most narcissistic fabric known to man. People who wear cashmere are always touching themselves" (BOB PAYTON)

sweaters. Marie Helvin thinks they're the best.

"I buy my knitwear from Joseph Tricot. I like the big long sweaters, the long skirts, the short skirts, I love the colours. I like the way the clothes are flexible. You can wear this with this, or this with that" (Joan Severance). Clientwise it's Amy Irving (Mrs Spielberg) and *"we've got Koo Stark in the dressing room now and we had Joan Collins in yesterday"*.

N PEAL, 37 Burlington Arcade, W1 ☎ (01) 493 5378. Everything in the shop is cashmere, body dresses, stoles, wonderful sweaters and twinsets with little pearl buttons. Colours like ivory, taupe, lapis, blood orange, white. Must haves. *"If you go to N Peal in Burlington Arcade in England, you'll always find one great style for the season"* (Diane von Fürstenberg).

BEST SHOES

♛ **MANOLO BLAHNIK, 49–51 Old Church St, SW3 ☎ (01) 352 3863** (see Shoes with souls).

BALLY, 116 New Bond St, W1 ☎ (01) 491 7062. Sangster likes to see his women shod here.

RAYNE, 57 Brompton Rd, SW3 ☎ (01) 589 5560 and 16 Old Bond St, W1 ☎ (01) 493 9077. They have shod Her Majesty for years in establishment royal court shoes. Bruce Oldfield has designed an exclusive collection for them; they also stock Ferragamo and Andrea Pfister.

BEST HATS

♛ **STEPHEN JONES, 34 Lexington St, W1 ☎ (01) 734 9666.** *The* best (see Crown him, crown him).

DAVID SHILLING, 44 Chiltern St, W1 ☎ (01) 487 3179. Romantic ribbons-and-bows showroom graced by just 2 or 3 striking hats *"in excess of £200"*. His witty couture extravaganzas adorn many noble heads.

HERBERT JOHNSON, 13 Old Burlington St, W1 ☎ (01) 439 7397. Traditional hatter to the Englishman. Men's jam-on trilbys and caps sold upstairs, feminine head-hugs downstairs.

KIRSTEN WOODWARD, Unit 26, Portobello Green, 281 Portobello Rd, W10 ☎ (01) 960 0090. Did Lagerfeld's upholstered hats of a few seasons back, and invents other pie-in-the-sky millinery to order.

SEAN BARRETT, 46 Hill Rise, Richmond Hill, Richmond, Surrey ☎ (01) 549 2753. This mad young hatter designed knock-out numbers for *Absolute Beginners.*

SHOES WITH SOULS

The master-designer of fancy footwork is the London-based Manolo Blahnik. At about £100 (US$145) and climbing, these shoes don't come cheap. But none comes more beautiful. *"He's a league above everybody else"* (Tina Chow). *"The very best must be Manolo Blahnik"* (Kailash Mishra). Joan Burstein, Lynne Franks, Katharine Hamnett, Arianna Stassinopoulos, Marie Helvin, all think he is divine. Bianca Jagger has worn Blahnik for more than 10 years. Once your feet have been cosseted by these whispers of lusciously concocted leather, it's hard to consign them to mere shoes.

Very much in the Vivier tradition, Manolo takes the best of what's in the wind, together with completely spontaneous ideas of his own devising, and sculpts them into the most sensitive real-life shapes. Moreover, they are beautifully made. Blahnik has tracked down the last of a breed of Italian cobbler-craftsmen who make his footly fineries entirely by hand. They come in soft kid, suede, leather, or satin, brocade, dark velvets, often incredibly simple. Others are more rococo delights like a silk and satin bootee lined in ruffled silk and punctuated by a series of bows. His shop in Old Church St, presided over by his formidably stylish sister Evangeline, is a Pandora's box of design ideas. Once swagged with baroque trifles like taffeta cabbage roses, at the time of writing it is *"a Napoleonic campaign tent"* (Hamish Bowles). Blahnik is a dyed-in-the-wool dandy. He hails from the Canaries, with Eastern European roots, and has a sleek, exotic face, narrowed eyes, and the oiled accent of a character from *Casablanca*. Has been seen strolling the streets of Mayfair in summer in a vanilla flannel suit, brown and white co-respondent shoes, Panama hat, gloves and a cane ... Cobbler Capone.

CROWN HIM, CROWN HIM

Overwhelmingly declared milliner of the moment, Stephen Jones is the man with a hat up his sleeve. *"He has the best designs and the most interesting hats. Obviously there are other hat designers but I think Stephen is constant. Others tend to come and go whereas Stephen constantly does beautiful hats"* (Lynne Franks).

The man who began cocking a snood at the world with his tat for tête designs for Blitz kid friends like Boy George now crowns the *tête royal* of the Princess of Wales. He is the supremely stylish end of the hat market, unfailingly witty, inspired, beautifully made, with a consummate sense of proportion and irony, the nascent all-time master milliner. His inventiveness never flags.

Stephen gets the vote of Azzedine "I'm free of any decoration" Alaïa: *"Apart from Stephen Jones in London, the best hats were made before. The whole spirit of the hat has almost been lost."*

Marie Helvin thinks he's best, so does Katharine Hamnett. *"He's No 1. Quality, originality, and flattering styles."* Even Margaux Hemingway knows what she's talking about, though not whom: *"The best hats are from the bald man in London."*

Stephen himself could be described as a light-hearted gadfly-about-town, sartorially inclined to the macaroni, and surmounted by a tender pate where nary a hair wanders, but whose perfect foil is one of his own untrad trilbies.

BEST ACCESSORIES

CHRIS TRILL at Liberty, Regent St, W1 ☎ (01) 734 1234. Lynne Franks swings a Trill bag: *"By far the best ... Chris Trill is small but very good."*

CORNELIA JAMES, 55 New Bond St, W1 ☎ (01) 499 9423/ 629 2176. A glove specialist with handsome fashion of every kind – silks, satins, leather, unadorned or ornamental. Her best gloves are made-to-measure extravagant handouts, from her showrooms in Bond St and Brighton, and on all the right hands on West End stages – theatre being her biggest made-to-measure customer.

BEST JEWELLERS

S J PHILLIPS, 139 New Bond St, W1 ☎ (01) 629 6261. A stock of fabulous riches makes this probably the best antique jewellery shop in the world. Only the rich and brave stride through the portals to face the intimidating scions of the Norton family, who run it. Once inside, you are privy to a powerhouse of Renaissance treasures and exquisite 18th- to 20th-century jewels.

BUTLER & WILSON, 189 Fulham Rd, SW3 ☎ (01) 352 3045. Innovators of costume jewellery as a style in its own right, rather than as a copy of real jewels. Among the best creative and directional design in the world, though workmanship can be slightly shoddy. Anouska Hempel loves B & W and Marie Helvin thinks they're No 1 for *"best fake accessories"*. *"Very good for fashion jewellery"* (Stephen Jones).

COLLINGWOOD, 171 New Bond St, W1 ☎ (01) 499 5613. Outstanding for antique and modern jewellery. They specialize in Edwardian pieces. 3 royal warrants – from the Queen, the Queen Mother and the Prince of Wales, who acquired Diana's engagement ring here.

DAVID MORRIS, 41 Conduit St, W1 ☎ (01) 734 5215. Oozes glamour – the best modern, glossy jewels. High-fashion, high-quality, continental style. A further attraction is the charming Morrises themselves.

EDITIONS GRAPHIQUES, 3 Clifford St, W1 ☎ (01) 734 3944. For art deco, run by world expert Victor Arwas, who wrote the best book on the subject – *Art Deco.*

GARRARD'S, 112 Regent St, W1 ☎ (01) 734 7020. Terrifically smart royal jewellers. Many a Garrard's gold cuff-link has graced a princely cuff.

JOHN JESSE & IRINA LASKI, 160 Kensington Church St, W8 ☎ (01) 229 0312. The best in art nouveau, deco and Forties jewellery. The legendary Jesse was one of the first devotees of art nouveau.

WARTSKI, 14 Grafton St, W1 ☎ (01) 493 1141. Fabulous Fabergé. Shopping ground for royals from all nations, run by the original Wartski's grandson, world specialist on Fabergé, A Kenneth Snowman. His secret weapon is world Giuliano and Castellani expert Geoffrey Munn, who can advise on the best in 19th-century jewels.

BEST LINGERIE

THE WHITE HOUSE, 51–52 New Bond St, W1 ☎ (01) 629 3521. The heady (and costly) heights of lavishment, ravishment and divine, die-for-it silk pyjamas, camisoles and further fine concoctions. A repro Victorian swing cradle (their children's stuff is just heaven) will set you back

£2,999 (US$4,339). But this is nothing to the silk satin negligées, a mere wisp of £1,032 (US$1,493). It's one of Betty Kenward's favourite shops, and Stephen Jones noses around for *"the best handkerchiefs, Irish Linen"*. *"The White House is where you get the most wonderful hand-embroidered [by nuns] silk garments"* (Meredith Etherington-Smith).

FOGAL, 36 New Bond St, W1 ☎ (01) 493 0900. *Real* luxury for the legs. *"The best selection of tights, the best colours,"* says Meredith Etherington-Smith, *"their mixture of cashmere and wool is exquisite."*

FUNN, at Liberty, Regent St, W1 ☎ (01) 734 1234. Silk stockings in nostalgic colours (leaf, sauterne, old ivory). Katharine Hamnett says *"Funn are the best stockings, apart from Father Christmas's."*

JANET REGER, 2 Beauchamp Place, SW3 ☎ (01) 584 9360. No, she has not gone bust. She has bought back the business and is still doing the frillies for Jackie Collins, who states: *"I adore Janet Reger in Beauchamp Place. It's just very beautiful."* Speciality: silk and sin.

Britain's Secret Weapon?

Marina Chaliapin, who said the best handbags come from Gucci, the best jewels Bulgari – all very *comme il faut* – adds, *"You want to know where I* really *like to shop? – Liverpool.* [Laughs uproariously]. *You don't believe me? A few years ago I used to buy everything there. Marks & Spencer? I adore it. I still go there. I shop there for all my nighties and dressing gowns. I just come back loaded like some kind of sherpa."*

RIGBY & PELLOR, 12 S Molton St, W1 ☎ (01) 629 6708. Upright, established old firm full of regal sales ladies. Corset-makers to the Queen (so that's what she wears under those outlandish Hardy Amies outfits ...). In fact, they do wonderful, subtle-hued made-to-measure satin corsets, boned, busked, the works; as well as bras in sizes no one else will stock. Really trustworthy, well made and often lovely. Marie Helvin gets undies here.

BEST MEN'S DESIGNERS

JASPER CONRAN, 37 Beauchamp Place, SW3 ☎ (01) 589 4243. The younger man's best bet for divinely different designer clothes. Jasper cuts with broad strokes on the canvas and cloth of fashion. He does the greatcoats that cut a dash down South Molton Street; the high-necked linen verandah suits that add Somerset Maugham to summer; the richly-coloured and textured tweeds that make you glad to be an Englishman – under 40.

KATHARINE HAMNETT, 124b King's Rd, SW3 and 50 S Molton St, W1 ☎ (01) 629 0827. Her men's collection this autumn is a knockout. Black mohair suits with a Fifties feel.

PAUL SMITH, 44 Floral St, WC2 ☎ (01) 379 7133 and 23 Avery Row, W1 ☎ (01) 493 1287. Smith sees himself primarily as a stylist. He takes classic menswear and updates it in more colourful and expansive form. Patronized by ad men, creative types and City boys who want a more seductive stripe in their shirt. The shirts, in particular, are beautifully made in snappy colours. But at about £55 (US$80) for a straightforward stripy, it'll cost the shirt off your back. Worth it, of course, to make you stand out from the crowd without looking an out-and-out outcast.

More modish things that the pinstripe brigade will find marches to the beat of a different drum: velvet duffle coats, pink soda or lime jackets, trays of gadgets and accessories for Modernist Man – lots of the old matt black, but battered leather and wood make a good showing. Jean Muir thinks they do the best menswear.

BEST MEN'S SHOPS

♔ **REGINE UOMO, 80 Brompton Rd, SW3 ☎ (01) 581 5873 and 44 New Bond St, W1 ☎ (01) 493 9960.** For the seriously designed man, 2 floors of uninterrupted style (interrupted, that is, only by a bar for fast recovery from vast investment on a Montana python-skin jacket). It's Milan central station marble with a ⅝ inch (17 mm) screen running round the walls, and racks of Soprani, Verri Uomo, Castelbajac, Foncel, Panchetti, Cerrutti 1881, Erreuno, Versace and Mugler, plus Tarlazzi swimwear. On the lower ground floor – a shop devoted entirely to the manly, machinations of **Gianfranco Ferre ☎ (01) 581 8732** who, as a former architect, designed it himself to look like a monster aeroplane with a wing speared through the shop's centre.

BAZAAR FOR MEN, 4 S Molton St, W1 ☎ (01) 629 1708. A closet collection of art for art's sake clothes: John Galliano, Gaultier, Nigel Preston, Valentino, and Stephen Jones's headcases.

BEST MEN'S TAILORS

ANDERSON & SHEPHERD, 30 Savile Row, W1 ☎ (01) 734 1420. Aloof and aristocratic tailors. Aniko Gaal's No 1. And: *"They are the best tailors"* (Lynne Franks).

"We don't advertise, mix or mention our customers. We have our own individual style which we have always kept to. No, I don't want you to say which style. We let people come to us." Clubby. You really need to be voted in by an insider.

“ London is the best for all men's attire. Italy is pretty good, but London is the leader ” (MEREDITH ETHERINGTON-SMITH)

"Tailors? It really does not matter as long as he is from Savile Row. They are the best tailors in the world. They make you a suit that you pay for with your blood, only to find out, the first time you put it on, that you have been wearing it for years"

(OLIVIER COQUELIN)

BURSTOW & LOGSDAIL, 8A Sackville St, W1 ☎ (01) 437 1750. David Hicks (on the Best Dressed List last year) has his suits cut here. "*I would say that my tailor was the best in the world.*"

DOUG HAYWARD, 95 Mount St, W1 ☎ (01) 499 5574. Dresses characters round London in immaculate mufti, and they're Lord Lichfield's No 1 tailors. "*For men, the best place to visit is Doug Hayward for stylish clothes*" (Michael Parkinson)."

GIEVES & HAWKES, 1 Savile Row, W1 ☎ (01) 434 2001. The military tailors. Upstairs, a cavalier array of brass buttons, insignia and dummies, resplendent in full parade-ground gear. Downstairs, civilians get fitted out in drabber City style. Having begun by making the best for 200 years of officers and gentlemen starting at the top with Nelson and Wellington, they are now sending suits over to the other side. Gorbachev, has one. (They balance it out by being naval tailors to the Duke of Edinburgh.)

HAWES & CURTIS, 2 Burlington Gardens, W1 ☎ (01) 493 2200. Tailors to the Duke of Edinburgh (when he's not messing about on battleships) and Princes Andrew and Edward. Mist-and-heather tweeds woven on their own looms in Scotland and Huddersfield. Also makers of superior shirts. "*I can't think of anywhere I would get as nice a shirt as I get from Hawes & Curtis*" (David Hicks).

HENRY POOLE, 15 Savile Row, W1 ☎ (01) 734 5985. Oldest and biggest establishment on the Row and once a thriving livery business (they still do natty velveteens for the Queen's footmen and other run-arounds). Noblesse prestige types like the Marquis of Tavistock and the Duke of Bedford come here. Poole makes the best field coats and jackets – but never breeches.

HUNTSMAN, 11 Savile Row, W1 ☎ (01) 734 7441. They have the cutting edge over the other tailors. "*The English make the best suits and Huntsman make the best suits in the world – sheer perfection*" (Katharine Hamnett). "*Italian or British tailors are the best. In London, it's Anthony Huntsman*" (Bill Blass). Beautiful, costly suits in fine cloths from their own mill in Scotland. They last for ever. A 3-piecer will set you back about £1,500 (US$2,170) and needs about 6 fittings. And they're *the* place to go for riding coat and breeches on a sober rein. Their worldwide reputation has earned them a cult following in the States and they visit Boston, New York and Washington each year to measure up their starry-eyed Stateside groupies, returning to Savile Row to make the suits.

TOM BROWN, 25 Prince's St, W1 ☎ (01) 629 5025. "*The best tailor for value for money. His suits are about £400, whereas Huntsman are about £750—£1,000*" (Meredith Etherington-Smith). Their Eton branch has a captive corps of customers requiring tails who grow up and come here for real-life uniforms.

TOMMY NUTTER, 19 Savile Row, W1 ☎ (01) 734 0831. "*Tommy Nutter is probably the best men's tailor. He has English tailoring with American loudness – a loudness and a humour done in the most tasteful and classic way. Wonderful brocade waistcoats and Edwardian suits in the most refined colours. You'll never find a navy and pinstripe there*" (Stephen Jones).

For the dandy element in established society – strictly no fogeys – Tommy Nutter's sensuous strokes of colour liven up the charcoal and blue to an aesthete specification. But nothing foppish, really quite natty. The evening waistcoats are of a particularly 18th-century splendour. "*If I want anything really special or ornate, I go to Tommy Nutter*" (Lord Lichfield).

BEST SHIRTS

HARVIE & HUDSON, 77 Jermyn St, SW1 ☎ (01) 930 3949. These ones don't come cheap – about £80 (US$116) for a silk one, and, of course, the minimum order is for a batch of 6. Well co-ordinated chaps like the Harvie & Hudson-designed striping with totally matching ties for City camouflage.

NEW & LINGWOOD, 53 Jermyn St, SW1 ☎ (01) 493 9621. Almost as famous as Turnbull & Asser for shirts of quality, perhaps with the best collars of all. Branches in Eton and Cambridge as well, to see a man through life, from babyhood through boyhood to bath-chair.

T M LEWIN & SONS, 106 Jermyn St, SW1 ☎ (01) 930 4291. "*I go to T M Lewin for ties and bow ties. It's great because you can design your own bow ties if you wish to, which is fantastic. It makes dressing for yourself very interesting*" (Benny Ong).

TURNBULL & ASSER, 71 Jermyn St, SW1 ☎ (01) 930 0502. The best bespoke shirts in London. "*The quality is good, the finish superb, they have a wonderful sense of colour. They are very British, yet exciting. The material is wonderful. What is so pleasing is that they haven't cut corners. It is a real pleasure to wear their shirts. Even if one has to pay a little more, it is worth it*" (Yuki Maekawa).

Everyone has a good word for Prince Charles's shirtmakers; they are the only Brits to get the thumbs up from Bill Blass; and they sum up "Best" to diverse male elements from Lord Lichfield to Stephen Jones ("*The best, just the best …*") and Bob Payton ("The *beginning and the end of fashion*"). Women in the business fall for the quality, too. "*Men's shirts? – Turnbull & Asser. Their variety of fabric is marvellous*" (Diane von Fürstenberg). Oldfield sums them up in a complimentary *non sequitur*: "*I have my shirts made here because I have very long arms and the prices are extremely reasonable.*"

BEST MEN'S SHOES

JOHN LOBB BOOTMAKERS, 9 St James's St, SW1 ☎ (01) 930 3664. The world-famous, hand-made-to-measure sober shoe. Royal bootmakers to Charles, Philip and Co. Dickensian shop which is also a workshop, piled high with soft and pungent leathers and old craftsmen, looking gnarled and authentic, plying their trade. Diane von Fürstenberg and Arnold Scaasi think it's world-best for men. *"The best-made English shoe, but extortionate"* (Lord Lichfield). Women come for walking shoes of a manly character but femininely tapering form.

FOSTERS & SON BOOT AND SHOE MAKERS, 83 Jermyn St, SW1 ☎ (01) 930 5385. Older than Lobb's, but they keep quiet about it in an English sort of way, and, anyway, their modern and entirely unexceptional-looking shop seems to give them the lie. Excellent, made-to-measure shoes for men – serious stuff, no footling around.

NEW & LINGWOOD, 53 Jermyn St, SW1 ☎ (01) 493 9621. Sleek, beautifully fashioned, expensive men's shoes in glorious woody tones (beech, chestnut and wonderful crème caramel shade). They do by far the best velvet slippers (with hand-embroidered crests, monograms, motifs).

COUTURE EXPOSEE

Couture is blatantly élitist, superbly put together and costs a fortune. A couturier (a word much abused) is no mere dressmaker: he is one who prepares twice-yearly collections of individually handmade clothes that are made to measure in the house's workshops. Paris has always been the capital of such mastery. The Paris design dictators, La Chambre Syndicale de la Couture, has decreed that a *maison de couture* must employ a minimum of 23 seamstresses in the *atelier*, present 2 collections a year of at least 75 models, custom make clothes and have 45 private fashion shows.

Up until the mid-Sixties, the couturier would tailor his collection principally to private clients, women born to or for elegance. Then mass-market manufacturers started cribbing designs and, while the couturier would sell a few hundred dresses a year, the copies would sell thousands.

Great secrecy followed in the couture houses – even private customers had to prove they weren't industrial spies. Many couturiers then gave in and went commercial, establishing their own ready-to-wear factories. Pierre Cardin was cannier – he licensed out his designs for royalties.

As couture in the 1980s booms, definitions become blurred. Who is a couturier, and what is a designer? The answer is: everyone is a designer, but couturiers, most of whom have a ready-to-wear line or two as well, specialize in the handmade garments for individual clients. Prêt-à-porter designers usually don't do for individuals, though nearly all of them will make to fit and even adapt designs for friends and celebs … so it really depends just as much on who *you* are as on what *they* are.

FRANCE

PARIS

HAUTE COUTURE

YVES SAINT LAURENT, 5 ave Marceau, 75008 ☎ (1) 4723 7271. *"YSL may not be daring or take chances like Ungaro does, but I think he is the best couture designer of our time"* (Bill Blass). *"YSL is the best because he is the most splendid: not necessarily everyone will wear it, but he does the big ballgowns and beautiful, delicious dresses that one dreams of"* (Stephen Jones). Diana Vreeland gets dreamy over his *"loose and dégagé tops, which are great"*; Meredith Etherington-Smith thinks he is *"the best contemporary couturier"*, and Marie Helvin, Jenny Gucci, the Marchesa Bona Frescobaldi, Arnold Scaasi and numerous other luminaries echo the view. *"Everybody imitates Saint Laurent. It's a very strong look, a complete mad fantasy"* (Eleanor Lambert). Tina Chow goes gaga for his *"small goodies, heavily flavoured by Loulou Klossowski,* Yves' Muse. The man who has dominated fashion since Balenciaga closed his doors in the Sixties is still King of Couture.

CHANEL COUTURE, 31 rue Cambon, 75001 ☎ (1) 4261 5455 and **42 ave Montaigne, 75008 ☎ (1) 4723 7412.** Diana Vreeland tells it like it is: *"Chanel's concept of clothes, and of wearing clothes, effected a revolution that changed fashion entirely, irrevocably, and with great élan."* Karl Lagerfeld re-invents the whole look in the tradition of the great Coco – those little tricot suits, braided and trimmed with the greatest of care, down to the last handmade button. Karl adds wit and insouciance to Coco's perennial basics. *"Chanel designed clothes that for the 20th-century woman are what the 2- and 3-button suit is for men"* (Karl Lagerfeld). Also gloriously conceived dressing-up dresses.

Meredith Etherington-Smith nominates their *"paillette sequin fantasies etc"* as the best. *"Their Watteau-inspired dresses cost from £25,000 a piece* up." Betty Kenward votes them No 1. Lynn Wyatt is a staunch devotee: *"I have a red, gold and black embroidered skirt and jacket from Chanel so divine I'll probably have to be buried in it."*

JEAN PATOU, 7 rue Saint Florentin, 75008 ☎ (1) 4260 3610. "You're the tops, you're a dress by Patou", sang Cole Porter way back when and now newcomer Christian Lacroix is bringing something worth singing about back to the House: fireworks, panache, youth and liveliness. Meredith Etherington-Smith thinks *"It's the best-made couture."* Katharine Hamnett votes it best because *"the clothes are so exciting and worth the money!"*

MADAME GRES, place Vendôme, 1 rue de la Paix, 75002 ☎ (1) 4261 5815. (See right).

EMINENCE GRÈS

"The best classic couture", in the words of Meredith Etherington-Smith, *"is at Madame Grès."* Known as Alix in the Thirties, she has been perfecting Grecian goddess dresses of mathematical purity and fluid form since then. Diana Vreeland wrote that her clothes were *"long, flowing, and often looked like carved marble"*. She was the first couturier to make silk jersey her medium (Jean Muir has gone on to make it hers) and once compared the difficulties of cutting a jersey dress to cutting a piece of sheet metal.

"I think to see really hand-made fashion at its most subtle and most pure," says Eleanor Lambert, *"you must go to the Madame Grès show – once every year. It's the highest level in taste and fashion. Very intricate dressmaking."*

Mme Grès is a beautiful, serene-looking woman of 88 who insists that no, things have not changed so much and that quality has not deteriorated. Her head is always bound in a length of cloth, her fingers encrusted with medieval rings. Her clients come from all over the world to find the *ne plus ultra* of line and simplicity.

CHRISTIAN DIOR, 30 ave Montaigne, 75008 ☎ (1) 4723 5444. Well-bred, understated clothes by Marc Bohan, though his predecessors, Dior and YSL, left him an impossible standard to live up to. The Monaco princesses have always dressed here (Caroline is not branching out in favour of Lagerfeld) and Stephanie worked in the *atelier* before launching her swimswear range. Pool Position. Lynn Wyatt comes here when she's not dying for Chanel.

EMMANUEL UNGARO, 2 ave Montaigne, 75008 ☎ (1) 4723 6194. An individualist with an audacious colour sense who trained with the maestro Balenciaga. He purveys a characteristically sexy shape: wide-angle shoulders, shorn at the knees, décolletage, fitted waist, in eyecatching, sugar-bright colours and prints. Americans go for it: *"I think each season is dominated by one creative personality, and in recent years it's been inspired by Ungaro. He gave us mixed patterns and strange proportions. He broke a lot of rules, and freed people from the frames they live in"* (Eleanor Lambert). Anouska Hempel, more restrained, likes his *"clean, neat lines"*. Dressy and outgoing.

GIVENCHY, 3 ave Georges V, 75008 ☎ (1) 4723 8136. Elegant, refined day and evening wear. Meredith Etherington-Smith recommends it for *"the more restrained evening dress"*. The real M Givenchy (Hubert) is still plying his pencil and scissors and Audrey Hepburn received a Fashion Oscar for her faithfulness to this one designer for 30 years.

JEAN-LOUIS SCHERRER, 51 ave Montaigne, 75008 ☎ (1) 4359 5539. Good, very French couturier who dresses *"dames officielles"* and the crowned and coroneted heads of Europe. *"Clothes for old money"* (Meredith Etherington-Smith). Among them, Mme Giscard D'Estaing and Christine Ockrent. Known for his lyrically embroidered evening dresses and his trouser suits.

PHILIPPE VENET, 62 rue François 1er, 75008 ☎ (1) 4225 3363. The best haute couture coats. Masterly cutting. The Queen of Jordan wraps up warmly here.

BEST DESIGNERS

AZZEDINE ALAIA, 17 rue du Parc-Royal, 75003 ☎ (1) 4272 1919. Alaïa does the best ready-to-wear ever. See box.

JEAN-PAUL GAULTIER, 6 rue Vivienne, 75002 ☎ (1) 4286 0505. The fashion funny man who got his big idea by taking a productive walk down the King's Road, London, in punky/New Romantic days. While the look languishes in London, Jean-Paul has invested it with Gallic whimsy and punch, and develops it on and on. *"One of the best off-beat young designers. He has a tremendous sense of humour based on a very solid classic understanding of clothing and what people like to wear"* (Stephen Jones). Yuki Maekawa rates him with Armani as a tailor. *"Because he's done some wonderfully inventive tailored clothes, not exaggerated like Montana, but fitting the body*

IT'S FASHION, IT'S ART – IT'S AZZEDINE

The Toulouse-Lautrec of the fashion world. Seriously small, seriously talented flavour of the decade. Though cheeky French fans call him "désigner de poche", Azzedine's a biggie. The list of the century's greats now reads Poiret, Chanel, Vionnet, Dior, Balenciaga, Saint Laurent – and Alaïa. What Alaïa has done is to re-invent the female shape as object of fashionable worship with his bodyclothes beautiful skimming and caressing the curves into the enshrinement of modern minimalism.

Fetish bodies who know what he can make of the female shape include Tina Turner, Grace Jones, Andrée Putman (who designed his new Paris place), Paloma Picasso, Raquel Welch, Greta Garbo, Marie Helvin. *"He's concentrated, precise, controlled, very much his own master"* (Tina Chow). *"The new image for women is Alaïa with the form-fitting clothes he really excels at"* (Joan Burstein). *"Alaïa truly loves the woman's body and respects it. I think that when a woman has a body to show she should wear clothes that accentuate her shape. With Alaïa a woman has to be so conscious of her body and it's actually difficult to cross her legs"* (Joan Severance).

Alaïa takes the art of dressing the female shape to an abstraction: *"One day I will stop designing fashion and will just design dresses in my head. I will imagine women and I will imagine the dresses I will make for them."* He is famous for his knits, invented the "body" – a very un-exercise leotard – and his working of leather was what brought him to the world's attention a few years ago. He's an alchemist designer who can turn a pantie girdle into gold: the seaming on his ski pants and skirts is inspired by some of the ugliest garments in history, the pantie hose of the Fifties and Sixties. He has made shaped seaming go public, sketching lightly round a woman's erogenous zones and transforming them into a thing of beauty and a joy forever.

really well and yet creating this off-balanced shape. He created the new way of unevenness in tailoring … he has incredibly clever ideas. He's a great creative designer, but because he treats life as fun I love it." Alaïa likes his style, Lynne Franks thinks he's second only to Alaïa among the French. His racy new collection is plastered with "Gaultier" in Sovietspeak. Darker colours, leathers and zip-up rubber are his brightest innovations, and A-line jackets over bouffant quilted taffeta skirts.

KARL LAGERFELD, 144 ave des Champs Elysées, 75008 ☎ (1) 4359 5750. The *homme-orchestre* with a finger in every pie. Does Chanel (and earns a reputed million dollars a year from this alone), designs the world's best furs for Fendi, as well as KL, his own line, inimitably witty, chic and stylish – for the woman with taste to waste. Chanel house model, the smoky-eyed Inès de la Fressange, insisting that *"I'm not just toeing the party line"*, votes him Best Everything: Best Couturier, Best Designer, Best Tailor, Best Costumier. And so it goes on, everything except Best Restaurant.

His irreverence and detachment from fashion are his secret (he wears tinted glasses, a little ponytail, and flirts behind a snap-to fan). Lynn Wyatt loves him, as does Paloma Picasso, and Princess Caroline of Monaco is his new Best-Beloved Customer.

"Karl Lagerfeld is the best designer in the world … He is totally in tune with his times with a wonderful attitude to fashion. He understands it, but does not treat it as sacred. He doesn't think he's pope. There is a spontaneous whimsy and a detached quality about him which means that he can design 4 completely different lines" (Aniko Gaal).

Lagerfeld's current collection is his mark *de triomphe*, accomplished and playful, with a carry-over of signature Chanel. Coco-esque chains ginger up long and easy day clothes; sequined dancers shimmy across his evening gowns; and he clinched it all with the year's flippiest accessory, a fake ponytail in velvet.

CLAUDE MONTANA, 131 rue St Denis, 75002 ☎ (1) 4222 6965. Sexy power-styling, delightfully bombastic with explosive colour. He has been strongly bitten by the Alaïa body bug of late and this season it has resulted in a superb collection, more pared-down and cool than usual. Everyone comes to him for leather, starting with Joan Burstein: *"I adore his leathers. His handling of leather is magnificent, it really is,"* right through to the *Dynasty* dressers, such as Catherine Oxenberg: *"I love Montana, especially his leather wear."* He's Jackie Collins's fave: *"I go to Montana for leather jackets with huge shoulders."*

AGNES B, rue du Jour, 75001 ☎ (1) 4508 5656. Fashion editor turned designer, Agnès B makes the sort of thing she and other working women like to wear – immensely chic, young, easy-to-wear separates. Successful items go on and on in different fabrics and colours – she's still turning out the same striped T-shirt as 15 years ago, because women still want to buy it. Lynne Franks rates her one of the top French designers. She hopes to set up in London soon.

JACQUELINE DE RIBES, 45 rue de la Bien Faisance, 75008 ☎ (1) 4562 5839. The best of the clothes'-horses now caparisons the rest of the field. Seriously glamorous French chic for the upper-echelon party people. Now sells privately to Paloma Picasso and big American clients.

PARVINE ET MURIEL, 13 rue Gustave-Courbet, 75016 ☎ (1) 4704 3626. On a different plane from Karl and Yves, of course, but worth a certain place in the pantheon. Parvine, an escapee Persian princess on the run from Iran's anti-ballgown régime, arrived in gay Paree with nothing but a fat address book and a sewing talent left over from finishing-school days.

SONIA RYKIEL, 4 et 6 rue de Grenelle, 75006 ☎ (1) 4222 4322. The secret of her collection is in the knitting (see Best Knitwear).

THIERRY MUGLER, 130 rue du Faubourg St Honoré, 75008 ☎ (1) 4256 1928. Purveyor of the high-class tart look and highly-structured Legend clothes to super-women. Satire plus sophistication. Alaïa worked with him in his early days, and admires him, as does Jean-Paul Gaultier.

VICKIE TIEL, 21 rue Bonaparte, 75006 ☎ (1) 4633 3380. *"She makes the sexiest dresses on earth"* (Catherine Oxenberg).

BEST OF THE YOUNG FRENCH

ADELINE ANDRE, 28 rue Léopold Bellan, 75002 ☎ (1) 4236 7519. She turned down a job as Marc Bohan's right hand at Dior to develop her own logic of dress. Simple, surprising clothes in the idiom of "less is more"

ELISABETH DE SENNEVILLE, 3 rue de Turbigo, 75001 ☎ (1) 4236 6303. *"The best off-beat young Parisian designer"* (Anne-Elisabeth Moutet). French singer France Gall and Caroline Kennedy shop here.

PREMONVILLE ET DEWARIN, 18 rue St Marc, 75002 ☎ (1) 4236 4168. New buzzword in French up-and-coming fashion. *"Everyone here in Paris is talking about them"* (Meredith Etherington-Smith). They do new-think tailoring with a Lagerfeld *chez* Chanel sense of wit.

JAPS IN PARIS

Most of the Japanese designers show in Paris, many are even based there. (See also Japan.) Here's a quick rundown:

Comme des Garçons, 42 rue Etienne Marcel, 75001 ☎ (1) 4233 0521.
Hanae Mori, 17 ave Montaigne, 75008 ☎ (1) 4723 5205.
Hiroko Koshino (cuts denim like silk), 43 rue du Faubourg St Honoré, 75008 ☎ (1) 4265 8315.
Junko Shimada, 54 rue Etienne Marcel, 75004 ☎ (1) 4278 8404.
Kenzo, 3 place des Victoires, 75001 ☎ (1) 4236 8141.
Tokio Kumagai, 32 rue de Grenelle, 75005 (satirical shoes) ☎ (1) 4544 2311.
Yohji Yamamoto, 24 rue du Louvre, 75001 ☎ (1) 4221 4293

IT'S FASHION BUT IS IT ART?

Le tout Paris is talking about the new Musée des Arts de la Mode tucked into the Pavillon de Marsan in a *coin* of the Louvre. This brainchild of one-time Minister of Culture, Jacques Lang (he has promised his notorious Mao-collared suit to the contemporary menswear section) is France's first comprehensive national costume museum. Not only does it share a roof with the Mona Lisa & Co, but the interior is by the brilliant young Jacques Granges, he who did the insides of the Lloyd's building in London.

At the opening of the first exhibition, *Moments de la Mode*, the *crème* in café society, fashion society, and M et Mme Mitterand ogled 3 centuries of style displayed in 19 set-pieces: Schiaparelli's dresses were done as circus lions and tigers on stools, reigned over by a high-booted and be-whipped ringmistress; mannequins in the bustle-backed dresses of the 1860s turned their well-decorated derrières to the spectators as they perused a picture exhibition within an exhibition. In short, *succès fou.* Coming up in '87: Yves Saint Laurent, Christian Dior and Roger Vivier exhibitions.

BEST STORE

GALERIES LAFAYETTE, 40 bvld Haussmann, 75009 ☎ (1) 4282 3456. Chic French women don't go department shopping much. Paris is small, easy to circumnavigate, and the designers all have their own shop or showroom. If they *do* end up in a store, though, it's this one, an art nouveau cavern with a stained-glass roof under which you find they stock *everything.* Lynne Franks shops here when she's in town.

BEST SHOPS

MUSEE DES ARTS DE LA MODE, 107 rue de Rivoli, 75001 ☎ (1) 4297 4728. Attached to the new Museum is a little treasure trove selling perennial classics, repro of the first Hermès scarf and first Chanel chain, plus Schiap and other blasts from the past, as well as pieces by young French hotcakes like Elisabeth de Senneville.

AU CHIEN ELEGANT, 67 rue Dames, 75017 ☎ (1) 293 1712. Collection *pour pooch*: the jewelled lead, the daycoat, the dainty dog-boots, the chic grooming bag, and all the right accessories for the couture-conscious canine.

BEST KNITWEAR

SONIA RYKIEL, 6 rue de Grenelle, 75006 ☎ (1) 4222 4322. The best knitwear in the world. A definite "look". The drop-waisted line, fine stripes and light texture hark back to the Twenties, golden age of tricot. "*The look she puts together is beautiful, it really is. Everything is wonderfully wearable, the colours are marvellous – the whole appeal. I mean, her look is not Chanel, but her whole image is a woman who has one feeling all through fashion. Everything is so well co-ordinated, it's so stylish. And then her evening wear is just superb. Everything is always very understated with her, but stunning*" (Joan Burstein). Bruce Oldfield admires her for her perfectionist techniques with knitted fabrics.

AZZEDINE ALAIA, 17 rue du Parc-Royal, 75003 ☎ (1) 4272 1919. The supremo of body-dressing does amazing, structured knits, cropped sweaters zoning in on the waist, architectural jackets shaped and strong as you never thought knitting could be. Yuki Maekawa think he's the best. "*He has uncanny timing. He made all those fitted sweaters just when people were looking for that closer-to-the-body silhouette. Beautifully made.*"

BEST STREETS

The best shopping areas are round *rue Tournon* and the *Faubourg St Honoré* for the Holy Chic, including Lagerfeld, YSL, Scherrer and Guy Laroche; *place des Victoires* and its environs for the more outlandish: Jean-Paul Gaultier, the Japs; le Marais in the new *branché* area with Azzedine Alaïa and the Musée Picasso; and the *place Vendôme* is *dripping* in diamonds. The French go to the individual designer shops for everything.

“ I tend to buy my shoes in Paris. Not from any particular shop ” (LYNNE FRANKS)

BEST SHOES

♔ **MAUD FRIZON, 81–83 rue des Saints Pères, 75006 ☎ (1) 4222 0693.** Butter-wouldn't-melt-like-my-leather shoes. Second only to Manolo Blahnik. She makes her own soles, which is unusual. *"She's right for the moment"* (Joan Burstein). Jean Muir wears her, David Shilling, Aniko Gaal think she's best. *"Manolo, and Maud Frizon, are just super. The styles are always the best. Yes, they're different"* (Anouska Hempel). Her bags in the same baby-soft leather are at *7 rue de Grenelle.*

CHARLES JOURDAN, 86 ave des Champs Elysées, 75008 ☎ (1) 4562 2923. Ubiquitous good design. *"I wear a pair of black Charles Jourdan pumps on the show"* (Shari Belafonte-Harper). Diane Freis echoes a paean of praise from Hong Kong: *"He does a lovely line of flatties for everyday wear. Great variety of materials, leather, patent. I have on a pair now, very smart and comfortable, with a simple textured heel." "I buy my shoes at Beltrami's and Charles Jourdan, I won't go anywhere else"* (Jenny Gucci).

WALTER STEIGER, 49 rue du Faubourg St Honoré, 75008. ☎ (1) 4265 1440. *"An inventive classicist"* (Pat Cantor). Knows how to take a simple pump and make it shine. *"A very exclusive, fashionable shoe"* (Meredith Etherington-Smith). *"I really like his high shoes"* (Jackie Collins).

BEST HATS

"There was a time when a woman would not consider going out without a hat and gloves, and I wish we could return to that time. I myself never go out without a hat, and I have taught my daughters to do the same" (La Comtesse de Paris). *"I never wore a hat in my life, except a little cap in the Thirties, maybe"* (Diana Vreeland).

♔ **JEAN BERTHET, 13 rue Tronchet, 75008 ☎ (1) 4265 3587.** Resounding worldwide reputation, has been a-hatting since 1949. Concocts classic little *folies de grandeur.* La Comtesse de Paris comes here, and Stephen Jones thinks he's the best, second only to the now-retired Lilian Daché.

JEAN-PAUL GAULTIER, 6 rue Vivienne, 75002 ☎ (1) 4286 0505. Would knock you into a cocked hat as soon as look at you. *Amusant* dream toppings arise from the same wellspring of irreverent genius as his clothes. *"A shot in the arm for the millinery industry"* (Pat Cantor).

PHILIPPE MODEL, 33 place du Marché St Honoré, 75008 ☎ (1) 4296 8902. Crowning glories for fantasy figures. Big bowed turbans, overweening toques, coronets, spirals and other dressing-up-box brouhaha. Martine Sitbon does chic chicanerie hats for the shop.

TETE-A-TETE, 183 rue du Faubourg St Honoré, 75008 ☎ (1) 4359 3989. Run by Josette, who worked 28 years for Paulette, Paris's Queen of Turbans (she could wrap a turban faster than a Turk). Josette continues the queenly tradition and also produces little *poufs* and insouciant caps for light-hearted occasions. Does a snooty haute couture *képi* for the likes of Lanvin.

BEST ACCESSORIES

"I really like designer accessories – I think the accessories are often the most interesting thing" (Lynne Franks).

♔ **HERMES, 24 rue du Faubourg St Honoré, 75008 ☎ (1) 4265 9648.** Established in 1754 and still one of the best shops in the world. *"The ultimate scarf, and gloves, and handbags. If you want the very best, you go there"* (Meredith Etherington-Smith). Stephen Jones votes them best for scarves. *"The huge cashmere ones are wonderful"* (Aniko Gaal). Inès de la Fressange and Mark Birley think they do the world's best luggage. *"Wonderful leather goods"* (Catherine Oxenberg). Tina Chow will go nowhere else for her shoe laces. *"For modern ties, Hermès is best, the colours are absolutely wonderful, as are the prints"* (Stephen Jones). *"Hermès have the cleverest designs, easiest to wear"* (Robert Sangster). Ex-princess Diane von Fürstenberg votes them Best Bags. *"I would still say Hermès is best for bags, because of the craftsmanship, the quality. I just got myself a beautiful alligator bag there that has a jewellery case underneath."* Diana Vreeland gets the last word on the world-best shop: *"The old-fashioned Hermès bag is a great bag. Their leathers and designs are superb, and their exhibitions of historic carriages and harnesses are marvellous."*

CHANEL, 31 rue Cambon, 75001 ☎ (1) 4261 5455. Gorgeous gloves that feel like butter and are lined with silk. Their speciality is driving gloves with keyhole back and the double "C". All the rage at the moment are their witty little quilted round patent bags on a chain. Bianca Jagger gave a baby-sized one from the latest collection to Paloma Bailey, daughter of David.

LOUIS VUITTON, 78b ave Marceau, 75008 ☎ (1) 4720 4700. Established in 1860, they have a history of wonderful, one-off wacky objects: a case that unfolds into a camp bed; a bureau-trunk made for Stokowski's Atlantic crossing. And they still make them for sybaritic time-travellers. *"They do 2 very popular things, the fleur-de-lys design in their standard beige on brown, and the modern-style sports luggage made of the same stuff as space capsules"* (Meredith Etherington-Smith). Nothing surpasses the effectiveness of their original brass locks, still to be seen on all their luggage.

YVES SAINT LAURENT, 5 ave Marceau, 75016 ☎ (1) 4723 7271. Great, big, strong scarves in wool and lurex; fab colours.

BEST JEWELLERS

Place Vendôme is perhaps the best setting in the world for buying jewellery.

BOIVIN, ave de l'Opéra 4, 75001 ☎ (1) 4296 0138. *"I don't like modern jewellery very much, but theirs is* incredible *and the craftsmanship is really beautiful and they have really beautiful designs. They are by far the best. Otherwise, I like old jewellery"* (Diane von Fürstenberg).

BOUCHERON, 26 place Vendôme, 75001 ☎ (1) 4261 5816. A solid, established name, recent creators of wonderful carved crystal jewellery. Margaux Hemingway's fave place to ogle the goodies.

CHANEL, 31 rue Cambon, 75001 ☎ (1) 4261 8335. For chains and wonderful, fake stone-encrusted decorations. The originators of costume jewellery, and the idea of upmarket inexpensive adornments. Marie Helvin and more go for it. *"Jewellery is not meant to make you look rich, it's meant to adorn you, and that's not the same thing at all"* (Coco Chanel).

CHAUMET, 12 place Vendôme, 75001 ☎ (1) 4260 3282. The oldest and most distinguished jeweller in France, now slightly living off its name. Classical jewels have crowned half the princely heads in Europe: now a more modern menagerie of animal-motif pieces satisfy chic clients who belong to what Pierre Chaumet has described as the *"époque animalière"*.

JEANNE D'ANJOU, 15 place Pont Neuf, 75001 ☎ (1) 4354 9932. Inès de la Fressange, embodiment of the Chanel spirit, also gets costume get-up here. *"It's really wonderful."*

MICHEL PERINET, 21 rue St-Honoré, 75008 ☎ (1) 4949 3566. Art deco and nouveau pieces.

VAN CLEEF & ARPELS, 24 place Vendôme 75001 ☎ (1) 4261 0236. One of the old guard along with Chaumet and Boucheron, greatly respected though perhaps lacking strong artistic direction. Betty Kenward is a staunch customer.

BEST LINGERIE

CHRISTIAN DIOR (see Best Designers). Stunning stuff, with the reputation for the best since their ruffle-breasted corsets for the New Look in '47. Marie Helvin's No 1.

CHANTAL THOMAS, 188 rue de Rivoli, 75001 ☎ (1) 4296 3065. Fêted in Paris for her lingerie above all: silks and satins to cocoon the body. Inès de la Fressange thinks it's the best (no, she did not vote Karl Lagerfeld best knickers man).

NINA RICCI, 39 ave Montaigne, 75008 ☎ (1) 4723 7888. More feathersoft satins in innocent colours, silks to sigh for.

BEST MEN'S DESIGNERS

CLAUDE MONTANA, 31 rue de Grenelle, 75007 ☎ (1) 4222 6956. For leathers, first and foremost – big, buttersoft flying coats, jackets, gloves. Also does trad gear (suits, shirts, ties), in noisy colours.

JEAN-PAUL GAULTIER, 6 rue Vivienne, 75002 ☎ (1) 4286 0505. Oh, the whimsy of it! Where else would you go for an Arran-knit romper suit or modern-day doublet and hose? Motley for Eighties jesters, but also more wearable ideas, re-vamped versions of the off-beat, always in good colours and patterns. Yuki Maekawa thinks he does the best coats and suits for men and women. This autumn, a play-it-cool collection inspired by post-Revo Russia. More sombre colours than heretofore, constructivist lines, "Gaultier" writ large here and there in Cyrillic letters.

BEST SHIRTS

CHARVET, 28 place Vendôme, 75001 ☎ (1) 4260 3070. These are the real specialists with the most incredible fabrics. At the same time, they have the answers to everything in a man's life from shirts to accessories. They have the rights to make up all the Dufy prints, which they do in his innocent colours on huge silk scarves. They used to sew de Gaulle's shirts and, earlier, those of Nazi officers, billeted during the Occupation at the nearby Ritz. *"The French equivalent of Turnbull & Asser. Luxurious and worn by the best dressed men in France"* (Pat Cantor). *"The best*

GETTING SHIRTY!

Robert Sangster struck a blow for the French shirt and pooh-poohed London's Jermyn Street: *"I wear Lanvin. They're the only ones that fit me, also the collars don't wrinkle after 3 hotel washes. These are usable after 3 years. The ones you get from Jermyn Street wrinkle after 3 washes, and that's useless for me as I travel so much."*

David Frost went fisti-cuffs with him: *"I don't agree with Robert Sangster, but I do agree with Roald Dahl who said that the greatest luxury would be to have a new shirt every day. There's nothing like the sensuous quality of an unwashed shirt."*

The French have carried off a significant coup with the world's first shirt-vending machine at the Frantel Hôtel, 20 ave Charles Lindbergh, Rungis 94656 ☎ (1) 4687 3636. Take the complimentary coach to procure a Brooks Bros button-down Oxford in blue, white or pink.

shirtmaker is Charvet in Paris. It's the collar of a Charvet shirt that is so good, a most flattering collar. Quite different to British shirts. Damn good shirt though" (Bill Blass). *"The best nightshirts and pyjamas, and for white cotton piqués – they must have a hundred different piqués"* (Tina Chow).

LANVIN, 22 rue du Faubourg St Honoré, 75008 ☎ (1) 4265 1440. *"They're the best, properly made shirts and they have very good fabrics. I've got Lanvin shirts going back more than 20 years. The make is very, very good and all the buttonholes are beautifully done, you know. They're made in an old-fashioned way"* (Mark Birley). *"The only one that has a size 44 that fits me"* (Robert Sangster).

ITALY

ROME

BEST COUTURIERS

Rome is home of the small but beautiful Italian couture.

VALENTINO, via Gregoriana 24, 00187 ☎ (06) 672011. All the seductiveness and glamour of screen goddess dressing *without* the kitsch. He does stylish *without rigueur* day clothes, but his laurels rest on his couture evening dresses. *"Valentino is still a romantic, still does the best"* (Anouska Hempel). Lynn Wyatt places him second only to Chanel: *"I have a bizarre, yellow, ruffled Valentino dress made for The Yellow Rose of Texas gala in Monte Carlo. It's wonderful, just wonderful." "If you want to go to a tea party and look like a prim miss aunt, he can do it. If you want to look really sexy, he can make you look really sexy"* (Jenny Gucci). He designed Jackie Kennedy's dress for her wedding to Onassis and 38 clients ordered the same dress – some sort of couture record. *"He's the best in Italy"* (Eleanor Lambert).

ROBERTO CAPUCCI, via Gregoriana 56, 00187 ☎ (06) 6792368. Best Black Sheep. Very little known couturier whose clothes are entirely a law unto themselves. Controlled and formal visions on an architectonic and breathtaking scale: his clothes are about sculptural cut, stand-alone forms, fabric – anything but the wearer. He has to be seen to be believed. *"Has to be the best, numero uno. Those flounces – divine"* (Jenny Gucci).

Best streets

ROME The **via Condotti** is where shopping starts and finishes: all the best tailors, shirt-makers, fash shops, plus Bulgari and Gucci a-plenty.

MILAN "Via Montenapoleone is the best street for shops in the world – the most satisfactory fashion street of all time" (Bill Blass). *"A wonderful shopping street is the via della Spiga in Milan"* (Bruce Oldfield).

FLORENCE the **via dei Tornabuoni** is the one, replete with Gucci, Valentino, Fendi, Armani, Versace, Ferragamo and the other classics. The more avant-garde edge (inspired by the *inglesi*) live on the tiny streets that riddle the city: via Porta Rossa, via della Vigna Nuova, via Condotti, via Roma.

BEST STORE

LA RINASCENTE, via del Corso, ang. P. Colonna 00186 ☎ (06) 6797691; Piazza Fiume, 00186 ☎ (06) 841231. The po-faced, pricey emporium that's tops for trad Romish goods. They try to do a Harrods and pack it all in, but nearly everything in the packaging is signature designer stuff – all emblazoned with a redeeming *name* Versace, Armani, Ferre.

BEST SHOPS

BALESTRA, via Gregoriana 36, 00187 ☎ (06) 6792917. A charmingly old-fashioned shop with all the beautifully worked timeless designer pieces that discriminating donnas love. *"I love their beaded sequin-y sweaters for evening"* (Catherine Oxenberg).

BATTISTONI, via Condotti 57, 00187 ☎ (06) 6795527. Just clothes, and the go-withs, but plenty of the best of both. Top Italian and French designers and their own made-to-measure and ready-to-wear as well. Where the snobs shop, especially for that essential little accessory that costs more than the dress.

CAMOMILLA, piazza di Spagna 85, 00187 ☎ (06) 6793551. Yuppy storehouse. It's the wicked difference of the French designer clothes that brings them in for an upmarket trendy edge over their Italian-buying rivals.

FUR AND AWAY

"The best furs for styling are in Italy. You go to Italy and your mouth drops open. They really are the masters" (Jenny Gucci). And the best? It's **Fendi, via Borgognona 39, Rome 00187 ☎ (06) 6797641.** The most inspired, the wittiest and most sumptuous furs in the world are designed by the irrepressible Karl Lagerfeld for the Fendi sisters. *"He has an Italian extravagance and grandeur, with an irreverence to wealth and opulence, a certain disrespect. At the same time he can create a totally exuberant design. He executes everything with German precision"* (Aniko Gaal).

His furry *tour de force* goes from mink T-shirts to lacquered sables, slit beaver trousers and shaved chinchillas, fur-cuffed evening gowns and floor-sweeping drama coats in fitch, squirrel or fox – drop-dead knockouts, every one. *"A great favourite, fabulous, wonderful because they are so different and imaginative. You can say goodbye to a quarter of a million dollars for those golden sables"* (Jenny Gucci).

MILA SCHON BOUTIQUE, via Condotti 64–65, 00187 ☎ (06) 6784805/6790326. Milanese designer of Austro-Hungarian birth who is at the classy end of the market and has the most *elegante* collection of wearables on the via Condotti.

BEST SHOES

DAL CO, via piazzatta Pinciana 16, 00187 ☎ (06) 486981. Best of the best in Italy, famed for their masterful handling of snakeskin.

MARIO VALENTINO, via Frattina 84a, 00187 ☎ (06) 6791246. Exquisite coquette evening slippers.

POLLINI, via Frattina 24, 00198 ☎ (06) 678 9028. Siren shoes and gorgeous little boots in silken leather, comfort to kill for.

BEST HATS

Italians don't go the whole hog on hats – why spoil those careful little coiffures?

BORSALINO, via IV Novembre 157B, 00187 ☎ (06) 6794192. Men's hats, superb classix with overtones of Al Capone shading into Marlon Brando and a more rakish continental cap. Homburgs, fedoras in the best felts and velours, for those who cultivate the beautiful boy look (but are really girls) as well as best-dressed men.

BEST ACCESSORIES

GUCCI, via Condotti 8, 00187 ☎ (06) 6789340. One of the world's most famous shops, knockout leather feverishly branded, stamped and inbred with the notorious double G. There has even been a custom-fitted Cadillac sports completely kitted out with a Gucci soft top, Gucci hub caps, and Gucci interior.

Those who don't want to go the whole way have their feet fitted with the Gucci shoe and logo and get bags, wallets and the works trademarked to match. Marina Chaliapin recommends.

❝ There's no place to wear jewels today, and because of it, the world has less colour and unfortunately a whole generation will come and go who have never seen a real pearl, and even cultured pearls are becoming rarer ❞

(DIANA VREELAND)

BEST JEWELLERS

BUCCELLATI, via Condotti 31, 00187 ☎ (06) 6790329. The best silversmith and goldsmith alive today. If Benvenuto Cellini were still with us, he'd be making his salt cellars for them.

BULGARI, via Condotti 10, 00187 ☎ (06) 6793876. World famous, with beautiful collars of crystal and gold studded with gems. Neo-classical stuff. Costly prestigious jewels change hands here. Marina Chaliapin and Marie Helvin think it's tops, but Stephen Jones, who's into costume stuff, says: *"I'm off Bulgari."*

MASENZA, via del Corso 410, 00186 ☎ (06) 6791344. Have the edge on setting and style, though the stones are not quite up to Massoni. A little more artistry here.

MASSONI, Largo Goldoni 48, 00187 ☎ (06) 6790182. No glitz, glam or fussiness, straight, simple, stunning silver and classic, serious jewels. Great stones.

BEST LINGERIE

"The Italians in my opinion make the finest lingerie. The same with hosiery" (Joan Burstein). *"I would say Italian lingerie was the best. The workmanship there is better"* (Diane von Fürstenberg).

BLANCHE DE SANVOISIN, via Crispi 109, 00187 ☎ (06) 6795365. Bijou, effete and irresistible shop, best of the very best for the Italian trousseau. The most luxuriously hand-embroidered linen and silks, made-to-measure, the modern continuation of medieval artisans.

PRATESI, piazza di Spagna 10, 00187 ☎ (06) 6790673. Not little rows of dear old ladies sewing little flowers on fresh linens, but gorgeous none the less, newer, and quality stuff. For more fashionable frillies.

BEST MEN'S CLOTHES

All the top tailors do superb shirts as well.

IBBAS, via Condotti 49, 00187 ☎ (06) 6791035. Made-to-measure sartorially imperative shirts for political bodies like President Craxi. The Turnbull & Asser of Rome, masses of beautiful cloth, plus Aquascutum jackets, sweaters and so on for a sense of English country.

RADICONCINI, via del Corso 139, 00186 ☎ (06) 6791807. Just the best, best shirts. They come (like eggs) by the dozen, hand-made-to-measure with *hand-embroidered* monograms. This swish service has been going since the last century.

MILAN

BEST DESIGNERS

This is Europe's home of superb prêt-à-porter. It's honed to a fine commercial art, which produces an ease of dress that spans the entire spectrum of Italian designers. *"The exciting fashion is in Milan, not Paris"* (Bill Blass). *"Italian designers are the best"* (Margaux Hemingway).

GIORGIO ARMANI, via Sant'Andrea 9, 20121 ☎ (02) 792757/709234. The *ne plus ultra* of tailored Italian chic. *"I think he is probably the best woman's tailor in terms of a ready-to-wear garment. His suits have that comfortable, slightly ruffled, lived-in feel of the Eighties about them"* (Bruce Oldfield). He reversed the usual order of things and designed for men first, then women. Translates the ease of menswear into very feminine,

“The cut of Italian design is so good. It makes you look so very good” (JENNY GUCCI)

whittled down clothes. The best little jackets here – stolen from men and reshaped and de-structured. Emporio Armani is his more affordable line. One of Vanessa de Lisle's faves, and Pat Cantor's. *"Armani makes the best tailored clothes. He understands co-ordination. Provides enormous scope for the consumer"* (Yuki Maekawa).

ROMEO GIGLI, via della Spiga 46, 20121 ☎ (02) 709380. The Italian new boy with a dress sense at odds with the rest of his Milanese peers. He calls his clothes "elemental" – *viz* a Japanese sense of proportion, tempered by Italian minimalist tailoring – plus a moodier palette completely different from the tonic Latin brights. He produces long and tapering separates, which he urges the wearer to rearrange at will, and the most beautifully cut-off-the-shoulder dresses ever.

BASILE, viale Lancetti 28, 20158 ☎ (02) 6071841. Relaxed, throwaway sportswear in the classic Italian vein, with that edge of dressiness that makes the Italians better at it than anyone else. Bruce Oldfield's No 3. *"I love Basile"* (Jenny Gucci).

CERRUTI 1881, viale Italia Corsica 16, 20122 ☎ (02) 440 1851. Bruce Oldfield places them second only to Armani, and they're Anouska Hempel's No 1: *"Always you can go in and there's a great suit, or a great hat or a mad pair of shoes that have that really elegant, simple look I particularly love. Every year there's something you can choose."*

GIANFRANCO FERRE BOUTIQUE, via della Spiga 11, 20121 ☎ (02) 794864. The Marchesa Bona Frescobaldi's fave Italian designer. Has an architectural approach to design

WHO'S DESIGNING WHO IN ITALY?

Never mind living in each other's pockets, the Italians are busy designing each other's pockets, and the French have a hand in it too. Next time you fall for a little black **Erreuno** dress with a detachable round collar, remember that that collar is the signature of **Armani.** What's it doing at Erreuno? It's entirely legit, because Armani designs on the side for them. In fact, almost everyone in Italy is really someone else as well. This is 1 reason why the design standard is so high there – the top few really do *pervade.* On the other hand, it's also partly why Italian style is so recognizable: a few influences go a long way. Here's your under-cover checklist of who's who:

Versace designs for **Genny** and the less well-known **Callaghan. Basile,** which was once done by Versace, has used **Luciano Soprani** since 1979. **Touche** is really **Enrico Coveri. Maxmara** is designed by **Annemarie Beretta.** And can you believe that **Complice** is the work of **Claude Montana?** This summer's Complice corset skirt shows his more-current-than-ever obsession with the body, but he usually designs them a look that is a lot milder than the aggressive style of his own-name clothes.

that usually finds expression in sharp, to-the-point city clothes for day, luxurious ease for night. But Benny Ong found him more than usually architectonic: *"I had the good fortune of doing a joint European show with him about 10 years ago. I represented Britain and he represented Italy, and he was so innovative, I thought it was fantastic. He designed a jacket that you could take off, zip up, and make into a tent."*

GIANNI VERSACE, via della Spiga 25, 20121 ☎ (02) 545 6201. The master of molten metal. *"No one can wrap cloth round a woman's body like Gianni Versace,"* Diana Vreeland has said. *"Every time I put on one of his blouses, I feel 20 years old again."* An innovator in cutting and sewing techniques, he's famed for his draped steel dresses as fluid as silk. *"Oh, of course, he's marvellous"* (Jenny Gucci). John and Chrissie Lloyd go overboard here. Bruce Springsteen comes looking for leather.

KRIZIA, via della Spiga 23, 20121 ☎ (02) 708429. Another of Marchesa Bona Frescobaldi's faves. Anouska Hempel preferred them in their less sleek and shiny days: *"They've changed and gone all sort of high fashion."* Krizia takes its name from Plato's Dialogue on Woman's Vanity.

LUCIANO SOPRANI, via Napoleone 2, 16134 ☎ (02) 701803. Cool sense of colour and studied ease, the Italian ideal again. Catherine Oxenberg goes for it: *"I think he does the best tailored clothes because he makes things which are wearable, as opposed to just looking good on the 6-foot model. And they're really flattering, because they're either snug at the waist or the hips which is really good for me. I like him for daytime."*

BEST STORES

The charm of Milan is that the old rich live in elegant and venerable houses dotted between the shops on the best shopping streets . . . it's as though Lord Lichfield were to live on London's Bond Street. Every other person works for one of the huge network of telephone-directory sized *Vogues* (*Vogue Pelle*, *Vogue Bambini* – even a *Vogue* for speedboats). Almost monotonously stylish.

CAFFE MODA DURINI, via Durini 14, 20122 ☎ (02) 791188. The top fashion store in the city, the latest *alta moda* from Ferre, Valentino, Krizia and felt-like Missoni knitlets.

COIN, 53 corso Porta Vittoria, Cinque Giornate 1, 20122 ☎ (02) 20129/792583. Milano's answer to Harvey Nichols with smashing little in-store designer boutiques for all your faves (Italians and French, that is) and the usual designer gewgaws that add on to the clothes.

BEST KNITWEAR

MISSONI BOUTIQUE, via Montenapoleone 1, 20121 ☎ (02) 700906. The best knits in the world, together with Sonia Rykiel. *"Missoni have always been considered the wizards of knitwear. Their coloration, their patterns, is quite distinctive, and also always copied"* (Joan Burstein). It's an old family business. Tai Missoni works out the Jacquard designs with water colours on graph paper, and his wife Rosita creates the line and shape. Stephen Jones votes them No 1: *"for the technology they put into their design. They have broken down the barriers that no other company has done in colour, texture, pattern, and type. They knit chenille thread in the most wonderful way so that it looks like moss. Beautiful and soft, very delicate shades of green all over. They cost a fortune."*

UMBERTO GINOCCHETTI, via Montenapoleone 5, 20121 ☎ (02) 790856. Clicks his needles to a young, modern, very pretty rhythm. *"I love his knitwear, he does a mixture of silky knit and linen with a wonderful pattern all on the same sweater"* (La Oxenberg again). *"The first thing I ever bought when I went to Italy was his, a beautiful green job which I still wear today"* (Jenny Gucci).

BEST LEATHER

PRADA FRATELLI, Galleria Vittorio Emanuele II 63, 20100 ☎ (02) 876979. Contemporary big-city look in natty little leather bits and bobs, with an exotic specialization in turtle-skin and elephant hide. What they are *really* famous for at the moment is their dolly little quilted patent leather circle bags hung on acres of loopy chain – *so* Coco! And, indeed, Chanel sued them for cashing in on their baggette and making a fat fortune.

BEST SHOES

"The best sole leather comes from Italy, because they really know how to finish it off" (Kailash Mishra).

ROSSETTI FRATELLI, via Montenapoleone ang. corso Matteotti, 20121 ☎ (02) 791650. An off-the-peg elegance to be found here, the Italian speciality. Willie Landels and Vanessa de Lisle, and *many* others think they are the best and Kailash Mishra agrees.

BEST JEWELLERS

LORENZO MARTIGNETTI, via Montenapoleone 10, 20121 ☎ (02) 701509. Pearly prizes (award yourself the outstanding sizes) of baroque opulence are to be found here. They do the best pearl necklaces in Italy: also cute little coral statuettes, and other *objets* of fashionable import.

ROMANI ADAMI, via Sant'Andrea 7, 20122 ☎ (02) 700804. Real specialists: art deco and art nouveau – all other periods are out of bounds. Pick up all the best Tiffany and Cartier trinkets from these periods plus silver with Papal scratchings. Versace, Armani, all the styleboys, shop here for toys, and there's a clique of knowing Swiss who come for period watches (brill Rolexes).

SUBERT, via San Pietro all'Orto 26, 20129 ☎ (02) 793220. A twenty-year period narrows it down to the best of the Thirties and Forties, when they really went in for show-stopping, diamond-spangled stunners. They sell mainly to collectors and walloping rich industrialists looking for a big little something for their molls. Not for those in search of the discreet charm of bijouterie.

BEST LINGERIE

"For lingerie, the best in Italy is the via Montenapoleone in Milan" (Meredith Etherington-Smith).

♔ **ARS ROSA, via Montenapoleone 8, 20121 ☎ (02) 793822.** The sort of swoonworthy satin and silk dream wear that sends shivers down Meredith Etherington-Smith's spine. Deeply feminine dainties, all brilliantly embroidered, including famous, well-wrought wedding dresses.

DONINI BIANCHERIA, via Verri 10, 20121 ☎ (02) 702568. Embroidery: Italians just can't get enough of their wildly accomplished workmanship, here to be found on pure and simple silks and cottons.

PRATESI, via Montenapoleone 21, 20121 ☎ (02) 709791. Stacks of satin knickers, silky smalls and other lovables to wear next to your designer dresses.

BEST MEN'S DESIGNERS

♔ **GIORGIO ARMANI, via Sant'Andrea 9, 20121 ☎ (02) 792 7575/709234.** The best men's designer (as opposed to tailor) is described in the English translation handed out with the programme of his latest collection as "the full-bodied fabric king". *"Giorgio Armani makes the best tailored clothes in the world"* (Yuki Maekawa). Marie Helvin is equally keen on the man in an unstructured Armani suit.

Nothing fancy, apart from the fabulously and subtly different fabrics (which are a closely guarded trade secret). Armani is after an uncluttered line, taking the pressing out of a pair of trousers. He wants what he calls "a very clean look", both in his top Couture collection (not couture in the strict sense of made-to-measure) and the cheaper, younger Armani, and Emporio Armani. *"I wear almost exclusively Armani – he cuts for big boys like me. I always have a problem with my suits and jackets and have to let down the sleeves to the absolute maximum, which is one reason why I stick with Armani as he cuts enough turning in the cuff for me ... I am 6 feet 2 inches, I have long arms, long legs, and a short bod!"* (Bruce Oldfield).

Armani also does the very best, most covetable and comfortable coats. *"Classic, but they have that little bit of extra detail which makes them interesting enough to be right. It's hard to beat an Armani overcoat. I have just bought an* incredible *one. Very generously cut navy blue cashmere, very nice and warm! They can be very dramatic"* (Bruce Oldfield).

♔ **GIANNI VERSACE (UOMO), via Verri ang. Montenapoleone, 20121 ☎ (02) 790281.** Italianate ease and unstructured shapes. Best in Europe for originally textured fabrics, chocolate brown crocodile-creased and oversewn suits, shirts with a light ripple running through, always nice, nobbly-textured jackets. Paolo Gucci comes here to be dressed.

BASILE DIFFUSIONE, viale Lanchetti 28, 20158 ☎ (02) 9 6071841. More Italian mufti in those very continental colours (catch an Englishman in tangerine?). All the stuff for the dapper young Latin exec. Bruce Oldfield shops here.

CERRUTI 1881, via G Di Vittorio 8, 20094 ☎ (02) 4476541. Oldfield's next fave to Armani. Together with Basile *"these are my top 3"*. Casual sports stuff with an upmarket feel, for lounging around the Med, the pool and the penthouse. And the clipped, cut-and-thrust tailoring of the archetypal Italian suit.

GIANFRANCO FERRE, via Sant 'Andrea 10, 20121 ☎ (02) 700385. Nice mix of colours. Simple pleasures like a buttonfront grey T-shirt, buttonless club silk jacket in salmon pink, slightly crumpled black linen suit. All part of the dressed-down-to-kill Italian look.

LUCIANO SOPRANI, via Santo Spirito 24, 20100 ☎ (02) 799019. A light touch with less familiar Italian stock-in-trade like updated duffle coats.

BEST MEN'S TAILORS

♔ **CARACENI, via Fatebenefratelli 16, 20121 ☎ (02) 655 1972.** *"The best suits in the world"* (Willie Landels). *"The best tailor is Caraceni in Milan. All made to order. He has a big clientele, but mostly men"* (Diane von Fürstenberg). On the list of snappy dressers who come to Caraceni are Gianni Agnelli, and hyper-discriminating Karl Lagerfeld who hides them behind his undulating fan. Undoubtedly the best in Italy, some would say in the world.

BOMBINO, at Mila Schön, via Montenapoleone 2, 20146 ☎ (02) 701803. Known as the Jean Muir of Italy, Mila Schön is of exotic Eastern European extraction, but Italian by design. When Bill Blass is in Italy, he comes here for suits made-to-measure by Bombino, which he ranks next to Huntsman of Savile Row.

FLORENCE

BEST SHOPS

♔ **VALDITEVERE, Lungarno Soderini 1, 50124 ☎ (055) 282707.** Ultra fashionable. They were among the first to show in the Salle Bianco of the Palazzo Pitti with Pucci and de Viti. An unfailing line of unremarkable but very well put together cotton, linen and silken chic. Marchesa Bona Frescobaldi shops here with all her aristo friends.

"You come back to Italy always for manufactured fashion – quality, highly wearable design, and they always get the proportions right" (BRUCE OLDFIELD)

LUISA VIA ROMA, via Roma 19–21r, 50100 ☎ (055) 217826. Stocks the raffish and refined avant-garde: Issey Miyake, Kenzo, Gaultier, Comme des Garçons. Kudos is a Luisa carrier bag. At their branch in via del Corso they sell their own designs in the same free spirit.

NEUBER, via Strozzi 32r, 50123 ☎ (055) 215763. What the Italians call "*tipo* Sloane Ranger" (though SW1 originals might not agree); in other words, no nasty surprises. SW1s will be relieved to find Burberry and Aquascutum ranked together with Cerruti and D'Avanza.

PARISOTTO, Calimata 33–35, 50123 ☎ (055) 214598. Oscar and Franco are the wizards of a certain look, irrevocably Italian with shades of London street (and known as Look Parisotto, of course). Cult following in Florence.

BEST SHOES

BELTRAMI, via Calzaiuoli 31, 50100 ☎ (055) 214030. Head-to-toe fetish leather, all in that ultra-well-made Italian idiom. Coats, shoes, bags, suits, would probably do leather sheets and pillow cases if asked. Made-to-measure and ready-to-wear Italian beauties. "*They make exquisite shoes, I have 3 or 4 pairs and winter boots with a matching handbag. All the rich Americans go there*" (Jenny Gucci). Anouska Hempel comes here.

FERRAGAMO, via Tornabuoni, 12–16r 50100 ☎ (055) 292123. Salvatore, once cobbler to the cognoscenti, is long gone, but his children carry on the business, turning out what Kailash Mishra calls "*the best mass-production designs*". He thinks Ferragamo do the world's best narrow-fitting shoe, and they are Marchesa Bona Frescobaldi's favourite. They also have a range of clothes to accessorize the shoes.

BEST HATS

MESSERI, Por Santa Maria 4, 50123 ☎ (055) 296563. Marchesa Bona Frescobaldi finds hats for a titled head here. Distinguished equivalent of an English garden party, racing day crowning glory.

BEST ACCESSORIES

CELLERINI, via del Sole 37/r, 50123 ☎ (055) 282533. Well known for smart accessories, and the Marchesa Bona Frescobaldi's fave for handbags. Florentine equivalent of Hermès in terms of lush leather and scarves. Everything is hand-stitched in their own workshops by swarms of Latin artisans. Cheapest item in the shop is 682,812 lire (US$434).

PIBRA, via Loggetta 26, 50135 ☎ (055) 652016. Beauty in the bag, all shapes and sizes of best, buttery leather.

BEST JEWELLERS

PICCINI, Ponte Vecchio 23, 50125 ☎ (055) 294768. This area round the Ponte Vecchio is just wall-to-wall jewels. Piccini are old, established, *comme il faut*, exquisitely and artfully worked. Their location brings them some foreign trade from richer tourists on the Dante trail. Rivulets of rubies, emeralds, diamonds, sapphires – the very best stones. "*They make up the jewellery my husband designs for me*" (Jenny Gucci).

SETTE PASSE, Ponte Vecchio 1–3/r, 50125 ☎ (055) 215506. Have decked out the Florentine nobility since 1860 in pomp and circumstance pieces to shout about. Classic gem-crowded gold and more modern showpieces.

BEST LINGERIE

LORETTA CAPPONI, Borgo Ognissanti 12, 50123 ☎ (055) 213668. Seduction here with the seal of approval of Marchesa Bona Frescobaldi. It's a contest with Garbo (see right) to see who's the best in town. "*Absolutely indescribable, inset lace, satin appliqué, heaven, heaven. It is* so *beautiful it intimidates you*" (Jenny Gucci).

GARBO, Borgo Ognissanti 2/r, 50123 ☎ (055) 295338. Womanly wonders, fantasy foundations, and angelic embroidery by a team of ladies on the premises who make and stitch the lot. Pristine, embroidered blouses and ornamental wedding gowns as well. While a number of these high-flown lingerie spots are very bra-di-dah, Garbo encourages customers right across the board.

BEST MEN'S TAILOR

PUCCI BOUTIQUE, via dei Pucci 6, 50122 ☎ (055) 283061. Remember Emilio? Marchese Pucci? You will if you wore Pucci prints in the Fifties and Sixties, bright and beautiful Capri pants and scarves with ravishing prints on fine silk jersey. Or if you've ever read Dante's *Divine Comedy*, which features several Pucci passés, Emilio's bona fide ancestors. Note that Pucci is the only designer esconced in a road named after him – you won't find Bruce Oldfield or even Lagerfeld getting away with that.

Born in 1914. The Marchese is still bold-printing with style on draped and flowing silks, foulards à la Botticelli. Charles and Diana drop in on the Pucci palazzo when in Florence – he's high (old) society bordering on the Royal.

D'ya know 'er?

Catherine Oxenberg comes to Odicini in Genoa for evening slinks: "*He has a kind of old-style elegance; he does really sexy clothes which are not tarty, and I think that that is the really fine line.*" He lives in Genoa and top ladies, Jackie Onassis and Mrs Sinatra, come for his very special brand of chic. **ANDREA ODICINI, via XXV Aprile 44r, Genoa 16123 ☎ (10) 293569.**

THE AMERICAS

UNITED STATES

NEW YORK

BEST COUTURIER

ARNOLD SCAASI COUTURE, 681 5th Ave, NY 10022 ☎ (212) 755 5105. Ready-to-wear: **SCAASI BOUTIQUE, 530 7th Ave, NY 10018 ☎ (212) 245 2683.** The *only* one. See box.

BEST DESIGNERS

TOP 5

★

1. DONNA KARAN, New York
2. GALANOS, Los Angeles
3. GEOFFREY BEENE, New York
4. CALVIN KLEIN, New York
5. BILL BLASS, New York

DONNA KARAN, 550 7th Ave, 14th Fl, NY 10018 ☎ (212) 398 1558. *"My woman of the moment is Donna Karan. A top designer who is fulfilling everybody's needs. Minimalistic and most wearable. Her clothes are edited superbly"* (Joan Burstein). *"She is the dominant figure. She was trained by Anne Klein. Donna brought out the body suit around which wraps skirts, pants: it works very well ... sensational. Very effective if you have a good waistline"* (Eleanor Lambert). From her first collection on her own in autumn '85, Donna has been the hit of New York and lauded everywhere else as well. The epitome of the American idea – a simple, wearable wardrobe that's right for a working woman. A few co-ordinating colours (black, grey, ivory – recently she updated black to navy blue) and interchangeable pieces – wool, cashmere, and jersey bodies that are soft, not structured like Azzedine's, a sarong skirt that you knot in front, pants, of course, *et voilà*. A longer, lusher sarong takes you on through the wee hours. Not cheap. A jersey headband clocks in at about $98.

GEOFFREY BEENE, 205 W 39th St, NY 10018 ☎ (212) 944 8080. "Uncluttered" is America's favourite fashion word, and Beene is uncluttered to the nth degree – evening T-shirts in glam fabrics like silk cloque. One of Joan Burstein's favourite US designers: *"He has that fabulous feeling for fabric – this sensitivity towards fabric is very great."* Some of these fabrics cost $300 a yard. Spare, lean, easy "energized" clothes in tune with that perennial US fashion basic – the working woman. Sophisticated but scrumptious pour-on evening dresses. *"Not for the tremendously 'best dressed' types"* (Nicholas Coleridge).

CALVIN KLEIN, 205 W 39th St, NY 10018 ☎ (212) 719 2600. It's all in the ads, from Brooke Shields' bottom proffered in Klein designer

LONE STAR SCAASI

Arnold Scaasi is the one and only true couturier in this vast continent still doing the time-honoured Paris thing of 2 couture shows a year to Press and potential clients. His forte is glorious, very sculptured evening clothes, what he calls "great occasion dressing", triumphant fantasies in taffeta and tulle. The couture prices are a cinch compared to Europe: $4,500–8,500; his ready-to-wear is $700–$1,800.

"Did you see Mrs Trump in the March issue of Town & Country*? She was wearing one of mine – a strapless gown that had a white velvet top with an apron all embroidered with diamond roses."* The list of other clients takes an hour or so to run through ... *"Lady Sarah Russell, sister to the Duke of Marlborough (Mall-bow-row) ... Diahann Carroll – I've dressed her for 22 years! ... Barbra Streisand, I dressed her before she went to California ... Arlene Francis – she was my very first client 28 years ago! ... Charlotte Ford, she buys my ready-to-wear, her mother buys the couture ... Mrs Adnan Khashoggi ... I think I'm the only person she buys from in America ... Joan Sutherland ... Joan Rivers ... and I've dressed 2 First Ladies ... Mrs Johnson and Mrs Kennedy ..."* He does a lot of début and wedding dresses, one-offs for his cliquey clientele, and lives the life of a super-rich Reilly. Scaasi, by the way, spells Isaacs backwards.

> **"Our ready-to-wear is spectacular. America has the best ready-to-wear in the world. That's why couture has nearly disappeared here"** (ARNOLD SCAASI)

denim to the octopus-bodies in the Obsession ads. Understated pieces that go well with the leggy, broad-shouldered American model. *"Calvin Klein designs for the lifestyle of the Americans – I really like him"* (Jenny Gucci). *"I love Calvin Klein because it is very comfortable and casual"* (Shari Belafonte-Harper). These are the unconstructed, easy-to-put-together separates in taupe, beige, black, ivory and red that best-dressed Middle America loves.

BILL BLASS, 550 7th Ave, NY 10018 ☎ (212) 221 6660. *"Blass is a great classicist. More than any other, Blass is aware of wealthy Americans and what they look like. He stands for wealthy women and good taste"* (Eleanor Lambert). He also stands for loud, pretty-bright colour statements, sugar candy colours, lemon, shocking pink (the first since Schiap to really carry it off), shrieking orange – all in the most demure, well-cut American clothes you ever saw. Solid colour head-to-toe with perhaps a sewn-in bolero of sweetie-pink silk on an otherwise sherbet-yellow evening gown. Hot, slinky beading, swish day clothes. Burstein approves his sense of fabric, he's Lynn Wyatt's No 1 American. *"He knows how to make a woman look truly feminine"* (Aniko Gaal). Does a small couture line. The man himself is America's No 1 fashion accessory, draped on the arm of the best society dames.

OSCAR DE LA RENTA, 550 7th Ave, NY 10018 ☎ (212) 354 6777. Known for his extravagant evening clothes with a certain conservative elegance. He's good on lace, might do an evening dress with an elaborate black lace top and plain long white skirt; puts assured black touches – bows, bands, edges – on textured whites all over his collection. *"Oscar does gypsy dresses, glamorous evening dresses, a lot of embroidery. Famous for ornaments"* (Eleanor Lambert). The famous French fabric firm, Lasage, do all Oscar's hand-beading. Dresses everybody: Lee Radziwill, Babe Paley, Marella Agnelli, Marie-Hélène de Rothschild, Nancy Kissinger … and that other Nancy.

THE BEST-DRESSED OF '86

At a certain time of the year, a little pamphlet is posted off to the chosen few at *Vogue*, *Harpers* and so on and to "others with the daily opportunity to see fashion at its best", inviting them to place their vote for the Best-Dressed List. In case they get stylist's block, a reference sheet of suggestions is usefully appended. The 84/85 sheet included Linda Evans (Queen of the Shoulder Pads) and Raquel Welch together with Princess Pia Ruspoli, Mme Arman de Borchgrave and the like; among the men Arthur Ashe and Issey Miyake rubbed shoulders with The Duke of Bedford and Prince Kyril of Bulgaria. Each contestant has at least 1 place (but it's chic-er to have 2) bracketed after their name. HM Queen Noor of Jordan and President Reagan were left with no fixed abode. On top of all this, the Reagans and Princess Diana were declared: "today's 3 greatest influences in the world on the way people dress." (Who do *you* know that models their dress sense on President Reagan?) P.S. According to Them, Jackie Onassis "remains consistently the woman other women want to look like". *Live* like, more like.

WOMEN
Mrs Sid Bass (Fort Worth, Texas and New York)
Mrs Dixon Boardman (New York and Palm Beach)
Helena Bonham Carter (British actress portraying Lady Jane Grey in Trevor Nunn's film *Lady Jane*)
Sra Maria-Pia Fanfani (vice-president, International Red Cross and wife of president of the Italian Senate)
Mrs Donald (Sybil) Harrington, philanthropist (Amarillo, Texas and New York)
Mrs John R Hearst Jr (an editor of *Connoisseur* magazine)
Mrs Francis Kellogg (New York hostess)
Miss Whitney Houston (young American singer and "Grammy" winner)
Mrs Charles (Carol) Price (wife of the American Ambassador to Great Britain)
Baroness Sylvia de Waldner (French socialite and famous gardener)

MEN
Thomas Ammann (Swiss art dealer)
The Duke of Beaufort (David Somerset) England
Mark Birley (London restaurateur and owner of Annabel's and Mark's club)
David Bowie (British actor and rock star)
Christopher Forbes (*Forbes* Magazine executive)
Mark Hampton (New York interior decorator)
HM King Hassan of Morocco
David Hockney (British-born artist)
James Hoge (New York newspaper editor)
Kevin Kline (American stage and film star)
Charles Pfeiffer (New York businessman)
Bobby Short (American nightclub musician)
Issey Miyake (Japanese fashion designer).

**Thanks to Eleanor Lambert for supplying the information.*

♕ **PERRY ELLIS, 575 7th Ave, NY 10018 ☎ (212) 921 8500.** This is what sportswear's all about. Perry has cornered the market in casual dressing that has its wilder moments. His Sonia Delaunay-inspired collection last winter walked off with all the awards. In general, though, you come here for beige linen culottes and halter dresses cut on the loose, a splash of chintzy prints, easy trousers and sweaters, bush hats, and emerge looking as though you've just come out of Africa.

♕ **NORMA KAMALI, 11 W 56th St, NY 10019 ☎ (212) 957 9797.** Kamali does amazing things with T-shirting and sweatshirt material. She's one of Jackie Collins's faves: "I like her separates" and Eleanor Lambert finds her "most intriguing".

Some rather tacky pieces of late, a bit pastiche, a bit awkwardly proportioned, but when she's good she's terrific – racy and young. She's got a best for her swimwear. Princess Stephanie of Monaco admires them, and Lynne Franks, among others, thinks they're the best. *"In terms of innovation, I think the Norma Kamali swimsuits are fabulous. They're all-black, hi-tech and rubberized – it looks as if they've come from a car factory! They sum up the sensuality and the aggression at the same time"* (Benny Ong).

ADOLFO, 36 E 57th St, NY 10022 ☎ (212) 688 4410. Natty little Coco-inspired suits for day, feathers, ruffles, bows and sequins for night are what "our darling Dolf" (as he's known to besotted clients) has been doing for years and years. He designs more than anyone else for Nancy Reagan, possibly even does exclusive First Lady outfits. No 1 with the society molls because Nancy loves him. She is not alone: *"At the Adolfo show people make a point of wearing suit X. 9 women in the same suit – like a class! They all adore him and are so glad to give him credit for what he does. He is a darling man. Nearly 50, but always looks like a little boy. He adores his work, he lives his work, he never goes to anything. He has a pug dog ... They wear their suits for him. It's all knits and tweeds. Adolfo is more a continuation of the spirit of Chanel than Lagerfeld"* (Eleanor Lambert).

CAROLINA HERRERA, 19 E 57th St, NY 10022 ☎ (212) 355 3055. The society queen turned dress designer who turns out little luxuries for her sort of party. And snobbish little day suits for her sort of luncheon party. She's in the mould of the other big Americans and pretty accomplished.

DIANE VON FURSTENBERG, Sherry-Netherlands Hotel, 783 5th Ave, NY 10022 ☎ (212) 935 0470. *"At this point I would have to say that the best evening wear is mine! I have opened this very special shop at the Sherry-Netherlands Hotel in New York and evening wear is what I specialize in"* (Diane von Fürstenberg).

MARY McFADDEN, 264 W 35th St, NY 10001 ☎ (212) 736 4078. McFadden has the same strict haircut, saucer eyes and geisha complexion as Jean Muir. She produces completely different clothes, but with the same timeless quality. Most desirable McFaddens: Fortuny pleated pale and interesting dresses.

■ BEST STORES ■

These are New York's best stores. Those stores with branches in New York are listed in their city of origin.

♕ **BERGDORF-GOODMAN, 754 5th Ave, NY 10019 ☎ (212) 753 7300.** The most incredible window displays in the world, and an uppity clothes climate inside to match. Anouska Hempel loves shopping here, and so does Joan Burstein. The chairman's a former doorman from the old Bonwit-Teller (now defunct department store). *"Walking through the store is like psychiatric therapy, they buy so brilliantly"* (Jenny Gucci).

BLOOMINGDALES, 1000 3rd Ave, NY 10021 ☎ (212) 355 5900. A New York landmark almost a block wide. It has everything the other big stores have. Bruce Oldfield (who's choosy about his socks) thinks it's best in that department: *"Bloomingdales has the best ever selection of men's socks. It's BRILLIANT! I spent about $200 there on socks."* Mark Birley comes here for functional luggage. *"It's the best department store in the US"* (Lynne Franks).

HENRI BENDEL, 10 W 57th St, NY 10019 ☎ (212) 247 1100. Elegant and intimate, more inviting than the usual stone-faced department store. One of Anouska Hempel's favourites. It was here that Geraldine Stutz originated the "street of shops" idea with cobblestones, *indoor* windows, and individual boutiques within the store ... Why not have a *real* street of shops, you ask? This is *New York*, this is a *shopping experience*, that's why. Jean Muir's first stop, and best place, she votes, for hosiery: *"They make their own stockings, and thick opaque tights, navy ... and other colours."*

MACY'S, 151 34th St, NY 10001 ☎ (212) 695 4400. Used to be a rather slummy store good for kids' prezzies, till it was spanked up and given a new image in '76. Now there's 2 *million* sq ft (185,800 sq m) the Western world's biggest department store) of chi-chi in-store designer boutiques.

SAKS FIFTH AVENUE, 611 5th Ave, NY 10022 ☎ (212) 753 4000. New York's well-dressed women come here for the really smart clothes of famous European and American designers.

■ BEST SHOPS ■

♕ **LOEHMAN'S, 9 W Fordham Rd, NY 10468 ☎ (212) 295 4100.** There's nothing like Loehman's anywhere else in the world. If you can brave the Bronx, you can cash in on superb designer clothes at 50 per cent off.

BARNEY'S, 106 7th Ave, NY 10014 ☎ (212) 929 9000. Once a discount men's store, now booming chic. Very upmarket, very young; it's where all the art/design/music/ film people shop. New women's store in the adjacent building stacked with European design names.

CHARIVARI, 2307 Broadway, NY 10024 ☎ (212) 837 1424. *"If you want to know what's going on in fashion, Charivari is the place to look. Ultra-modern, trendy, the most important store in Manhattan"* (Michael Catz). Eleanor Lambert recommends it to the young as "avant-garde", Shari Belafonte-Harper goes there for sweaters. Mick Jagger and Jerry

Hall are regulars at Charivari Workshop on 81st St. Stylish, exclusive, well-edited batch of mainly European designers, men's and women's collections.

MARTHA, 475 Park Ave, NY 10022 ☎ (212) 753 1511. Successful, selective New York style. *The* store in NY for anyone who is anyone. Martha collects a pantheon of the top names: Bill Blass, Carolina Herrera, Valentino and Zandra Rhodes. Plus less expected finds; people come into the shop and sell. She also has Pat Kerr, who does antique lace wedding dresses. *"I have 2 of her lace dinner dresses. People buy things like that for the rest of their lives. She does huge weddings – some of the dresses are $30,000"* (Eleanor Lambert). Martha has just been knighted by the Italian government for her services to the Italian fashion industry.

RALPH LAUREN, 867 Madison Ave, NY 10021 ☎ (212) 606 2100. Newly-opened world's first designer department store, a Ralph-aelite's dream in an out-and-out French neo-classic mansion built at the turn of the century for Gertrude Rhinelander Waldo, and still rather homey in the grand idiom with a grand entrance, fireplace and Scarlett O'Hara staircase. Everything from wallpaper to those all-American super-classic rough-and-tough clothes, safari-esque savannah suits, bush shirts. Ralph's on to a bumper year, thanks to Meryl Streep and Robert Redford modelling the Great White Hunter fashion scene. He's Lynn Wyatt's No 2 American designer. Payton thinks Lauren's Polo line is very good, and Lord Lichfield thinks *"it's the best casual menswear in the world"*.

SUSANNE BARTSCH, 456A W Broadway, NY 10012 ☎ (212) 674 3370. At one time this was the only place in the *world* where you could find some of the most outrageous young London designers. Susanne gave many of them their big break (Body Map, Tom Binns) – she loves the punky end of New Romantic. Her poppy Disneyland of a shop, designed by Michael Kostiff, is still strong on the British extremities.

TRUMP TOWER, 725 5th Ave, NY 10022 ☎ (212) 832 2000. Mr Trump's shrine to shopping is 10 floors of chi-chi shops in a knockout setting of a 10-floor atrium with a Tarzanian waterfall that plunges dramatically down to oblivion beside the coffee shop on the ground floor. Brass rails everywhere, and salmon pink marble – floor, ceiling, walls, 10 storeys of it ... it's like the bowels of 5th Avenue.

BEST KNITWEAR

ZORAN, 214 Sullivan St, NY 10012 ☎ (212) 674 6087. Remember "uncluttered", "understated", "easy", "pared down" – the bywords of Amerian prêt-à-porter? We-e-ell Zoran is *the* ultimate in uninflected simplicity – the very zero line of underexaggeration. It has its problems: *"1 woman in Zoran looks great, 2 are boring"* (Eleanor Lambert). It is the very best of a pure, fabric-orientated look that has turned turkey on buttons, buckles, zips and bows. Everything is soft, easy, minimal (but *never* stark) and usually ivory, white, black, mottled grey in silks and cashmere. Pyjama pants, swans-down sweaters, leggings. The shop, in the same minimal mood, is converted from Zoran's old SoHo apartment. It's appointment only, 1-woman-at-a-time. Winter customers are given sleek leather mules when they walk in (Zoran doesn't want his high-gloss epoxy floor scuffed) and offered a warming draught of Stolichnaya (Zoran hails from eastern Europe). Marie Helvin thinks he's the world's best for cashmere, he's Vanessa de Lisle's fave American designer. The prices are also out of this world. *"It's simplicity itself, very laid back. But two squares of crêpe de Chine cost $300"* (Tomasz Starzewski).

LOTTE GABERLE, 22 Greenwich Ave, NY 10011 ☎ (212) 741 9285. A true original and very little known. Does marvellous one-off knitted things like a great cobweb coat, ribbed and ballooned into an ankle-length doublet with equally Elizabethan sleeves. Designs to order and sells out of stock. Every piece is individually coloured and knitted in linen, cotton, silk, cashmere, mohair and wool.

BEST SHOES

ROGER VIVIER, 965 Madison Ave, NY 10021 ☎ (212) 249 4866. This is the world's first and only Vivier shop – up till now Vivier has come to your feet via Christian Dior and other couturiers. All the shoes, bags and scarves are designed by the spry, ingenious 74-year-old Vivier. No more made-to-measure, but if you want a shoe in a different colour, give them a couple of months.

BASS WEEJUNS, at major department stores and shoe shops, are the original and only penny loafers. The New England set have a Preppy love affair with them.

SUSAN BENNIS/WARREN EDWARDS, 440 Park Ave, NY 10022 ☎ (212) 755 4197. Swanlike evening slippers, chintzy summer mules with fan-pleated fronts, scalloped fantasies in crisp, light shoe leather. Margaux Hemingway (whose preference is a barefaced foot) thinks they're *"very good"*. *"I buy my shoes from Susan Bennis/Warren Edwards ... They fit my foot. I have a narrow foot and a high arch and they fit perfectly. I like the styles and their boots. They would do made-to-measure, but I don't have it"* (Joan Severance).

VITTORIO RICCI, 645 Madison Ave, NY 10022 ☎ (212) 688 9044. Fab and pricey shoe store with footwork for both men and women. Stephen Jones's No 1 men's shoe: *"They're modern but very well made, like a couture shoe, but in a modern vein. Like a little slipper type."* The shop has its own designers and the shoes are fashioned in Italy.

SHOE SAVVY

The best person in the world to talk to about shoes is Diana Vreeland. Ask what she thinks about shoes and she replies, "*Oh, but that's about the most important thing in a woman's life! – First of all the soles have to be perfect. And the heels have to be absolutely perfect – so there's never a worn spot on them. And then you must keep them so beautifully, in trees. I mean a pair of shoes should be kept as if they were diamonds.*"

This is at one end of the scale and at the other is Margaux Hemingway who announced, "*Shoes? I'd rather not wear any.*" Shari Belafonte-Harper was less decisive about the whole thing: "*I live in Reeboks – most of the time, but lately I've been wearing different-coloured shoes at the same time – I mean two different shoes that match the outfit.*"

Mrs Vreeland, meanwhile, expounded the importance of always having them made to measure. "*I've always had my shoes made to measure for me in Paris or Rome. I've never had a foot problem.*"

BEST HATS

FRANK OLIVE, 134 W 37th St, 9th Fl, NY 10018 ☎ (212) 947 6655. Less headiness, more classiness: "*One of the most enduring milliners in the world. Makes beautiful, ladylike hats, very classic, elegant, and rich. And not that expensive*" (Pat Cantor).

MAEVE CARR, 66 W 38th St, 4th Fl, NY 10018 ☎ (212) 840 6613. Designs for Donna Karan and, with her own label, heads for whimsy. "*Very whimsical. I don't think hats should be taken very seriously any more. When you think of a hat in the Eighties, it's not a lady-out-to-lunch hat. Hats should have an element of wit and fun, which Maeve Carr's have*" (Aniko Gaal). Head hat hunters get them from Bloomingdales and Neiman-Marcus.

PATRICIA UNDERWOOD, 37 W 39th St, NY 10018 ☎ (212) 840 6934. British, but working in New York. "*The colours are always right, the shapes are always right. She often designs for other people's collections ... Calvin Klein, I think, and Perry Ellis ... They're stylish, never outrageous. The magazines use her a lot*" (Joan Burstein).

BEST LEATHER AND ACCESSORIES

LA CRACIA, 389 5th Ave, NY 10016 ☎ (212) 532 7414. Marvellous, wicked gloves. "*They specialize in gold and silver gloves. Amusing designs*" (Aniko Gaal). The charming Stephen de Petri does couture gloves and gauntlets for them, frogged, baroqued, fringed and encrusted.

T ANTHONY, 480 Park Ave, NY 10022 ☎ (212) 750 9797. "*All the women wear T Anthony pants. They were the first ones to do canvas suitcases – they really are beautiful*" (Eleanor Lambert). Their signature piece: black canvas with Cognac-coloured leather trim. "*Classic and light and lasts forever*" (Aniko Gaal).

JUDITH LIEBER, 20 W 33rd St, NY 10001 ☎ (212) 736 4244. For lah-di-dah handbags. "*The best ones are evening bags by JL. She's very well known, very expensive, $3,000. These are not day bags – crocodile evening bags*" (Eleanor Lambert).

BEST JEWELLERS

FRED LEIGHTON, 781 Madison Ave, New York 10021 ☎ (212) 288 1872. Murray Mondschein runs the best period jewellers in the world, for late 19th- and 20th-century well-wrought rocks. Devilish little earrings for under $1,000, but blockbuster jewels are what it's really all about here. Murray has already had some million dollar sales – if you escape without spending over $50,000 you've done yourself proud. At the time of going to press he's selling possibly the best piece of art nouveau jewellery ever: the serpent bracelet-ring of gold, opal, enamel and diamonds that Mucha designed and Fouquet made for Sarah Bernhardt. A snip at half a million dollars. Murray also has, by the way, a bijou collection of adornments once owned (but ever worn?) by Diana Vreeland (who has sold all her jewels: "I never wore them – where could you wear them today?").

ARTWEAR GALLERIES, 456 W Broadway, NY 10013 ☎ (212) 673 2000; ROBERT LEE MORRIS GALLERY, 409 W Broadway, NY 10013 ☎ (212) 431 9405. Very best for exactly what it says, pieces of art to wear. Robert Lee Morris owns both shops and does marvellously understated ornaments of his own, plus sleek statements by other artists. *"Robert Morris is a very special jewellery designer. Best in New York"* (Lynne Franks). Eleanor Lambert thinks they're best for "fake" (basically non-important pieces). *"The No 1 is Ted Muhling. He sells through Artwear. Very sculptural and simple pieces for both men and women"* (Stephen Jones).

A LA VIEILLE RUSSIE, 781 5th Ave, NY 10022 ☎ (212) 752 1727. Wartski's counterpart across the Atlantic, a fabulous cache of Russian works of art and antique jewels, particularly Fabergé fantasies.

"A person looks well if they carry themselves beautifully and if they extend their necks. Even the mannequins don't extend their necks, but Marella Agnelli still has the best neck in the world. In the world. With a good neck a good pullover and a good pair of pants you can go a long way" (DIANA VREELAND)

ANGELA CUMMINGS AT BLOOMINGDALES, 1000 3rd Ave, NY 10021 ☎ (212) 355 5900. *"A marvellous American designer. She uses mainly silver and gold"* (Aniko Gaal). A very sleek modern style. Geometric shapes with the most wonderful, completely smooth semi-precious inlays.

ERIC BEAMAN, 218 W 37th St, NY 10018 ☎ (212) 947 4791. Chic jeweller of the moment, designs bead curtain belts for Jasper Conran among other colourful waterfall pieces. *"Very creative in design. Uses unexpected material like beads. Really inventive"* (Aniko Gaal).

HARRY WINSTON, 718 5th Ave, NY 10019 ☎ (212) 245 2000. You come to the Grand Salon more for the stupendous stones than the designs. For huge, Liz Taylor-sized diamonds and gems. *"The best, the only decent one in NY"* (Vivienne Becker). The Petit Salon at Trump Tower has less grand, more practical pieces, silk passementerie with ruby and sapphire ornaments, and semi-precious eye-openers as well.

JAMES ROBINSON, 15 E 57th St, NY 10022 ☎ (212) 752 6166. Elegant East-side number. More like a miniature department store and they choose the VERY BEST period pieces from all over the world. James II, upstairs, has the best of more whimsical and amusing late 19th-century trinkets.

KEN LANE, 20 W 37th St, NY 10018 ☎ (212) 868 1780 The well-known costume jewellery man. *"He's wonderful, just wonderful. He is a perfectionist who understands the value and glory of decorative jewels."* (Diana Vreeland).

TIFFANY, 727 5th Ave, NY 10022 ☎ (212) 755 8000. If you like to breakfast on "make it big" real jewels by Paloma Picasso, as Eleanor Lambert does, Tiffany still has something for you. But it's not what it was, though the eggshell-blue boxes are still a status symbol. They also do silver abstract pieces by Elsa Peretti that are well worth wearing. Margaux Hemingway does: *"I like her smooth lines, it's kind of modern." "Very organic looking, and now much copied"* (Vivienne Becker). (Opening in London in autumn 1986.)

VERONIQUE CARTIER, at Fred Leighton, 781 Madison Ave, NY 10021 ☎ (212) 288 1872. Side by side with the Victoriana and art deco at Fred Leighton are ravishingly bejewelled modern pieces by Veronique, grand-daughter of *the* Louis Cartier. *"Someone who makes beautiful jewellery is a girlfriend of mine who happens to be the daughter of Claude Cartier. She makes very classical, elegant jewellery, but with an original twist"* (Catherine Oxenberg). Once sued by Cartier (now owned by a South African firm) for using her own name, Veronique fashions rubies, diamonds, mother-of-pearl and startling marriages of sapphire and black steel (more expensive than gold), and signs them VC for victory.

BEST LINGERIE

CALVIN KLEIN, 205 W 39th St, NY 10018 ☎ (212) 719 2600. Calvin Klein started it and his is still the best. *"The best underwear in the world is Calvin Klein's ... I go there for cotton knickers"* (Lynne Franks). The Y-front for women, the little vest, the minimal, no-nonsense pioneering guy-'n'-gal ambisexual look America loves. *"Modern and very good ... Calvin Klein is really great"* (Stephen Jones). *"It lets across a certain sense of sensuality, of success if you are wearing his underwear"* (Benny Ong).

ORA FEDER, 171 Madison Ave, NY 10016 ☎ (212) 532 9236. The most exclusive in the USA. Exquisite silken smoothies and peignoir sets in heavy, creamy silk. Very Jean Harlow, biased cuts and sensational fabrics. *"Very in tune with the times. By far the best. Sensational. They fill a gap"* (Aniko Gaal). *"All I like is silk pyjamas. I wear Ora Feder"* (Catherine Oxenberg).

WIFE & MISTRESS, 1042 Lexington Ave, NY 10021 ☎ (212) 570 9529. On the other side of underwear. Joan Severance buys here.

BEST MEN'S DESIGNERS

BIJAN, 699 5th Ave, NY 10022 ☎ (212) 758 7500. A phenomenon – see right.

CALVIN KLEIN, 205 W 39th St, NY 10018 ☎ (212) 719 2600. The world's sexiest jeans plus lean-'n'-mean leisurewear.

RALPH LAUREN/POLO, 867 Madison Ave, NY 10021 ☎ (212) 606 2100. The all-American hero look for boys with a fresh-faced, hometown expensiveness.

BEST MEN'S TAILOR

WILLIAM FIORAVANTI, 45 W 57th St, NY 10019 ☎ (212) 355 1540. America's best: Fioravanti's up there with the Europeans. 30 craftsmen hand-handle suits for US captains of industry (Fioravanti says his suits have a "power look").

BEST MEN'S SHOP

PAUL STUART, 350 Madison Ave, NY 10022 ☎ (212) 682 0320. *"They've got some good styles in clothes"* (Bob Payton). Classic, but with an upbeat, more fashion-conscious idea. The best braces.

"There's a fabulous sock shop on the West side that just sells socks – it's brilliant! Imagine going in to a huge shop floor to ceiling socks! Fabulous, fabulous shop ... Perry Ellis spots, checks, Calvin Klein stripes..." (BRUCE OLDFIELD)

BEST SHIRTS

PEC, 45 W 57th St, NY 10019 ☎ (212) 755 0758. Famed far and wide for handmade shirts of the best quality, with mother-of-pearl buttons. All the US top cats get theirs here; customers have included Yul Brynner, John Rockefeller, Cary Grant, Robert Montgomery and Aristotle Onassis – who always ordered a white crêpe de Chine dress shirt.

BROOKS BROTHERS, 346 Madison Ave, NY 10017 ☎ (212) 682 8800. The classic buttondown Oxford shirt that clothes America's back. Best of a standard – simple, unexpected, widely worn. *"In America, I go to Brooks Brothers"* (Bruce Oldfield). *"I've really gone off Brooks Brothers, they're just too conservative. There's no sense of humour about them"* (Bob Payton). For some people, it's impossible to be too conservative.

TOTTING UP THE COST OF BEING A BIJAN MAN

Just where do you start with a one-man marketing phenomenon? With $100,000 a month. That's how much, Bijan reckons, you need to earn to be dressed by him. More, much more, would come in handy, particularly if you feel frequent hankerings for the chinchilla bedspreads, $98,000 a throw, or the 4-piece crocodile luggage set for $75,000 or chinchilla-lined boots at $5,500 with matching cashmere coat (chinchilla-lined, by the way) at $28,000. *And* the first ever men's perfume, selling at $1,500 for 6 oz (170 g) in a Baccarat crystal bottle, each one of which is insured at Lloyds.

Mr Bijan's speciality is the practical married to the extravagant. His suits come in at about $2,200 – prêt-à-porter – but the bulletproof lining comes free. Clients include, he says, King Hussein II, King Juan Carlos, Pierre Trudeau, the Saudi princes, and, on the other side of influence, Roger Moore, plus Julio Iglesias, Sammy Davis Jnr, Marcello Mastroianni, Jack Nicholson.

The first shop is in Beverly Hills and the new extravaganza is in the old Gucci shop in New York (both by appointment only). Once past the white-gloved doorman, it's champagne and a Scarlett O'Hara staircase. Obsessive Bijan has the shop painted every 10 days to keep it swanky.

You can always tell a man in a Bijan shirt – the third button down is a different colour. And if you just can't get to 5th Avenue this week, send the 727, as one Middle Eastern royal family did, to pick up the man, his assistants and 62 trunks of immaculate conceptions, and fly *him* to *you*.

BEST TIES

A SULKA, 711 5th Ave, NY 10022 ☎ (212) 980 5200. Best not just for ties, but also for shirts and fabulous brocade dressing gowns. When it comes to ties they have die-for-it fabrics, brocades, straight silks, riotously covetable patterns. And they do a tie in 18 ct gold thread for show-offs at $125.

DE CASI, 37 W 57th St, 10th Fl, NY 10019 ☎ (212) 421 3585. Decked out Rex Harrison for *My Fair Lady*. Henry Stewart is now going on 83, still doing suits, but prefers to concentrate on life's little details: silk Windsor, 4-in-hand and bow ties.

BEST MEN'S SHOES

BELGIAN SHOES, 60 E 56th St, NY 10022 ☎ (212) 755 7372. Henri Bendel's nephew started this shop up when he sold Henri Bendel's. Shiny dandy dance pumps with grosgrain bows, and excellent for made-to-measure monogrammed velvet or suede slippers.

E VOGEL, 19 Howard St, NY 10013 ☎ (212) 925 2460. Has been trundling along since 1879, making shoes, but especially custom-made riding boots, for New York's biggest cowboys. Paul Newman gets his footful here.

Sober business and smarter dress shoes in French calf, ostrich, snakeskin – even elephant.

BEST MEN'S HATS

JAY LORD HATTERS, 30 W 39th St, NY 10018 ☎ (212) 221 8941. The only place to go, Stateside. Tom Wolfe, he of the flamboyant fedora, comes here, as do Richard Avedon, Joseph Papp, and Miles Davis – all cool cats, no stuffed shirts! All manner of headgear from top hats, bowlers and deerstalkers to 10-gallon cowboys and a few plucky women's hats, including the Groucho, for incipient Annie Halls.

WASHINGTON DC

BEST SHOPS

GARFINCKELS, 1401 F St, DC 20004 ☎ (703) 628 7730. All the usual crowd of European designers from Missoni to Lagerfeld and a huge fur salon. Best thing about it: the Personal Shopper Service. Career women adore it.

INGEBORG'S, 117 N Henry St, Alexandria, Virginia 22314 ☎ (703) 836 0079. Carriage trade. A by-appointment-only store with a string of top European designers and its own couture line made up in yummy European fabrics. Lots of regulars among the embassy staffs. Will bring things to your house for you to try on.

BOSTON

BEST STORE

CHARLES SUMNER, 16 Newbury St, MA 02116 ☎ (617) 536 6225. Bijou department store that considers itself a baby Bergdorf-Goodman. Valentino boutique, Donna Karan and a department specializing in Rayne shoes.

BEST SHOPS

ROBERTS-NEUSTADTER, 69 Newbury St, MA 02116 ☎ (617) 267 2063. A riot of Fendi furs for chilly nose-in-the-air but tongue-in-cheek customers. They designed and made a kiddie mink for a 2-year-old child and a matching fur coat for her poodle. "*The place to buy fur is the US. There are sub-zero temperatures there ... even the poorest person has sheepskins*" (Jenny Gucci).

NANCY DRESS

Nancy Reagan trumpets the Star-Spangled Banner in her every outfit – by all-American designers Adolfo, Bill Blass, Oscar de la Renta and Galanos. She buys about 60 new dresses a year (that's 20 more than the Princess of Wales) and is generally held up as the picture of well-dressed America. Eleanor Lambert, organizer of the Best-Dressed Lists, expounds: "*She is the person most expressive of American taste today. She is not clothes-crazy, but she knows the part clothes play in any life where you're seen. She's a Californian beauty. She thinks Californian. She's a wonderful example of wearing clothes the way they ought to be worn.*"

Nancy is not alone on the Best-Dressed pedestal. Her pals Lynn Wyatt, Evangeline Bruce, Ann Getty, Betsy Bloomingdale (who's hot for Continental chic – Yves Saint Laurent, Dior, Chanel) *et al* always zipping in and out of the Best-Dressed Lists. Clothes-conscious if not -crazy, they subscribe to the fashion trade paper *Women's Wear Daily* (*WWD*) as well as glitzy, fortnightly, social *W*. Their designers, too, are big society fare in New York, lionized, lauded and loved. It's very cool to have Bill Blass on your arm, draped like the suavest cashmere shawl.

"And this is good old Boston. The home of the bean and the cod. Where the Lowells talk only to Cabots and the Cabots talk only to God" (JOHN COLLINS BOSSIDY)

PRISCILLA THE BRIDE'S SHOP, 129 Newbury St, MA 02116 ☎ (617) 267 9070. Celeb wedding gowns worn up and down the country by such luminaries as Luci Baines Johnson, the Nixon girls, Tricia and Julie. Custom-made and hand-beaded.

SARA FREDERICKS, Copley Place, MA 02116 ☎ (617) 536 8766. High-class clothes for the carriage trade with good, old-fashioned service. Sara Fredericks is in her eighties and still buying for 8 stores, including one in Palm Beach. Beene, Blass, Lagerfeld, Valentino, and a team of fitters and alterers. Has a client list that goes all the way to Europe and S America.

CHICAGO

BEST SHOPS

ULTIMO, 114 E Oak St, IL 60611 ☎ (312) 787 0906. *The* upmarket designer hunting ground for fash-conscious men and women in Chicago. A clubby kind of store, and enough Sonia Rykiel, Lagerfeld, Jean Muir and Giorgio Armani to keep anyone happy. Good accessories, and an alteration department.

CITY, 213 W Institute Place, IL 60610 ☎ (312) 664 9581. The first in the area to carry Memphis and Philippe Starck furniture and their clothes are the wearable counterpart. Most of them are by Hino & Malee, a Japanese designer team based in Chicago. Check out their Joseph Tricot, men's clothes and Arai fabric from Japan ... a definite Nip in the air.

STANLEY KORSHAK; 940 N Michigan Ave, IL 60611 ☎ (312) 280 9520. A Chicago institution that started as a couture house 70-odd years ago and now still carries the all-American stylebusters, such as Oscar de la Renta and Bill Blass. Also dressy European imports: Krizia, Ferre, Ungaro.

BEST MEN'S CLOTHES

MARK SHALE, 919 N Michigan Ave, IL 60625 ☎ (312) 440 0720. *"Mark Shale is a good place for big guys like myself"* (Bob Payton). Further updates of the man-sized traditionals. Suits, sportscoats, more shaped than most American menswear, and colourful. A big alteration and tailoring service for big guys like Bob.

LOS ANGELES

BEST DESIGNERS

GALANOS ORIGINALS, 2254 S Sepulveda Blvd, West, CA 90064 ☎ (213) 272 1445. Winsome pixie with the most flared nostrils in fashion who produces chic, beautifully handcrafted, outrageously expensive clothes. *"Marvellous ... he's always been an ivory tower designer. He doesn't see why he should get rich – a rare point of view"* (Eleanor Lambert). But it's hard not to rake in the dollars at $30,000 a dress ... ready-to-wear (though the quality is superb with a back-up

SOAPIES AND SWEATIES

Soapies are the Joan Collinses and the Joan Collins look-alikes, the Carringtons, Colbys and female JRs that muscle in on the US party scene in sizzling gowns in every shade of pillar-box, sequined, beaded and embroidered to the eyebrows, made up to the nines, with Grand Canyon cleavages and coat-hanger shoulders that could knock a small man flying. LA is their centre of emanation. *"The characters in the soap operas are caricatures and the clothes are caricatures of fashion. They've had a good influence in a way. They've made people feel dressy and I suppose you'll have to credit them someday with bringing back evening clothes ... The good influences are countered by the bad"* (Eleanor Lambert). Soapies like clothes by Nolan Miller, Bob Mackie and Ellene Warren, who dresses Cher, Donna Mills and the real soap queens off-set.

The other side of LA is the extreme casualness of the sweaties: *"I'm really into oversized clothes that I stole from my dad"* (Shari Belafonte-Harper). This is the look of the swingy young things that slouch down Rodeo Drive, offspring of LA aristocracy (old stars), born in Tinsel Town with a celluloid strip in their mouths. *"The Rodeo Drive kids don't dress formally. Jeans with expensive tops – more brassy and gaudy ... it's swimming pool parties with cowboy boots"* (Nicholas Coleridge). What they wouldn't be seen dead in are the dressy day clothes of Europe. *"I never wear hats, coats, suits"* (Jackie Collins). Ideal LA is to be a sweatie by day, a soapie by night: *"I live in sweat shirts and jeans during the day, and then evening gowns at night. That's all you need to live in LA"* (Shari Belafonte-Harper).

alterations service and made to order for special customers). *"You could look at his clothes inside out and they're as beautiful on the inside as they are on the outside. It's wonderful that someone can keep going, creating beautiful clothes at this level and not get taken over, not get greedy"* (Joan Burstein).

Classic clothes in stupendous fabrics, all with pure silk lining – this is the Galanos speciality. Plus his beading, which is done by former costume beaders at MGM. (He started out designing costumes for Rosalind Russell in *Never Wave at a WAC.*) An uncompromising "petite" is his sample size: *"He's not interested in fat women. They have to be very thin and very fine-boned. It's a ladies' club at his show. He doesn't encourage direct selling so only his very special clients go … Nancy Reagan is very faithful to him"* (Eleanor Lambert). And Gloria Vanderbilt, Ann Getty, plus Arianna Stassinopoulos: *"He did my wedding gown, partly because he's Greek."*

NOLAN MILLER, 910 S Robertson Blvd, CA 90035 ☎ (213) 655 7110. Exclusive designer to the *Dynasty* set – on the set, and Candy Spelling's No 1 fave. Think Krystle-clear shoulder pads, think sex-and-sensation dressing, think "vulgar!" and you're thinking your way towards Nolan Miller. Upfront, full-frontal and for diehard sequin freaks.

BEST SHOPS

Rodeo Drive is the shopping street of the stars.

LINA LEE, 459 N Rodeo Drive, Beverly Hills, CA 90210 ☎ (213) 556 2678. Where the Shoulder Set go for their Montana pads. *"They have a lot of good Italian designers and a lot of French designers and a lot of American designers"* (Jackie Collins). Chanel, Azzedine Alaïa, to name but 2.

MAXFIELD, 8825 Melrose Ave, CA 90060 ☎ (213) 274 8800. Melrose Ave is for the younger, wilder, wet-behind-the-ears-but-cool crowd in LA. Maxfield doesn't beat about the bush – Yohji, Comme des Garçons, Alaïa, Jean-Paul Gaultier, Lagerfeld, Hamnett, Joseph, Rifat Ozbek.

BATTLE OF THE SHOULDER PADS

On the West Coast, where Nolan Miller designs solidly sequined evening outfits that follow the American footballer silhouette, pads mean power. *"I love padded shoulders,"* enthuses Catherine Oxenberg, dynastic beauty and Joan's *Dynasty* daughter, *"I need them, otherwise I just vanish into oblivion."* This is understandable when you spend all day with Joan and Linda, each with shoulders sharpened to a point (a point somewhere out to *here*). New York model Joan Severance, however, just can't see shoulder to shoulder with the Hollywood build-up. She is the voice of East Coast realism: *"As I don't have big shoulders, I can't wear big shoulder pads."* Meanwhile, out West, the rage for power pads has the whole of LA queuing up for Montana's restructured shoulders. Oxenberg feels instant relief in one of his wing-shouldered numbers, as does Jackie Collins, who dies for his *"leather jackets with huge shoulders"*. The last word must go to Diana Vreeland, *"I'm very against shoulder pads. I think they're perfectly terrible. They have no femininity, no allure, and, in fact, I think we should forget the whole thing."*

BEST LEATHER

NORTH BEACH LEATHER, 8500 Sunset Blvd, CA 90060 ☎ (213) 652 3224. Hot leathers, included a fab collection of strapless, lace up the back dresses in butter-soft, creamy-coloured skins. A lot of special orders for stars and rock bands.

BEST JEWELLERS

CARITTA, 411 N Rodeo Drive, Beverly Hills, CA 90210 ☎ (213) 271 7443. *"I have 2 rings I love by a designer called Pepi. Square, enamel rings"* (Shari Belafonte-Harper). All the glam Hollywood crowd gather here for jewels. Jackie Collins pops in here as well.

FRED JEWELLERS, 401 N Rodeo Drive, Beverly Hills, CA 90210 ☎ (213) 278 3733. *"The best jewellery, I would say, is from Fred on Rodeo Drive. They have incredible design, I recently bought something there like a gold zipper. It's a diamond and ruby heart and you can zip it up and down on a chain with a zipper. It's great"* (Jackie Collins).

BEST LINGERIE

FREDERICK'S OF HOLLYWOOD, 6610 Hollywood Blvd, CA 90028 ☎ (213) 466 8506. Where you go if you *really* like it trashy: Jackie Collins does. *"If you want to go over the top, you go to Frederick's. They've got all the wildest things if you want wild lingerie."* For really slumming it up: peek-a-boo peignor sets, bras with cutout nipples, crotchless knicks, slingback mules.

TRASHY LINGERIE, 402 N La Cienaga, CA 90048 ☎ (213) 652 4543. America doesn't do things by halves. Trashy Lingerie (definitely *not* trashy) has 8,000 ways to undress you in everything from Victoriana to leather. They specialize in incredibly soft, silky leather corselets, bras and bustiers. They used to get so many sightseers and tour buses stopping to ogle that you now have to be a member to get in – $20 a year. Kim Basinger peeled off their body wares in the steamy *9½ Weeks*.

SAN FRANCISCO

BEST STORES AND SHOPS

I MAGNIN, 135 Stockton St, CA 94108 ☎ (415) 362 2100. They now have 26 branches, but this is the largest and first with a broad sweep of designer clothes and sportswear. An exclusive Chanel in-store boutique, also Ungaro, Valentino. A phalanx of "personal shoppers" will organize your wardrobe for you, sometimes bringing entire collections to your house.

JESSICA McCLINTOCK BOUTIQUE, 353 Sutter St, CA 94108 ☎ (415) 397 0987. Frothy lace wedding dresses designed by the eponymous Jessica. She did the bridesmaid's outfits for Marie Osmond and Victoria Principal. Twenties-line lace sheaths and other showpieces.

WILKES BASHFORD, 375 Sutter St, CA 94108 ☎ (415) 986 4380. Mostly men's stuff, with beautiful and expensive suits and a funkier department of Gaultier, Basile and Matsuda. The new store's women's department (they've just moved to above address) is big on come-on-strong beaded evening wear and Zandra Rhodes frilled-to-be-here numbers for California-style parties. They have just built a bar on every floor

DALLAS

In America, you don't just go into a shop to buy something, you go to have an *experience.* Shopping malls like indoor cities of the future, complete with fountains and statues, cover acres of the American city. The department stores are stupendous – best for sales bargains in the world. If something doesn't sell within a short, limited period, it goes on the sales rack and the price plummets ruthlessly week by week. It's all part of the hustle-hustle-bustle and the fine art of Consumerism.

The Dallas Galleria is the big, fashionable mall for serious spenders with 163 shops.

BEST STORE

NEIMAN-MARCUS, 1618 Main St, TX 75201 ☎ (214) 741 6911. Known in the US as "Needless-Markup". They do a broad band of designer things from Fendi and Versace to Chanel and Valentino, and Bottega leatherettes. Famous for "his-and-hers" Christmas pressies: in 1985 this was the "his-and-hers diamonds" that sold for $2 million the pair. *"The best department store in Texas"* (Lynne Franks).

BEST SHOP

LOU LATTIMORE, 4320 Lover's Lane, TX 75225 ☎ (214) 368 8915. Great for clothes: Donna Karan, Chanel, Geoffrey Beene, Montana and their own exclusive-design shoe boutique.

BEST JEWELLER

WHITESIDE, 7805 Inwood, TX 75209 ☎ (214) 358 0089. Fine pieces and art objects in precious and semi-precious stones, all custom-designed, many after Fabergé or in rococo high spirits. One woman had a 30 inch (76 cm) tall ivory camel for which they made a ruby and sapphire encrusted saddle, another local whacko came in with elk's teeth she wanted set in 18ct gold to wear as a ring.

CANADA

MONTREAL

“Canada is very, very chic. Oscar de la Renta will send a trunk show to Edmonton and everything will be sold. The mixture of English, French and American influences is just right” (JOYCE DAVIDSON)

BEST DESIGNERS

JEAN CLAUD POITRAS, 400 De Maison Neuve, Suite 1150, H3A1L4 ☎ (514) 849 8331. Going from strength to strength and dressing Mrs Mulroney, the President's wife. *“He has a lot of style, a lot of taste, he always makes beautiful coats. Very classy”* (Beverley Rockett).

SERGE SENECHAL AND REAL BASTIEN at “SERGE AND REAL”, 1456 Sherbrooke St, H3G1K4 ☎ (514) 282 0444. *“Custom-made clothes for wealthy women, the equivalent of couture in Canada”* (Beverley Rockett). 2 designers who work together on the grandiosely beautiful. Real started out as theatrical costumier, now he brings a sense of theatre to chi-chi Montreal. Mainly couture with a small prêt-à-porter line, and dressing the likes of the Governor-General and the top political females. *“We've worked for so many people, for young, for old, for in-between, for movie stars, for political people, for millionaires – I think by now we should know how to dress a woman”* (Real Bastien). *“Very elegant evening wear”* (Sondra Gotlieb).

WAYNE CLARK at EATON'S, 677 St Catherine St, H3B3Y6 ☎ (514) 284 8411 and leading stores. Well known as Canada's inventive edge on evening with fly-by-nights from ruffled and magnificent high society get-up to neat little cocktail shifts. *“His evening clothes are very wearable”* (Bernadine Morris). *“He's great, does elegant Joan Collins; very sexy, very, very feminine, alluring dresses. I have, for example, this deep maroon chiffon, off-the-shoulder dress – like a modern-day Juliet”* (Joyce Davidson).

“Has been designing exclusive evening wear for the last 40-odd years, but I believe I know what people want to wear on the street” (Wayne Clark). Consequently, here come Wayne's daytime lavishments, jackets in Japanese leathers (“because they are the most gorgeous”), bold-patterned little suits where the drama is all in the interplay of colour …

“He's original, very distinctive. You can look at a Wayne Clark and recognize it, which is more than you can say for a lot of designers” (Beverley Rockett).

> **Best Street**
>
> In what were once the stately homes of rich colonials on *Sherbrooke Street*, high fashion now jostles with smart-art galleries and fancy antique joints. Famous for both its haute cuisine and haute couture.

BEST STORES AND SHOPS

HOLT RENFREW, 1300 Sherbrooke St, H3G1H9 ☎ (514) 842 5111. The most beautiful shop in Canada. Lyrical art deco in the old heart of Montreal. Arnold Scaasi adores it. Very upmarket, classy fashion store with a very crisp and laudable designer selection that is wise to the news in European fashion. Prémonville et Dewarin, ultra-new pair of hot French designers, are here alongside well-established names like Ferre, Lagerfeld, Montana, Armani, beautiful things by Alaïa, charming knits by Joseph Tricot, plus Donna Karan. Oodles of kittenish Fernando Sancho lingerie. Of native Canadians they sell Alfred Sung and Jean Claud Poitras. *“I always go to Holt Renfrew, there's one in every city, very dependable and very good”* (Sondra Gotlieb).

EATON'S, 677 St Catherine St, H3B3Y6 ☎ (514) 284 8411. Old-fashioned, family-owned department store with a strong line in the top Europeans: Soprani, Montana, Chloë, Féraud, Ferre, Valentino and the gang. A fruity Fortnum & Mason sort of atmosphere with aeons-old shop assistants attending to your needs like geishas, and a famous bargain basement where designer togs are slashed to half price in 6 months; happy hunting ground for Pierre Trudeau, who is always skulking there, and other richies.

LES CREATEURS, 1442 Sherbrooke St, H3G1K4 ☎ (514) 284 2102. A really brave and characterful wonderland of wit – Jean-Paul Gaultier – and fit – Azzedine Alaïa – with further distinctive beauty from Versace's meshed metal, new Japan in the shape of Junko Koshino, and the spaciness of Jean Charles de Castelbajac. Avant-garde, strong and sure-refreshing antidote to monotonous businesswoman chic.

TORONTO

BEST DESIGNERS

♔ **ALFRED SUNG, 55 Avenue Rd; M5V2T3 ☎ (416) 968 8688/365 0330.** Best Canadian for easy, go-ahead separates in pared-away style. *“Alfred Sung does very good separates that are on the international level. They don't look Canadian, they don't look French, they don't look American – they just look nice. He puts colours together well”* (Bernadine Morris).

There's an echo of Armani ideals with a loosened sense of cut. Sung does boxy jackets in lightweight tweeds, slick little skirts, grey and black jersey tunics, *“the necklines always hit the right bones”* (Joyce Davidson).

For the high-profile career woman who wants a fast turnover in upmarket, complementary pieces. *“Alfred Sung is really the one, a brilliant tailor; I wear a lot of his things. To understand Alfred you have to see him. He wears great, baggy white silk pants, a big shirt and big belt. He's original. You don't look like anyone else when you wear his stuff. While everyone else is copying Chanel and Adolfo you look as if you are doing something very interesting on your own. It's sexy* and *elegant – you don't look as though you've just come out of the Hunt Club"* (Joyce Davidson). *"His daytime wear is very good for travelling for the high style working woman"* (Sondra Gotlieb).

CLOTHESLINES, Bernard McGee and Shirley Wickerbrod, 50 Bloor St W, M4W1A1 ☎ (416) 920 9340. Very up-and-coming husband and wife team with a fresh, clever sense of what works. *"They are* very *good, excellent, most famous for their trenchcoats. They don't bother trying to be trendy, they just keep making their versions of the classics – which is not all that classic"* (Beverley Rockett). *"They are really like 'wow'! They'll take an Armani-type suit and make it in gold lamé"* (Joyce Davidson).

MAGGIE REEVES, 108 Cumberland St, M5R1A6 ☎ (416) 921 9697. She's been dressing the rich and famous in well-turned gladrags for 25 years. Romantic and swish tailoring – she used to dress Vivien Leigh and now does sumptuaries like Ernest Borgnine's wife and draped Canada's prima ballerina Karen Kain as a modern Venus for her wedding. *"Expensive evening wear made with beautiful European fabrics"* (Beverley Rockett). *"I have a lot of her clothes, she's proper couture. If you get fatter, she makes it fatter"* (Sondra Gotlieb).

WINSTON KUNG, Winston Boutique, 158 Cumberland St, M5R1A8 ☎ (416) 924 8837. 16 years of concocting couture for Canada's noovs and Old Guard. Beautifully civilized clothes, especially the queenly gala and wedding numbers. He's a super-realist who designs with the client and the occasion in mind. *"Lovely clothes for society ladies. He and Maggie Reeves are the couture of Toronto"* (Beverley Rockett).

Best Street

Although stridently modern, glossy and glassy *Bloor Street* runs a close second, *Hazleton Lane* boasts the best European designer shops from Saint Laurent to Givenchy, Lagerfeld and Chloë, each in their own mini-Hall of Fame, plus Alfred Sung.

BEST STORES AND SHOPS

CREEDS, 45 Bloor St W, M4W1A4 ☎ (416) 923 1000. One of those old Canadian institutions, family-owned now for 3 generations. Creeds started out 70-odd years ago as a furrier of note and still do marvellous knee-deep furs that fans flock from all over N America for. *"In Canada a fur coat is a necessity, everyone has their secret furrier. Creeds have a wonderful fur section"* (Sondra Gotlieb).

Designer-wise, they have the slink to go with mink: Krizia and Valentino from Italy, Chloë, Vickie Tiel, Chanel and Ungaro from France. And they run the Sonia Rykiel, Ungaro and Krizia boutiques in town.

HOLT RENFREW, 50 Bloor St, M4W1A1 ☎ (416) 922 2333. An ultra-contemporary encore to the art deco palace in Montreal. The Toronto store, in stride with the mood of the city, is brand new, blazoned with glass and marble. *"the newest, the most good looking and the biggest in the street"* (Bonnie Brooks Young, Vice President).

IRA-BERG, 1510 Yonge St, M4T1Z6 ☎ (416) 922 9100. A Canadian cult that's been around for ever, now run by Michael Berg, grandson of the original Ira. It's newly renovated this year. Find Ungaro Parallèle, Genny, Byblos and Adrienne Vittadini here.

VANCOUVER

BEST SHOPS

BOBOLLI, 2776 Granville St, V6H3J3 ☎ (604) 736 3458. Opened this spring to a lah-di-dah press show with ice sculptures and champagne – the poshest nook in town. It's about *lifestyle* – clothes are minimal on the scene. Instead, eyes focus on the gargantuan ceramic dalmatian from Italy, a rare Chinese vase stuffed with jewellery, and furniture-cum-sculpture. A polished terracotta floor and leather sofa in radical plum make one want to move in immediately: instead it's home to Max Mara, Sports Max, I Blues, Della Roveres sweaters, Pollini costume prinkery, and other top, together Italian lines.

EXQUISITE BOUTIQUE LTD, 780 Park Royal, V7T1B9 ☎ (604) 922 5211. Exclusive little shop lorded over by Peggy Chroust, who shrewdly never stocks more than 1 of anything. She makes trips to Europe to pick up beaded and ruffled evening glamour (2 out of 3 of the ball gowns that graced the evening eventfulness for Charles and Diana were bought from Madame Chroust). Also a lot of little suits, silk dresses by Louis Féraud.

GEORGE STRAITH'S, 900 W Georgia St, V6C2W6 ☎ (604) 685 3301. One of the classiest shops in Vancouver. Doppelganger of Liberty's or Harrods: Liberty prints, Bally shoes – nostalgic of Old England, plus Sybil Connolly clothes from Ireland, beautiful mossy handknits, Hermès, Hardy Amies for men, fine French lingerie for women. Classic bests of Europe. *"I don't want to go to heaven when I die, I want to go to George Straith's"* (Kay Alsop).

Best Street

"Right now Robson Street *is the most exciting. We've got fashion from all over the world in a 3-block area"* (Kay Alsop).

AUSTRALIA

BEST DESIGNERS

★

1 ROBERT BURTON, Sydney
2 KATIE PYE STUDIO, Sydney
3 JENNY KEE, Sydney
4 LINDA JACKSON, Sydney
5 VANESSA LEYONHJELM, Melbourne

SYDNEY

BEST DESIGNERS

ROBERT BURTON, 104 Bathurst St, NSW 2000 ☎ (02) 267 2877. Australia's answer to couture, in wearable, play-it-down form. *"My favourite designer in Australia. His cut and his materials are very good. And he will design for you if you want"* (Patricia Coppleson). Also now does ready-to-wear.

KATIE PYE STUDIO, 89–97 Jones St, Ultimo, NSW 2007 ☎ (02) 212 1688. *"The most creative designer, I think, is Katie Pye. She is very clever. She's a great talent, and she's tremendously underestimated here. It's such a small market that she really would never be able to extend herself fully here"* (Nerida Piggin). Brave and beautiful clothes that re-proportion the body, loose and wide on top, draping, or tying up like origami. She always changes and stays ahead of the others.

LINDA JACKSON, 177 William St, PO Box 207, Kings Cross, NSW 2011 ☎ (02) 331 6911. Arty-smarty clothes here. The printed and sometimes hand-painted fabrics are a dream (Aussies have a talent for impressionistic printing). Jackson produces lovely colours – blue-purple, dulled silver, hot desert paint splashes. It's all in the cloth, shapeliness and cutting come second.

CARLA ZAMPATTI, 435 Kent St, NSW 2000 ☎ (02) 264 8244. Zampatti has the Australian fashion scene wrapped up with her lyrically draped jersey and silk evening dresses and breezy day clothes. This is real-life wardrobe-building – very laid-back, but stylish. Olivia Newton-John's fave and a rave right round the continent.

GEORGE GROSS, Viva, 19–27 Cross St Plaza, Double Bay, NSW 2028 ☎ (02) 322 485. *"George Gross does very elegant, subtly sexy, feminine clothes. Off-the-peg but very nice"* (Susan Renouf). George Gross has said that he likes making things that make women feel female, not feminine, but female – sexy and sensuous. His evening wear is a bit over the top, typically with Linda Evans bosom plumbline and knockover shoulders. The daywear, however, is less strident.

STUART MEMBERY, 188 Chalmers St, Surry Hills, NSW 2010 ☎ (02) 319 2766. Stuart *"I've never designed anything tight in my life"* Membery is a biggie here. Rather stylized clothes that play on an East meets West theme, but end up very West of somewhere. He designs for women and men and he's into everything, including shoes and hats. He shows 4 summer collections and gets all his best ideas on aeroplanes (so he says). Olivia Newton-John sports his skirts.

TRENT NATHAN, 129a Cathedral St, Woolloomooloo, NSW 2011 ☎ (02) 357 3288/3334. He's been designing for 25 years, and is still getting the image dead right. His ideal woman has a bang-up-to-the-minute edge with understated innuendo. Great tweeds dolled up with an Aussie sexiness, never the tweeded-out, sexless Sloane.

BEST STORES AND SHOPS

DAVID JONES, Elizabeth St, NSW 2000 ☎ (02) 266 5544. An edited and wide-ranging collection of homegrown and foreign-label clothes, and fab menswear department in the Market St branch across the road. It's the Aussie Harrods and has undergone a multi-million dollar facelift. They had to buy an Italian mountain top in order to obtain the marble they wanted. The Food Hall is where you stock up for post-shopping beanfeasts. Also for creamy silk and satin undies from home and away, plus goodies straight from America's Neiman-Marcus stores.

RHONDA PARRY, 19 Cross St, Double Bay, NSW 2028 ☎ (02) 320 584. Dressing for the Eighties summed up in 1 small but big-thinking shop that has the perfect, gloriously minimalist formula –

"Australians do casual fashion really well, but they fall short on elegance" (MICHAEL PARKINSON)

Best Street

Double Bay is where the toffs shop, and *Cross Street* is the best bit of Double Bay. *"Double Bay is the top shopping area in Australia, the smartest showplace. It's more* interesting, *with lots of outdoor eating and little arcades. You can buy everything – at a price"* (Elise Pascoe).

"As long as I'm close to nature I'll always be inspired. In Australia, we are guided by nature always; the sun makes you want to wear strong colours. My whole thing is earth and colour, and earth means every shade of opal. I just walk out into the bush and there is so much colour happening set against this extraordinary sky. That outback easy look is fabulous: little boxer shorts in my prints, big slouchy Hawaiian shirts, worn with a Drizabone, fantastic cowboy hats, R M Williams boots – I love wearing all of these things with my clothes" (JENNY KEE)

Issey Miyake plus Azzedine Alaïa plus Yohji Yamamoto – which adds up to the most exclusive fashion shop for the best-dressed. Jap accessories to go with, but the point is the sophisticated boom-boom of the stunningly stark clothes. Intellectual wear.

WORN OUT WEST-RANCHO DE LUXE, 94A Oxford St, Paddington, NSW 2021 ☎ (02) 331 7191. Owned by the well-rounded character Graham Webb: *"He's the most stylish man I know in Australia. He's tall, suave, he's lived in Europe for a long time. He's got a natural flair for design, a great eye for what suits him, and what suits other people."* (Nerida Piggin).

Style-king Webb does a unique and knockout line in Forties and Fifties filmic nostalgia. He buys in secondhand period cowboy kit from the American Old West. Vintage John Wayne, Magnificent Seven boots, spurs, denim and 10-gallon hats. It's Rockabilly, it's James Dean, it's Annie Get Your Gumboots. Not surprisingly, it's the only emporium of its kind in the continent, selling to toughboy rock bands like Australian Crawl, plus film-stars such as Greta Scacchi.

BEST KNITWEAR

JENNY KEE at FLAMINGO PARK, 2nd Fl, 102 Strand Arcade, George St, NSW 2000 ☎ (02) 231 3027. *"The most interesting knitwear designer in the world … really fantastic designs, very much for the summer. Very bright and strong."* (Lynne Franks). *"I admire Jenny Kee as a graphic artist … she's probably my favourite designer in Australia"* (Prue Acton). She's an icon of originality with stupendous, bold, rhythmic patterns in jungle colours. Her fabric prints on cotton and silk are just as dynamic. Best leggings ever.

DORIAN SCOTT'S AUSTRALIAN FASHION DESIGNERS, 105 George St, The Rocks, NSW 2000 ☎ (02) 274 090. Dorian herself knits up fine merino classics but is even better known as the forcing-house for young Aussie talent. Widely known ex-protégées include Jenny Kee and Linda Jackson, and her latest stock of embryonics starts with Maureen Fitzgerald, whose "armadillo" knitted coat hangs in the Melbourne Art Gallery, and Libby Peacock. Mint-new: Ruby Brilliant, who is just that, Christine Wilkes and Eleanor Laytham, who all do one-offs.

BEST SWIMWEAR

SPEEDO KNITTING MILLS, 269 Pacific Highway, Artarmon, NSW 2064 ☎ (02) 435 211. The solid gold Olympic medal special and the world's best sporting second skin is native Australian. Speedo launched 1,000 swimmers in 1929 with the deathless "Speed on in your Speedo" campaign. They are wonderful for serious swimmers, do beautiful straightforward but shape-conscious maillots, and also 2-pieces with a finger on the fashion pulse. Paula Yates swims in a Speedo, and so do an endless list of sports stars.

BEST SHOES

RAYMOND CASTLES SHOES, 7 Knox St, Double Bay, NSW 2028 ☎ (02) 327 3864. A fab shoe store chock-a-block with designer toelines like Charles Jourdan, and their own lines, which are carefree designer copies, just as nice and half the price.

BEST HATS

PETER JAGO, Flat 4, 19 Dellview St, South Bondi, NSW 2026 ☎ (02) 300 0492. He tailors a fine head. *"He does all the hats for my shoes. I've even got him making hats for Lady Fairfax. Judy Hirst wore one of his to the Melbourne Cup. He really is brilliant. He has a collection of over 200 hat pins all dated"* (Robert Burton).

MORAY MILLINERY, 306 Strand Arcade, George St, NSW 2000 ☎ (02) 233 1591. The best milliner in Sydney and one of the best in Australia. *"If you want a* Gone With The Wind *hat go to David. He's a very clever man"* (Elise Pascoe).

BEST JEWELLERS

ROX GEMS AND JEWELLERY, 31 Strand Arcade, George St, NSW 2000 ☎ (02) 232 7828. The best accessory excitement in Australia, and one of the world's best places for gilding the most fashionable ears. *"The best fashion jewellery in Australia"* (Lynne Franks). Spectacular costume counterfeit, Jezebel jewels and other outrageous ornament, all the way up to gold and diamonds. Tina Turner, Culture Club, David Bowie and Olivia Newton-John have all been bejewelled at Rox.

TONY WHITE, 52 Victoria St, Potts Point, NSW 2011 ☎ (02) 358 5467. *"The best women's jewellery in Australia"* (Kym Bonython). Beautiful, purist and wearable *objets d'art.*

GLASS ARTISTS GALLERY, 118b Windsor St, Paddington, NSW 2021 ☎ (02) 328 6013. Wonderful spare slivers of glassy-eyed ornamentation, by a small but sleek group of extremely modern, artists. Avant-garde, restrained but not overstrained.

BEST MEN'S DESIGNERS

HARRY THURSTON, 404 Oxford St, Paddington, NSW 2021 ☎ (02) 334 153. A real character and: *"He's the best Australian menswear designer"* (Nerida Piggin). Harry does an easy-breezy Italianate silhouette – sexy and bang-up-to-the-minute – with a subtle and highly developed colour sense (lavenders and greys, for example). The suits are mainly one-offs.

BEST MEN'S CLOTHES

RICHARD HUNT, 107 Pitt St, NSW 2000 ☎ (02) 232 6633. Sydney's burgeoning population of bow-tying connoisseurs (a strange anomaly in sportswear city) come here for little beauts. It's a shop for the pros – pre-tied bows are frowned on, but there are a few ready-mades for the perennially sticky-fingered. *"For classical men's clothes, you can't go wrong at Hunt's"* (Nerida Piggin).

TRELLINI MENS WEAR, 233 Pitt St, NSW 2000 ☎ (02) 264 6498. This is *the* manful trendspot, and boy, does it have clients ... from Billy Connolly to Sting to Gough Whitlam in outrageous mood, to Judy Davis. 100 per cent styleproof imported designer fandango, Comme des Garçons, Katharine Hamnett, Gaultier, Panchetti, Momento Due (great knits) ... it's all hot and ready to go, except the shirts, which are made to measure under their own label. Robert Burton recommends.

CHRIS HAND MADE SHIRTS, 4a Tank Steam Arcade, 175 Pitt St, NSW 2000 ☎ (02) 231 6094. For just what it says. They're well known and well worth wearing. Robert Burton recommends: *"You can have a shirt handmade, so it's a button-down collared shirt and yet big enough in the body so you can move about in it."*

FIVE WAY FUSION, 205 Glenmore Rd, Paddington, NSW 2021 ☎ (02) 331 2828. *"Beautiful imports for men"* (Nerida Piggin). *"Where to get your Cerruti suit"* (Robert Burton). For a shot in the arm of European up-style dressing. Zegna and Italians in particular, this is the place.

J H CUTLER, 33 Bligh St, NSW 2000 ☎ (02) 232 7351. *"We do an old English-style suit,"* says John Cutler proudly. John Cutler is fourth generation in the biz and doing a suit that is the Aussie equal of Savile Row in a land bereft of men of the cloth. Cutler also does a roaring trade with NZ upper-crust hungry for a decent pair of trousers.

JOHN LANE, 41 Knox St, Double Bay, NSW 2028 ☎ (02) 327 6198. Lane started at Hunt's and is now bringing a smart slice of Europe to the Aussies. *"Best for shirts. Also where you'd get your Hermès and Gucci ties, and good ready-to-wear men's suits"* (Patricia Coppleson). They stock Etienne Aigner, Cerruti, Fila sportswear, and Tacchini. Lane is for the classics and everyone ends up here: Michael Parkinson, Michael York, Gough Whitlam, Robert Sangster, Alan Bond, the newspaper Fairfaxes and more.

THE SQUIRE SHOP, 409 New South Head Rd, Double Bay, NSW 2028 ☎ (02) 327 5726. They edit down an eclectic bunch of the international and local designers to a few well-chosen pieces from designers such as Kenzo and Betty Jackson. At the back they have a cache of women's designer clothes, such as Jasper Conran and Kenzo. For men, they also make shirts and suits to measure. Tony Greig declares: *"There's only one place in Sydney to buy clothes and I'm a very good judge of that because I'm not easy to fit and that's the Squire Shop in Double Bay. And Tony Yeldham is the best salesman I've ever met ... if he can't fit you, he makes the clothes. He'll charge me $95 to make a shirt and do it in 2 days – it's Hong Kong treatment in Double Bay."*

MELBOURNE

BEST DESIGNERS

VANESSA LEYONHJELM, 382 High St, Armadale, VIC 3143 ☎ (03) 511 824. A good thing's happening to Australian fashion. Leyonhjelm does made-to-order with a rare breed of taste. Out of a Pandora's box imagination come beautifully appliquéd, rouléed and embroidered silk taffeta ballgowns, lavishly inventive coats, gauntlets, and swooping hats and mask-caps. A shining talent we'll hear more of.

ADELE PALMER, 671 Chapel St, S Yarra, VIC 3141 ☎ (03) 240 0611. Palmer's keynote is an insouciant style. People come here for casual printed cottons, the sportswear that Michael Parkinson so approves of, and the best jeans in Australia: Jag. All the American film-star tough guys like Redford and Newman wear Jag – and Cher and tough cookie Lauren Bacall as well.

DESBINA COLLINS, 1st Fl, 443 Little Collins St, VIC 3000 ☎ (03) 675 193. Drop dead evening oomph here in the shape of structured, jewel-coloured silks and taffetas. The best fly-by-night clothes are Desbina's. She lets fabulously constructed form do the talking and she knows when not to add unnecessary detail. Sticklers for form fall for her bouffant hip panels sharpened to wicked points, off-the-shoulder bows some 4 ft (1.2m) wide, and leg-o'-mutton sleeves big enough to keep a brood of baby wallabies in.

PRUE ACTON, 12 Bridge Rd, Richmond, VIC 3121 ☎ (03) 429 4122. She's been awarded an OBE and *"she is an original Australian motivator in fashion designing"* (Nerida Piggin). Susan Renouf notes that she *"designs good wearable clothes"* Acton is good for designer basics, and for plentiful, monotone appliqués.

BEST SHOPS AND STORES

FIGGINS DIORAMA, Collins St, VIC 3000 ☎ (03) 654 1744. Australia's best store (see box).

" Most of the best-dressed women in Australia are in Melbourne " (NERIDA PIGGIN)

EMME BOUTIQUE, 507 Chapel St, S Yarra, VIC 3141 ☎ (03) 241 5116. Best imported silks, cottons and linens from Europe and a fat fash file of Jean-Paul Gaultier (appeals to Aussie fun-loving exhibitionism), Dorothée Bis, Bobo Kaminsky, Nigel Preston.

GEORGES, 162 Collins St, VIC 3000 ☎ (03) 630 411. Genteel Australian exponents of *Are You Being Served* culture, where Miss Maree Hopkins has sold suits and coats for 40 years and Mrs Nancy Balding has reigned regal over the European mega-designers for many a fruitful season. The customers are equally dyed-in-the-wool diehards of Old Style Elegance. They come in search of a particular assistant, whose absence will cause them to postpone a purchase to some other day. The loos are a paradisal vision with free telephones, old sofas, magazines, flowers, tinkling chandeliers and an annexe for baby changing. Lagerfeld, Valentino, Saint Laurent, Ungaro, Montana, Yamamoto, Kenzo, Sonia Rykiel and Liberty scarves from London, plus musical ensembles of bow-tied violinists on the ground floor.

IN FULL FIG

"Figgins Diorama is the best store in the whole wide world. The look of the store, the beauty, the luxury. There is no store in the world, not even in Paris, that can match Figgins" (Lillian Frank). Relentlessly fashionable, pristinely beautiful, Figgins – *"I thought it was a new bowel disease"* (Dame Edna Everage) – has a post-modern atrium splicing through layers of designer shoplets, each individually designed, often by the fashion designer's chosen interiorist. Lagerfeld's is a stylish shoebox, restrained by Andrée Putman to black and grey with piquant touches of blue. Figgins has 'em all: Alaïa, Lagerfeld, Ungaro, Ferre, Versace, Chloë, Armani, Laura Biagotti, Issey Miyake. Carry it home in a status bag or have it delivered by their custom-built conker-coloured Rolls-Royce Phantom 6.

For the last word, Piggin on Figgins: *"Figgins Diorama have the best accessories in Australia. They have the most beautiful handbags I have ever seen."*

Best Street

Toorak Road is Melbourne's showcase, especially the South Yarra stretch with chi-chi little foreign designer stores nestling among chi-chi little Australian ones – Acton, Nathan and Weiss are all here for starters.

LE LOUVRE, 74 Collins St, VIC 3000 ☎ (03) 631 600. Very upmarket place to hoover up the best in French, English and Italian fashion with glitterbug evening wear and lavish wedding ensembles.

SABA, 131 Bourke St, VIC 3004 ☎ (03) 636 176. Amid on-line visual input from fash videos of the European collections, you can buy Yamamoto, Junko Sagawa (Aussies love her), Matsuda, Joseph Tricot, Saba's own clothes, and now Jasper Conran, too.

STAGGERS DIFFUSION, 37 Toorak Rd, S Yarra, VIC 3141 ☎ (03) 267 7850. Surreally named hideout of ex-Biba Queen, Barbara Hulanicki. From here she sells weird and wonderful one-of-a-kind make-up, plus a sharp line of latests: Issey Miyake, Jap and Italian shoes, Joseph, Saba and her own line.

BEST SHOES

EVELYN MILES, Shop 1, Tok-H Centre, 459 Toorak Rd, Toorak, VIC 3142 ☎ (03) 241 5844. The best women's shoes. European designer shoes, starting with Azzedine Alaïa (whose shoes are just as smashing as the rest of his body dressing), as well as Montana, Walter Steiger, Versace, Stephane Kelian, Dior, Valentino ... and the list goes on. *"Evelyn Miles is the biggest shoe store in the world! Where else could you sell some of the world's tartiest shoes at the most exorbitant prices?"* (Robert Burton).

McCLOUD'S, 120 Queen St, VIC 3000 ☎ (03) 673 386. Wallflower shop that looks like something undecorated (unwisely) since the Thirties. But it's a stomping ground for English, Italian and sturdy German shoes in kid and hand-tooled leather for the footwise, pound-foolish gourmet.

BEST HATS

RONALD BERNARDE, 66 Toorak Rd, S Yarra, VIC 3141 ☎ (03) 266 2890. A really wonderful harbinger of Hats to Australia, with a finger in every porkpie. Bernarde designs and makes his own bonnets, and imports a discriminating band of bests from abroad: Stephen Jones, Jean Berthet, Chloë, Georgette. *"I do casual hats and dressy hats, hats for weddings and bar mitzvahs. The big hat event here is the Melbourne Cup. We work for 5 months before for that alone"* (Ronald Bernarde). He learnt at the knee of Aage Thaarup, who makes all the Trooping the Colour hats, in London's Brook St, and concocted dishy little numbers for the Duchess of Gloucester, Moira Lister and Diana Dors.

WENDY MEAD HATS, 501 Toorak Rd, Toorak, VIC 3142 ☎ (03) 240 9093. Good current down-under headgear. Ready-to-head and custom-made one-offs, the latter in glorious fabrics that can cost A$120 (US$85) a metre. *"About 280 of my hats are worn to the Melbourne Cup"* (Wendy Mead). Baillieus, Myers, and all the top families head-dress here, plus Lady Stephen, the Governor-General's wife, and Tamie Fraser, wife of ex-PM Malcolm.

"The best hat designer in Australia is Wendy Mead, because she's got her fingertips on the look now *in hats. She doesn't bow down to the commercial demands so much"* (Nerida Piggin).

BEST JEWELLERS

KOZMINSKY GALLERIES, 421 Bourke St, VIC 3000 ☎ (03) 671 277. Antique silver, crystal and estate pieces from the last 120 years make this the place to go for trad rather than fad. And there are crystal decanters with silver stoppers to amuse you when all those ropes of dollars and diamonds begin to weigh you down. The richly carved antique showcases are worth a visit alone.

BEST LINGERIE

LA DONNA AT SHOP 3, The Place, 521 Toorak Rd, Toorak, VIC 3142 ☎ (03) 241 4172. Some of the best little silkies in Melbourne are found here. They have an exquisite treasury of Armonia silk lingerie and resort wear and La Perla, plus nightwear by both.

BEST MEN'S CLOTHES

HENRY BUCK'S, 320 Collins St, VIC 3000 ☎ (03) 679 951. Clothes that live happily in an environment of Persian carpets, polished timber and sniffy staff. *"Henry Buck's is the best in Australia for strictly classical men's clothes. Beautiful clothes, off-the-peg"* (Nerida Piggin). A 5-star wardrobe is available here for the conservative man, modelled by 2 rather stylish life-sized china dogs in the window.

Henry Buck's is Melbourne's mecca for bow ties. Fusspot touches like ready-tied bows adjustable at the back to fit collar size, and extra-wide bows for fatnecks, ensures a steady stream of the discriminating. Patrick McCaughey recommends.

WAYNE WATKINS, 403 Chapel St, S Yarra, VIC 3141 ☎ (03) 241 7980. Where to get spruce, Bruce. Best in Melbourne for classic but not conservative clothes, with deeply stylish moments. *"My favourite menswear shop. It's like Browns in South Molton Street in London – trendy and very, very stylish. A beautifully dressed man, to me, is a mixture of Savile Row and Milano"* (Nerida Piggin).

PERTH

BEST STORES AND SHOPS

ELLE, 56 Weld St, Nedlands, WA 6009 ☎ (09) 386 6868. Takes fashion in a broad stride from classy conservatism *à la* Yves Saint Laurent through to the avant-garde beattitudes of the Japs with lots of fab fashion to pore over and pour on in between: Zandra Rhodes (amoeba-inscribed party dresses), Bruce Oldfield (Big Brit Glam Dram), Giorgio Armani (top Italian tailoring), New York chic swim from Norma Kamali, hats, shoes, bags, and costume jewels from Britain's best decorators Butler & Wilson and Monty Don.

BEST SHOES

SCARPER'S, Shop 13, City Arcade, WA 6000 ☎ (09) 321 6941. Best imported feet in Perth, viz Robert Clergerie, Christian Dior, Rayne – the Queen's shoers – Sergio Rossi, and further Italian-crafted showy shoes.

BEST MEN'S CLOTHES

R M WILLIAMS, Shop 38 Carillon Centre, Hay St Mall, WA 6000 ☎ (09) 321 7786. "Will it wear well on the Birdsville Track?" If this is the priority, forget the others and come to R M Williams, "The Original Bushman's Outfitters", and very proper, too. Drover's moleskin trousers, grazier's and stockman's shirts, kangaroo hide belts and hats, wonderful elastic-sided riding and dress boots, and the famous Aussie oilskin Drizabone. The whole Jolly Swagman number for classy bushboys and townies with a sense of street swagger that incorporates the authentic chic of this Aussie equivalent of the Green Wellie brigade (before *that* went Sloany). In about 50 stores across the continent and by mail order to bushmen around the world.

THE FAR EAST

BEST DESIGNERS

★

(All in Tokyo)

1 **REI KAWAKUBO (Comme des Garçons)**
2 **YOHJI YAMAMOTO**
3 **ISSEY MIYAKE**
4 **JUNKO SHIMADA**
5 **HANAE MORI**

The Far East is a couturier desert, with only one outpost of merit and that's in Japan. But it's the world's best for quick-action tailors and dressmakers who specialize in *copying*.

JAPAN

TOKYO

BEST COUTURIER

HANAE MORI, 3-6-1 Kita-Aoyama, Minato-ku ☎ (03) 400 3301. This is haute couture in the grand European tradition by the woman Japs call "The Iron Butterfly". She was the *very* first Jap to make it – about 25 years ago, and she shows in Paris, has shops there and in London. She designs anything that moves – couture and prêt-à-porter, breakfast to ballgown, there are even Hanae Mori tights. Best are her evening clothes, seriously glamorous, with some overspill into the chi-chi. Never mind the clothes, she's also one of Japan's leading businesswomen, owns L'Orangerie, has her own building (called, of course, The Hanae Mori Building), and is a fashion diplomat, holding a big "London Comes To Tokyo" show each year, to introduce such insular imports as Stephen Jones to a hat-happy population of street-wise Orientals. She has also designed costumes for *Madame Butterfly* at La Scala, a job she describes as "*the icing on the cake*".

BEST DESIGNERS

COMME DES GARÇONS, 5-11-5 Minamiayamo, Minato-ku ☎ (03) 407 2480. Rei Kawakubo is the small, relentlessly bobbed matriarch of the bag lady look. The V & A has exhibited her holesome sweaters. "*The 1982 sweater with the holes people attacked again and again, but it has been copied all over. I like to praise the Comme des Garçons for having the courage to do such an outrageous thing and bear all the criticism and go on creating all those adventurous clothes … Comme des Garçons are serious – they have changed and challenged the way people think about clothes*" (Yuki Maekawa). Yuki also raves about her polyester taffeta evening dress that you shove in a bag and pull out wrinkle-free much later. "*No one ever made an evening dress for the contemporary working woman before.*" Her new shop in the Matsuya department store, designed by herself and Takao Kawasaki, is the holy-of-holies – all designer space, with the rare item of actual clothing displayed on a triangular shrine. After bringing black back into fashion, Rei is gingering up her collection with Japanese schoolgirl patterns. Best of her current look: long, lean layers of pattern mixes; tabard pinafores over longer dresses with houndstooth socks and sand shoes. Stiff foam-backed jersey is her significant new fabric.

YOHJI YAMAMOTO, 3F Maison Roppongi, 649 Roppongi, Minato-ku ☎ (03) 423 3200. Goateed ringleader of the gang of 3 we think of as "the Japanese" (Kenzo is entirely other). Does Holocaust Chic that is now mellowing from merciless black to fresh colour, even pattern. Origami-style clothes and great coats. He's the fave Jap of Vanessa de Lisle and Hamish Bowles, and one of Lynne Franks's all-time best designers. This year he actually played jokes at his Paris show, sending out fitted jackets with puffy peplums or very slender suits with a ghost of tongue-in-Chanel sense of wit. Tailoring is the autumn news, even at Yohji. "*I like his huge white shirts*" (Jenny Gucci).

ISSEY MIYAKE, Tessenkai Bldg, B1, 4-21-29 Minami-Aoyama, Minato-ku ☎ (03) 423 1408. Handsomest man in Japan, Art Incarnate, and progenitor of the zip-up plastic breastplate. Well known for his inventive synthetics like plasticized cotton. You'd never think it but he trained with Beene, Givenchy and Guy Laroche. "*He's brilliant, at times oddly like Balenciaga, and classical too. The best host in Tokyo*" (Tina Chow). Exhibited at the Boilerhouse and dressed 100 people from the Museum of Modern Art in giant paper butterfly jackets for the opening of the Buddhist temple in Kyoto. Does 2 less expensive lines, Plantation and Issey Sports (with the yen so high, Jap designer clothes are breathtakingly buyproof).

His new idea, Permanente, avant-garde in its anti-fashionism, is a collection of his best over the last 15 years made available in perpetuum. Best of his current collection: stunning red and white tweed coats, draped saffron and apricot cotton evening gowns.

JUNKO SHIMADA, Aobabai Terrace 1-1 Aobadai, Meguro-ku ☎ (03) 563 2346. *The* up-and-coming young Jap, funky and fun, a different parlance to the Big 3 altogether. "*She's less histrionic. Her clothes are more wearable, less wacky. Her biggest clientele are American women*" (Claudia Cragg). Her shop, in fact, is dubbed "Forty-Ninth Avenue" … bye bye Holocaust Chic.

> **"I love the Japanese designers, like Issey Miyake … I like almost all the Japanese because they have the oversized, baggy styles that I like"**
> (SHARI BELAFONTE-HARPER)

KENZO at Seibu, Annexe A, 2nd Fl, Udagawacho, 21-1, Suibuya-ku ☎ (03) 462 0111. The Jungle Jap of unfettered Seventies days. Extrovert folkloric clothes in great colours and pattern mixes. Clashes beautifully with the other 3 (he has no philosophy). Was first of the new wave Jap designers to succeed in Paris with his madcap materials and magpie tricot. *"I like Kenzo – all the Kenzo shirts and all the rubbish, and all the wonderful things that go with it. I'm not always this strict and straight"* (Anouska Hempel). *"I love Kenzo, he's one of my favourites. I have lots of his things. I love his colours and I think his materials are unique, all those flowered tweeds"* (Jenny Gucci).

BEST NEW DESIGNERS

HIROKO AND JUNKO KOSHINO, 6-5-36 Mininami-Aoyama, Minato-ku ☎ (03) 498 3404. Take wide-ranging inspiration from the kimono adding an element of modern Japanese uniform chic. Hiroko, sister No 1 cuts denim like butter into flowing, moulding forms. Junko, sister No 2 is less girl-of-the-Orient. They share a showroom, but Hiroko is often with the rest of Japan in Paris. *"Very hot here at the moment"* (Claudia Cragg).

JUKIKO HANAI, Roi Bldg, 2nd Fl, 5-5-1 Roppongi, Minato-ku ☎ (03) 404 5791. Not in the avant-garde mood of a Rei, nor yet the funkier edge of a Junko (either will do). Instead, she does the upmarket and conservative look for smart, young Tokyo. *"The Hanae Mori of her generation"* (Claudia Cragg).

KOSHIN SATOH, 3-24-22 Nishi-Azubu, Minato-ku ☎ (03) 401 7543. One of the freshly half-baked young Jap designers with spanking new ideas heavily infiltrated by Western ideology of dress. Another-worldly youngster who makes underground costume for bizarrely named design collective, Arrston vola ju. Mystic Orientalism by the coatload, and a first show in Paris in '86.

"Tokyo is very much like New York, but the difference is that the whole of Tokyo is like Disneyland and that's fascinating. It's one of my favourite places to shop in the world" (BENNY ONG)

Best Streets

Ginza is the established, pricey, conservative area. The big and brilliant Tokyo department stores are mostly here. *Aoyama* was the breeding ground for Yohji and the gang, and domestic designers still spring predominantly from this serious trend centre. *Harajuku* is *"purely fun. It has its chic area and it also has its cheap area. Imagine London's Covent Garden and the Portobello Road mixed together"* (Benny Ong).

BEST STORES

PARCO, 15-1 Udagawacho, Shibua-ku ☎ (03) 464 5111. Extremely stylish Japanese shopping phenomenon, belongs to Seibu. *The* shopping space for the under-25s (see 30 and die). Benny Ong is KO'd: *"The way they display their clothes is an art form. And the graphics are out of this world. I really love shopping there."*

Issier-than-thou shoplets rent individual floor space and customize it in marble, slate, ragged concrete, vying for Tokyo's most taste-ridden customers. Has its own exhibition space, cinema and theatre (avant-garde productions only) for inter-purchase taste-refining. The ads are almost more of a cult than the store (picture a horde of clay-caked warriors resurrected from the dead, caption: The Parco Succession). A bit of a mystery to Westerners, they are even more so to the Japanese, which is why, says Tsuji Masuda, originator of the whole concept, Parco succeeds.

SEIBU, 28-1 Ikebukuro 1, Toshima-kao ☎ (03) 981 0111 or (03) 462 0111. Unquestionably the biggest and the best. One of Lynne Franks's worldwide faves, she comes here looking for Jap designer shoes. The latest and the best of everything from everywhere. The Japs themselves come here for all their foreign name brands: Hermès, Vuitton, Sonia Rykiel, etc, but it also has the latest editions of Miyake, Rei Kawakubo and Yohji Yamamoto, and deeper into Japan. Kudos is carried in a Seibu bag. *"Seibu and Parco are the best … No one is after you, you are left to roam as much as you like … relaxed shopping and that environment is fantastic. I love it"* (Benny Ong). The devilishly ingenious ads use a starpack that includes Andy Warhol and Woody Allen to promote their products.

ISETAN, 3-14-1 Shinjuku, Shinjuku-ku ☎ (03) 352 1111. The eclectic one: for fashion extremists, Japanese wanting to ogle the British, and British wanting to ogle the Japanese. Issey Miyake, Bigi, Ichiro Kimishima, Junko, Kenzo and so on are met by Stephen Jones and Liz Claibourne: all beloved of the Japanese; Calvin Klein and Karl Lagerfeld add further *couture cordiale.* Bonus: the radically traditional (English, that is) Babington Tea Room has a 100-year history of serving 4 o'clock English tea.

BEST KIMONO FABRICS

BOUTIQUE YUYA, 3-10-12 Moto-Azabu, Minato-ku ☎ (03) 408 6749. The very best place to find contemporary clothes made up in traditional, out-of-this-world Japanese fabrics – for the Lady Nijo of the Eighties.

NUNO, Axis Bldg, B1, 5-17-1 Roppongi, Minato-ku ☎ (03) 582 7997. The best traditional fabrics. Beautiful hand-painted or printed silk kimono lengths are a good buy.

“ The best fabrics in Japan are the kimono silks and prints – I like the farmers’ rougher kimono fabrics, rather than the expensive hand-painted kimonos – kasuri ” (YUKI MAEKAWA)

BEST SHOES

COMME DES GARÇONS, 5-11-5 Minamiayamo, Minato-ku ☎ (03) 407 2480. Get top votes for the unbalanced shoe and leather bits and pieces. *“I love Comme des Garçons leather goods – wallets in particular. Quite simple workmanship but very good quality – particularly modern”* (Stephen Jones). *“I love their shoes. Really fab, mostly flat, so well engineered. Because they’re not shoe designers they have a different attitude. And the production possibilities in Japan are incredible”* (Lynne Franks).

JURGEN LEHL, 1-13-18 Jiayumae, Shibuya-ku, ☎ (03) 405 9737. German, but has been in Japan for years. Employs ancient Japanese technique of lacquering on deerskin. Does avant-garde bags for bag ladies. *“He made a Mickey Mouse out of the Vuitton pattern,”* laughs Yuki Maekawa. *“He made a very strange circular bag last year, it had a very heavy base like a rugby ball. It was very funny.”* For the kakkoii (Jap for cool, stylish) only.

TOKIO KUMAGAI, 3-51-10 Sendaga-ku, Sendaga, Shibuya-ku ☎ (03) 475 5317. Witty little Paris darling. Fey, funny and fascinating to know. Crazy shoes with a point: black courts with a white tape measure running across the toe; summer sandals bursting into fruit; mousy flatties with whiskers and upcurled tail. Beautifully made and totally frivolous.

YOHJI YAMAMOTO, 3F Maison Roppongi, 649 Roppongi, Minato-ku ☎ (03) 423 3200. Strong on the matt black designer shoe as well. *“One would never have imagined that Yamamoto made shoes. They are similar to Comme des Garçons, but not so unexpected”* (Yuki Maekawa).

BEST JEWELLERS

If you’re deep into the Big 3, you won’t want much more than a bared throat and black looks.

EMI FUKOZAWA (KEI ART INC), 3-32-5 Sendagaya, Shibuya-ku, ☎ (03) 470 3406. Updates the ancient Japanese art of lacquering on wood. *“Wonderful because she combines the modern with the old. To make the lacquer you must do a thin coat then wait for it to dry, then you do another and another one after another, it takes not only the technique, but the time as well. That’s why all the lacquered things are extremely expensive. Her bangles I was very impressed with”* (Yuki Maekawa).

BEST MEN’S DESIGNERS

The top designers for men are the same triumvirate of geniuses who dress the intellectually chic woman. The Japs specialize in the *total* look. You want a suit? Go to Yohji. You want a shirt? Yohji. You want shoes? Yohji. A wallet? Yohji ... and so on until you’re completely clothed. His label for men is “Y”. Why not, more like.

COMME DES GARÇONS HOMME (for the laid-back Jap-pack) and **COMME DES GARÇONS HOMME PLUS** (for the all-out bag man). **5-11-5 Minamiayamo, Minato-ku ☎ (03) 407 2480.** The whole designer “look” from odd little hats to clumpy sandals. Rei does the best alternative (not City stripes, in other words): modern shirt, pure cotton, washed, sometimes crinkled, sometimes with a wiggly row of mis-buttoning. *“A craze in Japan. When men put this on, they know it is the best shirt they ever owned”* (Yuki Maekawa). Lately, broad brushstrokes of eau-de-nil, Watteau pink, duck egg blue have diluted the black and white of Rei’s early canvas.

ISSEY MIYAKE FOR MEN, 5-3-10 Minami, Aoyama, Minato-ku ☎ (03) 499 3479. *“Very much better than his women’s collection ... he’s very into textiles. Cowlnecked shirts, very bold styling, more contrasting textures and colours. Earth-tones – he’s inspired by the Japanese who work on the land”* (Claudia Cragg).

YOHJI YAMAMOTO, Parco, Part 2, 4th Fl, Udagawacho, Chibuyu-ku ☎ (03) 476 2889. Either you’re going to England and perhaps Italy for suits, or you’re coming to Yohji for the best *other* way to look as a Man of the Eighties. He’s the best of his kind. Loose, but not sloppy clothes. Fab fabrics, heavy, textured in sombre tones with streaks of colour; hang-loose shapes, shake-down suits, zip-fronted shirts, buttonless crumpled jackets, sackcloth-esque tunics. It manages to look serious. The best coats, and hot on Rei’s heels for shirts. *“His are a lot more feminine than Comme des Garçons, the collars are a lot more dressy, and they’re prettier than the normal men’s shirt”* (Yuki Maekawa).

HONG KONG

BEST DESIGNERS

DIANE FREIS, 258 Lamma Gallery, Deck 2, Ocean Terminal, Kowloon ☎ (3) 7214342. Ubiquitous in the S China Sea, her clothes are to be seen adorning women of consequence. She specializes in the 1 size, uncrushable georgette dress; beaded evening wear; knits. Ex-President Carter and his wife visit the factory, Mrs Thatcher sends for Carol's dresses. *"I favour the feminine romantic look – my dresses are in soft fabrics, they drape nicely and travel well"* (Diane Freis).

EDDIE LAU, Shop C, Ground Fl, Mandarin Hotel, Central ☎ (5) 223997. The Honkers party crowd patronize him for his 14-yard (12.8 m) skirts. Day clothes more restrained. Sells little silk numbers through Chinese Arts & Crafts. *"He's a young Chinese designer, wonderful evening clothes – real BALL stuff! Trendy, for the older woman, not extreme"* (Winsome Lane).

JENNY LEWIS, Shop 214, Ocean Centre, 2nd Deck, Canton Rd, Tsimshatsui ☎ (3) 7233071. Interesting English designer who beads and embroiders *à la* antique Chinese. Bertolucci wants her to do the costumes for *The Last Emperor in China*, and Victoria Principal. Zsa Zsa Gabor and Stephanie Powers wear her clothes. Also in the Peninsula Arcade, Peninsula Hotel ☎ (3) 673750, and at Saks, New York and Harrods, London.

RAGENCE LAM, Shop 21, Swire House, Ground Fl, Central ☎ (5) 214646. Most promising young Chinese designer. *"Brilliant, slightly weird, innovative – a terrific image. He sells internationally and was trained at The Royal College"* (Winsome Lane). Has leanings towards Yohji and co.

RENE OZORIO, Star House, Kowloon ☎ (3) 698631. Oriental/Portuguese man of the cloth (silks and luscious brocades) who does simply structured evening wear. *"Great cocktail wear"* (Winsome Lane).

BEST SHOPPER

RIGGS SHOPPERS, Room 702 & 703, Ocean Centre, Canton Rd, Tsimshatsui ☎ (3) 696607. Hometown girl Mary-Lou Galpin will nip down to the local shops for you and pick up a nice batch of bargains if you are too busy wading into the local cuisine or whatever. Or she will act as automatic pilot, picking you up at your hotel, and driving you carefully from one best shop to another, fighting tooth and nail for the best prices along the way.

Best Shopping Areas

Hong Kong Island: If you're staying at *The Mandarin* start in its arcade, there's a bridge to *Princes Building* across the road; also try *Queen's Road*, with Lane Crawford and *The Landmark*. *"There they have the very best of Europe. Better value than in the States" (Diane Freis).* **Kowloon:** *Nathan Road* is the old, established shopping street; also the mammoth *Ocean Terminal* by the Star Ferry. *Harbour City* is the gargantuan extension to the complex, adding several hundred new shops. *Kwun Tong* is for the adventurous, but it's here that the *real* bargains start: *"This is the factory outlets area selling clothes made for the big French, US and UK design houses – wonderful bargains – especially silk dresses"* (Winsome Lane). The English-speaking *Community Advice Bureau*, 8 Garden Rd ☎ (5) 245444, provide a "Factory List."

BEST STORES

CHINESE ARTS & CRAFTS, Star House, Salisbury Rd, Kowloon ☎ (3) 674061, and **Chinese Arts & Crafts, Silvercord Building, 30 Canton Rd, Kowloon ☎ (3) 7226655.** Where you shop for mainland China's more capitalistic offerings. Bales of inexpensive, Chinese silk (solids better than prints). Also very good for jade. Quality is strictly government-controlled. *"Try the Silvercord Building opposite Harbour City before venturing into the smaller outlets to haggle"* (Claudia Cragg). Eddie Lau's slick little silk dresses at in-store boutiques. And glorious, madly desirable silk undies are here for peanuts. French knickers lavish on the lace for about HK$270 (US$35), and darling little slips, deep into embroidery, for less than 100 more baby smackers (the HK dollar is a small coin), plus silk with chiffon panels. Small shop-within-a-shop, Jen Pingping has beautifully ceremonial Oriental antique clothes (cheaper in Peking, if you can get in), the antique embroidered skirts are heirlooms-to-be.

LANE CRAWFORD, 74 Manson House, Nathan Rd, Kowloon ☎ (3) 7129668 and **Queen's Rd, Central ☎ (5) 266121.** HK Top People's store. Small, selective, chic, with everything in well-edited evidence from Mikimoto pearls from Japan (taxlessly) to a round-up of international designer clothes. Mondi, Escada, Jaeger, and the big end of French and Italian prêt-à-porter. Great accessories and shoes.

BEST SHOPS

Hong Kong is a tax-free port for just about everything you'll ever want. It's a shopper's seventh heaven, especially for decking yourself out in stunning, cut-price, cut-throat jewels.

BOUTIQUE BAZAAR, Rm 110, 11F The Landmark, Central ☎ (5) 242036. Evening wear of the wham-bam-sequined-*femme* kind, farouche sparklers that are the design equivalent of a bazooka – knock-'em-dead, farouche and fab, for international Krystle Carringtons.

HK FOR FAKE

Hong Kong is copy capital of the world. Show a Hong Kongese a Rive Gauche suit, a Jermyn Street shirt, an upper-crust shoe, and in the morning they'll have doubled it. The famous 24-hour made-to-measure suit is alive and kicking; but you pays your money and you takes your chance. Mark Birley warns of someone who *"got on to the 'plane in his just-cut HK special, and was reaching up to the overhead compartment, when, with a sudden rending sound, a great wad of newspaper shot out of the shoulder"*.

Startling verisimilitude of quality can be feigned, however. People in the know have their Turnbull & Asser shirts copied at A'Man Hing Cheong – no media padding there. Next-day jewels (it's better if you give them a more leisurely deadline though) and fake designer watches proliferate, too. Scandals over faux Rolexes, Omegas, etc, sold as the real thing by fast-buck local jewellers, have made people picky. The Tourist Board give a list of reliable jewellers, whose goods they'll guarantee as the real McCoy. The spin-off of the copy trade is that you can play Paloma Picasso or Carolina Herrera, design your own pieces, and have them made up specially for a pittance, at breakneck speed.

CHANEL BOUTIQUE, Peninsula Hotel Arcade, Kowloon ☎ (3) 686879. Only sells Chanel, but it's the completely Coco-ized look, from shoes to hats to handbags to all those pearls and gilty gadgets, even the make-up (which is excellent). And the clothes, of course, *mignon* little pieces for poodling around in.

CHARADE BOUTIQUE, Shop 120, Edinburgh Tower, The Landmark ☎ (5) 258888. The owner Nancy Miller does her own beaded thing for the cocktail hour (cocktails loom large in Honkers). Also Jindo Furs from Korea, Saga and other minks at very competitive prices.

JOYCE BOUTIQUE, 2nd Fl, The Landmark, Gloucester Tower, Central ☎ (5) 235236. A small stable of top European designer togs with Oscar de la Renta thrown in for graciously modern party gowns. Lagerfeld as Lagerfeld, and also as Fendi furs, Missoni and more. Plus bags, belts, shoes.

Silk Cut

Fabric is a good buy in Hong Kong. Lynne Franks thinks *"little shops in Hong Kong or India"* are the best places for cloth. There's Chinese silk, though this is no longer generally considered the best (it was the very first), though it's Katharine Hamnett's favourite, *"it's purer"*. Beautiful Thai silk can be found, however, *"it's the finest in the world, and it's a good buy in HK because there is no tax"* (Winsome Lane). Claudia Cragg finds Thai silk can be cheaper in the colony than on its native ground.

BEST FURS

"Leather and furs are great buys, no tax at all, so mink breeders from N America sell their pelts in Hong Kong, to be manufactured" (Winsome Lane). About 1 in 6 women in HK own a fur coat. Relative to the world fur market Hong Kong offers stupendous bargains – and made-to-measure is thrown in for good measure.

♛ **SIBERIAN FUR STORE, 21 Chatham St, Kowloon ☎ (3) 667039, and 29 Des Voeux Rd ☎ (5) 221380.** The very best in Honkers. They were famous in Shanghai before World War II, and now they are famous here. Really excellent quality (they have plenty of savoir fur). This is the place to bring your *Vogue* pictures of Fendi furs and have them made up matchlessly.

JINDO FURS, 1st Basement, Kowloon Hotel, Kowloon ☎ (3) 7391003. Extravagant individualism. If you want tie-dyed fox, it's here. The place is piled with great drifts of top-quality pelts, and you can choose your own and have them made up to your designs or a picture or photograph.

SINGER FURS, 163B Tai Shoh Gallery, Deck 1, Ocean Terminal, Kowloon ☎ (3) 677340. Marvelette minkies, great puffed-up jackets, and slim-priced leather coats.

BEST SHOES AND LEATHER

Best leather cheapos in the world are found here. Hong Kong is a made-to-measure paradise for the feet, as well as the rest of the body. The best cobblers will do all the exotics – alligator, crocodile, ostrich.

♛ **LEATHER CONCEPT, 11f 20 Hing Yip St, Kowloon ☎ (3) 899338.** Best leather in the Colony. Their own designer is Hannah Pang and they also have knockout bargains like Calvin Klein black leather pants at around HK$905 (US$116). *"A bit of an effort to find, so ask the concierge at your hotel to write the address down in Chinese for the taxi driver"* (Claudia Cragg).

♔ **MAYER SHOES, M-23 The Mandarin Hotel Arcade, Central ☎ (5) 243317.** Best made-to-measure shoes in the South China Seas. If it's got a skin, they can turn it into a shoe. Or a bag.

CHARLES JOURDAN, Eastern Arcade, Ground Fl, Peninsula Hotel, Kowloon ☎ (3) 693746. Best in Hong Kong for prêt-à-promener. Diane Freis goes there because *"they carry larger sizes"* (most HK shoe shops retain a bound-foot mentality to shoe size).

PARIS SHOES AND LEATHERWARE, Shop D5 and **6, Basement, Sheraton Hotel, Kowloon ☎ (3) 7237170.** The amazing 10-hour made-to-measure shoe (both), bag, briefcase – leather anythings, including clothes. For the jet-jetsetter on the run.

LO-PROFILE

The clean-living Hong Kong phenomenon and top Far East jewellery designer is stylish Shiatsu-freak Kai-Yin Lo (name means "dazzling revelation" in Chinese). *"I love her things. She uses a lot of semi-precious stones, her jewels are like creations – they are wonderful"* (Arianna Stassinopoulos). Her pièces de résistance are quietly incredible pieces of modern stamp, but with elements of Old China. New ornament to an old, old tune. Her big loves are semi-precious rocks, tourmaline, agate and jade most of all. She'll work old pieces into new designs, put carved coral beads with smooth, molten-edged modern ones, add 100-year-old slivers of wrought bone, Imperial jade archers' rings, gem-encrusted Tibetan bits to a plain-cut necklace. Her least expensive range is directly inspired by old pieces, with the ornament pared away for a minimalist line. Her philosophy is practical: nothing too expensive, there's no point keeping your strongbox well decorated. Beady-eyed buyers include Arianna Stassinopoulos, Natalia Makarova, Ann Getty, Imelda Marcos, various Hearsts and royal Brits, and she does bead-strewn shawls for the mother of all Japanese designers, Hanae Mori.

BEST JEWELLERS

Every second shop in Hong Kong is a jewellers, but deep discrimination is the prime prerequisite in this bijou beanfast.

JIMMY LAW GEMS CENTRE, 1 Lock Rd, Kowloon ☎ (3) 679218. Big and beautiful range of jewels of notable quality. Will try to match a lost stone or find a twin to an existing one.

KAI-YIN LO SHOWROOM, 6 On Ling St, 2nd Fl, Central ☎ (5) 248238. The very best jewellery designer – see Lo-profile.

K S SZE AND SONS, Mandarin Hotel Arcade, Central ☎ (5) 242803. An old Shanghaiese man, venerable and highly skilled, and his progeny here. Mr Sze is about 80 and still in the shop every day. They will make anything you desire to new designs or old or their own. Really consummate inlaid work (he is the well-guarded secret of a very well-known American jeweller who has her seamless inlays of semi-precious stones in gold done here).

MIRADOR JEWELLERY, 3A Ground Fl, Carnarvon Rd, Kowloon ☎ (3) 699730. Bring-and-buy jewellers who will make up little dazzlers from jewels in the shop, or from any you happen to have lying about at home. They specialize in stringing along big ropes of best and most beautiful pearls of the Orient, made-to-measure to match your length of neck and height of heel.

SATELLITE JEWELLERY, 18 Lock Rd, Kowloon ☎ (3) 680036. Ideal hunting spot for oystercatchers in search of Hong Kong's kingsized pearly bargains. Wide choice from best-quality white with a subtle bloom of pink to big, voluptuous creamy globes for lobes. Also, intricately carved coral beads sold individually, and will play copycat, plus redip worn settings.

SPH DE SILVA, Central Bldg, Pedder St ☎ (5) 225807. Best pearls in the Colony, by the river and rope. And some of the most trustworthy (key Hong Kong word in the jewellery trade) in terms of quality and prices for diamonds, jade (often a very tricky one, there's very little of the real McCoy around) and all kinds of glittering prizes. They make up and copy as a matter of course.

BEST LINGERIE

"Hand-embroidered Chinese silk lingerie is best" (Katharine Hamnett).

DIANE FREIS, 258 Lamma Gallery, Deck 2, Ocean Terminal, Kowloon ☎ (3) 7214342. *"I'm wearing my own designs at the moment. Georgette tunics, panties, short nighties in soft florals and pastels which I think are right for lingerie"* (Diane Freis).

MARGUERITE LEE, Gloucester Tower, The Landmark, Central ☎ (5) 256565. Beautiful, expensive flimsies especially the silkies, and hand-embroidered Swiss lace exquisitely done by young Aussie Anne Lewin.

BEST MEN'S CLOTHES

Hong Kong is basically a man's world with its population of tailors, shoemakers, shirtmakers, all making to measure at an uncommon rate.

DAVID'S SHIRTS, M7, Mandarin Hotel Arcade, Central ☎ (5) 242979. Best made-to-measure shirts in the colony. Broad-minded about cloth – everything from the respectable stripe to woven-in silk checks. Mark Birley gets his here.

A'MAN HING CHEONG, M-4, Mandarin Hotel Arcade, Central ☎ (5) 223336. Generally held to be the best tailors and they will forge a Savile Row suit remarkably well.

SAM'S TAILOR, Burlington Arcade "K", 92 Nathan Rd, Kowloon ☎ (3) 679423. A world-renowned tailor – in the right circles. Sam has done suits for the Duke of Gloucester, Duke of Edinburgh and son Charles, and Prince Rainier, who is mad about the shirts and had Winsome Lane deliver some when she was in Monte Carlo earlier this year.

Sarong way from Donna Karan ...

Best and most ravishingly original buys in Singapore and Malaysia are sarong lengths in lightweight cotton splashed with native prints and drenched with colour. *So* much cheaper than the New York equivalent in cashmere or silk jersey à la Donna Karan. Further fab fabric buy is silk, imported straight from China and sold in Singapore at *China Silk House, No 02-11/13 Tanglin Shopping Centre, 19 Tanglin Rd* and branches at *The Centrepoint* and *Lucky Plaza.*

INTO INDIA

1986 has been a bumper year for the Raj mob (as were '84 and '85 ...) with the huge interest generated by *Gandhi* piled on *Jewel in the Crown* piled on *Passage to India* piled on *Far Pavilions* (the further the better) culminating in America's Festival of India, the jewel in whose crown was Diana Vreeland's costumes of India spectacle at The Met. The priceless treasures purchased by the Maharajahs that are not popping eyes out at The Met are slowly finding their way to the market place. These are India's best bargains, but New York society figures who noticed the chic shoes gracing the feet of the Maharajah of Jaipur should take note of his bootmaker, Kailash Mishra, who also fits the royal feet of the Maharajahs of Udaipur and Kashmir, Princess Anne and the King of Jordan. He revealed stunning secrets of the Maharajah's shoe closet, *"I just made 6 pairs of the same model for him in different colours. He's fussy about his shoes, so when he finds one he likes he gets several pairs in burgundy, brown, black, white, suede and beige."* Kailash Mishra reckons *"The best upper leather in the world is from Madras, we even export vast quantities to Italy. Madras and Calcutta are the highest exporters of finest kid leather in the world."* The best *new* fashion find from India is Issey Miyake's little pet, Asha. She comes from a long line of Indian textile moghuls and carries on the tradition with her salwar-and-kameez-inspired clothes for the modern Indian aesthete; purist lines (hence Issey's interest) and crisp flowing cottons, with light moments of pattern and surface interest in rigorously controlled colours (black, white). Issey wears her, and Mrs Rajiv Gandhi felt inspired to buy the entire collection on her last visit to Tokyo – Asha's spirit-of-India clothes are not available at home, but are selling like hot cakes in Tokyo's Seibu store.

SINGAPORE

BEST SHOPS

Marooned in Singapore, you will be surprised to find some of Europe's most civilized pickings are there for the buying.

HILTON INTERNATIONAL HOTEL, 581 Orchard Rd, 0923 ☎ 737 2233. The best hotel shopping arcade with a handy supply of the best for homesick Europeans: Valentino, Gianfranco Ferre, Matsuda (for homesick Japs), Cartier, Alfred Dunhill, Gucci, L'Ultima (Italian shoes).

SCOTT'S SHOPPING CENTRE, Scott's Rd, 0922 ☎ 235 5055. The best shopping on the island. Etienne Aigner for clothes, handbags, shoes; a China Silk House; Diane Freis; Fellini; Ellesse for sports clothes. And a department store, *Metro Grand,* with a second floor chock-a-block with international fashion: Daniel Hechter, Christian Dior, Charles Jourdan, Givenchy Gentleman, Lanvin, Gucci, Calvin Klein and Guy Laroche ... and more.

HEALTH AND BEAU

by LESLIE KENTON

WORLD'S BEST HEALTH FARMS AND CLUBS

1
THE GOLDEN DOOR, California

2
FORT LAUDERDALE Intercontinental Spa, Florida

3
SHRUBLAND HALL HEALTH CLINIC, Suffolk, England

4
LES PRES ET LES SOURCES, Eugénie-les-Bains, France

5
THE GREEN BRIAR, West Virginia

6
TOKYO ONSEN-DIAMOND SPA, Tokyo

7
LA COSTA HOTEL SPA, California

8
THE GREENHOUSE, Texas

9
CHAMPNEYS HEALTH RESORT, Hertfordshire, England

10
MONTECATINI TERME, Pistoia, Italy

Being beautiful is all about being what you are. For what you are is far more interesting, vital and attractive than anything or anyone you might pretend to be. And each of us, man and woman alike, has a far greater capacity for glowing health and good looks than we ever use. The tools for health and beauty – from the knife of the plastic surgeon to the best anti-ageing cream – are merely the icing on the cake. They may add a decorative touch but they will never cover up the signs of neglect which come from a careless lifestyle. If you want to be healthy and beautiful, you need to *live* that way. You need to be *yourself*. And you need to love life.

A couple of weeks a year at a good health farm such as Shrubland Hall is a valuable start, as a spring clean. It gives you the opportunity to detoxify your body and establish new habits in eating, exercise and relaxation, to help you manage the stresses of every day life. That's the inside. On the outside, a good haircut is the single most important thing you can buy yourself to help you look great. For cutting and colouring hair, it is essential to have a good hairdresser. Beyond that, it is largely up to *you*.

In recent years, a new elite has emerged from the fast-moving mass of urban achievers and from the rut of a lazy country life. These highly individual men and women come in all different sizes and from myriad backgrounds, but they have some very important things in common: freedom of spirit, independence, fitness, masses of energy and an ability to live life for all it is worth. They have grasped the best of health and beauty – so can you.

Exercise. The new elite do, and not because some book on fitness tells them they should, but because they have found out that it heightens their sensitivity to all life's wonders – tastes, smells, beautiful objects, music – even sex. The fitness you gain from, say, running not only alters your body, but also your body image. It heightens your self esteem, can wipe

TY

Californian-born LESLIE KENTON is the most respected and original health and beauty writer in the world. Daughter of jazz musician Stan Kenton, she is Health and Beauty Editor of *Harpers & Queen*, and has written many best-selling books on the subject – *The Joy of Beauty, Raw Energy, Ultrahealth, The Biogenic Diet, The 10-Day Clean-up Plan* and *Ageless Ageing.* She lives in Wales with her 4 children, habitually rises at 5.30 am, wears white (for peace), eats raw foods, and runs 8 miles a day.

out addictions, produces high levels of energy, and frees your mind to be more creative.

Living fit brings tremendous benefits to the way you look as well as vibrant good health. The skin of someone who exercises regularly needs less make-up. It ages more slowly, and has a natural glow which artifice can never duplicate. Gifted beauticians can help too – by cleansing your skin thoroughly every now and then, and treating it deeply as only a specialist can.

Food too plays an important part. The way you eat helps create the foundation of lasting health and good looks. Yet most of the new elite are tremendous hedonists. They love to eat and they eat the foods they love. But they are not content with packaged, pre-cooked wondermeals. The foods they like best are unadulterated – nature's finest offerings of fruit, vegetables and grains.

You can search the world over for the best in health and beauty. It can be fun. I know – I've done it. But you'll find in the end that the very best comes from you alone. So use all the tools – visit the health farms and spas. But do it for the joy of it. Make this joy a part of everything you do, which costs nothing, yet promises a king's ransom in vitality and good looks. That's my recipe for health and beauty.

EUROPE

BEST HEALTH FARMS AND CLUBS

TOP 5

★

1. **SHRUBLAND HALL HEALTH CLINIC, Suffolk, England**
2. **LES PRES ET LES SOURCES, Eugénie-les-Bains, France**
3. **CHAMPNEYS HEALTH RESORT, Hertfordshire, England**
4. **MONTECATINI TERME, Pistoia, Italy**
5. **INSTITUT DE THALASSOTHERAPIE DE QUIBERON, Brittany, France**

"Beauty is from within – it is an attitude towards other people. Beautiful people are not those with lots of adornments. Beauty is to do with people's nature in being sensitive, loving and aware" (DEBBIE MOORE)

"Any diet is good if it rebalances the body and encourages better eating on a long-term basis. Anything cranky or short-term is a waster of time" (LESLIE KENTON)

ENGLAND

LONDON

AQUILLA, 11 Thurloe Place, SW7 ☎ (01) 225 0225. *"Very luxurious"* health club (members keep quiet about it because it's too good to share). Each dressing room has its *own* whirlpool bath and sauna, which accounts for other health clubs recommending it as the most upmarket in London. There are steam rooms for both sexes, an exercise room (for s-t-r-e-t-c-h-i-n-g, yoga, aerobics etc), swimming pool, gym with power jog, beauty therapy, massage – you name it. Full membership is £800 (US$1,157) p.a.; family membership (2 adults, 2 children) £1,200 (US$1,736); day membership: £500 (US$723).

CLUB ON THE PARK, 140 Battersea Rd, SW11 ☎ (01) 627 3158. New bright health club ("work, rest and play for social athletes," crackles the blurb). This place offers a fully fitted Schnell Gym: 2 studios with a varied programme of classes plus some of the newest sunbeds, sauna and a ladies-only whirlpool bath. A licensed bar helps to put back the calories you just burnt off and the CJ restaurant goes in for "light, nutritious and delicious meals". Wide range of membership packages, from £75–345 (US$109–500). On top of all that, a 10 per cent discount is available for "couples" – that's their quotes not ours.

CHAMPNEYS at Piccadilly, Le Meridien, Piccadilly, W1 ☎ (01) 734 8000. Newest of the best health clubs (only open since Sept 1985, so membership is still open). "A modern version of the old traditional club" (they say). Pretty enormous pool, 2 squash courts, Nautilus equipment, unisex Turkish bath, solarium, whirlpool bath, massage plus separate gym *and* library (to give your mind a work-out). Brasserie opens at 7 a.m. so you can eat breakfast after a first-thing swim. Membership: £900/US$1,302 (single), £1,250/US$1,808 (a couple), £4,000/US$5,787 (corporate membership – up to 6 execs, plus guests).

GROSVENOR HEALTH CLUB, Grosvenor Park Hotel, Park Lane, W1 ☎ (01) 499 6363. There are l-o-n-g waiting lists for this luxury work-out place managed by Mr John Hughes (membership currently stands at 800). Whirlpool bath, good gym with Nautilus, sauna, solarium, health-food bar, massage, 69-ft (21-m) pool. Shakira Caine recommends it (membership: £711/US$1,029 p.a.).

HOLMES PLACE HEALTH CLUB, Holmes Place, 188a Fulham Rd, SW10 ☎ (01) 352 9452. Proves that the best need not always be wildly expensive (membership: £452/US$654 p.a.). Very spacious club for men and women offering daily conditioning programmes plus individual exercise programmes. New

swimming pool and 2 new dance studios. Nautilus equipment, health-food restaurant and bar and, to top you off, a hair salon.

THE SANCTUARY, 11 Floral St, WC2 ☎ (01) 240 9635. Totally indulgent women-only club (recently taken over by Bridget Woods of the Fitness Centre next door and completely refurbished. Famous exotic haven swooping with parrots ("Who's a healthy girl, then?") and fish (don't worry, the carp are *not* in the wonderful 90°-heated pool you swim in). This club starred alongside Joan Collins in *The Stud* and won a design gold medal (1978) for the best pool environment in the world. Good salad bar with fresh juices. Membership: £575 (US$832) monthly, £17.50 (US$25) daily.

COUNTRY

SHRUBLAND HALL HEALTH CLINIC, Coddenham, Suffolk ☎ (0473) 830404. Lovely country house with gardens laid out by early Victorian architect Sir Charles Barry in style of the Villa d'Este (see the real thing near Rome). Owned and run by Lord and Lady de Saumarez with emphasis on relaxation (zzzz) and healthy eating (all diets veggie, except the last meal when carnivores can have meat). Best are the four-poster beds (£284/US$411 per person per week – same as a double room). Otherwise, prices run at £226–345 (US$327–499) per week. All the usual therapies, treatments and sports (including croquet) plus new Turkish bath with hand-painted tiles and stained glass window, officially opened in 1985 by Madam Rahmi Gumrukcügöglu, wife of the Turkish Ambassador to London. Offers a new exercise technique based on the Pilates method (see Alan Herdman – exercise therapist). *"Said by many to be the best of the best"* (Leslie Kenton).

CHAMPNEYS HEALTH RESORT, near Tring, Hertfordshire ☎ (04427) 3351. No flab on the slogan either ("positive health with personal attention"). This is one of England's most successful health farms (set in 170 acres/69 hectares of parkland) on which a further £2 million (US$2,893,400) will be spent on a super-luxurious update by November 1986. Offers 2-, 5- and 7-day courses at £60–£138 (US$87–200) per night. Indoor pool with aquajet, 2 whirlpools, gym, his and her spas, tennis courts, badminton. A beauty area shapes up the real you with Cathiodermie, aromatherapy, facials, paraffin-wax depilation, hairdressing and suntanning. Stars on the slab include John Cleese, Lord Lichfield, Lulu and media bon viveurs like Auberon Waugh. Snappiest stay is the "Day of Health & Beauty" – you book in at midday (greedy beast) and leave midday following (svelte beauty). See also Scotland.

ENTON MEDICAL CENTRE, Enton, near Godalming, Surrey ☎ (042 879) 2233. Run by Seventh Day Adventists (the healthiest people in the West), it has a charming, un-chi-chi atmosphere and a serious, holistic approach to health. Excellent food by the inventive vegan chef, and outdoor pool. From £322 (US$465) per week.

FOREST MERE, Liphook, Hampshire ☎ (0428) 722051. Georgian views (overlooking lake) outside, a new you inside. Top spot ("a great place for getting away from people" – *Lady Elizabeth Anson*) absolutely jumping with health pros trained in natural and allopathic methods. Massage, underwater massage, osteopathy, hydrotherapy, sauna, steam baths and physiotherapy, hairdressers and beauticians, plus visiting chiropodist and hypnotherapist. Prices vary according to the part of the house you stay in (best is around £800/US$1,157 per week for sole use of double room in a suite). Reservations of 7, 10 or 11 days are preferred (although a 3–4

THE MOST BEAUTIFUL WOMEN

Which comes first – the beautiful women or the beautifully taken photograph? In Lord Lichfield's picture book of modern-day stunners (*The Most Beautiful Women*) Sophia Loren perhaps provides one answer. *"Like all beautiful women she is not really difficult to photograph,"* he says. *"Beauty bestows confidence and makes people relax in front of the camera … she simply sat down on a sofa and, really, there was nothing else to do. I did not need to move or pose her and 2 rolls of film and 20 minutes later I was in the taxi and on my way back to the airport."*

Sometimes a photographer chooses to emphasize 1 particular quality or part of the body. In his book, Lord Lichfield concentrates on Mary Crosby's astonishing chestnut hair which *"seemed to go on for ever"* or on Iman, who has the longest, most swan-like neck in the world. But at other times, Lord Lichfield found it difficult to decide which beautiful bit to choose, as in the case of Shakira Caine. *"She has the sort of face which is so perfect in itself that I yielded to the temptation to come in close for a head shot and forgo the rest of her – which is equally beautiful."*

"A surfeit of surface beauty makes one long for something more. Without the glow of a warm spirit, a body is hollow. Without compassionate beliefs eyes lack real sparkle and faces are empty masks with a painted expression of glitter or gloss"

(MARIE HELVIN)

day visit is possible). A first visit of 10 days is recommended.

SCOTLAND

CHAMPNEYS AT STOBO CASTLE, Stobo Castle, Borders ☎ (07216) 249. It takes two to parafango (volcanic mud "deep heat" treatment) at this fairy-tale health castle (feudal splendour plus all mod cons). Swoony views plus local very healthy food (even the water comes from a freshwater spring). Beauty treatments include saunas, steam and spa baths, underwater therapy and algotherapy (be one of the seaweed people). Prices range from £72–89 (US$104–129) (single) to £120 (US$174) per person (double) plus VAT. Wide range of sports (riding can be arranged) plus Japanese water gardens (drink in serenity through your eyes) and hairdressing salon. Leslie Kenton recommends it as the best in Scotland.

JERSEY

PRIMROSE HILL HYDRO, rue du Froid Vent, St Saviour, Jersey, Channel Islands ☎ (0534) 26233. The first health farm for tax exiles (the only pounds they'll ever lose). Small (only 8 residential guests), friendly, super-equipped and has got top award from the Comité International d'Esthétique et de Cosmétologie (the health and beauty Oscar). Basic charge: £40 (US$58) per day.

BEST HAIRDRESSERS

LONDON

ANTENNAE, 27a Kensington Church St, W8 ☎ (01) 938 1866. Owner Simon Forbes was the first in the world to use hair extensions.

THE CADOGAN CLUB, 182 Sloane St, SW1 ☎ (01) 235 3814. Striding into traditional surroundings, Sloany ladies love the CC range of herbal-based products for skin and hair. The famous CC Pre-Raphaelite look is achieved with squashy Molton Brown rollers.

DEMOP, 7 Upper St James St, W1 ☎ (01) 437 2310. Top for streetwise style, this is a crazy place on the Soho fringes with Michelangelo-style ceiling, lighted candles and manic shopfront.

NEVILLE DANIEL, 175 Sloane St, SW1 ☎ (01) 235 2534; 4 The Pheasantry, King's Road, SW3 ☎ (01) 351 5227; 107–108 Marylebone High St, W1 ☎ (01) 487 5634. By appointment to HM The Queen. Owned and run by Neville Tucker and Daniel Hersheson (blonde, sleekly cut Leslie Kenton uses Neville).

EDMONDS, 40 Beauchamp Pl, SW3 ☎ (01) 589 5958. Small, friendly, chic salon which specializes in colour. It has pioneered a new "temporary permanent" colour which fades subtly over 6–8 weeks, so avoiding the dark roots problem. Clients include Elaine Paige, Rowan Atkinson, Annie Lennox, Derek Jacobi, Katie Boyle, Ringo Starr and Bruce Oldfield.

JOHN FRIEDA, 75 New Cavendish St, W1 ☎ (01) 636 1401. Also in The Ritz, Piccadilly, W1 ☎ (01) 493 8181. Famed for keeping up excellent rapport with clients, who include lots of royals. Charming JF does his wife Lulu, makes Paula Yates (Bob Geldof's wife) the "natural" blonde she is, Paul McCartney, Selina Scott, Jerry Hall, Marie Helvin, Koo Stark, Jacqueline Bisset, Faye Dunaway and *9 queens.*

DANIEL GALVIN COLOUR SALON, 42–44 George St, W1 ☎ (01) 486 8601. Famed as a leading British specialist in hair colouring. Vanessa de Lisle swears by his natural-looking auburn vegetable dyes when she is "feeling fragile"

HAIR COMES THE BRIDE

Who discreetly manages the silky locks of the wealthy low-profile ladies of London's best streets? Who advises the BBC for hair and make-up for major TV series? Who also does a manicure (and pedicure) with a mini-massage up to the elbows? Answer: CLIFFORD AUSTIN HUNT, 55 Kensington Church St, W8 ☎ (01) 937 2150/4084.

But this quietly successful London salon also offers the best bridal hairdressing service, managing you, your hair, your head-dress, veil and special make-up for the BIG DAY with specialist calm and skill. Clifford Austin Hunt's team consists of 5 "talented and imaginative hairdressers" plus an excellent beautician/manicurist.

First of all, the bride-to-be makes 4 visits to the London salon. Visit One offers a consultation on your hair and make-up; Visit Two offers hair-styling to complement your head-dress. Visit Three offers a bridal make-up and manicure (wearing white requires a very carefully thought-out make-up) and Visit Four offers a trial fitting of your head-dress plus a make-up run-through. Finally, comes Visit Five – it's your wedding day and this time both the hair stylist and beautician come to you in your home on the wedding morning.

The scale of fees for all that runs like this: London (£500/US$723); Home Counties (£750/US$1,085); provinces (£1,000/US$1,447); overseas (on quotation). Plus VAT.

HARI & FRIENDS, 30 Sydney St, SW3 ☎ (01) 352 2295. Hari is one of the best – and most modest – cutters in London. His non-chromy salon veers towards Victoriana: bare brick walls, antique mirrors, boudoir prints and soft lighting. Head cases Diane Keaton, Christopher Reeve and a well-heeled Chelsea set sip brasserie cups full of fresh-brewed coffee and lap up the calming atmosphere.

HARRODS HAIR & BEAUTY SALON, Harrods, Knightsbridge, SW1 ☎ (01) 730 1234. Now manely famed for its long-hair clinic, reputed to be the only one of its kind in the world. Rapunzels in the know let down their hair here for a 1-hour treatment, including shampoo and set (£29.75/US$43).

Face Magic

Less is sometimes more thinks top make-up artist CLAYTON HOWARD, Flat 6, 2 Colville Rd, London W11 ☎ (01) 229 9468. Clayton Howard has worked for 10 years with Lord Lichfield and has made up a spectrum of faces for the camera from royals to Kate Bush (on the cover of her latest album). The man is discreet, too. His clients (or friends as they quickly become) say that going to him is "better than going to a psychiatrist". And *6 months* before it was announced, he made up Lady Diana for her engagement photograph in *Vogue* (and kept the secret of the decade). *"He has made up Princess Anne for photo sessions and he was largely responsible for the make-up in my book,* The Most Beautiful Women", *says Lord Lichfield.*

Clayton Howard deplores the fact that women are often badly made up ("If you're not sure, use less" is his philosophy).

HUGH AT 161, 161 Ebury St, W1 ☎ (01) 730 2196. Looks after lots more hair on crowned heads and the aristos, including Lady Elizabeth Anson.

LEONARD, 6 Upper Grosvenor St, W1 ☎ (01) 629 5757. Rules the Mayfair waves in a very luxurious salon. Surprisingly enough, they only charge £80 (US$116) for a day-long hair and beauty makeover.

MICHAELJOHN, 23a Albemarle St, W1 ☎ (01) 629 6969 (women), (01) 499 7529 (men). Michael Rasser did Bo Derek's locks for the film *10* and is said to have turned Princess Anne punk pink (up to £100/US$145 for highlights and restyling).

MOLTON BROWN, 58 South Molton St, W1 ☎ (01) 629 1872. *Very* relaxing salon (you nod off almost the moment you walk in) with pretty South Seas waves painted on the walls upstairs. Specializes in totally natural looks and subtle colouring (whole head of low lights costs from £66 (US$96). Excellent own-brand products including travel-size packs.

VIDAL SASSOON, 60 South Molton St, W1 ☎ (01) 491 8848. Also at 44 Sloane St, SW1 ☎ (01) 235 7791; 130 Sloane St, SW1 ☎ (01) 730 7288. The darling of the sixties' geometrical cut, now famed for very good hair products.

SCHUMI, 8 Yeoman's Row, SW3 ☎ (01) 584 4070; 317 King's Rd, London SW3 ☎ (01) 352 9130; 16 Pont St, London SW1 ☎ (01) 235 3888; 4 Pont St, London SW1 ☎ (01) 235 6360. Uses a computer to ensure superb colouring and perming and will match your colouring for tints, make-up etc. Good range of natural hair products (clients include Jerry Hall and James Fox).

TREVOR SORBIE, 10 Russell St, WC2 ☎ (01) 240 3816. Bloomsbury in-place for the latest short cuts and new looks.

Best barber

TRUEFITT & HILL, 23 Old Bond St, ☎ (01) 493 2961. Established in 1805 (remember the Battle of Trafalgar?). Now owned by Alan Broughton and managed by Mr Beard (yes, truly). Opens early so that snappy young shavers can get "done" on their way to the City. Sir Winston Churchill had a short back and sides here and so did Field Marshal Montgomery. Other clients have included Herbert Wilcox, Alfred Hitchcock, Rod Steiger, Artur Rubenstein, Lord Olivier and Michael, Duke of Kent (they cut Prince Philip's hair "up at the Palace"). And prices don't slay a chap: cutting (£8.40/US$12); manicure (£5.50/US$8); beard trimming (£6.00/US$9); face massage (£5.50/US$8) plus other manly treatments.

CLIFFORD STAFFORD, 79 Duke St, W1 ☎ (01) 408 0898. Also at 7 Pavilion Rd, W1 ☎ (01) 235 9462. "Once a girl tipped us all £50 each, even the receptionist. We were amazed," he has claimed. That must have been a super hair cut. Lots of own hair products.

COUNTRY

MANTINI'S, 2 Bishop's St, Leicester, Leicestershire ☎ (0533) 555495. Best out-of-London hairdresser, run by owner Paolo Mantini. He is one of the world's top film and TV crimpers (currently hairing around on the new Madonna film in Hong Kong). Modest prices make you faint: £10/US$14 (cut and blow); £12–16/US$17–23 (perms, highlights); £5–£25/US$7–36 (over 20 different colouring techniques). Trained junior staff on second floor are even less expensive!

BEST BEAUTICIANS

"The most important part of beauty is that your skin should be very clean." (Aida Grey)

LONDON

THE BEAUTY CLINIC, 413a Fulham Palace Rd, SW6 ☎ (01) 736 7676. Good foot-work here using the famous German Sixtus products.

HARRODS HAIR AND BEAUTY SALON, Harrods 5th Floor, Knightsbridge, SW3 ☎ (01) 730 1234. Chiropody is offered by their qualified manicurists, who also do pedicures.

ARSHO GRIMWOOD, Steiner Salon, Royal Garden Hotel, Kensington, W8 ☎ (01) 937 8000. *"I treat people from the very highest society in London – royalty, film, TV people. The very* crème de la crème," says AG, who trained in medicine and then swapped to beauty therapy 27 years ago. Her treatments can be cosmetic, natural, psychological or scientific (usually a blend of all 4) according to a client's needs. She also did the UK a good turn by bringing René Guinot products into the country. A consultation (it can take up to 3 hours) is £30 (US$43); a treatment costs £40 (US$58); Cathiodermie £40 (US$58); Bio-peeling £28 (US$41); Liftodermie £55 (US$80), *but* she is fully booked 3 months ahead (so join that waiting list of 80–90 hopefuls).

JANET FILDERMAN, 15 Wyndham Pl, W1 ☎ (01) 262 7034. Barbara Daly says this lady is a cross between a beauty therapist and an agony aunt (*"I'm partly in a counselling situation. Yes, I'm known as a good listener"*). She specializes in facials and body work and also works with a nutritionist and dietician. (*"We will be able to offer inside and outside treatment, which is the only way to good health. You are what you eat, and you are only as good as you feel."* She always starts with a consultation (£16.50/US$24) and then offers the standard facial (£16.50/US$24); electrical toning of sagging muscles (£22.50/US$33) and sections off problem body areas (bust, abdomen etc) for special attention. JF uses her own skin-care range, but also all others to give clients the best possible choice.

EVE LOM, 3 Upper Wimpole St, W1 ☎ (01) 935 9988. Leslie Kenton recommends this therapist for wonderful lymphatic drainage, which eliminates all sludge from the skin. *"People have problems with their skin almost solely because they do not cleanse properly. Cleansing is all,"* says Eve, who describes herself as a "skin hygienist" rather than a beauty therapist. She spring-cleans necks and shoulders as well as faces (£35/US$51 per treatment) using her own products, plus the excellent peeling mask by Georgette Klinger. Usually booked up 10 days in advance.

NAILOMANIA, 1 Hinde St, W1 ☎ (01) 486 8079. The place for every aspect of nail care. The majority of clients are American rather than tatty Brits (*"they are better at looking after their nails than the English"* but gradually, we are getting better. Nail biters get a set of plastic tips, covered and sealed with acrylic (£38/US$55);

WHY THE PoW IS A PRM

When you've got *real* beauty and style, you go into the upper stratosphere of good-lookers that American fashion watchers call the PRM (Perennial Role Model). That means that from now until you sink gracefully into old age, your hair, make-up, clothes, shoes, the way you dance, walk, shop, bop, wear a miner's helmet, hold your baby or even kiss your husband in public, will be inwardly weighed up (and usually copied) from deepest suburbia to the Top.

To many Americans Princess Diana symbolizes THE DREAM they're reluctant to talk about – the magical-mystical-marvellous quality of being a commoner turned Royal. She is every little girl's idea of a real live princess whose life suddenly turned to gold.

Best of all, the PoW puts *proper English beauty* back on the international map. *"To me, and I think to many Frenchmen,"* said a French journalist, *"she is everything a man could wish for – beautiful, charming* and so English. *A rose . . ." "Her eyes,"* said the Australian Prime Minister, Bob Hawke, who was equally wowed, *"they're beautiful. And her skin . . . it's* so soft *and lovely."*

The PoW's hairdresser, Kevin Shanley, is one of the few people to see her without make-up. *"She looks great without it,"* he says. *"She has a terrific complexion and doesn't need blusher or foundation to give her colour, especially after she has done her exercises."* Looking back on her Australian tour, Kevin thought everything about her was just right. *"Her hair was full and looked perfect. She looked fresh, young and beautiful – everyone's fashion image of her."*

silk wraps to prevent breaking come at £28 (US$41); sculptured nails (£32/US$46); manicure (£8/US$12); pedicure (£11/US$16). Nailomania uses Sixtus products from Germany for the feet, Magic Sculptura products from California for hands and offers paraffin waxings for hooves and paws. Clients include Barbra Streisand, singer Grace Kennedy, Lesley Ash, Dusty Springfield and Sarah Brightman plus nobs anonymous. If you are so ashamed of your hands you can only go out wearing gloves, Nailomania will arrange a home visit. Better have strong, good-looking nails if you're clawing your way to the top.

MR BELL AT BEAUTY AT HARVEY NICHOLS, Knightsbridge, SW3 ☎ (01) 235 5000. Excellent chiropody say people who trotted in with hooves and walked out with feet. But you have to book well in advance (at least a month). Mr Bell comes in Thursdays, Fridays and Saturdays (£9.50/US$14 for half an hour).

GIVE US THIS DAY OUR DALY MAKE-UP

What Michelangelo did for ceilings and Botticelli did for botties, BARBARA DALY can do for your face – if you can find her. It's no use racing to the phone if you're getting married the day after tomorrow because she won't give her address or telephone number. But after a while, people still manage to find her. BD, the face ace, mostly works on photographic sessions (fashion, advertising, film work etc) and is very inventive, drawing most of her inspiration from paintings and art works in general. But don't despair, she does a few private clients (mostly friends or through recommendation). Prices vary – astronomical on advertising shoots to nothing if working with friends such as John Frieda (see Hairdressers). A wedding might take all day; a make-up lesson an hour, so price-wise "it all depends". From Sept 1986, the Body Shop chain sells her own brand of make-up ("my life-long ambition"), which is as natural and pure as possible. Up to now, she has used all brands of make-up quite indiscriminately, mixing everyone's up – just like us. (When it comes to cosmetics, few women are brand loyal either.)

WORKING OUT

"Exercise gives you more energy, not less. You can do so much more if you are fit!" (Debbie Moore)

LONDON

LOTTE BERK, 29 Manchester St, W1 ☎ (01) 935 8905; 465 Fulham Rd, SW6 ☎ (01) 385 2477. Now coaching and training in her 27th great year (she believes in *"exercising the muscles to provide a strong corset for good posture – good posture is all"*). The training is wonderful, but the facilities are *not* knock-out. Morning classes cost £4.11/US$6 (8 for £28/US$41); afternoon classes cost £3.50/US$5 (8 for £22/US$32).

THE FITNESS CENTRE, 11–12 Floral St, Covent Garden, WC2 ☎ (01) 836 6544. Currently the biggest and the best-equipped exercise studio in London (3,500-sq ft/325-sq m gym has *the works* from Nautilus to the bees' knees in computerized fitness equipment) plus classes for everything physical from martial arts to ballet and tap. Owner Bridget Woods also has beauty-treatment rooms offering nutritional counselling, Alexander technique, aromatherapy, chiropody plus saunas and Turkish steam rooms. BW pursues fitness with Californian fanaticism – if you can't find it here, you're in trouble.

ALAN HERDMAN, 17 Homer Row, W1 ☎ (01) 723 9953. *"The best,"* says Leslie Kenton (again). He specializes in Pilates technique where you lie flat, breathe correctly and work your body against the machine. Treats everyone from famous professional dancers to Mrs Housewife's Knee. This therapist only takes 2 or 3 people at a time on a one-to-one basis. It costs £6 (US$9) per lesson or 10 for £50 (US$72) (amazingly cheap considering the personal approach and professionalism).

MENTAL MUSCLE, c/o The London Indoor Tennis Club, Alfred Rd, W2 ☎ (01) 289 8771. Barbara Daly thinks the instructor, Daniel McMillan, is very good. Annual membership (£225/US$326) gives 7-days-a-week access to all equipment (including Nautilus, Universal and free weights, sauna, solarium and bar). Waiting list starts end of 1986.

PINEAPPLE COVENT GARDEN, 7 Langley St, WC2 ☎ (01) 836 4004. Where the pros go. Owned and run by sparkly Debbie Moore, it offers every type of exercise, dance and keep-fit facility you can think of plus saunas, showers and snack bar. There is a dance-wear shop next door at 6a Langley St. Basic membership is £29 (US$42) p.a.

“Eat fresh organic foods. Nothing tinned. Skimmed milk, unsalted butter, fresh vegetables, no red meat. Drink lots of herb teas and Evian water” (DEBBIE MOORE)

“I believe in natural eating – no new-fangled diets” (BARBARA DALY)

PINEAPPLE KENSINGTON, 38 Harrington Rd, SW7 ☎ (01) 581 0466. The poshest Pineapple – located in a lovely Victorian building with marble floors and stained glass everywhere. Same facilities and classes as the other 2 Ps, but annual membership takes a hike to £50 (US$72).

PINEAPPLE WEST, 60 Paddington St, W1 ☎ (01) 487 3444. Completely different atmosphere, with exercises , stretch and dance and the unique Hydra-Fitness system (beloved of Michael van Straten). Giles Webster (much praised) runs the gym. Hydra-Fitness (H-F) is like Nautilus, but much more sophisticated say users (it works 2 sets of muscles at a time, so you can do the course in half the time). Eventually, all Pineapple studios will have it. There is also a dancewear shop and snack bar here too. Annual membership is £29 (US$42) p.a.

The bouncy people

Mini-trampolines are a child's-play way to fitness and Leslie Kenton *swears* by them and bounce-bounce-bounce-bounces her way to fitness on the ones made by PT LEISURE, 57 Court House Rd, Maidenhead, Berkshire ☎ (0628) 28841.

ALTERNATIVE THERAPISTS

LONDON

IAN HUTCHINSON ☎ (01) 903 6455 (answering service). Offers smokers a 5-day course of aversion therapy based on a tried and proven American method (for 20 years chimney heads have been flying in specially to get it). IH works at CHAMPNEYS (see Best Health Farms and Clubs) in the mornings and visits smokers in their homes or offices afternoons and evenings. Course costs £245 (US$354) (if a client succumbs to the deadly nicotine during the treatment, they are not charged). Very high success rate.

LYN MARSHALL at Pineapple West (see Working Out). Lots of people say she is the very best (from accident cases to show-biz people to politicians). She teaches yoga on Thursday evenings and Saturday afternoons at Pineapple West but also takes private pupils. There is a waiting list of 2–3 months, but she will try to make an exception for genuine need. She devised her own yoga style 16 years ago, basing it on classical positions (but making them gentler and softer). Philosophy? *"Unification, tranquillity and serenity."* Fees for private pupils run from nothing at all to £25 (US$36) for a 90-minute lesson, depending on means.

CLARE MAXWELL-HUDSON, PO Box 457, London NW2 ☎ (01) 450 6494. Clare is so highly regarded she can rarely take on new clients these days. (She spends an increasing amount of time teaching so that her approach and technique can be passed on to as many as possible.) Tries to combine the best of traditional lore with the latest scientific research (latest treatments include manual lymphatic drainage and massage for high blood pressure). She charges from £20 (US$29); her team of girls charge from £17 (US$25) (a home visit can be arranged).

COUNTRY

DR GERALD HALES, 113 Church Green Rd, Bletchley, Milton Keynes ☎ (0908) 368628. Psychologist/psychotherapist dealing with habit disorders like smoking and obesity (and pain) through hypnosis. £15 (US$22) per session.

DR SHARMA at 97, 99 and 101 Seymour Place, W1 (called 101 Private Clinic Ltd) ☎ (01) 262 4507. Debbie Moore at PINEAPPLE (see Working Out) raves about his multi-purpose Magis Cream. Homeopath Dr Sharma and his son work together. 2 initial consultations (one to diagnose and one to draw up a scheme of treatment) cost £45 (US$65). Subsequent treatments cost £42 (US$61) (£15/US$22 if from one of 3 assistants).

MICHAEL VAN STRATEN, Glebe House, Cheddington, Leighton Buzzard, Bedfordshire ☎ (0296) 661215; 4 Treborough House, 1 Nottingham Place, W1 ☎ (01) 935 8911. MVS specializes in osteopathy, naturopathy and acupuncture (on the manipulative side he treats top dancers, athletes and DJs). Says: *"Holism is a consideration of all internal and external factors – mind, body and spirit."* Cost: £30 (US$43) for an initial treatment (cheaper at Glebe House); £20 (US$29) thereafter.

SCOTLAND

JAN DE VRIES, Auchenkyle House, Southwood Rd, Troon, Strathclyde, Scotland ☎ (0292) 311414. Runs a day clinic using naturopathy, acupuncture and osteopathy (plus wide range of other alternative treatments).

FRANCE

BEST HEALTH FARMS AND CLUBS

♔LES PRES ET LES SOURCES, Eugénie-des-Bains, 40320 ☎ (58) 511901. 3 stars in Michelin for the most famous spa in France (large white country house set in tropical park) on edge of spa village. Brits can't believe that in French health farms the food *really matters* (here Michel Guérard himself does the *cuisine minceur*). *"Fabulous and alarming"* treatments under strict medical supervision (strange array of hot springs, baths, pipes and caverns). Go there for digestive disorders (your liver needs a holiday); over-weight, cellulite, rheumatism, arthritis, spasmophilia. 2 price ranges (both exclusive of meals, treatments and service): 800 francs (US$113) per night for single room, 1,000 francs (US$141) per night for a suite. Think of 5,600 francs (US$789) per week plus (along with Catherine Deneuve, Isabelle Adjani and the Duchess of Bedford).

♔INSTITUT DE THALASSATHERAPIE DE QUIBERON, Pointe de Goulvars, 56170 Quiberon, ☎ (97) 502000. That long word starting with a T means treatment with seaweed. This is the only *hôtel diététique* in France. You are guaranteed to lose 6½ lb (3 kg) in 1 week on 4-star food (Michel Piot, food writer of *Le Figaro*, now eats nothing else). But no alcohol. *All* French politicians whether Right or Left go there (they say). Apart from aerobic riding and the usual sports, you can learn "sophrologie" – a technique to cure yourself of illness through sheer *concentration*. And being on a peninsula, surrounded by the majestic Atlantic on 3 sides helps you do just that.

BIOTHERM DEAUVILLE, blvd de la Mer, 14800 Deauville ☎ (31) 984811. Flash new hi-tech spa with accommodation at the nearby Normandy Hotel. If you like to feel robotic, this is for you (e.g. NASA metallic-film face masks, "bio-lift" facial stimulation, Zyderm injections to plump out wrinkles, plus lymphatic draining). You rest on blue-water mattresses or listen to underwater music ("acoustotherapy"). Prices are 840 francs (US$118) per day for treatments, plus 400 francs (US$56) per night for a room.

HOTEL MIRAMAR, ave de l'Impératrice 64, 200 Biarritz ☎ (59) 248520. Another top place for the sea cure (thalassa therapy). Princess Stephanie comes here (400–1,360 francs/US$56–192 per day for the room alone).

BEST HAIRDRESSERS

JACQUES DESSANGE, 37 ave Franklin Roosevelt, 75008 Paris ☎ (1) 4359 3131. Goes in for the natural look (those who do include Raquel Welch, Brigitte Bardot, Jane Birkin and Charlotte Rampling). One of 250 salons in the world, including one in NY run by Bruno Dessange. The place where "Molton Browners" (bendy soft curlers) were born. Shampoo, cut, blow-dry: 268 francs (US$38); perm: 190 francs (US$27).

ST GILLES, 1 ave du Président Wilson, 75016 Paris ☎ (1) 4723 7900. Lynn Wyatt likes it (family business plus very good pedicures).

“ Go to the best plastic surgeons, not clinics! It's too bad that people want to alter their looks. Plastic surgery should be a last resort – people seek it for all the wrong reasons. They should learn to respect themselves more for what they are ”
(LESLIE KENTON)

“ Avoid any type of surgery for cosmetic reasons unless you are very ill ”
(BARBARA DALY)

“ Plastic surgery, if done well, is necessary and very important psychologically. It also saves a lot of jobs! ”
(AIDA GREY)

A close shave with Dracula

CAPILODRÔME LUNAIRE, 40 rue Coquillère, 75001 Paris ☎ (1) 4233 2007. Run by Djelani Maachi, who thinks the full moon helps hair to grow, heal and hold a perm. He opens all night on full-moon nights (costs approx 400 francs/US$56). A Rolls-Royce will collect you and drive you home in the small hours for an additional 300 francs (US$42).

MODS HAIR, 7 rue de Ponthiou, 75008 Paris ☎ (1) 4359 0650. TV journalists like this chain of 100 salons (with 35 branches in Paris). Natural Look specialists with a very scientific approach to cutting hair (involves measuring the length of your neck, nose and forehead). Shampoo, cut, set: 250 francs (US$35); "mise en forme" (not quite a perm): 200 francs (US$28).

BEST BEAUTICIANS

PARIS

CARITA SALON DE BEAUTE ET COIFFURE, 11 rue du Faubourg St Honoré, 75008 Paris ☎ (1) 4265 7900. The most luxurious place in Paris for beauty and hair treatments (and that's saying something). Along with Catherine Deneuve, Isabelle Adjani, Nancy Reagan, Paloma Picasso, Queen Noor of Jordan, Olimpia de Rothschild, Marisa Berenson and Fanny Ardant, you work your way down 3 floors of sheer physical luxury. Every bit of you is scrubbed, epilated, nourished, massaged, made up, manicured, pedicured – all before a hair cut and set by one of the finest hairdressers in Paris. Anne-Elisabeth Moutet is prepared to wait 2 hours on a Saturday afternoon for the best – Jean-Michel Henry. (But try Maxime, Loïc, Noëlle or Régis.)

CENTRE PHILIPPE SIMONIN, 85 ave de Wagram, 75017 Paris ☎ (1) 4380 4069. Out damned spots – this is the place to go in Paris if you have troubled skin (said to be "remarquable").

INSTITUT LANCOME, 29 rue du Faubourg St Honoré, 75008 Paris ☎ (1) 4265 3074. The latest in luxury beauty treatments (*"the Institut of tomorrow"*) in spectacular grey, white and gold surroundings. A unique machine diagnoses your skin state and which Lancôme products can correct any faults. A dry massage (the Institut speciality) *"will set off all those beauty waves which lurk in everybody"* and release an inner glow. A course of treatment regenerates your skin in 10 days.

WORKING OUT

PARIS

CERCLE INTERALLIE, 33 rue du Faubourg St Honoré, 75008 Paris ☎ (1) 4265 9600. *"Lovely,* *understated, luxurious and full of nice polite people,"* says Anne-Elisabeth Moutet. (Full means 3 people in the chlorine-free indoor swimming pool.) Squash court, yoga, aerobics, saunas and whirlpool bath keep smart Parisians in shape, but there is a waiting list (and you need 2 sponsors to propose you as a member).

ESPACE VIT'HALLES, 48 rue Rambuteau, 75003 Paris ☎ (1) 4277 2171. Chic place to nip to for its superbly equipped gym, plus dance and body works.

THE KEN CLUB, 100 ave du Président Kennedy, 75016 Paris ☎ (1) 4647 4141. This is a vast sports complex which combines a sports centre with a health and beauty centre. Only recently opened, it is trendy, popular and has a very flashy décor.

MONACO

BEST HEALTH CLUB

LA CALIFORNIA TERRACE, Hôtel de Paris, Monte Carlo 98000 ☎ (093) 50 80 80. Stunning health complex with big indoor pool and sun terrace overlooking the Med. Offers low-calorie meals, exercise rooms, steam baths, saunas, underwater massage, whirlpool baths, spa and a beauty institute. Price for a de luxe double room for 6 days, 1 April–1 Nov, is 18,744 francs (US$2,642) (for the rest of the year, 18,000 francs (US$2,537). Personalized programme plus complimentary chips for the casino.

ITALY

BEST HEALTH FARMS AND CLUBS

HOTEL REVE, via Santuario, Monte Ortome, 35031 Abano Terme ☎ (049) 668633. Rich mythical place for fango (warm mud) therapy. Because Phaeton, child of the sun, fell to earth in these parts, the mud and waters are said to have special curative powers. Other pluses are indoor and outdoor thermal soaks, inhalations, massage and heavenly walks in the surrounding hills. Very relaxing. Prices for a single room, full board and treatments: 75,000–82,000L (US$48–52) (until March 1); 95,000–104,000L (US$60–66) (high season).

HOTEL CIPRIANI, Giudecca 10, 30123 Venice ☎ (041) 707744 (see also TRAVEL). Super location on the island of Giudecca in front of the Piazza San Marco (just looking does you good). Runs health programmes (from 3 days to 3 weeks) throughout the year, starting at 260,000L (US$165) for a single room with bath or whirlpool bath. Full board can include diet programme, use of gym, sauna, steam bath, sunbeds, whirlpool etc.

MONTECATINI TERME, c/o Local Tourist Office, viale Verde 66, Montecatini, Pistoia ☎ (0572) 70 109. The most elegant place in Italy to take the waters (said to be great for the liver and digestive system) with a superb selection of hotels, springs and parks. When mud baths and thermal soaks have done their work, smarties use Montecatini as a jumping-off pad for Florence, Pisa, Lucca, Siena. The best place to stay is the Grand Hotel (☎ (0572) 52801), but if the urge for a volcanic mud pack suddenly erupts but you don't want to make the trip, Montecatini products have been launched by Princess Marcella Borghese and are available in major department stores around the world.

REGINA ISABELLA E ROYAL SPORTING HOTEL, piazza Santa Restituta 80076 Lacco Ameno, Ischia, (Naples) ☎ (081) 994 322. The *"Island of Eternal Youth"* set in the Bay of Naples is a good place to regenerate your looks. Here, the thermal springs have been recommended since the 8th century for obesity, circulatory problems, rheumatism and phlebitis. This hotel is just next to the SANTA RESTITUTA SPA, which offers all the usual cures and treatments (facial mud packs for wrinkles; mud baths, massage) plus house doctor, chiropractor and qualified therapists.

THE SHERATON OROLOGIO, viale delle Terme 66, 35031 Abano Terme ☎ (049) 66 9111. Amazingly sumptuous hotel set in acres and acres of parkland and gardens. Dive into 3 swimming pools and 3 thermal pools and enjoy *"Italy's most up-to-date facilities for cures, physiotherapy and beauty treatments"*.

BEST HAIRDRESSERS

LUANA BENI, Lungarno Guicciardini 7r, 50132 Florence ☎ (055) 215240. The Marchesa Bona Frescobaldi likes this establishment.

MARIO DI VIA DELLA VIGNA, via della Vigna Nuova 22r, 50123 Florence ☎ (055) 294813. Beauty treatments also available.

SERGIO RUSSO, piazza Mignanelli 25, 00187 Rome ☎ (06) 678 1110. Top show-biz cutter – he is famous for short styles (the place is dense with Italian TV stars and actresses). Massage and waxing also available.

SERGIO VALENTE, via Condotti 11, 00187 Rome ☎ (06) 679 1268. *The* man – tops off the models for Italian couturiers Fendi and Valentino, plus visiting stars like Catherine Deneuve, Barbra Streisand, Placido Domingo, Marcello Mastroianni. Fantastic salon with marble staircase and for in-salon talkathons, each client has her/his personal telephone. Cut 60,000L (US$38); set 32,000L (US$16); perm 50,000L (US$32) plus. Massage, sauna and make-up too.

"A very good place is Montecatini near Florence, though you have to have doctors. It makes you like new – especially if you have been on a bit of a binge through the year. You can go there, you come out, then you can start all over again!"

(JACKIE COLLINS)

BEST BEAUTICIANS

ALDA ARELLI, via dei Tornabuoni 6, 50123 Florence ☎ (055) 294603. Recommended for massage and make-up by Marchesa Bona Frescobaldi.

GIL BEAUTY CENTER, via del Babuino 173, 60187 Rome ☎ (06) 361 3291. The male version of Barbara Daly waves his magic paint-brushes here – that's Cagné (make-up artist extraordinaire) and one of the Roman glitterati. But get the highly praised skin treatments first.

GERMANY

BEST HEALTH FARMS

BELLA MARE, Golden Linie 20, 2903 Bad Zwischenahn ☎ (04403) 1068. Very much a beauty farm (1,200 DM/US$520 single per week).

CHALET DE BEAUTE-HAUS FÜR SCHÖNHEIT UND GESUNDHEIT, Kurstrasse 14, 6478 Bad Salzhausen-Nidda ☎ (06043) 6061. Like most German beauty farms, this place will really make you diet (300 calories per day) or totally indulge you ("more cream on your strudel?") if you came to have fun. 1,090 DM (US$472) buys a week's stay (single) and use of all beauty and sporting facilities. Offers a special milk bath.

DIE SCHÖNHEITSFARM PANORAMA, Balgerhauptstrasse 101a, 7570 Baden-Baden ☎ (07221) 62051. Offers rejuvenation through special cell therapy (said to regenerate the body). The new you can then take advantage of the complete range of beauty treatments – massage, saunas, manicure, pedicure, hairdressing. The special costs 2,500 DM (US$1,082) for 6 nights single, inclusive of all the beauty treatments.

BEST BEAUTICIANS

HAMBURGERHOF-PARFUMERIE, Jungfernstieg 26, 2000 Hamburg 36 ☎ (040) 340 221. Top-to-toe salon offering their own make-up and skin-care products, many based on caviare extracts. A 1-hour make-over costs 37 DM (US$16); 1½ hours costs 50 DM (US$20). (Sounds fishy, but the caviare products cost extra.)

RENE KOCH, Helmstedterstrasse 16, 1000 Berlin 31 ☎ (030) 854 4023. Famous beauty salon, where Germany's top make-up artist, René Koch, puts the glitz on W Germany's show-biz stars (and glamorous Berliners).

KOSMETIKINSTITUT AN DER OPER, Residenzstrasse 7, 8000 Munich 2 ☎ (089) 222620. A beauty salon that also offers to glamorize you for a night out at the Bavarian State Opera (next door). You give them your evening dress (in the morning) and they devise a matching make-up. You are then prepared from top-to-toe – and utterly transformed.

BEST HAIRDRESSERS

HEADS, Marienplatz 11, 8000 Munich 2 ☎ (089) 229022. Ask for Manfred.

MARLIES MOLLER, Tesdorpstrasse 20, 2000 Hamburg 13 ☎ (040) 444001. The very best hairdressing salon.

WORKING OUT

BODY AFFAIR, Eppendorferweg 186, 2000 Hamburg 20 ☎ (040) 4203370. Gym, sauna, showers. Members only. Cost: 80 DM (US$35) to join: then 89 DM (US$39) per month.

CLUB VITATOP, Berg-am-Laim Strasse 91, 8000 Munich 8 ☎ (089) 433061. Gym, swimming pool, steam baths, solarium, restaurant and beauty salon. Members only (105 DM/US$45 per month for 2-year membership; 125 DM/US$54 per month for 1 year only).

CLUB VITATOP, Caffamachereihe 16, 2000 Hamburg 38 ☎ (040) 340491. Offers saunas, massage, Turkish bath, bodybuilding, stretching, power training, slow-motion training etc. Members only: 180 DM (US$78) to join; then 128 DM (US$55) per month for 1 year, 103 DM (US$45) for 2 years.

LET'S MOVE, Karlsruhëstrasse 7A, 1000 Berlin 31 ☎ (030) 8911221. Founded and owned by actress Sidney (*Not Just A Gigolo*) Rome in chic location just off Kurfürstendamm. Aerobics, stretch, jazz dance and ballet in one half, well-equipped gym with Nautilus etc in the other. Package deal of 4–32 classes costs 65–370 DM (US$28–160). To use the gym you can contract yourself for 6, 9, or 12 months, paying 90, 80 or 70 DM (US$39, 35 or 30) per month. 1 class costs 23 DM (US$10).

SPAIN

BEST HEALTH FARMS

BRISAMER SL, Fuente del Perro, Apartado 34, Alhaurin El Grande, Malaga ☎ (052) 490891. Easy-going place if you can't stand regimented or hi-tech health farms. Run by Leida Costigan and her daughter Anne (a physiotherapist trained in Vienna). Either indulgence or self-discipline – you choose. Exercise classes, steam baths, sauna, Swedish massage, facials, light and scrumptious organically grown food. Minimum stay is 1 week (from 57,000 pesetas/US$392 single). Greatest treat of all is the pure fresh air (scented in December with oranges, lemons and pine).

CURHOTEL HIPOCRATES Cha, San Pol, Sant Feliu de Guixols, Gerona, Costa Brava ☎ (072) 320662. Wonderful naturopathic place run by Dr Miguel Pros (says 80 per cent of our health problems are caused by bad diet). Day 1 you fast (that means *everybody*) and day 2 you

"Beauty is something in the eye of the beholder. It encompasses your total look from head to foot, the way you walk, your voice, your smile. Beauty is not just a pretty face or a good make-up. It's much greater than that. It's your attitude" (AIDA GREY)

go on mono-diet (1 kind of fruit only, to clear the system). After that you progress to fruit juices and simple good local fish and salads. Exercise programmes include yoga, callisthenics, riding, golf, tennis.

INCOSOL HOTEL & SPA, Los Monteros, Marbella, Malaga ☎ (052) 773700. Very fashionable place tucked away in fantastic scenery. Offers medical evaluation, monitoring, physiotherapy, dietics, revitalization, plus sports, beauty treatments and *wonderful weather.* Most clients come for Dr Augusto Gianoli's rejuvenation programme (cellular therapy and Gerovital H3). Ultra-luxury touch are the Kneipp showers (the best oils in the world).

REST OF EUROPE

HAIKKO HEALTH SPA, 06400 Porvoo 40, Finland ☎ (015) 153133. Ultra-modern health spa near 14th-century Haikko Manor (set in 24-acre/10-hectare park bordered by Gulf of Finland). Full range of health and beauty treatments include log-sauna on the beach and indoor salt-water swimming pool and energetic exercise (not for lazies) programme.

SOCIEDADE DA AQUA DO LUSO, Luso, 3050 Mealhada, Portugal ☎ (031) 93211. Peaceful thermal resort offering wide range of treatments, plus escape and rest. Guests at the Grand Hotel use the spa, swim, sunbathe, play tennis and – gamble.

SKODSBORG BADESANATORIUM, 2942 Skodsborg, Denmark ☎ (02) 803200. Biggest health resort in Scandinavia – set on the island of Sealand (12 miles/19 km north of Copenhagen). Really a sanitorium treating a wide range of disorders with diet, baths and exercise. Lovely walks in the surrounding beechwoods. From 485 krone/ US$57 (single).

SWITZERLAND

BEST HEALTH FARMS

BIRCHER-BENNER CLINIC, Keletenstrasse 48, 8044 Zürich ☎ (01) 251 6890. Founded by the famous morning-muesli man, Dr Max Bircher-Benner. He was light years ahead when he said at the turn of the century that bad diet was a major reason for bad health (this clinic is run on that principle). A diet is devised for you around raw and cooked veg, fruit, wholemeal products and dairy foods. Plus massage, breathing therapy, gymnastics, mud baths, hydrotherapy, swimming etc. Cost: 270 francs (US$141) single (lab tests, treatments etc extra).

GRAND HOTEL BEAU-RIVAGE, 3800 Interlaken ☎ (036) 224621. Stunning luxury hotel 1,870 ft (570 m) above sea level (not a speck of pollution in sight). Inside is a health centre called Belmilon offering 2 1-week programmes for men (sporty) and women (beauty orientated). And, of course, there is also skiing. Prices per person: 1,455 francs/ US$761 (single); 1,345 francs/ US$704 (double).

HOTEL THERME BAD VALS, 7132 Vals Graubunden ☎ (086) 50111. Modern spa hotel (4,265 ft/1,300 m above sea level) specializing in 2-week slimming and fitness cures. Hydrotherapy, massage, saunas, gym, parafango, 2 pools (outside one has artificial waves). Skiing in winter. The "Fat To Fit" programme (13 days) costs 1,326–1,911 francs/US$694–1,000 (single).

LE MIRADOR, 1801 Mont Pèlerin Vevey ☎ (021) 513535. Lovely hotel-cum-spa perched high in the Alps (reach it by twisty road or cable car). Founded by Christian Cambuzat to encourage complete r-e-l-a-x-a-t-i-o-n through massage and underwater jet therapy. Your individual schedule is prepared on arrival. 250 francs (US$131) per day (single); 245 francs (US$128) per person per day (double); 600 francs (US$314) per day for 2 (suite).

ELIXIR OF LIFE

CLINIQUE LA PRAIRIE, 1815 Clarens-Montreux ☎ (021) 643311. The area round Lake Geneva is one big Valley of Youth. Within 30 miles/48 km of Lac Leman you can find virtually *every* type of beauty treatment for turning mutton into lamb. Way back in 1931, this clinic pioneered Dr Paul Nieman's "youth serum" injections of cells from foetal lambs. It has attracted celebrities for many years, such as Charlie Chaplin, Gloria Swanson, Marilyn Monroe, Somerset Maugham, Sir Winston Churchill . . . so perhaps it doesn't work? At 9,555 francs (US$5,000)per week plus, why not grow old gracefully and give the woollies a chance?

"I do think the upkeep of the human being and their spirit towards their own life and their own appearance is the essential point today. You've asked me what's the best, and this is the best thing anyone can do. It takes spirit, determination, and maintenance of health, figure and hair plus character, imagination and total concentration" (DIANA VREELAND)

THE AMERICAS

UNITED STATES

BEST HEALTH FARMS

TOP 5

★

1 THE GOLDEN DOOR, California
2 FORT LAUDERDALE Intercontinental Spa, Florida
3 THE GREEN BRIAR, West Virginia
4 LA COSTA HOTEL SPA, California
5 THE GREENHOUSE, Texas

COUNTRY

THE GOLDEN DOOR, PO Box 1567, Escondido, CA 92025 ☎ (619) 744 5777. No phones, no TVs, no stress (except effort). This place offers pampering personified in a Japanese Garden of Eden (oriental robes are provided). Famous for its "Da Vinci" class – 45 minutes of perpetual motion to relentless disco music. Women only (but with 9 men's weeks and 7 couples' weeks per year). Offers Deborah Szekely's "Inner Door" programme for positive energy ($3,000 single, Sun–Sun).

FORT-LAUDERDALE INTERCONTINENTAL SPA AT BONAVENTURE, 250 Racquet Club Rd, Fort Lauderdale, FL 33326 ☎ (305) 389 3300. Pretty new spa with innovative programmes devised by Lisa Dobloug. Looks like a small town set amid palm trees and waterways in 1,250 acres (506 hectares). Treatments and treats range from Swiss needle showers to shiatsu massages, Lancôme skin care and herbal wraps, plus full range of exercise action-action-action. One place that keeps Linda Evens looking good.

THE GREEN BRIAR, White Sulphur Springs, WV 24986 ☎ (304) 536 1110. Also a historical spa (going for 208 years) with up-to-the-minute equipment and facilities. 6,500 acres (2,630 hectares) offer an amazing range of sports and exercises (in winter, cross-country skiing, skating, sleighing). Past mineral-water drinkers have included 22 American presidents, Joe 'n' Rose Kennedy (on honeymoon) and the Duke and Duchess of Windsor. Costs start at $116–140 per person per day (based on double occupancy).

LA COSTA HOTEL & SPA, Costa del Mar Road, Carlsbad, CA 92008 ☎ (619) 438 9111. Startlingly good mix of high-living, low-calories with 30 miles (48 km) of Pacific beaches to walk or ride along. Imagine 6,700 acres (2,711 hectares) of facilities (everything from nightclubs to biking path) plus individually tailored diets, Roman pool, aqua-thinics and *cuisine minceur* food. Framed by the Chocolate Mountains, but you won't be getting any of *that.* Prices start at $310 single for 4 days.

THE GREENHOUSE, PO Box 1144, Arlington, TX 76010 ☎ (817) 640 4000. *"Wonderful,"* says anyone who has stayed here. It's the answer to every woman's prayer (shelter and care in a luxury setting). Even the temperature is controlled in your private sanctum and you need never go outside if you can't stand all that ghastly sport. Diet programmes are prepared by Bertja Shields. Cost: $2,625 inc (Sun–Sun).

THE ASHRAM, PO Box 8, Calabasas, CA 91302 ☎ (818) 888 0232. Run by Swedish fitness-guru Anne-Marie Bennstrom (only 6–8 guests share the Bennstrom experience at any one time). Diet of juices, raw veggies and fruit, plus meditation, 3-mile (4.8 km) hikes and more yoga under a geodesic dome. Fitness without frills at $1,500 per week.

CANYON RANCH, 8600 E Rockcliffe Rd, Tucson, AZ 85715 ☎ (602) 749 9000. Co-ed spa for men and women, built by Mel Zuckerman. Enormous 28,000-sq ft (2,601-sq m) fitness centre offers every type of exercise and fitness machine imaginable. Recommended by Shakira Caine, there's everything you could possibly want for fitness and beauty – and no alcohol.

THE DOWNINGTON PRITIKIN CENTER, 975 E Lincoln Highway, Route 30, Downington, PA 19335 ☎ (215) 873 0123. Stay at the Tarabas Hotel and follow Nathan Pritikin's famous high-complex carbohydrate, low-fat, low-cholesterol diet (strict medical supervision). Not the place to go for un-serious slimming. Starts at $4,375 for 13-day programme.

GREEN MOUNTAIN AT FOX RUN, Box 164, Fox Lane, Ludlow, VT 05149 ☎ (802) 228 8885. Takes obesity seriously. Offers 2-week programme on *resolving* (yessir!) obesity in women. The staff think of a 30-lb (13.6 kg) weight loss as a failure if pounds creep back after 6 months to a year. 1 month recommended as the basic unit ($3,800 single, inc).

THE HOMESTEAD, Hot Springs, VA 24445 ☎ (703) 839 5500. Heritage-style health centre offering peace, escape and privacy. 17,000-acre (6,880-hectare) resort with all the latest treatments. Superb sporting and trout-fishing facilities. Prices start at $120–160 per person per day.

THE INTERNATIONAL HEALTH & BEAUTY SPA, Gurney's Inn, Old Montauk Highway, Montauk, Long Island, NY 11954 ☎ (516) 668 2345. On the edge of the Atlantic, spa for people on the edge of being fat. Owner Nick Monte combines European-style water therapies with holistic approach and the great American outdoors (massage is often done outside). Stressed execs choose from Swedish massage, shiatsu, polarity, reflexology, herbal kelp wraps, salt rubs, fango therapies, hatha yoga and 23 classes daily. 7-day spa plan costs $740.

THE KERR HOUSE, Grand Rapids, OH 43522 ☎ (419) 832 1733. Good for getting away from it all – cosily decorated Victorian mansion with a high ratio of staff to guests. After breakfast in bed, you start on relaxation and s-t-r-e-t-c-h-i-n-g exercises, mineral baths, herbal wraps and massage. Delicious dinners. Price: $2,350 single (inc) for 1 week.

MAINE CHANCE, Phoenix, AZ 85018 ☎ (602) 947 6365. Women-only beauty farm opened by Elizabeth Arden with country-house atmosphere and Arden-style pink petunias and palms (not pink) outside. Wonder at the scenery, wander in the grounds and *gently* lose weight (900 calories per day).

THE NEW AGE HEALTH FARM, Route 55, Neversink, NY 12765 ☎ (914) 985 2221. Only 2 hours from Manhattan in scenery that looks like something from *The Sound of Music.* Sharp focus here on controlled fasting and cleansing (Miss Piggies come here for a physical spring clean). The Water Diet (guess what that is) needs a letter of approval from your doc: or you could try Fresh Juice Fasting (350 calories a day); the Spartan Diet (450–500 calories a day) or the Light Diet (600–650 calories per day). Or (to hell with it all) there is the Gourmet Plan (calories no object). Lots of other non-food activities too – yoga, biofeedback, aromatherapy, holistic health service, or just lots of lovely walks. De luxe single starts at $968.

NEW LIFE HEALTH SPA, Liftline Lodge, Stratton Mountain, VT 05155 ☎ (802) 297 2600. Offers a programme to revitalize mind and body (yoga is key therapy) but saunas, slimnastics (600–800 calories per day) are also key elements. Very close supportive staff coping with only 20 guests at a time. Private tennis available at the John Newcombe Tennis Center. Cost starts at $930 single (Sun–Sat).

THE OAKS AT OJAI, 122 Ojai Ave, Ojai, CA 93023 ☎ (805) 646 5573. Showbiz and media people come back here year after year. Emphasis is on exercise and 500–750-calorie meals rather than beauty (though beauty treatments are available). Just 80 minutes from LA and close to the sea.

THE PALMS AT PALM SPRINGS, 572 N Indian Ave, Palm Springs, CA 92262 ☎ (619) 325 1111. Total health and holiday resort run by Sheila Cluff in a lush setting. Once inside the wrought-iron gates, expect stiff walks, exercise and every form of beauty treatment imaginable. In between the 750-calorie meals are "broth breaks", "happy hour juices" and herb teas (before bed). Prices start at $160 (single) for 2 nights.

THE PHOENIX, 111 N Post Oak Lane, Houston, TX 77024 ☎ (731) 680 1601. Caters for people serious about fitness. This spa shares 24 acres (10 hectares) with the Houston Fitness Center, so you can enjoy the best of both worlds. Diet of 850 calories is quite an experience (try banana ice-box pie and stuffed cantaloup flowers). $2,000 for a week's stay.

RANCHO LA PUERTO, Tecate, CA 92980 ☎ (619) 478 5341. Easily qualifies as America's first modern fitness resort founded over 40 years ago by Edward and Deborah Szekely. (THE GOLDEN DOOR is its younger sister.) Offers well-planned programmes for those seriously interested in getting into shape (very relaxed atmosphere, sun bins, Kneipp herbal wraps, Roman baths, veggie meals and accommodation in a *casita*).

RITZ CARLTON CLUB, Chicago, IL 60611 ☎ (312) 266 1400. Famous social club with spa facilities for its members. Rena of Rena's Gym has 2 instructors here teaching small classes (a 1-hour work-out is said to exercise 600 muscles in the body). Cost: $1,200 (corporate membership, plus $70 per month); $1,000 individual membership (plus $60 per month).

SEA PINES BEHAVIORAL INSTITUTE, Hilton Head Island, SC 29988 ☎ (803) 785 7292. Director Dr Peter Miller is dedicated to helping people lose weight and stop smoking (without putting on a pound). His "Center for Weight Control" offers a 26-day residential programme with 700-calorie diet. The Smoking Programme also takes 2 weeks. Other goodies on offer include 65 tennis courts and miles of Atlantic beach. Total cost of both programmes: $3,800.

THE SPA AT PALM-AIRE, 2501 Palm-Aire N, Pompana Beach, FL 33060 ☎ (305) 327 4960. Wonderful sun, sea and seriousness about fitness and slimming. A complete medical check-up is given to determine which form of exercise will be suitable. Your jaws work out on 600–1,000 calories per day.

SPA AT SONOMA MISSION INN, PO Box 1094, Boyes Hot Springs, CA 95416 ☎ (707) 966 1041. Very secluded and surrounded by the spectacular Sonoma Mountains. Diets are based on American nouvelle cuisine (*and* you can drink the local wines). Keep-fit philosophy here centres on aerobics, endurance, muscle toning, flexibility and learning to relax (in surroundings strikingly decorated with lots of pinks).

THE SPA AT TURNBERRY ISLE, 19755 Turnberry Way, N Miami Beach, FL 33180 ☎ (305) 932 6200. Being near a world-class marina, this place is the darling of the international yachting set. Very modern and glamorous, but with classic health and beauty treatments. Complete Nautilus centre plus latest crazes in fitness (want to try gravity guidance inversion boots?). 1 beauty special is the papaya enzyme face peeling. $435 single for a 3-day, 2-night spa package with private whirlpool bath.

BEST HAIRDRESSERS

NEW YORK

GERARD BOLLEI AT THE GALLERIA, 115 E 57th St, NY 10022 ☎ (212) 759 7985. The French darling of young trendies like Cornelia Guest. Everything is available from the simple trim to the full make-over (from Gerard himself, a cut, shampoo and finish costs just over $100).

JULIUS CARUSO, 22 E 62nd St, NY 10021 ☎ (212) 759 7574.

Comfortable salon with clients such as Lauren Bacall, Gloria Steinhem and the Baroness de Rothschild. Julius charges $100 for a first trim, $75 thereafter.

LA COUPE, 694 Madison Ave, NY 10021 ☎ (212) 371 9230. One of NY's most dynamic salons (the glitzy reckon this salon has the best colourists in town thanks to Colour Director Louis Licari). Other stars to ask for are Susan Campbell (she extends hair by weaving extra bits into your own) and Antonio Costa.

BRUNO DESSANGE, 760 Madison Ave, NY 10021 ☎ (212) 517 9660. One of the traditional tops in NY (lovely, white, airy salon). Bruno cut Raquel Welch's hair when she went from long to short; other regulars are Catherine Deneuve (who seems to have her hair done everywhere), Donald Sutherland and Christie Brinkley. $100 for a cut.

GAD, 49 W 57th St, NY 10022 ☎ (212) 593 5445. Left La Coupe to set up his own salon. *"He is the best blow-dryer and setter on earth,"* swears Catherine Oxenberg. *"you come out feeling like a lioness!"* Gad likes hair to be feminine – *"not too dramatic or strong. Pretty hair, that's what I'm after."* Let him run his fingers through yours for $150.

KENNETH, 19 E 54th St, NY 10022 ☎ (212) 752 1800. Reigns supreme over NY's most elegant heads from his luxury town house (you ring his secretary Victoria for an appointment). People who dial his number are Jackie O and Diana Vreeland.

RENE AT THE PIERRE HOTEL, Suite 413, 2 E 61st St, NY 10021 ☎ (212) 838 7950. Lynn Wyatt's favourite man. He concentrates his Cuban charm on chic conservative styles (plus full range of beauty treatments).

SUGA, 115 E 57th St, 10022 ☎ (212) 421 4400. Sleek uncluttered salon in white, pale grey and peach owned by Suga and Sandy Vargas (he shot to fame with the wedge-shaped haircut he invented for Olympic ice star Dorothy Hamill). Excellent manicurists, pedicures and make-up by Hiromi Ando. Much recommended by Shari Belafonte-Harper.

“ If you're happy you look good. If you're healthy you tend to look good. Beauty is smiling a lot and meaning it. I'm really into laughter lines ” (JANE BIRBECK)

“ My own diet programme is the best – no smoking, no alcohol, no drugs, no sugar, no oil, no fat ” (no fun) (BROOKE SHIELDS)

Best men's salon

GIO AT THE PIERRE HOTEL, 2 E 61st St, NY 10021 ☎ (212) 308 7600. Marble, mirrors and clubby atmosphere in this salon where superstars like Frank Sinatra, Guy de Rothschild and George Steinbregger come for the facial works. The boys sip a glass of wine as they wait for the cut, colour, perm, manicure, pedicure, speciality massage or the famous seaweed cleansing mask.

XAVIER, 692 Madison Ave, 10021 ☎ (212) 751 8588. New very hi-tech salon concentrating on short practical styles (clients include Jamie Lee Curtis and the rock band Kiss). A separate floor for colour, run by top colourist Marian, opens in 1987. First visit costs $100, subsequent visit, $75.

LOS ANGELES

ARMANDO'S, 607 N Huntley, CA 90069 ☎ (213) 657 5160. Intimate black and turquoise salon with nice bits of Art. He does Catherine Oxenberg's hair for *Dynasty* and is a rare find, doing both hair *and* make-up. *"A good make-up artist must be sensitive enough to allow you to contribute,"* she says. *"You have to like them enough to trust them to experiment to make you look good."* Jackie Collins, Bette Midler, John Travolta and Linda Evans all rate Armando.

RILEY'S, 9159 W Sunset Blvd, CA 90069 ☎ (213) 274 2131. Owned by Emile Riley, part English, part Lebanese (from same town as Shakira Caine and a regular at the Caines' tea-parties). Emile does not do hair, he just reads clients' coffee grounds (the Lebanese way of telling your fortune). Jackie Collins says he's a *wonderful* soothsayer. Cut for women costs $40; for men $25.

BEST BEAUTICIANS

NEW YORK

ACCENT, 1498 First Ave, NY 10021 ☎ (212) 472 3220. Very pretty pale-pink shop specializing in problem nails. Russian-born owners Mila and Bela use no acrylics (special vitamins and creams are the answer, they say).

ADRIANA'S SKIN CARE CORPORATION, 34 E 67th St, NY 10021 ☎ (212) 772 0488. Absolutely the best place for the treatment of acne. Personal care and attention in a small and sympathetic salon. A 1-hour basic facial costs $45 and means you can go out minus the yashmak.

ELIZABETH ARDEN, 691 Fifth Ave, NY 10022 ☎ (212) 407 7900. Arden's "Maine Chance Day" is the ultimate revitalizer and best for 1-day beauty. You start with a work-out, relax in a steam cabinet, then go through all the beauty treatments from hair to make-up (costs $208 per day). Alla does waxings using natural beeswax.

ELENA DE DAMIAN, 24 E 64th St, NY 10021 ☎ (212) 734 2562. Elena uses lots of lovely natural recipes from Romania. A 1-hour facial is given here with such fragrances as freshly pressed walnut oil, mint, cucumber (and apricots, almonds and rose-water).

DENSUKI, 730 Fifth Ave, NY 10019 ☎ (212) 265 5445. Salon set high in the Penthouse of the Crown Buildings with stunning view of Manhattan. Here, Ling offers you the normal range of beauty treatments plus shiatsu massages ($50 per hour) or her crushed pearl and rose-oil facials – *"very pure and natural,"* she says. $50.

DINMAR, 35 E 65th St, NY 10021 ☎ (212) 249 9268. The *only* one says Margaux Hemingway – *"she puts on silk nails, fake nails, is a pedicurist too and will come to your house."* Run by Margaret Din, who sets the pace for nail fashion every season.

EVA OF NEW YORK AT THE HELMSLEY PALACE, 455 Madison Ave, NY 10022 ☎ (212) 888 7738. Fancy being "Queen for a Day"? Hungarian-born sisters, Eva, Ari and Zsizsi, offer royal treatment here from French mud-packs to make-up. Farrah Fawcett owes her "natural" sun-kissed looks to stylist Eddie, who offers a special 24-carat gold treatment. Queenly treatment costs $222.50. Men (like Adnan Khashoggi and Mr T) opt to be "King for a Day" for $146.64.

GARCIA, 240 E 27th St, NY 10016 ☎ (212) 889 3028. This great make-up artist believes every woman is beautiful in some way – it's his job to identify and accentuate it. Gives make-up lessons ($300 for 1½ hours) and makes you up at home or hotel for $175 per hour.

GEORGETTE KLINGER, 501 Madison Ave, NY 10022 ☎ (212) 838 3200. A day of health and beauty here (plus a good lunch) costs $200. The new salon at 978 Madison Ave features an "Intensive Curriculum" of individualized treatments including stress management.

IL-MAKIAGE, 107 E 60th St, NY 10022 ☎ (212) 371 3992. All the work of this salon (manicures, hair-care, make-up) is henna-based. They produce the henna range Avigal. There is a work-shop atmosphere – *"We want to teach people what to do, to unravel the mystery,"* says owner Ilana Harkavi.

KLISAR SKIN CARE CENTER, 18 E 53rd St, NY 10022 ☎ (212) 838 4422. Offers Klissar's Dead Sea Spa Treatment (lasts 2 hours for $125).

Blusher to go

KIEHL'S PHARMACY, 109 Third Ave, 10003 ☎ (212) 475 3400. This 132-year-old pharmacy is a real find. Its latest service is to make up your favourite lipstick, nail varnish, blusher – you name it – and a new batch of your fave products will reach you in 1–2 weeks. (And surprisingly cheap too.)

PABLO MANZONI, 465 Park Ave, Suite 261, NY 10022 ☎ (212) 355 5700. Italian charmer. Pablo was Beauty Director at Elizabeth Arden for 15 years before going solo. He has made up some of the most famous faces in the world and will do yours for $300 (1½-hour consultation plus detailed chart, so you can do it at home).

TRISH McEVOY, 800a Fifth Ave, NY 10021 ☎ (212) 758 7790. Madonna and Kim Alexis like this salon's no-nonsense approach. Trish does the therapeutic work, while her dermatologist husband (Dr Ronald E Sherman) tends to medical disorders.

MONSIEUR MARC, 22 E 65th St, NY 10021 ☎ (212) 861 0700. Marc de Coster has so many celebs gliding into his salon that a guard is posted to fend off the *paparazzi*. Wide range of beauty treatments includes palm-oil therapy for hair (said to be very good).

MOI, 498 West End Ave, NY 10024 ☎ (212) 877 6128. Pronounced "Moy", this lady is very popular with fashion and movie people. Amazing manicures and pedicures, plus her own range of nail-care products (76 colours of nail varnish alone).

ORLANE INSTITUT DE BEAUTE, Bloomingdale's, 1000 Third Ave, NY 10021 ☎ (212) 705 2828. French-trained "esthéticiennes" analyse your skin and devise a skin-care programme specially for you. A 1-hour treatment costs from $55.

PAYOT, Bloomingdale's, 1000 Third Ave, NY 10021 ☎ (212) 705 2829. Uses the Payot method (a special massage using 40 movements) developed by this Russian dermie for her friend Anna Pavlova. Dead duck skins go in, radiant complexions swan out.

RAYMOND & NASSER, 747 Madison Ave, NY 10021 ☎ (212) 737 7330. This salon send a limo to pick you up from home or office – then a day of cosseting begins (all for $366). Or they will come to you – a pedicure in the office for the exec on the run is the ultimate in fancy foot-work.

JANET SARTIN, 480 Park Ave, NY 10022 ☎ (212) 751 5858. This lady has been looking after the thin-skinned social set for decades – her skin-evaluation treatments keep a bloom on the cheeks of Princess Elizabeth of Yugoslavia, Gloria Vanderbilt, Diana Vreeland, Betsy Bloomingdale, Princess Ira von Furstenberg, Yves Saint Laurent etc.

LIVIA SYLVA CLINIQUE DE BEAUTE, 133 E 54th St, NY 10022 ☎ (212) 759 9797. Hive of activity for skin-care treatments centred around bees. A special 4-layer heat treatment (Livia's Bee Pollen Miracle Mask) gets rid of tiny lines caused by the sun. (Costs $55.) Offers the Magnaderm Mini-Treatment (shark-liver-oil-based cream is applied to the face and removed with a magnet).

RICHARD STEIN SALON, 768 Madison Ave, NY 10021 ☎ (212) 879 3663. Korean nail specialist Yoomi does very good manicures and pedicures for $30 each.

CHRISTINE VALMY, 767 Fifth Ave, NY 10153 ☎ (212) 752 0303. One of 500 salons world-wide. Miss Valmy's latest skin-care products are based on Dr Christiaan Barnard's anti-ageing research.

HAWAII

LES BEAUX, 1750 Kalakaua, Century Center, Honolulu 96826 ☎ (212) 941 0325. Super place for skin-buffing (consists of rubbing aloe-based exfoliator all over the body; $35 for 1½ hours). Candy (Marie Helvin's favourite beauty therapist) also does super facials.

HOUSTON

CLAY ELLISON STUDIOS, 4100 Westheimer Rd, TX 77027 ☎ (713) 850 8441. Some people think this man is the best make-up artist in the world (he does Queen Noor of Jordan and Princess Mary Obelinsky for starters). Everyone has a consultation and skin-sensitivity test before any treatment or make-up. Cost: a make-up lesson ($45).

LOS ANGELES

BEVERLY HILLS HOTEL SALON, 9641 Sunset Blvd, Beverly Hills, CA 90210 ☎ (213) 278 2011. Nail-care top spot used by Catherine Oxenberg and Jackie Collins (*"everyone goes there"*). A manicure costs $10 (and they will wash and gas your car).

JESSICA'S NAIL CLINIC, 8627 W Sunset Blvd, CA 90069 ☎ (213) 659 9292. Jessica Vartoughian analyses the nails and uses her own bases and top coats to correct problems. She suggests a special daily programme of nail care. Her pedicures let you put your feet in a herbal whirlpool.

THE LA TALKATHON

Sharing exercise (and making a social event out of it) doubles the pleasure of keeping fit. Walking lonely as a cloud o'er hill and dale certainly suits some (it suited Wordsworth), but apparently not Arianna Stassinopoulos, who likes company on her hikes.

"Since I moved to LA," she chatters, *"I've found a new way to exercise and see friends at the same time. I go hiking. Instead of having lunch with a girlfriend, we walk round the canyons. If you're one-to-one you can talk really intimately, and you're not putting on unnecessary calories.*

"I hike every morning with a different friend," confides Arianna. *"Whoever's in better shape talks on the way up and whoever's in worse shape talks on the way down! I love going at 6.45–7.00 a.m. when it's still quiet and the smells are wonderful. LA is anyway an earlier city than London. We get up earlier and go to bed earlier."*

WORKING OUT

NEW YORK

LYDIA BACH, 23 E 67th St, NY 10021 ☎ (212) 288 6613. Fantastic studio on three floors (*"great and very together"* says Margaux Hemingway). Basing her programme on Lotte Berk's method, Lydia incorporates dance movements into exercises (9 women per class). Prices: $15 for 1 class, $398 for 30.

BROADWAY BODY BUILDERS, 2162 Broadway, NY 10023 ☎ (212) 496 2444. Very serious gym with all types of body-building equipment (Joan Severance works out here with a pumping iron under supervision). Membership costs $500 per year (you can pay for 1, 3 or 6 months).

PINEAPPLE BROADWAY, 599 Broadway, NY 10012 ☎ (212) 219 8860. Debbie Moore's newest place in the heart of NY's theatre-land (15 studios and a huge gym on 4 floors). And it also features a *huge* dance-wear shop (*"You can even learn belly-dancing,"* she warns).

“Daily exercise is a must. The most practical exercise is the one which fits most conveniently into an individual's lifestyle but, certainly, stretching is one of the most essential as one progresses into life. Personally, I am a devotee of the Pilates machine, originally designed by a dancer for dancers. But when my travels take me to a city where one is not available, I resort to a routine of floor exercises and yoga, all directed again towards stretching in order to retain the youthful suppleness. My own particular method of preparing for a busy day includes an immersion in ice water following an exercise. If you think it sounds brisk then you're on the right track, for briskness adds to your physical and mental well-being and can best be described as zestful”

(VIDAL SASSOON)

THE VERTICAL CLUB, 330 E 61st St, NY 10021 ☎ (212) 980 0939. Where Arnold Schwarzenegger gets his muscles – simply *everyone* goes here from tennis stars (McEnroe, Borg and Billie-Jean) to showbiz people (Diana Ross, Catherine Oxenberg, Brooke Shields). 300 pieces of equipment, plus swimming pool, whirlpool, steam baths, sauna, sun deck, juice bar, racquet ball, squash and tennis courts.

HOUSTON

THE HOUSTON FITNESS CENTER, 1535 West Loop S, TX 77027 ☎ (713) 627 8500. Does all types of exercise, but caters specially for the over-40s and certain medical conditions. (Lynn Wyatt thinks it's *splendid.*) Best instructor is Melany Murphy.

BEST MASSEUSES

NEW YORK

CHRISTIANA AND CARMEN, 128 Central Park S, NY 10019 ☎ (212) 757 5811. Mother and daughter massage team from Romania. Christiana is best known for her shiatsu massage (working in complete silence) finishing with a Swedish massage to smooth away knots. A 1-hour session costs $48 (5 for $218).

ANN KEANE, 29 E 61st St, 10021 ☎ (212) 644 0755. Masseuse using aromatherapy as the basis of her technique (mandarin oil relaxes, sage detoxifies etc). Facial massages use geranium, sandalwood, ylang-ylang and rose oils.

LOS ANGELES

BELLA KRUPER, 320 N Town Drive, Beverly Hills, CA 90210 ☎ (213) 859 0393. Bella is a Russian doctor who has been in the States for 7 years. Offers excellent Turkish massage (recommended by Shakira Caine). Men as well as women ($50 an hour).

GET THE MASSAGE

"My exercise teacher gives me massages. After having tortured me, he massages me. He is no one well known but he is wonderful because he does Tai Chi, then archery, massage, karate, exercise, weight-lifting, muscle toning – and he comes to the house. He is called Eric Allen and he works with Audrey Hepburn's son, Sean. He is just starting up, so he is not pretentious or expensive" (Catherine Oxenberg).

"In LA, the masseuse I use is Betsy Taylor, a wonderful woman. The best time to have one of her massages is late at night before you go to bed. Her massages last 2 hours. She's an incredibly loving woman like an earth mother. Love is poured into her massages" (Arianna Stassinopoulos).

CARIBBEAN

BEST HEALTH CLUBS

THE ROYAL BAHAMIAN HOTEL, West Bay St, Cable Beach, Nassau, Bahamas ☎ (809) 327 6400. De luxe hideaway with club-like atmosphere (but serious about health and fitness). The $7 million re-vamp includes a multi-station gym, whirlpool, sauna, steam baths, massage and facials plus tennis courts, fresh-water swimming pool and lovely private beach of fine white sand. $225 per night.

SPA AT THE HOTEL PLANTATION DE LEYRITZ, 97218 Basse-Pointe, Martinique ☎ (596) 755392. Converted rum distillery in an 18th-century sugar plantation housing ultra-modern equipment for all forms of beauty and health therapy. French Colonial décor, 100 per cent fresh diet and all on the tropical slopes of a dormant volcano! Cost: 8,200 francs/$1,164 inc (single) for 1 week.

SPA AT SONESTA BEACH, Southampton, Bermuda ☎ (809) 298 8122. Classic programme of low-cal loofah scrubs, herbal wraps, saunas, exercise classes and beauty treatments. 3 private beaches, scuba diving and, of course, the sun. Starts at $878 inc for a 4-day programme.

A keep-fit pome

Robert Redford is a runner (he had to be doing something pretty energetic to keep on looking like that). And Jamie, one of his three children, is a poet in the making, whose framed four-liner hangs on the wall of father's office. This is what it says:

I call my Dad Redford the
Runner,
There are few things he
thinks are funnier.
But everyday he goes to the
trouble,
To keep his body from turn-
ing to rubble.

"I know I'll inevitably get wrinkles. I don't look for them every morning but that doesn't mean I'm looking forward to seeing them develop. For the moment, though, I still find myself quite cute." (RAQUEL WELCH)

AUSTRALIA

BEST HEALTH FARMS

TOP 2

★

1 WARBURTON HEALTH CARE CENTRE, VIC

2 BERRIDA MANOR HEALTH RESORT, NSW

COUNTRY

WARBURTON HEALTH CARE CENTRE, Yuonga Rd, Warburton, VIC 3799 ☎ (059) 662404. Tucked away near Healsville in the hills outside Melbourne, this place is reckoned by Lillian Frank to be the best in Victoria. Unlike the US, the totally sybaritic health farm is unknown in Australia (here the emphasis is on offering a quiet retreat rather than an ultra-glam experience). Book in here for diet and health programmes, plus sauna, body massage and spa. Offers Melbourne's best stop-smoking course, and exercise in the form of bush walks.

Best health and beauty moan

"Frankly, health farms here are a joke compared with those in America. They have no gyms. In the US, in Florida, they offer exercise classes, massages, aerobics, facials, body scrub, rest, herbal wraps – very luxurious. Health farms here are too spartan, not enough to keep your mind off food, make you feel good. So if you live in Australia and can afford it, go to one overseas!" (Patricia Coppleson).

"Australian women age much quicker – though they hate me for saying that – because of the sun. But they do play a lot of sport, they ski, they play tennis. Some Australian women play tennis *every* day of their lives, at any rate, 3 times a week. 40 per cent of Australian women play tennis that much. Their bodies are fabulous. They do aerobics, the lot. But they age"

(LILLIAN FRANK)

BERRIDA MANOR HEALTH RESORT, David St, Bowral, NSW 2576 ☎ (048) 611177. This up-market health resort has been going for 8 years (you find it 81 miles (130 km) south-west of Sydney). The owner is Alex North (the Sydney property developer who specializes in retirement homes and villages). On offer are dieticians to plan your weight-loss individually, a sports instructor, massage, sauna, aromatherapy and a doctor. But in true Aussie fashion, you come here for the *social mix*. That means people who come for the R&R: podgies and CDs (conference delegates who come to use the smartistic conference centre and indulge in a little health farming between the yak sessions). Princess Anne and Captain Mark Phillips have stayed here, plus top South Pacific politicos such as the Prime Ministers of Fiji, Samoa, New Zealand, Tonga, plus India's. Aussie showbiz people also pile in to throw off the pounds. Prices run at A$156 (US$110) per single room per day (inclusive of meals): A$250 (US$177) per double.

BEST HAIRDRESSERS

SYDNEY

JOHN ADAMS, 1/F, Dymock's Bldg, 428 George St, NSW 2000 ☎ (02) 233 7656 and 35 Bay St, Double Bay, NSW 2028 ☎ (02) 326 1722. Salon with pale minimalist interiors, attracting a chic, business-orientated clientele. Lady Rowland, Lady (Sonia) McMahon, Wendy Hughes, Peta Toppano and Carla Zampatti come to Adams to be cut and blown by French- and English-trained hairdressers.

GIORGIO BARONI, 55 Bay St, Double Bay, NSW 2028 ☎ (02) 32 3316. *"A very good cutter,"* says Patricia Coppleson of scissors wiz Baroni who does all the girls for *Vogue Australia*. Elegant salon has a sleek interior of black, grey and white Italian marble and attracts many of Sydney's non-stop socialites. Baroni's team offers the full range of hairdressing services (strong slant on individuality and up-to-the-minute cutting). Good relaxing scalp massage and conditioning treatments.

JEAN LOUIS DAVID AT THE CUT ABOVE, Angel Arcade, NSW 2000 ☎ (02) 231 2003. One of the many franchised Jean Louis David salons around the world (innovative styling and colouring ideas).

GET SMART, 52–58 Clarence St, NSW 2000 ☎ (02) 294249. Post-punk tribal interior of this salon attracts an eclectic set of clients (from male and female business execs to young students with an eye for a wild hair-do). Staff of "excellent" cutters include the owner, Paul Guttenbeil (plus top-notch colouring department). Beauty services are also on offer.

LLOYD LOMAS, 13 Bay St, Double Bay, NSW 2028 ☎ (02) 328 7085 and 1/F, Suite 80, Strand Arcade, Pitt St, NSW 2000 ☎ (02) 231 4411. Lomas, trained with Sassoon, looks after Marisa Berenson, Lord Lichfield, Kate Fitzpatrick, Neil Sedaka and Martina Navratilova. In between he dresses hair for *Cosmopolitan*, and *Harper's Bazaar* models and is in attendance for top fashion shows, such as Sydney's Valentino Fashion Parade.

CARALYN TAYLOR, 19 Cross St, Double Bay, NSW 2028 ☎ (02) 32 1771. An experienced and renowned stylist with a loyal following (*"the best in Sydney,"* says Susan Renouf). CT's appointment schedule runs *weeks* ahead, so it's best to book early.

JASON VILLA SALON, 1 Transvaal Ave, Double Bay, NSW 2028 ☎ (02) 327 3074. Takes care of the Double Bay smarties.

MELBOURNE

LILLIAN FRANK HAIR STYLISTS, 521 Toorak Rd, Toorak, VIC 3142 ☎ (03) 241 9179. *"I am the best hairdresser in Australia. I say that without modesty. I don't believe modesty has anything to do with it. I train the best hairdressers and there are 10 salons run by them in Melbourne. I am the Vidal Sassoon of Australia."*

BEST BEAUTICIANS

SYDNEY

ELLA BACHE INSTITUT DE BEAUTE, 29 Cross St, Double Bay, NSW 2028 ☎ (02) 320602; or 3 Spring St, Chatswood, NSW 2067 ☎ (02) 411 5126; or JEAN HALLAS, 118 Walker St, NSW 2060 ☎ (02) 957 2004. All 3 of these salons are owned and managed by the importers of Ella Baché products in Australia. They offer excellent products plus very well-trained beauticians. (The Jean Hallas salon is the most luxurious and comprehensive – offers facials, nail care, hairdressing and body massage.)

BAY COTTAGE BEAUTY CENTRE, 18 Manning Rd, Double Bay, NSW 2028 ☎ (02) 327 3659. Housed in a quaint cottage off the (very) beaten track of Double Bay, this small salon offers the best in relaxation therapies (aromatherapy, reflexology and massage). Also renowned for expert waxing.

CHAMPS ELYSEES COSMETICS INSTITUT, 100 William St, NSW 2000 ☎ (02) 358 6797. Run by Mme Koby, a Lancôme graduate and passionate on beauty matters. She offers facials, biological "face lifting", Cathiodermie and various skin miracles.

MADAME KORNER BEAUTY SALONS, Royal Arcade, Hilton Hotel, 428 George St, NSW 2000 ☎ (02) 264 1241. (And at other city and suburban locations.) The *grande dame* of Sydney's beauty salons offering plush interiors, s-o-o-t-h-i-n-g ambience and Madame Korner's "excellent" own-label products. Services range from facials and massage to capillary or pigmentation treatment.

ALI HAMYLTON AT LLOYD LOMAS SALON, 13 Bay St, Double Bay, NSW 2028 ☎ (02) 328 7085 or 326 2226. Perched on the first floor of this hairdressing salon, Ali works minor miracles on broken, bitten and generally abused nails and hands. *But* if you want acrylic or porcelain nail extensions don't come here (Ali is keen on nail health as well as looks). Some of the best fingertips in the An-tip-odes come here.

EMILIE PETROVIC, 302 Pitt St, NSW 2000 ☎ (02) 267 6461. Fashion people love this salon. Designer Linda Jackson and her friends swear by Emilie's treatments based on a system of hydrotherapy and using her own-label products (lovely, lovely water).

PAUL POSHOGLIAN PODIATRY, 10th Floor, Dymock's Bldg, 428 George St, NSW 2000 ☎ (02) 232 7694. Smart Aussies don't have chiropodists – they have podiatrists to keep their sporty feet going strong. This man is the best – used and recommended by those in the fashion and cosmetics industries.

A TOUCH OF GENIUS, 20 Cross St, Double Bay, NSW 2028 ☎ (02) 328 7689. Internationally stocked parfumerie offering special make-up services as well (you get your latest Chanel colours here).

COUNTRY

FACE TODAY MAKE-UP STUDIO, 211 Ben Boyd Rd, Neutral Bay, NSW 2089 ☎ (02) 908 1277. Owned by Petrina, the fashion magazine make-up artist, this place offers make-up classes (plus 1-time make-overs for special occasions). Professional make-up artists stock their kits here.

JANETTE'S BEAUTY THERAPY, 57 Thomas Drive, Chevron Island, Surfers Paradise, QLD 4217 ☎ (075) 382231. Provides laser therapy, collagen treatment, aromatherapy and cellulite treatment.

WORKING OUT

SYDNEY

CITY GYM, 107 Crown St, NSW 2000 ☎ (02) 357 6247 or 33 4947. No Yuppy frills or juice bars here – this is the spot for *serious* weight-lifters and those training for world titles. *Not* for the faint-hearted.

THE FITNESS NETWORK, 46 Oxford St, Darlinghurst, NSW 2010 ☎ (02) 332 2422. Trendy aerobic classes to fast and furious music, plus big weights area, sauna and snack bar.

HYDE PARK CLUB, 170 Castlereagh St, NSW 2000 ☎ (02) 267 3255. Running a mile ahead – this is the most glam fitness club in Sydney (owned by Kerry Packer) so it's full of media people working off ex-account lunches.

OXFORD GYM, 200 Goulburn St, Darlinghurst, NSW 2010 ☎ (02) 211 2799. Small weights area, but interesting and imaginative floor classes. On Saturday afternoons, Mark's Marvellous Motivational Movement Class merges ballet, modern dance, and aerobics into a huffing 'n' puffing 2-hour work-out. (Steady and loyal following.)

FAR EAST

BEST HEALTH CLUBS

TOP 2

★

1 **TOKYO ONSEN-DIAMOND SPA, Tokyo**

2 **ORIENTAL, Bangkok**

JAPAN

TOKYO ONSEN-DIAMOND SPA, 3rd Floor, 6-13-6 Ginza, Chuo-ku, Tokyo ☎ (03) 541 3021. Onsen are Japanese hot springs (the country is full of them). Tokyo Onsen is Japan's oldest and biggest (has served more than 12 million bodies since it opened in 1951). This place offers the best shiatsu (pressure-point massage) in town and is best visited in the late afternoon or early evening when least crowded. Open 10 a.m.–9.30 p.m. there are separate facilities for men and women. The King Course includes sauna, whirlpool baths, bodywashing and massage (3,800 yen/US$21); the Royal Course also includes an invigorating body scrub. Staff are used to dealing with foreigners and yes, they do walk up and down your back.

THE GOLDEN SPA, The New Otani Hotel, 4-1 Kioi-cho, Chiyoda-ku, Tokyo ☎ (03) 447 3111. Open to all (the Japanese *love* spas) the hours here are 9 a.m.–10 p.m. Facilities include wet and dry saunas, hot whirlpool, cold pool, plus gym and indoor swimming pool. A 45-minute regular massage in a room along with a dozen others costs 3,900 yen (US$22) (private massage rooms are available for an extra fee). A powder massage with oil is 4,800 yen (US$27).

BEST HAIRDRESSERS

BIJIN, 25–8 Sarugakucho, Shibuya-ku, Tokyo ☎ (03) 464 3419. The name of this place means "Beautiful People" and Mr Honda, the man with the blades, cuts hair for Japan's rich and famous. That includes Ryuichi Sakamoto, star of *Merry Christmas Mr Lawrence* and of Yellow Magic Orchestra.

PEEKABOO, Belaire Garden Building B1, 2-11, Jingumae 4-chome, Shibuya-ku, Tokyo ☎ (03) 402 8214. Fumio Kawasaki (who speaks English) is said to be the greatest crimper in Tokyo and he certainly leaves some idiosyncratic marks on the heads of the local fashion and music glitterati. Strictly for those who want to be noticed sporting the latest and most courageous styles (cut and blow dry starts at 3,500 yen/US$20).

Y S PARK INTERNATIONAL SALON, 1st Floor, Yaguchi Building, 5-10-31 Roppongi, Tokyo ☎ (03) 423 2244. The man here is Mr Park, a Korean who is expert in dealing with foreign (wavy) or difficult hair. This is the place for nervous ex-pats who want to stay unscathed by the latest "buzzing" or other weird hair techniques of some Tokyo salons.

BEST BEAUTICIAN

SHEISEIDO, The Ginza, 7-9-10 Ginza, Chuo-ku, Tokyo ☎ (03) 572 2121. Headquarters of the world-famous Japanese beauty company (artistic director is the celebrated ex-Dior Frenchman Serge Lutens).

WORKING OUT

CLARK HATCH PHYSICAL FITNESS CENTRE, Azabu Dai 2-1-3, Roppongi, Tokyo ☎ (03) 584 4092. This health club (only 8 minutes from Roppongi Station) is part of a world-wide chain and charges only 15,000 yen (US$84) for a month's unlimited use of its excellent facilities – track suit, towel and shoes are all provided. MD Tony Allman gives individualized diet and exercise advice.

DO SPORTS PLAZA, SHINJUKU, Sumitomo Building, Annexe 2-6-1 Nishi-Shinjuku, Tokyo ☎ (03) 344 1971. Unlike the majority of exercise clubs in Tokyo, this place is open to non-members and visitors alike for a flat 7,000 yen

Reach for the spas

Beppu, Kyushu, is about 7 hours by bullet train or "shinkansen" from Tokyo, but it's worth the effort for hundreds of geothermal baths. (It has an added plus of deep-sand baths for an alternative sauna treatment.) Stay at the SHUSUI-EN JAPANESE INN, 27-27 5-chome Yunohama ☎ (0977) 23 3201 (across from the hot sand beach). This has been described as the best alternative health farm in the world.

"Oriental beauty is not so much physical but a mental attitude that makes people different. The world has become so small because of good communications that cosmetics and make-up have become uniform. But inner things last longer and reflect beauty whatever your age. You should be emphasizing your best parts instead of changing yourself with plastic surgery"

(YUKI MAEKAWA)

Japanese trot-spot

Run round the moat surrounding Emperor Hirohito's sumptuous home – that's the Imperial Palace Course (about 3 miles/5 km) and a hard slog for smarties who like to push themselves. Take a subway to either Nijubasshi-mae on the Chiyoda (green) line, or to Hanzomon (mauve) line and join the national "Beautiful Human Life" get fit campaign. If you feel like running only half that distance, head for Yoyogi Station (on the Chiyoda line) and run round Yoyogi Park – less exhausting and *more fun*.

(US$39) fee. Open daily 10 a.m.–10.30 p.m., it offers a gym, sauna, diving pool and indoor jogging track. (There is another branch at Harumi 4-41 Toyosu 5-chome Koto-ku ☎ (03) 531 8221.)

SIETAI KYOKI, 1-9-7 Seta Setagaya-ku, Tokyo ☎ (03) 700 5550. Currently the chic-est exercise studio in Japan (futuristic bliss)

HONG KONG

BEST HAIRDRESSERS

ANDROS AT LA COUPE SALON, 104 Hutchison House, 10 Harcourt Rd ☎ (5) 214386. Andros is the owner and chief hairdresser at this salon for "western high-class expatriate community". Cutters are trained at London's Sassoon Academy, and specialities include an exclusive range of scalp treatments for a whole range of troublesome hair.

ELYSEE INSTITUT DE BEAUTE LTD, Ground Floor, Hilton Hotel Arcade, Queen's Rd Central ☎ (5) 268271. Lymphatic drainage and all sorts of other exotic beauty techniques are offered here by Paris-trained health expert Frederick Deleage. Showbiz people passing through town always drop in here. This salon has the usual treatments (facials, waxing, massage, manicure, pedicure) plus the Phytomer Method (beauty packs based on lyophilized seawater and seaweeds to restore the body's natural balance). This salon also does three kinds of make-up – day-time, night-time and a fantastic Fantasy Face (a "special" for parties, dances or just a time when you want to look *very* exotic). A manicure here costs HK$45 (US$6) and a 1-hour body massage costs HK$180 (US$23) and the quickie tension-relieving massage of your back, neck and shoulders costs HK$85 (US$11).

PHILIP GEORGE, Bank of East Asia Building, 10 Des Voeux Rd, Central ☎ (5) 243143. European and Chinese upper-crusties lie in reclining chairs here and have a manicure and pedicure as their hair is being done. The voluptuous shampoo and head massage is "absolutely the thing after a day's shopping". Philip is the top stylist, but if you can't get him, book Mark. This place is so keen to give you what you want that if you are not satisfied with your hair style after a few days, you can go back and have it re-done free of charge! Prices for cut and blow-dry range from HK$150–220 (US$19–28).

LE SALON, 67 Wyndham St, Central ☎ (5) 247153. This place is frequented by resident Europeans who depend on wonderful Kenneth for non-terrifying highlighting and colouring techniques. The artistic director is Kim Robinson, who heads a snippy team of European-trained cutters (they cut and style Miss Hong Kong, plus a milky way of Hong Kong showbiz starlets). In congested HK, smarties also come here for the car-parking as well as the crimping (the doorman takes your keys and whisks your car away to a safe spot).

THAILAND

BEST HEALTH CLUBS

THE BANGKOK HILTON, 2-14 Wireless Rd, Bangkok 10500 ☎ (2) 513 0123. Set in 8½ acres (3.4 hectares) of tropical gardens, waterfalls and lily ponds (called Nailert Park) this hotel offers comprehensive facilities for health, beauty and exercise. The sports complex lines up with 2 squash courts, a gym with Nautilus equipment, stress-testing and saunas, plus 2 all-weather tennis courts (it can't half rain in Thailand), a whirlpool bath and massage. After exercising or swimming in the pool, guests can slow down with an iced drink in the Chuan Chom Pool Pavilion.

DUSIT THANI, Rama IV Rd, Bangkok 10500 ☎ (2) 233 1130. Offers a large freshwater swimming pool (in a romantic garden setting) and a health club with fitness machines, squash and tennis courts and a sauna. Joggers run the circuit in Lumpimi Park directly opposite the hotel.

HYATT CENTRAL PLAZA, PO Box 10-182, Phaholyothin Rd, Bangkok 10900 ☎ (2) 270 1820. This hotel has 4 superb restaurants including Chom Talay, the open-air seafood restaurant. Guests who pig out can work out in the 2 fitness centres, jogging track, tennis courts, outdoor pool and saunas (and then go back to the 21,528 sq ft/2,000 sq m of banqueting space)!

ORIENTAL, 48 Oriental Ave, Bangkok 10500 ☎ (2) 236 0400. This is rated as one of the great hotels of the world ("an island of calm in a cacophony of sound" in their own words) and it certainly caters for the health and beauty requirements of its international guests. (As in Hong Kong, the plethora of massage parlours outside cater mainly for men.) The Oriental offers a top-glam beauty salon with good hairdressing, pedicure, manicure, waxing and body massage. In the same complex, a sports centre and health club have a wide range of facilities, including 2 tennis courts, swimming pool, exercise equipment, saunas, gym, jogging track and golf driving-range.

ROYAL GARDEN RESORT, 107/1 Petkasem Beach Rd, Hua Hin 77110 ☎ (32) 511 881. This hotel is set in the Thai royal family's traditional coastal resort. Swimmers and sun-worshippers luxuriate on the private beach on the Gulf of Siam. Championship tennis courts, a pool with whirlpool bath and an international-class 18-hole golf course are also on offer.

SINGAPORE

BEST HAIRDRESSERS

CASEY HAIRDRESSING SALON, 02–04 Pavilion Intercontinental Hotel, 1 Cuscaden Rd, 1024 ☎ 235 5328. Where ex-pat wives are going this year. Set in a beautiful modern hotel, this place has a reputation for good and reliable cutting. (But it is usually unwise for Westerners to think of having perms – even here. Chinese hair is coarser and this is what local stylists cater for.)

MOSCHE SALON, 4th Floor, Dynasty Hotel, Orchard Rd 0923 ☎ 737 6593. The other good hair salon in Singapore. Has a reputation for creative cutting (frequently used by locally produced fashion magazines).

AN INSTANT PHILLIP

Hong Kong jumps with specialist private exercise clubs where you either have to be a member (it could take time) or you take out temporary membership (at around HK$250/US$32 a throw). But, if you want *instant exercise*, going-for-the-burners who are just passing through HK, head straight for the chain of exercise studios run by PHILIP WAIN (the male Debbie Moore of Hong Kong). Wain has done for this part of the world what Pineapple has done for London – top-quality exercise facilities and *fun* without too many membership hassles. He runs three exercise spots where you can drop in on spec for a set fee of HK$120/US$15 (for this you can use all the facilities and stay as long as you wish). On offer are dance and aerobic classes, saunas, steam baths and whirlpool baths. Find it all at Philip Wain, 7 Sunning Rd, (opposite Lee Gardens Hotel), ☎ (5) 7906363 *or* at Philip Wain, New World Tower (5th Floor), 18 Queen's Road, Central, ☎ (5) 255025 *or* at Philip Wain, 3rd Basement of Regal Meridian Hotel, Tsimshatsui East, Kowloon ☎ (3) 699111.

WORKING OUT

DANCEWORKS, THE FITNESS AND DANCE PLACE, B1-34-37 Paiklane Shopping Mall, 35 Selegie Rd, 0718 ☎ 337 2555. Sanctuary for women – beauty, fashion, fitness and dance in luxurious surroundings. There are 2 large dance exercise studios (with classes), shower, sauna, snack and juice bar, cosmetic and body shop.

SHANGRI-LA HOTEL HEALTH CLUB, Shangri-La Hotel, Orange Grove Rd, 1025 ☎ 737 3644. The most comprehensive health-club facilities in one place with fully equipped gym (plus computerized jogging machine); hot and cold hydra-pools, sauna, steam room, 2 swimming pools and golf and squash facilities. Facials, manicures and massage are also on offer Membership fees: S$1,000 (US$466) per year (plus S$75/US$37 per month); hotel guests pay a limited fee.

Far East beauty shock

Health and beauty has its own culture shock (what is a Number One priority in the West may be far down the list as you shoot East). *"The Thais and Chinese put hair first, nails and feet second, and colour and make-up third,"* says beauty explorer Nicki Smith of Britain's glossy *Woman's Journal*. *"Exercise ranks very low on the health and beauty stakes, since culturally it is extremely bad manners for women to appear discomposed or flustered in any way."*

SPORTING LIFE

by STIRLING MOSS

THE WORLD'S BEST EVENTS

1
ROYAL ASCOT, England

2
AMERICA'S CUP, Perth, Australia

3
ALL ENGLAND LAWN TENNIS CHAMPIONSHIPS, Wimbledon

4
PRIX DE L'ARC DE TRIOMPHE, Longchamp, Paris

5
MONACO GRAND PRIX, Monte Carlo

6
ADMIRAL'S CUP, Cowes, England

7
DERBY, Epsom, England

8
US OPEN, Flushing Meadow, USA

9
THE ASHES, Lord's, London

10
HENLEY ROYAL REGATTA, Oxfordshire, England

Sport is, above all, entertainment. Motor racing is a very exacting sport where the stakes can be high. If you have talent and control, you endeavour to play as hard as possible and yet never cross the very fine line to disaster. It is because of my involvement with my own sport that I enjoy watching others, provided they are played really well.

To see a downhill skier like Franz Klammer balancing his speed and manoeuvrability, or cyclist Eddy Merckx put every ounce of power through his legs to pedal up the Pyrenees, or watch snooker genius Hurricane Higgins pot a near impossible black, all excite me. To have seen Pelé or Maradona play football, Fangio drive a racing car, or, indeed, any athlete at the top of his profession demonstrate exactly how it should be done, with timing, balance and concentration – that's exhilarating.

One of the things about motor racing's best events, and other top sporting events where you get so many people together, is that they become big occasions. Le Mans is a spectacle that happens around a motor race and it is undoubtedly very prestigious and very dramatic. People like to see competition – they like someone who will fight and fight and come back again from behind. I know that I would always drive as hard as I could – whether leading or losing – and people like to see that supreme effort.

From a competitor's point of view a great sporting event usually requires tradition. Wimbledon will always remain *the* tennis championship to win and attend. The Admiral's Cup at Cowes is the most prestigious yacht race in the world (though Perth will surely be the place to be for the America's Cup next year), while Royal Ascot, the Derby and the Prix de L'Arc de Triomphe run neck and neck in the racing world.

The other side of sport is the social one. I think a lot of people enjoy skiing because it is an activity which makes them reasonably fit and it also has the après-ski. The great thing about skiing is that you can continually improve. My favourite resorts are mainly in France where they appear to be more geared up for skiing than other places. At Courchevel, there are lots of lifts, so you spend more time skiing and less time queueing.

At the top level of sporting event, everyone goes because everyone else goes. Part of the performance involves staying in the best places. In Monaco if it's not the Hôtel de Paris or The Hermitage, the right place is a private yacht in the harbour. Few actually offer a good view of the race, but the prestige is enormous. In the old days, Onassis would arrive on his yacht, which had a mosaic dance floor on deck that sank at the press of a button to reveal a swimming pool.

In 1974, which was the first year Lord Hesketh's extravagant Formula I racing team hit Monaco (with James Hunt in the hot seat), his was the only team to have two yachts but only one racing car! His was the last of the old-style, work-hard/play-hard teams, financed with private money. Grand Prix is big business now, with corporations footing most of the bills, and much of the drivers' time spent at sponsor functions.

Monaco still comes alive for those few days in May, and you can't help being caught up in the urgency of the moment – the colour, the sound, the people, the action. To be there, to be at the most splendid event in the world for your favourite sport, is to experience the very best of sporting life.

STIRLING MOSS, OBE is perhaps the most famous racing driver ever. Between 1947 and 1962, he competed in 496 races and won 222 including the Grand Prix in Monaco 3 times and in Britain and America twice. He was given his first car, an Austin 7, at the age of 10. A champion showjumper as a child, his current other love is skiing. Stirling Moss is now Motoring Editor of *Harpers & Queen*, and runs his own company.

CRICKET

WORLD'S BEST EVENTS

★

1 **THE ASHES, Lords, London**

2 **THE ASHES, Sydney**

EUROPE

BEST GROUND

LORD'S, St John's Wood Rd, London NW8, England ☎ (01) 289 1615. *"The home of cricket, where cricket nuts from all over the world long to go either to watch or play"* (David Gower). Best event: The Ashes (5-day Test series, England v Australia). *"The ultimate cricketing contest"* (Tony Greig). Members of Lord's-based MCC (see below) socialize (or fall asleep) in the Pavilion or Q Stand, but the ideal place is a private box, procured by ballot.

BEST CLUBS

I ZINGARI, c/o MCC, Lord's. A century-old club whose motto is: *"Keep your word, keep your temper, keep your wicket up."* Members, who include ex-captains of England Colin Cowdrey, Ted Dexter and Peter May, are divided into regular players, emergency players, and aged and decayed non-players. They wear gaudy black, red and yellow ties (with the yellow stripe falling first from the knot; only when in mourning for the monarch does the black stripe fall first). These pull rank over MCC ties at Lord's, enhanced by equally flamboyant hand-me-down blazers. One nonagenarian Brigadier only recently relinquished his 1912 vintage blazer in case he was called upon to play.

MARYLEBONE CRICKET CLUB (MCC), c/o Lord's. 40-year waiting list for the privilege of wearing a tie that looks like you've spilt eggs and orange juice down it.

BEST GEAR

GRAY NICHOLLS, Station Rd, Robertsbridge, E Sussex, England ☎ (0580) 880357. Best bats (Tony Greig, David Gower).

AUSTRALIA

BEST GROUNDS

ADELAIDE OVAL, North Adelaide, SA 5006 ☎ (08) 513759. *"The most beautiful Test ground in Australia, if not the world. A great occasion – a garden party atmosphere, champagne at the back on the grass tennis courts, a bit like Wimbledon"* (Henry Blofeld). Best party: when there's a rest day, the Hill-Smith family of Yalumba Winery transport bus-loads of cricket types to the Barossa Valley.

MELBOURNE CRICKET GROUND, St Kilda Rd, VA 3000 ☎ (03) 511913. Good atmosphere, with crowds of over 80,000, though the stadium is nothing to chant about.

SYDNEY CRICKET GROUND, Moore Park, Sydney, NSW 2021 ☎ (02) 357 6601. Australia's answer to Lords, though, sadly, the old stands with their Victorian ironwork have been replaced. However, the pavilion and a maze of dressing-rooms with wooden benches and old lockers do remain. Best event: England v Australia Test (Jan). *"A magnificent playing surface – it aids fast bowlers and also spinners. I used to love fielding at third man, in front of the Hill [the grassy area where ockers drink]. I kept being called a Pommy bastard, when the truth is I was born in South Africa. So I got a lot of pleasure using sign language to tell the Hillites they were a collection of convicts!"* (Tony Greig). Best party: Diana Fisher and Peter Doyle's (of the restaurant) on a boat on the rest day of the England v Australia Test.

"It's a great game artistically. When you watch someone like David Gower bat at his best, it makes you think perhaps of Nureyev and Fonteyn dancing *Swan Lake*. There's a sumptuousness about the movements. There's also something rather romantic about white-flannelled fools on green grass" (HENRY BLOFELD)

FAR EAST

BEST GROUND

EDEN GARDENS, c/o Cricket Association of Bengal, Calcutta, India ☎ (33) 232447. The world's largest ground, with crowds of about 100,000 every day. *"The most enthusiastic of cricket nations – the crowd goes wild and the stadium resounds with firecrackers when India takes a wicket"* (David Gower). *"My favourite cricket ground. The only Test I've played in where it was packed to capacity every day. I love India"* (Tony Greig).

FISHING

EUROPE

BEST RIVERS

★

SALMON

1 **SPEY, Scotland (at peak in spring)**

2 **TWEED, Scotland (peaks in late autumn; best stretches: the Duke of Roxburghe's and Junction Pool)**

3 **TAY, Scotland (peaks in spring and autumn)**

4 **DEE, Scotland (where the Queen Mother fishes, at Birkhall)**

★

TROUT

1 **TEST, England (best stretch owned by the Houghton Club; at peak early June)**

2 **ITCHEN, England**

BEST CLUB

HOUGHTON CLUB, c/o Grosvenor Hotel, High St, Stockbridge, Hampshire, England ☎ (0264) 810606 on the Test. The most exclusive club in England, founded in the 1820s. Only 12 (life) members – it's a long wait.

BEST LETS

The salmon famine has sent rents sky-high. A week on the Dee could cost £5,000 (US$7,234). The best stretches of river are leased through:

STRUTT & PARKER, 13 Hill St, London W1, England ☎ (01) 629 7282.

P D MALLOCH, 259 Old High St, Perth, Scotland ☎ (0738) 32316.

BEST GEAR

HOUSE OF HARDY, 61 Pall Mall, London SW1, England ☎ (01) 839 5515. For the best (graphite) rods. Suppliers to Royals – from Queen Victoria to the Queen Mother and Prince Charles – and makers of the Zane Grey big game reel that drew in the biggest-ever blue marlin (1,265 lb/575 kg), off Hawaii.

C FARLOW & CO, 5 Pall Mall, London SW1, England ☎ (01) 839 2423. Specialists in clothing and tackle for trout and salmon fishing.
Will make up rods, flies, etc. from customers' own designs. The Prince of Wales is a client.

ORVIS, Nether Wallop Mill, Stockbridge, Hampshire, England ☎ (0264) 781212. Best mail-order suppliers of rods, reels, flies, waders, nets, specialist clothes and oddities such as Vermont maple syrup. Fishing tuition arranged here too.

AMERICAS

Far-flung fishing

BRISTOL BAY, Alaska The best Pacific salmon fishing. It's almost as much of a struggle – and a delight – getting to the rivers as it is hauling in the fish. You fly to Anchorage, then on to Dillingham, where you are met and whisked to your lodge. Bristol Bay Lodge is the best – friendly; good food; lots of hot water.

HUNTSVILLE, Ontario *"You're flown to a lake all of your own with a canoe, fishing tackle and food, and left for the day. There are hundreds of lakes – it's wonderful"* (Cliff Michelmore).

GOLF

EUROPE

BEST COURSES

ROYAL AND ANCIENT GOLF CLUB, St Andrews, Fife, Scotland ☎ (0334) 72112. The Old Course is *the* best. *"No 1 in the world without a doubt – ask any golfer, and that's where they'll most want to play"* (Cliff Michelmore).

QUINTA DO LAGO, Almansil, 8100 Loulé, Algarve, Portugal ☎ (089) 94271. The Algarve is indisputably the best golf resort area of Europe. The best club, with lush fairways of Bermuda grass and a superb clubhouse with swimming pool. Golfers stay at Hotel Dom Pedro, 8125 Vilamoura ☎ (089) 35450.

WORLD'S BEST COURSES

★

1 **ROYAL AND ANCIENT, Scotland**

2 **CYPRESS POINT CLUB, California**

3 **QUINTA DO LAGO, Algarve**

AILSA COURSE, Turnberry, Strathclyde, Scotland ☎ (06553) 202. Fabulous position by the sea.

CRANS GOLF CLUB, Crans-sur-Sierre, Valais, Switzerland ☎ (027) 412168. A gem of a golf course, unmatched in Switzerland. Crystal clear air concentrates the mind, tightens the grip, and sends the ball rocketing over the fairways. Tranquil and lovely, with views of the Rhône Valley and the Alps beyond.

GLENEAGLES HOTEL & GOLF COURSES, Auchterarder, Tayside, Scotland ☎ (07646) 2231. Glorious course in moorland setting, and 5-star après-golfing indulgence. The only thing that disturbs the peace (and the deer) is a flock of loud checked trousers. 4 courses, including the championship King's and Queen's. (See also TRAVEL.)

GOLF DE MORFONTAINE, MORTEFONTAINE 60520 La Chapelle-en-Serval, Ile de France, France ☎ 4454 6827. One of the great courses of Europe, peaceful and surrounded by pines.

LA MANGA CLUB, Los Belones, Cartagena, Murcia, Spain ☎ (068) 569111. Resort golf.

MUIRFIELD, Gullane, Lothian, Scotland ☎ (0620) 842123. The oldest golf club in the world, founded in 1744. Golfing bon viveurs stay at glorious Greywalls Hotel (see TRAVEL).

PEVERO GOLF CLUB, Porto Cervo, Sardinia, Italy ☎ (0789) 96072. A Trent Jonesian masterpiece. Challenging course amid rugged mountains, with magnificent views over the Med. Within putting distance of the sailing set's playground.

ROYAL BIRKDALE, Southport, Merseyside, England ☎ (0704) 69903. The finest links in England, though a little bleak.

SUNNINGDALE, Sunningdale, Berkshire, England ☎ (0990) 21681. The most beautiful inland course in England.

VILLA D'ESTE, Montorfano 22030, Italy ☎ (031) 200200. One of the finest clubs and courses in Italy, lined with chestnuts, pines and birches. Excellent lunches and local wines on the terrace of the distinguished clubhouse, which add a certain *je ne sais quoi* to your swing in the afternoon.

AMERICAS

BEST CLUBS

CYPRESS POINT CLUB, PO Box 466, Pebble Beach, CA 93453 ☎ (408) 624 6444. Exclusive club which has hosted 3 presidents, a king and the Prince of Wales.

AUGUSTA NATIONAL, PO Box 2086 Augusta, GA 30913 ☎ (404) 738 7761. Fabulous course built on a floral nursery, designed by architect Dr Alister Mackenzie, but overseen by the ubiquitous Trent Jones. Venue of the Masters tournament in April.

LOS ANGELES COUNTRY CLUB, 1010 Wilshire Blvd, Los Angeles, CA 90024 ☎ (213) 276 6104. A country atmosphere amid the urban sprawl of LA. Prestigious, private, stuffy, chauvinistic (women have not been allowed to wear trousers). The North Course is one of the best in the US. Membership in the region of $75,000 with an endless waiting list.

PALM BEACH BATH & TENNIS CLUB, Palm Beach, FL 33480 ☎ (305) 832 4271. The best lunch in town – lobster and crabmeat salad. Dress cotton and casual, women may wear trousers. This club is keener on cordiality than wealth.

AUSTRALIA

BEST CLUBS

AUSTRALIAN GOLF CLUB, Bannerman Crescent, Rosebery, NSW 2018 ☎ (02) 663 2273. The best golf course in Sydney, but more nouveau than the RSGC. Redesigned by Jack Nicklaus in the seventies at the behest of Kerry Packer, who wanted juicier viewing when he televised the Australian Open. *"One of two outstanding courses in my mind [the other's Gleneagles]. It's a pleasure to walk around"* (Tony Greig).

ROYAL ADELAIDE GOLF CLUB, Tapley's Hill Rd, Seaton, Adelaide, SA 5023 ☎ (08) 356 5511. Championship course with a railway line running through the middle. In the top league in Australia, and sometime home of the Australian Open.

ROYAL SYDNEY GOLF CLUB, Kent Rd, Rose Bay, Sydney, NSW 2029 ☎ (02) 371 4333. Currently updating its course in order to wrest the Australian Open from the AGC in Bicentennial Year, 1988. Magnificent setting, difficult to get in to, expensive, cliquey. About 6,000 members, mostly men; after 6pm in the club, men must wear jacket and tie, and women skirts. Acres of coiffed lawn also accommodate croquet, bowls and tennis. Difficult to tell when the fairway ends and the green-carpeted clubhouse begins. Reciprocal arrangements with other Australian clubs – the Royal Adelaide, Royal Melbourne, Royal Brisbane, Royal Perth and Royal Hobart – plus St Andrews in Scotland and Hurlingham in London.

FAR EAST

BEST CLUBS

DISCOVERY BAY GOLF CLUB, Valley Rd, Lantau, Hong Kong ☎ (5) 987 7271. Designed by guru of the fairways Trent Jones. Reputedly the best course in SE Asia.

JURONG COUNTRY CLUB, 9 Science Centre Rd, Singapore ☎ 560 5655. Brand-new, carefully landscaped course of international standard.

KOGANEI, Koganei-shi, 184 Tokyo, Japan ☎ (0423) 811221. Japan's most expensive club at 100 million yen (US$ 559,284) membership.

NATIONAL COUNTRY CLUB, Fujinomiya, Shizuoka Prefecture, Japan ☎ (0544) 541051. Membership, which includes the octogenarian former prime minister Nobusuke Kishi, as

Golf club sandwich

The Japanese are obsessive about golf. There are millions of regular golfers in the country. The best – only – golf in jam-packed Tokyo is in any one of hundreds of tiered "chicken-coops". There you can practise your golfing drive in a 6½ ft (2 m) cubicle on top of a skyscraper (a bit like practising in a bunk bed on top of the Eiffel Tower).

well as the more infamous ex-PM Kakuei Tanaka, costs about 40 million yen (US$223,714) with threats of fees rising to keep out undesirables.

ROYAL HONG KONG GOLF CLUB, Fan Kan Rd, Fanling, New Territories, Hong Kong ☎ (0) 901 211. The most exclusive, expensive club in Hong Kong. 3 extensive courses here, plus a small 9-holer in Deepwater Bay. About HK$7,300 (US$935) membership.

SHEK O COUNTRY CLUB, Shek O, Hong Kong ☎ (5) 94429. A snooty, old-established club with mainly oldish gweilo members. Chinese have only been allowed to join in the last decade. A (green) young Briton once slipped on to the green and was spotted by his boss, who proclaimed: *"I don't come here to meet my subordinates. I never want to see you here again."*

SINGAPORE ISLAND COUNTRY CLUB, Island Club House, 180 Island Club Rd, Singapore ☎ 459 2222. 4 18-hole courses, the result of the combined strength of the Royal Island and Singapore Island clubs. The S$150,000 (US$69,897) membership makes it exclusively for the rich and powerful.

WACK WACK GOLF AND COUNTRY CLUB, Shaw Blvd, Man D, Manila ☎ (2) 784021. Lovely course in lush tropical gardens. Serious, wealthy Filipinos.

RACING

WORLD'S BEST EVENTS

★

1. **ROYAL ASCOT, Ascot, June**
2. **PRIX DE L'ARC DE TRIOMPHE, Longchamp, Oct**
3. **DERBY, Epsom, June**
4. **GRAND NATIONAL, Aintree, March/April**
5. **KENTUCKY DERBY, Kentucky, May**
6. **MELBOURNE CUP, Melbourne, Nov**

ROYAL ASCOT, Ascot Racecourse, Ascot, Berkshire, England ☎ (0990) 22211. June. The crème de la crème (more like cram de la cram) of the social racing year. The royal procession by carriage is a spectacle in itself, though nothing beats the Ladies' Day Silly Hat Parade led by Gertrude Shilling, rivalled on occasion by Dame Edna Everage. The Royal Enclosure (for habitués of at least 8 years and those they sponsor in) is the only place to be – with your name tag (for all except Betty Windsor), your dark morning suit (or service or national dress) and grey top hat. Women must wear a hat that covers the crown. *"Wonderful picnic parties given by Charles Benson"* (Taki); *"I love the whole thing – the glamour, the procession, the racing, and I meet masses of friends"* (Betty Kenward); Lady Elizabeth Anson adores it too.

PRIX DE L'ARC DE TRIOMPHE, Hippodrome de Longchamp, Bois de Boulogne, 75016 Paris, France ☎ (1) 4772 5733. Oct. The Arc is the most prestigious race in the world and the most valuable in Europe – the winner takes FF2,659,250 (US$374,806). The race that determines the international champion of champions among horses aged 3 and over: the winner is worth a mint in stud fees. Held at elegant Longchamp, which draws international horsy glamours. A whirlwind of social gatherings, especially at the Ritz.

DERBY, United Racecourse, Racecourse Paddock, Epsom, Surrey, England ☎ (03727) 26311. June. The most prestigious race in England, with total prize money of over £350,000 (US$506,345) and a soaring stud value – up to £40 million (US$57,868,000) – for the winner. A tremendous sense of occasion, morning suits, black toppers, picnics – and champers, of course – are *de rigueur*.

GRAND NATIONAL, Aintree Racecourse, Liverpool, England ☎ (051) 523 6520. March/April. Long, 4½ mile (7.24 km) race with 30 jumps which prove the supreme test of daring and endurance. For racing connoisseurs rather than socialites, though the view's more complete on telly. *Everyone*, however, should go once.

CHELTENHAM GOLD CUP, Cheltenham Racecourse, Prestbury Park, Cheltenham, Gloucestershire, England ☎ (0242) 23102. March. The National Hunt Festival displays steeplechasing and hurdling at their best. Crammed with ardent enthusiasts headed by the Queen Mother, all oblivious to the weather. Strong Irish contingent – the Cup runneth over with Guinness and Irish Whiskey.

GOODWOOD, Goodwood Racecourse, Chichester, W Sussex, England ☎ (0243) 774107. July. Delightful summer event, though it's madly windy. The scenic course is owned by a bunch of aristos – the Richmond/March/Settrington/Gordon-Lennox family. Light suits and panamas for men, straw hats and frocks for women. Pimm's is *the* drink.

HENNESSY GOLD CUP, The Racecourse, Newbury, Berkshire, England ☎ (0635) 40015. Nov. A very drunken day – more than any other meeting. Start of the jumping season.

BEST CLUB

TURF CLUB, 5 Carlton House Terrace, London SW1, England ☎ (01) 930 8555. Well-bred club for the higher echelons of the racing world. *"Fun, upper-class sporting crowd; racy, raunchy types who have drinks and debts. Grace, the head porter, has been there 55 years and knows every single person in London. The club is Grace"* (Taki).

AMERICAS

BEST EVENTS

KENTUCKY DERBY, Churchill Downs, 700 Central Ave, Louisville, KY 40208 ☎ (502) 636 3541. May. The race everyone would like to win; for 3-year-olds, with $500,000 in prize money. First leg of the Triple Crown (horse must go on to win the Preakness and Belmont Stakes – only 11 horses have succeeded in the past century). In 1985, three ex-Presidents, a mint of Hollywood stars and 120,000 others attended before trotting off to lunch on home-made Derby Pie, real Kentucky fried chicken and beaten biscuits washed down by mint juleps and bourbon.

BELMONT STAKES, Belmont Park, Long Island, New York, c/o PO Box 90, Jamaica, NY 11417 ☎ (718) 641 4700. June. Third leg of the Triple Crown. Racing continues for 4 months of the year, 6 days a week.

BREEDERS CUP, Los Angeles Turf Club (see Clubs). Recently established but immediately important, with an inordinately high $10 million in prize money – the biggest in the world. The Superbowl of racing.

ECLIPSE AWARDS, Grand Ballroom, Fontainebleau Hilton, 4441 Collins Ave, Miami Beach, FL 33140 ☎ (305) 538 2000. Feb. Oscar-style presentations for the best racehorse performance of the year, nominated by press and pundits. A flurry of film stars and celebs.

HIALEAH, Box 158, Hialeah, FL 33011 ☎ (305) 885 8000. Preparatory races for the Kentucky Derby are run for 2 months each winter, when the climate of the Sunshine State sees the making or breaking of horses. The Flamingo Stakes are celebrated by the Flamingo Ball.

TRAVERS, PO Box 564, Saratoga Springs, NY 12866 ☎ (518) 584 6200. August. The highlight of the Saratoga racing season, which takes place over 1 month in upstate New York. A charming old town and track with the original wooden stands. *"The entire racing scene moves up there. A national magnet for Kentucky horses, some Californian stables, and racing society – including Vanderbilts, Bostwicks, du Ponts, Guests, Mellons and Phippses. The best-quality racing in the year. Parties every night, private and charity"* (Steven Crist).

BEST CLUBS

LOS ANGELES TURF CLUB, Santa Anita Park, 285 W Huntingdon Drive, Arcadia, CA 91006 ☎ (818) 574 7223. The only other private club of racing, set in one of the most scenically beautiful courses in the world.

TURF & FIELD CLUB, PO Box 62, Jamaica, NY 11417 ☎ (718) 641 4700. Established in 1895, the oldest private racing club in the USA, with bases at Belmont Park and Aqueduct Racecourse. Daniel Wildenstein and William S Paley are members; new hopefuls must be true aficionados, personally introduced and then voted in.

Bloodstock bucks

The United States is the golden source of thoroughbreds (ever since blinkered Britons wiped out their own stud population by selling to the States). The sales pavilion at Keeneland, Lexington, in Kentucky is the powerhouse for buyers and sellers in July. The Selected Yearling Sale is the most important bloodstock auction in the world. Investors from Europe, Japan and the Middle East (but it's mainly Arab sheikhs and Robert Sangster) flock to buy. Every year sees record-breaking sales. The latest was $13.1 million.

AUSTRALIA

BEST EVENTS

MELBOURNE CUP, Flemington Racecourse, Melbourne, VIC 3031 ☎ (03) 376 0441. Nov. *"Melbourne comes alive that week – for once. Equal best with the Epsom Derby for sheer visual appeal and because they're people's days"* (Susan Renouf). Special luncheon for the élite and a public holiday for all – even Parliament stops to listen. *"The most exciting racing event. Adrenalin is built up by the media for 3 months in advance. Afterwards, every cab driver and porter could tell you who the winner is"* (Robert Sangster).

MEMORIES OF MELBOURNE

"One Melbourne Cup there was the most enormous thunderstorm, and this fantastic mud-runner from New Zealand won. The jockey was totally unrecognizable – you could just see his eyes when the goggles came off. And then, out of the pouring rain, this character appeared in wet-suit and flippers and stole the front page of every paper worldwide." (Susan Renouf)

THE AUSTRALASIAN, Ascot, Perth, WA 6000. Jan. To be held for the first time on Australia Day, 26 January 1987, this is one of the mega-bucks pre-America's Cup crowd-pullers. Can't fail to impress, with A$1 million (US$706,614) at stake.

GREAT EASTERN STEEPLECHASE, Onkaparinga Racing Club, Adelaide, SA 5000 ☎ (08) 212 6179. The best *fun* event – true carnival spirit. Blends the panache and style of Ascot with the friendliness of a country picnic.

FAR EAST

BEST EVENT

JAPAN CUP, Tokyo Race Course, Fuchu City, Japan ☎ (0423) 633141. Nov. Thoroughbreds from 8 countries around the world vie for the laurels and a hefty 148,800,000 yen (US$832,214) plus in prize money.

BEST CLUB

ROYAL HONG KONG JOCKEY CLUB, Sports Rd, Happy Valley, Hong Kong ☎ (5) 837811. They used to say that in HK hierarchy, the Jockey Club came first, Hong Kong Club second and the Government third. Country annexe for horsy types is at Bees River on the New Territories. Racing, all operated by the RHKJC, is frantically important in Hong Kong – partly as a staple in the social diet and partly because, in a small community of wealthy would-be gamblers, it is the only legal form of betting. Consequently, staggering sums of money change hands (a turnover of HK$19.6 billion [US$2.5 billion] in 1985). Regular weekend and midweek evening meetings at the racy new grass track at Shatin or the old, sandy racetrack at Happy Valley. The cuisine in the Derby Room of the main clubhouse is among the best in Hong Kong. Prestige spot is the Stewards' Box; slap-up dinner brought to the box, bets taken from the box, action all there on the box (futuristic 66 × 20 ft (20 × 6 m) TV screens) – you need never stir.

HUNTING

EUROPE

BEST HUNTS

TOP 5

★

1. BEAUFORT, Gloucestershire
2. QUORN, Leicestershire
3. PYTCHLEY, Northamptonshire
4. BELVOIR, Lincolnshire
5. ZETLAND, N Yorkshire

BEAUFORT, c/o Major Dallas, Primrose Hill, Westonbirt, Tetbury, Gloucestershire, England ☎ (066 688) 252. The Duke of Beaufort's hunt has the finest pack of hounds. Immensely smart – the POW rides with this pack. No red coats here – they're known as the blues and buffs, and the hunt servants' green livery is lavished with buttons. Glorious hunting: the countryside (all 760 sq miles [1,968 sq km] of it) makes it – lovely undulating land without too many steep hills, acres of good grass to gallop over, hedges with no barbed wire and plenty of woods.

QUORN, c/o Major C J Humfrey, Newbold Farm, Burrough-on-the-Hill, Melton Mowbray, Leicestershire, England ☎ (066 477) 329. Hailed as the best hunt, certainly the most prestigious of the 5 Shire packs (Shires are the home of hunting). But expensive – the cap is about £60 (US$87) a day; a long waiting list of prospective subscribers. Joss Hanbury is joint-master of both the Quorn and the Cottesmore. Star huntsman (the best in the country) is Michael Farrin.

PYTCHLEY, c/o Major Cheyne, Manor House, Badby, Daventry, Northamptonshire, England ☎ (0327) 702374. Hunt servants wear a plummy Padua red coat. Senior master Dick Saunders is a former Grand National winner.

BELVOIR, c/o Mr Henson, Ermine House, Boothly, Gaffoe, Lincolnshire, England ☎ (0522) 810206. The Duke of Rutland's is the hardest-riding pack – fall off and you'll be trampled by over-eager Belvoirs.

ZETLAND, c/o Mrs Reynolds, Spencer Cottage, Gilling West, Richmond, N Yorkshire, England ☎ (0748) 2759. The Quorn of the North. Marvellous hunting country, hard riding, and a cracking pack of hounds.

CATTISTOCK, c/o Mr R Unwin, Mary Jane, Toller Porcorum, Dorset, England ☎ (0300) 20641. The "true blue hunt". Happiness in hunting is a 5-letter word: GRASS. In rural England, ravaged by the plough, this is becoming a luxury, but there's still masses of unadulterated green stuff in the West Country.

FERNIE, c/o Mr R G Watson, Springfield Farm, Smeeton, Westerby, Leicestershire, England ☎ (053 753) 2271. The best-mannered hunt, with a good quota of peers to keep up the tradition, among them the Earls of Verulam, Onslow and Inchcape.

HEYTHROP, c/o Major J Ballard, Worton Heath Farm, Middle Barton, Oxfordshire, England ☎ (0608) 83237. The smartest meet is during the Cheltenham National Hunt Festival, in between racing days. Otherwise *un peu nouveau riche.*

Huntin' red coats

Hunting etiquette requires you to have a *red* coat (it's now suburban to say "pink", and one hopes you never said "jacket"), breeches (not "jodhpurs"), stock (not in a million years a "cravat"), hard hat, and *good boots.*

BEST HUNT BALL

HORSE & HOUND BALL, Grosvenor House Hotel, London W1, England ☎ (01) 261 6741. Royal horsies Princesses Anne and Michael go. Ever-growing in grandeur. Provincial balls are to be avoided, with the possible exception of the Belvoir and Heythrop.

BEST GEAR

HUNTSMAN (see FASHION) for the very best coats.

HENRY MAXWELL, 11 Savile Row, London W1, England ☎ (01) 734 9714. Perfect riding boots (pushing £1,000/US$1,447 a pair, plus nearly £200/US$289 for the trees) unless you're bandying new money – it's said they can spot the gait of a nouveau as he walks through the door.

JAMES LOCK, 6 St James's St, London SW1, England ☎ (01) 930 5849. For hard hats, silk top hats that'll knock you back £250 (US$362) if you're not knocked unconscious first, and – more practically – safety hats with chinstraps.

FRANK HALL, 30 St Mary's Rd, Market Harborough, Leicestershire, England ☎ (0858) 62402. Best gear in the country. Royal warrant for PC's hunting coats, etc.

S MILNER & SON, Belgrave Gate, Leicestershire, England ☎ (0533) 56733. Hunting gear is an investment. Shops that are local to the big hunts produce top-notch kit.

SWAINE ADENEY BRIGG, 185 Piccadilly, London W1, England ☎ (01) 734 4277. Handmade riding whips made to any specification – crocodile with an ivory top, for example – saddles, hunting horns and flask cases. (They are perhaps better known for their umbrellas, which shelter the royal family, James and Edward Fox, Paul Newman and Dustin Hoffman. They also made the frog mascot that Prince Andrew gave to Princess Diana, and the chrome owl he gave Fergie.)

BERNARD WEATHERILL, Kilgour, French & Stanbury, 33a Dover St, London W1, England ☎ (01) 629 4283. Best breeches in town – makes for the royals.

AUSTRALIA

BEST HUNT

OAKLANDS HUNT CLUB, Sherwood, Somerton Rd, Greenvale, Melbourne, VIC 3047 ☎ (03) 333 1533. Not the oldest, but the toffiest, strictest and most traditional hunt in Australia.

MOTOR RACING

WORLD'S BEST FORMULA I RACES

★

1. **MONACO GRAND PRIX, Monte Carlo, May**
2. **AUSTRALIAN GRAND PRIX, Adelaide, Oct**
3. **BRAZILIAN GRAND PRIX, Rio de Janeiro, March**
4. **BRITISH GRAND PRIX, Brands Hatch or Silverstone, July**
5. **AMERICAN GRAND PRIX, Detroit, June**

EUROPE

BEST EVENTS

MONACO GRAND PRIX The grand social event of the circuit. The entire town turns into the racing arena, presided over by the Monégasque royals and a glittering entourage of film and pop stars, playboys and socialites. Non-stop partying culminates in cocktails at the Hôtel de Paris, *"a bejewelled, star-studded, multilingual extravaganza not to be missed"* (Stirling Moss). It's also the best place to stay, in a balconied room overlooking the course.

BRITISH GRAND PRIX Lots of clout, an entertaining day with RAF fly-pasts, helicopters, Concorde even. ... But, since you can't prolong the party 50 miles (80 km) out of town (nightclubs aren't a feature of Brands Hatch), socializing is of the on-track corporate kind.

BEST AMATEUR CLUB

96 CLUB, Gate House, Oak Grange Rd, W Clandon, Surrey, England ☎ (0483) 222741. Track them down at Brands Hatch or Silverstone, in their hospitality suites. Founded by Michael Scott for fast-car enthusiasts with money to burn. They rent circuits to thrash around on and have lessons. *"Very exclusive, very social, a self-indulgence for the professional guy who'll never make it in racing"* (Stirling Moss). Best binge: le camping weekend to Le Mans (96ers are honorary members of the 72 Club du Mans for ex-Le Mans drivers). Tents are pitched in serried ranks at the Tertre Rouge garage on the first corner of the circuit. British teams are entertained in lavish style by the 96 squad; they later flash their lights in acknowledgement as they zip past.

AMERICAS

BEST EVENTS

BRAZILIAN GRAND PRIX Important event as it marks the start of the season. Carnival country plus big money means muchos festivities.

AMERICAN GRAND PRIX The heartland of American automobiles. Important, a big social deal for enthusiasts, and film/pop stars.

AUSTRALIA

BEST EVENTS

🏆 **AUSTRALIAN GRAND PRIX.** The first event, in 1985, was organized with professionalism and panache. Street circuit, like Monaco.

DALLAS GRAND SPREE

A glistening social event held infrequently. Last time, most of the cast of *Dallas* went – JR *et al* – and Jimmy Carter with full bodyguard. A celebrity race before the big day attracted crowds. Neiman Marcus held a stupendous in-store cocktail party (barbecue extraordinaire, Rolls-Royce auctioned for charity) and magnanimously offered to organize ladies' wardrobes for the event – they choose, you pay. *"The only time I've ever been in an air-conditioned tent, silk-lined, like Arabian Nights, and carpeted throughout. Drivers and cars were incidental to the pomp and circumstance"* (Stirling Moss). *"Everything that happens in Dallas has a social side to it. If you have an ingrowing toenail operation there's an extravaganza attached"* (Susie Moss).

POLO

WORLD'S BEST EVENTS

★

1. ARGENTINE OPEN, Palermo, Nov/Dec
2. WORLD CUP, Palm Beach, March
3. BRITISH OPEN, Cowdray Park, July
4. GOLD CUP, Deauville, Aug
5. GOLD CUP, Sydney, Easter

EUROPE

BEST EVENTS

🏆 **BRITISH OPEN, Cowdray Park Polo Club** (see below), July. Best event for players (2 Brits minimum to a 4-man team), and for spectators – if they can share Lord Cowdray's little box with its wicker chairs and royal guests. Otherwise they're mainly dressed-down country British stock, with touches of cosmopolitan glamour, such as when Dallas porcelain millionairess and patron Helen Boehm flew in with 300 of her best customers for the occasion. Cowdray Ball on final night is very grand.

GOLD CUP, Polo de Deauville, Calvados 14, Deauville, France, Aug. At the same time as the races and thoroughbred sales. Niarchos and Rothschild own local stud farms. Imported players and attendant society. Patrons, their teams and hangers-on stay at the Hotels Normandy and Royal, where it's one long party. Flashy, racy; no one ever notices who wins.

INTERNATIONAL, Guards' Club (see below), July. Most loudly trumpeted event in Britain, though it's not a *proper* international – teams are thrown together specially, and some players scoff that they don't even change ends after each goal. But it's *"the best polo to be seen in Europe – teams in excess of 30 goals"* (Lord Patrick Beresford). Bands, parades, the Princess of Wales with fingers crossed for Charlie (who plays in the second, lower-calibre match), superior Army officers and their Golf GTIs. Run by Prince Charles's polo manager Major Ferguson, Prince Andrew's father-in-law.

BEST CLUBS

♚ **COWDRAY PARK, Midhurst, W Sussex, England ☎ (073081) 3257.** Most prestigious club, with 9 polo pitches, in the lovely parkland of Lord Cowdray's stately home.

CIRENCESTER PARK, Cirencester, Gloucestershire, England ☎ (0285) 3225. In the top league, although Cowdray players complain that every time there's a drop of rain Cirencester cancels.

GUARDS', Smiths Lawn, Windsor Great Park, Englefield Green, Egham, Surrey, England ☎ (0784) 34212. Thinks it's the best. Long waiting list, expensive bar.

ROYAL COUNTY OF BERKSHIRE POLO CLUB, North St, Winkfield, Windsor, Berkshire, England ☎ (0344) 886555. Newly opened by ex-manager of Deep Purple Brian Morrison, with Norman Lobel. Blends American plush with English roots. Smart clubhouse, tennis courts, croquet lawn and gym. Only 30 members, including high-goaler Howard Hipwood.

BEST GEAR

LOCK (see Hunting) for helmets.

LOBB (see FASHION) for boots

RICE BROS, 6 West St, Midhurst, W Sussex, England ☎ (073081) 3395. One of the best saddlers in the world, used by the Cowdray set.

J SALTER & SON, 23 High St, Aldershot, Hampshire, England ☎ (0252) 20692. Best sticks, made to measure – you specify length, weight, width, finish. Players get through about 15 a season.

AMERICAS

BEST EVENTS

♚ **ARGENTINE OPEN, Cancha de La Victoria, Palermo, Argentina.** Gigantic stadium with mammoth crowds. Top event to win. Polo is the premier sport of Argentina – everyone learns out on the estancias; it's second nature. Their best teams are 40-goalers, which means every player has a 10-goal handicap – the ultimate.

♚ **WORLD CUP, Palm Beach Polo & Country Club,** (see below), April. $100,000 match, sponsored by Piaget, with teams of pros whose standard is second only to that of the Argentine Open. A glitzy, global, garden-party-style gala that attracts Rolls-Royces and convertible Mercedes-full of Florida Fluorides in Porsche sunglasses. Crab, caviare and champagne are conspicuously consumed in the Polo House.

GREAT GATSBY DAY, Will Rogers State Park, 14253 Sunset Blvd, Pacific Palisades, CA 90272 ☎ (213) 454 8212. A refined summer event with Hollywood lookers-on. (On a normal day in this park, you can see members of the select Will Rogers Polo Club practising, including surgeons with bleepers on their breeches.)

BEST CLUBS

♚ **PALM BEACH POLO & COUNTRY CLUB, 13198 Forest Hill Blvd, W Palm Beach, FL 33411 ☎ (305) 793 1113.** A 1,650-acre (668 hectares) resort complex for the chic. Superb tennis courts and golf course. Best pitches in the world – purpose-built (over a swamp) with ultra-efficient drainage and Bermuda grass which grows *horizontally* across the ground producing a spongy carpet – the ultimate surface.

SANTA BARBARA POLO & RACQUET CLUB, 3375 Foothill Rd, Carpinteria, CA 93013 ☎ (805) 684 6683. Manicured fields nestle between the Santa Ynez mountains and shimmering Pacific Ocean. Many charity extravaganzas.

WILLOW BEND POLO & HUNT CLUB, PO Box 1010, Plano, TX 75074 ☎ (214) 248 6298. Set up by local fast-food supremo Norman Brinker, patron and player. The best medium-goal polo club, playground for the Dallas set.

AUSTRALIA

BEST EVENTS

GOLD CUP, Sydney Showground, Moore Park, Sydney, NSW 2021 ☎ (02) 331 9111. Held on the small ground in the middle of the Royal Easter (Agricultural) Show. Unusual event – 3 a side, very fast. Floodlit final on Easter Monday draws 25,000 spectators. Aussie players are largely farmers, in the same mould as Argentinians; both nationalities have the advantage of being able to play virtually all year round.

POLO BALL, Sheraton-Wentworth Hotel, 61 Phillip St, Sydney, NSW 2000 ☎ (02) 230 0700. Held on Maundy Thursday. Smartest table: that of NSW's former, 10-goal, player Sinclair Hill (who has coached and hosted the Prince of Wales) and his wife Wendy. Their guests include visiting English jackaroos, impresario and sometime polo player Harry M. Miller, and the Hills' son Noel and his wife Annie (née Bolton, ex-flatmate of the Princess of Wales). There is a "Calcutta", in which favoured players change hands for up to A$2,500 (US$1,766).

BEST CLUBS

ADELAIDE POLO CLUB, Rose Park, SA 5067 ☎ (08) 42 7757. Informal polo – bushies turn up in boots, Akubra hats, ties and moleskins, all from R M Williams (see FASHION, Perth). BYO (Bring Your Own) refreshment – cucumber and pâté sandwiches (sangers) and Pimm's.

HEXHAM POLO CLUB, c/o Terang Sporting Club, Main St, Terang, VIC 3264 ☎ (055) 998218.

LILYDALE POLO CLUB, Flowerfield, Coldstream, Melbourne, VIC 3770 ☎ (03) 654 5216. Melbourne polo is the snootiest in Australia.

ELEPHANT POLO

Picture, if you can, a curious gathering of elephants, elongated polo sticks and a sea of internationally known faces. Each December, the World Elephant Polo Championships take place at Meghauli in the Royal Chitwan National Park, Nepal. Competitors include the Tiger Tops Tuskers, Pan Am Jumbos, Gurkha Gladiators, and imported celebs such as the firm-seated Lucinda Green and Virginia Holgate and their husbands, following in the heavy hoofprints of the unlikely Ringo Starr, Barbara Bach, Billy Connolly and Steve Strange. The merry band take over Tiger Tops Jungle Lodge. Go via ExplorAsia (see TRAVEL).

ROWING

WORLD'S BEST EVENTS

★

1. **HENLEY ROYAL REGATTA, Oxfordshire, Jun/Jul**
2. **LUCERNE REGATTA, Lucerne, July**

EUROPE

BEST EVENTS

CAMBRIDGE UNIVERSITY MAYS, on the Cam, Cambridge, England. June: **OXFORD UNIVERSITY EIGHTS WEEK,** on the Isis, Oxford, England. May. Crews row in divisions, and try to bump the boat ahead (a gentle touch constitutes a bump, and the cox's hand shoots up to acknowledge it: ramming the cox in the back is frowned upon). It's a week of constant partying in the boathouses, and romantic twilight theatre productions and grand May balls in college quads and gardens. On the final night, members of the winning – Head of the River – crew ceremoniously burn their boat and hurl themselves through the flames. Nursing singed eyebrows, they go on to massacre a decadent bump supper. Best bump supper ever: at Merton, when the chef (the best university chef in Britain) concocted a boat-shaped Baked Alaska complete with crew and oars.

OXFORD & CAMBRIDGE UNIVERSITY BOAT RACE, Putney to Mortlake, London, England. March/April. Fit-as-fit though weatherbeaten varsity boys vie to win this historic race, while drinking enthusiasts line the banks of the Thames. Best spectacle ever: in 1984, when the yellow Cambridge boat accidentally rammed a barge and sank like a squashed banana into the murky river.

LUCERNE REGATTA, Rotsee Lake, Lucerne, Switzerland ☎ (041) 502255. July. The hub of international rowing – the regatta in which every pro wants to row. Perfect conditions – deep water, no wind, fast rowing – the connoisseur's dream. Rowers congregate at the Pickwick Pub. Best crew: the East Germans, who practically always win. The secondary aim of the event is to acquire an East German vest. Russians happily swap theirs for foreign currency, cameras, etc, but the EGs cling on to theirs for grim death – they're impossible to replace back home.

BEST CLUB

LEANDER, Henley-on-Thames, Oxfordshire, England ☎ (0491) 575782. The oldest rowing club in the world with the most ludicrous emblem: a pink hippo. Members (all oarsmen) wear Leander-pink socks, ties and blazers, and look like they've been whizzed up in a Magimix with the smoked salmon and strawberries. At Regatta-time, since the clubhouse is but a stagger away from the Stewards', crews who have been knocked out meander down to Leander for a change of Pimm's.

HENLEY: REGATTA CHATTER

HENLEY ROYAL REGATTA, Regatta House, Henley-on-Thames, Oxfordshire, England ☎ (04912) 2153. June/July. *"The best, most traditional regatta in the world – the heart of rowing in an emotional way"* (Dan Topolski). A glorious summer event, the epitome of all that is English: lavish picnics, a Champagne Lawn, marquees, bunting, a bandstand, the river, the sun (sometimes), a speech-giving Royal (occasionally) – last year it was Prince Andrew. The place to be (if not a member of the Leander club), is the Stewards' Enclosure (members and guests only), amid a sea of boaters and panamas, crisp white cotton frocks, stripes – endless stripes, and pea-green Eton blazers. Men must wear jacket, tie and never jeans; women never trousers – even nattily culotted ladies are told to leg it.

SAILING

WORLD'S BEST EVENTS

★

Points for the best events go towards the Champagne Mumm World Cup. They are:

1 **AMERICA'S CUP, Australia, Feb '87**

2 **ADMIRAL'S CUP, England, Aug**

3 **SARDINIA CUP, Italy, Sept**

4 **KENWOOD (formerly Clipper) CUP, Hawaii, Aug/Sept**

5 **SOUTHERN CROSS CUP, Australia, Dec/Jan**

EUROPE

BEST EVENTS

ADMIRAL'S CUP, c/o RORC (see Clubs), Aug, odd years. The best ocean-racing team event (countries enter 3 yachts), held biennially during Cowes Week, sponsored by bubbly Mumm. Three 1-day and one 2-day races culminate in the famous 4/5-day Fastnet Race. Aussie yachties say it's cold, foggy and terrible sailing, but it's *the* series to win because the competition's so good. Prince Philip and sons are there on the royal yacht *Britannia*, guarded by a Naval vessel. Streets, pubs and clubs (the Island and the Royal London) teem with riotous yachties, a sea of navy blue. When the Brazilians last won a race, the marina vibrated to the rhythm of the crew's impromptu band.

SARDINIA CUP, c/o Yacht Club Costa Smeralda (see Clubs). Sept. The most glamorous series in the sailing world. *Everyone* attends, from the King of Spain to Alan Bond. Each visiting nation throws a party, and yachties go wild. However, Porto Cervo is purposely way beyond the means of the average crew, which means it attracts the richest, not necessarily the best.

COWES WEEK, Cowes Combined Clubs, 18 Bath Rd, Cowes, Isle of Wight, England ☎ (0983) 295744. Aug. A virtual ghost town out of season, Cowes leaps into life in summer – especially Admiral's Cup years. All classes of boat are catered for, including the historic X boats. International crews and their entourages rent every square foot of sleeping space; Juliana's brings along a disco; yacht clubs host, in turn, a different ball each night, and, as a finale, fireworks explode over the sea and culminate in a pyrotechnic portrait of Her Majesty.

BEST CLUBS

ROYAL OCEAN RACING CLUB (RORC), 20 St James's Place, London SW1, England ☎ (01) 493 5252. Organizers of most British-run international offshore races; more seriously sailing-orientated than the Royal Thames. Based in two small Georgian houses.

ROYAL THAMES YACHT CLUB, 60 Knightsbridge, London SW1, England ☎ (01) 235 2121. The commodore is the Prince of Wales, the vice-commodore, Owen Aisher, sailing luminary and Marley tileman. Smart premises shared, incongruously, with the Anglo-Belgian Society. Challengers for the America's Cup.

ROYAL YACHT SQUADRON, The Castle, Cowes, Isle of Wight, England ☎ (0983) 292743. The marine version of White's – smart, stuffy, faded grandeur. Used to blackball everyone in trade, but though the tea set were kept out (Sir Thomas Lipton), the beerage have trickled in (Whitbreads and more). The main traditions of Cowes Week emanate from the Squadron – the start and finish of each race marked deafeningly by *their* shiny brass cannons; the royals slipping in via *their* slipway; *the* ball of the week being *their* ball.

KIELER YACHT CLUB, Hindenburgufer 70, Kiel, Germany ☎ (0431) 85021. Produces consistently strong racing teams, which sweep up the best cups.

ROYAL BURNHAM YACHT CLUB, The Quay, Burnham-on-Crouch, Essex, England ☎ (0621) 782044. Put on the international map after Peter de Savary launched his Victory '83 syndicate from here. Popular, upmarket, active.

ROYAL LYMINGTON YACHT CLUB, Bath Rd, Lymington, Hampshire, England ☎ (0590) 72677. The best local club, in a smart little town. Overlooks sea and an ever-growing marina. Home of the turn-of-the-century X boats, *"floating vintage Bentleys"* (Col D German). Active royal patronage in the shape of Princess Anne, who choppers in several times a year.

YACHT CLUB COSTA SMERALDA, 07020 Porto Cervo, Costa Smeralda, Sardinia, Italy ☎ (0789) 92590. Built by the Aga Khan with a consortium of wealthy Italians such as Gianni Agnelli. Like a Hollywood film set with a swimming pool on the roof and more ritzy yachts than anywhere else. As challengers for the America's Cup, an area has been designated for 12-metre antics; Italy is awash with *Azzurra*mania.

YACHT CLUB DE FRANCE, 6 rue de Galilée, Paris 75016, France ☎ (1) 4720 8929. Most prestigious club in France, the equivalent to the Royal Thames.

AMERICAS

BEST EVENTS

KENWOOD CUP, Royal Hawaiian Ocean Racing Club, PO Box 88648, Honolulu, HA 96830 ☎ (808) 941 1273. Aug/Sept. Formerly the Clipper Cup, well organized, and the best fun of all the international series. (It has to be for the Aussies, who have beaten into the hellish wind for over a month to get there; some arrive with bent keels from being on one tack for so long.) The main race is the Round the Island. Big seas, big crowds, big US participation, crazy crews.

ONION PATCH SERIES, c/o New York Yacht Club (see below). June. The series ends up with the oldest ocean race in the world, the magnificent Bermuda Race. A test of navigational skills – 635 miles (1,022 km) of nothing but sea, the Gulf Stream and reefs to pit one's wits against.

SOUTHERN OCEAN RACING CONFERENCE, c/o Lauderdale Yacht Club, 1725 SE 12th St, Fort Lauderdale, FL 33316 ☎ (305) 524 5508. Feb. The joint effort of this and several other clubs, ending up with the big Miami to Nassau race. The chief US series, on Admiral's Cup lines only more parochial.

BEST CLUBS

IDA LEWIS YACHT CLUB, PO Box 479, Newport, RI 02840 ☎ (401) 846 1969. A ramshackle wooden clubhouse belies the expensiveness and exclusiveness of this club. On its own tiny island. Scenes of revelry during the Onion Patch series.

NEW YORK YACHT CLUB, 37 W 44th St, New York NY 10036 ☎ (212) 382 1000. Elegant gentlemen's club (women cut no ice here) with leather chairs, fine paintings, models and trophies. Spending $15 million on their challenge campaign for the America's Cup.

ROYAL BERMUDA YACHT CLUB, PO Box HM 894, Point Pleasant Rd, Hamilton 5 ☎ (809) 295 2214. An old colonial-style royal club, with an active fleet.

ST FRANCIS YACHT CLUB, Marina Blvd, San Francisco, CA 94123 ☎ (415) 563 6363. Perfect blend of city and harbourside club. Reciprocal privileges with the New York YC and the Royal Thames in London. Holds an annual Stag Cruise for 700 yachtsmen (men being the operative word) to the private retreat of Tinsley Island.

SAN DIEGO YACHT CLUB, Foot of Talbot St, San Diego, CA 92106 ☎ (619) 222 1103. Modern, laid-back, sunny club overlooking yachts. Respected contender for the America's Cup, since their commodore is the determined 1980 winner Dennis Conner, who, though the wind was taken out of his sails last AmCup, is generally regarded as the greatest 12-metre sailor in the world.

AUSTRALIA

BEST EVENTS

SOUTHERN CROSS CUP, c/o CYC, Sydney (see below). The Admiral's Cup of the southern hemisphere, with lots of grass-roots support plus UK, HK and NZ. The series, spaced out over Christmas, equals two weeks of non-stop raging. Sunny Boxing Day, start of the important Sydney to Hobart race, sees a jostle of sleek pointed bows and a flourish of colourful spinnakers. This race is almost a puberty rite for young Aussies. Riotous New Year's Eve on the boats in Hobart followed by mega-hangovers and a remedial QLD – nothing to do with Queensland, but a Quiet Little Drink.

BEST CLUBS

ROYAL SYDNEY YACHT SQUADRON, Peel St, Kirribilli, NSW 2061 ☎ (02) 927 171. Old-established, senior club of Australia, fine house and grounds. Small sailing membership, large eating membership (one stalwart felt it was his job to keep the public *off* the water). Difficult to penetrate – has been known to blackball good but belligerent sailors.

CRUISING YACHT CLUB OF AUSTRALIA (CYC), New Beach Rd, Sydney, NSW 2000 ☎ (02) 329 731. Arriviste, active, informal, raucous, full of characters. Clubhouse right on the waters of rich Rushcutters Bay. Yacht owners include vending-machine king Jack Rooklyn (whose maxi *Apollo* – with its fiery rocket spinnaker – won the Sydney to Hobart last year) and the man who started Sydney's coolest radio station, Rod Muir (of *Dr Dan*). Twilight Races in summer mean laid-back, drunken socializing on and offshore over crates of Bundi (rum) and coke, XXXX beer and local Seaview champagne followed by the best quayside barbecue in the world.

AMERICA'S CUP FEVER

Since the Australians got their blistered hands on the Cup in 1983, this race has turned into an international battle of power and money, waged by syndicates that employ the very best sailors in the world to compete in spanking new 12-metre yachts. Designed specially for the event, they are no more than alloy shells – pure racing machines – useless for cruising or offshore racing. Australian entrepreneur Alan Bond is spending A$150 million (US$106 million) on his defence campaign; when the rival Perth yacht, *Kookaburra II* (designed and helmed by 18-ft Skiff world champion Ian Murray) beat his *Australia I, II* and *III*, he set about building No. IV. No one who's anyone will dare skip the extravaganza of the February '87 final. Hotels will be humming (among those you should have already booked are the ritzy new Merlin and the good ol' Parmelia Hilton), the new casino will be swinging, and planes will be rushed off their runways. BUT, should the Western Australians lose, Perth will be the blushing white elephant of the century.

ROYAL FRESHWATER YACHT CLUB, Keanes Point, Peppermint Grove, WA 6011 ☎ (09) 384 9100. "The Freshie." The club that refused Alan Bond membership and then wished it hadn't. Regular harbour racing; young, fun crowd.

ROYAL GEELONG YACHT CLUB, Eastern Beach, Geelong, VIC 3220 ☎ (052) 91418. Go-getting club with comparatively recent royal patronage, excellent in sailing terms.

ROYAL MELBOURNE YACHT SQUADRON, Lower Esplanade, St Kilda, VIC 3182 ☎ (03) 534 0227. Fine traditional old club with modern policies. Great rival of the RYC of Victoria.

ROYAL PERTH YACHT CLUB, Pelican Point, Crawley, WA 6009 ☎ (09) 389 1555. Bondie's club; winning the '83 AmCup put it on the map and has jolted it into the 20th century. Go-ahead club with a good fleet of dinghies, offshore keel boats and, of course, 12-metres.

ROYAL PRINCE ALFRED YACHT CLUB, Mitala St, Newport, NSW 2106 ☎ (02) 997 1022. The upper North Shore club for Pittwater yacht owners. Smart, suburban, more family-orientated.

ROYAL SOUTH AUSTRALIAN YACHT SQUADRON, Outer Harbour, SA 5018 ☎ (08) 248 1063. Rightfully royal, since Queen Adelaide's husband was William IV, the Sailor King. Civilized social outings with excellent local wine.

ROYAL YACHT CLUB OF TASMANIA, Marieville, South Bay, Hobart, TAS 7000 ☎ (002) 234599. *The* club in Tazzie for all seafaring sorts – sailing, power and fishing boats. Small, active, social, with excellent men-against-the-sea races.

ROYAL YACHT CLUB OF VICTORIA, 120 Nelson Place, Williamstown, VIC 3016 ☎ (03) 397 1277. Tries to be stuffier than the RSYS. Heavyweight on sporting politics but not very active on the water.

FAR EAST

BEST EVENT

CHINA SEA RACE SERIES, c/o RHKYC (see below). The Admiral's Cup of the Orient. The finale runs from Hong Kong to Manila. A frustrating finish, as the wind often drops near Manila. Piracy is also a real danger. Terrific reception at the Manila Yacht Club (for those who make it).

BEST CLUBS

MANILA YACHT CLUB, 2351 Roxas Blvd, Manila, Philippines ☎ (2) 593897. Lovely clubhouse on stilts in the sea.

ROYAL HONG KONG YACHT CLUB, Kellett Island, Causeway Bay, Hong Kong ☎ (5) 833 2817. On an island off Hong Kong Island. Regular racing in winter; in the unreliable summer months, they hold the prophetic Typhoon Series and Sunset Series.

SHOOTING

BEST MOORS

★

1 ABBEYSTEAD, Lancashire

2 DALLOWGILL, Yorkshire

EUROPE

BEST BIRDS

BEST GROUSE There are many more grouse in the north of England than in Scotland, where the species has declined by more than 50 per cent over 10 years. Frantically expensive – can be from £3,000 to £7,000 (US$4,340 – 10,127) for 8 or 9 guns.
1. ABBEYSTEAD, Lancashire (the Duke of Westminster's moor). The record bag for England in 1985; with upstepped management and manpower, the bag has increased from 400 to 3,500 over the last 6 years (recommended by Lord Lichfield).
2. DALLOWGILL, N Yorkshire. The barometer by which other moors are measured. Lord Ripon, perhaps the greatest shot of all time, died here during a drive.
3. GUNNERSIDE, N Yorkshire (Lord Peel's moor).

BEST PHEASANTS The best commercial lets for top quality high-flyers (for skilled shots).
1. GURSTON DOWN, Dorset
2. POWYS CASTLE , N Wales
3. SIX MILE BOTTOM, Cambs.

BEST WILDFOWL
1. SOLWAY
2. MEDWAY
3. NORFOLK

BEST PARTRIDGES
1. TOLEDO and VALDEPEÑAS, Spain. For the best red-legged partridge in the world. Wild rocky terrain. Roxton (see opposite) arrange lets. King Juan Carlos is a fine shot. He recently shot the best bag in 10 years.
2. EAST ANGLIA, England, for wild partridge
3. EXMOOR, England. Milton's (see below) reared partridge.

DEERSTALKING

Only in the Highlands of Scotland where they have to shoot 60,000 deer to keep the population steady. Very expensive, solitary sport (only the stalker, ghillie and you). The ultimate trophy is a Royal, a stag with 12 points on its antlers.
SEAFIELD ESTATES, Teesside (the Countess of Seafield's land). The best deerstalking, via Major Neil Ramsay (see opposite).

LETS AND AGENTS

MILTON'S, Exmoor Shoot, Hollam Farm, Britchtown, Dulverton, Somerset, England ☎ (064 385) 300. *"Good shooting let – the highest pheasants and partridges, a discerning crowd. Two poachers could probably find as good birds in a Welsh valley and have just as much fun though!"* (Lord Lichfield).

MAJOR NEIL RAMSAY & CO, Farleyer, Aberfeldy, Tayside, Scotland ☎ (0887) 20523. Fine letting agent for Britain and Eastern Europe. Deerstalking too.

ROXTON SPORTING, 10-11 Bridge St, Hungerford, Berkshire, England ☎ (0488) 83222. 450 letting days a year over 175 top British and Spanish estates.

STRUTT & PARKER (see FISHING). Snooty agents for all the top shoots (and rivers too).

BEST GEAR

♔ **JAMES PURDEY & SONS, 57 S Audley St, London W1, England ☎ (01) 499 5292.** The best gunsmiths. Their intricately hand-built (never "made") walnut guns cost about £30,000 (US$43,400) a pair. A better investment than gold, but a longer waiting list to obtain. The best green wellies (Royal Hunter) and French Le Chameau leather-lined boots are stocked here too.

ALMOST UNWEAROUTABLE SOCKS, Piper Close, Corbridge, Northumberland, England ☎ (043471) 2283. Brightly coloured shooting stockings – lavender, primrose, turquoise – which don't seem to frighten the birds.

WILLIAM EVANS, 67a St James's St, London SW1, England ☎ (01) 493 0415. The best calf cartridge bags, with canvas straps made up in your old school or regimental colours.

HOLLAND & HOLLAND, 13 Bruton St, London W1, England ☎ (01) 499 4411. Made-to-measure guns with high-quality engraving on the trigger and lock. They have practice shooting grounds near London. Letting agents too.

JOHN RIGBY & SONS, 13 Pall Mall, London SW1, England ☎ (01) 734 7611. Old-established makers of the finest rifles; royal warrant.

Hot shots

You won't get shot by this lot:

The Earl of Pembroke
Nicholas Cobbold
Duke of Roxburghe
Duke of Westminster
Lord Ramsay
Earl of Lichfield
Lord Stafford
Duke of Abercorn
David Douglas-Home
Hugh van Cutsem
Jocelyn Stevens
Noel Cunningham-Reid

SKIING

WORLD'S BEST RESORTS

★

1 ST MORITZ, Switzerland
2 GSTAAD, Switzerland
3 VAL D'ISERE, France
4 ZERMATT, Switzerland
5 KLOSTERS, Switzerland
6 COURCHEVEL, France

EUROPE

BEST RESORTS

♔ **GSTAAD, Switzerland** Pretty village crawling with furred and bejewelled international names: Prince Rainier *et famille*, Audrey Hepburn, Roger Moore, Gunther Sachs, Boucherons, Bulgaris and Buckleys (Pat gives the most splendid parties). *"It's the most divine getaway holiday at the end of February"* (Lynn Wyatt). The Palace Hotel is the place to stay and meet, the Green Go to whoop it up by night, the Eagle Club for civilized, sophisticated lunches. PS The skiing's only so-so.

♔ **VAL D'ISERE, France** The finest ski area in the world, thinks ex-ski champion Killy, who learnt here. Killy ski-suits from the Killy shop are almost obligatory in Val now. A largely Sloane Ranger population *live* in Les Petites Anglaises (home-made English teas), and the Members' Bar of Dick's T-Bar (more glam than it sounds: global ski gossip). Best lunch: high up on the Tignes/Val borders, upstairs at Tovière.
Best hotel: Sofitel.

♔ **ZERMATT, Switzerland** Romantic setting in the shadow of the Matterhorn. Only horse-drawn sleighs and electric taxis allowed in town. Brilliant, varied skiing – open pistes and powder runs; some of the best helicopter skiing in Europe. Best place to slope into for afters is Elsie's Bar – Irish coffee, oysters, escargots or just drinks. Dozens of fine restaurants. Best dinner: at the Pollux. Best disco: at the Hotel Alex for lethal cocktails and heavy-duty dancing (three floors); Le Village at the Hotel Post; Schweizerhof. Best hotels: Mont Cervin; Zermatterhof (smart, with indoor pool). *"I've been to Zermatt 8 times and it's the best"* (Robert Sangster).

♔ **KLOSTERS, Switzerland** Small, smart, old-fashioned. Sometime habitués include the Prince and Princess of Wales, Deborah Kerr, and the Duke of Gloucester. Best skiing at nearby Davos. Best hotels: Wynegg (excellent cuisine); Chesa Grischuna (room for only 55).

♔ **COURCHEVEL, France** *Le plus chic* resort in France for young French and British, plus the likes of Giscard d'Estaing, Roman Polanski and Roger Vadim. Jetters wing in by private means to the Altiport. Immaculately kept runs – broad and gentle for debutantes, steep and narrow for experts. The best base for off-piste skiing too. Luxury chalets. Best hotel: Hôtel des Neiges. Best bar: Jump Bar, frequented by British aristos. Best clubs: Caves de la Loze (mainly French); St Nicolas (mainly Brits).

CORTINA D'AMPEZZO, Italy The Italian St Moritz. Dynamic at

GLITZ HITZ ST MORITZ

Grand Victorian resort, home of the 101-year-old Cresta Run (the treacherous, men-only toboggan run invented by the Brits), the fabled Badrutt's Palace Hotel (now slightly living on its name), Stavros Niarchos, Baron Thyssen, the Aga Khan, and the exclusive Corviglia Club, where any amount of Agnellis, Rothschilds, Heinzes, Guinnesses or Weinbergs might ski in for lunch. There's also bobsleighing, curling, polo on the lake (on ponies with spiked hooves) and heli-skiing on untracked glaciers.

Best hotels: the imperial Carlton (built for Czar Nicholas of Russia), the Külm (pop stars), Suvretta House (generations of aristocratic families), Badrutt's Palace.

Best lunch in the Alps: true haute cuisine cooked by Hartley Mathis at La Marmite, at the top of Corviglia. Sensational Lady Curzon soup, truffles, foie gras, gravad lax, caviare, and salt and pepper from battery-operated grinders. Cool people book for the 2pm sitting; the negligent – of whom Princess Caroline has been one – must wait.

Best tea: delectable hot chocolate and nut tortes at Hanselmann's, where you sit on the ground floor. *"My favourite café in Switzerland – excellent coffee, a wonderful place to meet people"* (Anton Mosimann).

Best bars: Cresta Bar in front of the Steffani Hotel, where the February Cresta set slip in for a cosy drink; lower bar of the Chesa Veglia.

Best clubs: Gunther Sachs's Dracula Club is the place on New Year's Eve (when Sachs dons cape and fangs); Kings' Club at the Palace.

Carnival, Easter and Christmas time. Royals, film stars and families such as the Pirellis, Buitonis, Cicognas and Colonnas. Best ski hotels in the country are the Miramonti Majestic (luxurious, with indoor pool) and Cristallo Palace (houses the Monkey Club), Hôtel de la Poste (tiny terrace where the fashionable bask). Mountain binges on pasta and seafood. Varied skiing with access to more than 500 lifts in and around the Dolomites.

CRANS, Switzerland *Très snob, très français*. Draws royals and aristos from Benelux, Denmark and Italy. Lofty, with spectacular views over Rhône Valley and acres more sun than most resorts. Best shopping in the Swiss Alps (rue du Golf). Best Alpine Glühwein (fruity and spicy, served in silver teapot) from Des Vignettes; best fondue and raclette from Le Cave.

KITZBUHEL, Austria Medieval walled city, weekend resort for Munich café society (worth the trip for Praxmair's hot chocolate). Too low for expert skiing but good for families. Fine shopping.

MEGEVE, France Where the ultra-smart French go. Inès de la Fressange loves it. Hotter on nightlife than skiing. Best hotel: Chalet Mont d'Arbois (best food from its Grill).

MERIBEL-LES-ALLUES, France Attractive chalet resort for smart, private British, like the Dukes of Kent and Bedford. Extensive skiing – it's at the hub of the largest ski-lift system in Europe, in the Trois Vallées. Best lunch: a buffet on the terrace of the Hôtel Tarentaise in Mottaret; best dinner: at Chez Kiki. No après-ski, only the duty-free.

ST ANTON, Austria Serious skiing, serious queues, excellent instruction (over 300 instructors at the ski school). Picturesque but crowded. Mark Birley goes. Best dinner: at Hotel Hospiz; nightspot: the Krazy Kanguruh (KK).

VERBIER, Switzerland Sunny, post-war trad-style chalet resort teeming with bright young Brits. Challenging skiing – steep jet black runs, and terrain for powder buffs and mogul bashers. Heavy après-ski and après-diner drinking at La Luge, a rustic bar which draws some of the best skiers in Europe. Best hotels: the Rhodania (dancing in the sophisticated Farm Club in the basement) and Le Mazot. Best *croûtes au fromage*, swilled down with Fendant or Dole, upstairs at Ruinettes, on the south-facing terrace overlooking the Rhône Valley. Amusingly mad waiters.

BEST GEAR

MOUNTAIN AIR, 907 Fulham Road, London SW6, England ☎ (01) 731 5415. The best shop in England for real skiers (a branch of the original in Verbier). You can smell the wax. Event and Powderhorn ski gear.

TOP SKI, BP 41, Val d'Isère 73150, France ☎ (79) 061 480. Best equipment. Kastle skis a speciality. Excellent guiding service for off-piste skiers.

SKI SERVICE, La vallée Blanche, 1936 Verbier, Switzerland ☎ (26) 75772. Run by Dale Anderson, the most laid-back man in the Alps. Ski fashion trends start here. Powderhorn. Jet Set and K2 skis, among others.

AMERICAS

ASPEN, Colorado, United States An old mining town with a proper established feel, though any hint of Victoriana is countered by lines of private Lear jets at the local airport. The most social resort in the USA. Commuters include Jack Nicholson, powder-skier John Denver, Christie Brinkley and Billy Joel. Four mountains – Ajax (the steepest), Aspen Highlands, Buttermilk (for beginners) and Snowmass.

SUN VALLEY, Idaho, United States Mainly steep runs for expert skiers only. Isolated, but Californians struggle to get here: so do the top men at AmEx, James D. Robinson III and the Sid Basses. Favourite resort of Brooke Shields and of powder-hound Margaux Hemingway, who was brought up here and adores the place.

BANFF, Alberta, Canada Best resort, divided into Mount Norquay (famed for its steep runs, in particular the Lone Pine, one of the meanest in the world), Sunshine Village (masses of snow, and you can ski across the Great Divide into British Columbia) and Lake Louise (two mountains, long runs). Currently limbering up for the 1988 Winter Olympics.

PORTILLO, Chile Chilean society and North American ski freaks descend from May to October. First-class skiing – fine powder snow on a desolate moonscape: vast, remote, thrilling. Everyone stays at the social Hotel Portillo with its sundeck, swimming pool, anti-avalanche power plant and water system.

STOWE, Vermont, United States The best in the East. Steep narrow runs for mogul-bashers.

VAIL, Colorado, United States Sixties resort fashioned after an Alpine village. The accumulation of wonderful snow and trails is matched by a pile up of names from the Social Register – ex-President Gerald Ford, Texas clans of Bass, Murchison and Wyatt, and Denver doyennes. Centralized, sleek, high altitude, with the fastest ski-lifts in America. Skiing for all abilities: great off-piste snow.

WHISTLER, British Columbia, Canada Trendy, fast-growing resort with the longest vertical drop in the Americas (4,278 ft/1,304 m). Nearby Blackcomb mountain has recently opened. Gorgeous powder-bowl skiing above the treeline, and heli-skiing.

BEST CLUB

CALEDON SKI CLUB, PO Belfountain, Ontario L0N 1B0, Canada ☎ (519) 927 5221. Family-orientated ski club, with a comfortable clubhouse and weekend activities. Usually private, but open to the public 2 days a week.

AUSTRALASIA

BEST RESORTS

MOUNT COOK, South Island, New Zealand Stunning scenery on a grand scale. Uncluttered slopes. Exhilarating heli-skiing down the 8 mile (13 km) Tasman Glacier. Cheap ski passes and heli-hire. Skiwis and European pros visit in July and August for training. Best (only) hotel: The Hermitage.

THREDBO, Australia Alpinesque resort where Aussie surfers head for winter and European pros train during their summer (June to end-Sept). Glühwein from the Keller; best hotel: Thredbo Alpine (spas, saunas, bistro, piano bar).

FAR EAST

BEST RESORTS

GULMARG, Kashmir, India Primitive, modest slopes, but the most exotic all-round experience. A bearer carries your skis while at least six instructors clamour to help you – they're crying out for skiers. Masses of virgin snow, panoramic Himalayan views.

NAEBA, Japan Site of the 1973 world championships, surrounded by luxury natural hot springs (après-ski in Japan consists of lolling around in a steaming bath). The Crown Prince takes his family here every year.

SAPPORO, Japan Near Hokkaido For hardy ski enthusiasts – difficult to get to, bitterly cold, but worth it to escape a billion kamikaze skiers elsewhere, and for the excellent snow. Site of the celebrated annual Snow Festival, when some 150 skyscraping sculptures are carved out of gigantic blocks of ice.

ZAO-ZAN, Japan In one of Japan's most beautiful natural parks. Best hotel: the nearby Yamagata Grand Hotel.

SURF, WIND AND FLIER

Keen and hulky Australian rich kids surf all year. They talk about faces, walls, tubes, lefts, rights and close-outs, and socialize at the local Surf Club. In the Sydney area, NORTH NARRABEEN gets the best waves – long, peeling walls with an occasional tube (hollow) of surfers. WHALE BEACH kicks up a brutally powerful wave known as "The Wedge" PALM BEACH at the non-trendy northern end produces a good wall. (Down the other end you might get mown down by Tony Greig or Kerry Packer on water skis or jetskis.) In W Australia, the best surf beaches are TRIGG and STRICKLAND BAY on Rottnest Island. Around Perth, beaches are brilliant for surfing in the morning; in the afternoon, a wind called the Fremantle Doctor gets up and so do the windsurfers. Best winds are at LANCELIN, GERALDTON, and the BLUFF area. Most exclusive club: **CABBAGE TREE CLUB, Ocean Rd, Palm Beach, NSW 2108 ☎ (02) 919 4087.** For surf life-savers only, with lots of eminent members.

TENNIS

WORLD'S BEST EVENTS

★

1. **WIMBLEDON (ALL ENGLAND LAWN TENNIS CHAMPIONSHIPS), London, Jun/Jul**
2. **U.S. OPEN, Flushing Meadow, Aug/Sept**
3. **FRENCH OPEN, Paris, May/Jun**
4. **AUSTRALIAN OPEN, Melbourne, Jan**

EUROPE

WIMBLEDON, All England Lawn Tennis & Croquet Club (see Clubs). June/July. The ultimate for players and spectators alike. *"There's nothing else like it in the world, with so many courts and so much happening; the Centre Court is unique, and the organization is excellent"* (John Lloyd). Best place to be, when not on the Centre Court, is the Members' Enclosure. Freeloaders bounce from hospitality tent to tent, eating corporation strawberries and meeting the cream of the tennis circuit. Mark McCormack's tent is best – he owns most of the top players. At dusk, chauffeuses (date fodder) transfer the stars to the Gloucester Hotel in Harrington Gardens, SW7, or to their homes (the Lloyds, Navratilova, Mats Wilander, McEnroe and Peter Fleming all rent or own pads in London). Rub tennis elbows with players at PONTE VECCHIO, 256 Old Brompton Rd, London SW5 ☎ (01) 373 9082, and ALEXANDER'S, 138a King's Rd, London SW3 ☎ (01) 581 4254.

FRENCH OPEN, Le Stade Roland Garros, 2 ave Gordon Bennett, 75016 Paris ☎ (1) 4743 9681. May/June. Part of the Grand Slam. Stylish from end to end, the athletic counterpart of the rue du Faubourg St Honoré. Best-looking ball boys in the world. On court, the Americans fail dismally – they can't get to grips with *terre battue*. European youngsters shine through, with lots of celebrated upsets when they smash the old hands. Borg won his first French title here at the age of 18. The sports media cover the social side as much as the tennis, cameras spying people like Karl Lagerfeld and Princess Caroline of Monaco in the stands. "The *sports event of the Parisian season. You simply must be a guest of Philippe Chatrier, the charismatic president of the World Federation of Tennis, in the official stands of the central court, where you'll meet everyone in Parisian life, from Jacques Chirac to film director Claude Lelouch and actor Jean-Paul Belmondo"* (Anne-Elisabeth Moutet).

MONTE CARLO OPEN, Monte Carlo Country Club (see Clubs). April. The most glorious social tennis event, though the actual game is eclipsed by the stars – Princesses Caroline and Stephanie, David Niven Jnr, Nabila Khashoggi – and a frenzy of cocktail parties. All the top tennis names are there too. As a tax haven, Monte has lured players like Borg and Boris Becker, who are then required to play at the Open.

XLII CAMPIONATI INTERNAZIONALI D'ITALIA, c/o Federazione Italiana Tennis, viale dei Gladiatori 31,00194 Rome, Italy ☎ (06) 361 9041. May/June. *The* Italian tournament. Scene of wild parties and tennis hooliganism – a passionate crowd throws coins at players.

BEST CLUBS AND RESORTS

ALL ENGLAND LAWN TENNIS & CROQUET CLUB, Church Rd, Wimbledon, London SW19, England ☎ (01) 946 2244. The most prestigious club in all England – only those steeped in tennis ancestry belong. Nearly impossible to get in (except to watch at Championship time).

HURLINGHAM, Ranelagh Gdns, London SW6, England ☎ (01) 736 8411. The country club comes to town – acres of rolling

English garden, grass and hard courts, and Pimm's on the terrace after a taxing match. A younger membership than the All England, but old-timers nevertheless rule with a rod of iron. The lovely Georgian house is the scene of many summer receptions and dances. Long waiting list.

♔ **MONTE CARLO COUNTRY CLUB, BP 342, MC 98006, Monaco ☎ (93) 782045.** A spectacular setting on the Med. 24 fine clay courts. Full of cosmetic tennis types who whiff of Etienne Aigner Sport Fragrance and wear an all-over honeyed tan, topped with Cerruti *on* court and Ellesse *off*. *"Probably the best amateurs' club – a most special place"* (John Lloyd).

HOLLAND PARK, 1 Addison Rd, London W14, England ☎ (01) 603 3928. *"A very private outdoor club where we practise in the summer"* (John Lloyd).

QUEEN'S, W Kensington, London W14, England ☎ (01) 385 3421. Civilized, established club, a hide-out for bridge players, mid-Europeans and deposed royals. Princess Michael of Kent practises here twice a week. Wonderful outdoor grass courts – *"the pros don't shear them up as much as they do at Wimbledon"* (Jake Eberts).

ROGER TAYLOR TENNIS CENTRE, Vale de Lobo, Almansil, Loulé, Algarve, Portugal ☎ (351) 899 4779. A tennis resort for rich kids set in 1,000 acres (405 hectares) of natural valley, surrounded by pines.

AMERICAS

BEST EVENTS

♔ **US OPEN, 1212 Ave of the Americas, New York NY 10036. ☎ (212) 302 3322.** Aug/Sept at Flushing Meadow Stadium. One of the Grand Slam events. Serious tennis in this bleak concrete complex.

US MASTERS, 4th Floor, 437 Madison Ave, New York, NY 10022 ☎ (212) 838 8450. Dec, at Madison Square Garden. The best event in the tennis year for players – important for picking up points that decide world ranking.

TOURNAMENT OF CHAMPIONS, WCT, 21st Floor, 150 E 58th St, New York, NY 10022 ☎ (212) 980 0660. May at Forest Hills. The best all-round event now that the US Open has moved. The tennis establishment loves this old, ivy-clad, English-style club. *"An absolute delight, the finest courts in America, wonderful atmosphere"* (Jake Eberts).

BEST CLUBS AND RESORTS

BEVERLY HILLS TENNIS CLUB, 340 N Maple Drive, Beverly Hills, CA 90210 ☎ (213) 273 4130. Hollywood stars flex their face-lifts.

CANEEL BAY, PO Box 120, St John, US Virgin Islands ☎ (809) 77-66111. Lovely national parkland hideaway for Hollywood stars at Christmas. Alan Alda and Charlton Heston go.

JOHN GARDINER'S TENNIS RANCH, Box 228, Carmel Valley, CA 93924 ☎ (408) 659 2207. The smallest and most exclusive tennis "clinic" with the great guru Gardiner. Superb food.

MEADOW CLUB, PO Box 11968, Southampton, NY 11968 ☎ (516) 283 0425. A private tennis club with 37 courts. The finest grass courts in the world, say some.

PALM BEACH POLO & COUNTRY CLUB (see POLO). The best tennis in the southern states. Safe, affluent, sanitized.

PETER ISLAND HOTEL, PO Box 211, British Virgin Islands ☎ (809) 49-42561. On its own island with private marina.

AUSTRALIA

BEST EVENT

♔ **AUSTRALIAN OPEN, c/o Lawn Tennis Association of Australia, PO Box 343, South Yarra, Melbourne VIC 3141 ☎ (03) 267 4277.** Jan. Important as a Grand Slam event, and 1987 is special – the last year of grass, at Kooyong Stadium. From 1988 the Open will be held at the new National Tennis Centre on synthetic courts.

BEST CLUBS

MEMORIAL DRIVE TENNIS CLUB, War Memorial Drive, N Adelaide, SA 5006 ☎ (08) 514371. Floodlit courts for matches in the cool of the evening. Home of the SA Open.

WHITE CITY CLUB, 30 Alma Rd, Paddington, NSW 2021 ☎ (02) 357 4111. Private tennis club with excellent grass courts and small membership. Scene of the NSW Open.

TRAVEL

by RENÉ LECLER

WORLD'S BEST HOTELS

1
MANDARIN, Hong Kong

2
ORIENTAL, Bangkok

3
CONNAUGHT, London

4
CIPRIANI, Venice

5
CARLYLE, New York

6
BEVERLY WILSHIRE, Los Angeles

7
OKURA, Tokyo

8
HOTEL DU CAP, Cap d'Antibes

9
REGENT, Sydney

10
REGENT, Melbourne

Oscar Wilde, summed it all up for me when he wrote: 'My tastes are very simple: I only like the best.' Quite. Let all those who like frozen fish and wine in a box have them. I will have the Beluga to start with the Château Cheval Blanc to follow with the pheasant.

Some might say that all this costs money. Of course, most of the really good things do, and if I can't have them I would rather go without than compromise because for me there is no possible comparison between the great and the indifferent. This certainly applies to travel. Personal, memorable and unique, its high points belong to you only.

After 26 years of travelling in 104 different countries, to ask me about the high points of my voyages is rather like asking 'When did you last see your father?' But I remember, oh yes, I remember. The Taj Mahal in the middle of the monsoon; the Acropolis when a sharp wind sent puffy clouds scurrying across the Attic sky; standing in the middle of the Queen of Sheba's palace; my first sight of the Emerald Buddha; landing on Bora Bora. And, naturally, sipping mulled wine at the bar of the Palace in St Moritz, studying the menu at La Tour d'Agent in Paris or raising an eyebrow for service at the Hassler in Rome.

I get as much fun sampling seaweed in a Japanese motorway café as I get watching snow flurries descending onto the canyons of Manhattan. Apart from England, which became my home so many years ago, and France, the most universally beautiful country in Europe, I would say that the two countries which have had the greatest influence on me have been Greece and India.

I have loved Greece to perdition for years. For me, this unique little country is the perfect marriage of land and sea, the perfect blend of historical inebriation and present-day simplicity. I like almost everything about Greece, except the Greece which travel agents try to sell you.

India? It is a huge cornucopia from which all things flow: infinite colour, humanity and togetherness, the magic and the turbulence, the unbelievable poverty and the incredible wealth. Although I am basically Western/materialistic-orientated, somehow India has changed my life values. I can never forget this. And I still don't understand India. That's part of the appeal.

My favourite means of transport is anything that moves. I would just love Concorde to fly wherever I am going but I also like being poled in a boat from one island to another in the Venice lagoon. I must admit that big ships bore me (especially cruise ships), but help me sail in and out of the Grenadines, those heavenly microdots of the Caribbean.

On reflection, my favourite holidays have been spent pootling about Crete and lying on a beach in the Tobago Cays, watching the lace tablecloth of tide spreading over the blond sand. Add to that walking around a Sumatra garden where, unbeknownst to me, some rogue tiger had just eaten the local mayor and you might get a measure of my own delights and surprises.

In my book, what makes perfection is two things. The first is total communion, body to body, soul to soul, between myself and the place I am in. The second lies in the infinite materialistic well-being of, say, a suite in the Mandarin or having scrambled eggs brought up to me on a silver tray at 2 am at the Ritz in Paris. The combination of both is, of course, rare but the best of either makes me feel that I am about as near to heaven as I am ever likely to be.

BELGIAN-BORN RENÉ LECLER was Travel Editor of *Harpers & Queen* magazine for 28 years until his retirement this year, during which time he has travelled millions of miles in more than 100 countries and stayed in over 3,000 hotels. His books include the discerning traveller's bible *The 300 Best Hotels in the World* (in its 12th year in print) and *The World Shopping Guide.* René Lecler once stayed in a beach hut in the South Pacific which fell into the sea during his visit.

EUROPE

BEST HOTELS

TOP 5

★

1. CONNAUGHT, London
2. CIPRIANI, Venice
3. HOTEL DU CAP, Cap d'Antibes
4. RITZ, Paris
5. GSTAAD PALACE, Gstaad

ENGLAND

LONDON

CONNAUGHT, Carlos Place, W1 ☎ (01) 499 7070. Distinguished and refined, the undisputed best *"for overall quality, excellent food, politeness and very, very good management. A small hotel which doesn't really want to know you if you don't belong – a special place"* (René Lecler); *"if you've been going there all your life, not if you haven't"* (Edward Carter).

BERKELEY, Wilton Place, Knightsbridge, SW1 ☎ (01) 235 6000. The only one of London's best with a swimming pool (on the roof). Terrifically discreet, with the atmosphere of a gentlemen's club. Favourite of Nigel Dempster, Lynn Wyatt (*"I like a hotel with a small lobby"*) and René Lecler (*"well situated and very English"*).

CLARIDGE'S, Brook St, W1 ☎ (01) 629 8860. *"The Rolls-Royce of London hotels. By far the nicest, with frightfully good service"* (Betty Kenward). The oldest and most dignified of the fleet, in operation since 1855. A divine slice of old-style elegance, with carpets you sink into and dining chairs you don't (Victorians didn't slouch). A quartet plays in the dining room. Tea, so refined, is all porcelain and silver and liveried service. Hosts visiting royals and premiers.

LE MERIDIEN, Piccadilly, W1 ☎ (01) 734 8000. One to watch: fabulously refurbished – gleaming marble lobby, glass-domed Terrace Restaurant, luxury bedrooms and bathrooms, and automatic membership of Champneys at Piccadilly (see HEALTH AND BEAUTY).

RITZ, Piccadilly, W1 ☎ (01) 493 8181. The swansong of César Ritz, a grandiose affair from the moment you enter the bleached pine doors. Gloriously decorative in *fin de siècle* style, pastel-toned and *"very special, with gilt angels climbing up the walls"* (René Lecler). Tea at the Ritz is still a wonderful institution, and cabaret has been reinstated (*"I love cabaret: the Ritz is making a brave attempt to bring it back"* – David Frost). The Grill Room and wine list are exceptional. A suitably ritzy guest list includes Rex Harrison, Sophia Loren, Ginger Rogers and Joan Collins. Best suite, overlooking Green Park, £580 (US$839).

SAVOY, Strand, WC2 ☎ (01) 836 4343. Grand old hotel overlooking Embankment Gardens and the Thames. David Hicks has revamped the River Room, and superb art deco mirrors have been uncovered in the bar. Its proximity to the theatre and Covent Garden entices entertainers such as Elton John and Placido Domingo, and Jerry Hall is a model guest. *"It'd take a lot of beating"* (Frederic Raphael).

Room service?

47 PARK STREET, W1 ☎ (01) 491 7282. The alternative to a hotel: luxury serviced apartments above Le Gavroche (see FOOD AND DRINK). A double-bedroom suite costs £165 (US$239) a night (3 nights minimum), so you can munch your way through its menu via room service.

COUNTRY

CHEWTON GLEN, New Milton, Hampshire ☎ (04252) 5341. *"Enormously beautiful, a great success story, and always full"* (René Lecler). In the New Forest, it's one of the most famous country hotels, an undoubted crowd-puller. Luxurious if unhomy, with attentive service and exemplary cuisine that has earned toques, turrets, stars and rosettes galore.

GRAVETYE MANOR, near East Grinstead, W Sussex ☎ (0342) 810567. Refined 16th-century house in well-tended gardens. Leo Schofield's favourite. *"Gets our family vote for superb food, wine and service. It is our very favourite 'celebration' restaurant. Lovely gardens for a pre-dinner drink of champagne. Food is French, the wine list elegant"* (Cliff Michelmore).

HAMBLETON HALL, Hambleton, Oakham, Leicestershire ☎ (0572) 56991. A Victorian hunting lodge, still in the perfect position for such pursuits. Interior chintzified by Nina Campbell and hung with sporting prints. Delicious updated old-English fare – fabulous game and fish in inventive sauces cooked by Nick Gill, *"one of the best chefs in Britain"* (Elisabeth Lambert Ortiz).

HUNSTRETE HOUSE, Chelwood, Bristol, Avon ☎ (07618) 578. *"A very nice manor house with lots of character, beautifully run by very pleasant people"* (René Lecler). The epitome of the English country house – Georgian, with walled garden, croquet lawn, tennis court and heated swimming pool – where it feels as though you are a private guest.

LORDS OF THE MANOR, Upper Slaughter, Cheltenham, Gloucestershire ☎ (0451) 20243. A 17th-century manor set in one of the prettiest villages in England – of mellow golden Cotswold stone, with a stream running through and rolling pastures around. Run very much as a private house with friendly, personal service under the

THE COUNTRY-HOUSE HOTEL

The English country house made accessible to everyone (who has the lolly). Gentleman hotelier is the new smart profession: it has to be when old families are financially embarrassed by death duties, and when, in any case, maintaining a large ancestral home costs a small fortune. If the gentleman doesn't fancy playing hotelier, there are plenty of astute entrepreneurs and restaurateurs ready to step in. Increasing numbers of would-be crumbling piles are being transformed into orgies of glossy-magazine-style decoration and cuisine (*The World of Interiors* meets *Gourmet*). In the best of these hotels, service is as it was in the beginning (impeccable), comfort is better (carpets, heating, efficient plumbing, warm sumptuous towels), while old-fashioned customs and characteristics remain (four-poster beds – re-sprung – brass taps, ancestral portraits, hearty breakfasts with the papers, fresh flowers, crackling log fires, home-made nibbles at the bedside).

Staple diet

STAPLEFORD PARK, near Melton Mowbray, Leicestershire ☎ enquiries (01) 581 7933. Pizza King Bob Payton's 16th/17th-century country-house hotel and sporting estate is due to open in spring 1987. His select bunch of co-directors range from Richard Shepherd of Langan's to Joss Hanbury, master of Bob's hunt, the Cottesmore. You'll be able to heli in to hunt, shoot, fish, ride, play polo, tennis and croquet, work out in the gym, and lap up the indoor pool, sauna, fine cuisine and wines.

impeccable management of James Gulliver of the Argyll Group. Chintzily and warmly decorated in apricots and buttermilks. A very fine menu and wine list. Roaring trade during Cheltenham Gold Cup week.

MIDDLETHORPE HALL, Bishopthorpe, York, N Yorkshire ☎ (0904) 641241. A very elegant William and Mary house overlooking York racecourse. Punters put all their money on this one. *"Certainly the best country hotel in England – it's like staying in a private house"* (Serena Fass).

MILLER HOWE, Rayrigg Road, Windermere, Cumbria ☎ (09662) 5236. *"Like a private country house. The beds are really comfy. Delicious food; biscuits and Malvern water waiting for you in your bedroom and bowls of fruit in the corridor in case you are still hungry. You can borrow binoculars to look over the lake and take in the magnificent view, and they give you books to read in your room"* (Richard Compton-Miller). Food as performance art by the amazing John Tovey.

ROYAL CRESCENT HOTEL, Royal Crescent, Bath, Avon ☎ (0225) 319090. Superb building in the centre of the crescent, with more rooms in a Palladian villa round the back. Suites have spa baths with water from the famous hot springs. *"The chef Michael Croft's starter of quails' eggs with truffles is one of the most gorgeous things in the world"* (Elisabeth Lambert Ortiz). Under the slick management that has turned Cliveden into a hotel (see Folie de Grandeur).

STON EASTON PARK, Chewton Mendip, Bath, Avon ☎ (076121) 631. A grand-scale Palladian stately home which really feels like home. Well restored, elegantly decorated, fine cuisine, and in a good position for investigating the West Country.

* *For the especially Foodie hotels, Le Manoir aux Quat' Saisons in Oxfordshire and Gidleigh Park in Devon, see FOOD AND DRINK.*

WALES

BODYSGALLEN HALL, Llandudno, Gwynedd ☎ (0492) 84466. The first of clever Richard Broyd and Nicholas Crawley's Historic House Hotels. An imposing 17th-century stone mansion high on the hills above Conway, with oak-panelling and solid fireplaces within. Bedrooms are both sumptuous and pretty. Steaming scented baths and wraparound towels to sink into, and scrumptious traditional food to sink your teeth into.

SCOTLAND

CROMLIX HOUSE, Kinbuck, Dunblane, Strathclyde ☎ (0786) 822125. A softly elegant house amid the austerity of baronial Scotland. Decorated with a light and sympathetic touch by Designers' Guild, retaining features such as wooden-seated commodes, and highlighting others, such as a circular corner turret which is now an exotic window-seat. Very fine gourmet cooking.

GLENEAGLES, Auchterarder, Strathclyde ☎ (07646) 2231. Souped-up Scottish pile that will please all international golfers – a multitude of extra sporting facilities, restaurants, a hairdresser, bank, whirlpool baths, solarium, helipad, etc etc. *"Marvellous indoor swimming pool, very good food, a comfortable place to stay"* (Cliff Michelmore).

GREYWALLS, Muirfield, Gullane, Lothian ☎ (0620) 842144. The best thing about this honey-hued house designed by Lutyens (a welcome incongruity in grey Scotland) is the cosy panelled library with plumped-up sofas, wall-to-wall collectors' editions of books and a roaring log fire. Golfers can step straight out on to the famous Muirfield course: walkers can wend their windswept way over tufty grass to the sea before returning for a welcome noggin by the fire.

INVERLOCHY CASTLE, Fort William, Highland ☎ (0397) 2177. Number 1 in Scotland and *"one of the great country house hotels – I like to get away from places to somewhere secluded"* (Bob Payton). Inverlochy is certainly that, set in gorgeous rhododendron-filled grounds by a loch, in the shadow of Ben Nevis. Grand-scale magnificence, frescoed ceilings, superlative food and local spring water – it's all totally awesome, as Brooke Shields will vouch.

EIRE

ASHFORD CASTLE, Cong, Co Mayo ☎ (094) 22644. *The* Irish stately, set by a lake in 300 acres (121 hectares) of gardens, 4,000 (1,619) of wooded nature reserve and 27,000 (10,926) of shooting land. Rooms are rather lofty and grand but unpretentious.

FRANCE

PARIS

♔ **RITZ, 15 place Vendôme, 75001 ☎ (1) 4260 3830.** The grand, sumptuous testament to haute hôtelier César Ritz. This is what ritziness is all about – supremacy of setting, comfort, service and cuisine. *"It's a question of knowing what's right, what's worth looking at. When the Ritz found they couldn't get the right door handles in the shops, they had them made specially in a country town. If you can have scrambled eggs brought up to your room at 2 in the morning, you know that's the right place to be"* (René Lecler). *"So aware of their clients' comfort. They very much try to please. I used to stay many years ago and they literally romanced me back"* (Lynn Wyatt). International fashion luminaries like Bill Blass stay when in town.

HOTEL LE BRISTOL, 112 rue de Faubourg St Honoré, 75008 ☎ (1) 4266 9145. Newish and exclusive, it's already gained a reputation for style and discretion, rather like the Lancaster. Where prominent Americans and diplomats stay. *"The best town hotel in the world"* (Leo Schofield).

HOTEL DE CRILLON, 10 place de la Concorde, 75008 ☎ (1) 4265 2424. Grand 18th-century palace built for Louis XV, in suave surroundings, with the American embassy next door. Tapestries, columns and marble baths that ooze super-luxe, but a sadly horrendous modern bar.

L'HOTEL, 13 rue des Beaux-Arts, 75006 ☎ (1) 4325 2722. A 4-star joker in the pack – the sublime fused with the ridiculous, famous as the place where Oscar Wilde died. Some rooms are hysterically tasteless, a symphony in leopardskin. But it's got sex appeal: it's fun, it's different, it's Rive Gauche. *"The one I enjoy most – a mistress hotel, a great feeling of sin about it"* (Lord McAlpine).

LANCASTER, 7 rue de Berri, 75008 ☎ (1) 4359 9043. Discreet, personal and individual. Like a very well-run private house, where movie stars can be normal and everyone is cosseted. *"My favourite – it's terribly cosy, and has a wonderful un-hotel feeling"* (Lady Elizabeth Anson).

HOTEL PLAZA-ATHENEE, 25 ave Montaigne, 75008 ☎ (1) 4723 7833. *Très huitième*: this could only be Paris. The Plaza has style, and it attracts people with style. Lustrous silk couches, marble surfaces, a little courtyard profuse with plants. Audrey Hepburn stays, Lady Elizabeth Anson admires its panache and Taki used to live there. Olivier Coquelin knows *"it's still Jacques Demoulian, the head concierge, who pulls the strings"*.

LA RESIDENCE DU BOIS, 16 rue Chalgrin, 75116 ☎ (1) 4500 5059. A very beautiful house, very Paris, very dainty, very discreet, with original Third Empire décor and a charming garden. Run by an ample French madame. Tessa Dahl and fashion designer Tomasz Starzewski adore it.

RIVIERA

♔ **HOTEL DU CAP-EDEN ROC, blvd Kennedy, Cap d'Antibes, 06604 Antibes ☎ (93) 613901.** A glowing legend of the between-wars era, when Scott and Zelda Fitzgerald and Noel Coward would stay. *"La grande dame of them all. When you've had breakfast and admired that most wonderful allée [a pink gravel path] taking you to Eden Roc, La Mare Nostra and the world, it is worth finishing your glass of Cristal and dying, for you've seen it all"* (Olivier Coquelin). *"My favourite hotel in the world because it's the most romantic and glamorous"* (Marie Helvin).

BEACH CLUB, Monte Carlo Beach Hotel, Roque Brune Cap Martin, route du Bord de Mer, 0690 France ☎ (93) 782140. The only place to be, languishing, bronzed, around the swimming pool (the beach itself is totally passé), paying well over the odds for cocktails and a season's worth of green and white candy-striped tent, and clocking Princess Stephanie's legs rather more than

❝ The place which has made the most lasting impression on me is Scotland. I was there in the autumn and the textures and colours were totally captivating. I was entranced by the myth of the Loch Ness monster ❞ (WARREN HOGE)

her Pool Position swimwear. When not being cool by the pool, the royal family hold court by their tent on the sea front, with 2 guards on standby.

CAP ESTEL, 06360 Eze-sur-Mer ☎ (93) 015044. *"Half-way between formal and informal, the only hotel in the South of France to have very large gardens [and an indoor and outdoor pool]. Well managed, very personal; excellent food"* (René Lecler). Clubby atmosphere, set on a promontory with its own tiny beach.

HOTEL DE PARIS, place du Casino, Monte Carlo, Monaco ☎ (93) 508080. *"One of the very few unforgettable hotels that enrich your bloodstream every time you see them – though you are sure to meet every bore you have been successfully avoiding for years"* (Olivier Coquelin). Oozing gloss and glamour during the Grand Prix and Red Cross Ball week, when the jetset stay in harbourside suites, watch the motor-set and wave to the yacht-set.

Bourgogne en luxe

Barge through Burgundy in deluxe style: 3 state suites with king-size beds; central heating, a grand piano and a helipad (add £400/US$578 to hover down from Paris). For you and 5 buddies, the 3-day trip from Montbard to Tanlay costs £1,204 (US$1,742) apiece including exceptional food and service. Abercrombie & Kent (see Tours).

HOTEL MAJESTIC, PB 163, 060403 Cannes ☎ (93) 689100. *"The best formal resort hotel – it would need a great deal of beating"* (René Lecler). Splendid, sparkling white, runs like a dream. The place to stay for the Film Festival.

HOTEL NEGRESCO, 37 Promenade des Anglais, 06000 Nice ☎ (93) 883951. Queen of the Riviera, reigning in grand Edwardian style. Perhaps the best cuisine in the South of France (see FOOD AND DRINK).

LA COLOMBE D'OR, St-Paul-de-Vence, 06570 Alpes-Maritimes ☎ (93) 328002. *"Everybody knows this is the loveliest hotel, but you can't get in unless you've been staying there for years. They're not snooty, just conscious that regular guests rebook every year and they hate to turn them down"* (Frank Lowe). Smart people pull strings to get in – the Duke of Roxburghe had to enlist help last year. The attraction is its individuality and rusticity (set in the hills behind Nice). *"It's just terribly relaxing. When you arrive, you feel you're home again. There's not a bad room in the place, they're all filled with lovely tiles and antiques"* (Frank Lowe). And paintings. Artists who couldn't afford their bills and didn't fancy washing up donated pieces of work instead. They just happened to be people like Matisse, Picasso, Braque, Utrillo and Miró.

LA RESERVE DE BEAULIEU, 5 blvd Général Leclerc, 06310 Beaulieu sur Mer ☎ (93) 010001. *"Probably the best hotel in the world"* (Lord McAlpine). Elegant apricot-tinted building decorated in light summery pastels. *"Wonderful, though it tends to be full of film people"* (Frank Lowe).

Is the Med dead?

Yes, yes, it's dead. Or so trendies like to think. But there's a time and a place for everything, and, in season, the right resorts sizzle with the right sort of life. If it's April it must be Marbella, or Monte Carlo (Open tennis); in May it's Marbella, Capri, Cannes and most definitely Monaco (Grand Prix); June – Marbella, Mallorca and Biarritz; July – Sardinia (the Cup), Monaco (Bal de la Croix Rouge) and St Tropez; duck out in August when the natives are at play, and head for the culture of Salzburg and the races at Deauville; September – back to Marbella or Mallorca, and, after that, the Rest of the World's your oyster.

❝ There's never a dull day in the South of France. There are wonderful gardens to visit and private houses which you can make an appointment to see. The palace in Monte Carlo looks like a palace for a fairy princess. The Matisse Chapel in Vence is so simple, a tiny empty thing with white walls and a window, but you get a sense of something very special ❞ (FRANK LOWE)

ITALY

ROME

EXCELSIOR, via Vittorio Veneto 125, 00187 Rome ☎ (06) 489031. Opulent hotel with glitzy clientele – movie magnates and stars, heads of state and royals. Favoured by Nigel Dempster, and by Olivier Coquelin *"for its caravanserai-type atmosphere"*.

LE GRAND, via Vittorio Emanuele Orlando 3, 00185 Rome ☎ (06) 4709. Truly *le grand*, in all its finery of gold leaf, brocade, tapestries, mirrors and chandeliers. *"You can't go wrong"* (Taki). *"I adore the Grand, I am devoted to it. There's nothing better. It was built on very ancient Roman baths and was a monastery in the Middle Ages. The rooms are lovely, with hand-painted wallpaper and beautiful furniture."* (Marina Chaliapin).

HASSLER VILLA MEDICI, Trinità dei Monti 66, 00187 Rome ☎ (06) 678 2651. Gloriously sited at the top of the Spanish Steps, discreet, civilized and tasteful. Impeccably run, faultless service. *"One of the three best hotels in Europe. Very special – a matter not just of glamour, but a feeling that you're in the very top place. It's a question of service, of attention to personal wishes"* (René Lecler). *"A frightfully good, old-fashioned hotel"* (Quentin Crewe).

FLORENCE

VILLA SAN MICHELE, via Doccia, 50014 Fiesole, Florence ☎ (055) 59451. Part of the James Sherwood (Orient-Express) empire, *"the best historic house hotel in the world"* (Serena Fass). A former Franciscan monastery with a private, frescoed chapel, and cells that have been sumptuously converted into bedrooms. Princess Margaret has stayed in the Michelangelo Suite with its canopied bed, stone fireplace and irreverent whirlpool bath. Set amid cypresses and oleander, with gorgeous misty views over the red-tiled roofs of Florence and *"the best sunsets in the world"* (Marchesa Bona Frescobaldi). *"My complete highest praise. It's heaven, simply lovely"* (Nicholas Coleridge).

VENICE

CIPRIANI, Giudecca 10, 30123 Venice ☎ (041) 707744. An island haven, a short glide from San Marco by private launch. Stylish, relaxing, with excellent cuisine. *"I can't think of anything nicer. Superb, beautifully run, frightfully comfortable"* (Betty Kenward). Nigel Dempster, David Frost and Mark Birley concur. *"The best because of its swimming pool – the only one in Venice. It's Olympic size because it was approved in feet and built in metres!"* (Nicholas Coleridge). *"The pool is like a cocktail party – everybody waving at each other"* (Frank Bowling). *"It's the closest you get to swimming in a cocktail. Also the pool snacks are wonderful – they have some of the best hamburgers in the world"* (Barbara Kafka).

GRITTI PALACE, Canal Grande 30100, Venice ☎ (041) 26044. *"The best formal, grand resort hotel"* (René Lecler). Confident, charming, the very model of quality and taste. *"I love it. The first floor corner apartment is sheer beauty: a couple of bedrooms join on to a big drawing room with parquet floor; there are bits of Biedermeierish furniture with little black bands that I always like. It looks down over the restaurant, with tiny canals to the left and the Grand Canal to the right. It hasn't been changed for years, and that's divine, and they keep up the standards, the old style, the quality of staff. The atmosphere is first rate; there's a feeling of belonging to something great – they feel it and you feel it. It's Venice, it's magical, it's lovely"* (Anouska Hempel).

AMALFI COAST

"The view, of course, is the best in the world. I've really travelled all over the world, and I can't find anything more beautiful. It has a history in it, an antiqueness. It lives. It isn't just the beauty of nature, but the beauty of every stone, every thing" (Marina Chaliapin).

SAN PIETRO, via Laurito 2, 84107 Positano ☎ (089) 875455. Chiselled into the cliff face, with terracotta-tiled terraces overhung by grapevines, lemon trees and bougainvillea. A lift runs down through the cliff to a tiny private beach. *"The best and most beautiful hotel. Exclusive because they don't take in people they don't know. Very much frequented by the English, people who don't like to be mixed up with the crowds"* (Marina Chaliapin). *"The most exquisite suites, very discreet staff, extravagant food and the most magical ambience"* (Marie Helvin).

LE SIRENUSE, via C. Colombo 30, 84017 Positano ☎ (089) 875066. A maze of rooms and terraces on 7 levels with a colossal swimming pool. *"A charming, rather old-fashioned hotel"* (Mark Birley).

CAPRI

GRAND HOTEL QUISISANA, via Camerelle 2, 80073 Capri ☎ (081) 837 0788. The best hotel on Capri, *"still marvellous to go to"* (Mark Birley). Statuesque, with antique furnishings and individual terraces.

COMO

VILLA D'ESTE, via Regina 40, 22010 Cernobbio, Lake Como ☎ (031) 511471. Grand palazzo at the fashionable, upmarket end of Como. That ancient, historical, misty feel of all Italian towns harmonizes with clear air and colours reminiscent of the Swiss lakes. Both civilized (antique furnishings, follied gardens) and sportif (water-skiing, sailing and tennis).

SARDINIA

PORTO CERVO is the best resort of all, where God (the Aga Khan) reigns omnipotent. He has only a handful of guests on *Shergar* (and stays at home himself); berthed as near as they dare are the swinging yachts of Stavros Niarchos (*Atlantis II*), Heini Thyssen (*Hanse*), Robert Stigwood (*Jezebel*) and Tommy Sopwith (*Philante*), all brimming with guests such as Princess Margaret, Prince Rainier and clan, Koo Stark, Mick Jagger, Mark Weinberg and Anouska Hempel. Sardinia Cup time is the highlight (see SPORTING LIFE).

"I love Sweden in the fall – it has tremendous mood, a great feeling for nature … the colours and the first snow – it's very dramatic" (JENNIFER KRAMER)

"I especially love Sardinia, because although it seems to be very worldly, one can be alone and at peace, even in the most crowded months. It is a place where nature is still intact and the sea is one of the most limpid blues I've ever seen" (GIANNI VERSACE)

HOTEL CALA DI VOLPE, 1-07020 Porto Cervo, Costa Smeralda ☎ (0789) 96083. Part of the Aga empire. *"Like a film set. A big hotel and chalets, a beautiful bay and wonderful sailing boats. Everything is Sardinian – things like the bedspreads, though they may have been manufactured in Milan, look as if some peasant wove them. It's dreadfully expensive but terribly good"* (Prue Leith).

BELGIUM

HOTEL DUC DE BOURGOGNE, Huidenvettersplaats 12, 8000 Bruges ☎ (050) 332038. A canal-side jewel of a hotel, laced with tapestries and fabulous bibelots. Small and soigné: luscious food.

NETHERLANDS

AMSTEL HOTEL, 1 Professor Tulpplein, 1018 GX Amsterdam ☎ (020) 226060. Super-grand hotel overlooking the river, clogged with local and visiting high society – royals, film stars and heads of state.

HOTEL DES INDES, Lange Voorhout 54-56, 2514 EG The Hague ☎ (070) 469553. *"The one in this region I like best. A very old-fashioned grand hotel. The first time I went, years ago, the oldest staff wore felt slippers in the evening so they wouldn't make a noise when walking up and down the corridors. It was lovely – very special"* (René Lecler).

SWEDEN

GRAND HOTEL, S. Blasieholmshamnen 8, PO Box 16424, S-103 27 Stockholm ☎ (08) 221720. Imposing hotel on the edge of the harbour, where multinational yachts pull in for smörgåsbord and home-made pastries on the verandah. Elegant, clean interior design. You could find yourself rubbing shoulders with Ingmar Bergman and Liv Ullman in the sauna.

GERMANY

BRENNER'S PARK, An der Lichtentaler Allee, 7570 Baden-Baden ☎ (07221) 3530. *"One of the three best hotels in Europe"* (René Lecler). A hangover from Edwardian days – people still flock to take the waters, down the wine, trot along in the coach and four and sip tea to the strains of the string quartet.

BRISTOL HOTEL KEMPINSKI, Kurfürstendamm 27, 1000 Berlin 15 ☎ (030) 881091. The best place to stay if you're checking out Checkpoint Charlie.

BURGHOTEL TRENDELBURG, 3526 Trendelburg ☎ (05675) 1021. *"Everybody's idea of what a German* Schloss *should be. Perched high up over the Rhine, it looks like a million dollars – really great!"* (René Lecler). Dates from the 13th century, timbered everywhere – real *Sleeping Beauty* stuff.

HOTEL VIER JAHRESZEITEN KEMPINSKI, Maximilianstrasse 17, 8000 Munich 22 ☎ (089) 228821. A bastion of Bavarian hospitality. Muncheners munch lunch in the top-notch Walterspiel restaurant.

AUSTRIA

IMPERIAL, Karntnerring 16, 1015 Vienna ☎ (0222) 651765. Palatial rooms lined with marble and adorned with chandeliers and rococo furniture. No sooner do you ring room service, than a waiter waltzes in with your order, accompanied always by a red rose. *"Almost too grand. It has a bedroom where Gaddafi, Nixon and the Queen have stayed"* (Eric Newby).

"I am very fond of Vienna in winter. Unlike London, they are prepared for the cold and you can totter into a cellar and have a rum or a sausage. You know that you can dress up in warm clothes and be able to keep them on all day, whereas you sally forth in Sloane Street in your sheepskin coat and the sun comes out.

There are such amazing museums. There's the undertakers' museum, and the psychopathic museum within a tower that used to be the loonybin, which is rather macabre. There is a lifetime of museums in Vienna. The nastiest is the anatomical museum. There you find ladies in crinolines whose dresses have been ripped from top to bottom and all their innards exposed. They are all dressed up with pearly necklaces. You can also visit the Central Cemetery, where Beethoven and Schubert are buried. It's a long ride, but at least you are coming back from it! And you can visit Freud's consulting room" (ERIC NEWBY)

SCHLOSS DURNSTEIN, 3601 Durnstein, Donau ☎ (02711) 212. Here you can realize the Austrian dream, and indulge in figure-licking pastries while gazing from the terrace over the beautiful blue Danube.

SWITZERLAND

GSTAAD PALACE, 3780 Gstaad ☎ (030) 83131. A splendid affair. the hub of Alpine society in February, when those who aren't staying at least are swaying in its Green Go disco. Excellent service. Satisfied punters include Anton Mosimann, Taki and Frank Bowling.

The Armleder of the pack

It is no coincidence that so many managers of top hotels around the world have names that sound Swiss or German. More than likely they are far-flung graduates of the legendary Ecole Hôtelière at Lausanne. The Swiss connection automatically connotes precision, discretion and all-round immaculateness. The school, designed like a hotel, was founded by Black Forest ex-pat Adolphe-Rodolphe Armleder, who also created the Hôtel Richemond in Geneva, which is still in the family. Kurt Wachtvietl flies the Swiss flag at the Oriental, Bangkok (see Thailand), where he presides at the helm; a number of his old shipmates are posted at Hong Kong in the Peninsula, Regent and Mandarin.

BADRUTT'S PALACE, 7500 St Moritz ☎ (082) 33916. A glorious winter palace in which the cool people ensconce themselves for the month of February. *"It just has a sort of snootiness and snobbiness and showbiziness – everything about it is unique"* (Diana Fisher). Own ski school, kindergarten, and private rail link (see also SPORTING LIFE).

BEAU RIVAGE, 13 quai du Mont-Blanc, 1201 Geneva ☎ (022) 310221. Immaculate lakeside family-run hotel where the Duke of Brunswick once lived.

DOLDER GRAND HOTEL, Kurhausstrasse 65, 8032 Zurich ☎ (01) 251 6231. Sporting bankers chopper in, take a dip in the oscillating swimming pool, a jog in the forest, play a round of golf, a set of tennis, and wind up with a triple axle on the ice before winding down in the solid splendour of the hotel. Frank Bowling and Anton Mosimann clock in from time to time.

HOTEL DE LA PAIX, 11 quai du Mont-Blanc, 1201 Geneva ☎ (022) 326150. More 5-star lakeside luxury with lovely views of Mont Blanc and distant Alpine peaks. *"A very fine hotel"* (Frederic Raphael).

RICHEMOND, Jardin Brunswick, 1201 Geneva ☎ (022) 311400. Owned and run by 4 generations of Armleders, the original of whom set up the hotel school at Lausanne (see left). Grand, antique-ridden, refined in every respect, with eagle-eyed attention to detail.

SUVRETTA HOUSE, 7500 St Moritz ☎ (082) 21121. Anton Mosimann's favourite skiside hotel.

PORTUGAL

AVENIDA PALACE, Rua Primeiro de Dezembro 123, Lisbon ☎ (01) 360151. *"The best in Lisbon. An amazing turn-of-the-century hotel. Especially nice in winter, with an air of faded grandeur"* (Eric Newby).

HOTEL PALACIO, Estoril ☎ (011) 268 0400. Palatial hotel near the beach with marvellous airy halls and corridors. Impeccable, attentive staff.

SPAIN

HOTEL FORMENTOR, Puerto de Pollensa, Formentor, Mallorca ☎ (71) 531300. Gracious, relaxed, edging towards the geriatric, set in gorgeous hillside gardens amid acres of pines. A great sense of well-being, which the King of Spain has sampled. Paths lead down to a private beach dotted with straw umbrellas.

MARBELLA CLUB HOTEL, Carretera de Cadiz, Marbella ☎ (52) 771300. Andalusian-style bungalows around pools and gardens. *"Jazzy sort of society people, but it's a very good hotel, no doubt about it"* (René Lecler). Khashoggi has an apartment here.

“ The most awe-inspiring public event is Holy Week in Seville. Statues representing the virgin and the crucified Christ are carried through the streets on the backs of artisans, preceded by men in long hoods carrying candles and looking like members of the Inquisition. Some of the statues are so heavy that it takes 40 men to lift them and the rough artisans who carry them emerge at the end bleeding where the wooden supports have cut into them. It's an amazing demonstration of the power of church and state. There are also penitents who are hooded and carry heavy crosses. Of course, they wear hoods so they will not be recognized, and there are lots of shouts in church beforehand of "Got a safety pin?" if there is a bit of head showing ”

(ERIC NEWBY)

and Baron Thyssen a plot of land (so far), but the recent sheikh-up has disturbed some people, and it's sent former host Prince Alfonso von Hohenlohe off to Mallorca, where he runs the Anchorage Club. Bendinat (for residents, not travellers).

Khashoggi would never miss a Marbella summer. As *Nabila* glides in, Puerto Banus starts swinging. At his birthday party on board one year, each guest was served a slice of cake studded with rubies and pearls.

RITZ, Plaza de la Lealtad 5, 28014 Madrid ☎ (01) 521 2857. Its recent revamp has pushed it back into the top league. Importantly decorated: acres of hand-woven bespoke carpets are tended by their own personal carpet-wallah. Garden terraces with flower-covered pergolas and fountains. *"So grand, with liveried staff"* (Bruce Oldfield). *"Forget the Paris one – I prefer the Ritz Madrid for old-world graciousness"* (Olivier Coquelin).

GREECE

AKTI MYRINA, Myrina Beach, Myrina, Lemnos ☎ (0254) 22681. Individual stone villas clustered around a lovely beach. Relaxed, holiday-ish, watersportif: delicious spreads of food laid out in the garden. *"I love it. It's the last good holiday I had. The food is marvellous, which is unusual for Greece, and the choice is enormous. Very informal – you dress up only if you feel like it"* (René Lecler).

ASTIR PALACE, Vouliagmeni Beach, Vouliagmeni 166 71 ☎ (01) 8960602. The only place to stay in the neighbourhood of Athens. A sophisticated, spacious resort hotel.

KHASHOGGI'S DREAMBOAT

Adnan Khashoggi has three boats: the famous 287-ft (148 m) *Nabila*, named after his daughter (based at Brunei, in company with the Sultan's), and 2 named after his sons, plus a new Bannenberg-designed $95 million 417-footer (127 m) on the way. Not only hotels and nightclubs, such yachts are also offices (uninterrupted big biz, where the client can't walk out on you), nuclear shelters (many yachts carry anti-missile radar) and even hospitals (*Nabila* has 2 operating theatres – for choppy days?) Most have satellite mushrooms to scoop up the international calls (*Nabila* has 296 telephone lines), helipads, ballrooms, swimming pools. On other yachts, fantasies emerge in the form of solid gold and marble bathrooms, dazzling modern art collections, a cold store for furs, and a motorized gangway for the Bentley.

ATHENS HILTON, 46 Vassilissis Sofias Avenue, 106 76 Athens ☎ (01) 720201. A class above the usual run of Hiltons, well run and decorated, with fabulous views of the Acropolis and Hymettus.

GRANDE BRETAGNE, King George I St, Athens 10210 ☎ (01) 323 0251. An Athenian landmark, the oldest hotel in town. There may be flashier and more luxurious hotels, but the old money and cognoscenti remain faithful.

TURKEY

BODRUM Although the Tomb of Mausolos – one of the Seven Wonders of the Ancient World – crumbled to its foundations centuries ago, the sailing set, who flock increasingly to this port, find the cradle of civilization is still rocking. Those who rock along include Mick Jagger (gathering no moss in one of several holiday hideaways, this one is owned by Ahmet Ertegun of Atlantic Records), Nureyev (who can be spied doing wheelies round town on a bicycle), Phil Collins (who can be spied doing keelies round the harbour on a chartered yacht – not *Drum*), David Dimbleby and Robin Day (both of whom find even Turkish food preferable to that of the Beeb canteen).

"The in place to be is Turkey. You find half of Knightsbridge there. Eventually it will become like the South of France. Go in spring – it's too formidably hot in summer, and jam-packed with Turks in August" (Eric Newby).

RUSSIA

NATIONAL, 14/1 Mark's Prospect, Moscow ☎ 203 6539. A charming hotel that overlooks Red Square. *"One of my favourite hotels – where Lenin lived, with all sorts of accoutrements that date from Imperialism"* (Warren Hoge).

GETTING THERE

AIR

BRITISH AIRWAYS Their efforts have been noted, and the consensus is they're the best in the world. *"I love them, I think they're great. They've actually turned themselves around in the last 5 years. Their philosophy of putting people first actually works, and to get the average Brit to care about somebody else is an amazing accomplishment"* (Bob Payton). *"They had gone down, but since Lord King cracked the whip they've risen again. Cabin service is very good"* (Betty Kenward). *"Improved seats, very comfortable, the service is more mature than on other airlines. They cut out the frills, the deluge of special toothbrushes, and give you more of the service you need"* (Lord McAlpine). *"I think they are more concerned about safety. Concorde may sometimes be late, but it's because they are checking some technical query. In the end, I think BA are the best"* (David Hicks).

SWISSAIR Very highly regarded (it's the inimitable Swiss precision, inherent also in their hoteliers and timepieces). *"Always punctual – they never let you down"* (Serena Fass). *"The best. Cabin service is absolutely immaculate. They are very intelligent about airline food. They understand the appetite of the airline passenger better than other airlines"* (Mark Birley).

AER LINGUS *"I always fly to Shannon and pick up the Aer Lingus jumbo. It's the best way to go to the States and the crew are among the best – all racing-orientated. About 12 of us travel up front and there was an incident a few years ago. The hot towels ended up in a throwing match, and one of them landed slap on the back of some American's neck. He immediately stood up and said: 'WHO threw that?' The whole crew got up! It's that kind of camaraderie I like – we're a great team"* (Robert Sangster).

AIR FRANCE The best airline food, according to the well-travelled tastebuds of Lynn Wyatt and Betty Kenward. Champagne doled out even in economy, melt-in-the-mouth fillet steaks. Their subsidiary, UTA, produces similar delicacies.

BRITISH CALEDONIAN Super – friendly staff who really do try harder. British Caledonian ferry stars to and from B.B.C.'s *Wogan* show (via not-too-public Gatwick – A plus for celebs like Phil Collins and Eric Clapton).

LUFTHANSA *"Teutonic efficiency and wonderful service. One of the few airlines that always seems to be everywhere you want it to be, and on time. I'm not taken in by all that ridiculous orchids stuff on the Asian airlines. Very tiresome"* (Leo Schofield).

Cruising along at a slightly lower altitude are ALITALIA (*"Makes you feel at home"* (Marchesa Bona Frescobaldi), KLM and SAS.

Best aircraft

CONCORDE *"The best way to travel to England"* (Jackie Collins). *"Just superb – the service, the courtesy and everything that goes with it"* (Joan Burstein). *"If Concorde took off on time it would be the supreme flight, the crème de la crème"* (Robert Sangster). *"The best way of travelling? Concorde. That's that. When you need to get somewhere very elegantly, very fast"* (Anouska Hempel).

CRUISE LINES

SEA GODDESS CRUISES, Dronningen 1, 0287 Oslo 2, Norway (0472) 437500. A plushy new line with 2 identical small ships, more like floating clubs, carrying only 70 guests apiece and nicely kitted out in subdued pastels, with pale oak furniture and linen and crystal. They visit the ports other ships cannot reach, such as Portofino, Capri, Puerto Banus, Patmos, Tobago Cays,

Virgin Gorda, Casa de Campo in Dominica and many Brazilian ports. Swimming pool, whirlpool and health spa; occasional unscheduled stops to air the windsurfers, snorkelling equipment and speedboats (for water-skiing) that are carried on board. Al fresco breakfasts and lunches, formal dinners and nightclub-casino. Around £3,000 (US$4,340) for a week.

SUN LINE CRUISES, 2 Kara Georgis Servias St, 10562 Athens ☎ (01) 322 8883. Cruise around the Med on *Stella Maris*, leaving from Piraeus. Immaculately organized. 160 people. Best in May/June or Sept/Oct.

QE coup

The QE2 consumes one-third of the world's annual production of Beluga caviare. Enjoy it in the comfort of the Queen Elizabeth Suite, a gulp-worthy £98,730 (US$142,833) for the 108-day world cruise. Cunard Line, 38 Pall Mall, London SW1 ☎ (01) 491 3930.

YACHT CHARTER

CAMPER & NICHOLSONS, BP 183, Port Pierre Canto, 06407 Cannes ☎ (93) 431675. Hundreds of luxury crewed yachts, motor and sailing, modern and old-fashioned, stocked up to your requirements and steered where you will. Baron Thyssen's *Hanse* is on their books for 442,018 francs (US$62,300) a week, sleeps 12. The most expensive is *Maria Alexandra*, at 670,477 francs (US$94,500) (sleeps 22); nothing much below 35,475 francs (US$5,000).

CRUISE AND CHARM, 104 rue du Faubourg St Honoré, 75008 Paris ☎ (1) 4266 6400. Ultra-exclusive cruises aboard the good ship *Maxim's des Mers*, owned and decorated by Pierre Cardin. The salle à manger is a replica of Maxim's in Paris; there are 16 extravagant suites and a mosaic pool.

TOP YACHT CHARTER, Andrew Hill Lane, Hedgerley, Buckinghamshire ☎ (02814) 2640. Specialists in bareboat (non-crewed) sailing around Turkey and Greece, plus some crewed boats.

YACHTCLUB CHARTER CO, 307 New King's Rd, London SW6 ☎ (01) 731 0826. Smart, young company operating out of Bodrum with a fine fleet of sailing yachts for bareboat and flotilla holidays. Also crewed old-style wooden cruising boats for up to 12 people.

RAIL

VENICE SIMPLON-ORIENT-EXPRESS, Sea Containers House, 20 Upper Ground, London SE1 ☎ (01) 928 6000. The legendary Orient-Express, sumptuously re-created in 1920s style, from the polished inlaid wood panelling to the crystal and linen napiery. Dressy and elegant: gourmet cuisine and a good many cocktails murdered daily. Dig-a-dig-diggers include Margaux Hemingway, Eric Newby, Serena Fass and Frank Bowling. 30-hour overnight trip via the Swiss and Austrian alps. £520/US$752 (£612/US$885 for the Guinness Suite).

TGV (Train à Grande Vitesse) The fastest train in the world whisks you at 168 mph (270 km/h) from Paris to major French towns, Geneva and Lausanne. From usual stations; must reserve a seat. *"The best train in Europe – so quick they don't need to have a restaurant car"* (David Hicks). They don't: meals are served at your seat, depending on which first-class carriage you're in. *"Very exciting, absolutely wonderful. The food is like going out to dinner in one of France's better restaurants"* (Frank Bowling).

ROYAL SCOTSMAN, c/o Abercrombie & Kent (see Tours, Villas and Agents). 6-day tour of Scotland for 28 people, visiting private houses, castles and gardens. Some Edwardian carriages, which for part of the journey are pulled by steam locomotive. The best food on any train – *and* the best sleep, since it stops in a siding for the night. A 6-day trip costs an all-in £2,290 (US$3,313) in the State Cabin.

TRANS-SIBERIAN EXPRESS. From Moscow, it's 8 days across the steppes of Siberia, past forests and hills thick with wild flowers, before arriving at Khabarovsk, near the Chinese border. It's a romantic notion, if rather under-patronized by the beautiful people. Book via Intourist.

Moscow Metro

Built under Stalin, it took dissidents (otherwise Siberia-bound) over 12 back-breaking years to complete (in 1943). Stations are more like ballrooms, art deco masterpieces lined with marble, adorned with stained glass mosaics, bronze plaques and chandeliers, and scrubbed scrupulously clean. This metro is the cheapest, most efficient, and has the least crime and vandalism in the world.

London taxis

"The best in the world. It's one of the few professions left in this country. They have to know the town and it takes them 3 years of going round on a motorbike to learn. Everywhere else, you want to be a taxi driver? Sure, here's the car. You go to New York and say take me to the Empire State Building, and they say where's that? They know Fifth Avenue's Fifth Avenue – what's so difficult about Fifth Avenue? But you say 1049 Fifth Avenue and they don't know whether it's between 52nd and 53rd or 72nd and 73rd. London is the most difficult city in the world to get around, and yet all these taxi drivers know all of it. They're just light years ahead, the taxis are big, they're comfortable, they're fun to travel in" (Bob Payton). *"Far and away the best, particularly the owner-drivers. They always know where you want to go, they don't mind waiting if you want to go into a series of shops"* (David Hicks).

TOURS, VILLAS AND AGENTS

ABERCROMBIE & KENT, Sloane Square House, Holbein Place, London SW1 ☎ (01) 730 9600. All sorts of worldwide luxury tours, specializing in things African: safaris, Egyptian exploration, Nile cruises, hotels on the Kenyan coast, Mauritius and the Seychelles. Marketeers for top British country-house hotels under the Pride of Britain partnership.

CARIBBEAN CONNECTION, 93 Newman St, London W1 ☎ (01) 930 8271. Upmarket hotels and villas all over the Caribbean.

CONTINENTAL VILLAS, 38 Sloane St, London SW1 ☎ (01) 245 9181. Luxury villas, mostly with pools, in the South of France, Spain, Portugal, Palm Beach and the West Indies.

COUNTRY HOMES & CASTLES, 118 Cromwell Rd, London SW7 ☎ (01) 370 0259. Susie Worthy arranges stays at privately-owned stately homes on a paying guest basis. Somerley in Hampshire and Winslow Hall in Buckinghamshire are on her books.

CV TRAVEL, 43 Cadogan St, London SW3 ☎ (01) 584 8803. The smartest selection of villas (and villa girls) on Corfu. The Duchess of Kent and her family have stayed in one of theirs. Also villas on other Greek islands, the Algarve and the South of France, and their DIFFERENT WORLD division offers cushy villa and hotel hols in the Caribbean.

EXPLORASIA, 13 Chapter St, London SW1 ☎ (01) 630 7102. Smart treks in India and Nepal. They have arranged elephant polo championships, climbs up Everest, a trek for Prince Charles, and lunch in February 1986 for Prince Philip in Tiger Tops Jungle Lodge.

KUONI TRAVEL, Kuoni House, Dorking, Surrey ☎ (0306) 885044. Luxury tours around the world, including the Concorde and Sandy Lane Spectacular (7 spectacularly expensive nights in Barbados).

SERENISSIMA TRAVEL, 21 Dorset Square, London NW1 ☎ (01) 730 9841. Incorporates Heritage tours. Chaired by John Julius Norwich, with a string of scholarly lecturers and a grand clientele. Refined cultural tours of Europe, Russia, the Middle East, South America, Africa and Asia. Serena Fass's personal favourites are the North Yemen tour, Nile cruise aboard *MS Helio* and Moghuls & Maharajas. Not all are cocoons of luxury: the Silk Road and From Kathmandu to Lhasa are billed as "strenuous". Brochures have no gaudy photographs, only watercolours.

TRAILFINDERS, 42 Earl's Court Rd, London W8 ☎ (01) 937 9631; first and business class **☎ (01) 938 3444.** Upmarket they may not be, but the most comprehensive and knowledgeable agents on worldwide air travel they are. Tailor-made itineraries at the best value.

TWICKERS WORLD, 22 Church St, Twickenham, Middlesex ☎ (01) 892 7606. Tours and treks to outlandish places with the accent on wildlife. Intense stuff accompanied by experts – Amazon safari, Patagonia overland, Antarctica and the Falklands, Papua New Guinea.

VACANZE IN ITALIA, Bignor, Pulborough, W Sussex ☎ (07987) 368. Incorporates Vacances en Campagne and Heritage of England – superb privately owned villas, châteaux, cottages and country houses for rent in Italy, France, their islands, and England.

The right place at the right time

The essence of good-time travel is being in the right place at the right time. According to Prince Alfonso von Hohenlohe, this means: January – the Caribbean; February – St Moritz or Gstaad; March – Florida and California; April to September – Europe (see Is the Med dead?); October – New York; November – shooting in England and Spain; December – home.

"The best way to travel is the quickest. The actual business of travel is no fun, unless you do it in a grand manner with a string of 20 camels behind you. My idea of heaven would be to see the whole of Rajasthan in a vintage Rolls-Royce"

(RENÉ LECLER)

THE AMERICAS

BEST HOTELS

TOP 5

★

1. CARLYLE, New York
2. BEVERLY WILSHIRE, Los Angeles
3. BEL AIR, Los Angeles
4. MANSION ON TURTLE CREEK, Dallas
5. REMINGTON, Houston

“Europeans have all been to America now, and they've said: ‘Hey, it's OK over here – it's not all McDonalds and it's not all flash and trash – it's fun and it's nice, it's easy and it's casual.’ What Americans have got is an unbridled enthusiasm; we're so unashamedly brash, so disarmingly nice and friendly, and when you go abroad, that's what you want” (BOB PAYTON)

UNITED STATES

NEW YORK

CARLYLE, 36 E 76th St, NY 10021 ☎ (212) 744 1600. Intelligent management, loyal staff, loyal guests – it's got *class. “It's a left-over lovely sort of English hotel that we don't actually have any more. It's all rickety – for a designer it's not right – things don't match up, bits of chintz don't work – but it's like a home, and lots of homes don't quite work on a design level. The staff are sensational, old-fashioned, full of chat and charm. It has a touch of magic ... it's the owner Peter Sharp's attention to detail, caring year after year after year.”* (Anouska Hempel).

ALGONQUIN, 59 W 44th St, NY 10036 ☎ (212) 840 6800. A character hotel that distils the very essence of New York. Its restaurant is where the legendary wits of the *New Yorker* magazine Round Table (Dorothy Parker *et al*) would sharpen their tongues, while the lobby bar is a frothy cocktail of natives and visitors. *“I always stay at the Algonquin. It's lovely and old-fashioned, and has that perfect touch of their always remembering you. If I don't go there for 10 years, I'll arrive and they'll say, ‘Good afternoon, Mr Crewe.’ They know exactly what you want in your room and send up the drink you're accustomed to – they note it all down on a card. Extremely friendly”* (Quentin Crewe).

ELYSEE, 60 E 54th St, NY 10022 ☎ (212) 753 1066. Small, eccentric, with named not numbered rooms. *“A very dear place to me. The owners are like family when greeting their guests. Furthermore, they always manage to materialize a room when the rest of the city is packed”* (Olivier Coquelin).

HELMSLEY PALACE, 455 Madison Ave, NY 10022 ☎ (212) 888 7000. Grand and new. A soaring tower block of bedrooms sits on top of the 19th-century Villard Mansion which houses the lobby and dining rooms. *“The best. You stay in the tower in a suite, like staying in a glorious private apartment, with a fantastic view of the city. I usually stay on the 48th floor. The décor is beautiful – a cross between modern and antique*

THOROUGHLY MODERN MORGANS

MORGANS, 237 Madison Ave, NY 10016 ☎ (212) 686 0300. Small and *so* chic, it's clannish and club-like – and co-owner Steve “Palladium” Rubell should know all about that. It has been designed to within an inch of its life (although it's probably not true that the bath taps run Perrier) by Parisian style guru Andrée Putman, who apparently “dislikes aggressivity”. In her quest for passivity – to soothe a heady clientele – she has splurged out with neutrals and achromatics. At Morgans, the furniture wears the trousers. Chairs are upholstered in grey flannel, bedclothes in Brooks Bros shirting. The staff, aspiring young thespians (performing in their first runaway success), are decked out in Calvin Klein and Giorgio Armani uniforms which they top off with designer haircuts. The hotel's integral restaurant has been described as a “synthesization of the Morgans image”. Rod Stewart ordered a steak at 5 a.m. and got it. The rooms have been adorned with an original Warhol and the roll call is pure *People* magazine: Brooke Shields, Bette Midler, Mick Jagger, Cher and Azzedine Alaïa. *“It's like being at home – great kids as waiting staff, a wonderful young atmosphere”* (Margaux Hemingway – who would far rather be here than propping up her family's namesake bar at the Ritz). And, though guests like these would have no problem getting into Palladium, admission is guaranteed with the price of the room.

– and they don't stint on space" (Jackie Collins).

MAYFAIR REGENT, 610 Park Ave, NY 10021 ☎ (212) 288 0800. Known to its intimates as Dario's (Dario Mariotti is general manager), it can't go wrong as long as it houses Sirio's (Le Cirque – see FOOD AND DRINK). Handsome and spacious, with 199 rooms (all of luxurious suite calibre) and almost as many umbrellas for those who come unprepared for showers.

PIERRE, 5th Ave at 61st St, NY 10021 ☎ (212) 838 8000. *"La grande dame of New York hotels. If you stay there, everybody knows who you are"* (René Lecler). Peaceful, discreet, secure, with ultra-attentive service, it attracts New York glamorati. Best view over Central Park is from the elegant Presidential Suite. The Café Pierre, revamped by Valerian Rybar, is a local landmark.

RITZ-CARLTON, 112 Central Park South, NY 10019 ☎ (212) 757 1900. Opened in a blaze of hype and glory in 1983: decorated in manorial splendour by "Sister" Parish (see HOMES AND PROPERTY) : fabulous views over the Park: superb position shop-wise: personal service: managed by the hotelier with the best CV, Frank Bowling: houses the mock-historic quasi-English Jockey Club dining room, and, according to Nigel Dempster, *"it's the latest* in *hotel in New York"*.

UNITED NATIONS PLAZA, 1 UN Plaza, 44th St, NY 10017 ☎ (212) 355 3400. Not to be confused with the plain old Plaza. A superb position overlooking the United Nations and the East River, and all sorts of lavish facilities. *"A great sporty hotel – indoor tennis courts [24-hour], swimming pool and gym, and always a taxi available outside"* (John Lloyd).

WESTBURY, 15 E 69th St, NY 10021 ☎ (212) 535 2000. *"They always make you welcome and are happy to see you. They cosset you like a 5-year-old. They have the best concierge, Anthony"* (Inès de la Fressange).

WASHINGTON DC

FOUR SEASONS HOTEL, 2800 Pennsylvania Ave NW, DC 20007 ☎ (202) 342 0444. On the border of historic Georgetown, a building that is modern but not unsimpatico, with a plush-carpeted lofty lobby full of antiques and plants. *"The combination of all one needs – comfortable rooms, a good restaurant,* and *it's located in Georgetown"* (Aniko Gaal).

MADISON, 15th and M Sts NW, DC 20005 ☎ (202) 862 1600. Quiet and tasteful; owner-driver management that means extra-special service. *"The owner collects fabulous antiques, furniture and art, so the hotel has a fantastic interior – you feel like you are part of the Renaissance"* (Aniko Gaal). Teeming with foreign ministers and ambassadors, who read their favourite paper over breakfast and make use of the hotel's interpreter service.

MARRIOTT, 1331 Pennsylvania Ave NW, DC 20004 ☎ (202) 393 2000. *"It's the best modern hotel, very exciting, space age, with a really zippy feeling. It's in an extremely good location – 2 minutes from the White House – and is extremely comfortable, with thick carpets, modern tapestries, very good lighting, masses of potted plants and beautiful flower arrangements. The staff are delightful, really efficient – you are given your messages immediately in about 4 places"* (Serena Fass).

RITZ-CARLTON, 2100 Massachusetts Ave NW, DC 20008 ☎ (202) 293 2100. *"The best old-world hotel, definitely as good as the one in New York. It gets all the glitterati, and there are masses of functions there"* (Aniko Gaal). Chilly glitterati can warm themselves by the log fire in the oak-panelled bar.

BOSTON

RITZ-CARLTON, 15 Arlington St, MA 02117 ☎ (617) 536 5700. Proud and dignified, the uncontested best in Boston. *"The same homy, protected feeling as the Connaught – it has great quality"* (Bill Blass). Impeccable service and every nicety, including the loan of ice skates to guests who wish to glide across Swan Lake in the adjoining public gardens.

CHICAGO

MAYFAIR REGENT, 181 E Lake Shore Drive, IL 60611 ☎ (312) 787 8500. At the best address in town, with scintillating lake views and a penthouse restaurant for elevated locals. *"It is the businessman's perfect hotel – an example of the American hotel at its best"* (Lord Lichfield).

LOS ANGELES

♛ **BEL AIR, 701 Stone Canyon Rd, Bel Air, CA 90077 ☎ (213) 472 1211.** A heavenly pink California mission with red tiled roofs and a courtyard of foliage, palms and fountains, crowned by a pond of swans. The smallest and purportedly the most difficult of the LA greats to penetrate, it was "done over" by Caroline Hunt-Schoellkopf (see Rosewood raptures) to the tune of $12.7 million. Though a subtler sanctum than its Hills neighbours, there's no stinting on necessities like private outdoor whirlpool baths. Dolly

Parton and Robert Wagner are frequent visitors. The late Princess Grace of Monaco stayed frequently and a suite is named after her.

BEVERLY WILSHIRE, 9500 Wilshire Blvd, Beverly Hills, CA 90212 ☎ (213) 275 4282. *"One of the top 3 in America. A one-man creation, a bit of a Hollywood madhouse, but it works beautifully. Why not? This is America! I think it is a great hotel"* (René Lecler). The one man is Hernando Courtright, self-styled Padrino (Godfather) of Beverly Hills. The bar is called El Padrino (*"you always meet people you know in there"* – Robert Sangster); the number plate of his Rolls-Royce says Padrino. You enter the lavish neo-Renaissance building through Louis XV gates of wrought iron and bronze, on the private cobbled street, El Camino Real, that divides the older Wilshire wing from Padrino's new Beverly wing. His wing is a nutty confection of French, Mexican, Spanish and Californian floors, topped with Italian marble, French tapestries, Spanish furniture, and bubbling with suites named after champagnes. The most opulent suite in the hotel is the two-storey Christian Dior, where Prince Charles and Co have stayed. The question is who *hasn't* stayed here. A few of the glitterati who have are the stars of *Amadeus* and *A Passage to India*, Michael Caine, Rudolph Nureyev, Alain Delon, Warren Beatty, the King of Tonga (who ordered McDonald's cheeseburgers) and Emperor Hirohito (who ordered peeled grapes).

BEVERLY HILLS, 9641 W Sunset Blvd, CA 90210 ☎ (213) 276 2251. A magnificent pink stucco Spanish villa, surrounded by lawns and palm trees, dotted with cottages. This is the old-Hollywood hang-out, as much a landmark as the sign in the hills, where *le movie monde* sip cocktails from the casting couches of the Polo Lounge (see FOOD AND DRINK). *"A very special place, hard to get in to and inhabited mainly by movie stars. You run into the biggest celebrities on the West coast there. I'd call it American quaint"* (Craig Claiborne).

CHATEAU MARMONT, 8221 Sunset Blvd, Hollywood, CA 90046 ☎ (213) 656 1010. A glorified bed and breakfast (no bar or restaurant): slightly déclassé 1920s gothic with infinite charm. Robert de Niro and Roman Polanski follow the train of Hollywood greats that included Garbo and Valentino in their heyday.

LAS VEGAS

CAESAR'S PALACE, 3570 Las Vegas Blvd, NV 89109 ☎ (702) 734 7110. *"The most fun hotel in Las Vegas – wonderfully over the top, I mean everyone dresses in Roman togas – it's* quite *bizarre. There are Roman statues everywhere, and the biggest swimming pool you have ever seen. It is real Americana. I just like sitting in the hotel lobby watching America come and go"* (Jackie Collins).

SAN FRANCISCO

FAIRMONT, Atop Nob Hill, CA 94106 ☎ (415) 772 5000. Still holds an exalted position among nobs as well as on Nob Hill. This is the grand hotel of the small screen, as seen on *Hotel*. In real life, it's old-fashioned and sophisticated. Its rooftop restaurant is reached by an outdoor glass lift.

Tiptop suite

The Penthouse Suite atop the Fairmont Hotel in San Francisco with 3 bedrooms, a kitchen, secret-passage library, game room, cable TV, maid and butler will hit you for $4,000 – the most expensive suite in the States.

HUNTINGDON, 1075 California St, CA 94108 ☎ (415) 474 5400. *"The best hotel in America – the quietest, most discreet, least vulgar; they are friendly, intelligent, and it's in a lovely location"* (David Hicks).

STANFORD COURT, 905 California St, CA 94108 ☎ (415) 989 3500. *"One of the loveliest hotels in America – very fine indeed"* (Craig Claiborne). It stands resplendent on "Snob" Hill, in Governor Leland Stanford's former family mansion. *"One of the top 3 in the USA – a quiet and peaceful atmosphere, and the food is probably the best of any hotel in America – quite something. You won't go hungry there"* (René Lecler).

WESTIN ST FRANCIS, 335 Powell St, CA 94102 ☎ (415) 397 7000. Where Californians prefer to stay because, being down in the square, there aren't any tourists hankering after the view.

PALM BEACH

BREAKERS, South Country Rd, FL 33480 ☎ (305) 655 6611. A palatial Italianate resort hotel with Venetian arches and Roman courtyards in palm-filled gardens. If you don't have a pad in Palm Beach, this is the place to stay.

NEW ORLEANS

PONTCHARTRAIN, 2031 St Charles Ave, LA 70140 ☎ (504) 524 0581. Post-Mardi Gras Shangri-La.

DALLAS

MANSION ON TURTLE CREEK, 2821 Turtle Creek Blvd, TX 75219 ☎ (214) 559 2100. The Rosewood blueprint, a cleverly converted Twenties mansion that has an established country-house feel, with log fires, leaded windows and fresh flowers. The Terrace Dining Room plays host to dozens of Dallas do's. (See Rosewood raptures.)

HOUSTON

REMINGTON ON POST OAK PARK, 1919 Briar Oaks Lane, TX 77027 ☎ (713) 840 7600. *"Fabulous – everyone flips out when they stay. Absolutely wonderful, you feel you're in your own home. Beautifully decorated, not overdone, in very good taste. Mrs Hunt-Schoellkopf is a very refined lady"* (Lynn Wyatt). (See Rosewood raptures).

Rosewood raptures

"America has more good hotels coming out than any other country I know. They are very special and there are always new people going into the business, who are not bound by tradition. Rosewood Hotels are the pioneers – everything they do is absolutely magnificent, tastefully done" (René Lecler). Rosewood is the brainchild of Dallas oil heiress Caroline Hunt-Schoellkopf, the second-richest woman in America, worth an estimated $1.3 billion. Her projected spending on Rosewood Hotels is $350 million, lavished so far on the Mansion at Turtle Creek, the Remington, Bel Air, Hana-Maui, and one in progress in Washington DC.

No mere caprice, these hotels represent a solid gold real-estate investment. And they are a thumping success. Every room is a designer showpiece: the Mansion lobby has polished floorboards, warm pink walls, a domed ceiling, tall arched windows, and masses and masses of foliage brimming from terracotta urns; the Remington is more velvety grand with business accoutrements; the Bel Air bar is wood-panelled and homy. Endless extras allure – hand-milled soap, shiny brass razors, bedroom feasts of fresh berries, cream, cookies and chocs."

ARIZONA

"I love the American South West in winter or summer – there's great skiing and great air at high altitudes or a lovely desert climate at lower altitudes. Cool nights and hot days in summer ..." (Jennifer Kramer).

ARIZONA INN, 2200 E Elm St, Tucson AZ 85719 ☎ (602) 325 1541. *"The perfect example of a good, small-town inn with very high standards. Arizona/Mexican-style bungalows in lovely gardens"* (René Lecler).

NEW MEXICO

RANCHO ENCANTADO, Rt 4, Box 57C, Santa Fe, NM 85701 ☎ (505) 982 3537. Small ranch-house and cottages in a hotch-potch of Spanish-cum-Indian-cum-American styles. For outward-bound gringos who wanna ride and swim and explore the wild South West.

HAWAII

MAUI *"Haleakala volcano is a fantastic place – you can wander around for days in this moonscape-type atmosphere"* (Warren Hoge). *"The prettiest island in the world"* (Lord Lichfield). *"Kapalua Bay is the most peaceful beach and very private too"* (David Frost). *"Whale-watching at Maalaea Bay and Lahaina Bay is wonderful. In Hawaii some of the islands have beautiful white sand beaches, and some black lava sands"* (Marie Helvin). *"If I suddenly had one wish, I would go to Maui"* (Marina Chaliapin).

KAHALA HILTON, 5000 Kahala Ave, Honolulu, Oahu, HA 96815 ☎ (808) 734 2211. *"A huge, terrific hotel where they have a swimming pool as well as the beach, so you have the choice. And then there is another big pool full of dolphins; you can watch them being fed. And there are several restaurants – I love the open one on the beach. It really is wonderful. A good weekend place"* (Jackie Collins).

GETTING THERE

AIR

REGENT AIR, 5757 West Century Blvd, Suite 220, Los Angeles, CA 90045 ☎ (213) 216 7566. A private airline, currently having a bumpy time, that has luxuriously kitted out a 727 with whirlpool baths, gold finishes – the works. Like a flying hotel. *"It's like having your own private jet. They send a limousine to pick you up at home, and there are no more than 35 people in the plane. You have your own cabin, like in a train, and food from the best restaurants. You can have a pedicure or make a call to anywhere in the world"* (Jackie Collins). *"You can sleep – there are curtains that can be drawn to separate you, there's beautiful china, lovely crystal, champagne and a choice of 6 movies. At the other end, you step into a bus, and by the time you reach your limousine in a remote part of LA airport, all the Filipino*

"My most vivid childhood memory is my first glimpse of Honolulu. Standing on the ship's deck, I suddenly noticed a cluster of mysterious bright lights glittering in the distance. I asked the steward if he knew what they could be. He had seen the sense of magic in my eyes, and told me that everyone in Hawaii had switched on their house lights to welcome us. I was 8 then, and my family have lived in Hawaii ever since. The islands are paradise. On Kamaaina, you can go barefoot to school, see Baryshnikov dance, eat huli-huli chicken or ulua and ahi fish raw, seconds after they are caught. Our beaches are the cleanest and most beautiful in all the world. You can get wiped out surfing at Banzai Pipeline or go snorkelling at Hanauma Bay, where you can hand-feed hundreds of tame colourful reef fish" (MARIE HELVIN)

chauffeurs are standing with your name on a placard and your luggage is already in the back of the car. It's terrific!" (Patricia Coppleson). *"It's the neatest, just like being on someone's private jet. Every day they say it's their last trip – I just hope it never is"* (Margaux Hemingway).

TWA The best way to fly across the Atlantic business class because they send you a boarding pass with your ticket – half the check-in time.

"I hate cruises. I used to go quite often to write about them in *Brideshead Revisited* style, and even then I found them boring. I think the food is overrated, the amusements are so childish – who wants to listen to Captain Foot on the organ? It is all very well if you are engaged in fornication, but for everybody else there is nothing but silly hat competitions. The most ghastly thing is being invited to the Captain's table. You don't just go once, but you're stuck there for the whole cruise: a group of ill-assorted people who have no desire to talk to each other. One poor Captain had a nervous breakdown. As an ex-sailor I always feel as if I should be scrubbing the deck, not wrapped up in a blanket drinking beef tea" (ERIC NEWBY)

CRUISING AND TOURS

ROYAL VIKING LINE, 1 Embarcadero Center, San Francisco, CA 94111 ☎ (415) 398 8000. *"By far the best in the world. All one class, better than first class. Any cruise is good, but the Hebridean one is very interesting"* (Lord Lichfield). A great variety of cruise durations (from 7 to 106 days), ports and areas – such as the Coral and Java Seas, Wine Country, the Holy Land, the Black Sea, Alaska, Panama Canal-Gatun Lake and the North Cape. An eclectic crew – officers are Norwegian, stewardesses Scandinavian, chefs Swiss, Austrian or German, waiters European and the launderers Chinese.

ABERCROMBIE & KENT, 1420 Kensington Rd, Suite 111, Oakbrook, IL 60521 ☎ (312) 954 2954. Worldwide tours and cruises (see Europe, Getting There).

HEMPHILL HARRIS, 16,000 Ventura Blvd, suite 200, Encino, CA 91436 ☎ (818) 906 8086. Highly exclusive tours for rich old fogeys. Guarantee the best of everything – the best rooms with the best views in the best hotels. Trips all over the world (except for their own doorstep – North America) include helicopter cruises, ballooning and a world tour in a private jet.

LINDBLAD TRAVEL, 1 Sylvan North, Westport, CT 06881 ☎ (203) 226 8531. Fabulously expensive trips for the intelligent élite; conservation-loving regulars have formed an exclusive travellers' club, the Intrepids. Cruises to the Antarctic, private river trips in China, extravagant safaris with four-poster beds provided.

SEA GODDESS CRUISES, 5805 Blue Lagoon Drive, Miami, FL 33126 ☎ (305) 266 8705. Superb cruises (see EUROPE, Getting There).

SUN LINE CRUISES, 1 Rockefeller Plaza, Suite 315, NY 10020 ☎ (212) 397 6400. The best cruises in the Med and Aegean (see Europe, Getting There).

CANADA

"Canada is where I most like to visit. From the Rockies across to Vancouver Island it's really lovely – glorious – especially when the tourists aren't there. You have to go in May or September – May to catch the thaw, September to catch the fall. Then you miss the Japanese, who don't come out of the woodwork until May, and have gone back in by September – but this is hard luck too because you also miss the Calgary Stampede in July" (Cliff Michelmore).

FOUR SEASONS, 21 Avenue Rd, Toronto, Ontario M5R 2G1 ☎ (415) 964 0411. Smart hotel in the heart of Yorkville. Indoor and outdoor pools, and the award-winning Truffles restaurant.

MANDARIN, 645 Howe St, Vancouver, BC V6C 2Y9 ☎ (604) 687 1122. In Canadian condo style, it's all things to all men – living quarters, gourmet restaurant, health club and business centre – but all the essence of the Mandarin is there to reassure: pure plushiness, taste, and faultless service.

RITZ-CARLTON, 1228 Sherbrooke West, Montreal H3G 1H6 ☎ (514) 842 4212. Luxurious continental-style hotel, the best in Montreal. Near all the fashionable boutiques, galleries and restaurants.

GETTING AROUND

RAIL

THE CANADIAN The train runs across Canada from Halifax to Vancouver. *"Pick it up in Calgary or Banff to do the most fascinating part of the journey. It curves its way up through the mountains and goes through a complicated series of tunnels, where the front of the train is coming out as the back of the train is going in. It's a smashing train"* (Cliff Michelmore).

TOURS

WAYFARER HOLIDAYS, 235 Yorkland Blvd, Suite 610, Willowdale, Ontario M2J 4W9 ☎ (416) 498 5566. Adventure tours around Canada. One of their best is to the Grand Pacific Circle, through the Rockies to Banff and Vancouver, on to the wild stream country of N Vancouver Island, and finally to Port Hardy, a protected area for killer orca whales. This huge blubbery population swims up the Johnstone Strait, indulging its expensive taste by eating salmon, and making appreciative noises that can be heard on hydrophones by the eager boat-trippers. Next on the itinerary is a voyage to Prince Rupert, via hundreds of islands.

MEXICO

LAS BRISAS, Carretera Escenica Clemente Mejia 5255, Acapulco ☎ (748) 41650. Glorious resort in gardens splurged with violet bougainvillea and scarlet hibiscus, high on a hill above Acapulco Bay. The best thing is that the 300 individual "casitas" each have their own pool, garnished daily with fresh orchids.

HOTEL GARZA BLANCA, PO Box 58, Puerto Vallarta, Jalisco ☎ (322) 21023. The *in* place in the *in* place – Liz Taylor and John Huston have pads nearby. Suites right on the little bleached sandy beach or Mexican villas with their own garden and pool.

CARIBBEAN

BEST ISLANDS

1. **DOMINICA – most beautiful**
2. **MUSTIQUE – most secludedly social**
3. **PETIT ST VINCENT – most peaceful hideaway**
4. **ANTIGUA – most showily social**

DOMINICA

An island with *sights*: waterfalls, sulphur springs, freshwater lakes, a gorge, botanic gardens and rain forests. *"My favourite island in the West Indies. So beautiful and lush. It feels like an undiscovered country, not yet destroyed by tourism. It rains an awful lot, but it means the vegetation and flowers are wonderful.* **REIGATE HALL HOTEL** [**Roseau ☎ (809) 44-54031**] *is very comfortable, very good"* (Quentin Crewe). The secluded **PAPILLOTE WILDERNESS RETREAT ☎ (809) 44-52287** is near the Trafalgar Triple Waterfalls and natural hot mineral baths.

GRENADINES

32 islands and cays dotted about between Grenada and St Vincent, including BEQUIA, MUSTIQUE and PETIT ST VINCENT. The best winter cruising waters (under sail) in the world.

MUSTIQUE Playground of royals and super-rich, who own colonial-style houses designed by Oliver Messel. The best way to stay here is to know or be related to Princess Margaret or Lord Glenconner or Mick Jagger and Co. That's what Viscount Linley, Prince Andrew, Raquel Welch and Margaux Hemingway do. Otherwise it's book way ahead for the **COTTON HOUSE, Mustique ☎ (809) 45-84621**, an 18th-century former cotton storehouse made of stone and coral. *Everyone* eats there, at Basil's Bar.

BEQUIA 6 sq miles (15.5 sq km) of exclusivity, where the Queen and Bob Dylan have stayed.

PETIT ST VINCENT Hide away here and you might never be found. Privately owned and traffic-free except for Mini mokes that scoot round the island tending to guests' every whim. As none of the 22 cottages has a telephone, guests hoist a yellow flag to summon room service (guaranteed to vroom up within 15 minutes) or a red flag to keep the mokes at bay. *"My idea of paradise. No culture on the island whatever, so you won't feel guilty about not seeing the ruins. Perfect beaches and sailing"* (Prue Leith). **PETIT ST VINCENT RESORT ☎ (809) 45-84801.**

PALM ISLAND John and Mary Caldwell sailed round the world to find this little Garden of Eden and now keep a sloop for sailing parties. Local Créole cooking. **PALM ISLAND BEACH CLUB ☎ (809) 45-84804.**

ANTIGUA

Largest of the Leewards, with a beach for every day of the year, as they say. *"The best holiday is spent lying in a hammock on a beach in Antigua – fantastic!"* (Margaux Hemingway).

ST JAMES'S CLUB, PO Box 63 ☎ (809) 46-31430. Sister to Peter de Savary's London club, though it bears no resemblance, some lament. Nevertheless, it couldn't be more *in* nor getting more hype. The latest line-up of sun-worshippers includes Madonna, the Prince Michaels of Kent, Prince Andrew, Princess Margaret, Joan Collins and Liza Minnelli.

COPPER AND LUMBER STORE, PO Box 184 ☎ (809) 46-31058. A converted Napoleonic warehouse overlooking English Harbour in Nelson's Dockyard. Furnished in Georgian style which goes down a treat with visiting celebs.

MILL REEF CLUB, Mill Reef ☎ (809) 46-32081. Namesake of the racehorse *Mill Reef*, which is owned by chief club member Paul Mellon. For the in crowd, and intent on keeping it that way.

ANGUILLA

MALLIOUHANA, PO Box 173, Maids Bay ☎ (809) 49-72111. This hotel is the most exclusive and expensive in the Caribbean (to stay in *and* to build – the 20-villa complex cost US$35 million). Quiet and privacy are so respected that the bar is 5 miles (8 km) from the hotel. Kissingers and Onassises take advantage of a bit of peace, at £1,680 (US$2,430) each a week without meals.

BAHAMAS

WINDERMERE ISLAND CLUB, Rock Sound, Eleuthera ☎ (809) 33-22538 is the most exclusive and pretty resort, surrounded by candy-coloured beaches, where Charles and Diana sunbathe in peace. **LYFORD CAY** is a private resort for Bel Air types who are used to being locked away from the outside world.

BARBADOS

Traditional favourite of the British, often referred to as "Little England". The smart part is St James's Beach, on the west coast, although some smarties are packing up to find less developed spots. Those who have been Barbados-way include Paul McCartney, Mick Jagger (who rents a villa at Bathsheba on the east coast), Elton John, Princess Margaret, Omar Sharif and Bryan Ferry (who stays at the **COLONY CLUB, St James ☎ (809) 42-22335**).

CASUARINA BEACH CLUB, St James ☎ (809) 42-83600. More a meeting- than a staying-place, although Prince Andrew and Vicki Hodge stayed here in a splash of publicity. Sting and local folk hero Eddy Grant would drop in for a cocktail or two when Sting was recording *Dream of Blue Turtles*.

CORAL REEF CLUB, St James ☎ (809) 42-22372. *"One of the finest resort hotels in the Caribbean"* (René Lecler). Cottages set in tropical gardens: endless watersports – water-skiing, catamaran sailing, snorkelling, skuba diving – plus tennis, golf, riding and polo.

SAM LORD'S CASTLE, Parish at St Philip ☎ (809) 42-37350. An exclusive hotel on the Atlantic side of the island, near the airport: ritzy Mustique-bound travellers stay the night here before continuing their journey. The Queen dined here with Richard Rowntree during her Caribbean tour some years ago.

SANDY LANE HOTEL, St James ☎ (809) 42-21311. Where it *has* all been happening …

SETTLERS BEACH HOTEL, St James ☎ (809) 42-23052. Landing spot of the first settlers in Barbados. *"The best place in Barbados – it's self-catering in little chalets. All the big, famous ones are dreadful"* (Prue Leith).

BERMUDA

"The best fishing I've ever done. Bermuda has 2 wonderful continental shelves that form an underwater plateau and suddenly slope off into deep water, which is the resting and feeding ground of a wide range of fish – dogfish, tuna, marlin, wahoo and dolphins" (Anthony Watson).

CAMBRIDGE BEACHES, Mangrove Bay, Sandy's Parish ☎ (809) 29-40331. A cottage colony on a peninsula. *"Altogether charming. Very sophisticated and very well run, with a beautiful beach and very high standards"* (Anthony Watson).

GRAND CAYMAN

"A 7-mile beach. It's unbelievable – goes on and on. Beautiful pink to white coral sand, superb swimming, and very good fishing in the south-east" (Anthony Watson).

GRENADA

"The prettiest capital town is St George's. A lot of it is 18th century. The trouble with most of the West Indies is the buildings get blown down in hurricanes" (Quentin Crewe). **SPICE ISLAND INN, St George's ☎ (809) 44-44258** has luxurious suites directly on Grand Anse Beach, one of the best in the Caribbean.

HAITI

GRAND HOTEL OLOFFSON, Port-au-Prince ☎ (509) 120139. A superb hideaway hotel decorated by Oliver Messel in collaboration with the owner, Suzanne Seitz. Rooms are named after the celebrity who first stayed in them. Erstwhile guests who love the privacy include Mick Jagger, Anne Bancroft, Sir John Gielgud, Harold Pinter and Lady Antonia Fraser, Marlon Brando and Graham Greene.

RELAIS DE L'EMPEREUR, Petit Goave ☎ (509) 240318. Luxurious, private, palatial and exotic, this retreat is run by the flamboyant Olivier Coquelin and Michael Febrarro. They attempt to materialize the whims of guests before they are expressed. King-size suites, private beach, Olympic pool, and gardens in which Coquelin strolls with his Burmese leopards, Sheba and Raj.

JAMAICA

"The Blue Mountain range is incredibly beautiful with all the waterfalls, forest and wild flowers – it's absolutely magic. The marlin fishing tournament off Port Antonio is very exciting" (Anthony Watson).

HALF MOON CLUB, PO Box 80, Montego Bay ☎ (809) 95-32211. Superbly run, one of René Lecler's top 3 in the Caribbean. A profusion of tropical vegetation and 1 mile (1.6 km) of private sandy beach.

PLANTATION INN, PO Box 1, Ocho Rios ☎ (809) 97-42501. Set on twin white crescent beaches with a spectacular coral reef a short flipper away.

ROUND HILL HOTEL, PO Box 64, Montego Bay ☎ (809) 95-25150. Elite social resort. Local-style villas with high ceilings and verandahs, set in more lush greenery.

TRYALL GOLF & BEACH CLUB, Sandy Bay Post Office, Hanover Parish ☎ (809) 95-25110. A sedate shangri-la for American retirees.

MONTSERRAT

"Unspoilt, casual with its own charm and character" (Carol Wright). A floating recording studio – Police, Stevie Wonder, Duran Duran, Paul McCartney and Wham have all crooned their way round George Martin's studios.

NEVIS

Separated from St Kitts by a 3-mile (4.8-km) channel known as the Narrows. Sleepy, but *"a very civilized island"* (Quentin Crewe).

MONTPELIER PLANTATION INN, PO Box 473 ☎ (809) 46-55462. Small, on the slopes of Mount Nevis. Fruit and veg grown in the hotel grounds. *"So informal and friendly. Everyone eats together and mixes in, and they're all such civilized, interesting people – artists and writers from everywhere. I thought I'd hate it, but it works very well"* (Quentin Crewe).

ST KITTS

Forested volcanic hills slope down to exquisite sheltered beaches, some of soft black volcanic sand. Less souped-up to international standards than the larger islands.

GOLDEN LEMON, Dieppe Bay ☎ (809) 46-57260. *"One of the top 3 hotels in the Caribbean – small and quite beautiful"* (René Lecler). An elegantly decorated haven with its own walled garden. Colonial ceiling fans, canopied beds and candlelit dinners. Where Kennedys and other well-known faces hide away, often booking under an assumed name.

ST LUCIA

"Very lush. The Pitons must be a wonder of the world – 2 strange volcanic mountains that shoot out of the sea, rising abruptly in a cone shape. You could trot around the base of them in about 25 minutes. Lord Glenconner has bought a plantation between them, which must be one of the most beautiful spots in the world" (Quentin Crewe). Destined to become the next Mustique.

TOBAGO

Robinson Crusoe's island: smaller and more exclusive than its sister island, Trinidad. Miles of white sandy beaches and a tropical interior with mountains rising to 2,000 ft (610 m). It's also Norman Parkinson's retreat from society smiles. MOUNT IRVINE BAY HOTEL ☎ (809) 63-93871 has a golf course and a 200-year-old converted sugar-mill restaurant. HOTEL ROBINSON CRUSOE ☎ (809) 63-92571 is *"an old colonial hotel which is tremendous, unspoilt and just like a christening cake"* (Katharine Hamnett).

VIRGIN ISLANDS

"The best getaway holiday I've ever experienced was a cruise by private yacht through the Virgin Islands. The whole sea is at your command, and you don't have to sail for long before you reach another beautiful island. The swimming and snorkelling are unbelievably wonderful and the Rockresorts, Little Dix and Caneel, are both superb" (Anthony Watson).

LITTLE DIX BAY, PO Box 70, Virgin Gorda, British Virgin Islands ☎ (809) 49-55555. 300 acres (121 ha) of paradise, Laurence Rockefeller style. Stilted thatched cottages, an open air dining room and marina.

CANEEL BAY, PO Box 120, St John, US Virgin Islands ☎ (809) 77-66111. More Rockefeller glory. Both the rooms and beaches are squeaky clean and ultra-spacious.

GETTING THERE

AIR

AIR MUSTIQUE, PO Box 870, King's Down, St Vincent, Grenadines ☎ (809) 45 84380. A tiny fleet of 5-seater Beach Barons and 9-seater Islanders which run scheduled flights from St Vincent to all the islands or can be chartered to meet clients direct from Barbados.

BWIA INTERNATIONAL *The* airline that serves the Caribbean, flying out of the USA, Canada and the UK. Hostesses hail from all the different islands, rum punches are served, steel band music vibrates over the airwaves and part of the menu is devoted to ethnic Caribbean dishes. They team up with LIAT (see below) for smaller island hops.

LIAT, Antigua The local airline that serves the West Indies. *"Tiny little planes that have to land in the most hazardous places – quite frightening, but it's fun. Every flight's a short haul – 25 minutes is the longest. The pilots are charming"* (Quentin Crewe).

YACHT CHARTER

CAMPER & NICHOLSONS (see Europe) have over 400 crewed sailing and motor-yachts for charter, from small boats to turn-of-the-century schooners.

NICHOLSON'S YACHT CHARTER, English Harbour, Antigua ☎ (809) 46-31059 and **CHARTER SERVICES, PO Box 9998, St Thomas, US Virgin Islands ☎ (809) 77-45300** have a fine range of sailing yachts.

Cruise with SEA GODDESS and ROYAL VIKING (see United States, Cruising and Tours).

TOURS AND RENTALS

ALLEYNE, AGUILAR & ALTMANN, Rosebank, Derricks, St James, Barbados ☎ (809) 43-20840. Rent top-notch properties on Barbados.

ABERCROMBIE & KENT (see Europe, Tours, Villas and Agents). **1420 Kensington Rd, Suite 111, Oak Brook, Il 60521 ☎ (312) 954 2944.**

CARIBBEAN CONNECTION, 93 Newman St, London W1 ☎ (01) 245 9181 and **DIFFERENT WORLD, 43 Cadogan St, London SW3 ☎ (01) 584 8803** Arrange plushy villa rentals.

BRAZIL

"The best antidote to life in New York. I love the weather, the language, the attitude to life, the music, the size of the country, the variety of people and the immediate feeling of warmth." (Warren Hoge). Everyone goes nuts in Brazil at carnival time: *"There are carnivals all over Brazil. Every little town has its own. Recife's is very nice, and Salvador's is smashing"* (Dan Topolski). The most spectacular carnival in the world is, of course, at Rio. *"It really is quite thrilling. It's a 24-hour festival. You can grab an hour or two's sleep on the beach in the morning and then it's all go again. There's nothing to beat the Rio Samba School parade. It's like a football league, and each school produces a theme and a song and a colour and a show with 3 or 4,000 people involved in the rehearsals for 6 months in advance, making costumes and so on. The 10 top Samba Schools parade through Rio from 8 pm on Sunday through until the next morning – thousands and thousands of people – just glorious. Competition is really intense and people lose their lives. The president of one Samba School was assassinated before the Carnival in 1980. It raises the passions"* (Dan Topolski).

RIO DE JANEIRO

"Rio has a fantastic physical setting, with Sugar Loaf Mountain and great bits of rock coming out of the sea like fingers poking up to a dramatic sky" (Elisabeth Lambert Ortiz). When the Carnival is over, there's always Copacabana, with its equally striking and jostling beach parades. *"Copacabana Beach is an extension of the city, raucous, vibrant and colourful"* (Warren Hoge).

COPACABANA PALACE, Ave Atlantica 1456 ☎ (021) 542 1887. The best hotel on the best beach, chock-a-block and full of beans at carnival time.

BAHIA

Bahia, or Salvador, is *"the heart and soul of Brazil. It's where all the black magic and makumba and slaves emanated from"* (Dan Topolski). *"The churches are simply splendid, so elaborate with twisted gold ropes, carvings, walls of gold leaf – everything but the kitchen sink. It's breathtaking"* (Elisabeth Lambert Ortiz).

BUZIOS

"The *glamour place where the rich and smart set go to get away from Rio"* (Dan Topolski). Laid-back would be an understatement: *"In Buzios, breakfast is taken around 2 pm, lunch at 7 and dinner never before 3 am. It has never been recorded that anybody was able to get to the beach (a minuscule one at that) in less than 4 hours, when it is only 20 minutes' walk from any point in this tiny fishing village. You see, the houses in Buzios have no doors and what with the percussions blaring all over the place, the cha cha cha, the batida des limoẽs and the joie de vivre des cariocas, when you finally reach the beach, you've forgotten why you went!"* (Olivier Coquelin).

MACEIO

"The most gorgeous place. There are miles and miles of deserted beaches, where you find little stands selling freshly cooked crabs and shrimps" (Warren Hoge).

TOURS

CLASSIC TOURS, Ave NS Copacabana 1059, Office 805, Rio de Janeiro 22050 ☎ (021) 287 3390. Made-to-measure holidays within Brazil – you could embark on an expedition to Manaus, where the Amazon proper begins, a boat along the river to the island of Marajo at the delta and a stay at a lodge in the heart of the jungle. Carnival parties, too, where they teach visitors to dance.

LINDBLAD TRAVEL (see United States, Getting there). Luxury Amazon cruises on the *MS Lindblad Explorer* sail from the river mouth at Belém in Brazil to Iquitos in Peru. Rubber dinghies diverge up little waterways to check out the vegetable and animal life (howler monkeys, dolphins, butterflies, leaches).

Amazin' Amazon

"The best adventure is to fly over the jungle in a little aeroplane – it's fantastic" (Margaux Hemingway).

"Manaus is the centre point for the Amazon, but you want to get away from there. It's built up and the forest is cut down. You have to go a long way upriver and along little tributaries to get into the jungle. I recommend that. That's what Brazil is" (Dan Topolski).

PERU

LAKE TITICACA *"The highest navigable waterway in the world – the most fantastic place. The clarity of the water and the islands are captivating"* (Warren Hoge).

CUZCO to MACHU PICCHU by train *"The best train ride, on a narrow-gauge railway, riding along the crest of the Andes. The most extraordinary train journey I've ever been on. Cuzco is 1,200 ft up and absolutely astonishing, the main centre of Inca culture. As you travel along, you pass these marvellous people, until you finally arrive at the Lost City of the Incas"* (Frederic Raphael).

AUSTRALASIA

BEST HOTELS

TOP 5

★

1 REGENT, Sydney
2 REGENT, Melbourne
3 SEBEL TOWN HOUSE, Sydney
4 ROCKMAN'S REGENCY, Melbourne
5 MERLIN, Perth

“The Australians and the Chinese and the Americans achieve that marvellous mixture of being perfectly good at service but still equal and friendly. The English tend to be either haughty and you feel a fool or subservient and you feel embarrassed. Aussie staff will chat to you if you want to chat and won't if you don't, and they bring your laundry back in 5 seconds. At the Mandarin the service is fantastic – you've hardly put your phone down before the chap is at your door. The English hotelier will say it's because they have all these Chinese coolies, but they don't have them in Australia and they don't have them in America. It's training and it's confidence and it's money – they redecorate all the time – their hotels are very big and brash and beautiful” (PRUE LEITH)

AUSTRALIA

The 1980s have produced a fertile crop of 5-star hotels, each desperate to outdo its elders in looks, service, cuisine and personality; to keep in the running, the oldies have had dramatic facelifts. The frenzied competition is generally healthy, pushing standards up – *"They're just* very *confident. They do things with so much panache"* (Prue Leith) – but the question is, are there enough takers for all this enthusiasm? Sydney may be enjoying year-round boom occupancy rates, but business at the Sheraton Ayers Rock is tepid, while at Perth and Adelaide, it may cool off altogether after the America's Cup and the Grand Prix.

SYDNEY

TOP 4

★

1 REGENT
2 SEBEL TOWN HOUSE
3 INTER-CONTINENTAL
4 SHERATON-WENTWORTH

REGENT, 199 George St, NSW 2000 ☎ (02) 238 0000. Its brilliant position overlooking the Opera House and sparkling harbour shoots it into the top class. Sleek and glossy, with excellent rooms-with-a-view (except for the too-small lowest-priced ones). Best are the Royal Suites, on the 33rd floor, with dining room, sitting room, dressing room, marbled bathroom, and butler. *"The only truly international hotel in Sydney. The service is as good as you'll encounter anywhere in the world"* (Leo Schofield). *"Just terrific"* (Prue Leith). *"All due to Ted Wright, the general manager, who pays the* greatest *attention to detail. Everything is so personal – when you open your door to a waiter, they know your name"* (Patricia Coppleson). *"The styling and the approach to their clients is very good"* (Anouska Hempel). Jetting journos, media bigwigs and businessmen stay there.

SEBEL TOWN HOUSE, 23 Elizabeth Bay Rd, Elizabeth Bay, NSW 2011 ☎ (02) 358 3244. Smaller, more intimate hotel where all visiting rock and showbiz stars are pampered. At the quiet, harbour end of razzy King's Cross, it's tastefully, sombrely plushy with excellent service. Whenever a star is in town – Spandau Ballet, Dire Straits, Bob Dylan – fans keep vigil outside the foyer. Wall-to-wall signed celeb photos in the bar. *"I absolutely adore the Sebel. My room had a writing table – that's fundamental. It's somewhere between America and England. In America it would be much more over the top, and in England much more uncomfortable. One's entire cultural history, from the Fifties onwards, stays here: Max Bygraves, Cilla Black, Warren Mitchell, Robert Morley – it's utterly thrilling"* (Peter York).

INTER-CONTINENTAL, 117 Macquarie St, NSW 2000 ☎ (02) 230 0200. The façade of this 3-storey Victorian building, former HQ of the NSW Government Treasury, has been preserved and topped with a A$150 million (US$106 million) towerful of bedrooms. Fine setting, 5 minutes from the Opera House, city, and art gallery; wonderful views over the Botanic Gardens, the sea glinting beyond. Very good management, and foodwise, it's *"treading on the toes of the Hilton"* (Max Lake).

“Half the point of Sydney is knowing people. What you must do is go out on a private yacht at 6 or 7 at night, have dinner on board with champagne, wonderful wines, and watch the sun go down. Get asked to cocktails or breakfast by someone who lives on the water – those things can only happen here. I sit on my wall at night [in Rose Bay] and have a glass of champagne before dinner and it's wonderful, magical. Meet people, see their houses and how they live, and what Australia is about” (PATRICIA COPPLESON)

SHERATON-WENTWORTH, 61 Phillip St, NSW 2000 ☎ (02) 230 0700. Its apologetic exterior conceals a thoroughly well-run hotel with many loyal guests. New-jetters would go to the Regent, but diehards swear by this one. *"It's brilliant. Very much a club atmosphere, a great continuity of staff. Everyone's lovely, from the switchboard operator to the chap who brings me a cup of coffee at 6 in the morning. Tony Facciolo is without doubt the greatest concierge in the world – a Venetian – and one of the great features of Australia"* (Henry Blofeld).

Sydney slow boats

Sydney offers the best ferry rides in the world. From Circular Quay to Manly is the longest. On a sparkling summer's day, the sun dances on the sea; at dusk, the cavernous sky lights up in a blaze of colour, and at night there is the sensation of being in a slow-motion rocket launch, the twinkling city skyline rising as you draw away. The Woolwich Ferry, which sails under the bridge to Hunters Hill, is also brilliant. Best event: Sydney is the only place in the world to have a ferry race, the Ferrython in January. Punters pay to ride on their chosen ferry and the harbour goes mad. Not so long ago the oldest ferry in the fleet sank, just as it reached the quay, thus not drowning any passengers.

RUSSELL, 143a George St, NSW 2000 ☎ (02) 241 3543. Small private colonial-style hotel where Bryan Brown and Rachel Ward stay. Run by Tory Alexander; very good personal service. *"A charming small hotel – enchanting, not grand"* (Leo Schofield).

Sydney's best views

- ☆ From the sea, looking back at the Opera House and Bridge – better than the tame view from Mrs Macquarie's Chair in the Botanic Gardens.
- ☆ From Centrepoint Tower – the suburbs, beaches and inlets laid out like a map.
- ☆ From the Sydney Opera House, watching a cruise liner depart at night. Little lights shine from every porthole as she sails past the green-lit big-wheel of the Harbour Bridge. Just like the art deco posters.

MELBOURNE

TOP 5
★

1. REGENT
2. ROCKMAN'S REGENCY
3. WINDSOR
4. MENZIES AT RIALTO
5. HILTON INTERNATIONAL

REGENT, 25 Collins St, VIC 3000 ☎ (03) 630 321. A 50-storey modern architectural classic, built around a soaring sky-lit atrium. The actual hotel is based on the top 15 floors. *"It has a fantastic hollow in the middle – all black glass and little white bulbs, like living inside a Christmas tree. You look down and there's a torch-singer on the mezzanine floor, and the acoustics are so fantastic that you hear her as you step out of the lift on the 50th floor. It's just magic!"* (Prue Leith). At the top are ten suites – Jackie Collins stayed in the Kensington – and the best loo view in the world, with windows from floor to ceiling.

ROCKMAN'S REGENCY, Corner of Lonsdale and Exhibition Sts, VIC 3000 ☎ (03) 662 3900. Brand new, smallish (some rooms *too* small), good position, and Sebel-like personal service that attracts celebs (John McEnroe, Sean Connery). *"My favourite in Australia. Brilliant rooms – suites have a private Jacuzzi, an enormous [whirlpool] bath which can hold 5 people. There's a very good bar rule: they only serve people who are eating or staying there, so it doesn't become one of the city's main pick-up places"* (Henry Blofeld).

WINDSOR, 103 Spring St, VIC 3000 ☎ (03) 630261. Long-established Victorian hotel, now run by the Oberoi group. *"Everyone got up in arms about it – 'the smell of curry … impossible!' but a great deal of money was spent on reworking it to its original state. The result is unbelievable"* (René Lecler). The domed Grand Dining Room has silk wallpaper and crystal chandeliers – *"it's the best – such splendour …"* (Lillian Frank). Visiting Prime Ministers stay here.

MENZIES AT RIALTO, 495 Collins St, VIC 3000 ☎ (03) 620111. Curiously based in 2 Victorian buildings linked by an atrium, under the shadow of the new twin-towered Rialto, tallest building in Australia. Restored to the tune of A$40 million (US$28.2 million), it has Gothic arches and a wood-panelled ballroom with ornate ceiling.

HILTON INTERNATIONAL, 192 Wellington Parade, E Melbourne, VIC 3002 ☎ (03) 419 3311. Outside the city centre, overlooking Melbourne Cricket Ground and gardens. *"The best bar in the city, and the hotelier, Frank Christie, is the best in Australia – he's from the old school of hoteliers, and runs a very tight ship"* (Lillian Frank). Susan Renouf goes overboard about it; Prince Philip and Margaret Thatcher have had first-class cabins.

ADELAIDE

ADELAIDE CASINO, North Terrace, SA 5000 ☎ (08) 212 2811. Spanking new 5-star hotel/restaurant/casino, built in the old Victorian railway station, with a modern skyscraper addition. Good position, near the arts centre, overlooking the Torrens River and Adelaide Oval.

HILTON INTERNATIONAL, Victoria Square, SA 2000 ☎ (08) 217 0711. New, spacious 'n' gracious. The best in Adelaide, with pretty views over the square.

“On arrival at the very best hotels, you feel the warm vibrations surrounding you – as if you have been dearly expected and finally you are coming home. Unfortunately, these places are, like Sheba my pet Burmese leopard, on the endangered species list. They are usually owned and managed by the same person. The more congenial ones are run on a paying-guest basis where you pay not according to what you consume but an all-in rate for the number of days you stay. Then there are the palaces, where it is always a tremendous pleasure to stay, if for no other reason than to massage one's ego. Visiting frequently assures your status of being welcomed warmly” (OLIVIER COQUELIN)

PERTH

TOP 3
★
1 MERLIN
2 PARMELIA HILTON
3 SHERATON

MERLIN HOTEL, 99 Adelaide Terrace, WA 6000 ☎ (09) 323 0121. Sparkling 5-star hotel that will trap the most glamorous hangers-on during the America's Cup. The lobby has a pink Italian granite floor and an atrium that soars 13 storeys to a domed glass roof. Rooms are equally grand, a dove grey and pastel theme.

PARMELIA HILTON, Mill St, WA 6000 ☎ (09) 322 3622. Still the favourite for consistent service and a good position. It's Sydney's Sebel Town House equivalent for visiting celebs who want individual service. *“Excellent in terms of personal service. They always remember who you are”* (George Falkiner).

SHERATON, 207 Adelaide Terrace ☎ (09) 325 0501. A fine 5-star hotel overlooking the Swan River; Test cricketers stay here. Lovely views and superb tucker from the River Room restaurant.

BRISBANE

SHERATON, 249 Turbot St, QLD 4000 ☎ (07) 353535. Superbly decorated, some say it's the best hotel in Australia. Lovely views of Brisbane River.

HOBART

WREST POINT CASINO, Country Club Ave, Prospect Vale, TAS 7000 ☎ (003) 448 855. Not super-luxe, but big rooms with 7-ft (2.1-m) beds, in a circular building. Good view of Derwent River. The first legal casino in Australia, opened in the mid-1970s.

COUNTRY AND RESORT

BURNHAM BEECHES COUNTRY HOUSE, Sherbrooke Rd, Sherbrooke, VIC 3789 ☎ (03) 755 1903. An art deco mansion built by a ship-mad family, hence the vast sun decks (terraces). The sitting room has a feel of the old *Queen Mary*, its chairs are replicas of those on the QM. Moored in a garden of English trees in the Dandenong Hills. Fine cuisine.

JUPITER'S CASINO-CONRAD INTERNATIONAL, Gold Coast Highway, Broadbeach, QLD 4551 ☎ (075) 502546. Resort hotel newly opened in a blaze of razzmatazz: a shock to Queenslanders who thought their right-wing Premier Joh was anti-gambling. *“The best hotel in the world. It outdoes Caesar's Palace in Las Vegas. There's nowhere else in the whole wide world with a pool like that – tropical, with palms and fountains and half a dozen spas. There's a sort of Coliseum at the back with pillars, all in South Australian sandstone. It should win an architectural prize. The rooms are beautiful, the beds 9 foot wide. The discotheque is superb”* (Lillian Frank).

MIETTA'S QUEENSCLIFF HOTEL, 16 Gellibrand St, Queenscliff, VIC 3225 ☎ (052) 521 066. A gracious hotel with one of Port Phillip Bay's most delightful sea views. Refined, relaxed and classic Victoriana, to the extent of going down the hall to the wood-panelled, brass-fitted bathroom. Run by Mietta O'Donnell (of Mietta's restaurant in Melbourne, see FOOD AND DRINK). Old-fashioned breakfasts go on for ever.

NOOSA HEADS By far the best mainland resort town – upmarket, with chic shopping and eating. Visiting Europeans come in January and February, when it's too hot and wet to hit the Barrier Reef. The area is surrounded by heavily treed National Parkland, with hills rising behind the shore, surf beaches, and low-rise development only. *“Condominium style, like Hawaii – not the outback, but part of what I call the international look of Australia”* (Susan Renouf). Best hotel: **NETANYA, Hastings St, Noosa, QLD 4567 ☎ (071) 474 722.**

PEPPERS GUEST HOUSE, Ekert Rd, Pokolbin, Hunter Valley, NSW 2321 ☎ (049) 987596. A restful country-house atmosphere, though it is new and plushly fitted out. Looks out on to vineyards.

SHERATON AYERS ROCK, Yulara Drive, Yulara, NT 5751 ☎ (089) 562200. A wonderful sight, painted in rich Ayers Rock hues, with desert-toned furnishings. On a scorching site just outside the official Ayers Rock limit (now Aboriginal property,

Ayers and Graces

"I'm wonderfully happy leading a simple, primitive life in the centre of Australia – the absolute utter quiet and peace, no sound, nothing, just an ancient feeling that comes to you … I haven't had that sense anywhere else in the world. I, and a number of my friends, are beginning to feel really part of the land: the space, the heat, the quiet, the history, the colour, the light, the sun" (Prue Acton)

leased back to the central government for touristic pursuits), it is kept cool by a series of white windsurferesque sails that form a parasol over the low-level complex. Some think it sacrilegious, others incongruous, to build in the spiritual heart of Australia, but it's certainly the only way to see the Rock in style.

BEST ISLANDS

TOP 3

★

1 **LIZARD ISLAND**
2 **ORPHEUS ISLAND**
3 **BEDARRA ISLAND**

LIZARD ISLAND, (see Tours and Agents). The most northerly and most exclusive island in Australia, on the fringe of the Outer Reef. *"Excellent food, small, intimate, a house-party atmosphere. No fawning attention from flunkies. You don't go for the service"* (Claudia Rossi Hudson). No playground either, just superb Marlin fishing, scuba diving, snorkelling and sunbaking, as the Aussies say. Bob Hawke is on the guest list.

ORPHEUS ISLAND, Townsville, QLD 4850 ☎ (077) 777 377. Privately owned by 2 Italians and run by Frenchman Kolke Muller, it's a chic blend of Tropics and Mediterranean. No day-trippers allowed; a dead quiet getaway where famous faces can choose to ignore or fraternize with each other. Lots of honeymooners. Only 24 serviced units (rooms or bungalows), Italian-tiled, whitewashed, cany, airy. Those who have been lured into the underworld include Bob Hawke, Prince Charles, and the Duke and Duchess of Westminster.

BEDARRA ISLAND, (see Tours and Agents). 2 separate resorts (Hideaway and Bay) with 16 villas apiece. A proper Pacific island idyll, unquestionably hidden away, like a private club. No entertainment (a mercy, since Aussie resort entertainment takes the form of toad races and bingo), just a spread of tropical goodies and a beach to yourself. About A$219 (US$155) a day all-in, though once on the island, it's a cashless society where bankers cool down.

GREAT KEPPEL ISLAND, (see Tours and Agents). Not at all exclusive, but the best island for young, footloose international trendies. Laid-back, with much spontaneous partying (instead of regimented fun), since itinerants can sail in and stay on their yachts or at the free-for-all youth hostel, rather than being bound to a 24-hour resort existence. 17 miles (27 km) of brilliant, sweeping, firm sandy beaches; pretty wooded island.

TURNING OVER A NEW REEF

Australia has been slow to exploit the wonders of the Great Barrier Reef, a 1,200-mile (1,931-km) semi-submerged causeway of live coral that lies in splendour off the Queensland coast, home of 1,900 varieties of tropical fish. Until recently, most resorts remained downmarket, catering either to geriatric/18–30s package-trippers from Victoria, or to diving and snorkelling enthusiasts. (The best diving is off Heron Island.) Communications were the major problem, now being resolved by new airstrips and swish launches. Ansett, TAA and one or two entrepreneurs are currently pouring millions into the development of islands to standards that international travellers understand. Best time to visit is after the sea wasps (poisonous jellyfish) have gone: March–Sept.

WHITSUNDAY ISLANDS

"Last year I flew from Lizard Island down to Hayman and Hamilton by private helicopter. It was fantastic because we could see the whole of the Barrier Reef stretched below us. Who wants to go to the Aegean when you have the Whitsundays? In 2 hours from Sydney you're in seventh heaven – just magic" (Susan Renouf).

The islands, a series of gentle, matted green peaks, are remnants of a drowned valley, some 550 miles (900 km) north of Brisbane. Many are uninhabited, with names like Plum Pudding Island. Others are resortified. The plushiest are:

HAMILTON ISLAND HIP HOP

The most social (not the most refined) time to hit Hamilton is in April for Race Week, when the island rocks under the weight of boisterous ocean sailors and a flashy entourage – Rod Muir, rock hero Richard Clapton (no relation to Eric), cricket captain Allan Border, and enough sparsely clad, anonymous girls to go round. Fast-living, chauvinistic stuff. A week of Mai-Tai-sipping in the pool, spas under the stars and dancing in a coke-driven frenzy. Last year's dramatic fire, which razed the central resort buildings, left a fraught Bob Bell (British owner of the star maxi-yacht *Condor*), whose safe-deposited A$10,000 (US$7,066) went up in smoke, and a thrilled bunch of yachties, who'd watched their bills go the same way. The *planned* highlight of the week is the lay-day exodus to Whitehaven Beach on Whitsunday Island (the largest in the group), a boundless stretch of squeaky white sand, normally deserted save the odd goanna (a gnarled and nobbly prehistoric-style lizard). A barge transplants marquee, barbecue, band and beer, while yachts stream in, bulging with party-goers, who wind up dancing semi-bikini'd and barefoot on the beach, or wallow like hippopotami in the shallows, sun visors and shades down, lager in hand.

HAMILTON ISLAND, Shute Harbour, QLD 4007 ☎ (079) 469 144. Keith Williams's multi-million dollar dream, a lump in the ocean that has undergone plastic surgery in the shape of a man-made beach and lagoon, a passenger jet-sized airstrip and a marina. Cosmetic highlight: Polynesian-style bures (bungalows) and central complex (with expensive restaurants, shops, bars etc – a A$7 million (US$4,946,297) rebuild after last year's tragic fire). Scar: the gauche medium-high-rise condos that mar the hillside and raise accommodation levels to 1,200 (rocketing to 3,000 by 1988). Some privately owned apartments. A favourite haunt of David Gower and the John Lloyds: George Harrison has built a mansion set in 5 acres (2 hectares), one of 14 private sites here. Williams has also launched a floating hotel, *Coral Cat*, which goes out to the Reef, and has plans for a motor-racing circuit.

MIDDLE PERCY A wild, enchanting island accessible only by private boat. It has only 1 inhabitant, Andy, an Englishman, who lives in a colonial-style stilted homestead among unkempt flowering trees and shrubs of violent purple and raspberry pink. One coconut rationed to each visiting yacht; you can buy home-made preserves, fruit and bread (if it's baking day). Fresh-water shower, hot from its hosepiped voyage down the hillside. Everyone's invited to hike the 3 miles (4.8 km) up to the homestead, through bush, stream and swamp, spotting birds and kangaroos, following Andy's witty signs (a sort of Disneyland assault course). Fresh lime juice and lunch are your reward. Back on the beach are a hut and shelter filled with yachtie mementoes – it's a tradition for all boats to leave their name inscribed on to whatever is dispensable at the time, ranging from a broken paddle and a T-shirt to a guitar and a chest X-ray.

BEST BEACHES

Around Sydney
PALM BEACH and WHALE BEACH have stretches of sand studded with nymphets (daughters of the rich and, southern-hemispherically speaking, famous) and hulky surfers in zazzy board shorts. In the Eastern Suburbs, TAMARAMA ("Glamarama"), a stage for macho Mr Universes and topless Miss Worlds, is the prettier, tinier neighbour of the well-trodden and sewage-infested BONDI, which, none the less, retains its style, with surf lifesavers lording it from their stripy tent, and its admirers: *"For all the hideousness and ugliness, it is a wonderful beach. All human life is there, that's what's so interesting"* (Leo Schofield). *"When there's a moment, I dash to Bondi. I love*

surfing, sunbaking and playing porpoises – it's glorious for me to go out and lie on a golden beach under a sky that is the brightest blue and as seemingly endless as ever" (Diana Fisher). The best harbour beach, BALMORAL, Mosman, has comforting – though probably ineffectual – shark netting, and teems with trendy windsurfers.

Best escapist beach
"STANMORE PARK on the south coast – very beautiful" (Leo Schofield).

Best surfing beaches
HARBORD, a freshwater beach just up from Manly, and CALOUNDRA in Queensland" (Max Lake).

SURFERS' PARADISE *"The air is wonderful and fresh, and there are the most beautiful surf beaches. There's* miles *of beach and the water's lovely and clean. Where else can you walk along mile after mile of glorious beach without finding a cliff or something in the way?"* (Gloria Staley). *"It licks Honolulu, it leaves it for dead"* (Blyth Staley).

Pom voyage!

Celebrate Australia's bicentenary in 1988 by sailing there in a square-rigged ship. On 24 April 1987, 11 ships sail from London, carrying up to 220 passengers and crew. Ports of call include, Tenerife, Rio de Janeiro, Cape Town, Mauritius and Fremantle, finally reaching Botany Bay on 26 January 1988. It won't be quite the same as the original Pom voyages to the penal colony: you have a £23,000 (US$33,274) fare to pay on top of your labours. Cox & Kings Travel, 46 Marshall St, London W1 ☎ (01) 734 8291.

NEW ZEALAND

No Mecca for hotel-goers, gourmets or shoppers (unless it's for the best camping gear in the world), but a paradise for sportif, outdoorsy types. Some of the most thrillingly beautiful scenery you'll ever see. South Island is the most spectacular, boasting the finest walk in the world – the Milford Track (you book and pay to go on it), which winds up at Milford Sound, a magnificent fjord with cruise boats that take you gasp-makingly near the sheer mountain walls and waterfalls which plummet down them. Queenstown, a ski centre in winter, offers jet-boat and white-water rafting in summer; Fox and Franz Josef are glacial, yet flanked by rainforest. Superb sailing from Auckland, whose harbour compares well with Sydney's. International yachties bob around the Bay of Islands area, catered for by ambitious new restaurants. NZ has 70 million sheep (and 4 million people) and on a driving holiday you'll meet most of them.

CHATEAU TONGARIRO, Mount Ruapehu, North Island ☎ (081 223) 809. The best in the north, in National Parkland.

HERMITAGE, Mount Cook, South Island ☎ (05621) 809. A luxury chalet hotel at the foot of the highest peak in New Zealand. Cocktails are poured over ice from the highest, purest glaciers in the country.

HUKA LODGE, PO Box 95, Huka Falls Rd, Taupo, North Island ☎ (074) 85791. At the heart of the North Island, on the banks of Lake Taupo. *"Equal to the best 5-star accommodation in the world"* (Tony Greig).

PACIFIC

VANUATU

HIDEAWAY ISLAND *"The whole family loves snorkelling and scuba diving here. Your roof is of leaves; you fall out of your hut on to the beach and there's the most beautiful underworld, equivalent to the Barrier Reef. The water, in fact, is a little clearer, more consistent than the Reef. Also, as a result of the French influence, they have some very good restaurants"* (Tony Greig).

FIJI ISLANDS

REGENT OF FIJI, PO Box 441, Nadi Bay ☎ 70700. Typical tropical set-up of modern town precinct meets the jungle village: a central lofty lobby opening on to restaurants, bars and shops, set in a lush Garden of Eden dotted with simple, stylish villas. Humorous, friendly staff with bushy hairdos. The barman is called Sam Meat Pie. Each day, a plane glides up the beach and whisks you away to your chosen island, there to feast until nightfall.

TOBERUA A 4-acre (1.6 ha) microdot, undetected by rainclouds and mosquitoes. Fresh water is brought over by barge from Fiji. Peaceful days of sunning, windsurfing, snorkelling and fishing and nights in your private thatched bure (bungalow) – on land or floating.

TAVEUNI *"Beautiful, tiny, exotic island, and rather inaccessible"* (Lord Lichfield). It's on the 180° longitude line, the true International Date Line (although in practice, the line skirts it). The only place where you can stand with one leg in today and one in tomorrow.

“My favourite holiday place in the world is Huka Lodge in Taupo. It's on a river with magnificent trout fishing. There are Lancastrians and Yorkshiremen who have never gone home after fishing in that area. I tie in the trip with one to Queenstown. We stay on a big sheep station by the glacial lake. Anyone who hasn't been in a jet-boat up and down the Shotover Gorge hasn't lived. Around the lake are mountains called the Remarkables, and they have these incredible slides – stainless steel troughs – down the sides. To go down from the top is marvellous”

(TONY GREIG)

FRENCH POLYNESIA

The best thing about these islands is the aerial view: the inky blue ocean, studded with green volcanic islands, each ringed with a reef that is marked by white surf. Within the reef, the lagoon water is still and translucent, shaded from aquamarine to indigo. Best view from terra firma: from the top of Mount Tapioi on Raiatea.

It's sadly true that Papeete, capital of Tahiti, is dirty and noisy, a let-down after the amusing arrival at its airport, Faaa, when you are serenaded by rotund, jolly native musicians got up in flower leis and pareus. More amusingly, the band can later be seen scarpering on mopeds, ukuleles over one shoulder and blue jeans on. After that excitement, it's best to grab the first plane out to a smaller isle, or cruise around by private yacht.

BORA BORA The only island that really caters to the rich, mainly American market, with a series of hotels and clubs set in private gardens with their own stretch of beach. Guests at the **OA OA, PO Box 10, Bora Bora ☎ Tahiti 27870**, stay in floating huts and have breakfast rowed out to them. **HOTEL BORA BORA, BP 1015, Papeete ☎ 19689** has nabbed the best site on the island, on a promontory, where the beach always looks magically picture-book white and palm-fringed (even though the adjacent shoreline is shabby). Thatched bungalows in lush gardens, terrace restaurant, outrigger canoes, reef and motu views.

HUAHINE The best island to cruise to – quickly, before it gets too developed. Unsophisticated, with some perfect little jewels of beaches in the south (the Tahitian islands don't have the expanses of sweeping sand of the Caribbean) with clear-as-clear luminous turquoise waters). Best resort: the legendary **BALI HAI, Fare ☎ Tahiti 29068**.

MOOREA *"One of the natural wonders of the world is the first sight of Moorea, sailing in to Cook Bay from Papeete"* (Marie Helvin). Stay at CLUB MED, BP 575, Papeete, PF Tahiti, newly renovated in a strange mixture of styles (the main building is Japanese) and occupying the most glorious corner of the island. Lavish feasts, their own private atoll just off the coast, and all watersports on tap.

GETTING THERE

AIR

QANTAS is in the very top league. Its impeccable safety record speaks for itself. *"The best in the world. Great service, comfort and Australians looking after you. I like that"* (Gloria Staley). *"The best first-class in the world. Most efficient. I prefer stewards [Qantas has more male than female cabin staff] to stewardesses – they can get very crotchety at times. The stewards are more professional"* (Patricia Coppleson). *"All stewards are fanatical racing people. I can always get updates on any results. I manage to yak all the way through a 24-hour flight, even with 3 crew changes – something you couldn't share with a BA crew, who also have silly rules regarding drink. They make you wait until airborne for your first glass of champagne, whereas Qantas are very efficient and sensible on that score"* (Robert Sangster). *"... Because the Australian wines are quite outstanding"* (David Frost). *"The best way to travel is first class, up front, in a 747 flown by a Qantas captain who is about 45"* (Michael Parkinson).

AIR NEW ZEALAND. Since they are not a worldwide concern, they put all they've got into their Pacific routes. Cliff Michelmore's favourite.

ANSETT AIRLINES. The better of the 2 main internal airlines, half-owned by Rupert Murdoch. Voted top by all free-enterprise-loving Aussies (George Falkiner, Patricia Coppleson, etc), though Henry Blofeld says: *"I always fly TAA because I don't find any cricketers on board. They all travel with Ansett. What used to happen is that, say, Dennis Lillee would kick Javed Miandad [1981 incident] and I would write the most frantically strong piece in the paper. Next morning I'd find myself sitting next to Lillee, with my piece open on his knee. I really could see no future in that."*

LE CLARE, Building 400, Comper Street, Bankstown Airport, NSW 2200 ☎ (02) 700038. Exclusive light-aircraft charter from David Le Clare. Mostly used by businessmen, but can be hired to fly wherever you want around Australia. Double the cost of normal first-class air fares.

YACHT CHARTER

EASTERN SUBURBS SAILING CENTRE, New Beach Rd, Rushcutters Bay, Sydney, NSW 2000 ☎ (02) 328 7666. 24-ft (7-m) and 36-ft (11-m) yachts can be hired by the day (until 8 p.m. in summer to allow for twilight tipples).

HAMILTON ISLAND CHARTERS, Hamilton Island, QLD 4802 ☎ (079) 469 144. A slick fleet of cruising yachts with self-furling sails, talking depth sounders and all mod cons. Crewed motor-yachts too – Robert Holmes a'Court hired one last year. The Whitsunday Passage provides perfect cruising waters, but the most delightful island, Middle Percy, lies further south.

TOURS AND AGENTS

ANSETT, 501 Swanston St, Melbourne, VIC 3000 ☎ (03) 668 2222 (and in all Australian capitals). For Hayman island and other tours.

MARY ROSSI TRAVEL, Suite 1501, CML Building, 14 Martin Place, Sydney, NSW 2000 ☎ (02) 231 3633. All arrangements for upmarket globetrotters are made by Mary and 6 members of her family. Agents for Serenissima (see EUROPE, TOURS).

TAA, 50 Franklin St, Melbourne, VIC 3000 ☎ (03) 665 1333 (and in all the Australian capitals). Arrange trips to Bedarra, Lizard, Great Keppel and other islands. Also inland tours.

FAR EAST

BEST HOTELS

TOP 6

★

1 MANDARIN, Hong Kong
2 ORIENTAL, Bangkok
3 OKURA, Tokyo
4 PENINSULA, Hong Kong
5 REGENT, Hong Kong
6 TAJ MAHAL, Bombay

"There's a tremendous energy in the East. Everything in Tokyo is very modern, all made of rock and steel. They're preparing for the next century there. Get out on the bullet train to Kyoto, via magical cities like Nara, one of the ancient capitals, or Kobe, the port city. Kobe has incredible hills covered with lace cap hydrangea – all blue. Go to Hakone, to the hot springs and pine forests. Just below, on the Izu Peninsula, there are really wonderful beaches – you go to the hot sulphur springs and then the sea" (TINA CHOW)

"The best thing to see anywhere in the universe is the Terracotta Warriors in Xi'an. They're in what looks like an aeroplane hangar – it is absolutely the most amazing spectacle. I used to think Michelangelo's David was a real wow but these are being unearthed in the side of a hill. It's absolutely spellbinding" (BOB PAYTON)

JAPAN

OKURA, 10-4 Toranomon, 2-chome, Minato-ku, Tokyo 105 ☎ (03) 582 0111. A mini international city, eclectic in all spheres. *"The best in the world. The best services – telex, telephones – the best European food in Japan, and the best flower arrangements in the hall – it's staggering! A complete flowering cherry will be sawn off and brought into the hotel. It's the combination of service and cuisine that puts it at the top. Swimming pool, shops, varied restaurants, everything – I never go out – I just stay there 3 days and then go back to the airport"* (David Hicks). *"The Japanese restaurants in it are really wonderful"* (Tina Chow). *"They cope with hordes of people, but it's not impersonal. It's perfection. They'll remember you even if you haven't stayed there for 5 years. Attention is enormous, and what I love about Japan is there's no tipping ... such a relief"* (Joan Burstein).

GAJOEN KANKO HOTEL, 1-8-1 Shimo-Meguro, Meguro-ku, Tokyo 153 ☎ (03) 491 0111. *"Old-fashioned and run down, but some wonderful carving on the elevator doors; oriental design of the 1940s"* (Yuki Maekawa).

Ski stops

The best winter resort hotels are: SAPPORO PARK, 3-11 Nishi Minami-IO, Chuo-ku, Hokkaido 064 ☎ (011) 511 3131; SAPPORO GRAND HOTEL, 4 Nishi Kita-I, Chuo-ku, Hokkaido 060 ☎ (011) 261 3311; YAMAGATA GRAND, 1-7-40 Honcho, Yamagata 990 ☎ (0236) 41 2611. See also SPORTING LIFE.

A shot in the park

Japan's bullet train runs from Tokyo to Omiya, Morioka, Nigata and – the best route, whizzing at 130 mph (210 km/h) through national parkland beneath Mount Fuji – to Hakata, via Kyoto, Nagoya, Osaka and Hiroshima.

CHINA

JINLING HOTEL, Xinjiekou Square, Nanking ☎ 44141. Built by a shoeshine boy who escaped from Nanking in the 1940s to Singapore, made his fortune, returned shiny-shoed, and magnanimously built this 36-storey hotel – a floor for each year of his absence – on the corner that was his boyhood beat.

HONG KONG

"My favourite city – such excellent shopping for food, clothes, bags – everything imaginable" (Serena Fass).

MANDARIN, 5 Connaught Rd, Central ☎ (5) 220111. Sleekly turned out, like an elegant woman in a little black dress, the Mandarin is the very best hotel in the world, provoking ecstatic reactions from one and all. *"The joy of being awoken with tea in a wafer-thin porcelain cup ..."* (Billy Hamilton). *"The comfort and the energetic gaiety of the whole place"* (Olivier Coquelin). *"A standard of service that very few people can emulate"* (Mark Birley). *"If you want anything delivered or collected there's somebody there instantly; if you have a torn garment, the houseboy's there with a needle and thread. Very courteous management, who make a fuss of their guests"* (Anthony Watson).

"One of the most comfortable hotels in the world. Superbly run" (Betty Kenward). *"The quintessence of service, style and understated chic elegance"* (Diana Fisher). More accolades showered on the Man Wah Chinese restaurant and the Grill (see FOOD AND DRINK), and the standard of its shops (the tailor, the cobbler, the splendid shirtmaker).

PENINSULA, Salisbury Rd, Kowloon ☎ (3) 666251. Revered hotel where the original Taipans would stay, still loved by latterday Very Important Businessmen. In operation since 1928, it remains as stately and superb as ever. Its gastronomic trump card is Gaddi's (see FOOD AND DRINK).

REGENT, Salisbury Rd, Kowloon ☎ (3) 721 1211. Built with typical Hong Kong panache right beside what must be the most exciting harbour in the world. The Lobby Bar has a panel of glass 146 by 60 ft (44.5 by 18.3 m), so that wherever you sit, there is a stunning view. The octagonal swimming pool is the largest in Hong Kong. Each room has its own butler, rather like a steward on board ship. *"One of my favourite hotels, along with the Regents in Kuala Lumpur, Sydney and Melbourne. They have the best service and seem to keep their staff a long time. I spend a lot of time in my room writing and editing, and I eat my meals there. They are very quick to adapt the room to your needs. In most hotels they have more room for a TV set than for a desk"* (Bryan Montgomery).

THAILAND

ORIENTAL, 48 Oriental Ave, Bangkok 10500 ☎ (2) 234 8621. The minute you step out of the steam bath that is Bangkok and into the cool lobby, you know it's of the very highest calibre. The Authors' Wing (1876), with suites named after the likes of erstwhile residents Somerset Maugham and Joseph Conrad, is full of colonial character, while the modern block is supremely plush and comfortable. Enormous corner suites overlook the sampan-filled river from two angles. You're offered fresh fruit juice and a basket of fruits so exotic that a leaflet of explanation accompanies it. Blue silk bath wraps, fat white towels that are changed constantly, and at night a pair of padded slippers upon a white linen mat placed by the bed, and a single chocolate truffle in a tiny basket on your pillow. They have the art of presentation taped, and the staff hop to before you even have to ask. Al fresco barbecue feasts and Thai food on the riverside Verandah; exquisite French cuisine at the Normandie. Best for: *"its mysterious sensuality"* (Olivier Coquelin); *"its enormous staff-to-guest ratio"* (Lord Lichfield); *"the wonderful Lord Jim's [seafood] restaurant"* (Prue Leith).

DUSIT THANI, Rama IV Rd, Bangkok 10500 ☎ (2) 233 1130. A traditional Far Eastern hotel with delectable Thai, Chinese and Japanese restaurants, and an enormous freshwater swimming pool. See also HEALTH AND BEAUTY.

ROYAL GARDEN RESORT, 107/1 Petkasem Beach Rd, Hua Hin 77110 ☎ (32) 511 881. A beautiful hotel with its own private beach on the Gulf of Siam, plus championship tennis courts, a pool and Jacuzzi. Hua Hin is the coastal resort of the Thai royal family, who bolt when possible to their summer palace, Klai Kangoom, for a bit of peace (the railway station still has a royal waiting room).

MALAYSIA

SHANGRI-LA, 11 Jalan Sultan Ismail, Kuala Lumpur 04-01 ☎ (03) 222388. A new member of the same group as the Singapore Shangri-La, and fast gaining a similar reputation.

Getting around Hong Kong

It has the densest harbour traffic in the world – a mêlée of barges, tugs, junks, sampans, hovercraft and a 1,000-strong fleet of ferries (admittedly not all out on the harbour at the same time). The Star Ferry ride between Central and Kowloon is short but sweet, and best for a night-time look at the wondrous skyline. A longer journey to Lantau takes you past ramshackle, tumbledown corrugated iron huts on the far side of the island, past sampans, junks and little floating raft-homes. The boat of the moment is the jetfoil, the gambling-mad Chinaman's saviour – a high-speed night service from Macao to Hong Kong, using special vision that can produce a screen image 50,000 times brighter than the night outside. And it does the trip that takes the ferry 3½ hours in 55 minutes.

Hong Kong's new super-swish air-conditioned underground is controlled by a central computer that tells the train when to accelerate, coast, stop, and when to leave the platform – down to the last second. A failsafe will override the computer to prevent a collision.

There are 2 good funicular trips: to the Peak on Hong Kong Island, and up the hill on Penang, off the west coast of Malaya. When building the Penang railway, the only thing that induced the natives to hack their way up the jungle was firing gold coins from a cannon to the summit.

“ My favourite holiday place is an island called Rawa, off the east coast of Malaysia. It has the most beautiful coral reefs, and a little village community who will look after your basic needs. I don't want to go from comfort to absolute nothingness, so Rawa is a happy marriage between the two. You do what you like there – climb coconut trees if you must. It's like the land of the Lotus Eaters ” (BENNY ONG)

HYATT, Telok Champedak, Kuantan ☎ (095) 25211. The only other hotel of international standard in this part of the world, built on a fabulous beach overlooking the South China Sea. Squash, tennis, swimming pool and health club, plus a chance to spot the rare and elusive sea turtle.

Getting around Malaysia

The air-conditioned train up the Malaysian peninsula as far as the Thai border, or beyond into Bangkok, is a marvellous way to see the vastness of the rubber and palm oil plantations (and a great deal safer than driving, when you are likely to be held up by robbers). The train from Kota Kinabalu to Tenom, in Sabah, north Borneo, takes you through thrilling country.

SINGAPORE

♔ **MARCO POLO, Tanglin Rd, 1024 ☎ 474 7141.** *“The best in Singapore”* (Lord Lichfield). Switched-on service and a mass of facilities – 2 semi-Olympic-size pools, gym, sauna, shops, discotheque and various restaurants.

GOODWOOD PARK, 22 Scotts Rd, 0922 ☎ 737 7411. Colonial building modernized with perfect taste. High-tech security: each guest has a unique key which is destroyed when they leave. *“The Brunei Suite is the best hotel suite in the world – very large, well furnished, and it must be the only suite with its own library and desk – a real den, surrounded by books”* (David Frost).

RAFFLES, 1–3 Beach Rd, 0718 ☎ 337 8041. Though it's showing its years, it's still a delight to stay in the Somerset Maugham or Rudyard Kipling rooms and take a curry in the fanned coolness of the Tiffin Room. *“It may be rather run down but I still like it best because it's very colonial – you get huge bedrooms with fans on the ceiling”* (Nicholas Coleridge).

SHANGRI-LA, 22 Orange Grove Rd, 1025 ☎ 737 3644. A luxurious haven, one of the few landed gentry in Singapore, with pools, tennis courts, a putting green and tropical gardens. The balconies of the Garden Wing, in the Japanese garden, cascade with vibrant bougainvillea and overlook a waterfall. All guests are greeted by name and with a pot of Chinese tea in a little basket. Impeccably run. *“Superb, American-type hotel”* (René Lecler).

BALI

BALI OBEROI, Kuta Beach, PO Box 351, Denpasar ☎ (0361) 51061. Beautifully laid-out losmen (bungalow) complex by the beach, set in jungly green gardens with tropical flowers that stand out in 3D-plus. Interesting sunken baths and little private patios. One of the best positions in the world for experiencing incredible skies and sunsets.

NUSA DUA BEACH HOTEL, PO Box 1028 Denpasar ☎ (0361) 71210. One of the best hotels on Bali, it's *“like driving into a temple”*. Huge pool and 4 restaurants. The hotel was taken over entirely in 1986 for President Reagan's stay with his staff. *“Combines the best of traditional Balinese style with immaculate modern oriental service”* (Lord Lichfield).

PHILIPPINES

MANILA HOTEL, PO Box 307, Rizal Park, Metro Manila ☎ (02) 470011. One of very few surviving old buildings in Manila, used by General MacArthur as his headquarters for part of World War II. *“One of my great favourites”* (Warren Hoge). *“A magnificent place, filled with the most marvellous antiques, carvings and paintings – it really is something!”* (René Lecler). Auberon Waugh and Mark Birley are erstwhile guests.

“ I love exotic events such as the Bali festival, where they have wonderful dancing. They dig up the dead after 10 years and bury them again. It is very colourful and you don't find any tourists there ” (FRANCIS YEOH)

“ One of the best beaches I have ever known is Kuta. I like walking on beaches, and at low tide you can walk for miles. It is totally unspoilt except for a few bungalows and it faces west so you get the most wonderful sunsets ” (BRYAN MONTGOMERY)

“ Bali is my favourite holiday place. I've found some rather fascinating artifacts there – not the traditional Balinese carved heads, but wood carvings. Sanur Beach is the best, but I like getting off the beaten track on the island ” (KYM BONYTHON)

INDIA

DELHI

The hotels in central New Delhi are short-stay, business-orientated and impersonal. The most friendly and comfortable is the **OBEROI NEW DELHI, Dr Zakir Hussain Marg, New Delhi 110003 ☎ (011) 699571,** while the vast new **TAJ PALACE, 2 Sardar Patel Marg, New Delhi 110021 ☎ (011) 344900** has *"the most imaginative décor – very evocative with excellent workmanship."* (Serena Fass).

HOTEL OBEROI MAIDENS, 7 Sham Nath Marg, Old Delhi 110054 ☎ (011) 252 5464. The best place to stay in Delhi if you want a relaxing hotel rather than to be on the spot in New Delhi. Airy, colonial palace set in pretty gardens. Exceptionally helpful staff. The best swimming towels in India – enormous black and white striped affairs (which match the décor of many of the rooms). Ultra-spacious suites with bathrooms of marble.

"The most unusual transport I've taken was a succession of boats down the Ganges. We started at Pandua, when the water is at its lowest ebb in winter, and ended up in the Bay of Bengal. It was very exasperating as the first boat we hired had no bottom and the one we eventually got kept running ashore. It took 26 people to lift it. Every time we came to a waterfall we had to empty the boat and carry it down over red hot stones for anything up to a mile. We would sleep on sandbanks and drink water from the river, which is full of corpses" (ERIC NEWBY)

BOMBAY

TAJ MAHAL HOTEL, Apollo Bunder, Colaba, 400039 ☎ (022) 202 3366. The finest hotel in India – as long as you stay in the old palatial part with its sweeping staircases, antique furnishings and enormous bathrooms with big, plain shelves (not glass: toothmugs on glass set the teeth on edge). Lovely waterfront setting. *"It's like something out of* 1001 Nights. *It may not be 2,000 years old, but it feels like it. It's got columns and pillars and it's entirely baroque, and the smell is marvellous"* (Charlotte Rampling). Indophiles Quentin Crewe, Willie Landels and Billy Hamilton adore it.

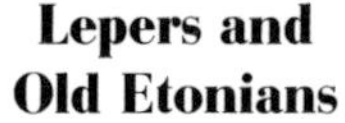

Lepers and Old Etonians

Every 12 years, a Kum Mayla takes place, a ritualistic bath in the Ganges to cleanse away sins. It occurs at 4 places, where on each, in Hindu mythology, a drop of nectar (the potion for immortality) was spilt on the earth – Allahabad, Hardwar ("Door to Heaven"), Nasik and Ujjain. Up to 12 million people join in – even the hermits come down from the mountains.

"The River Ganges is holy. One of the greatest goods you can do is give people water from the river. Everywhere you go, people are worshipping by the river. It is littered with little shrines. People bring offerings of marigolds. You see great manifestations of joint faith when they have a Kum Mayla, with millions of people bathing from a sandbank at the same time. It does lead to terrible accidents. The actual day is determined by astrologers as everything in India is determined. Lepers bathe with Old Etonians – it's an amazing spectacular" (Eric Newby).

"One thing's for sure, if you go and see the Taj, no matter what picture you build up before you arrive, you will never, never be disappointed! It defies description" (VICTOR BANERJEE)

AGRA

MUGHAL SHERATON, Taj Ganj, 282001 ☎ (0562) 64701. Welcoming garland of marigolds: exotic fruit and home-made biscuits in the room. The décor is rather too modern-Indian, but charming service, an ocean of blue swimming pool and some of the best *tikka* to be tasted in India make up for it. Film stars, such as Peter O'Toole, stay there when they're taking in the Taj.

JAIPUR

"Jaipur is my favourite city. The idea of a unified city designed by one man appeals to me. Rajasthan is one of the most fascinating places – a whole group of princely states. The purest beautiful things are the private houses known as Havelis, in the province of Shekawati within Jaipur state. The houses (some are inhabited, but haphazardly so) are marvellously painted with dramatic fresco work" (Quentin Crewe).

HOTEL NARAIN NIWAS, Kanota Bagh, Narain Singh Road, 302004 ☎ (0141) 65448. Gorgeous decaying ochre-tinted colonial villa, built by the Rajput noble Narain Singh-Ji in 1881. Not the height of luxury, but the most authentic small-scale palatial living, with all the original decorative fresco-work, tapestries, chandeliers, portraits, four-poster beds, dhurries and weaponry. You can breakfast on the verandah with the grandson of Narain himself. The best hot-buttered *nan* in India.

RAMBAGH PALACE, 302005 ☎ (0141) 75141. Built in 1727 for Maharajah Sawai Jai Singh II – after whom the city is named – it is truly palatial. Lofty and cool, painted in creams and buttermilks, with marble floors, loggias and verandahs giving on to gardens. Icy indoor swimming bath, all pillars, swings and golden mosaics. *"I would like to live 6 months of the year there – you can afford to live in considerable comfort for less than it would cost to stay in some miserable hotel in Wiltshire if your car broke down."* (Nicholas Coleridge).

UDAIPUR

LAKE PALACE HOTEL, Pichola Lake, 313001 ☎ 23241. The glory of this hotel is in the setting – one of the most splendid in the world. Floating resplendent on a shimmering lake, the white marble palace, double-deckered and turreted, is reminiscent of a Mississippi paddle steamer. It is reached by private launch. Once aboard, there are little formal flower and water gardens, walkways, terraces and follies with mirrored mosaics that glint in the sun. The tiny swimming pool terrace is surrounded by white turrets, cupolas and arches (and overhung by a mango tree where many pigeons nest: beware). One to look at rather than stay in.

Sweet Chariot

"A million people flock to the fantastic Jagannath Chariot Festival, Puri – it takes over 4,000 professional car-pullers to move these huge chariots. The main one is 14 metres high, over 10 metres square and rides on 16 wheels. At some point, every one of those million shoulders will have helped pull the chariot" (Victor Banerjee).

GETTING AROUND INDIA

PALACE ON WHEELS, Central Reservation House, 36 Chandralok, Janpath, New Delhi 110001 ☎ (011) 322332. A luxurious (by Indian standards) old-fashioned train that steams round Rajasthan, packing in the sights, with over-night stops at top-class hotels. Lovely atmosphere of faded grandeur, in tiny narrow-gauge carriages that once belonged to sundry Maharajahs. Exhausting, however: one American woman refused to get back on after a night in the Mughal Sheraton at Agra.

The trains in India are, of course, among the worst in the world (snail-paced, stuffy, dusty, uncomfortable, late). However, if you *must* travel by train, the best way is ACC (Air Conditioned Class, one above first class).

"I travel first class because it is difficult getting on the train if you travel third class. It's difficult enough in first as you find an Indian ambassador sitting in your reserved seat who will not move. The only answer is to arm yourself with a letter from the head of Indian Railways and present it to every station master as soon as you get there. Hopefully, he will ensure you get on" (Eric Newby).

"One of the best train rides is through the plantations of Karnataka" (Serena Fass). The mini railway runs through the hills from Ootacamund (Ooty) to Mettuppalaiyam through coffee, tea and eucalyptus plantations.

“The welcoming charm of the Goans is really something – they have a quiet, elegant, smiling way with them. The beaches are still natural: it's hard not to enthuse with travelogue clichés – the Arabian Sea, golden-blue, rides in swinging broad scimitars of silver surf. Afonso de Albuquerque was obsessed by it 500 years ago – as shall all the West be again soon I fear”
(SIR PETER PARKER)

“India has wonderful beaches but you get people coming up to stare at your navel”
(ERIC NEWBY)

GOA

FORT AGUADA BEACH RESORT, Sinquerim, Bardez, 403515 ☎ 3401. *“The best villa resort”* (Bob Payton). Perfect combination of airy villas, the main hotel, lawns, pool and glorious beach in laid-back Portuguese India. “The *place to relax, completely lost in another world, forgetful of the problems and projects that assail one in the normal round of life. The restaurant is excellent too”* (Gianni Versace). The AGUADA HERMITAGE stands in the hills above, where rich Indians go with servants in tow.

Newby's India

“I tend to stay in railway waiting rooms, where you can get a bed with a mosquito net if you are lucky. Otherwise, the best thing is a civil-service-owned bungalow or a Tourist Bungalow [government-run hostels, about £2 (US$2.9) a night – one of the prettiest is the Sarovar, on the lake at Pushkar, a palace once owned by the Maharajah of Jaipur]. It is too expensive to go to a hotel as there are so many other things to spend your money on – such as huge, multi-handed goddesses made in Birmingham” (Eric Newby).

Sweet tooth

At the Festival of the Tooth in Kandy, Sri Lanka *“parades of elephants are ornately caparisoned, some of them spangled with light bulbs (their owners proving their wealth in the number they can show); fire-eaters, dancers, musicians all circle the great glittery lake. The tooth of the Buddha is extracted from its temple for the annual celebration. Huge crowds sit under the trees with their umbrellas to keep off the droppings of the birds, which are wildly excited by it all”* (Sir Peter Parker).

KASHMIR

HOTEL OBEROI PALACE, Gupkar Rd, Srinagar ☎ (0194) 75641. Another opulent princely pile, set in fountained gardens above Dal Lake. A train of liveried staff.

KASHMIR HIMALAYAN EXPEDITIONS, Boulevard Shopping Centre, Dal Gate, Srinagar ☎ (0194) 78698. The most luxurious houseboat is *1001 Nights*, berthed on Dal Lake, with its own glorious garden. 4 bedrooms with private bath and three living rooms, all decorated according to traditional themes and folk fables, with Kashmiri carved oak furniture. The number of guests is matched by staff: a cook, pantry boy, house boy, dust boy, log boy, gardener and 2 bearers.

NEPAL

TIGER TOPS JUNGLE LODGE, Royal Chitwan National Park, Meghauli ☎ (0977) 212706. Wildlife resort in the Royal Chitwan National Park, erstwhile host to a safari-suited British royal family, and to the elephant polo championships (see SPORTING LIFE). Sleep in thatched tree-houses on stilts or in a tented camp (intrepidly deeper into the thick of things). Elephant safaris, on the track of rhinoceroses (like the one Prince Philip undertook earlier this year), and tiger-spotting. Open Sept–June.

GETTING THERE

AIR

The oriental airlines are highly favoured by all, for efficiency, attentive service and thoughtful little extras.

BEST AIRLINES
★
1. CATHAY PACIFIC AIRWAYS
2. SINGAPORE AIRLINES
3. JAPAN AIR LINES
4. THAI INTERNATIONAL
5. PHILIPPINE AIRLINES

CATHAY PACIFIC AIRWAYS *“Blissfully comfortable to the Far East”* (Betty Kenward). *“The only airline I know that serves bowls of fresh fruit no matter what class you are travelling in”* (Marie Helvin). *“British maintenance with Oriental service, and food as good as it can be”* (Lord Lichfield). *“The first-class wine list is formidable, the food delicious, the hostesses so kind and helpful”* (Henry Blofeld).

BANERJEE'S INDIA

Roof of the world: Mussoorie, near Dehra Dun, at the foot of the Himalayas. *"Without doubt the best place on earth. It's what I am working for, to retire to. I have a house there with Tibetan prayer flags all around – every time there is a breeze, a prayer flies to heaven. I go there every spare moment I have. The best trekking is around the source of the Ganges, in the Garhwal area. All the pilgrim points up to Gomukh, the source, are beautiful."*

Garden on top of the world: The Valley of the Flowers, near Badrinath, in northern Uttar Pradesh. *"When in bloom it's an unforgettable experience. Carpets of flowers,* hill upon hill *of flowers – when you have found that you don't need anything else."*

Caves: the Ellora and Aurangabad Caves, famous for their erotic sculptures. *"The best guide is* Ajanta, Ellora and Aurangabad Caves: An Appreciation *by T. V. Pathy, for its delightful use of English. One statue is described as: 'a semi-nude dryad with slender waist, pouting lips and abundant mammalian equipment …'"*

Elephants: The Khedas ceremony. *"The most exciting thing to do is ride bareback on an elephant through virgin jungle and catch wild elephants. The leaders go ahead with 2 trained elephants. They grasp the trunk of the wild elephant, entwine the legs and catch him. The Khedas follows. There is nothing like being in the jungle at midnight, hearing the sounds as you circle the elephants. Bundles of straw are burnt and waved in front of them, tears roll down their faces, and all the while we sing elephant songs that have been passed down generations to soothe the elephants and make them realize they will be looked after: 'You're our bride, son, our family now!'"*

🏆 **SINGAPORE AIRLINES** They have been known to send boxes of chocs to regular travellers on their birthdays. One businessman was presented with a chilled bottle of Dom Pérignon when he sat down in the aircraft at Heathrow – the staff had somehow noticed it was his birthday. *"They actually live up to their advertisement. The stewardesses really are very nice to you and the food is wonderful – satays on sticks and stuff. You can lie down upstairs in sheets and blankets and they only wake you at Bahrain if you want to be woken – otherwise, they put a belt over you to land. I'm a great sleeper on aeroplanes, and they don't come and talk to you all the time. The pilot isn't forever telling you that underneath the clouds 30,000 feet down, if you could see, there's a town you don't want to know about"* (Prue Leith). *"Terrific; very, very nice staff"* (Patricia Coppleson).

JAPAN AIRLINES Margaux Hemingway's favourite commercial airline.

THAI INTERNATIONAL *"Consistently good, with excellent food and service"* (Victor Banerjee).

PHILIPPINE AIRLINES *"Sufficiently rich for their planes to be modern, but sufficiently beleaguered politically for them to be trying terribly hard. The hostesses are sufficiently modern to understand what is expected of them on a luxurious flight, but sufficiently unliberated to be ludicrously cringing and bowing. In the first-class-plus, you sleep in proper beds in the bubble of the 747. You have that immensely luxurious feeling of waste in that your incredibly large chair is sitting idle downstairs while the poor people in coach class are, at this point after a 26-hour flight, buckled like napkin rings"* (Nicholas Coleridge).

AIR INDIA *"Very efficient, good vegetarian meals. I love the smells"* (Willie Landels).

SEA

CV CHIDAMBURAN An Indian Civil Vessel which sails from Madras to Singapore. *"Rather oddly hilarious. You must go first class out of the eight different classes. It's a luxurious way of travelling in this part of the world"* (Nicholas Coleridge).

BEST TOURS

COX & KINGS, 404 Deepali, 92 Nehru Place, New Delhi 110019 ☎ (011) 641 4306. Veterans of Indian travel who once made the travel arrangements for the British Army in India. Tailor-made itineraries or set tours around the Indian subcontinent.

EXPLORASIA (see EUROPE, TOURS) arrange Nepalese safaris and visits to Tiger Tops at elephant polo time.

TOUR EAST, Suite 730-731, 7th Floor, Ocean Centre Building, Canton Rd, Kowloon, Hong Kong ☎ (3) 663311. The best and most exclusive tour company in the Far East. A worldwide network of contacts means they can arrange anything, any time, any place.

AFRICA

BEST HOTELS

TOP 5

★

1. **MOUNT KENYA SAFARI CLUB, Kenya**
2. **LA GAZELLE D'OR, Morocco**
3. **MENA HOUSE, Egypt**
4. **MOUNT NELSON HOTEL, South Africa**
5. **MEIKLES HOTEL, Zimbabwe**

MOROCCO

LA GAZELLE D'OR, PO Box 60, Taroudannt ☎ (085) 2039. An exotic *"oasis of splendour"* (Olivier Coquelin) created near a fortified town in the Atlas Mountains. *"I absolutely love it there. It's like a film set. I like fantasy resorts. I don't care if it's not genuine – I don't need original ethnic blankets, but I do like it to be pretty. The Gazelle d'Or has little tiny Moroccan chalets among the orange groves and an Olympic swimming pool. You eat outside – the central dining room is a huge tent"* (Prue Leith).

LA MAMOUNIA, Ave Bab Jdid, Marrakech ☎ (04) 32381. "Beautiful *gardens and pools. The first time I was there, 20 years ago, I was having breakfast in bed, and I saw this little swoop of birds coming in one after the other. I couldn't realize what was happening. I thought I was going crazy. Then I spotted an envelope on my breakfast tray that said 'Pour les petits amis de Mamounia.' I opened it and it was full of breadcrumbs. It was divine"* (Diana Vreeland). A Moorish extravaganza where Churchill loved to stay, and much admired by Olivier Coquelin *"for its opulence"*. But those who knew it in the old days mourn the fact that the old magic – the ricketiness, the rattan screens you peep through, the rush matting, the suite with the velvet drapes and old gold tassels – has gone. Now it's a mite too flash.

EL MINZAH, 85 rue de la Liberté, Tangier ☎ (09) 35885. The best hotel in the heart of the only resort city where the Med and Atlantic meet. Here you can come to the Kasbah, set on a plateau overlooking the Straits of Gibraltar.

PALAIS JAMAI, Bab-el-Guissa, Fez ☎ (06) 34331. *"The most lovely hotel with one beautiful, beautiful room – the King's Suite – which still exists just as it was"* (Anouska Hempel). Other parts have suffered the Moroccan revamp, but the service, the food and the gardens are still sensational.

EGYPT

Land of the Pharaohs, home of the Pyramids, the Sphinx, the tomb of Tutankhamun and countless other magnificent tributes to an ancient civilization, all now treated with a sad irreverence. Tourists scramble over pyramids, while guides scrape at wall paintings in tombs that have withstood their first 5,000 years but may not hold out for the next 5,000. And in the Cairo Museum, the treasures of Tut's tomb are displayed offhandedly (rumour has it, in any case, that the originals were long since sold to Russia).

MENA HOUSE OBEROI, Pyramid Rd, Giza, Cairo ☎ (02) 855444. For claustrophics who aren't so mad about chock-a-block Cairo. *"Fancy opening your windows in the morning and having breakfast looking at the pyramids! You can't beat it. This is an old hotel that had become a wreck. Oberoi Hotels rebuilt and restored it completely, using people who were willing to work hard. It's marvellous"* (René Lecler). The old colonial weekend palace where Army and diplomatic bigwigs would meet.

SALAMLEK, Kasr El-Montazah, Alexandria ☎ (03) 860585. A converted wing of Al-Montazah Palace, summer residence of the former Egyptian Royal family. On high ground overlooking an exquisite beach on the eastern tip of Alexandria, surrounded by colossal gardens and woods.

"The glories of Egypt unravelled by the most romantic river in the world" (William Golding, *An Egyptian Journal*). The Nile, an estimated 40 million years old, is Egypt's lifeblood. In this corner of the Dark Continent, it rains perhaps 5 times a year.

Travelling upriver from 2,318-year-old ALEXANDRIA, with its superb beaches, you reach CAIRO, a sand-tinged, crumbling, traffic-jammed bedlam, the largest city in all Africa. *"I love it for its madness*

THE SANDS OF TIME

DIANI BEACH, south of Mombasa, Kenya *"The best beach in the world – the most perfect stretch of sand with palm trees and a reef. It's miraculous – there's nothing I've seen yet to compare in the Caribbean"* (Quentin Crewe).

MARSA MATRUH, west of Alexandria, Egypt A small port on the Mediterranean, with one of the best beaches in the world. 4½ miles (7 km) of soft white sand and calm azure waters. A wide bay enclosed by a chain of rocks and reefs, with a narrow channel for boats.

LA DIGUE, Seychelles *"The most spectacular piece of sunshine in the world. White sand, the bluest ocean, big beaches with nobody on them. The rock formations and palm trees look just like a Hollywood movie set – there are places you think must be made of papier mâché. It reminds me of the movie,* The Emerald Forest*"* (Bob Payton).

LAMU ISLAND, Kenya *"An extraordinary magical place, almost empty, except for the old town and the old culture. There are miles and miles of deserted beach running all round the island – it's a delight"* (Dan Topolski).

HURGHADA, Egypt On the Red Sea, a wonderland of coral reefs, exotic sea creatures and submarine flora that beats even the Great Barrier Reef. The best skuba diving in the world.

MAURITANIA *"One of the best sights in the world is men fishing with dolphins. It's unique. They both think the other is working for them"* (Quentin Crewe).

SAHARA *"Walata is the best place because it's so remote. It's the one village in the whole desert with decorations on the walls – strange mud patterns in different colours. You still see camels and tribespeople"* (Quentin Crewe).

and chock-a-block fullness" (Dan Topolski).

Onward to LUXOR, on the East Bank of the Nile, a calm winter resort, dry-aired, clear-skied, with a staggering conglomeration of temples and monuments. Stay where William Golding stays, at the **WINTER PALACE, El Nil St, Luxor ☎ (095) 755216.** Just upriver at Thebes is the Valley of the Kings, where lie the tombs of Tutankhamun and Rameses VI. Past Edfu and Kom Ombo to ASWAN, salubrious and beautiful. Plant Island is its showplace for rare, exotic flora. Stay, again in company with Golding, at the **CATARACT HOTEL, Abtal el Tahrir St, Aswan ☎ (097) 23510.**

TOURS

HELIOTOURS EGYPT, 105 Higgaz St, Heliopolis ☎ (02) 87708. Arrange cruises locally on *MS Helio*, the best, most up-to-date boat on the river.

BALES TOURS, Barrington Rd, Dorking, Surrey, England ☎ (0306) 885991. These old-established operators do long cruises from Cairo to Aswan on their *Death on the Nile*-style steamer, *Nefertari*. *"The best tour I've ever been on. An old paddle steamer with all the servants dressed up in blue and gold uniforms"* (Auberon Waugh).

KUONI TRAVEL (see Europe) have their own extended Nile cruise aboard *MS Neptune*, from Cairo to Aswan and back.

SERENISSIMA (see Europe) run a comprehensive 17-day tour taking in Cairo, Giza, and all major monuments, winding up with a cruise on *MS Helio* between Luxor and Aswan. *"Unsurpassed – it's impossible to do it as an individual"* (Serena Fass).

KENYA

Land of Safari, land of sun (8 hours a day all year round), Kenya straddles the Equator, stretching from the Indian Ocean to the shores of Lake Victoria, the largest lake in Africa. Scenery is wildly varied – hot dry bush country in the northern plains; the gaping valleys and sparkling lakes of the Great Rift Valley; the gently rolling downs of the cool Central Highlands with their forests, moorlands and trout streams; rippling grass plains of the savannah; lush tropical vegetation on the coast.

MOUNT KENYA SAFARI CLUB, PO Box 35, Nanyuki ☎ (0176) 333232. The brightest star in the vast Kenyan constellation, very *Out of Africa*. On the slopes of Mount Kenya, it's set in 100 acres (40.5 hectares) of rolling turf with ever-blooming flower-beds, ponds, shady trees, babbling brooks, a walled rose garden, vegetable and nursery gardens and a mountain stream with waterfalls. With its own airfield and satellite communications to the world, international royals, aristos, premiers and celebs home in from afar. Bob Hope, Charlton Heston, Trevor Howard, Connie Booth, John Travolta, Lucinda Green and Maud Adams have been drawn. The club organizes air and land safaris.

Azure allure

Lake Turkana (aka Rudolf) is *"the most beautiful lake in the world. A brilliant bluey-green jade colour, the winds blow hot and the water is icy cold and very clear – it's the most marvellous place to swim"* (Quentin Crewe). *"Remote, deserted and very beautiful. It's exciting because of its very rarity and beautiful because of the blueness of the lake. To the west, light aircraft fly in to Eliyi Point with exclusive tourists – Prince Michael of Kent and the more adventurous young royals go there. You can stay in some comfort in mud and wattle huts done up nicely as cabins"* (Dan Topolski).

"The Great Rift Valley is all multicoloured pink sandstone – it's extraordinary, particularly from the air" (SERENA FASS)

NORFOLK HOTEL, PO Box 40064, Nairobi ☎ (02) 335422. Turn-of-the-century hotel with bandas (cottages) in the gardens. The Lord Delamere Terrace is the most chic eating place in town. It even has its own private aviaries.

TREETOPS The famous lodge where royals and other elevated guests dine 10 ft (3 m) above the animals. This is an overnighter only – you transfer from your longer-stay hotel and sip cocktails at the bar, while observing a veritable menagerie swigging at the waterholes. A sheet of glass divides man and beast, for those pesky baboons have acquired more of a taste for Wallbangers than water. Book via Block Hotel Central Reservations Office, New Stanley House Arcade, PO Box 47557, Nairobi ☎ (02) 335807.

TANZANIA

A vast country south of Kenya and equally rich in National Parkland and game reserves, including the SERENGETI NATIONAL PARK and the NGORONGORO CRATER.

"Ngorongoro is the most awe-inspiring natural wonder. Inside are all sorts of animals – elephants, lions, rhinos and hippos, wildebeest, hyenas – just everything: it's their world and you're the alien. You edge into it carefully down the sides in a jeep ..." (Sir Peter Parker).

On the island of ZANZIBAR you can visit the houses of Dr Livingstone and of the notorious slave trader Tippu Tip. The best hotel is **BHAWANI, PO Box 670, Zanzibar ☎ (054) 30200.**

MALAWI

A tranquil country, unspoilt, unpolluted and untamed. Its national parks and rain forests boast over 300 species of birds and over 400 species of orchid.

SOCHE TOURS, PO Box 2225, Blantyre ☎ (0265) 620777. The premier grand tour operator in Malawi. Explore the Zomba Plateau in the wake of various queens and emperors, seeing forests, flowers, the Mulunguchi Dam. Reel men go fly-fishing here: 3-day courses, staying at Brian and Jane Burgess's fabulous mountain home. Also mountaineering, flying and, oddly, dressage – the Burgesses keep schooled Lippizaners and run courses.

ZIMBABWE

MEIKLES HOTEL, PO Box 594, Stanley Ave, Harare ☎ (00) 707721. One of the best hotels in Africa, first class in every sense, with a pool on the roof.

LAKE KARIBA 5,000 sq miles (12,950 sq km) of water, created by the famous Dam that was built in 1961 to provide hydro-electric power. **BUMI HILLS SAFARI LODGE, PO Box 41, Kariba ☎ (063) 353** offers its own water wilderness safaris. Their boat has double beds and bathroom and is purportedly insect-proof.

VICTORIA FALLS Livingstone described "scenes so lovely they must have been gazed upon by angels in their flight". The Mosi oa Tunya ("smoke that thunders") are indeed best viewed from the air, and you can charter a light aircraft to embark on what is known as the Flight of Angels (see Getting Around). Stay at the **VICTORIA FALLS HOTEL, PO Box 10, Victoria Falls ☎ (040) 203,** which has nightly African dance displays, brilliantly staged in a floodlit amphitheatre.

SOUTH AFRICA

The best way of doing South Africa is to know people, but anyone with the loot can venture forth on gambling safaris to SUN CITY, Bophuthswana, a millionaire's playground with the largest casino south of the Equator; gourmet safaris to JOHANNESBURG (delicious seafood from the Zoo Lake Restaurant); or on surfin' safaris to DURBAN.

CAPE OF GOOD HOPE The most beautiful part of South Africa. On the Atlantic side of the Cape peninsula, the best beaches are CAMP BAY, LLANDUDNO BAY and AFTON BEACH – for bathing in the sun and not the sea, which is cold with dangerous undercurrents. On the Indian Ocean side, where the sea is warmer and safer, MUIZENBURG BEACH is the best. Hedonists go on wine safaris round the Stellenbosch Paarl and Franschoek Wine Estate areas, lunching and quaffing at wonderful farms such as the former home of Cecil Rhodes, and nurturing several senior hangovers a day. Tours arranged via SARTravel, PO Box 1111, Johannesburg 2000 ☎ (011) 774 4204.

MOUNT NELSON HOTEL, Orange St Gdns, PO Box 2608, Cape Town 8000 ☎ (021) 231000. The best hotel in town – thoughtfully run; gorgeous gardens. *"Timeless, terribly old-fashioned, very colonial – the complete antithesis to modern horrors"* (Lord Lichfield).

GETTING AROUND

SAFARIS

EAST AFRICAN WILDLIFE SAFARIS, PO Box 43747, Nairobi ☎ (02) 331228. If you want exclusive, luxury, tailor-made safaris, Jock Anderson's your man. All the best game reserves (as above) are his stamping grounds. You can fly over them on a Wing Safari, and set up private camp in them too. Jock arranged for Jackie Onassis to go ballooning over the Masai Mara from Naivasha (rising at dawn, touching down in time for champagne breakfast) and has sent Lucinda Green, Charlton Heston and John Travolta off on various jaunts.

MASAI MARA GAME RESERVE One of the greatest wildlife areas in the world, where a spectacular migration of wildebeest and zebras arrives from the Serengeti, accompanied by numerous predators. Stay at **KEEKOROK LODGE, PO Box 40075, Nairobi ☎ (02) 331635.**

SAMBURU GAME RESERVE A wild, semi-desert area bordering the Uaso Nyiro River, where zillions of animals and birds stop by for a quick one. Rare species include Grevy's zebra, oryx, reticulated giraffe, and the graceful gerenuk. Stay at SAMBURU LODGE, where members of the local Samburu Tribe perform dances daily. (Via London agents ☎ (01) 734 4246.)

SILK CUT TRAVEL, Meon House, Petersfield, Hampshire ☎ (0730) 65211 can arrange a camel safari in Kenya with good guest-to-camel ratios (6 for riding and 20 for baggage), camping out for 14 nights, by which time your body will be attuned to the agony.

TEMPO TRAVEL, 337 Bowes Rd, London N11 ☎ (01) 361 1131. Arrange riding safaris at Sangare Ranch near Mweiga, one of the most beautiful private properties in Kenya. Owned by Mike and Jane Prettejohn, a 6,500-acre (2,630-hectare) farm with a stable of hospitable horses, mules and zebroids.

TSAVO NATIONAL PARK Stay at KILAGUNI LODGE, where, on a clear night, you can observe game at illuminated watering holes and, on a clear day, you can see the snow-capped summit of Mount Kilimanjaro. (Via London agents ☎ (01) 541 1199.)

AIR

AIR KENYA, PO Box 30357, Nairobi, Kenya ☎ (02) 501601 and **SAFARI AIR, PO Box 41951, Nairobi, Kenya ☎ (02) 501211.** Flights to remote and inaccessible parts of Kenya.

CAPITAL AIR SERVICES, PO Box 14, Zomba, Malawi ☎ 2700 fly you from Lake Malawi with its hippos and bird island to the Zomba Mountains and beyond.

FLIGHT OF ANGELS A fleet of tiny aircraft set off from a small airstrip beside the Victoria Falls to give passengers the most spectacular views of the 5 separate waterfalls – the Devil's Cataract, Main Falls, Horseshoe Falls, Rainbow Falls and the Eastern Cataract. Arranged by UNITED AIR CHARTERS, PO Box 2177, Harare, Zimbabwe ☎ (00) 21240, who also arrange air safaris over game parks in Zimbabwe.

SA AIR TOURS, PO Box 3268, Kenmari 1745, South Africa ☎ (011) 659 1246. Personalized South African safaris.

RAIL

Steam locomotives are still used on a grand scale in South Africa. The best routes are the BANANA EXPRESS (Port Shepstone to Izingolweni), the APPLE EXPRESS (Port Elizabeth to Loerie), and TOOTSIE (Mossel Bay to Knysna). Best of all is the BLUE TRAIN, South Africa's answer to the Orient-Express. Streamlined and confident, it glides at 40 mph (64 km/h) from Cape Town over the Hex River Mountain Pass, across the Karoo to Johannesburg and Pretoria. *Le style bleu* means cuisine that is fittingly Cordon Bleu, a formidable cellar, private valets, plushy suites and windows tinted with pure gold to tone down the glare.

HOMES AND PROPI

by DAVID MLINARIC

WORLD'S BEST AREAS

1 BELGRAVIA, London

2 UPPER EAST SIDE, New York

3 7 ème, Paris

4 KNIGHTSBRIDGE, London

5 8 ème, Paris

6 POINT PIPER, Sydney

7 HOLMBY HILLS Los Angeles

8 BEL AIR, Los Angeles

9 CHIYODA, Tokyo

10 THE PEAK, Hong Kong

The ideal place to live in any city is in an area that is reasonably central, but not too grand, with a mix of shops and residential buildings: this makes a community. The best houses are characteristic of their city: such buildings have, through centuries of experiment, proved to suit the conditions of that place best. One of the best building formulas ever is the small 18th-century town house.

In London, Chelsea is a village in the city: quiet streets, flowering trees, small town houses built on human scale, with old brick, sash windows, lovely gardens. No other city has a residential suburb quite so close to the centre.

In Paris, the Palais Royal must be one of the most civilized arrangements for town living ever, with its arcaded ground floor around a central garden. Or the Place des Vosges – the first square in the world – which was built with shops on the ground level, nobility on the first floor, merchants above them, and artisans on the top. Jane Birkin's house in Passy has a feeling of complete privacy and calm in the middle of Paris. You go through a door in an ordinary street wall and into a courtyard, to find two small, classic French houses with grey mansard roofs and shutters. Best of all, perhaps, are the houses on the Ile St Louis and the Ile de la Cité where, as in Venice, there is practically nothing ugly.

In Rome, the Isola Tiberina – an island in the Tiber – is hard to beat, as is Trastevere, with its artisans and markets, and its Indian red and yellow ochre buildings. The way houses are painted in shades of these colours complements the architecture; details are picked out in different colours.

In New York, the East 60s have something of the same character as Chelsea in London, and they are also near the centre. The point of living in New York is to live high up, overlooking Central Park, and the best apartment I know is Mrs Richard Rogers's immaculate flat above the Pierre Hotel. The view at night is much more exciting from half way up than from the top of any skyscraper: buildings, brightly lit at all levels, surround the blackness of the park.

RTY

DAVID MLINARIC was born in Britain and has been an interior decorator since 1964. Renowned for his precise knowledge of period styles, he is consultant to the National Trust. Besides NT properties such as Beningbrough Hall and Nostell Priory, he has worked on embassies in Washington, Paris and Brussels, the houses of Lord Lichfield, Mick Jagger and Eric Clapton, Le Gavroche restaurant and the Curzon Club. He lives in a 19th-century studio house in Chelsea with his wife Martha and 3 children.

Houses of all periods are best if the structural form is left as near to the original as possible. Alterations are nearly always disappointing. That is not to say that one must keep slavishly to the period of the house when decorating, which usually looks self-conscious. One of the buildings I like best is Desmond Guinness's house, Leixlip Castle, in County Kildare, where the bright, rich palette of colours and the mixture of styles and periods create a festive and theatrical atmosphere. It has the quality that is hardest of all to achieve, of a beautiful house that looks as though it has always been there, and has slowly grown and developed out of itself, and where the hand of the interior designer, of taste imposed from without, is not visible to the eye.

When doing up a house, if you choose antiques and furnishings that you really like yourself, even if the things do not appear at first glance to belong together, and even if they are not valuable or in fashion, the general effect will be harmonious. Taste is always an individual thing. When I first saw the unnamed shop of Madeleine Castaing in Paris, in 1961, I stayed for ages looking through the windows. The unexpected colour combinations – toothpaste green, Sèvres blue, black – and the strange, improbable shapes of the furniture gave me an idea of how things could look and made me feel that there was something to interpretative decorating that I wanted to pursue.

EUROPE

ENGLAND

The compleat house

A sauna, Jacuzzi, swimming pool and tennis court are standard accessories, but, according to Anne-Elisabeth Moutet: *"A house should have an indoors and outdoors swimming pool, private Jacuzzis in every bathroom, a dish antenna to catch every possible TV station direct from the satellite [now hitting the world in a big way, but attracting distress signals from country planners in village England], a gym with Nautilus machine, a screening room with Dolby equipment, central heating (how can the English survive in those glacial piles?), a helicopter pad, the perfect couple of servants/caretakers to see that everything runs smoothly and, most essential, his and hers bathrooms."*

"In a city you should have a conservatory, filled with camellias and heavily scented plants. In the country a walled garden, symmetrically planted with flowers, fruit and vegetables in the manner of Villandry" (David Mlinaric).

LONDON

BEST AREAS

TOP 10

★

1 BELGRAVIA
2 KNIGHTSBRIDGE
3 CHELSEA
4 KENSINGTON
5 MAYFAIR
6 ST JOHN'S WOOD
7 HAMPSTEAD
8 REGENT'S PARK
9 HOLLAND PARK
10 SOUTH KENSINGTON

BELGRAVIA WILTON CRESCENT for houses; EATON SQUARE (and roads off) for enormous, grand flats. Part of the Duke of Westminster's estates, inhabited by a chunk of nobility – Northamptons, Lady Lucan, James Ogilvy – plus Astors, Conrans, a Mountain and a Tree. Apsley House, belonging to the Duke of Wellington, situated at Hyde Park Corner, is here – it's address is No.1, London.

KNIGHTSBRIDGE Encompasses monstrous redbrick Victorian mansion blocks in the Harrods style (old families keep on pieds-à-terre for their daughters' coming out), some stately high-ceilinged terraces, plus some of the prettiest, tree-lined, cobbled mews in London. The CADOGANs, and MONTPELIER SQUARE are tops.

CHELSEA A maze of delightful, individual streets from pastel-painted Victorian to grand Georgian terraces. CHEYNE WALK's view over the Thames is marred somewhat by the deafening Embankment traffic, but *"It's leafy, and the houses have great proportions and beautiful walled gardens. The Guinness house is marvellous"* (Anouska Hempel). CHEYNE ROW and CARLYLE SQUARE are also top addresses. Younger arty/actor/media types like Rupert Everett live in cottagy terraces and flats round King's Road and Fulham Road.

KENSINGTON KENSINGTON PALACE GARDENS Immense houses on Crown Estate leases just round the corner from the Palace (where Charles and Diana, Princesses Alice, Margaret and Michael and the Gloucesters all have apartments). London's most prestigious address must be the last private house here, belonging to the Marquis of Cholmondeley. Otherwise mostly embassies and societies, but a few are privately owned and the odd one comes on

" I'm a north London person. I don't hold with south-west London. I find Belgravia incredibly cold – it seems like living in a sanatorium. If you have a vision of Chiswick or Parson's Green, a cold hand grips your heart. I dearly love Hampstead and Highgate. People make fun of them, of course, because they envy them. Are there trendy liberals in Hampstead and Highgate? There are. But the houses are so delicious and the way they're townscaped on to hilly bits is absolutely wonderful. It's prettier overall than any other part of London "

(PETER YORK)

the market. Everything on the check-list – all 8 bedrooms, 5 bathrooms and 4 receptions' worth – plus a private, gated drive with guard. Minimum £5 million (US$7,233,500) plus the same again for renovation. UPPER PHILLIMORE GARDENS has outsize family houses.

MAYFAIR Too full of shops, businesses and flashy foreigners to remain in the uppermost bracket, but expensive and plushy, and some old families stay on in GROSVENOR SQUARE, MOUNT STREET, etc.

ST JOHN'S WOOD and **HAMPSTEAD** CAVENDISH AVENUE, ("The Avenue") and THE BISHOP'S AVENUE (between Hampstead and Highgate Golf Courses) are lined with personalized number-plated, gold-handled Rolls-Royces and Mercs. Ultimate deluxe detached pads with pools and tennis courts. One estate agent recently sold a client the adjacent house for his staff. Though properties are sold in pristine, freshly tarted-up condition, it's not unusual for buyers to redo them completely.

Gilding the 'Dilly

The best block of flats in London is Albany, set in a spruce courtyard off fume-filled Piccadilly. Children and dogs are not allowed; prospective residents have to be vetted by committee. Stamping ground of Terence Stamp and David Hicks, who thinks: *"The flats are compact and elegant, and the rooms tall and airy. It has the best situation – I can walk anywhere from it, the best atmosphere, and it's extremely quiet. It also has the best porters anywhere in London – they are loyal and helpful."*

INTERIORS

DAVID MLINARIC, 38 Bourne St, SW1 ☎ (01) 730 9072. Respected for his attention to historical detail. Work for the National Trust involves re-creating designs from original documents for houses such as Dunham Massey. He is working on the exquisite British Embassy in Paris, revamping rooms that once belonged to Pauline Borghese, sister of Napoleon. His own house, Thorpe Hall in Suffolk, is restored unswervingly to its original 16th-century state. Mlinaric has designed everything Lord Lichfield has ever lived in: *"He has an extraordinary sense of style and a flexibility that enables him to work on everything from the smallest London flat to a major stately home"* (Lord Lichfield).

DAVID HICKS, 101 Jermyn St, SW1 ☎ (01) 930 1991. Designs the whole caboodle – from architecture (influenced by neo-classical masters such as Robert Adam) to furnishing fabrics. Renowned for rich colours and bold patterns, as shown in the varied and vivid reds he has used for his chambers in Albany. Recently designed a palatial house in Portugal, on a Palladian theme. Garden designs too. *"I like a rather international, eclectic mixture of old and new. It doesn't matter how grand or inexpensive things are – as long as they have style and quality they will work together"* (David Hicks).

JOHN STEFANIDIS, 6 Burnsall St, SW3 ☎ (01) 351 7511. Born in Patmos, his work is divided between there, England, Paris and New York. With a team of architects and craftsmen, he undertakes building, landscape gardening, designing of woven and printed fabrics, and of furniture. His country home, in converted cowsheds in Dorset, remains rustic – whitewashed brick walls, red brick floors – but not primitive. An uncluttered look, with muted colours, bare walls and plenty of light and space. *"He understands about comfort, space and harmony. He's clever at devising good bones on a simple background"* (Christopher Gibbs).

ARAM DESIGNS, Kean St, WC2 ☎ (01) 240 3933. *"Along with Ciancimino, they have continued single-mindedly with their classic modern designs through all the changes of a quarter-century"* (David Mlinaric).

CIANCIMINO DESIGN, 307 King's Rd, SW3 ☎ (01) 352 2016. (See *Aram.*)

CIANCIMINO LTD, 99 Pimlico Rd, SW1 ☎ (01) 730 9950. *"The best Indian antiques"* (David Hicks).

COLEFAX & FOWLER, 39 Brook St, W1 ☎ (01) 493 2231. Chief exponents of the English country-house look, much copied. Internationally known for their traditional 17th-, 18th- and early 19th-century chintzes taken from originals. Tom Parr and Imogen Taylor are the senior designers. *"The best people to rearrange a huge country house – they have generations of experience, plus craftsmen who know exactly how things should be done, and valuable resources unavailable to anyone else"* (Christopher Gibbs).

LENYGON & MORANT, 30 Lyme St, NW1 ☎ (01) 482 2156. *"The best traditional sofas and armchairs in the world"* (David Mlinaric).

LONDON LIGHTING CO, 135 Fulham Rd, SW3 ☎ (01) 589 3612. *"A wonderful selection of contemporary lights"* (John Stefanidis).

ART AND ANTIQUES

COLNAGHI & CO, 14 Old Bond St, W1 ☎ (01) 491 7408. Founded in France in the 18th century. Serious, quality stuff. Excellent prints and paintings by Botticelli, Raphael, Rubens and Rembrandt sell internationally.

THOS AGNEW & SON, 43 Old Bond St, W1 ☎ (01) 629 6176. Best reputation for old masters, including works by Reynolds, Gainsborough and Turner. Also a wide range of drawings and watercolours at modest prices. Frequent exhibitions, some contemporary – they have shown Lucian Freud, Emma Sergeant and Julian Opie.

Under the hammer

CHRISTIE'S, 8 King St, SW1 ☎ (01) 839 9060 and SOTHEBY'S, 34 New Bond St, W1 ☎ (01) 493 8080 rule the world. Christie's may *slightly* have the edge in popularity. The grandest of the grand in furniture, fine art, sculpture, antiquities, porcelain, glass, silver, jewellery, costume, books, sporting guns, armour, vintage and veteran cars, wine – virtually anything of intrinsic and unusual value – reach new homes via the hallowed portals of these two houses, both in London and overseas. They direct many important country-house contents' sales.

CRUCIAL, 204 Kensington Park Rd, W11 ☎ (01) 229 1940. New, young craftspeople working in sculpture, ceramics, textiles, etc. *"The best for post-punk originality and style"* (David Mlinaric).

FINE ART SOCIETY, 148 New Bond St, W1 ☎ (01) 629 5116. *"Outstanding, the best gallery of its kind – mainly English pictures of the last 100 years. Intelligently run with interesting exhibitions, and they know how to hang pictures"* (Mark Birley).

CHRISTOPHER GIBBS, 118 New Bond St, W1 ☎ (01) 629 2008. Old Etonian antique dealer, a flamboyant character with clear ideas and unerring taste. Buys for the Sainsburys and the National Trust. *"The best antique shop in the world – it's like visiting a museum. The standard never drops and I have never not wanted something"* (David Mlinaric).

MALLETT & SON, 40 New Bond St, W1 ☎ (01) 499 7411. The ultimate ritzy dealer in England. 18th-century furniture, decorative *objets* and *bibelots*. **MALLETT AT BOURDON HOUSE, Davies St, W1 ☎ (01) 629 2444** is their showcase for Continental furniture and garden statuary.

MARLBOROUGH FINE ART, 6 Albemarle St, W1 ☎ (01) 629 5161. Light, spacious gallery, joint-best with Waddington for modern art. Shows Henry Moore, Barbara Hepworth and John Piper.

GUY NEVILL, 10 Bramerton St, SW3 ☎ (01) 351 4292. *"The best English sporting pictures"* (David Mlinaric).

PARTRIDGE, 144 New Bond St, W1 ☎ (01) 629 0834. John partridge is in the very top league. Grand-scale pieces – colossal chandeliers; French furniture displayed on brilliant carpets. Everything is highly restored. Main market is foreign, but he did provide Althorp with some antiquities.

WESTENHOLZ ANTIQUES, 68 & 80-82 Pimlico Rd, SW1 ☎ (01) 730 2151. Owned by Piers von Westenholz. *"His shop shows his ability to combine furniture and objects of value and quality with simpler, no less stylish antiques"* (David Mlinaric). *"He works very hard, has a keen eye and finds the most unusual things. I've never bought anything from him which I've regretted"* (Mark Birley).

WADDINGTON GALLERIES, 11 Cork St, W1 ☎ (01) 437 8611. Four galleries in Cork St plus a fifth devoted to graphic art. Leslie Waddington buys the best modern and contemporary art and sculpture – Picasso, Miró, Matisse, Ben Nicolson, Elisabeth Frink, Allen Jones and a galaxy of younger painters.

WILDENSTEIN & CO, 147 New Bond St, W1 ☎ (01) 629 6861. This sumptuous gallery with its thick pile carpets and velvet walls offers an even richer selection of masterpieces than the others. More stock than any other gallery. Daniel Wildenstein and his sons (including polo patron Guy) buys anything from Giotto to Bonnard. Go here to build an important collection. Galleries in New York and Tokyo.

COUNTRY

BEST AREAS

★

1 GLOUCESTERSHIRE
2 HAMPSHIRE
3 WILTSHIRE
4 BERKSHIRE
5 OXFORDSHIRE

BEST STATELY HOMES

BLENHEIM PALACE, Oxfordshire (1722, Duke of Marlborough, open March–Oct). *"The best country house to stay in, without doubt. Nowhere do you find a more generous host and hostess who pay more attention to detail. They really care. They bottle their own water from a nearby spring. You get a hottie in your bed, chocolates, lavender bags in the drawers and by your pillow, and fresh flowers. They have lovely old-fashioned staff who unpack for you and turn back the bed. They do it beautifully"* (Anouska Hempel).

CHASTLETON, Gloucestershire (1603, Mrs Clutton-Brock, open March–Oct). *"Not a symmetrical house, nor a house of great architectural beauty, but it's terribly romantic, like something out of* Alice in Wonderland *– tumbledown walls, overgrown grass, oaky rooms leading off each other, a long gallery upstairs with old nurseries off it"* (John Brooke-Little).

CHATSWORTH, Derbyshire (1680s, Duke of Devonshire, open March–Oct). *"Enormously grand,*

beautifully proportioned classic building. And they still live there, which makes it a little more interesting. Magnificent grounds, built in the grand manner – a touch of Versailles. In a sense, it's a house of the 17th-century parvenus. The Cavendishes were rather late-comers on the nobility scene" (John Brooke-Little).

LONGLEAT HOUSE, Wiltshire (1570s, Viscount Weymouth, open all year round). *"It may be a corny choice, but I like it better than Woburn Abbey or even Castle Howard. It just happens to be a very elegant house – and very modern for a 16th-century building. It has what was the first pull-plug loo in the country. It was a highly civilized place at the height of the Renaissance (which came late to such a Philistine country)."* (John Brooke-Little).

West is best

Royal GLOUCESTERSHIRE is the ultimate, around TETBURY and CIRENCESTER, in company with Princes Charles and Michael, and Princess Anne. Some truly glorious, impeccably maintained houses and grounds. HUNGERFORD, OXFORD, SALISBURY and WINCHESTER are fashionable towns to be near but not in.

BEST GARDENS

PENSHURST, Kent (Viscount de L'Isle, open Easter–Oct) *"The best – well-kept, formal gardens"* (John Brooke-Little).

SISSINGHURST CASTLE GARDEN, Kent (created by Vita Sackville-West, 1930s; open April–Oct). *"I'm very keen on gardens. This is the best in England – it has the best design, layout and planting for a garden of its size and for the climate. The whole concept is the best"* (David Hicks).

FRANCE

PARIS

BEST AREAS

TOP 6

★

1 7ÈME
2 8ÈME
3 16ÈME
4 1ER
5 6ÈME
6 4ÈME

7ème Ultra-chic embassyland: quiet, stately buildings, laid-out boulevards and gardens. RUE DE VARENNE, the ESPLANADE DES INVALIDES and streets on either side of the PARC DU CHAMP DE MARS such as AVENUE ELISEE RECLUS and AVENUE EMILE ACOLLAS. The most interesting place to live is in a convent or monastery with a communal garden and the sound of church bells to wake you.

8ème Chic central area on la Rive Droite rising as far as PARC DE MONCEAU with its private streets, AVENUES RUYSDAEL, VAN DYCK and VELASQUEZ. The best houses are on AVENUE GABRIEL looking over the gardens of the Champs Elysées, and on AVENUE MONTAIGNE.

16ème Ritzy residential area. The north is *le plus chic*; the south is *pretty* chic except around Porte de St Cloud. AVENUE FOCH, the most expensive street in Paris – sometime home of Grimaldis, Khashoggis, Onassises and Rothschilds – is now overrun with Lebanese, prostitutes and traffic. The even numbers still get the sun. Villas (private areas cut off to traffic with detached houses and gardens) are *très désirable* – VILLA DE MONTMORENCY and VILLA BOILEAU, where the Comte de Paris used to live. Anything giving out on to the JARDIN DU RANELAGH.

1er Quieter than the 8e with 17th- and 18th-century town houses. The best garden to overlook is the JARDIN DU PALAIS ROYAL, where Colette lived. PLACE VENDOME is a bijou residence – the immaculately groomed base of the top jewellers. RUE DE RIVOLI, from nos 180 to 250, is lovely.

La crème du septième

Karl Lagerfeld has a whole wing of an 18th-century town house on rue de l'Université in the 7ème, with electricity only for the video – otherwise it's candlelight and perishing winters among the lavish Louis XV furniture. In the 1er, 2ème, 3ème and 4ème you live in a 17th- or 18th-century town house in its entirety or on one storey. Ceilings are at least 12 ft (3.7 m) high, walls are wood-panelled or have intricate Louis XIV or XV cornices; some have paintings over the door lintels. Rooms are painted white or off-white with mouldings highlighted in gold. The best floor is a *parquet de Versailles.*

6ème Fashionable narrow streets steeped in arts and academia. The tiny PLACE DE FURSTEMBERG off rue Jacob is a delight in spring when the wisteria is in bloom. Trendy place to live is art gallery-lined RUE DE SEINE, which runs from the Seine into RUE DE TOURNON and to the gates of the Palais du Luxembourg.

4ème Anywhere on the ÎLE DE LA CITE; or on the ÎLE ST LOUIS, especially the QUAI D'ORLEANS, is very exclusive. Guy de Rothschild lives at Hôtel Lambert, a complete 17th-century house (most are duplexes) on the Île St Louis.

BEST PARIS SUBURBS

★

(Suburbia is the French commuter belt – they don't have country houses)

1 LE VESINET
2 ST CLOUD
3 NEUILLY
4 GARCHES
5 CROISSY-SUR-SEINE

INTERIORS

MADELEINE CASTAING (see ART AND ANTIQUES).

FRANÇOIS CATROUX, 20 rue du Faubourg St Honoré, 75008 ☎ (1) 4266 6925. Contemporary designer – combines modern elements with classical grace – and a high-profile, vibrant jetsetter.

JACQUES GRANGE, 32 avenue Raymond Poincaré, 75116 ☎ (1) 4727 1779. Skilful and organized, he trained under Henri Samuel. Recent accomplishments include a château in Normandy for Philip Niarchos, a 19th-century house in Deauville for Yves Saint Laurent and a mansion in the South of France for Mick Jagger. He was the main designer for the Musée des Arts de la Mode in the Pavillon de Marsan, the new fashion wing of the Louvre. *"The best – he's the only one who will do up a place so it doesn't look as if the decorator has been round"* (Inès de la Fressange).

SABINE IMBERT, Techm'Art, 23 rue Galilée, 75116 ☎ (1) 4720 6605. Terrifically social, works with husband Didier, who deals in antiques. Her clients include Karl Lagerfeld, Princess Caroline and Régine. In Monte Carlo, she has done Frank Sinatra's apartment and the Portanovas' suite at the Hôtel de Paris.

PRELLE, 5 Place des Victoires, 75012 ☎ (1) 4236 6721. *"For warp-printed silks and damasks made from their archives on the old looms"* (David Mlinaric).

ANDREE PUTMAN, Ecart Internationale, 111 rue St Antoine, 75004 ☎ (1) 4274 0840. Very *in, très aujourd'hui.* Chicly turned out, a minimalist who goes for a monochrome, clean, sophisticated look. Did Yves Saint Laurent's showrooms in San Francisco and Philadelphia and the hip Morgans Hotel in New York (see TRAVEL). Designs furniture. *"My favourite interior designer – she has ideas and taste similar to my own, and a wonderful spirit"* (Azzedine Alaïa).

PHILIPPE STARCK, 5 rue de Dion, 78490 Montfort l'Amaury ☎ (1) 3486 8474. Much admired· *"for his restraint ... for linear order and discipline, for the clarity of his colours, like watercolours – Perrier water green, lemon yellow. Also for the material he uses – real things – ecologically produced raw materials"* (David Mlinaric). Incorporates symbols and hidden messages into designs. The latest is the Café Costes, Place des Innocents, Paris, which has been described as beautiful and as melancholy as the railway station in Prague. Other works as diverse as a chain of wine bars for Eric de Rothschild, the private apartments of President Mitterand at the Elysée Palace, and the trendy Starck Club in Dallas.

ART AND ANTIQUES

Paris hosts the world's best antiques show, the Biennale Internationale, at the Grand Palais (Sept/Oct, even years).

DIDIER AARON, 32 avenue Raymond Poincaré, 75116 ☎ (1) 4727 1779. Premier Paris dealer for 17th- to 19th-century furniture. A chief participant at the Biennale.

AVELINE & CIE, 20 rue du Cirque, 75008 ☎ (1) 4266 6029. Very grand, has super-cachet. Mainly 18th-century stock.

BRAME & LA RENCEAU, 68 blvd Malesherbes, 75008 ☎ (1) 4522 1689. The best art dealer for Impressionist paintings.

MADELEINE CASTAING, 21 rue Bonaparte, 75006 ☎ (1) 4354 9171. *Antiquaire au goût anglais* – both dealer and decorator. *"Third empire decoration – she brought back the ornate interior. She won't sell you anything from her shop unless she feels like it"* (Eleanor Lambert). She is a fabulous but extraordinary-looking person, spotted once in wig with elastic under the chin, three pairs of woollen tights and a velvet battle jacket.

GALERIE CAMOIN, 9 quai Voltaire, 75007 ☎ (1) 4261 8206. Alain Demachy's splendid shop has a double staircase that leads to room after room of dramatic 18th- and 19th-century pieces.

GALERIE DU LETHE-LETAILLEUR ALAIN, 50 rue de Seine, 75006; 1 rue Jacob, 75006 ☎ (1) 4633 2517. The best art galleries for Post-Impressionist works.

GALERIE TEXBRAUN, 12 rue Mazarine 75006 ☎ (1) 4633 1457. This gallery, run by Texarian and Braunschweg, deals in the best of contemporary photographers, such as Robert Mapplethorpe and Jöel Peter Witkin and in rare 19th-century early French photographers such as Le Gray, Baldus, Salzmann and Atget. Clients include the biggest private collectors and institutions, such as Howard Gilman in the States and the Musée d'Orsay in Paris.

JACQUES KUGEL, 279 rue St Honoré, 75008 ☎ (1) 4260 8623. The finest, most important Baroque works in France.

Sous le marteau

HOTEL DROUOT, 9 rue Drouot, 75009 ☎ (1) 4246 1711. Labyrinth of showrooms crammed with curiosities, grand and minor, all jumbled up together. There are no major or thematic sales, so it's up to the 8,000 customers a day to sift out the real bargains.

“ The best place in the world to live is where I live, in a tiny hamlet in France, near Apt and Forcalquier, in the foothills of the Alps. The house is surrounded by lavender fields grown for soap and scent. It lies to the east of the fashionable area, so one has the charm of living somewhere completely remote, with places like Gordes and lots of friends close by but not swamping you ” (QUENTIN CREWE)

JACQUES PERRIN, 3 quai Voltaire, 75007 ☎ (1) 4260 2720. Exceptional 17th- and 18th-century French furniture and objets d'art.

BERNARD STEINITZ, 4 rue Drouot, 75009 ☎ (1) 4246 9898. Has been described as an exuberant, extravagant, over-excitable, bearded, Svengalian character who pays about 10 times the norm and has his own ideas about what's wonderful. An idiosyncratic buyer, he will indeed pay over the odds for a piece if he wants it badly enough, and resell for as much as possible. The Getty Museum and the Met are among his undaunted clients.

THE RIVIERA, a sunny place with shady people, is generally out, residentially speaking. The only place is CAP D'ANTIBES, full of movie stars, and *"Freddie Heineken lives there, next door to Lambsie Norman's wonderful Château de la Garoupe on the tip of the Cap, with the most staggering gardens in the south. It's loveliest in spring, when the mimosa and wisteria are in flower"* (Frank Lowe). MONTE CARLO has three apartment blocks that tower above the rest in prestige terms: Rockabella, Soleil d'Or and Shuykill, which you could rent for £5,000 (US$7,235) a month.

COUNTRY

The LUBERON region of Provence is the smartest country area to live in or bolt to. Between Avignon and Apt, around Gordes (land of asparagus and artichoke), people such as conductor Pierre Boulez, a host of duchesses including the Duchesse de Sabrin, Herbert von Karajan, Mitterand and a côterie of Britons such as Jeremy Fry have houses (and Woody Allen has toyed with the idea).

NORMANDY is out for old French money, but in for Deauville playpeople and for Britons attempting to get that bit nearer the Equator (the Ashley château – decorated *partout* in Laura Ashley – is here). Karl Lagerfeld has a jewel of a 16-roomed château in BRITTANY, filled with rococo furniture and a library full of books on fashion and literature. In the area around PERCHE and south-west of Chartres in the LOIRE VALLEY, you can pick up a decent 25-roomed château for about 10.6 million francs (US$1.5 million). Nice secret places are LA BAULE, with the largest sandy beach in Europe, ÎLE DE NOIRMOUTIER and ÎLE DE RE.

ITALY

ROME

BEST AREAS

TOP 5

★

1. **From PIAZZA DEL POPOLO to PIAZZA DI SPAGNA**
2. **PALAZZO BORGHESE**
3. **PARIOLI**
4. **VIA GIULIA**
5. **QUARTIERE MUSICISTI**

PIAZZA DEL POPOLO to **PIAZZA DI SPAGNA** Where the oldest, most established lire live. A network of delightful, fashionable streets of which the VIA DEL

“ The VATICAN is surely the best address in the world – they don't bomb you or blitz you or anything – you just sit there in peace and quiet. Good air. Nothing better! ” (MARINA CHALIAPIN)

BABUINO, VIA CONDOTTI and VIA SISTINA are the most exclusive, and the VIA MARGUTTA, where Zeffirelli used to live, the most attractive – a narrow cobbled lane flanked by grand mansions (mostly apartments now), art galleries and antique shops.

PALAZZO BORGHESE, off the Piazza Borghese Sumptuous apartments with noble occupants such as the Duchessa Salviati, Principe Camillo Borghese, Principessa Ercolani.

PARIOLI An elegant if nouveau riche district north of the Villa Borghese. Aimless rich kids from the area are known as *i Pariolini*.

VIA GIULIA Built by Pope Giulio at the beginning of the 16th century, it runs dead straight from Michelangelo's San Giovanni de' Fiorentini to the Palazzo Farnese (a smart place to have an apartment). Now colourful and trendy. *"Everybody has always lived there from Renaissance days. My old flat there was out of this world, on the top floor of an old palace. I even contributed to the lighting in that street – it used to be very badly lit and we formed a committee to put those ancient-looking lantern lights in – we brought it back to life"* (Marina Chaliapin).

QUARTIERE MUSICISTI Any of the streets, named after musicians, around the Piazza Giuseppe Verdi.

ART AND ANTIQUES

GALLERIA CLAUDIO GASPARRINI, via Fontanella di Borghese 46, 00187 ☎ (06) 679 0954. Specializes in very high quality oil paintings of every period. Gasparrini runs a television programme on antiques.

MARCO GOBBI, via Monserrato 126, 00186 ☎ (06) 654 5307. Winner of the most elegant chair award, Marco Gobbi supplied most of the articles in the Bulgari home. He is known for his famous collection of aeroplane and polo paintings and likes "to create 20th-century antiques", when not finding them for interior designer Lorenzo Mongiardino.

CESARE LAMPRONTI, via del Babuino 67, 00187 ☎ (06) 679 5800. One of the most successful dealers in paintings in Europe. Sells paintings of every period to grace the interiors of rich and beautiful homes.

FLORENCE

BEST AREAS

PIAZZALE MICHELANGELO or one of the grand houses on the VIALE MICHELANGELO are the most OK addresses. It's more chic, however, to live in a crumbling Renaissance palazzo in a little town like SETTIGNANO, or FIESOLE in the hills above Florence, surrounded by olive groves and vines (which you inspect from time to time in the traditional peasant-wear of the region – Armani and Bulgari). Sir Harold Acton leads the Anglo-Tuscan clique, in Villa La Pietra just outside Florence. He occasionally conducts idiosyncratic tours around his beloved gardens, with their follies and sculptures. Others living in exiled splendour include Lord Lambton and Teddy Millington-Drake.

ART AND ANTIQUES

GIUSEPPE & MARIO BELLINI, Lungarno Soderini 5, 50100 ☎ (055) 214031. Superb stock of fine furniture, marbles, bronzes, sculptures, tapestries and paintings.

GIOVANNI GENTILINI, via Santo Spirito 5, 50121 ☎ (055) 214256. Established 100 years ago, this firm specializes in 18th-century Venetian art, including furniture, paintings, objets d'art and mirrors.

BERTALOZZI GUIDO, via Maggio 18R, 50100 ☎ (055) 287570. Deals in high quality furniture and 16th- to 18th-century Italian paintings, 14th- to 18th-century sculptures, majolica of the 16th and 17th centuries, and tapestries from France and the Netherlands.

MILAN

BEST AREAS

MONTENAPOLEONE is *the* place – PIAZZA SAN BABILA and VIA MONTENAPOLEONE. Many smart Milanesi – the least showy of all the Italian people – live centrally in hidden courtyards behind closed doors. But they refer to their weekend houses on the shores of Como and Maggiore as "home". Baron Thyssen's Villa Favorita on Lake Lugano, with its stunning international art, is the ultimate weekend retreat.

INTERIORS

LORENZO MONGIARDINO, viale Bianca Maria 45. The best designer in Italy. Works mainly for friends, like the Agnellis, Heinzes and Baron Thyssen. *"From the world of theatre design into design for living. An opulent vision of wonderful colours and materials, an imaginative mixing of styles, and a great team of craftsmen – marblers, stencillers, embroiderers …"* (Christopher Gibbs). *"A true artist because his houses seem to have existed for a long time, they have a past and a history which is identified in those who live there"* (Gianni Versace).

ART AND ANTIQUES

NELLA LONGARI, via Bigli 15, 20100 ☎ (02) 794287. 15th- to 18th-century furniture is their speciality. Also sells bronzes and paintings to international clients and Italian collectors.

ALESSANDRO ORSI, via Bagutta 14, 20100 ☎ (02) 702214. Specializes in collectors' pieces of furniture, paintings and sculptures.

DOMENICO PIVA, via Sant' Andrea 8a, 20100 ☎ (02) 700678. Nearly everything in the shop is Italian, such as Italian furniture and paintings from the 17th and 18th centuries, majolica of the 18th century, fine procelains from Naples and Venice, and silver and bronzes from the renaissance and baroque periods. His clientele ranges from industrialists to the haute bourgeoisie.

THE AMERICAS

UNITED STATES

NEW YORK

BEST AREAS

TOP 6
★
(always on Manhattan)

1 UPPER EAST SIDE
2 UPPER WEST SIDE
3 SUTTON PLACE
4 RIVERSIDE DRIVE
5 GREENWICH VILLAGE
6 SOHO

UPPER EAST SIDE Grand, stuffy, establishment wealth. Families with *names*. Almost repulsive to those who don't fit in, but the only place to live for those that do. Penthouses on FIFTH AVENUE are the ultimate, overlooking Central Park, between 60th Street and the mid-90s (though the lower the street number the better). At 834, near 64th Street, live a Rockefeller, a Taubman and a Whitney in cosy co-operation. Jackie Onassis lives on Fifth, as do fish-out-of-water Paul Newman and Robert Redford. The Kissingers live at River House, on E 57th St, overlooking the river.

The blocks between Fifth and Madison (the next Ave along) from 65th to 82nd, and PARK AVENUE (2 away from Fifth) are ultra-plushy. Parksiders include Paloma Picasso, Diana Vreeland (in a small but perfectly formed all-red apartment), Brooke Astor, Jackie O's sister Lee Radziwill, Barbara Walters, and model Carmen. These are apartments-plus: financier Saul Steinberg's 34-roomed triplex, for one, is more akin to a baronial country mansion. Top co-ops from $4 million.

UPPER WEST SIDE Diverse people, stores, eating and architecture; a younger, homier image than the East Side – professionals-trying-to-be-artsy, models and media types. The mirror image of Fifth Avenue is CENTRAL PARK WEST; the smartest address is the Dakota Building at 72nd (where John Lennon was shot and where Yoko still lives, in company with Lauren Bacall). Madison Avenue is mirrored by Columbus Avenue, a more youthful, less pretentious version. More brownstones, less high-rises. It's now OK to live as far up as 103rd Street – the Hispanics are being forced further away.

SUTTON PLACE overlooks the East River. Elegant apartment blocks house luminaries such as Irving Berlin, Valerian Rybar and the Morgans. 1 Sutton Place South is a very desirable address.

RIVERSIDE DRIVE runs along the west side of Manhattan. At its smartest between the 70s and 90s, overlooking Riverside Park and the Hudson River.

GREENWICH VILLAGE The Village entertains an avant garde mix of types, has its own distinct atmosphere and ungridded streets with names not numbers. *"It's a very civilized place, small enough to be a community and for one to know people"* (Seymour Britchky).

SOHO Arty-trendy types who have been converting lofts and opening galleries for so long that they are part of the establishment, and attract an influx of weekend tourists. TRIBECA (TRIangle BElow CAnal Street, would you believe?), CHELSEA and the LOWER EAST and WEST SIDES are up-and-coming hang-outs for architects/designers/ photographers/models of the eighties.

INTERIORS

MARIO BUATTA, 120 E 80th St, NY 10021 ☎ (212) 988 6811. The English country houses – cluttered, lived-in – moulded to the States. Supervises the NY Winter Antiques Show, and shines at the gala opening night. WASPish clients include Sir Rudolph Bing, Henry Ford II, Ogden Phillips Jr, Nelson Doubleday.

MARK HAMPTON, 46 E 56th St, NY 10021 ☎ (212) 879 9006. Worked with David Hicks, and is greatly influenced by English taste. Patterned walls stir him. He redecorated the Governor's mansion in Albany, New York.

PARISH-HADLEY ASSOCIATES, 305 E 63rd St, NY 10021 ☎ (212) 888 7979. "Sister" Parish and Albert Hadley. *"'Sister' Parish does beautifully finished and traditional rooms – the best for quality, comfort and easy elegance"* (David Mlinaric). Clients include Ann Getty, Mrs Nelson Rockefeller, Brooke Astor and William Paley.

VALERIAN RYBAR & DAIGRE DESIGN CORP, 601 Madison Ave, NY 10022 ☎ (212) 752 1861. Reputedly the most expensive designer in the world. Rybar's style is *no* distinct style. He flits from monochrome severity to rich colours, from high-tech to Palladian, from marbled and mirrored surfaces to embroidery and tapestry. A glittering, global list of clients – Guy de Rothschild, Nicholas DuPont, Sir James Goldsmith, Christina Onassis, Pierre Schlumberger, Stavros Niarchos.

“ Everybody in New York wants to be a New Yorker. Most of them aren't native New Yorkers, but they like the whole 'New York, New York' fantasy. Chicago's more like London in that it's a big city made up of small-town people. They come up from Iowa or Michigan or Indiana, but they're all from the neighbourhood. On the West Coast, they're 'wow, surf, sand, *LA*!' Denver's a lovely place – I wouldn't mind settling there, or just outside it. Colorado is nice too – it's great out there – everybody is going through the cowboy thing again. *That's* the new America ”

(BOB PAYTON)

ART AND ANTIQUES

DIDIER AARON, 32 E 67th St, NY 10021 ☎ (212) 988 5248. Didier's son Hervé has cultivated a shop that is, if anything, even more interesting than the Parisian one. Specializes in French, Austrian and German 19th-century furniture, and decorative arts.

LEO CASTELLI GALLERY, 420 West Broadway, NY 10012 ☎ (212) 431 5160; 142 Greene St, NY 10012 ☎ (212) 431 6279. Best dealer of contemporary American art – Warhol, Lichtenstein, Stella Rosenquist. The SoHo gallery (Greene Street) has modern sculpture.

OK HARRIS, 383 West Broadway, NY 10012 ☎ (212) 431 3600. The capacious 11,000 sq ft (1,022 sq m) gallery is ample room for 4 simultaneous exhibitions of contemporary artists, photographers or sculptors.

MICHAEL KNOEDLER & CO, 19 E 57th St, NY 10021 ☎ (212) 794 6269. Respected gallery for mainly contemporary art plus the odd old master.

MARLBOROUGH GALLERY, 40 W 57th St, NY 10019 ☎ (212) 541 4900. The largest art gallery on 57th Street. European and American works by Henry Moore, Botero, Lipchitz, and photographers Brandt, Brassai and Penn.

JAMES ROBINSON, 15 E 57th St, NY 10022 ☎ (212) 752 6166. The best in the world for rare antique silver and crystal from the 16th century onwards.

ISRAEL SACK, 15 E 57th St, NY 10022 ☎ (212) 753 6562. The best American folk art and antiques outside Boston's Museum of Fine Arts. Albert Sack is a fund of knowledge.

STAIR & CO, 59 E 57th St, NY 10022 ☎ (212) 355 7620. London-New York firm, but both branches are more US-orientated – impressive 18th-century English furniture to fit rooms with 9ft 6in (2.9 m) high ceilings.

Under the star-spangled banger

Super-important auctions of worldwide interest are held at the two greats:

CHRISTIE'S, 502 Park Avenue, NY 10022 ☎ (212) 546 1000

SOTHEBY'S, 1334 York Ave, NY 10021 ☎ (212) 472 3400

GARRICK C STEPHENSON ANTIQUES, 50 E 57th St, NY 10022 ☎ (212) 753 2570. Individual taste, top-quality, unusual pieces. Specializes in 18th-century furniture and porcelain.

WILDENSTEIN & CO, 19 E 64th St, NY 10021 ☎ (212) 879 0500. (See LONDON.)

DANIEL WOLF, 30 W 57th St, NY 10019 ☎ (212) 5868432. Handled the historic sale of the major photographic collections from André Jammes, Arnold Crane and Sam Wagstaff, the world's leading private collectors, for a reputed sum of $20 million plus to the J Paul Getty Museum.

BOLT-HOLES

CONNECTICUT Old money flutters off at weekends to country towns like SALISBURY, LAKEVILLE and CORNWALL in the north-west, and coastal towns such as OLD LYME and ESSEX. On FISHER'S ISLAND there are no hotels, only rambling Victorian houses with wraparound Porsches and a view of the ocean (except for one, named House Without A View).

Company presidents may even commute from the NY/CT border towns of GREENWICH (Round Hill Road and Belhaven), NEW CANAAN (Weed St), DARIEN (large estates at Tokeneke) and WESTPORT (more artistic).

THE HAMPTONS The south shore of Long Island – miles of sand dunes, surf, luke-warm sea, and architectural wonders and monstrosities from potato barns and windmills through revival anything to Stanford White success stories. A wonder is the Roundhouse in East Hampton, based on an African village – cone-shaped with an open ceiling at the apex, white plaster walls and quite bare. *"It's the best house, owned by Jack Lenor-Larsen who has perhaps the best taste in the world"* (Stanley Marcus). Hamptons are hell to get to unless you have a helicopter or seaplane. Best Hamptons are Southampton, exotic-cum-WASP, but turning trade (Ahmet Ertegun, Gloria Vanderbilt, Tom Wolfe, Taki); East Hampton is twee-cum-media (Sidney Lumet, Craig Claiborne; actors and artists).

WASHINGTON DC

BEST AREAS

There are no highrises, no TV aerials in evidence, just wide roads, signifying a grand, laid-out diplomatic quarter.

GEORGETOWN The old colonial city centre with cobbled streets and Federal houses. A mix of intelligentsia, university students, Yuppies and cave dwellers (Washington DC aristocracy) – Robert E. Lee (whose great-grandfather built his Greek Revival mansion), Evangeline Bruce, Susan Mary Allsop, Katharine Graham (*Washington Post*-owner) and the Basses. The grandest streets are NORTH STREET, 28TH STREET and nearby FOXHALL ROAD. *"To have a real house in Georgetown has ambience and history, it's quaint and grand, public and private – a marvellous counterbalance to the rest of the city"* (Aniko Gaal).

"New York is stimulating but exhausting. People burn out in the city. They have become very much like Londoners – they disappear to the country at weekends. I go to an 18th-century stone town called Washington, in Connecticut" (BILL BLASS)

WATERGATE TOWERS apartment block is still smart, the smirch forgotten; CAPITOL HILL is on the rise (the nearer the Capitol, the better). The richest district is ALEXANDRIA, a 17th-century town. Teddy Kennedy lives at ARLINGTON.

BOLT-HOLES

Virginian ranches, particularly the horse-farming country of MIDDLEBURG, where the art-collecting Mellons live.

BOSTON

More like England than England. The tone is set by families whose forebears floated in with the *Mayflower*, and by privileged young WASPs at Harvard, though some say the inner city has lost its soul. The oldest bucks are on BEACON HILL, which is like something out of a Henry James film set.

BEST AREAS

TOP 3

★

1. **MOUNT VERNON STREET**
2. **LOUISBURG SQUARE**
3. **BEACON STREET (between Beacon Hill and Back Bay)**

Commuter belt is mainly on the north shore, rocky, hilly, more densely populated and butcher than the south. MARBLEHEAD (yachty set) and MANCHESTER-BY-THE-SEA (palatial mansions) are the chief towns.

BOLT-HOLES

The more far-flung reaches of the south shore, CAPE COD, where the folks are flasher and the land flatter and sandier than in the north. CARVER, DENNIS, BREWSTER and CHATHAM (away from the over-developed drag) are key weekend haunts, but the gilt key gets you into the compound at HYANNISPORT (Kennedy-land), which is patrolled by bronzed bouncers. From here it's a hop to the islands of MARTHA'S VINEYARD ("the Vineyard", where Jackie Onassis, Carly Simon and New York media celebs like Walter Cronkite have retreats) and NANTUCKET (a quaint old whaling centre, where the "clabberd" (clapboard) houses are long and low, and building regulations will keep them that way).

NEWPORT, RHODE ISLAND

Eastern seaboarders have been making the pilgrimage since the 1860s. Stunning Astor and Vanderbilt mansions are now open to the public. Oldies continue in civilized style while a Preppy young sailing set invades for wild, debauched party weekends.

CHICAGO

The near north of Chicago is the best. NORTH DEERBORN, NORTH STATE PARK and ASTOR STREET are lined with civilized old mansions built by the rich mid-Western industrialists. The spectacular LAKE SHORE DRIVE stretches for miles along the banks of Lake Michigan.

Arizona loner

"The best house in America is William Emphie's in carefree Arizona, 30 minutes from Phoenix. It's built in the midst of five gigantic boulders (about 20 ft high). As you approach, you think there are only the boulders, but up close you are faced by the front door. Brilliant construction and design by Charles Johnson. The view is of wild saguaro cacti, which are about 15 ft high and 125 years old" (Stanley Marcus).

LOS ANGELES

Film stars and their ilk monopolize the western suburbs of Los Angeles, in the foothills and flats below the Santa Monica Mountains, as far east as the Beverly Hills/Hollywood border, and as far west as the Pacific coast. It all started with Douglas Fairbanks and Mary Pickford. Modern-day dwellers dice with disaster – Hillspeople face their houses tumbling off the cliff when the big quake comes, while Malibuites regularly have to rebuild those parts of their timber houses that have slid into stormy seas.

BEST AREAS

TOP 5

★

1. **HOLMBY HILLS**
2. **BEL AIR**
3. **BEVERLY HILLS**
4. **MALIBU**
5. **PACIFIC PALISADES**

HOLMBY HILLS The smartest, because it's cooler and clearer above the polluted smog that pervades even the enshrined Bel Air. Old stars like Loretta Young and beefcakes like Burt Reynolds don't seem to realize that when the earth trembles, the Hills will be the worst place for their health. Best address: CAROLWOOD DRIVE.

BEL AIR and **BEVERLY HILLS** Hollywood is nothing – just litter, tourists, dead memories. Carry on down Sunset, and you'll glide into the Beverly Hills and Bel Air film sets – pristine, manicured, empty; sweeping roads, swaying palms, baize lawns, and *outrageous* houses. Simply dream it up and build it. It's as if you're still on the ersatz streets of Universal Picture Studios: olde-worlde English farmhouses, half-timbered Tudors and Georgian redbricks face French baroque châteaux, sunny Spanish villas and whitewashed weatherboard mansions.

“ Beverley Hills and Bel Air houses are all beautiful, on about an acre of land – sumptuous, comfortable, big. Berry Gordy’s house is particularly wonderful [he runs Motown and discovered Michael Jackson and Diana Ross] – it’s Mediterranean style, and the grounds are fabulous (about 5 acres). I doubt whether he goes out a lot – he stays there and has everything he could possibly want ” (SHAKIRA CAINE)

Beverly Hills covers the hills (mainly Canyon addresses) and the flats, between Santa Monica Boulevard and Sunset Boulevard (mainly Drive addresses: houses, shops and restaurants). Smartest Canyons: COLDWATER, LAUREL and BENEDICT (where Michael and Shakira Caine live). Lucille Ball, George Burns, Charlton Heston and James Stewart are Hillspeople.

Bel Air oozes even more wealth and exclusivity (it’s for media heads and mega-stars). Adjacent to Beverly Hills on the flats, it’s fenced and gated, with closed-circuit TV, the odd alsatian, and signs on houses stating “armed response”, lest you felt like tapping on the door uninvited (residents must warn security of impending visitations). Cars must not loiter or park: kerb-crawling would be pointless since the only people to walk the streets are posses of guards.

Beverly Hills cop

Kenny Rogers sold his hill-top house to 20th Century-Fox-owner Marvin Davis for $20 million. A huge building, covering over 10,000 sq ft (929 sq m) with a basement laundry that could service a hotel. About 6 bedroom suites plus the servants’ quarters.

On Bel Air Road, the late Arnold and Carlotta Kirkeby’s house (TV home of the Beverly Hillbillies), set in 7.5 acres (3 hectares), is on the market for $27 million.

Palm Springs eternal

Palm Springs, a clear-aired patch of cultivated desert, 40 miles by 3 (64 km × 5 km), where washed-out LA glitterati have second homes for R & R, and where burnt-out stars go to restore their chemical independence at the Betty Ford Center (see HEALTH AND BEAUTY). A chequer-board of golfing greens, swimming pools and handsome houses belonging to ageing eminent figures such as Walter Annenberg, Bob Hope, and, of course, Gerald Ford.

MALIBU For funkier types – they have to be to spend millions of dollars on wooden shacks that are liable to fall apart when the big waves come. You must live in the Colony – right by the sea, cordoned-off, exclusive. John McEnroe bought Johnny Carson’s old house when he upgraded himself, Steven Spielberg, Dyan Cannon, Linda Ronstadt, and Rachel Ward and Bryan Brown have houses here.

PACIFIC PALISADES Great houses on the cliffs. People who have dug themselves out of the Valley (San Fernando) but can’t quite make the Hills yet, plus more singular types like the director of the Long Beach Museum of Art, Stephen Garrett, whose house overlooks the beach.

SAN MARINO Not all business is showbusiness. San Marino, near Pasadena, means older money, more refined, professional families: some live in authentic old Spanish villas with oleander-scented gardens and swimming pools – like a heavenly slice of the Med.

WESTWOOD UCLA campus area for the funky, hip, smart young (not necessarily students) – a self-contained quarter with shops and eateries.

BOLT-HOLES

Out of the smog and off to ranches of about 150 acres (60.7 hectares) around SANTA BARBARA, in company with the Reagans.

SAN FRANCISCO

Despite being shaken to its knees in 1906, there remain more 19th-century houses and fewer apartments than in most other American cities. Home town of the Hearsts and the Gettys.

BEST AREAS

TOP 4

★

1. PACIFIC HEIGHTS
2. PRESIDIO HEIGHTS
3. RUSSIAN HILL
4. NOB HILL

PACIFIC HEIGHTS The best apartments are in the all-white Spreckels Mansion at 2080 Washington St, which takes up an entire block.

PRESIDIO HEIGHTS The most elegant area, teeming with the most prominent people. Mansion houses with land (from $2 million).

RUSSIAN HILL 945 Green St is the best apartment block in town – an architectural gem with great views.

NOB HILL Snob Hill has been deposed from its original No. 1 slot for town houses of the wealthy: now some hotels and aparments. BROCKLEBANK is the best apartment block (the best penthouses sell for up to $6 million).

BROADWAY The last mile (1.6 km) from Fillmore St onwards has old mansion town houses – home of Gordon and Ann Getty, George Jewett and Marianne Booth.

TELEGRAPH HILL Arty area with bags of character.

INTERIORS

TONY HAIL, 1055 California St, CA 94108 ☎ (415) 928 3500. Traditional style, likes muted beigy colours. Will shop for antiques in Europe for clients.

MICHAEL TAYLOR, 9 25th Ave N, CA 94121 ☎ (415) 668 9090. A theatrical, gardeny look. Mixes modern and ancient, lacing specially made furniture with overscaled 18th-century pieces and antiquities.

BOLT-HOLES

The west shore of LAKE TAHOE is the best. Smart houses in the wooded national parkland north of San Francisco, in MARIN COUNTY, and in NAPA VALLEY, wine district of California – though too many people have developed a taste for the area. CARMEL is chic and sophisticated, with a network of pretty, shady streets that perch above the Pacific.

PALM BEACH

"God's waiting room" (Nigel Dempster). *"The nicest place to live is Florida, extremely well controlled, safe and beautiful"* (Rodney Dillard). A new(ish) town on an island connected to the mainland by 3 bridges. Geriatric bon viveurs such as members of the families DuPont, Kennedy, Lynch and Ford, Douglas Fairbanks Jr and Estée Lauder whoop it up at the various beach and country clubs. Unsurprisingly, the most police per capita and the lowest crime rate in the US. Garbage is collected daily. Houses from $500,000 to $10 million. Best street: OCEAN BOULEVARD.

NEW ORLEANS

With the swamps on one side and the Mississippi on the other, New Orleans has nowhere to go. Residents make do with the historic Pontalba Apartments on JACKSON SQUARE or a mansion in the garden district on SAINT CHARLES AVENUE.

DALLAS

To some, Dallas is miles from anywhere, but to Stanley Marcus, it's "equidistant from everywhere". Super-rich, super-glitzy, super-ostentatious Dallas, where fantasy houses are a reality.

BEST AREAS

TOP 3

★

1 HIGHLAND PARK
2 UNIVERSITY PARK
3 PRESTON HOLLOW

HIGHLAND PARK Near the city centre, run as a private incorporated town with its own schools, police and fire departments and local government. It's smartest to live by TURTLE CREEK, which runs through this and UNIVERSITY PARK. America's second richest woman, Caroline Hunt-Schoellkopf – her sister's the richest – lives here, as does Stanley Marcus and H Ross Perot.

The ultimate estate, on the ultimate road, TURTLE CREEK ROW, belongs to $350 millionaire Edwin Cox. A small palace in walled grounds, with a lovely gazebo, huge indoor swimming pool and a soundproofed tennis court that the pros clamour to practise on: worth $20 million.

On Armstrong Parkway there's a house run by computer. From poolside or armchair, you can operate the security system, lawn sprinklers, heating, air conditioning, and the piped music of the moment. Dive into the pool, and the sound waves switch to underwater mood. And, should you have an accident, there's a paramedical emergency system.

Palm peach

A *faux* French Regency house of marble, built in the sixties on a valuable site on the beach, home of Mrs Robert Young (deceased), went on the market earlier this year for $25 million.

BAYOUD INTERESTS, 400 North St Paul St, Suite 1100, Dallas, TX 75201 ☎ (214) 470 9496. Twinkle Bayoud is the star of upmarket real estate.

HOUSTON

RIVER OAKS is the place, although sinking oil prices have devalued the houses. But the Wyatts still live there in style.

CANADA

TORONTO

The richest city in Canada, with the longest street in the world: Yonge Street (the city's main artery), which runs north for 1,000 miles (1,609 km) from Lake Ontario, through the city, and beyond to Thunder Bay.

BEST AREAS

TOP 3

★

1 ROSEDALE
2 FOREST HILL
3 PARK LANE CIRCLE

ROSEDALE WASPy, blue-blooded. A civilized country nucleus of gracious, traditional homes and gardens, parks, tennis courts and shops, 10 minutes from the centre. Home of Lord Thomson, the Heiseys, Hal Jackman, Gordon Lightfoot, Donald Davis, Catherine Leggett and university eggheads.

FOREST HILL Mansions with pools and tennis courts. Dyed-in-the-wool Torontonians intimate it's nouveau riche. Inhabitants such as the Eatons, premier of Ontario David Peterson and Galen Weston disagree.

PARK LANE CIRCLE Super-rich suburbia – opulent houses with all garden accoutrements. Home of Conrad Black and Elvio Del Zotto.

YORKVILLE "The Village" is the best downtown area for over-achievers, singles and jetsetters who don't want or need the drag of a huge house in Forest Hill. Smart town houses on HAZELTON AVENUE and chic apartments on AVENUE ROAD. The most expensive condos (C$1–2 million/ US$716,332–1,432,665) are in the brand-new RENAISSANCE PLAZA; the facelifted MANULIFE CENTRE is very smart.

Canadian condos

Living in the best condominium blocks in Toronto is living by machine. On top of standard fittings – washing machine and dryer, microwave, coffee-maker, smoke alarm and thermostat air-conditioning – buildings have porterage, parking, car-wash facilities, shopping, dry-cleaning, pool, roof terrace, cinema, bar, restaurant and subway-link so that you need never step outside in winter.

BOLT-HOLES

"Farms" in the wild rolling hills an hour north of Toronto. CALEDON, CLAREMONT and KING have the ritziest, with staff, pool, sauna, tennis court and stabling (horses are about the only thing to authenticate these farms). Caledon, home of Norman Jewison and Peter Monk, has a glamorous ski club (see SPORTING LIFE, Skiing); King is the horsiest area, where Joe Zentil has a 250-acre (101-hectare) farm.

Summer cottages are in the GEORGIAN BAY area in breathtaking lakeland wilderness, dotted with endless islands. Outdoorsy and sportif. The rich have their own islands and do the back-to-nature bit. The best places are BEAUMARIS, which draws the Mellons, and POINT AU BARIL.

MONTREAL

WESTMOUNT is the oldest part of town. Bronfmans, Eatons, Geneviève Bujold and Paul Desmaries live there in Beverly Hills style. Best streets: BELVEDERE CIRCLE, SUMMIT CIRCLE.

Real estate on a plate

HARRIET "SIS" BUNTING WELD, 104 Kilbarry Rd, Toronto, Ontario M5P 1K8 ☎ (416) 488 0272, or c/o Johnston & Daniel, 414 Mount Pleasant ☎ (416) 489 2121. Sis caters for the choicest slice of the market. A workaholic, she coddles her clients with lunches, dinners, the works before settling them into dream homes.

VANCOUVER

SCHAUNESSEY is the home of old-established Vancouverites. Professors and businessmen live in POINT GREY. NORTH VANCOUVER is a notch down from Point Grey, but is romantically served by sea bus to Downtown and is only 20 minutes from the Grouse Mountain ski slopes. WEST VANCOUVER is for smart up-and-comings who enjoy the view. Smart highrises with water and mountain views on ENGLISH BAY, Downtown.

CARIBBEAN

Jetsetters wing in to exclusive little pre-fab enclaves on certain islands (see also TRAVEL).

BARBADOS Sandy Lane – sometime residence of the Reagans, Jackie Onassis and Jerome Zipkin – could be all washed up: top houses are up for sale. One Barbadian house that *isn't* – just – belongs to Robert Sangster: *"I was going to sell it last year, but my 4 children persuaded me not to. It must be the best house there, on the beach, and spread out. It's made up of private cottages – enough to accommodate 14 people in their own private quarters, and we all meet in the dining room and sitting room."*

BAY CAY and **SPANISH CAY** are the most valuable islands. Bay Cay is the most developed private island with roads, houses, hotels and navigable waters, owned by Mrs Seward Johnson. Properties from US$300,000 to US$3 million for 25 acres (10 hectares).

The lesser-known ST MARTIN (Leeward Is), TORTOLA (British Virgin Is), TURKS and CAICOS (both Bahamas) are the best investments.

JAMAICA: ROUND HILL, TRYALL and **PORT ANTONIO** are the places. Baron Thyssen has a fabulous place at Port Antonio. Ralph Lauren and Paul McCartney at Round Hill, and US congress types at the luxurious Tryall. Reasonable properties – around US$500,000.

LYFORD CAY, New Providence, Bahamas Gated-off, in one corner of this druggy island Bohemia: own golf course, rolling hills, about 200 varied houses with gardens, tight security, armed police. Bernard Ashley, Arthur Hailey, Sean Connery, Ringo Starr and Barbara Bach have plots there.

MUSTIQUE Small, exclusive, private atmosphere (though Lord Glenconner has sold the major shareholding to a Venezuelan consortium). Christmas getaway homes of Mick Jagger and Jerry Hall, and (post-Christmas) Princess Margaret. *"Where public people can be private. You have to buy large plots of land. The houses are spaced out – I can't see a single one from my window. The island isn't on the Jumbo landing list; it's relaxed, not grand, but has that fundamental Caribbean atmosphere"* (Lord Lichfield).

WINDERMERE, Eleuthera, Bahamas A lower-key, more aristocratic resort with about 30 houses, belonging to people like David Hicks, the Duke of Abercorn, the Brabournes, and the Astor girls (who designed and built their sleek villa). *"It's islandy, not cocktaily; you don't notice the buildings, only the colours ... the pink sand, the sea, the trees"* (Pauline Astor).

AUSTRALIA

SYDNEY

BEST AREAS

TOP 5

★

1 POINT PIPER
2 VAUCLUSE
3 DARLING POINT
4 WOOLLAHRA
5 BELLEVUE HILL

POINT PIPER Exclusive waterfront area with *"very little commercial development, not many blocks of flats, no shops, hardly any downmarket buildings at all"* (Leslie Walford). Among the best streets in Australia are WOLSELEY ROAD (including 1920s houses converted into spacious flats – Lennox "Dinger" and Joan Bode, and Sir Bob Crichton-Brown have magnificent apartments) and WOLSELEY CRESCENT (Susan and Frank Renouf's famous house, Toison d'Or – see box). Peter and Edwina Baillieu live in WINGADAL PLACE.

VAUCLUSE Established, upmarket, quiet, clubby suburb, bang on the harbour. Superb views back to the city without being in the thick of it. Lots of European Jewish refugees who fled to Sydney in the Forties, just as the pale-faced Pommies were fleeing their swish Vaucluse homes for fear of air raids. Top streets are VAUCLUSE ROAD, WENTWORTH ROAD (good boating facilities) and THE CRESCENT. COOLONG ROAD (level blocks of land, a few steps from the sea, where there's deep water access) is home of Sir Alexis Albert (Forties house with a Georgianesque atmosphere) and the Earl of Portarlington, whose house is *"lovely because of the English collection of paintings, books and furniture. One of the rare places where you really would see a Gainsborough on the wall. It's more like walking into a good English country house than you'd see anywhere in Australia"* (Leslie Walford).

DARLING POINT Home of newspaper magnate James Fairfax in LINDSAY AVENUE and the Anthony Oxleys' stone-built Victorian Gothic House in CARTHONA AVENUE. YARRANABBE ROAD and GREENOAKS AVENUE have fine views, but the best are from the LONGWOOD penthouse in Thornton Street. Michael Parkinson has an apartment overlooking the next-door bay, Rushcutters Bay: *"Water adds an extra dimension to life – it is like living in a movie set with the scenario changing constantly."*

WOOLLAHRA Upper-class suburb with everything but the views. ROSEMONT AVENUE is *"grand as a street – an interesting curve to it, and those absolutely magical plane trees"* (Leslie Walford). Smart serviced mansion flats, set back. *Everybody* (except Diana Fisher, who lives in Holdsworth Street) lives in QUEEN STREET – Premier Neville Wran, radio king John Laws and tastebud king Leo Schofield, whose 1890s house, St Kevins, has been historically restored, Morris for Morris, stained glass for stained glass, to *"that rather dark and gloomy look of the period"* (Leslie Walford). *"It's fabulous – west Woollahra is like a little village – a tiny triangle bounded by Oxford*

"The best real estate investment in the next 2 years will be in residential waterfronts – houses with an ideal lifestyle. In Sydney, north- or north-easterly-facing waterfronts offer the best sun in the southern hemisphere. The eastern suburbs are one of the few waterfront areas in the city with fabulous views to the north. They have intimate views with expansive views beyond. The combination of the two is outstanding"

(ANDREW GIBBONS)

Street, Ocean Street and Jersey Road. All the embassies and consulates are in that triangle. There are shops on the corners, and pubs, and it's terrifically handy for the City. I've lived there for 20 years and I can't conceive of living anywhere else" (Leo Schofield).

BELLEVUE HILL Quietly residential, hilly, tree-filled. *"Sydney's a hidden city – everything is round corners and down steps"* (Leslie Walford). Best streets are ROSE BAY AVENUE (where the Bond Corporation and mining magnate Tony Grey have houses), VICTORIA ROAD and GINAGHULLA ROAD.

Other smart areas are CENTENNIAL PARK (MARTIN ROAD, ROBINSON ROAD and LANG ROAD); HUNTERS HILL (some smart stone houses dating from the 1870s in WOOLWICH ROAD, reached by a wonderfully different ferry ride under the bridge and up the harbour); and DOUBLE BAY (flash Beverly Hills-style shops, but less residential – BEACH STREET is the best).

PADDINGTON is the place for young British Sloanes and Aussie Bushies – irregular streets of old Victorian terraces with iron balustrading smack of the Motherland. Conversely, it's also a gay enclave. The best city penthouses are on top of the REGENT HOTEL in George Street and THE QUAY in Phillip Street (where Susan Renouf has a pied-à-terre).

Anyone for space-age tennis?

The current craze in Sydney is for synthetic grass tennis courts with none of the old chicken-wire netting – you press a button and a mesh frame pops up around the court. People are filling in swimming pools to make courts (which were there in the fifties before they made them into pools).

Toison d'Or – je t'adore

The fabled Point Piper house of Susan and Frank Renouf (the richest man in New Zealand) was bought for A$8 million (US$5,653).

Set on 3 blocks (houses worth) of land with 315 ft (96 m) of waterfront, a saltwater swimming pool by the sea, a grass tennis court (resurrected by Susan), expansive views and the right aspects, it's one of the best properties in Australia. Susan supervised the redecoration (tented ceilings and padded walls in the drawing room), aided by Michael Love (see INTERIORS). Despite others' sour-grapes comments on its being "in a windy position"/"not great architecturally"/ "not that extraordinary inside"/having a "difficult entrance", Toison d'Or is to Susan Renouf: *"My love and joy. It combines everything – the most fantastic site on the most fantastic harbour in the world."*

INTERIORS

MICHAEL LOVE, 4 Milson Rd, Cremorne Point, NSW 2090 ☎ (02) 902389. Interior designer who worked on Toison d'Or with Susan Renouf. Belgravia-cum-Seizième in style. His own house, close to Cremorne jetty, is prim and polished, a showroom.

MARSH FREEDMAN ASSOCIATES, 129 Bourke St, Woolloomooloo, NSW 2011 ☎ (02) 358 4522. *"The best interior designers"* (Leo Schofield).

ART

ROBIN GIBSON GALLERIES, 278 Liverpool St, Darlinghurst, NSW 2010 ☎ (02) 331 6692. The best of contemporary Australian art – Brett Whiteley, Tim Storrier and co.

BOLT-HOLES

PALM BEACH Sydney's answer to Malibu, California, but less spoilt, more discreet. The fantastic hammerhead Barrenjoey Peninsula has one of the best ocean beaches in the world on one side, and a quieter harbour beach the other. Hidden homes in the gum-treed hillside have extraordinary views, some over both sides of the spit. Best roads: the dress circle – twisty PACIFIC ROAD (home of Bryan Brown and Rachel Ward) and FLORIDA ROAD; SUNRISE ROAD; and the front row of the stalls – BARRENJOEY ROAD (Pittwater side) and OCEAN ROAD (Palm Beach side, where the Joys and the Kerry Packers live).

TOWLERS BAY, MACKEREL BEACH and **PEARL BEACH**, on Pittwater, are only accessible by boat. Lovely wooded national parkland, where properties are 25 per cent of the price of Palm Beach. Adventurous politicians and businessmen who seriously want to get away.

In the south-west, BOWRAL has regained its fashionable country weekend status of the thirties. Families, flowers, gardens, horses. Two fine houses are Redford Park, owned by James Fairfax, and, nearer Sydney, Camden Park, home of the Macarthur-Onslows. Also BUNDANOON, MITTAGONG and MOSS VALE for stockbroker farmers.

MELBOURNE

BEST AREAS

TOP 4
★
1 TOORAK
2 SOUTH YARRA
3 SOUTH MELBOURNE
4 EAST MELBOURNE

"The residential architecture is much better than in Sydney, and the gardens are superb. You have beautiful homes in Toorak, South Yarra and Kew with very English gardens, in flat, lovely wide boulevards with beautiful trees. It's what I call an establishment city" (SUSAN RENOUF)

TOORAK *"The houses are grand and gracious, often with great flat gardens (which Sydney seldom has), so you get elegance and space around the house. Original houses with a Georgian or Queen Anne look to them"* (Leslie Walford). Best streets: ALBANY ROAD (graceful, curving, lined with oak trees), LANSELL ROAD (leafy: masses of mansions), ST GEORGES ROAD, ORRONG ROAD, WHERNSIDE AVENUE, IRVING ROAD and CLENDON ROAD.

SOUTH YARRA Smart Yuppy area – young trendies preparing for Toorak.

SOUTH MELBOURNE ST VINCENT'S PLACE is a delightful curved street of terraced houses with iron lacework balconies, all facing a central park.

EAST MELBOURNE Very toffy. Fine Victorian architecture. DARLING SQUARE looks just like a London garden square.

ART AND ANTIQUES

ANTIQUE PRINT & MAP GALLERY, 546 High St, Prahran, VIC 3181 ☎ (03) 529 8011. Spencer Sandilands stocks marvellous prints depicting Aboriginal, military, mining and other scenes from Australian history.

DAHLENBURG & HARPER, 1009 High St, Armadale, VIC 3143 ☎ (03) 205 943. The best source of English, and some French, 18th-century furniture.

BOLT-HOLES

POINT ADDIS *"I stay in my house here for a month over the Christmas holidays to rejuvenate. I am very happy getting an all-over suntan, surfing, eating simply and painting using the local ochres"* (Prue Acton).

PORTSEA is a real getaway place. There is a windsurfing bay, but the ocean can be treacherous. Best investments are tucked away in quiet streets away from the waterfront.

ADELAIDE

With its international Grand Prix *and* a new casino, Adelaide is now the best place in Australia to invest in – catch her on the upswing. Springfield, Glen Osmond, N Adelaide and Medindie are the best bets.

BEST AREAS

TOP 2
★
1 SPRINGFIELD
2 MEDINDIE

SPRINGFIELD The most exclusive suburb at the foot of the Adelaide Hills. The biggest houses have 9 bedrooms, large gardens, stables, servants' quarters, swimming pool, and tennis court. SPRINGFIELD AVENUE is the key street, boasting the "little bit established" Cockses of the concrete and Rainsfords of the seat-belts. Also BROOKSIDE ROAD and DELAMERE AVENUE.

MEDINDIE The old Adelaide establishment. Those with the oldest bucks (the likes of property-owning Greenslades) are safety deposited in streets such as ROBE TERRACE.

WALKERVILLE and **GILBERTON** The refuge of established Adelaiders when a deluge of nouveaux riches forced them out of North Adelaide. Barr Smiths and McLachlans live here.

ANTIQUES

HANNIBAL BONYTHON, 105 Unley Rd, Adelaide, SA 5000 ☎ (08) 441404. Everything from 18th-century English and French antiques to arts nouveau and deco. A trendsetter for Adelaide's cultural set.

HAROLD QUIGLEY ANTIQUES, 12 Wyatt St, SA 5000 ☎ (08) 223 7994. Quigley's aim is to push Australians farther back in time, to before the late Victoriana which they most admire. 18th-century English and French provincial furniture, plus silver, paintings and porcelain.

MEGAW & HOGG, 26 Leigh St, SA 5000 ☎ (08) 231 0101. The Victoriana side of Quigley's empire: bowing to demand. Mostly British-born antiques bought by a mainly British-born clientele.

BOLT-HOLES

PORT WILLUNGA Establishment port on the way to Victor Harbor. Royal Adelaide golfers have houses here.

VICTOR HARBOR An hour south of the city. Young and social over New Year. Good waves at BOOMER BEACH and CHITON ROCKS.

PERTH

Is Perth booming or has it boomed? It's been through enormous pre-America's Cup expansion and development, but estate agents reckon it's no longer the best place to invest. It could be a question of overkill.

Home sweet Holme

Robert Holmes à Court, possibly the richest man in Australia (with at least A$300 million (US$212 million)), has just overkilled himself and his family by constructing two huge houses that have different exteriors, but are virtually identical within – so that they should always feel at home.

BEST AREAS

DALKEITH Equivalent to Sydney's Vaucluse. Smart, waterfront houses. Alan Bond lives here.

PEPPERMINT GROVE Grand: old-established (as far as it can be), on the waterfront, lovely views, and less flash than Dalkeith.

BRISBANE

BEST AREAS

Old Brisbane families and racing sorts live in northside suburbs, ASCOT, HAMILTON and CLAYFIELD. Stone or brick houses (rather than the heat-reducing stilted timber buildings) overlook the Brisbane River. Qintex chairman Christopher Skase and his wife Pixie have bought two neighbouring colonial houses in Hamilton because they couldn't decide between them. They live in one, and her 4 daughters by a previous marriage live in the other.

BOLT-HOLES

Brisbane's main bolting possibilities are to places where the whole of Australia bolts to – the ghastly Gold Coast (Surfers Paradise highriseland) and the Sunshine Coast, where NOOSA is the only unspoilt resort left.

LIE OF THE LAND

There is a rural depression in Australia. Sons who, in the old days, would have taken over the family "property" (an Australian ranch) now look to the bright lights and high finance of the cities. That a slump in agricultural exports and high interest rates forced many old families to sell up or apportion properties.

Meanwhile, a new breed of city-rich have created a demand for properties within a 3-hour radius of their work (and rocketing prices, particularly in NSW, reflect that fashion rather than the superiority of the land). There always have been property-owners who lived and worked in the city – Pitt Street (Sydney) and Collins Street (Melbourne) farmers – but they were in it for tax concessions. The new absentee landlords enjoy the kudos of a weekend estate, and the latest trend is in timeshare farming. A 3,000-acre (1,214-hectare) property may be divided into 30 lots, and each investor gets the use of the homestead for part of the year, while a manager runs the farm. Ideal if you want your own bit of dirt, horses ready and champing at the bit, and beds turned down when you turn up.

NEW SOUTH WALES

The best, richest country area is MOREE. *"The Moree Club is the only one in country NSW where some of the members drive Rolls-Royces rather than Holden Commodores"* (George Falkiner). BUNGENDORE, near Canberra, is élitist, with its own little polo field; Bungendore Bushies include the Gordons, Davieses, Rutledges and Osbornes (on the royal circuit). WALLAMUMBI, near Armidale (David Wright), is the best property: beautifully maintained, runs lots of cattle, good house and land. BELLTREES, Scone (Michael and Judy White), is the most social property; the Prince of Wales had a whale of a time here. WALLENDOON (the Baldrys) covers 5,000 acres (2,023 hectares) of the best land in Australia, at Wallendbeen, near Young. *"Beautiful soil, capable of running a lot of sheep to the acre, superb crops, the right climate"* (Bill Ranken). GLEN ROCK HOUSE, Marulan, near Goulburn, is the loveliest country house: a perfect Georgian building, beautifully restored, with 2,000 acres (809 hectares) . PJAR PARK, Crookwell, near Goulburn, has the best country garden. The best sheep are from URADRY, Hay; the best cattle from WEEBOLLABOLLA, near Moree. The best Peppin Merino sheep parent studs in the world are the 60,000-acre (24,281-hectare) HADDON RIG, Warren (George Falkiner, pure Merino himself and the most eligible bachelor in the Bush, worth about A$20 million (US$14 million)), BOONOKE, Hay (Rupert Murdoch – the stud is part of News Corp), and MERRIVALE, Yass (the Merrimans).

NORTHERN TERRITORY

This part of the bush is only for the big boys, like Sam Vestey and Kerry Packer. Individuals can be wiped out if the rains don't come, but big companies can write off the bad years as tax losses, and on a good year, make a mint. The scale of properties leaps into square miles, and cattle-mustering

"If you're looking for a weekender in NSW, go for the Yass area near Canberra or the Hunter Valley [see opposite]. These areas offer quality of life, lovely homes, proximity to Sydney (within 3 hours' drive), interesting neighbours, and enough water to have a good garden and grow yourself roses. It's a temperate climate, so you don't have raging dust-storms, where the crows fly backwards to keep the dust out of their eyes, or the sort of heat where you can fry an egg on a sheet of corrugated iron if you park it in the sun for too long"

(GEORGE FALKINER)

(rounding up) is done by helicopter. The largest station is Peter Sherwin's VICTORIA RIVER DOWNS (4,772 sq miles/12,360 sq km), followed by BRUNETTE DOWNS (4,730 sq miles/12,250 sq km – with 2,983 miles/4,800 km of roads and 1,367 miles/2,200 km of fencing): and NEWCASTLE WATERS (3,995 sq miles/10,347 sq km), bought by Kerry Packer from Peter Baillieu (his cousin) and Tony Chisholm for A$5.6 million (US$4 million).

QUEENSLAND

The best bush investment in Australia is in central Queensland – cheap to buy: good income from sheep (minimum staff, mobs of sheep = maximum money). Best property is Pam Bell's at COCHIN COCHIN – a beautiful 19th-century building on stilts, where Prince Charles has stayed.

S AUSTRALIA

The best properties are those owned by the McLachlans (who shear a million sheep and own about a third of the state), the Rymills and the MacGregors.

VICTORIA

The smartest bit of the Bush is the Western District of Victoria. Western District Graziers (equivalent to British Sloane Rangers) include the Clarks (who own the best station in the area, DEVON PARK, where visiting English royals have stayed), Manifolds, Kellys, Landales, and ex-PM Malcolm Fraser. *"The closest thing to smart people in the English countryside. A closed book, very snobbish and grand. The most fertile country in Australia, and lots of it"* (Bill Ranken).

WESTERN AUSTRALIA

Wild and empty, despite current world hype. Just a few rich developers have built themselves homesteads in the outback. Lord McAlpine's more ambitious 60-acre (24-hectare) zoo near BROOME is an attraction to the public and a delight to him. *"The rock formations and wildlife in the area are wonderful. North-west Australia is the best place in the world to buy. Travel is getting quicker and quicker – only one stop to Perth from London – and communications are so good now. It's an area of enormous growth, with offshore gas, diamonds, minerals and huge pearls and, though it's adjacent to a densely populated part of the world [Asia], it's vastly underpopulated and has no racial tension. The Japanese are currently putting A$11 billion (US$7.8 billion) into offshore gas and carting it back to Japan in ship-loads"* (Lord McAlpine of West Green).

TASMANIA

CONNORVILLE is the best property in Australia, owned by Ros O'Connor and son Rod, who have hosted British royals. Superb Saxon Merino sheep (super-fine wool) and cattle. *"One of the prettiest houses I've ever been in, and one of the few sheep stations that has bitumen roads on it and a polished wood floor in the shearing shed"* (George Falkiner). *"It's run like England – forelocks are touched. Beautiful outbuildings, lovely house and country, well fenced. Connorville and the O'Connors are the embodiment of civilization"* (Bill Ranken).

HOW GREEN IS MY (WINE) VALLEY?

The smartest old wineries flourish in South Australian valleys (Henschkes and Rymills are among the established Bacchanalians). The BAROSSA VALLEY, 35 miles (56 km) north-east if Adelaide, is the most prestigious.

Property-wise, however, the HUNTER, NSW, is the valley of the future. Set in lush, rolling country on a scale that makes English landscape look like toytown, it's already the home of many rich Aussies who own a vineyard or two and whose forbears were wine-makers in the 1820s.

Where the grapes grow there build I. Beaverish Len Evans mourns the fact that the Hunter is becoming urbanized (from his house you can make out 1 or 2 other buildings – and you can see for miles).

He designed his E-shaped outsize bungalow on classic English country-house format, building it around period architectural relics such as door-frames and stained glass windows, like a homy mini-San Simeon (the knock-out Spanish-plus castle on the Big Sur coast of California, built by W Randolph Hearst). Inside, it's like a traditional country farmhouse, peppered with local and European antiques – a French Provincial refectory table, Welsh dresser, Australian range. The whole family had a hand in creating mosaic terraces. The guest quarters are wittily arranged as a French boudoir, an Elizabethan bedroom (the tub in the bathroom is a converted wine barrel) and an old Colonial room (with an immense copper bath). One by one, Evans's ideas are realized – a croquet lawn, swimming pool, mini-cinema, tennis court, stables, 9-hole golf course, and, naturally, a wine store.

FAR EAST

Hot property in the Far East is divided between affluent European banking and trading companies (for bigwig employees, who reside in colonial splendour), rich orientals, and, more recently, Americans.

JAPAN

TOKYO

BEST AREAS

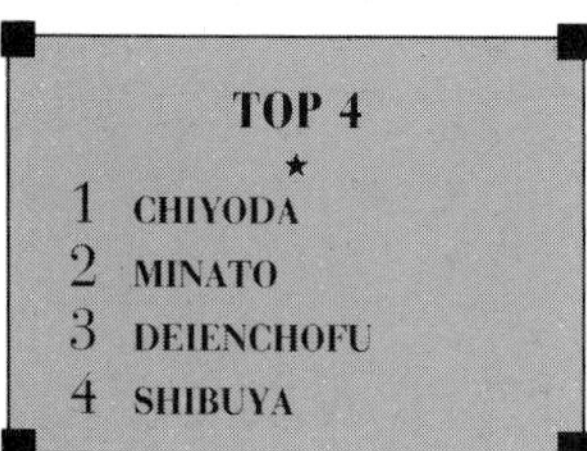

TOP 4

★

1. CHIYODA
2. MINATO
3. DEIENCHOFU
4. SHIBUYA

CHIYODA Home of the Imperial Palace (where Emperor Hirohito lives), the superlative British Embassy, the best hotel in Japan (Okura) and, at 2-3-1 Nagata-cho, the sprawling 1928 manor where Prime Minister Yasuhiro Nakasone lives. KOJIMACHI and ICHIBANCHO are expensive residential areas for high-level businessmen: the famous high school for eggheads is in Kojimachi.

MINATO Trendy area, brimming with boutiques and restaurants. Hiroo is the best residential part, where rents have shot up by 40 per cent (to over 1 million yen (US$5,600) a month for a 4-bedroom apartment). The most luxurious foreigners' accommodation is at 2-1 Roppongi – the Mitsuiyama Residences, built for the United States Embassy in 1983. The 12-storey towers and 2 townhouses are built on land once owned by the Mitsui family. The grandest Western-style house is also here: the Akasaka Rikyu in Moto Akasaka, modelled after the Château de Versailles. It is now used to house visiting heads of state.

DEIENCHOFU The Beverly Hills of Japan, where many actors live. The only part of Japan where "enormous" houses really *are* big. Old-style and imaginative architecture with mod cons inside, tennis courts and pools.

SHIBUYA Rowdy young students and Yuppies. The exclusive bits are SHYOTO and HATSUDAI.

HONG KONG

BEST AREAS

TOP 3

★

1. THE PEAK
2. SHEK O
3. REPULSE BAY

THE PEAK The Taipans of Hong Kong (merchants like the Swires and Jardines) were the first to build their homes on the Peak back in 1851. The higher altitude served as a retreat from the frenetic city, displayed in physical terms their exalted position in society, and provided knock-out panoramas. The HK ethos of if it's not tall enough, knock it down and rebuild it in ultra-modern, higher-rise style, means there are few old detached houses left – just a handful, and they are still in the hands of latter-day Taipans. The smartest have 6 bedrooms, guest quarters, a swimming pool and space for a retinue of cars and servants; they rarely come on the market. What you *can* buy (at head-of-company level) is a luxury house and patio in a complex with pool and tennis court. The best is a group of 7 on PEAK ROAD (up to HK$60,000 (US$7,688) a month rental); then STRAWBERRY HILL and KELLETT VIEW (HK$5 million (US$640,656) to buy: HK$50,000 (US$6,407) to rent). Next down the line, for second-rung execs, are towering apartment blocks in Mid Levels. The most prestigious are GARDEN TERRACE and ESTORIL COURT.

SHEK O Snobby village-style residential area for old colonials, who live in spacious private bungalows with *gardens*. A coveted change from the tall, thin house-plus-patio norm. Houses are numbered according to age.

1997 : THE YELLOW PERIL

At the very pinnacle of the property market in 1981, prime houses on the Peak were selling for up to HK$40 million (US$5 million). That was before the Chino-British agreement that Hong Kong should be surrendered to the Chinese in 1997. Many old colonials saw this as the end of their dealings in the Far East, and sold up. Hong Kong slumped into depression (not that this deterred developers), from which it is just emerging. Property prices rose by 30 per cent in 1985, though the top-drawer residences wouldn't budge and have stayed at half to two-thirds of their peak price. (Punters are expected to move in soon and snap them up on the cheap.) There is a distinct shift in the Hong Kong population – more Americans, who see a great future in China opening up, but fewer Brits, who liked the old days too much, and are cutting their losses and running.

“One of the loveliest, most prestigious homes in Hong Kong is BROADWOOD PARK – an exclusive development in a tree-lined road on a wooded hillside above Happy Valley. It's secluded, in landscaped gardens, with pool, terrace, squash and tennis courts. The master bedroom has a dressing room and marbled bathroom with antiqued brass fittings”

(DAVID DAVIES)

REPULSE BAY Primarily a resort, on the south, rather Med-like, side of the island. Apartments are highly sought-after, mainly for families who want to be close to the beach.

LANTAU ISLAND Villages, countryside and long white beaches. The place for ex-pat retreats.

INTERIORS

KENNETH KO, 15th Floor, On Wah Industrial Building, Fo Tan Village, Shatin ☎ (0) 604 9494. The best architect and interior designer in Hong Kong. Modern and flamboyant. Remodels old houses. His own home has a swimming pool half in and half out of the house.

On a world scale, every property in Hong Kong is a box – it's only when you see some of the smaller boxes [right down to the Chinese stallholders' – they close the shutters on their 5 ft (11.5 m) square stalls and sleep in them] that you appreciate your super-deluxe box.

HK BANK'S RISING ASSETS

The Hong Kong Bank raze-and-replace programme involved two major works. One was the new premises for the bank, the other the controversial new residence for their chairman. This opulent neo-Spanish-Muslim-Chinese palace is nicknamed “Sky High” for its cost as well as its situation (it's the highest building on the island). Its rumoured appointments include an art gallery and a vegetable patch.

The bank building, designed by British architect Norman Foster, is a 52-storey (4 subterranean) feat. Completed at last in 1985, it is two and a half times the size of its Thirties predecessor (which superseded the 1886 original), cost in the region of HK$15.6 billion (US$2 billion), and has been likened to an incomplete oil rig. If not aesthetically pleasing from the outside, it is the sum of its custom-made parts – an eclectic mass of the very best and latest in technology and design. To keep pace with the next 50 years, floor panels lift, partitions move, units wheel away. A computerized communications system operates the workings of the building and express glass lifts (the intention being that Jo Pub Lik should be able to see for himself the awesome mechanics of the bank). Seawater is pumped through pipes to warm or cool the building, and a sunscoop reflects natural light into the dramatic Banking Hall. Despite all this technology, the most indispensable consultant was a fung shui expert who ensured the site and aspect of the building were right, according to Chinese mythology. And there could be no dispensing with the two bronze lions from Shanghai, which still guard the entrance, their noses worn down by locals, who rub them for luck.

MALAYSIA

CAMERON HIGHLANDS Space is not a problem in Malaysia. Sweltering heat is. While properties in Kuala Lumpur are unremarkable, second homes in the hills above the city are havens. North of KL, in the rarefied cool air of the Cameron Highlands, stand, incongruously, pseudo-Tudor houses. From the heat of jungly rubber plantations to the quasi-Surrey hills, a network of villages, flower gardens and vegetable farms. These prestigious residences were built on tea plantations for the hill station managers of Somerset Maugham's heyday. Inside, they reproduce faithfully features such as beams, open fireplaces and horse brasses.

GEORGE TOWN, Penang Palatial houses in the old colonial heart of this island. Beautiful beaches.

SINGAPORE

BEST AREAS

A tiny island where space is at a premium. Ambassadors, millionaires and corporate chiefs live in “black and whites” (which refers to the paintwork), built during colonial days in elegant, 2-storey verandah style – allowing the breeze to flow through. Tennis courts and swimming pools are standard accoutrements.

INDEX

ACKNOWLEDGEMENTS

Lord Lichfield and the publishers would especially like to thank the following people for their invaluable help in putting together this book:

Vida Adamoli, Jock Anderson, Richard Ashworth, Josh Astor, Amanda Atha, Michael Belmont, Catherine Bond, Hamish Bowles, Bonnie Brooks-Young, Michael Catz, Richard Caws, Victoria Collison, Claudia Cragg, William Cranfield, Sherri Creed, Tiffany Daneff, William Davies, Lucinda de Laroque, Lucy Elworthy, Anne Fulwood, John Galbreath, Robinder Garewal, Marilyn Garrow, Col David German, Fred Gill, Kathie Gill, Juliet Gosling, Charles Gregory, Janet Grosvenor, Billy Hamilton, Gillian Haslam, Keith Holland, Gillian House, Deh-Ta Hsiung, Sally Ievers, Angela Jeffs, Miranda Kennedy, Anna Kythreotis, Debbie Le Foe, Denice Lewis, Felicity MacDonald, Tina MacFarlane, Katy McGuinness, Victoria Mather, Michael Matthews, Bobbi Mitchell, Sarah Murray, Tristram Murray, Robin Nydes, Nigel Oakes, Christopher Orssich, Ricki Ostrov, Camellia Panjabi, Elisabeth Pedersen, David Pyott, Clement Rioux, Claudia Roberts, William Roberts, Ann Ross-Smith, Fiona Ross-Smith, Alistair Scott, Alan Shelley, Kate Sheridan, Caroline Silver, Anne Snell, John Spearman, Tomasz Starzewski, Catherine Tennant, Samantha Todhunter, Shortie Trimingham, Shelley Turner, Karin Upton, Michael van Straten, Maria Louisa Wahlberg, Hilary Walden, Kate Waldy, Annabel Walker, Susie Ward, Annie Young.